W9-AHY-996
3 1230 00593 2385

6-05

THE BEST PLAYS THEATER YEARBOOK 2003–2004

JEFFREY ERIC JENKINS
Editor

THE BEST PLAYS
THEATER YEARBOOK

○ ○ ○ ○ ○ ○ ○ ○ ○ ○ ○ ○ ○ ○ ○

THE BEST PLAYS THEATER YEARBOOK 2003–2004

○ ○ ○ ○ ○ ○ ○ ○ ○ ○ ○ ○ ○ ○ ○

EDITED BY
JEFFREY ERIC JENKINS

Illustrated with production photographs

○○○○○

LIMELIGHT EDITIONS

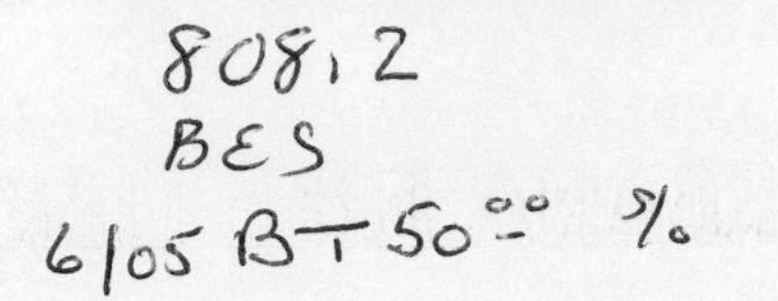

ISBN: 0-87910-315-9

ISSN: 1071-6971

Printed in the United States of America

The work of The Best Plays Theater Yearbook *has been generously underwritten, since 2001, by a multiyear grant from the Harold and Mimi Steinberg Charitable Trust.*

Published in 2005 by
Limelight Editions (an imprint of Amadeus Press, LLC)
512 Newark Pompton Turnpike
Pompton Plains, New Jersey 07444, USA
www.limelighteditions.com

For sales, please contact:
Limelight Editions
c/o Hal Leonard Corporation
7777 West Bluemound Road
Milwaukee, Wisconsin 53213, USA
Tel.: 800-637-2852
Fax: 414-774-3259

Website: www.limelighteditions.com

The Best Plays Theater Yearbook 2003–2004 is dedicated to the memory of Isabelle Stevenson.

For decades, Isabelle served as the elegant public face of New York theater through her good works at the American Theatre Wing and her determined support for excellence in the theater. She and her generous family routinely made theater people of all types and talents feel warm, welcome and valued in the community of artists.

INTRODUCTION

AS THE CYCLE OF theater seasons turns, we are often reminded of the theater of the Greeks and the centrality of it to understanding the earthly cycles of life. For *The Best Plays Theater Yearbook*, seasons run June to May, June to May; year in, year out. Although this is the 85th volume of the series begun by Burns Mantle in 1920, it is only the fourth such edition under the stewardship of the current editor. Four editions complete with a fifth on the way and the seasons continue: June to May, June to May. We hope with this series to provide a picture of the theater season both in overview and microcosm. Our season essays are meant to take the long view of the year, tease out currents and offer a bit of perspective. The essays on the Best Plays, on the other hand, are meant to assess worthy texts and their productions more closely, and to locate them in their particular cultural moment. When we succeed, the satisfaction is great. When we do not, there is always next year.

It would be thrilling to report that a revolution took place in the 2003–2004 theater season. In our fantasy inversion of the theater world, brilliant new plays and musicals on Broadway might supplant a steady diet of revivals populated with film stars. This dream sequence might report that solo performance pieces—often demonstrations of theatrical narcissism and producers' aversion to risk—were now an endangered dramatic species. Alas, that dream world does not exist. There was one producer in the 2003–04 season who decidedly was *not* risk-averse. Rosie O'Donnell put $10 million of her own money (and her reputation) on the line. The musical she produced, *Taboo*, had problems ranging from the aesthetic to the logistical and closed after 100 performances. Her show was not, however, without its pleasures in performance. There was also, though, the small musical starring unknown puppets that managed to upset a megashow for the top Tony Awards. So, even if it wasn't a revolutionary year, it also wasn't quite business as usual.

As we have said in this space before, this book is but the second draft of theater history in the US—theater journalism, of course, is presumed to be the first. We'll leave it to others to perform finer interpretations of the statistics we glean from a variety of primary sources (including *Variety*) and print herein. Note this, though: since the attacks of September 11, 2001, there is a bit of "fiddling while Rome burns" feeling in our theatrical culture. This feeling of unease may well be due to the amount of time it takes to let events settle in the artistic consciousness before new dramatic works take shape. And, perhaps, given the brutality and suffering we see daily on our television and computer screens, we should just be happy for a few moments of entertainment. (We'll set aside for the moment questions about the quality of that entertainment.)

II

WHEN THE BEST PLAYS of the 2003–04 season were chosen, by the editor in consultation with the editorial board, no thought was given to a thematic construct—despite our stated intent to provide an overview of the season. As we consider the 10 Best Plays for the season under review, though, several strands emerge to weave a cloth in which we might wrap this season.

A glance at the list of authors brings a pleasant surprise: women playwrights are well represented. To the best of our knowledge, this is the strongest representation of women writers in the history of the series. Including a play co-authored by two women (*Omnium Gatherum*) and a musical co-authored by a man and a woman (*Caroline, or Change*), there are eight women represented among the Best Plays honorees. Indeed, it is no stretch to say that women characters and women's issues are prominently featured in the subject matter of the majority of the plays.

In Nilo Cruz's *Anna in the Tropics*, which draws on Tolstoy's *Anna Karenina* for its underlying themes, women are central to the action of the play. Their needs and desires provoke male passions, but there is also an undercurrent of violence—rape and murder committed by one man—that marks males as transgressors, as victimizers in modern culture. Remarkably, the play does all of this with a literate, poetic sense that delivers a not unexpected emotional blow in the final moments. In Tony Kushner and Jeanine Tesori's musical *Caroline, or Change*, an African-American maid is torn between the material realities of raising children alone and a longing for something more from life in a time when change (literal and figurative) surrounds her. Bryony Lavery's troubled production of *Frozen* (see editor's note with essay) eventually overshadowed the diametrical positions of two women who struggle with understanding violence, psychopathology and guilt when they encounter a serial child-killer. But the play is likely to continue finding productions (and audiences) as the controversy over intellectual property fades away.

The central character of Lynn Nottage's *Intimate Apparel*, an African-American seamstress with a thriving business at the turn of the 20th century, finds herself victimized by someone she should be able to trust before finding emotional intimacy with an orthodox Jew. *Living Out* by Lisa Loomer sympathetically confronts issues that face today's overachieving parents—particularly women—who need adequate child care to obtain their piece of the American dream. But it also looks incisively into the plight of those who do the caregiving: Who's raising their kids? Paula Vogel's *The Long Christmas Ride Home* returns to familiar ground for the Pulitzer Prize-winning playwright as she addresses family expectations, dysfunction and the role of memory in constructing identity. Although the play is not limited to the concerns of women, it certainly illuminates the roles women play in their own domestic captivity.

With *Omnium Gatherum*, by Theresa Rebeck and Alexandra Gersten-Vassilaros, we shift gears to consider the work of two playwrights who traffic in ideas related to American fascination with "bread and circuses." The dark comedy of this play is a move in the direction of understanding how we ignore larger issues (terrorism, racism, cultural hegemony) as we focus on those of lesser significance (what is the interesting flavor in this appetizer?). In *Small Tragedy*, Craig Lucas asks that we all consider our complicity in the savage acts human beings visit upon one another, but especially those committed in the name of religious or ethnic purity. Richard Greenberg invites us to think about the construction of history as an agglomeration of "facts" viewed through whatever critical lens is fashionable in a particular moment. In Greenberg's *The Violet Hour*, life is merely fodder for a machine in the future that will digest and convert us to its own purposes. Finally, Lisa Kron's *Well* enables a woman to create her own paradigm for personal agency. Through a feminist lens—interestingly, a lens not unlike those satirized in *Violet Hour*—Kron envisions an identity for her character (her "self") that stands apart from peculiarly American ideologies surrounding "illness" and "health."

By now, the wise reader of *The Best Plays Theater Yearbook* series knows that Broadway theater is often more about economics than a regenerative experience of the mind and spirit. Indeed, one of the Best Plays for this season came from Off Off Broadway, increasingly the home for much of our finest writing. Of the rest, all started elsewhere: in the UK, in resident theaters or Off Broadway. Four of them made it to Broadway after following the twisting route that often accompanies art wed to commerce.

In addition to the plays celebrated in these essays, we also hope that readers enjoy the volume's expanded statistics and index. Whenever possible we track all Broadway and Off Broadway revivals back to their original presentations in New York and abroad. In the case of William Shakespeare and others of his ilk, we employ George C.D. Odell's *Annals of the New York Stage*—which links with the *Best Plays* series to chronicle New York theater back to the 18th century—back issues of *The New York Times* and other source materials in an attempt to locate plays in their original context.

With our colleagues in the American Theatre Critics Association, we also keep close tabs on the developing new plays that arise in theaters across the US. Through the good offices of the Harold and Mimi Steinberg Charitable Trust, we recognize the honorees and finalists of the American Theatre Critics/Steinberg New Play Award and Citations. The Steinberg Charitable Trust has also supported the *Best Plays* series since 2001. We extend our deepest thanks to the Trust and its board (William D. Zabel, Carole A. Krumland, James D. Steinberg, Michael A. Steinberg and Seth M. Weingarten) for making *The Best Plays Theater Yearbook* a priority for their support.

Honorees for the 2004 American Theatre Critics/Steinberg New Play Award and Citations include Lynn Nottage's *Intimate Apparel*, which won the Steinberg top prize ($15,000) before its New York opening. As noted above, it was later selected as a Best Play. Nottage's play is discussed by Lenora Inez Brown. The 2004 American Theatre Critics/Steinberg New Play Citations (along with $5,000 each) went to Carson Kreitzer for *The Love Song of J. Robert Oppenheimer* (detailed here by Rick Pender), and August Wilson for the latest in his exploration of 20th century African-American history, *Gem of the Ocean* (essay by Christopher Rawson).

III

AS WE MOVE FORWARD with the 85th volume of this chronicle of theater in the United States, we celebrate not only the season past but also the beginning of a new partnership. Limelight Editions, publisher of *The Best Plays Theater Yearbook* since the 1992–1993 edition, changed ownership when Melvyn B. Zerman sold his interest in Limelight to John Cerullo of Amadeus Press. Zerman deserves the thanks of all who toil in theater history and research for all of his efforts on our behalf. We welcome Cerullo and his team to the *Best Plays* family and look forward to a fruitful collaboration.

The collection of data for a volume such as this relies on the labors of many people. Our thanks to Paul Hardt for his efforts on the Cast Replacements and Touring Productions section, and to Mel Gussow for his expanded essay of the Off Off Broadway theater. Rue E. Canvin, who has worked on the *Best Plays* series since the early 1960s, continues to make the USA section a "must-read" for those interested in theater around the country. Lara D. Nielsen, a colleague at New York University, has assumed the difficult task of tracking new productions Off Off Broadway. Jonathan Dodd, the longtime publisher of the *Best Plays* series, continues to provide important background information and good advice. My good friend Henry Hewes, himself a former editor of this series and my invaluable consulting editor, never stops thinking of ways to help improve the series.

We are also deeply indebted to all of the press representatives who assisted in the gathering of information for this volume, but we particularly want to acknowledge Adrian Bryan-Brown and Chris Boneau of Boneau/Bryan-Brown for their unflagging support of the series and its editors.

Thanks also are due to the members of the *Best Plays* editorial board, who give their imprimatur to our work by their presence on the masthead. Thanks as well to those who have offered and provided extra support and assistance to this edition: Charles Wright, John Istel, Christopher Rawson, Caldwell Titcomb (Elliot Norton Awards), David A. Rosenberg (Connecticut Critics' Circle Awards), Elizabeth Maupin (American Theatre Critics/Steinberg New Play Award and Citations), Edwin Wilson (Susan Smith Blackburn Prize), Michael Kuchwara (New York Drama Critics' Circle Awards), Henry Hewes (Theater Hall of Fame Awards) and Ralph Newman of the Drama Book Shop (New Plays and Publications).

We congratulate and thank all of the Best Plays honorees who made the 2003–04 season so invigorating to contemplate. Nilo Cruz, Alexandra Gersten-Vassilaros, Richard Greenberg, Lisa Kron, Tony Kushner, Bryony Lavery, Lisa Loomer, Craig Lucas, Lynn Nottage, Theresa Rebeck, Jeanine Tesori and Paula Vogel all enriched our lives during the season under review. The photographers who capture theatrical images on film and help keep those ephemeral moments alive for historical perspective are also due thanks for their generous contributions to the greater body of theatrical work. Building on our work from past years, we have included credits with each photograph and indexed the photographers' names for easier reference. Similarly, we continue offering biographical information about each of this volume's essayists and editors in a brief section at the back of the book.

A personal note: In addition to serving as editor of this book, I teach full-time in the Drama Department at New York University's Tisch School of the Arts. In addition to superb students who inspire me to strive for excellence in my teaching, research, editing and writing, I have the support and friendship of as fine a faculty as I have known. Each member of the senior faculty has, in ways large and small, provided the kind of encouragement one needs to do an annual compendium of critical perspective and historical reference that runs nearly 500 pages. My thanks to Awam Amkpa, Una Chaudhuri, Jan Cohen-Cruz, Laura Levine, Carol Martin and Edward Ziter. For the season under review, I especially want to thank our department chair, Kevin Kuhlke, and our director of theater studies, Robert Vorlicky, for their continuing support of my work as a teacher, researcher and writer.

My wife, Vivian Cary Jenkins, continues to serve the theater and *The Best Plays Theater Yearbook* as a tracker of what's happening in the New York theater. Although I repeat these thanks each year, one thing remains true: It is largely through her efforts, and her love and support, that the series continues to appear.

As we were about to go to press with this edition, our beloved silent partner in this enterprise—a cuddly 93-pound Rottweiler named Lady—died at the age of 11. The challenges of producing a book in each of the past four years were always mitigated by Lady's willingness to take us for long, restorative walks and by her insistence on sprawling among whichever massive stack of papers we were using to edit or proofread the listings in this and the past three volumes. To the end, she was an active, cheerful, loving spirit: a muse who was marvelously amusing. We sorely miss pulling research from beneath her warm, sleeping mass.

JEFFREY ERIC JENKINS
NEW YORK

Contents

THE SEASON ON AND OFF BROADWAY

THE SEASON: BROADWAY AND OFF BROADWAY

○○○○○ *By Jeffrey Eric Jenkins* ○○○○○

AFTER THE CURTAIN FELL on the 2003–2004 season, the 2004 Tony Award ceremony offered enough surprises to keep even the most jaded Broadway observer's interest. And that's not counting the spectacle of Carol Channing and LL Cool J doing a brief rap number while presenting the award for best score. The Little Show That Could, *Avenue Q*—which owes much of its charm to audiences' familiarity with *Sesame Street*, perennial show business joke (and former gubernatorial candidate) Gary Coleman and 20-somethings saturated in ironic detachment—knocked off the heavily favored *Wicked* to win the major musical categories (book, score and show). *Wicked*'s director, Joe Mantello, managed to win, but for another musical: the revival of *Assassins*.

With its no-name cast, tongue-in-cheek adult lyrics and simple musical compositions—many of which echoed *Sesame Street* thematics—*Avenue Q* mounted an election-style advertising campaign asking Tony voters to vote with their hearts. And it worked.

Even the graphics operators in Radio City Music Hall were caught off-guard by *Avenue Q*'s win for best musical. When the show was announced as the winner, *Wicked*'s title first appeared on the stage's proscenium before it was changed to the correct winner.

Heaping irony upon irony, though, a few days after the big win the producers of *Avenue Q* announced an exclusive deal for an extended engagement in Las Vegas. Why is that ironic? The exclusive engagement meant that road presenters—a significant bloc in the Tony Awards' voting structure—would not enjoy the fruits of their voting. And they were hopping mad. As Chris Jones wrote in *Variety*, "Better not to dwell on what that says about the integrity of the road voters."

But *Avenue Q* wasn't the evening's big winner, that honor fell to the revival of the John Weidman and Stephen Sondheim musical, *Assassins*, which earned five Tony Awards in the musical category (best revival, director,

BROADWAY SEASON 2003–2004

Productions in a continuing run on May 31, 2004 in bold

Productions honored as Best Plays *selections in italics*

Best Plays *from prior seasons are noted with a date in parentheses*

NEW PLAYS (10)

The Retreat From Moscow
Six Dance Lessons in Six Weeks
The Violet Hour
(Manhattan Theatre Club)
Anna in the Tropics
I Am My Own Wife *(02–03)*
Drowning Crow
(Manhattan Theatre Club)
Match
Sixteen Wounded
Frozen
Prymate

NEW MUSICALS (7)

Avenue Q
The Boy From Oz
Wicked
Taboo
Never Gonna Dance
Bombay Dreams
Caroline, or Change

PLAY REVIVALS (10)

Master Harold . . . and the Boys (81–82)
(Roundabout Theatre Company)
Cat on a Hot Tin Roof (54–55)
The Caretaker (61–62)
(Roundabout Theatre Company)
Henry IV (Lincoln Center Theater)
King Lear (Lincoln Center Theater)

PLAY REVIVALS (*cont'd*)

Twentieth Century
(Roundabout Theatre Company)
Sly Fox *(76–77)*
Jumpers *(73–74)*
A Raisin in the Sun *(58-59)*
Sight Unseen *(91–92)*
(Manhattan Theatre Club)

MUSICAL REVIVALS (5)

Big River: The Adventures of Huckleberry Finn
(Roundabout Theatre Company)
Little Shop of Horrors
Wonderful Town *(52–53)*
Fiddler on the Roof *(64-65)*
Assassins
(Roundabout Theatre Company)

SOLO PERFORMANCES (4)

Golda's Balcony
Sexaholix . . . a Love Story
The Oldest Living Confederate Widow Tells All
Barbara Cook's Broadway!
(Lincoln Center Theater)

SPECIALTIES (2)

Laughing Room Only
Marc Salem's Mind Games on Broadway

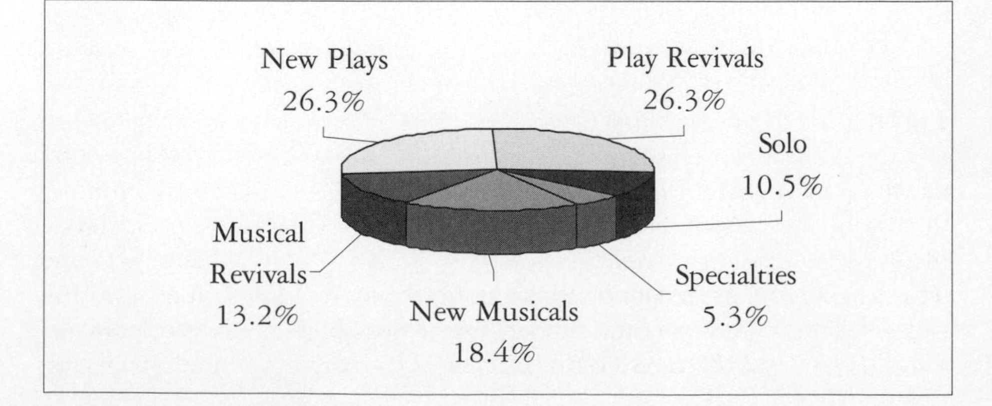

featured actor, lighting and orchestrations). The heartstopping power of *Assassins*—with its pointed commentary on US politics and its satire of the American fetish for fame and notoriety—might have made it an even greater force with which to contend had it been considered a "new" musical. The musical, of course, had a brief initial run at Off Broadway's Playwrights Horizons in 1991 (25 performances), which excluded it from "new" contention. This might make sense except for the 2000 production of Sam Shepard's *True West*—which enjoyed a long run Off Broadway (762 performances) in the 1980s—and the 2002 production of a 19th century Ivan Turgenev play, also deemed "new" in translation by Mike Poulton. In fairness to the Tony Administration Committee, Roundabout Theatre Company, which produced the revival did not petition to be considered a new musical. Artistic director Todd Haimes told *The New York Times*'s Jason Zinoman, "We felt that the committee makes the rules and they should interpret them." Some in the theater community also felt that the dark themes of *Assassins* made it stronger in the revival category—and, it seems, they may have been correct.

Despite the excitement generated by movie star Hugh Jackman hosting the awards ceremony (and winning best actor in a musical for *The Boy From Oz*), there was a big hole at the center of the evening in the absence of Isabelle Stevenson—who died midway through the season in December 2003. Stevenson, to whom this volume is dedicated, led the American Theatre Wing for nearly 40 years. Generously giving her time and resources to the theater community, she was a strong proponent for education and excellence in the theater. For generations of young theater fans, she was emblematic of the glamour of the theater in her sweeping gowns and elegant presentation during the annual Tony Awards television broadcast. Those lucky enough to know her, found her always to be welcoming, warm, gracious—a great ambassador for the American theater.

Broadway's Dog Days

BEFORE THE INK WAS dry on the Tony Award ballots from the previous season, the summer closings began on Broadway this season. Eddie Izzard's star turn in *A Day in the Death of Joe Egg* ended its limited run June 1, 2003—the first day of the season for *The Best Plays Theater Yearbook*. June also saw the closings of *Salome* (June 12), *A Year With Frog and Toad* and *The Play What I Wrote* (June 15), *La Bohème* and *Life (x) 3* (June 29). The only closing in July was the limited-run revival of Athol Fugard's *Master Harold . . . and the Boys* (1981–82 Best Play), which opened six weeks earlier on June 1. It was a respectable production—starring Danny Glover and Michael Boatman—of Fugard's play on corruptions of the human spirit that result from institutional racism.

By the end of August, an innovative revival of *Big River: The Adventures of Huckleberry Finn* had opened (July 24) in a joint production of Roundabout Theatre Company and Deaf West Theatre, using actors who were hearing and deaf. *Avenue Q* staked its first claim to part of the Broadway audience with a July 31 opening at the Golden Theatre after its initial run at Off Off Broadway's Vineyard Theatre. By the end of August, *Say Goodnight, Gracie* departed for a national tour (August 24), with *Man of La Mancha*, *Long Day's Journey Into Night* and *Enchanted April* all dimming their lights August 31. (In fact, everyone dimmed their lights on August 14, when a massive power failure darkened the northeast. Broadway missed one performance, but some downtown theaters missed shows into the weekend.) With those late August closings, Richard Greenberg's *Take Me Out* (2002–03 Best Play) became the lone play running on Broadway until *Golda's Balcony*, a solo performance piece, opened October 15.

Although *Avenue Q* opted for a summer opening on Broadway—traditionally a time when tourists make their way to established productions—it had a good model in a previous Tony Award-winning musical, *Hairspray*, which opened in mid-August 2002. Indeed, *Hairspray* and its more virtuosic sibling, *Movin' Out*, are the only two shows to open during the 2002–2003 season and then survive the trials of 2003–2004.

Force of nature: Tovah Feldshuh in Golda's Balcony. *Photo: Aaron Epstein*

Perhaps other Tony Award hopefuls will begin to follow this summer-premiere trend in the near future and stop loading the March and April schedule with last-minute openings. In the two months and five days leading up to the 2004 Tony Award nominations deadline, 13 of this season's 38 Broadway shows opened (34 percent). It's also worth noting, though, that unlike some recent years, most new Broadway productions this season opened in the first six months.

Other shows from prior seasons that succumbed during 2003–04 included *Nine* (December 14), the long-running revival of *Cabaret*—at 2,377

> Will summer opening become the new model for successful Broadway musicals?

performances, more than double the original production's run—and *Take Me Out* (January 4), *Urinetown* (January 18) and *Gypsy* (May 30).

Most closings during the 2003–04 season also opened during the 38 new productions, 20 didn't make it to May 31. *The Oldest Living Confederate Widow Tells All*, a solo performance piece starring Ellen Burstyn, opened and closed the same night. *Prymate*, which featured the estimable André De Shields as a gorilla (and enough said about that), eked out but five performances. *Bobbi Boland*, starring Farrah Fawcett, closed in previews amid rumors of unstable behavior on and off stage (it is not included in any of our numbers). The last time that a majority of new shows remained open at season's end was 2000–2001, which saw only 28 new productions—10 fewer than this season. Of those 28 new productions, 17 (60 percent) remained open on May 31 (more than a third of which opened in the first six months of the season). Since that season—which was also the last full season before the 2001 terrorist attacks—most new productions of Broadway shows have failed to make it to the end of the season in which they premiered. Does this mean that the streets of the Theater District are running red with accounting ink? For some hapless producers, yes, but hope springs eternal as backers pray for the next *The Lion King*, *The Producers* or *Hairspray* (in the best-case scenario) or a Tony Award nomination (in the least).

Meanwhile, *Variety* reported that box office revenues for the Broadway season reached an all-time high of $771 million, an increase of nearly 7 percent over the previous season. Attendance grew by less than 2 percent (to 11.6 million), however, leading to the conclusion that increased ticket prices—up $3.20 on average this season—accounted for the gains. Broadway attendance has yet to return to the heady days of 2000–01, when attendance reached its high point of 11.9 million. Since that time, the US has reeled under fears of terrorism, a weakened domestic economy and costly wars fought in two foreign nations. The logical argument made again and again by producers is that fear, a shaky economy and war keep people at home. Nathan Lane and Matthew Broderick attempted to counter that argument when they rejoined the cast of *The Producers* for a hand-over-fist moneymaking spree—particularly for the two stars who each earned approximately $100,000 a week—that lasted three months. But even the hyperbole surrounding those appearances couldn't raise *The Producers* from its winter doldrums and the show averaged approximately 77 percent attendance until the two stars' last few weeks, when sellout business became routine.

The Case of Musicals v. Plays

WHEN THE AVERAGE AMERICAN thinks of Broadway theater—*if* he or she bothers to think of it at all—it's a safe bet that the musical is the first thing to come to mind. Despite its roots in the blackface minstrel shows of the early 19th century, the musical has come to represent the American theater (for good and ill). Big, glitzy musical hits are what attract tourists and drive the economy of the Theater District, which employs thousands of performers, technicians, hotel and restaurant workers—and help New York City itself to glow more brightly. These days, though, mounting a Broadway musical is a quick way to lose $10 million. If the pieces of the puzzle that is Broadway success do not align, then a lot of investors lose a lot of money or, as in the case of Rosie O'Donnell's star-crossed production of *Taboo*, one person loses a fortune (an estimated $10 million in O'Donnell's debit column).

These financial risks lead to conservative programming, not only in the political sense but in the sense of investment safety. By Broadway standards, there was nothing "safe" about *Taboo*—a musical based on the lives of singer Boy George and artist Leigh Bowery in 1980s London. But it wasn't as bad as the Times Square touts would have had us believe. Problems? Yes, it had many, but the production was not without its rewards. A "second-night" performance found O'Donnell giving a performance of her own: as the intermission drew to an end, she acknowledged the audience's applause for her, saying to the critics present that night, "We love you."

Risky Boy: Euan Morton as Boy George in Taboo. *Photo: Joan Marcus*

Then, motioning toward the street outside the theater, she went on, "As for the rest of them . . ." (the first-night critics who had not been kind) O'Donnell offered her feelings in a two-handed digital salute. But even relative conservatism has its pitfalls. *Never Gonna Dance*, a pastiche musical based on the film *Swing Time*, was heavy on dance—choreographed by Jerry Mitchell—and otherwise just plain leaden. It was similar to watching a master class in classic theatrical dance steps absent the theatrical spark. Audiences agreed and the show closed after 84 performances.

In fact, though, musicals—new and revived—are more likely to survive to the end of the season (due partly to the promise of summer tourists). In the summer of 2003, only one musical closed (*Man of La Mancha*) and it lasted to the end of August—for our purposes, *La Bohème* (June 29 closing) remains an opera. Of the 12 musicals to open during the 2003–04 season, only *Taboo*, *Never Gonna Dance* and *Big River: The Adventures of Huckleberry Finn* did not survive into the summer of 2004. After its closing, though, *Big River* had embarked on a national tour.

Much has been written about the dearth of plays on Broadway, but this season sported 20 plays—10 new, 10 revivals—as well as two solo performance pieces (*Golda's Balcony* and *The Oldest Living Confederate Widow Tells All*) that were treated as if they were plays. As noted above, of course, the term "new" is relative. Among the new plays were William Nicholson's moving drama about the unraveling of a family, *The Retreat From Moscow*, which was first presented at the Chichester Festival Theatre in 1999. John Lithgow and Eileen Atkins played a couple estranged by decades of emotional battles. Ben Chaplin was the son who finds himself uncomfortably sandwiched between his parents. Bryony Lavery's restrained 1998 play, *Frozen* (a 2003–04 Best Play), had runs at the Birmingham Repertory Theatre and London's National Theatre before MCC Theater opened it in New York and, eventually, on Broadway. Lavery and her play ultimately were tainted by accusations of plagiarism from a doctor who believed her work (and life) had been pillaged in the play's creation. Anne Marie Welsh discusses the contretemps in her essay in this volume and an editor's note addresses the issue directly.

The only play that opened on Broadway without a tryout run abroad, in an institutional theater or Off Broadway was Stephen Belber's *Match*. Starring Frank Langella as a dance teacher with a past, the play also featured Ray Liotta and Jane Adams as a married couple researching dancers of an

Fabulous Frank: Frank Langella in Match. *Photo: Joan Marcus*

earlier generation. Liotta was a tough cop raised by his mother—a former dancer—but it doesn't take a detective to figure out the point of the research. Adams provided a steadying hand as the cop's wife, but the production was all about the acting genius of Langella. Despite the predictability of Belber's conceit, it was a pleasure simply to settle in and be entertained by Langella and company. Belber is a talented young writer who—though he relies on twisting plot points in plays such as *Match* and *Tape*—hasn't yet mastered the art of keeping his audience interested and off-balance. A shakeout production might have helped *Match* before grabbing for the Big Show.

But shakeout productions didn't do much for *Six Dance Lessons in Six Weeks*, which started at the Geffen Playhouse in Los Angeles with Uta Hagen as an aging Floridian and David Hyde Pierce as an irritating dance instructor who makes house calls. The play received tepid notices in Los Angeles, but the pairing of Hagen and Hyde Pierce made critics take note. A planned Broadway production was halted after Hagen had a stroke and was unable to continue. A March 2003 production in Florida, again directed by Arthur Allan Seidelman, featured Rue McClanahan and Mark Hamill. McClanahan withdrew before the Broadway bow—apparently over contract issues—and the indefatigable Polly Bergen joined Hamill. The musical chairs casting of the play as it wound it way to New York was, unfortunately, the most interesting part of the story. As for the great Hagen, she never completely recovered from her illness. When she died January 14, 2004, at age 84, Hagen left behind an immense legacy as an actor of brilliance and as a teacher who provided inspiration to generations of young artists.

What Makes a Best Play?

FOUR OF THIS SEASON'S Best Plays opened on Broadway: *The Violet Hour*, *Anna in the Tropics*, *Frozen* and the musical *Caroline, or Change*—which transferred from Off Broadway. As has become the trend, most of this season's Best Plays came from Off Broadway (six including *Caroline*) and Off Off Broadway (*The Long Christmas Ride Home*). Returning to the topic of programmatic safety once again, if we include revivals there were 14 current and former Best Plays in Broadway theaters. *I Am My Own Wife*, while not technically a revival, was named a Best Play after a run at Playwrights Horizons in 2002–03. Why, the close reader might ask, is *I Am My Own Wife* considered a play and not *Golda's Balcony*? It has to do with the structure of *I Am My Own Wife*, which interweaves characters in a manner that shift it from monologue to play. It is imaginable that *I Am My*

Own Wife might be played, at some point in the future, by an ensemble of actors performing the dozens of characters that Jefferson Mays renders with such virtuosity. The same does not hold true for pieces such as *Golda's Balcony* and its ilk—despite one's eagerness to (twice) see Tovah Feldshuh metamorphose from an attractive middle-aged woman into the force of nature that was Golda Meir. It apparently takes a force of nature to play a force of nature and Feldshuh did so with characteristic power.

Manhattan Theatre Club opened its new Broadway space at the handsomely refurbished Biltmore Theatre with Richard Greenberg's *The Violet Hour*. A 2003–04 Best Play, with an essay by Michael Feingold in this volume, *Violet Hour* was beset by difficulties when two actors (out of five) were replaced during rehearsals. Laura Benanti left the cast over "creative differences," as reported by Robert Hofler in *Variety*. Benanti was replaced by Dagmara Dominczyk. Television star Jasmine Guy departed during previews for what were cited by the company as "medical reasons." One report had Guy slurring her speech and seeming to have difficulty standing—she was replaced at an intermission by her understudy, Robin Miles, and never returned. The melodrama behind the scenes overshadowed Greenberg's haunting drama about consciousness, the effects of time and how "history" is constructed. Adding to the distractions was a character, Gidger, that Greenberg reportedly wrote for Mario Cantone. A hilarious (and wildly self-dramatizing) comedian, Cantone played the role at the South Coast Repertory premiere in 2002 before reprising it on Broadway. Unfortunately, the character of Gidger came across as a gift only for the actor playing the role. Cantone was lively and fun, but neither his character nor his performance meshed with that of Robert Sean Leonard and the others. Still, the play is a worthy drama and likely to find a better production down the road.

Even though we're now considering the Broadway Best Plays, we should pause here to explore what some believe was a cursed season for the Manhattan Theatre Club. With Broadway successes under its belt in recent years (*Proof*, *The Tale of the Allergist's Wife*), MTC had been riding high in press and popular esteem. But with the opening of the Broadway space at the Biltmore this season, the company seemed to stumble every time it took a step. Even before the casting problems with *The Violet Hour*, MTC artistic director Lynne Meadow had engaged in a feud with longtime collaborator Terrence McNally. A producer of no small vision, Meadow commissioned a play from McNally for the opening of the Biltmore, *Dedication*, which she then rejected. As she told Alex Witchel of *The New York Times*, "I read a draft and did not feel it was ready for production."

Dedication was the first play of McNally's scheduled to appear on an MTC stage since the company's 1998 production of *Corpus Christi.* MTC ignited a fiery protest from the arts community when it first announced the cancellation of *Corpus Christi* due to complaints (and threats) from fundamentalists over its intertwined Christian and gay themes. MTC relented and ran the production amid intense security. Theatergoers passed through a gauntlet of pastel-bereted, kneeling protesters that surrounded City Center and prayed loudly. Once past the protesters, theatergoers were then screened by metal detectors and security guards before entering the theater space. McNally did not take the rejection of *Dedication* well, a breach emerged in a longtime artistic relationship and his play was replaced with *The Violet Hour.*

Then, only a month after *The Violet Hour*'s tempestuous pre-opening process (and lukewarm reviews) on Broadway, the company had artistic troubles Off Broadway. Just two weeks before Mary Tyler Moore was slated to open in Neil Simon's new play, *Rose's Dilemma*, the star withdrew from the show after receiving harsh criticism from the playwright for not knowing her lines during previews. Jason Zinoman reported in *The New York Times* that Moore had been wearing an earpiece through which she received prompting. She was replaced by understudy Patricia Hodges, but the play—about a woman who cannot escape her dead lover's ghost—never gained its footing.

In February, Regina Taylor's *Drowning Crow*, a quasi-hip updating (and relocation) of Chekhov's *The Seagull*, opened to droves of aging Manhattan Theatre Club subscribers departing the theater during the show. Some couldn't understand the Gullah dialect of the island characters, others found the shifting style of the dialogue (hip-hop rhymes, blank verse, realism) to be unsettling. It might be argued that Chekhov's meditation on art, death and the death of art needs no updating. Still, a more coherent, focused production of Taylor's adaptation might have illuminated these issues for a new generation. Despite a spirited ensemble led by Anthony Mackie and Alfre Woodard, the production never rose above its muddled direction.

There were high points in the MTC season Off Broadway, but the first show out of the blocks in June 2003, *Last Dance*, provided a hint of the bumpy road ahead. Marsha Norman's play about a romantic, middle-aged novelist living abroad was dismissed by critics for the florid quality of its dialogue and its plot. The outlook improved with the October opening of Rona Munro's *Iron*, a prison drama about a woman confronted by her teenage daughter 15 years after she murdered the girl's father. Where *Last Dance* managed only 40 performances, *Iron* exactly doubled that number

OFF BROADWAY SEASON 2003–2004

Productions in a continuing run on May 31, 2004 in bold
Productions honored as Best Plays *selections in italics*
Best Plays *from prior seasons are noted with a date in parentheses*

NEW PLAYS (36)

Last Dance (MTC)
A Bad Friend (LCT)
The Notebooks of Leonardo da Vinci (Second Stage)
Flesh and Blood (NYTW)
Portraits
Omnium Gatherum
Recent Tragic Events (Playwrights)
Living Out (Second Stage)
Rounding Third
Beckett/Albee
Iron (MTC)
Private Jokes, Public Places
The Beard of Avon (NYTW)
Juvenilia (Playwrights)
Nothing but the Truth (LCT)
The Story (Public)
Rose's Dilemma (MTC)
Eden (Irish Rep)
Valhalla (NYTW)
Roulette (EST)
Magic Hands Freddy
Big Bill (LCT)
Bug
The Moonlight Room
Wintertime (Second Stage)
Small Tragedy (Playwrights)
Embedded (Public)
From Door to Door
Ears on a Beatle
Well (Public)
Sarah, Sarah (MTC)
Intimate Apparel (Roundabout)
Between Us (MTC)
Guinea Pig Solo (Public/Labyrinth)
Light Raise the Roof (NYTW)
Chinese Friends (Playwrights)

PLAY REVIVALS (10)

The Persians (NAT)
Ghosts (BAM)
The Importance of Being Earnest (Aquila Theatre Company)
Henry V (Public)
The Two Noble Kinsmen (Public)
Hamlet (New 42nd/Jeune Lune)
Pericles (BAM/TFANA)
A Midsummer Night's Dream (BAM)
The Normal Heart (Public/Worth Street)
Homebody/Kabul (01–02) (BAM)

NEW MUSICALS (8)

The Thing About Men
Wilder (Playwrights)
Fame on 42nd Street
Caroline, or Change (Public)
Ministry of Progress
Johnny Guitar
Bare: A Pop Opera
The Joys of Sex

MUSICAL REVIVALS (5)

The Prince and the Pauper
Iolanthe (G&S Players)
H.M.S Pinafore (G&S Players)
The Mikado (G&S Players)
Sweeney Todd (NYC Opera)

REVUES (6)

Mack the Knife
Capitol Steps: Between Iraq and a Hard Place
Listen to My Heart: The Songs of David Friedman
Our Sinatra: A Musical Celebration
The Musical of Musicals–The Musical (York)

REVUES (*cont'd*)
They Wrote That?

SOLO (21)
Bad Dates (Playwrights)
Edge
That Day in September
The Love-Hungry Farmer (Irish Rep)
Berkshire Village Idiot
Flow (NYTW)
A Rooster in the Henhouse
Nobody Don't Like Yogi
Lypsinka! As I Lay Lip-Synching
Women on Fire (Cherry Lane)
Sholom Aleichem–Now You're Talking!
Addicted . . . a Comedy of Substance
Dinner With Demons (Second Stage)
The Last Letter (TFANA)
Max Morath: Ragtime and Again (York)
Bridge and Tunnel
My Kitchen Wars
More
The Tricky Part
Biro (Public)
The Two and Only (Atlantic)

SPECIALTIES (9)
Trumbo
Can-Can (Encores!)
Cookin'
Silent Laughter
Pardon My English (Encores!)
The Marijuana-Logues
Chef's Theater: A Musical Feast
Loudmouth
Bye Bye Birdie (Encores!)

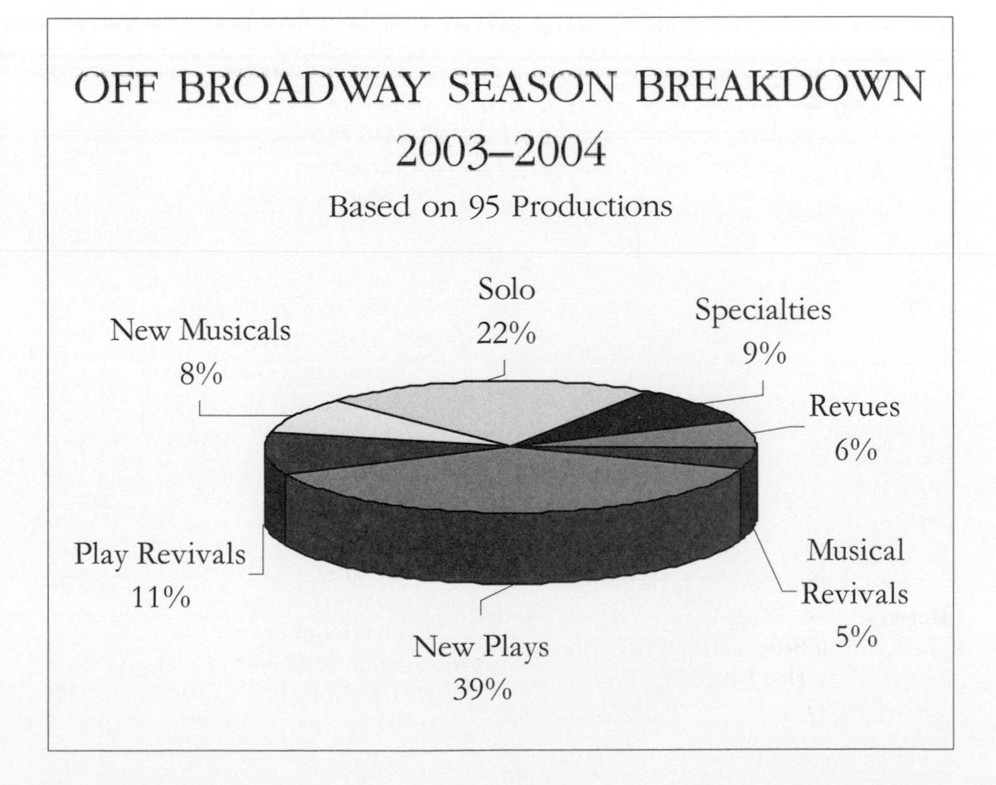

on the strength of Lisa Emery's powerful performance as the mother—and better word-of-mouth than critical reaction. With the March production of Daniel Goldfarb's *Sarah, Sarah*, which pits immigrant dreams against the power of love for a child, MTC offered yet another play with a challenging female role. J. Smith Cameron portrayed the domineering title character in the first act and her own granddaughter in the second. Ably supported by Richard Masur in both halves of the play, Cameron shined a light on the paths to healing and forgiveness—even if they sometimes lie only in imagination. *Sarah, Sarah* continued its run through the end of our season. Finally, Joe Hortua's *Between Us* explored the familiar terrain of college friends who travel divergent paths and find themselves polar opposites in middle age. The strong cast of Kate Jennings Grant, David Harbour, Daphne Rubin-Vega and Bradley White teamed with director Christopher Ashley to keep the audience interested and amused—but the shadow of Donald Margulies's Pulitzer Prize-winning *Dinner With Friends* hovered nearby.

With Margulies's *Sight Unseen* (a 1991–92 Best Play), MTC ended its first Broadway season at the Biltmore on a more positive note than had sounded earlier. Laura Linney, who played a young interviewer in the original production—a turning point in Margulies's playwriting career—returned in the role of a woman left behind by an artist who has turned his life into a commodity. While the focus of the play should be on the artist and the compromises he makes to attain success, only Linney managed to hold the audience's interest in a performance of uncommon richness—though we have come to rely on that sort of work from her. The talented Ben Shenkman—a late replacement for Liev Schreiber, who reportedly departed to direct a film—played the artist overmatched by his moral choices. One quick question: What's happening in the MTC casting department?

Back to Best Plays

IN COMPILING A LIST of Best Plays this season, perhaps the most interesting outcome was the enthusiasm among members of the editorial board for a play that lasted a scant 113 performances on Broadway: Nilo Cruz's *Anna in the Tropics*. It is particularly puzzling given the critical reception to the play when it opened in November. Although many criticized Emily Mann for static direction and some even indulged in fantasies that one male character was having an (unscripted, unmentioned, unlikely) affair with another man (unpresent), apparently critics privately thought more highly of the play than was published in their various outlets. Can this be a late reversal of the out-of-town Pulitzer Prize backlash? The reference here, of course, is to the critical carving of plays that manage to win a Pulitzer before New York critics get (or is it "take"?) their shot(s) at new work. In addition to *Anna in the Tropics*, *The Kentucky Cycle* (1993–94) experienced a similar fate.

The Broadway production of Cruz's play, which opened at the Royale, was admittedly a bit slight for a theater of that size. But a reading of the play at South Coast Repertory in May 2003 was held in a similarly sized space and it impressed its audience, which included a group of critics seated in the last row. A romance about the rise of industrialization in the Florida cigar industry—and a concomitant loss of humanity—*Anna* first appeared at the tiny New Theatre in Coral Gables, Florida. That version of the play was nominated for the American Theatre Critics/Steinberg New Play Award, which it won before the Pulitzer committee's deliberations. Although *Best Plays* published an essay on the Steinberg-winning play last year, editorial board member Christine Dolen was asked to expand her thoughts and consider the development of the play from that first production in Florida.

Other present and past Best Plays on Broadway this season included a new musical (*Caroline, or Change*), six play revivals (*Master Harold . . . and*

Southern beauty: Ashley Judd in Cat on a Hot Tin Roof. *Photo: Joan Marcus*

the Boys, *Cat on a Hot Tin Roof*, *The Caretaker*, *Sly Fox*, *Jumpers*, *A Raisin in the Sun*) and two musical revivals (*Wonderful Town*, *Fiddler on the Roof*). Although this seems to underline the "investment safety" argument made above, it cannot be asserted that the revived Best Plays were as well received this season as they were in their respective premieres.

The latest new production of *Cat on a Hot Tin Roof* (a 1954–55 Best Play) came—like so many other Broadway productions over the past several decades—via London where American actor Brendan Fraser starred in late 2001 as Brick with Frances O'Connor as Maggie. Ned Beatty played Big Daddy in both productions (and, it turned out, offstage). The New York production starred Jason Patric as Brick and Ashley Judd as Maggie. Patric seemed to e-mail his performance from a hotel across town and Judd's luminous screen presence was so light onstage that it evaporated. As a result, the critics were not kind—but neither were they brutal. The Times Square ne'er-do-wells left that task to none other than Big Daddy himself: Ned Beatty. In a *New York Times* interview with Robin Pogrebin titled, "Movie Stars Onstage: Big Daddy Speaks Out," Beatty made some less-than-politic comments about his young costars. However dead-on his remarks were, they were widely believed to be the reason why Beatty's convincing performance received no Tony Award nomination. Beatty on Judd:

> She is a sweetie, and yet she doesn't have a whole lot of tools. But she works very hard.

And on Patric:

> He's gotten better all the time, but his is a different journey.

Beatty, a stage veteran, expressed regrets at needing film actors to draw an audience to the theater:

> The reality is, we have a lot of actors out there doing theater. In theater you want to go from here to there, you want it to be about something. [. . .] Stage actors learn how to do that. Film actors often don't even think about it. They do what the director wants them to do, and they never inform their performance with—call it what you wish—through-line, objective. I think we've got those actors out there, and I think Broadway could be richer if it exploited that.

And then he lowered the boom:

> I lucked out because I drew Brendan Fraser the first time. [. . .] He's great at stagecraft, knows how to go from the beginning to the middle to the end. I must tell you, that can be lacking in what we're doing.

In rehearsal halls (and restaurant kitchens) all over the country, one could imagine struggling stage actors thinking, by turns, "You go, Big Daddy," and "Thank God, I'm not working with that guy."

Roundabout Theatre Company's production of *The Caretaker* (a 1961–62 Best Play) joined Patrick Stewart, Kyle MacLachlan and relative newcomer Aidan Gillen in one of Harold Pinter's classic tales about the terror underpinning human relationships. Gillen generated positive notices for his portrayal of the dark, aggressive Mick. But the production languished in an almost lazy mode of domestic comedy: call it *Two Guys and a Bum*. Without the terror—or at least some menace—the Pinteresque quality disappeared. The production itself did so after 63 performances.

Among the revived Best Plays, *Sly Fox* (1976–77), *Jumpers* (1973–74), *A Raisin in the Sun* (1958–59), *Wonderful Town* (1952–53) and *Fiddler on the Roof* (1964–65) are the ones that managed to last through the end of the season. The cast for Larry Gelbart's *Sly Fox*, was a remarkable collection of comic talents led by Richard Dreyfuss, Eric Stoltz, Bob Dishy, Rene Auberjonois, Bronson Pinchot, Peter Scolari and Professor Irwin Corey. Add to the mix saucy Rachel York with Elizabeth Berkley as a sweet young thing, and it seems a recipe for box office magic. Unfortunately, this Old West adaptation of Ben Jonson's *Volpone* staggered under the weight of an intricate plot that did not mesh with a mélange of acting styles—each traveling down slightly different tracks.

In Tom Stoppard's *Jumpers*, Simon Russell Beale played a befuddled philosopher with a gorgeous wife (Essie Davis) who tries to make sense of the notion of God, the universe and humanity's place in it. After approximately 20 minutes of the intellectual humor, the luster dimmed even for the more philosophically inclined and many orchestra seats were vacant for the second act.

One of the great shames of the Broadway theater community was corrected when Sean Combs—a hip-hop star and entrepreneur who has also gone by the names of Puff Daddy and P. Diddy—led a cast of superb women in the first Broadway revival of Lorraine Hansberry's classic, *A Raisin in the Sun*. The shame is that it took more than 45 years for this marvelous play about human aspiration and the struggle for a piece of the American Dream to come back to Broadway. (As John Leguizamo said some years ago, "They don't call it the Great *White* Way for nothing.") Combs, a novice actor, gave a performance that lacked the depth and nuance of someone with more experience—for instance, the superb actor who played Asagai in this production, Teagle F. Bougere. What emerged under Kenny Leon's increasingly reliable direction, though, was a new interpretation highlighting the struggles of the women played by Phylicia Rashad, Audra McDonald and Sanaa Lathan. Although there were times when it felt as though Rashad was "working the audience" a bit, she and

Hansberry's women: Phylicia Rashad, Audra McDonald and Sanaa Lathan in Raisin in the Sun. *Photo: Joan Marcus*

McDonald richly deserved their Tony Awards—it was McDonald's fourth for a featured role.

Although it took more than 50 years to mount the first revival of the musical *Wonderful Town*, it wasn't the same sort of cultural oversight mentioned with regard to *A Raisin in the Sun*. Where *Raisin* is a distinguished cultural artifact, *Wonderful Town* is a charming tale about two sisters from Ohio who get into all sorts of adventures in New York City. Based on Joseph Fields and Jerome Chodorov's long-running 1940s comedy, *My Sister Eileen*—itself based on stories by Ruth McKenney—the musical version included lyrics by the venerable Adolph Green and Betty Comden with music by maestro Leonard Bernstein. Although the original received five 1954 Tony Awards (best musical, actress, scene design, choreography and musical director), the current production managed only to win for Kathleen Marshall's choreography. Donna Murphy, who won previous Tony Awards for *Passion* (1994) and *The King and I* (1996), missed quite a few performances when Tony voters where scheduled to attend. The theater-gossip columnist for the *New York Post*, Michael Riedel, helped to lead a campaign (of sorts) against Murphy due to her frequent absences—which were reportedly due to vocal problems. The columnist needn't have bothered, though, because Murphy's illness kept her from being seen by enough voters. Idina Menzel (*Wicked*) took home the Tony.

Riedel was again to be part of the story after the opening of *Fiddler on the Roof*. Jason Zinoman reported in *The New York Times* that the *Post* columnist was pushed to the floor by director David Leveaux after "insulting English directors who, [Riedel] said, ruin classic American musicals." That Riedel was merely expressing a widely held opinion didn't make it any less painful for the British director, who had been pummeled in print for his production's supposed lack of "Jewishness." Featuring Alfred Molina as a decidedly unstereotypical Tevye, this *Fiddler* aimed to open the audience's eyes to other possibilities for the portrayal of life in the Jewish *shtetl*. But American audiences—Jewish and otherwise—will brook no trifling with their cherished theatrical icons. As one elderly Jewish legend of the theater was heard to say, "You want my review? No Jews, no Tevye, no heart, no show."

Tony, Tony, Tony

EVEN *CAROLINE, OR CHANGE* by Tony Kushner and his musical collaborator, Jeanine Tesori, was such a risky venture that it took more than 20 producers above the title to get it transferred to Broadway. Although it continued to run at the end of the season, it is unlikely to recoup its investment (neither did *Angels in America*, though it finally entered profit on the road). Kushner's semi-autobiographical tale about a Jewish boy in 1963 Louisiana whose mother has died and whose father is emotionally distant puzzled critics and divided audiences. The musical breaks ground in a thrilling way by first employing an innovative device in which household appliances come to life and perform songs that reflect the frustrations of the boy's African-American housekeeper, Caroline. These innovations continue in several other scenes focused on African-American life amid the civil rights struggle. But when *Caroline* (a 2003–04 Best Play) shifts to the concerns of the Jewish family, the narrative becomes a mush of Oedipal anxiety and identity confusion.

Despite these flaws, which were only minimally amended for the Broadway transfer, the musical's childlike rhyme schemes and its recitative style, the raw power of the piece made it a natural choice for *Best Plays*. That it is a deeply personal work for the playwright is underlined by his advocacy for transferring the Off Broadway production from the Public Theater to Broadway—he reportedly "made the rounds" himself to convince chary producers to open their wallets and rolodexes. According to Robert Simonson of Playbill On-Line, Kushner also served as keynote speaker for the Spring Road Conference of the League of American Theatres and

Producers early one morning just before the Tony Award voting—during which he skewered critics with doggerel not unlike some of the recitative lyrics in *Caroline*. He even engaged in a heated exchange with *Chicago Sun-Times* critic Hedy Weiss, who wrote in the May 9 edition of her newspaper, in part:

> Unfortunately, Kushner, in the classic style of a self-loathing Jew, has little but revulsion for his own roots. You can hear it and feel it throughout, most notably when the Gellmans, modestly successful first generation Jews, sing their Hanukkah songs.

After an e-mail exchange between playwright and critic, which was not published, Kushner wrote a letter to the *Sun-Times*, which said, in part:

> I don't respond publicly to reviews. I've wanted to, of course, but it can't be done to any good purpose. I've learned that a good play lasts a lot longer than a bad review. So I keep my irritation to myself.
>
> [. . .]
>
> *Caroline* has received many reviews—some great, some mixed, some negative. None has accused me of me being a Jewish anti-Semite.

Kushner argued that there is no specific corroboration for "her charge" and continued:

> It goes beyond the bounds of criticism, and indeed of ethical behavior, to make such a charge without accountability.

He later concluded:

> I am immensely proud of being Jewish—a sentence I should not have to write in response to Ms. Weiss's ugly and baseless charge. I have written extensively about being Jewish. Nothing makes me prouder than hearing, as I often do, that my work is identified as Jewish-American literature. My anger at this critic and her editors for accusing me of hatred for the Jewish people—for my people—exceeds my abilities to express it.

The clash made news in Chicago where the weekly *Chicago Reader* noted that Kushner and Weiss had clashed before on matters of Mideast politics. In an April 10, 2002, article for the *Sun-Times*, for instance, Weiss wrote about a Kushner appearance in nearby Evanston:

> If only he had posed a few more complex questions to himself before launching into a stock anti-Israeli diatribe that no one—either among the distinguished panelists onstage or the students and general public in the audience—attempted to probe further.

Clearly, this critic and this playwright have issues that go beyond aesthetics and right into the heart of identity politics.

Blake Eskin, editor of Nextbook.org—the website of "a national initiative to promote books that illuminate 3,000 years of Jewish civilization" sponsored by Keren Keshet (The Rainbow Foundation)—brought a more thoughtful perspective to the dispute. In an article published after the Tony Awards, Eskin said he couldn't "stop thinking" about the controversy. He wished that Weiss had not employed the "self-loathing Jew" term—it's probably fair to say that, by now, she wishes she'd never used it—because, Eskin wrote, it stifled "further critical conversation about the play or the viewer's reactions."

Eskin's final paragraph is reprinted here, in total:

> Kushner complained that "there is not a single line of text to corroborate her charge," but musical theater is more than text, and this production of *Caroline*, held together by director George C. Wolfe's swift, inventive staging, yields supporting evidence in harmony and gesture. In January, before *Caroline*'s transfer to Broadway, I left the Public Theater dazzled by the soulful singing appliances, but wondering what klezmer music had to do with the assimilated Gellmans of Louisiana, and why 9-year-old Noah exhibited such an insensitivity to rhythm when he dances with the children of his family's black maid. This was rehearsed awkwardness, not a failing of actor Harrison Chad. Noah's body language communicated a fundamental discomfort with himself and an anger at his dysfunctional family (empty widowed father, hopeless Northern stepmother, grandparents with cartoonish old-country manners). For Noah and for theatergoers, the Gellman family defines the Jewish universe. And I could easily imagine him growing into someone like Louis Ironson, the self-conscious to the point of self-flagellating gay intellectual of Kushner's *Angels in America*. Louis is Jewish and full of self-loathing, which is not necessarily the same as being a self-hating Jew; this may be what Weiss is getting at.

John Istel's essay on the musical in this volume offers further perspective on what's at stake in this musical, how it reflects a moment in time and how it may project our own theatrical future.

It was a big year for Kushner on the small screen as well. The Mike Nichols version of *Angels in America* first played on cable television's HBO in December 2003 as a two-part, six-chapter production with a screenplay by the playwright. *The New York Times* pulled out the stops in its coverage of the epic drama about the AIDS crisis in the Age of Reagan with a Sunday Arts and Leisure cover featuring a photo of Kushner that covered nearly half of the page. The accompanying texts included nearly 4,000 words on the playwright's life and work, and a 1,500-word appreciation of the HBO film. But the *Times* was hardly alone, in the two months leading to the premiere of both parts nearly 100 articles appeared in publications around the country.

Some who had seen multiple stage productions found the film version awkward in its use of fantasy sequences and special effects (although this may be a minority opinion)—and a large number of devotees were nonplused by the elimination of the line, "*Very* Steven Spielberg" at a crucial moment. The HBO production, however, did introduce the play and writer to a larger constituency than is ever possible onstage. Missing from the film version, though, are the simultaneously staged scenes of love and betrayal that drive right into the theatrical heart of the play. Kushner, in collaboration with Nichols, also made the gay Republican character of Joe Pitt much more sympathetic in the film—in the play he appears irredeemable. An element that seemed to be de-emphasized in the HBO version is that described in the play's subtitle: *A Gay Fantasia on National Themes*. This subtitular inversion of the heteronormative American experience is essential to support the perspective Kushner ultimately espouses in the final moments of the epic. It may have been mere coincidence, but a reissue of the printed play—which accompanied the HBO film—eliminated the subtitle from the outer cover. The film had an impact on the critical community that was not unlike the stage version: it won five Golden Globe Awards from the Hollywood Foreign Press Association. It later received a record 11 Emmy Awards in the television miniseries category.

We cannot complete our Kushnerian homage, before noting the return of *Homebody/Kabul* to New York. A 2001–02 Best Play following its initial run at New York Theatre Workshop, the play was revised for productions around the country and is now in what must be considered its final form. In its return to New York during the Brooklyn Academy of Music's spring season Off Broadway, the play again featured Linda Emond in the role of the stifled Homebody who dreams of a mystical Afghanistan of the mind. Although members of the NYTW company returned to the production—notably Rita Wolf and Bill Camp—the biggest improvement was in the casting of Maggie Gyllenhaal as the Homebody's daughter, Priscilla, who struggles to find her own identity in a world that tends to de-voice women. The shift from Homebody's loquacious, meandering monologue to the Afghan setting made better dramatic sense in Frank Galati's new production. Despite the exquisite Emond's detailed performance, however, there almost surely is another 30 to 45 minutes throughout the play that could be trimmed without harming its dramatic intent—indeed, it might well enhance the effect.

More on Broadway

WHEN IT WAS ANNOUNCED that Hugh Jackman would star in a 2002 New York workshop of *The Boy From Oz*—which had been rewritten for American consumption by Martin Sherman after a successful two-year run (1998–2000) in Sydney, Australia—they might as well have engraved his 2004 Tony Award on the spot. As loose-limbed showman Peter Allen, Jackman finally satisfied the theater community's desire to see him on a Broadway stage. Many had been disappointed when Jackman did not join the 2002 transfer from London of Trevor Nunn's clunky revival of *Oklahoma!* The handsome Aussie apparently took a respite from the stage to earn a few million dollars in films—and good for him. Though *The Boy From Oz* had little to recommend it other than Allen's delightful pop songs and a dead-on Judy Garland impersonation by Isabel Keating, Jackman's persona charmed audiences and made him a lock for the top theater awards. Even his wife was convinced. According to Robert Hofler in *Variety*, Jackman's wife had told him that if he didn't win the Tony Award she would "run down Broadway naked."

The other show from "Oz" was an entry more literary than literal. Based on the Gregory Maguire novel *Wicked: The Life and Times of the Wicked Witch of the West*, Stephen Schwartz and Winnie Holzman's musical

Persona grata*: Hugh Jackman in* The Boy From Oz*. Photo: Joan Marcus*

was a monstrous machine of a show. It seemed as though every trick of the designer's trade was employed in the Tony Award-winning work of Eugene Lee's scenery and Susan Hilferty's costumes: monkeys and witches flew, the Wizard's clanking head was a frightful (and amusing) invention. Audiences—particularly teenage girls, it seemed, on two separate visits to the show—were mesmerized not by the production itself but by the overpowering pop-style singing of Tony winner Idina Menzel and her pixieish counterpart, Kristin Chenoweth. More and more, there is less and less singing on Broadway, with the vacuum filled by relatively on-pitch wailing to the rafters aided by zealous sound designers.

The last (and least) of new Broadway musicals to consider is *Bombay Dreams*, a parody of "Bollywood" movies: Indian films that conform to a conventional structure in their storytelling. The problem *Bombay* faced, though, was that the mainstream Broadway audience (i.e., the white middle class) was unlikely to be in on the joke—when there was one—or to understand when the show slipped from "honest" Bollywood form into parody. The show bumped along into the summer.

Little Shop of Horrors, which was overshadowed by the revivals of *Wonderful Town* and *Assassins*, also managed to survive the season with a lively production starring Hunter Foster and Kerry Butler. *Little Shop* may have suffered from overexposure in the various forms it had previously appeared: the original Roger Corman film in 1960, the long-running 1982 Off Broadway musical and the 1986 film of the musical. Perhaps, though, it was that original Off Broadway run of more than five years (1982–87) for a total of 2,209 performances inspired producers to invest $10 million. After an initial run in Coral Gables—with generally positive reviews by Florida critics, who were also supportive of the prior season's dreadful *Urban Cowboy*—the show was closed, director Connie Grappo and other key cast members were fired (except Foster), Jerry Zaks was hired to direct, roles were recast and the show was retooled. For many who were familiar with the original *Little Shop*—or at least the film version—the memory of the spectacular original Audrey, Ellen Greene, was never overcome. The New York critics were mixed, but audiences must have figured out that this would be one case where a rented video might be preferable to a live performance (particularly at $99 per ticket). The musical never did sellout business. Its best weeks were during the Christmas and New Year's holidays. Maybe there was room for only one puppet show on Broadway. Sorry, Audrey II.

Playwright Eliam Kraiem's topical Broadway debut, *Sixteen Wounded*, was an odd coupling of a "sleeper" Arab terrorist—one waiting to be activated by his handler—who is befriended by a Jewish Holocaust survivor. The terrific cast included Judd Hirsch, Jan Maxwell, Martha Plimpton, Omar Metwally and Waleed F. Zuaiter, but the playwright's contrived relationships and moral quandaries offered little in the way of subtlety or nuance. It closed after 12 performances.

Two bona fide classic plays and one American comedy that aspires to those heights round out the play revivals on Broadway this season. We'll start with the least and end on a higher note: Ben Hecht and Charles MacArthur's *Twentieth Century*, which first premiered in December 1932, was regarded by Brooks Atkinson—that most generous of *New York Times* critics—as "something less than perfect entertainment" in the original staging by George Abbott. A 1950 revival by the American National Theatre and Academy was directed by José Ferrer with Gloria Swanson and Ferrer starring. Eighteen years after the original, Atkinson softened his stance somewhat calling it, "hilarious when it was new [and . . .] still uproarious." The latest *Times*man to hold the "hot seat," Ben Brantley, waxed rhapsodic over the charms of co-star Anne Heche before settling on, "you start to realize there are reasons it hasn't been revived on Broadway in more than 50 years." The usually astute Alec Baldwin—his *Macbeth* at the Public Theater

Wacky crew: Alec Baldwin, Dan Butler, Anne Heche, Julie Halston and Tom Aldredge in Twentieth Century. *Photo: Joan Marcus*

aside—played Heche's opposite number in this Roundabout Theatre Company revival about the con-artist nature of theater producers. Unfortunately, Baldwin seemed always a bit behind the comic beat—as if he hadn't the stamina to push through to the punch. Heche, however, continued to shine her Broadway star, which first rose as a replacement in *Proof*.

It is hard to choose which of the classics offered by Lincoln Center Theater was the greater production. Jack O'Brien's staging of *Henry IV* featured a fine adaptation by Dakin Matthews of the two-part saga into a single, unified work. O'Brien's cast also had higher wattage in terms of star power: Kevin Kline, Dana Ivey, Ethan Hawke, Audra McDonald, Richard Easton and Michael Hayden carried the larger roles in the production. Jonathan Miller's version of *King Lear* featured the superb Christopher Plummer as a great king who de-legitimizes his entire kingdom and throws society into chaos. The *Lear* cast was composed mostly of Canadian actors—the production first played at the Stratford Festival of Canada. Besides Plummer, the best known to many eyes was Broadway musical star (and Canadian) Brent Carver in the unlikely role of Edgar. Instead of focusing on comparisons, though, it is far wiser to acknowledge the achievement of André Bishop and Bernard Gersten in bringing these truly remarkable productions to a New York theater audience—even if the large subscription rolls at LCT kept a more general public from seeing either show.

Solo performances were down this Broadway season when compared to the past couple of years. Only four solo shows opened—*I Am My Own Wife* counts as a play—two of which were discussed above. As for the other two, John Leguizamo returned with his *Sexaholix . . . a Love Story* and Barbara Cook returned to croon for fans onstage at Lincoln Center's Vivian Beaumont Theater. Jackie Mason eschewed the solo route to Broadway this season with a musical revue, *Laughing Room Only*, which closed after only 14 performances. It was Mason's eighth Broadway show going back to the ill-fated *A Teaspoon Every Four Hours*, which played one performance in 1969. As the season drew to a close, a final specialty act opened with mentalist Marc Salem in *Marc Salem's Mind Games on Broadway*, which ran on Monday evenings when *I Am My Own Wife* was dark.

Theater for One?

THE NUMBER OF NEW Off Broadway productions rose by 20 percent this season from 79 in 2002–03 to 95 in 2003–04. Although new-play production accounted for a substantial percentage of the increase (36 new plays this year, 30 last), solo performance pieces jumped from 14 in 2002–03 to 21 in 2003–04. Taken alone a 50 percent increase is pretty impressive, but when one considers the increase over the past two seasons the trend is even more remarkable: the number of new solo productions Off Broadway has *tripled* across three seasons. Meanwhile, play revivals were down (slightly) as were new musicals. Without the Gilbert and Sullivan Players and a New York City Opera revival of *Sweeney Todd*, the category of musical revivals would not exist this season—as it did not last year. Specialty productions were up slightly, but is that a good thing? (And if one removed shows with chefs, the number would be flat from the previous season.) Despite the increase in new-play production over the previous season, Off Broadway is still down when compared with the 2001–02 season (44 new plays that season)—which was the season of the terrorist attacks on the World Trade Center. Why are producers continuing to shift toward solo shows? Is it because there are too few multicharacter plays to produce? Are playwrights writing for "the marketplace"?

The monodrama often presents an opportunity for the playwright to unburden his or her secret heart to a willing audience in a public confessional. During the 2003–04 season, 9 of the 21 solo pieces involved writers telling stories from their own lives. Imagine for a moment that Eugene O'Neill decided to do *Long Day's Journey Into Night* as a monologue or envision Tennessee Williams sitting at a table regaling an audience about the Gentleman Caller in *The Glass Menagerie*. Too ridiculous? Perhaps. But how many possible dramatic masterpieces are being channeled into events that might be better handled in a therapist's office? The personal travails recounted Off Broadway this season ranged from the effects of September 11, to the humiliations of growing up in New England, to a Mr. Mom scenario, to a variety of issues relating to self-esteem, sexual abuse and/or political oppression. Anyone who thinks this all sounds hyperbolic can look it up in the Plays Produced Off Broadway section of this volume. Even when the writer was not present onstage, solo performance pieces often carried an overtone of victimization—some real, some contrived for dramatic effect.

Among the monodramas that rose above the mundane were Theresa Rebeck's *Bad Dates* in which delightful Julie White kept audiences amused with edgy tales of dating (and life) chaos. Anyone who loves Yogi Berra could not have failed to enjoy *Nobody Don't Like Yogi* by Thomas Lysaght. While it was a pleasure to see Ben Gazzara's return to the stage—he was the original Brick in *Cat on a Hot Tin Roof* and has performed in several other Broadway shows—there was little in the piece that was new or fresh.

American dreamer: Sarah Jones in Bridge and Tunnel. *Photo: Brian Michael Thomas*

John Epperson returned as Lypsinka in *Lypsinka! As I Lay Lip-Synching*, which moved to an Off Broadway run at the Minetta Lane after a month at Show nightclub. Judith Ivey brought heat to a lackluster collection of monologues by Irene O'Garden, *Women on Fire*. O'Garden's dramatic ruminations on the lives of middle-aged women, unfortunately, dealt in predictable stereotypes giving the text little in the way of sizzle. A woman of quiet fire, Kathleen Chalfant, gave life to Frederick Wiseman's adaptation of a Vasily Grossman novel in *The Last Letter*. Produced by Theatre for a New Audience, the piece was a searing (if brief) tale of life in a wartime Jewish ghetto. Sarah Jones's *Bridge and Tunnel*, frequently rumored to be bound for Broadway, was a tour-de-force of powerful performance and witty observation. Framed as a "poetry slam" in a borough of New York City, Jones unearthed personal stories that reflected an international culture of aspiration. It was a poignant demonstration of what Mayor David Dinkins used to call the "gorgeous mosaic" of our great metropolis.

New Space, New Plays

BUCKING THE MONODRAMATIC TREND was Roundabout Theatre Company in its new Laura Pels Theatre. Located in the former American Place Theatre on West 46th Street, the renovation of the theater and the building were largely underwritten by the Harold and Mimi Steinberg

Charitable Trust. In honor of the trust, which has been an significant supporter of *The Best Plays Theater Yearbook*, the building itself was named the Harold and Miriam Steinberg Center for Theatre. During a marquee lighting ceremony in the theater, Roundabout artistic director Todd Haimes told the gathering that, when the company was forced to close *Cabaret* at the old Henry Miller Theatre due to a construction problem in the neighborhood, an unsolicited (and generous) check arrived from the trust.

Playwright Paula Vogel, who started her life in theater as Wynn Handman's assistant in the same building, spoke passionately about the connections in the theater that night. It was a Vogel play, *The Mineola Twins*, that closed the old Laura Pels Theatre when Roundabout was evicted from the Criterion Center several years ago. The playwright was excited, however, that the first tenant of the new Laura Pels Theatre would be *Intimate Apparel* by Lynn Nottage—the first undergraduate student whose work Vogel produced at Brown University. Vogel went on to remind the audience that the Steinberg Trust had helped facilitate much of her work as a teacher through its grants for student productions.

The Pulitzer Prize-winning playwright (and *Best Plays* honoree) also said:

> Playwrights in the theatre need, not the light of a new day, but the light of a new marquee, the light of a single spotlight, the mesmerizing half-light and whisper of the backstage—where we can crouch in the wings and watch the stage lights and glimpse people in the first row in the dark.
>
> There is a paradox in our field. As playwrights, we forsake the camera, the perpetually documented and frozen work on film for the ephemeral moment shared between the living actor onstage and the living spectator only feet away in the audience. But it takes a great deal of matter to produce the ephemeral[. . . .] And when all of these people and things [. . .] come together, the miraculous often occurs. All of us melt, in that moment onstage, into spirit alone.
>
> We give our lives for that moment. But it takes so much more for us to get there. It takes the vision, the faith and love in this strange endeavor[. . . .] It takes the gift to us in the here and now, and more importantly, the gift to the young artists 10 and 20 years in the future. It takes a Laura Pels. It takes Harold and Mimi Steinberg.

When *Intimate Apparel* opened, it was warmly received by critics and audiences, going on to win the New York Drama Critics' Circle Award—but not before it was named winner of the American Theatre Critics/Steinberg New Play Award after productions in Baltimore and at South Coast Repertory. The powerful tale of an African-American woman's journey through the thickets of love, race and business enterprise in New York City at the beginning of the 20th century, it was finely directed by Daniel Sullivan—despite a ludicrous review from the *Times*'s Margo Jefferson. (It wasn't the first time this season that the Pulitzer Prize-winning Jefferson demonstrated an appalling lack of critical aptitude—see Charles Wright's essay in this volume for another example.) Lenora Inez Brown offers a clearer view of this 2003–04 Best Play and its affect on today's women in her essay in this volume.

Lincoln Center Theater got its new-play season started with Jules Feiffer's *A Bad Friend*, which located a family melodrama against the backdrop of leftist ideology in the early 1950s. A deeply personal play for Feiffer, whose family members were part of "the cause," it ultimately reflected the great cartoonist's flair for working in the more unidimensional media of paper and ink. Tony Award-winner John Kani returned to New York with *Nothing but the Truth*, in which tensions caused by apartheid threaten to tear a family apart. Kani, who wrote the play, also starred. A.R. Gurney's *Big Bill* told the story of a great tennis player who eschewed commercialism in sport but was finally destroyed by his relationships with young men. John Michael Higgins was a charming force as William T. Tilden II.

Mary Zimmerman revisited Second Stage, home of her success a couple of seasons ago with *Metamorphoses*. This season Zimmerman staged *The Notebooks of Leonardo da Vinci* in a characteristically inventive production that featured nine performers all playing characters named Leonardo. Part whimsy, part intellectual discourse on the ideas and consciousness of da Vinci, the play never managed the warm humanity of Zimmerman's *Metamorphoses*. When Lisa Loomer's *Living Out* opened to generally enthusiastic critical and audience response—and a 2003–04 Best Play citation—it was believed that the play might move to Broadway. *Living Out* is a poignant (and very funny) exploration of the demands made on families—both native and immigrant—who struggle to attain the American Dream but need someone to care for their children. As Charles Wright discusses in his essay, the play's power was dismissed by *The New York Times*'s Margo Jefferson and the production never got the traction needed to expand and transfer. It is unfortunate that the *Times* continues to wield this sort of life-and-death power over theatrical work, but it really says more about our theater community—mainly producers who follow the dictates of the newspaper—than it does the media giant itself. Playwright Jonathan Reynolds followed Loomer's play with a solo cooking show that doubled as personal memoir. Audiences came, smelled and left hungry (in more ways than one). Charles L. Mee's *Wintertime*, which has made the rounds of resident theaters, came to the Second Stage directly from the McCarter Theatre Center in New Jersey. Starring Marsha Mason, Michael Cerveris and Marylouise Burke, the production was received as a deconstructed sex farce—with a bit of Mee's beloved Greek philosophy added for spice.

Downtown at New York Theatre Workshop, Peter Gaiten's adaptation of Michael Cunningham's novel *Flesh and Blood* was a by-the-numbers vision of the changes wrought on dysfunctional family relationships over time. Cherry Jones, Martha Plimpton, Jessica Hecht and Peter Frechette led the estimable cast directed by the ubiquitous Doug Hughes. The director also staged the next new play at NYTW—"new play" again a relative term because the play had numerous productions around the US—*The Beard of Avon* by Amy Freed. The comedy purports to question the true identity of William Shakespeare the writer as it toys with modern re-visions of Elizabethan sexuality. Although remarkably well received by the critics, the play ties itself in knots trying to make connections among Shakespeare's various patrons, then pulls itself apart arguing both sides of its polemic. Paul Rudnick's latest comedy, *Valhalla*, centered on the particular (and parallel) lives of a gay boy in 1940s Texas and a 19th-century madman, King Ludwig II. Critics found it to be a jokebook—a good one—without a coherent thematic line. The final new play at NYTW was a Kia Corthron curiosity, *Light Raise the Roof*, about a man who works tirelessly to help build habitats for the homeless. Marilyn Stasio argued tellingly in *Variety* that the production raised "unsettling questions about [play development] workshops in general[. . . .] Was no one able to keep this simple urban fable from becoming so theatrically bloated?"

Playwrights Horizons began its new-play season with Craig Wright's award-winning *Recent Tragic Events*, starring Heather Graham and Hamish Linklater. Graham was widely seen as miscast in this seriocomic take on the aftermath of September 11, 2001. Before the play even begins, a "stage manager" introduces a metatheatrical device apparently meant to distance the audience from the powerful emotions stirred by the play (other distractions follow). In this iteration of the play, though, there was plenty of alienation as soon as the miscast Graham began to speak. The season continued with a country-ish musical, *Wilder*, by Erin Cressida Wilson, Jack Herrick and Mike Craver. John Cullum starred as a man who returns, in memory, to the frontier brothel where he first felt love for a woman (played by the fetching Lacey Kohl). Wendy MacLeod's *Juvenilia* brought yet another rites-of-passage tale to the stage. What more can we learn from substance-abusing college kids about sex, race and religion? Not much, except to wonder, perhaps, at how ridiculous *we* must have looked at that age. *Small Tragedy* by Craig Lucas—a touching tale of struggling theater artists who think in terms of the "real," until confronted with reality—was the gem of the Playwrights season and earned a 2003–04 Best Plays citation. Charles Isherwood discusses the play and production in this volume. The final piece of the Playwrights season, *Chinese Friends* by Jon Robin Baitz, ran aground on the rocky shoals of politics and Oedipal conflict. Directed by Robert Egan, the production featured Peter Strauss as a former politician—in the future—who is attacked by his son and the son's friends. The plot's twists and turns are more torturous than what the kids do to Dad, but the production sank under the weight of the playwright's political rants.

Change was in the air at the Public Theater this season, and not just because of *Caroline*. George C. Wolfe, talented producer and brilliant director at the Public for a decade, announced that he would retire from his leadership post—a move that had been rumored for some time as one top administrator after another resigned over the past several years. In his final full season, though, Wolfe managed to provide an eclectic mix of programming and to lead the company into a new partnership with the Labyrinth Theater Company. Labyrinth is the Off Off Broadway company—led by Philip Seymour Hoffman and John Ortiz—that produced an updated version of Georg Büchner's *Woyzeck*: Brett C. Leonard's *Guinea Pig Solo*. Collaborations at the Public also included the Worth Street Theater Company's fine revival of Larry Kramer's *The Normal Heart* and a production from the Los Angeles-based Actors' Gang. The company brought to the Public Tim Robbins's *Embedded*, a scathing Brechtian satire on the media's role in selling as the US war in Iraq. It is worth noting that two of the Best Plays came from the Public Theater this season. In addition to *Caroline*, there was Lisa Kron's thrilling new play, *Well*—an exercise in metatheatricality and autopsychoanalysis that works beautifully as theater. It is discussed in Michael Sommers's essay in this volume. Other productions at the Public included *The Story* by Tracey Scott Wilson, about a young, African-American woman journalist for whom ambition is everything; and the seldom seen collaboration of William Shakespeare and John Fletcher, *The Two Noble Kinsmen*. The Off Broadway season for the Public started back in the summer of 2003, of course, at the Delacorte in Central Park where Mark Wing-Davey directed Liev Schreiber in a flashy, unfocused production of Shakespeare's *Henry V*.

Of the 10 play revivals Off Broadway this season, 8 were of plays that were at least 100 years old. Among those not previously mentioned in this essay were a National Actors Theatre production of Aeschylus's *The Persians*, adapted by Ellen McLaughlin (NAT's production of *Right You Are* is listed under Off Off Broadway); Ingmar Bergman's revisionist production of Henrik Ibsen's *Ghosts* at BAM; Aquila Theatre Company's lively and popular *The Importance of Being Earnest*; Theatre de la Jeune Lune's all-too-brief New York visit with an imaginative *Hamlet*; the Theatre for a New Audience production of *Pericles*, in association with BAM; and Edward Hall's production of *A Midsummer Night's Dream* at BAM.

Theater and Commerce

IN JUNE 1974, W. McNeil Lowry of the Ford Foundation spoke to the First American Congress of Theatre—a collection of commercial theater producers and nonprofit theater leaders—about foundations funding private enterprise. He said, in part, "There is not necessarily a dichotomy between Broadway and art, but there is a dichotomy between commerce and art." Commercial theater producers in those straitened financial times were looking for ways to enhance their revenue streams and to build bridges to the nonprofit theater because as Bernard Jacobs of the Shubert Organization said, "We are interested in doing everything we can to help your kind of theater, because theater will not otherwise survive in this country."

Both of these grand men of the theater were correct. Nonprofit theater nowadays feeds the machine that is commercial theater and commercial success can enliven a nonprofit's fortunes. On the other hand, expending valuable resources to create a commercial success can gradually erode a nonprofit institution's mission and its soul. The commercial theater—as in any risky enterprise—is averse to the big gamble. That's why Broadway grows more and more corporate (and somnolent) each year—Rosie O'Donnell was the wild card this season. When risks are taken on Broadway, they are generally taken by institutions such as Roundabout Theatre Company, Manhattan Theatre Club and Lincoln Center Theater, all of which have their own Broadway theaters (and more favorable union contracts than commercial producers).

Off Broadway also has more new plays produced by nonprofit institutions than commercial producers. In the 2002–03 season, 30 percent of new plays Off Broadway were commercially produced. This season the commercial percentage fell slightly to 28, but that number is down from nearly 45 percent in the 2000–01 season. Seventy-two percent of new plays Off Broadway were produced by nonprofit entities in the 2003–04 season. But even among the nonprofits, almost every new play Off Broadway got its start somewhere else. Bernard Jacobs had it almost perfect: theater doesn't come *from* New York, it comes *to* New York. New plays (and musicals) arrive from London and Louisville, Chicago and Los Angeles, Denver and San Francisco, Seattle and Austin—and Coral Gables.

Following a run at Actors Theatre of Louisville's Humana Festival of New American Plays in spring 2003, *Omnium Gatherum* by Theresa Rebeck and Alexandra Gersten-Vassilaros opened Off Broadway in September. Rebeck and Gersten-Vassilaros explore issues of terrorism and political instability through a dinner party from hell (literally). Stocked with talking heads from various points on the political spectrum, the play satirizes our willingness to continue consuming even as Rome burns—or perhaps it is only the rack of lamb. Those who saw both productions argued that the arena staging in Louisville—aided by a turntable—allowed the action to unfold more smoothly than the Last Supper arrangement in the Variety Arts Theatre. Although critics were resistant to its chat-show hedonism aesthetic, even Ben Brantley at the *Times* noted its charm, "What makes the play sing and sting is its radical yet perfectly organic shifts in tone." But cultural potentate Frank Rich disagreed, calling *Omnium* (along with *Recent Tragic Events*, which opened three days later) "miserable failures" and denouncing the play as "part of the problem, not the solution" to our current cultural and political situation. Despite Rich's damnation of the work—no wonder Rebeck told a public forum a few years ago that she does not allow the Arts and Leisure section of the *Times* into her home—*Omnium Gatherum* is a 2003–04 Best Play. Chris Jones discusses the play and its impact in this volume.

Just before the openings of *Omnium Gatherum* and *Recent Tragic Events*, another September 11-themed play premiered at the Union Square Theatre. *Portraits* by Jonathan Bell, featured monologues on grief, guilt and fear experienced in the aftermath of the 2001 terrorist attacks. Bell reportedly collected newspaper items about the tragedy and constructed an amalgam of personal stories from them. Unfortunately, the result was a bunch of stories many in the audience had heard, seen or read dozens of times before. What was most clear in the presentation of the September 11-themed productions is that the definitive theatrical statement has yet to be made. It may take years of distance from those horrifying events to attain the kind of perspective needed to provide a clear vision—which is why there is that cliché about hindsight. In the meantime, artists will continue to try to make sense of it all to greater and lesser degrees of success.

Elsewhere on the commercial Off Broadway stage, Matthew Arkin and Robert Clohessy starred in Richard Dresser's *Rounding Third*, a comedy that brought together Little League baseball coaches from different ends of the social spectrum for some laughter and some learning. Edward Albee and Samuel Beckett were together again at Century Center for the Performing Arts for a collection of one-acts titled *Beckett/Albee*. With the superb Marian Seldes and Brian Murray in the leading roles, the evening ranged from darkly evocative (Beckett) to the sprightly and sophisticated (Albee). Maverick producer Scott Morfee presented a 1996 Tracy Letts play, *Bug*, at the Barrow Street Theatre. A sci-fi thriller about people living at the margins of society—and the government's dominion over them—the play survived through the end of the season. Tristine Skyler's teens-in-trouble tale, *The Moonlight Room*, transferred from a Worth Street Theater Company production at Tribeca Playhouse to a run at the Beckett Theatre on Theatre Row. The move appeared to be made largely on the strength of a good review by *The New York Times*'s Bruce Weber. Weber was later transferred from the critical beat to the cultural beat and he was replaced by Margo Jefferson—causing an uproar in the theater community that grew when Jefferson questioned the competence of director Daniel Sullivan's work on *Intimate Apparel*. As faithful readers of *Best Plays* may recall, Weber was called a "sick bastard" by Jackie Mason for his review of Mason's 2002–03 show, *Prune Danish*. Mason's 2003–04 show, *Laughing Room Only*, tanked after 14 performances, closing just a few days before Weber's transfer was announced. Mason gleefully told the *New York Post*, "Now I'm going to Miami but he's going to be reporting on Siberian dance festivals." There were, however, no reported sightings of Weber anywhere in the former Eastern bloc.

New Off Broadway musicals declined to eight productions this season, which started with *The Thing About Men*. Created by the same folks who did the long-running *I Love You, You're Perfect, Now Change*, the new musical followed in a similar, what's-the-matter-with-relationships mode. Marc Kudisch anchored the cast and the production played for 199 performances. *Fame on 42nd Street* finally brought to New York the musical based on the film, which has been touring the US on and off since 1988. After years of repeated exposure to the film version, the stage version seemed flat and almost amateurish. It managed, however, to run 232 performances during the season and to continue into the summer. *Ministry of Progress* had a short life (30 performances) at the Jane Street Theatre after the director, Kim Hughes, was reportedly barred by Actors' Equity from interacting with performers for alleged abusive behavior. *Johnny Guitar* spoofed a 1954 Joan Crawford film and its gender-bending themes with only the gentlest of tweaks. Yet another teen story, *Bare: A Pop Opera*, arrived at American Theatre of Actors by way of Los Angeles. Set in a Catholic boarding school, the coming of age musical played 43 performances and was scheduled for an expanded Off Broadway run that has yet to materialize. The final new musical of the Off Broadway season, *The Joys of Sex*, was most notable for a threatened protest by the musicians' union when producers planned to use a synthesizer that simulates an orchestra for the show. After the producers agreed to let the union have a say in whether or not the machine might be used, the protest was cancelled and the union allowed the use of the synthesizer. As for the prurient interest in this show ostensibly about sex, let's just say that the union contretemps had more arousal in it.

The Human Condition

THE END OF EACH theater season brings with it the echoes of high points and low. As the 2003–04 season gasped toward its end, though, the mean season of political theater was in full swing as the quadrennial presidential election drew nearer. There was chatter on the airwaves, in newpapers, periodicals and on the internet about the heroism of this candidate or the cowardice of another. Spring also marked various anniversary dates related to war in Iraq with the media feeding on body and casualty counts of young people in harm's way. There was talk of death tolls among innocent civilians in a foreign land and speculation on notions of heroes and heroism—often indulged by those who never wore the country's uniform.

But we are concerned with a more genteel type of theater, which itself saw a kind of heroism demonstrated by press agent Bill Evans when he donated a kidney to an ailing friend, playwright Neil Simon. Evans and Simon were both reluctant to discuss the transplant until doctors convinced them that public education might help others. In an interview in *The New York Times*, Evans cited "the glop factor" when discussing his generous gift, expressing a desire to avoid talk of heroism, bravery and the like. The press agent made self-effacing jokes about his kidney's new homes on Park Avenue and in Southern California, according to *Times* gossip writer Joyce Wadler, and yet Evans's selfless act reminded the community just how tenuous is our grasp on health and life.

Indeed, we lost many from the theater community during this season. The deaths of Isabelle Stevenson and Uta Hagen are noted above, but we also lost such productive members as Tony Randall, Joseph Chaikin, Hume Cronyn, Spalding Gray, Katharine Hepburn, Earl Hindman, Gregory Hines, Ann Miller, young Jason Raize, playwright John Henry Redwood III, playwright Jerome Lawrence, director Gerald Gutierrez, critic Elliot Norton, press agent Mary Bryant and many others who made valuable contributions to our theatrical life.

When Adolph Green died in 2002, a memory of him came to mind that bears recounting. At a conference in 2001, Green had just participated on a musical book-writing panel and was making his way gingerly through a mass of lighting cables and set pieces backstage at Circle in the Square Theatre. He hummed a nondescript tune as he moved among the mess, seemingly oblivious to the hazards all about him. A concerned party offered assistance to the elderly writer, saying, "Mr. Green, take my hand." Without missing a beat, he replied, "Why? Are you a stranger in paradise?" It was a delicious moment of exquisite comic timing that will live as long as someone continues to tell the story.

And so it is as we prepare for another season: The house lights dim, we breathe in the darkness, our faces turned toward the warm light about to emanate from the stage. We hope for magic, for grace, for human connection—or even just a passing moment of exquisite comic timing.

THE BEST PLAYS OF 2003–2004

2003–2004 Best Play

ANNA IN THE TROPICS

By Nilo Cruz

○○○○○

Essay by Christine Dolen

> MARELA: We can always dream.
>
> OFELIA: Ah yes. But we have to take a yardstick and measure our dreams.
>
> MARELA: Then I will need a very long yardstick. The kind that could measure the sky.
>
> CONCHITA: How foolish you are, Marela!
>
> MARELA: No, everything in life dreams. A bicycle dreams of becoming a boy, an umbrella dreams of becoming the rain, a pearl dreams of becoming a woman, and a chair dreams of becoming a gazelle and running back to the forest.

LIKE THE SINUOUS, curling smoke from a fine cigar, dreams have enveloped everything about Nilo Cruz's lovely and lyrical *Anna in the Tropics*, the surprise winner of the 2003 Pulitzer Prize for drama.

Set in 1929 in Ybor City near Tampa, Florida, the play examines the catalytic effect that a new *lector*, or reader, has on a family of Cuban-American cigar makers. Lush and theatrically poetic, Cruz's script intertwines passages from Leo Tolstoy's *Anna Karenina*—which the play's *lector* reads to the workers as they roll cigars each day—with the playwright's own story of passionate men and women at the end of an era, just before mechanization and the Depression would bring the tradition of the *lector* to a close.

Commissioned by New Theatre in Coral Gables, Florida, Cruz's breakthrough play had been staged only in that intimate, 104-seat space (for 23 performances in October–November 2002) when the script won both the ATCA/Steinberg New Play Award and the Pulitzer in the space of three days in early April 2003. But even before members of the Pulitzer board—none of whom had seen the play's only production, as had no one on the drama jury—made Cruz the first Latino playwright to win the prize, three major regional theaters had already committed to their own productions of *Anna in the Tropics.*

Dream rollers: Vanessa Aspillaga, Jimmy Smits, Daphne Rubin-Vega and Priscilla Lopez in Anna in the Tropics. *Photo: Joan Marcus*

So in September–October 2003, the unprecedented happened: three different productions of a Broadway-bound play ran simultaneously in the United States. Juliette Carrillo staged a production at South Coast Repertory in Costa Mesa, California, one of Cruz's theatrical "homes." Chicago's Victory Gardens Theater produced a version directed by Henry Godinez. And McCarter Theatre Center artistic director Emily Mann—another of Cruz's champions in regional theater—chose the play to open the company's new $14 million Roger S. Berlind Theatre in Princeton, New Jersey. It was Mann's production that producers Berlind, Daryl Roth and Ray Larsen chose to move to Broadway's Royale Theatre in November 2003.

ANNA IN THE TROPICS begins with contrapuntal scenes, energized exchanges that introduce the characters, their yearnings, their strengths, their flaws. In alternating between masculine and feminine passions at the beginning of the play, Cruz gives equal focus to two strands of his plot: the ambitions of a flawed man who represents change, and the allure of another who embodies imperiled tradition.

Both of these cross-cutting scenes involve gambling; both involve men and women betting money on their passions. The men wager on cockfights, addictively in the case of Santiago (a gruff Victor Argo), who insists on the win that will not come. The women scan a seaport dock anxiously, matriarch Ofelia (the vibrant Priscilla Lopez) having forwarded passage money so that the factory's new *lector* might arrive by ship from Cuba.

Handsomely attired in long-sleeved, white linen guayabera shirts, white slacks and two-toned shoes, Santiago and his Cuban-American half-brother, Cheché (a conniving David Zayas), drink and wager on evocatively named fighting birds—Espuela de Oro (Golden Spur), Picarubio (Red Pike) and others. Santiago loses but cannot walk away from the fevered high of the

> "I'm writing music for the stage: Language is theatrical music."

hopeful gambler. He asks Cheché, whose luck has been far better, for a loan. Cheché is reluctant but relents after Santiago pulls out a knife and carves his IOU on the sole of his brother's shoe. Predictably, the sour luck continues; predictably, Santiago asks for more money.

Cheché balks, but Santiago persuades him with a sentence: "If I don't pay you, part of the factory is yours." Cheché walks home with just one shoe on because "this here is our contract, and I don't want it erased." Though this first scene is boozy and gently funny, Cruz uses it to efficiently establish Santiago's weakness and Cheché's self-serving character.

At the other side of the stage, the women of the Alcalar family are also dressed in their best, elegant clothing in whites and creams to stay cool(er) in the brutal Florida sun. They have brought white handkerchiefs to wave, and they take turns gazing at a photograph of Juan Julian Rios (the playfully suave Jimmy Smits), a *lector* known as the "Persian Canary" for his deft, sonorous way of transporting listeners to other places. Girlish Marela (the giddy, gushing Vanessa Aspillaga), a 22-year-old with a teenager's propensity toward crushes, is already half in love with him—a connection Cruz sharpened with second-act restructuring and rewriting in his post-premiere revision of *Anna in the Tropics* for the McCarter. Worldly, married Conchita (the powerful, smoky-voiced Daphne Rubin-Vega) warns her sister to avoid trying to influence love and destiny.

A revised Scene 2 begins with a brief but illuminating exchange between Cheché and Juan Julian, who have arrived for work before the rest of the family. Cheché behaves as though he's running the place, and when Juan Julian affirms that he's a *lector*, Cheché dismissively says, "If you're looking for a job, we're not hiring." Then Ofelia arrives and establishes in a sentence—"He's been hired by me, Chester"—that she's in charge and Cheché has no say in the matter.

At the factory, the women offer snippets of biography about various workers to Juan Julian, who doesn't understand Cheché's immediate dislike of him. Marela enthusiastically supplies the historical context, revealing that her uncle's wife "disappeared one day with the *lector* that was working here. She was a Southern belle from Atlanta, and he was from Guanabacoa. Her skin was pale like a lily, and he was the color of saffron. [. . .] Cheché thinks the love stories got under her skin. That's why she left him."

Asked his impressions of Tampa, the *lector* is both diplomatic:

> JUAN JULIAN: It seems like it's a city in the making.

And vivid:

> JUAN JULIAN: It's curious, there are no mountains or hills here. Lots of sky I have noticed . . . And clouds . . . The largest clouds I've ever

Desperate love: Daphne Rubin-Vega and Jimmy Smits in Anna in the Tropics. *Photo: Joan Marcus*

seen, as if they had soaked up the whole sea. It's all so flat all round. That's why the sky seems so much bigger here and infinite. Bigger than the sky I know back home.

The scene ends with another tart exchange between Cheché and Ofelia, who deepens her brother-in-law's frustration by dismissing the value of his "promissory" shoe.

SOON, USING TOLSTOY'S classic novel, Juan Julian transports these Cubans who toil in a steamy, aromatic factory to snowy Russia. Like the best *lectores*, he has an actor's gift for bringing the many characters to life—passages read in the play were crafted by Cruz from different translations of the novel. In the style of today's telenovela, Juan Julian knows just where to stop each day to leave the women—though not the dismissive men—hungry for more. Anna's illicit affair with Count Vronsky inflames the female workers' imaginations, yet *Anna Karenina* works as a kind of auditory air-conditioning.

OFELIA: He chose the right book. There is nothing like reading a winter book in the middle of summer. It's like having a fan or an icebox by your side to relieve the heat and the caloric nights.

Alone with her husband Palomo (a gruff John Ortiz) in the factory after hours, Conchita decides to speak openly about the source of her unhappiness: his infidelity. Verbally, Palomo feints and dodges, dancing around his wife's questions. Until, finally, a woman who still loves her husband vows to change—to "try to love you in a different way"—and to think about taking a lover of her own.

The play's other married couple uses Marela as an intermediary in dealing with the small crisis caused by Santiago's gambling and the larger one of his lingering depression. Grandly, theatrically, the two aren't speaking—until a winded Marela gets tired of repeating comments her parents can hear perfectly well and walks out. The tone abruptly shifts from a funny mock battle to a tender, touching conversation on subjects ranging from the trivial to Santiago's inertia and despair.

It is at this point that Cruz made a major shift in revising his Pulitzer Prize-winning script for the McCarter production. Working with director Mann and dramaturg Janice Paran, he decided to heighten Marela's attraction to Juan Julian and her rejection of Cheché as the motive for murder. In Cruz's original, a scene in which Cheché chides a dreamy, dismissive Marela for turning out sloppy work as she listens to *Anna Karenina* served to set up Cheché's second-act rape of Marela, an act that would bring tumult and death to the factory. In the revision, the rape is eliminated, and the prickly Cheché-Marela scene moves to the second act. Though the changes accomplish Cruz's intention, they also drain some of the emotional intensity from *Anna in the Tropics*.

Act I ends with the beginning of Conchita's affair with the *lector*. Their mutual seduction entwines talk of nature and romantic ritual, with an apt passage from *Anna Karenina* leading to a kiss of surrender. In the script, Act II begins with Conchita and Juan Julian making love on a table in the factory, the *lector* atop his half-naked lover. Mann's staging moved the two onto the floor downstage center, with the strapping Smits on the floor and tiny Rubin-Vega moving on top of him, neither as exposed as the script suggests because, after a brief exchange, they cut short their tryst before other characters enter the scene. Though both erotic and playful, the beginning of the scene on Broadway was also less passionate than the text suggests.

Again shifting the order of the action for the New York production, Cruz introduces an element that signals the end of seas of workers hand-rolling cigars as well as the end of the *lector* tradition: the cigar-rolling machine. Trying to assert himself as both a manager and a man, the entrepreneurial Cheché brings a rolling machine into the factory, causing a storm of protest—particularly from Ofelia. In contrast to the rest of the family—Cubans who value tradition—Cheché is an American drawn to efficiency, cost-cutting, progress. He also knows that the *lector*'s job is among those the machines will eliminate, since readers can't be heard over the mechanized din. This, to Cheché, is a bonus.

Juan Julian, who likens the workers to Taino Indians listening quietly as a chief translates the sacred words of their deities, speaks up for tradition, for the ritual pleasures of smoking a fine cigar: "The truth is that cars, machines, are keeping us from taking walks and sitting on park benches smoking a cigar slowly and calmly. [. . . Y]ou want modernity and modernity is actually destroying our very own industry."

His words easily persuade everyone except Palomo and Cheché, the only workers who raise their hands when Santiago appears and asks who wants to get rid of the *lector*. Then the re-energized Santiago announces he has decided to launch a new brand called the Anna Karenina, and that he wants Marela to pose as Anna for the label. Santiago then deals Cheché two more blows by demanding his brother return the rolling machine and by repaying the loan that would have given Cheché a greater stake in the business. Cheché expresses his frustration and misery: "I can't stand it. Working here is like hitting my head against a wall."

Tropical Anna: John Ortiz and Daphne Rubin-Vega in Anna in the Tropics. *Photo: Joan Marcus*

As he finishes with angry talk of his runaway wife and of the *lector* who serves as a daily reminder of her betrayal, Marela returns dressed in fur and ready to model for the new label. Her father exits to find the finishing touch for her, a flower for her hair, and Juan Julian enters looking for his copy of *Anna Karenina*. His compliment thrills her, and after he exits, she mutters, "I wish you would take a picture of me with your eyes."

Cheché has watched this exchange, registering Marela's attraction to the *lector*, and it's here that Cruz inserts the scene in which the uncle chides his niece, then expresses his incestuous desire for her, only to have her angrily and haughtily reject him.

Scene 2, which begins with Juan Julian upstage reading a passage about propriety from *Anna Karenina*, explores the effect of Conchita's affair on her marriage. Agitated, Palomo demands details. Conchita complies and denies, in ways both graphic and metaphoric. Gradually, steamy talk about the man who has awakened Conchita's sensuality re-ignites passion between husband and wife.

The party to celebrate the launch of the new cigar is a masterly scene: amusing, threatening, moving. It touches on Palomo's jealousy and Cheché's burgeoning anger as well as the ritualistic pleasures of smoking a great cigar. Palomo asks Juan Julian questions about the adulterous affair in *Anna Karenina*, but the "literary" conversation is really aimed at getting information from his rival.

After everyone has taken turns puffing on the very first Anna Karenina cigar—and gone into a poetic frenzy to describe its taste, aroma and distinctive qualities—Palomo and Conchita remain behind while the others go outside to fire a gun in celebration. She expresses her puzzlement over his lust for details of her affair; he orders her to tell Juan Julian "you want to make love like a knife." And when she says, "Why a knife?," he replies, "Because everything has to be killed."

The scene ends with a giddy Marela expressing her happiness to—and conveying her crush on—Juan Julian. Gently, the *lector* acknowledges her sweetness and innocence without returning her romantic feelings. After he exits, Cheché—who has been watching from afar, seething during the tender exchange—grabs Marela's arm.

In the penultimate scene, as everyone tries to begin working while dealing with hangovers, Marela enters wearing her fur coat and hat. Something is wrong, but all she will say is that she wants to be like the winter months in Russia, "layered and still." As Juan Julian begins reading a passage about Anna's husband and his fantasies about murdering his rival, the missing Cheché enters, listens, pulls out a gun and shoots Juan Julian. The *lector* dies, and with him a tradition.

The final scene, a coda both mournful and hopeful, finds the workers rolling in silence. Marela, still wearing her coat, says, "we must look after the dead, so they can feel part of the world. So they don't forget us and we could count on them when we cross to the other side." Conchita and Marela suggest they read to end the silence, to honor the lost *lector*. Picking up *Anna Karenina*, Palomo begins a new chapter in their lives.

CRITICS EMBRACED ALL three 2003 productions, small reservations notwithstanding. In Chicago, the *Tribune*'s Michael Phillips noted the "disarming blend of prose and . . . trademark poetic dreaminess" of Cruz's writing, and the *Sun-Times*'s Hedy Weiss pronounced his imagery, his grasp of varying kinds of love and his "sense of the heart's willfulness" faultless. *The Orange County Register*'s Paul Hodgins, though he felt Carrillo's South Coast staging magnified the script's "sometimes forced sense of melodrama," nonetheless praised Cruz's "compelling and ingenious story in which life and art intertwine." In *The Los Angeles Times*, Reed Johnson called the play "a beautifully written period piece, which conceals subterranean strata of thought and feeling beneath its alluring, seemingly transparent surface." Reviewers also praised Mann's spare, poetic Princeton production, with its all-Latino cast headed by television and movie veteran Smits. But knowing that the production was headed for Broadway, the major New York critics—who might otherwise have seen it at the McCarter—waited for it to reach the Royale.

There, the critics were largely appreciative—more so than for Robert Schenkkan's *The Kentucky Cycle*, the only other play to win the Pulitzer before reaching New York—if not enthusiastic. The *Times*'s Ben Brantley noted the Chekhovian tone of Cruz's script, his "densely lyrical language" in a play "as wistful and affectingly ambitious as its characters." He complained that Mann's "straightforward staging," however, didn't suit Cruz's style and that the performers (who represented the multitude of workers one would have found in such a factory) looked "small and adrift against Robert Brill's stark wooden set." *Newsday*'s Linda Winer called *Anna* "a nostalgic cultural tone poem, wrenching labor history and a full-blown old-fashioned bodice ripper," though she found Mann's production "lovely if somewhat inert." Critics who didn't enjoy *Anna in the Tropics*—which managed a Broadway run of 15 previews and 113 performances before closing on February 22, 2004—saw it as florid melodrama, a libretto looking for a score.

What they were responding to, perhaps, is a quality Cruz—who doesn't see *Anna* as melodramatic—strives for in his writing. "I see it as full of musicality," he says. "Music must have emotions. Characters must have emotional levels. I'm writing music for the stage: Language is theatrical music. Latinos understand the emotional flow of the language."

One of Cruz's goals in creating *Anna in the Tropics* was to illuminate the lost tradition of the *lector* for a broader audience—and in so doing remind people that Cubans were part of American culture long before Fidel Castro came to power. The playwright pointedly did not want to get into the very real role *lectores* played in inspiring workers to help liberate Cuba from Spain at the end of the 19th century. Rather than focusing on the newspapers or left-leaning political tracts *lectores* read, Cruz wanted to explore the transformative power of great literature on the lives of the workers. Once he chose the romantic, tragic *Anna Karenina* (a logical pick, since the cigar workers would have been exposed to Russian art as well as its politics), he imagined its effect on his characters—and transformed himself into a Pulitzer Prize-winning playwright.

2003–2004 Best Play

CAROLINE, OR CHANGE

Book and lyrics by Tony Kushner
Music by Jeanine Tesori

○○○○○

Essay by John Istel

CAROLINE: I'm gonna slam that iron
down on my heart
gonna slam that iron down on my throat
gonna slam that iron
down on my sex
gonna slam it
slam it
slam it down
until I drown
the fire out
till there ain't no air left
anywhere.

AT THE TOP of Act I, when we first meet Caroline Thibodeaux, a black maid for a Southern Jewish family—and the title character of *Caroline, or Change*—she's presented as a besieged monarch presiding over a modest underground kingdom. Her dominion? A Lake Charles, Louisiana, basement laundry room: "sixteen feet below sea level," she sings. It's 1963, and although the first lines of this sung-through, lyrical fairy tale of a musical by Tony Kushner (book and lyrics) and Jeanine Tesori (music) are, "Nothing ever happen underground / in Louisiana," anyone with an inkling of American history knows that a flood of social change is about to sweep the nation off its feet. Everything is changing.

Caroline is determined to stay afloat amid these tidal transformations without sinking too far into her own misery. Her travails are due partly to her lousy poverty-level pay and are partly the result of being beaten and abandoned by the husband she once loved. She's a single mother trying to make it on $30 a week.

In my gloom: Tonya Pinkins in Caroline, or Change. *Photo: Michal Daniel*

Since this is a musical, one produced eventually on Broadway, audiences might naturally assume that if Caroline starts the show so down and out—literally underground in a hellish laundry room—surely by the second act curtain she will rise like Cinderella.

But *Caroline, or Change* disrupts almost every convention that audiences, particularly on Broadway, have come to expect. Much of the piece takes place in a living-room set similar to those that audiences have seen in dozens of domestic dramas—but it's a setting where this title character rarely finds herself. There's little or no dancing and no chorus for crowd scenes, except for a surreal chorus of inanimate consumer appliances that surround Caroline in the laundry room—talk about Brechtian alienation!—as well as a singing Bus and a crooning Moon. Each object has a personality and a distinctive vocal part. Neither can the show be considered a "concept musical"—such as *A Chorus Line* or *Cabaret*—in which an overarching theatrical device ties the narrative together. The nonhuman characters simply create a fantastical dialectic with the domestic lives of the 11 human characters.

THE STORY DETAILS Caroline's relationships to the Gellmans, for whom she works, and to her own family consisting of Larry, who is in Vietnam, and three others, for whom she struggles to provide. It's told relatively chronologically over the course of two epic months, November and December, in 1963. Each of the two acts consists of six scenes; each scene has a title, as does the second act epilogue.

The plot focuses on Caroline's relationship with Noah Gellman, the 8-year-old boy who idolizes her, as well as with her own friends and family. Yes, everything changes; but in this musical, their relationship smashes in a climactic second act scene. Meanwhile, monumental changes are happening

Caroline's only sense of identity or "I" is the one found in "I-ron."

in the world at large. In "Scene 4: Moon Change," Caroline's friend, Dotty, goes to college, a harbinger of Southern blacks' burgeoning pride of accomplishment. We hear about the locals who have toppled a statue of a Confederate soldier in the town square as a protest, Martin Luther King Jr. is marching and President Kennedy is murdered.

Caroline refuses to let these larger tremors rock her world, which makes the toughened maid's rigid refusal to change with the times the *Lear*-like spine of the musical. Instead, her soul is wrenched from its moorings by a fight over some "loose change" that Noah absent-mindedly leaves in his pants' pockets. Rose, Noah's stepmother, insists that Caroline keep the money in order to teach her stepson a lesson. But Noah begins leaving coins in his pants on purpose, hoping this will endear him to Caroline, whose attention he craves. (At the beginning of the musical, Noah's mother has recently died of cancer.) At first Caroline stubbornly refuses to accept the change and continues to put it in the bleach cup, but then, figuring she's underpaid, angrily begins taking it. That slip of pride comes back to haunt.

THE PECULIAR, IDIOSYNCRATIC style and tone of this "musical" isn't surprising considering the book and lyrics are by Kushner, an avowedly political playwright, and an artist influenced equally by Bertolt Brecht and Maurice Sendak. The music was composed by Jeanine Tesori, who came to prominence via her 1997 Off Broadway musical *Violet,* also set in the South during the 1960s with an interracial relationship at its center. For *Caroline,* Tesori told an interviewer that she listened to Etta James to help hone Caroline's voice, while the rest of the score was influenced primarily by 1960s musical vernaculars like doo-wop, R&B, and Motown. But there are also swirling klezmer riffs (Noah's dad is a professional clarinetist), beautifully rearranged Christmas and Chanukah tunes for the December holiday scenes at the top of the second act, and Noah's second act sing-song, child-like playground chant.

According to Kushner's introduction to the published script (TCG, 2004), the two collaborators did not originally choose each other. He had been commissioned by San Francisco Opera to write a libretto. The original opera composer decided to back away, and Kushner's friend and colleague, George C. Wolfe, who had directed Kushner's *Angels in America* on Broadway, suggested he turn the nascent script into a musical. Initially, Tesori turned the project down, feeling the script, based on Kushner's own childhood in Louisiana, was already complete. But after working together briefly on a song for a compilation CD, and enjoying the experience, Kushner

Friendly debate: Chandra Wilson and Tonya Pinkins in Caroline, or Change. *Photo: Michal Daniel*

and Tesori began to collaborate on *Caroline, or Change*. After several years of workshops, under the guidance of Wolfe, the show began performances at the Public Theater in October 2003. It opened on Broadway in May 2004 and garnered five Tony Award nominations: for best musical, book (Kushner), score (Tesori), and actress and featured actress in a musical (Tonya Pinkins as Caroline and Anika Noni Rose as Emmie). Rose was the only winner for a role that unexpectedly becomes the heart of the show.

Is it coincidence that Emmie is the harbinger of social change in the musical? She's the "cockeyed optimist" who holds onto her belief in nonviolent protest and closes the show with an epilogue entitled "Emmie's Dream." It is of a future in which she acknowledges her roots but refuses to abide the redneck racists that surround her in Louisiana:

> EMMIE: I'm the daughter of a maid,
> in her uniform, crisp and clean!
> Nothing can ever make me afraid!
> You can't hold on, you nightmare men,
> your time is past now on your way
> get gone and never come again!
> For change come fast and change come slow but
> everything changes!
> And you got to go!

In the end, Kushner gives us this emotional satisfaction, but it's at a distance, the distance of one generation removed from the title character. Caroline begins the musical as a maid, a lonely laundry queen barricaded in a basement of pain and anger; she ends the show having doffed her crown of thorns, although she remains a maid.

AT THE BEGINNING of the show, Caroline's chorus of courtiers includes a Washing Machine, a deep basso Dryer and a Radio consisting of three Supremes-like soul singers. While the actual appliances sit stolidly onstage, the actors representing them appear and sing either in harmony or counterpoint, commenting on the events in the world—and on Caroline's troubled life. "Caroline! Mercy me!," sings the Radio, "39 and divorcee." But the most devoted sycophant to the maid's royal presence is sad-faced Noah whose few joys include coming home from school and lighting Caroline's daily cigarette. As we soon see, not only has he lost his mother, but Stuart, his father, is distant and preoccupied ("as remote as Tibet," he sings of his son, "The bigger he grows, the stranger we get"). Not surprisingly, Noah turns his grief-blind devotions to his housekeeper, as he sings in "Scene 2: Cabbage":

> NOAH: Caroline
> the President of the United States.
> Caroline who's always mad!
> Caroline who runs everything!
> Caroline who's stronger than my dad!

Of course, eight-year-old Noah doesn't realize how romanticized a portrait he's painted of this sad, desolate single mother of four. "Caroline is king / and Caroline is queen," he tells his stepmother, Rose, in the pivotal fourth scene, "Moon Change." To Noah, Caroline is god-like; to her daughter she's a dinosaur; and to the rest of the world, she's almost invisible.

The first act is the weaker of the two because its six scenes are laden with exposition and set pieces that characterize peripheral players in Caroline's drama. No matter how carefully wrought or beautifully written, by intermission the momentum has slowed. "Scene 3: Long Distance" is an exquisite character monologue in song, for example, in which Rose phones her father in New York City to talk about her new life in the South:

> ROSE: I'm fine, just fine, I'm learning the lingo:
> Magnolia, camellia, azalea, y'all.
> The Temple—get this—has Sunday night bingo—
> just like the goyim.

During the call, Rose spells out her problems with Noah and how his habit of leaving change in his pockets embarrasses her, especially because "The negro maid, she's making bupkes." Dramatically, however, this single-character, phone-call scene is inert.

The next scene, "Moon Change," is more complex, filled with new characters and story lines. It establishes Dotty as Caroline's upwardly striving friend who fills her in on the shenanigans with the Confederate soldier statue that's missing a head. It introduces the Moon as a character in the form of a Cassandra-like Aisha de Haas singing of "moon change." And as the two friends wait for the bus home, the character of "the Bus" arrives and sings, according to the stage directions, "in a terrible voice of apocalypse" about the death of JFK.

In the fifth scene, "Duets," Caroline and her daughter Emmie tussle about the world events. Emmie couldn't care about the assassination, for example:

Prexy and proxy: Tonya Pinkins and Harrison Chad in Caroline, or Change. *Photo: Michal Daniel*

EMMIE: Just some old white man
sent Larry off to Vietnam.
Sorry he dead.
I ain't killed him.

When Emmie goes off to bed, Noah calls to her from his window: "President Caroline!" He wants to know what she's going to do now that she's the only president left. She magically hears his queries and sings a litany of laws she'd enact:

CAROLINE: Gonna pass me a law
that night last longer.
Gonna pass me a law
Larry come home from Vietnam
wherever that is
gonna pass me a law
no woman can be my age

and not know enough
to read a map.

This peaceful, yearning scene doesn't exclude the realities of class consciousness for Kushner, however. When Noah asks if his hero will wish him goodnight, Caroline replies, "That not my job."

The last scene before intermission tightens the deal: Caroline decides she could use the spare change she finds in Noah's pockets and Noah purposefully plants more and more coins. When he tries a dollar bill, however, Caroline hands it back to him. The act ends with Caroline's children and the Moon singing a fanciful fairy tale about some imaginary character named Roosevelt Pernicious Coleslaw while Noah imagines them talking about him and his coins. The act's close is the weakest part of the musical as it sags under the weight of all the exposition Kushner has been intent on including.

THE FIRST SCENE of Act II begins as the first act did: Caroline is in the laundry, only now the extra change she's finding is allowing her to dream a little, cracking her hardened heart, and she allows herself to relive the memory of being married and having her first children. The Radio and the Washing Machine sing along and fill in her story.

In the next scene, "The Chanukah Party," conflicts that have been festering start to boil. Noah's paternal grandparents and Rose's father from New York arrive for the big holiday dinner. The older southern couple are accommodating and assimilationist; Mr. Stopnick is a stereotypical New York social progressive who would seem plenty radical to much of the country. Meanwhile, Caroline has Emmie and Dotty helping her prepare and serve the food. The scene cuts back and forth between the blacks in the kitchen and the Jewish holiday rituals. Tesori facilitates the switches by mixing rhythm and blues with antic, percussive arrangements of traditional Chanukah songs. The tension from the outside world eventually intrudes: Emmie lets her devotion to Martin Luther King's nonviolent movement for civil rights—and her resentment at Northerners who come down to "help the Negroes"—air in front of the Gellmans. Emmie's behavior horrifies Caroline even as it thrills Mr. Stopnick. A veteran of the union struggles, he urges Emmie to drop the pacifism. Caroline hustles her out of the room. Then Mr. Stopnick gives Noah his gift with a little hardline economic lecture (in song):

MR. STOPNICK: What's the meaning of this Gelt?
For peace sometimes, blood must be spilt.

> For life, sometimes, a good man dies.
> What means this money, Noah boychick?
> You won't learn this in Arithmetic.
> [. . .]
> Think of someone who is poor:
> and know, you stole this gold from them.
> Especially here in the Devil's South!
> You rip your gold from a starving man's mouth!

This imagery is almost made literally true in the next scene, titled simply "The Twenty Dollar Bill." Of course, Noah forgets the gift in his pants pockets. He runs home from school and demands that Caroline give it back. She refuses. "Now I can take my boy to the dentist," she says. And as Noah screams at her to give it back, time slows down and then everything changes between the two. Noah, in a fury, claims "President Johnson has built a bomb / special made to kill all Negroes." He then repeats, "I hate you," over and over. Caroline pauses and then lets all her anger and hate rise up. She sings, "Hell's so hot it makes flesh fry / and hell's where Jews go when they die." She then leaves the $20 bill in the bleach cup—and walks out of the house and doesn't come back—for five days.

THE LYRICS IN the epigraph to this essay appear in what would be called the "11 o'clock number" in a traditional Broadway musical. However, because this work was never meant to be a commercial tourist attraction on the Great White Way, these words are part of a sung dramatic soliloquy that was performed by Pinkins, both at the Public Theater and at Broadway's Eugene O'Neill Theatre under Wolfe's direction. Pinkins, in both venues, transformed this sung-through soliloquy into a bit of bust-your-guts bravura.

In "Scene 11: Lot's Wife," after Dotty urges Caroline to call her employer and quit, and wonders where the happy friend she once knew has gone. Caroline tells her friend to get lost. She's on her way to church and God will be the only one to whom she speaks. Dotty rebuts: telling her to "change or sink . . . this ain't no time for prayin. You got to think." When Caroline basically throws her out, she's left alone onstage, and Caroline becomes completely distraught for having spoken her "hate to a child." She blames her situation on the spare coins.

> CAROLINE: Pocket change change me, pocket change change me,
> can't afford loose change, can't afford change,
> changin's a danger for a woman like me. [. . .]

Why does Caroline, in this soliloquy also quoted in the epigraph, suddenly refer to herself in the third person? Just after we experience her virago of fury and pain as she suggests she can "iron" out her problems, slamming it down on her "heart," her "throat," her "sex," she sings,

> CAROLINE: [. . .] Now how 'bout that then?
> That what Caroline can do!
> That how she re-arrange herself,
> that how she change!

Is she so unhinged by this second act climax that she's actually contemplating the ultimate "change"—from life to death? That would indeed be revenge on all—her friend Dotty, her daughter Emmie, and her boss, Rose—who are trying to make her adapt her hardheaded ways.

This 11th scene is like a harrowing abdication. It recalls the one in Shakespeare's *Richard II*, where a similar identity disjunction occurs when the eponymous monarch abdicates his crown to Bolingbroke with one of the strangest lines in the canon: "I . . . no; no . . . I." In some editions, the line is written as a vacillation: "Ay, no; no, ay," which in contemporary English would be rendered, "Yes, no; no, yes." (Coincidentally, Kushner's early musical play for children, which this work resembles in tone, was titled *Yes, Yes, No, No.*)

Of course, Shakespeare's line can be read many ways. Change the first "no" to its homonym "know," which is how audiences might hear it, and you have "I know no I." That's not far from the truth: Richard without a crown is a man without an identity. Likewise, Kushner suggests, Caroline would not know herself if she dared to embrace change, if she abdicated her old sense of self no matter how shattered and turned upside down it may be, no matter if her soul feels tumbled in a permanent rinse cycle. Her regal steadfastness has pulled her through past crises, even after her offstage, never-seen ex-husband deserted her and their four children. So her refusal to change gives her the only sense of royalty she can claim. As the Dryer intones in "Scene 7: Ironing": "You the queen of keep-at-bay / what-was-once or might-have-been."

Caroline's only sense of identity or "I" is the one found in "I-ron."

I can imagine some readers muttering, "What is he talking about?" So throw my theory away like loose change—it doesn't ultimately matter. The point is: When has any musical libretto or lyric in memory invited such speculation and dissection? In addition to the tragedy connotations, there are the Brechtian overtones as well. Singing appliances become alienation effects, amusing audiences even as they realize that Caroline's mechanical "friends" are a capitalist consumer culture's sweet music played for every manual laborer on his lemming-like march to death.

Kushner has always embraced excess—just never in a musical. With the help of Tesori's R&B anthems and Motown imitations, Wolfe's silky direction and a stellar cast, *Caroline, or Change* carries its audience to the end like a slow, meandering Mississippi raft ride while stopping to make references to issues like Jewish-black relations; capitalist-communist notions of wealth redistribution; domestic violence; blacks' poverty and unemployment; the effect of a mother's death on a child; the notion of black-white friendship amid an inequitable work situation; and there's probably more—lots more. The music and lyrics bear repeated listening. It's rich and fertile silt and eminently worth sifting.

2003–2004 Best Play

FROZEN

By Bryony Lavery

○○○○○

Essay by Anne Marie Welsh

EDITOR'S NOTE: *As this volume entered the final editing process, 2004 Tony Award nominee and* Best Plays *honoree Bryony Lavery was alleged to have lifted substantial portions of the text of* Frozen *from a 1997 article by Malcolm Gladwell in* The New Yorker *magazine and from a book by Dorothy Otnow Lewis,* Guilty by Reason of Insanity. *That Lavery borrowed from Gladwell and Lewis seems not to be in dispute. In a* New York Times *article by Jesse McKinley, press agent Chris Boneau asserted that "the discussions are amicable."*

It is the position of The Best Plays Theater Yearbook *that although Lavery relied on the words and work of others—without, we are sorry to note, careful acknowledgment of all of her underlying sources—it was she who constructed a narrative that we felt made for such compelling theater. As we were going to press, Gladwell published a thoughtful appraisal of the controversy in* The New Yorker *that is largely consonant with our assessment.*

NANCY: Actually, nothing's unbearable.

THE NEW YORK production of Bryony Lavery's *Frozen* began life Off Off Broadway at the East 13th Street Theatre March 18, 2004. Positive reviews of the MCC Theater production sparked a transfer to Broadway's Circle in the Square Theatre. It opened there May 4, 2004, the day before the deadline for the 2004 Tony Award nominations. *Frozen* garnered four—for best play and for all three speaking actors. Brían F. O'Byrne, nominated previously for his role as the shy suitor in Martin McDonagh's *The Beauty Queen of Leenane*, won the featured actor Tony Award for his blunt, chillingly restrained portrayal of the serial murderer, Ralph Wantage.

In 30 short scenes on an unadorned stage, *Frozen* explores the impact on a bereaved mother of her daughter's abduction, rape and murder. The mother's name is Nancy and, in the MCC Theater production, the role

Parent's nightmare: Swoosie Kurtz in Frozen.
Photo: Joan Marcus

brought from Swoosie Kurtz a performance of profound intensity. The play is the first by British writer Bryony Lavery to be produced in New York, and it was her first produced at London's National Theatre in 2002. Although she has written more than 20 other plays, Lavery told Matt Wolf in *The New York Times* that *Frozen* was her first "grown-up one."

As Nancy moves from numbing grief toward solemn forgiveness, her daughter's murderer, Ralph, and the forensic psychologist who examines him, Agnetha (Laila Robins), begin their own thaws from emotional freezes. In creating these dynamics, Lavery neither sensationalizes the crime of child rape and murder, nor sentimentalizes the spiritual anguish this mother suffers. Without trivializing or undermining her subject, the playwright often commits the kind of "mischief in the darkest moments"—as she told London's *Daily Telegraph*—that she admires in the mordant wit of Alan Bennett. Nancy's ultimate forgiveness proves more torturous to the killer than revenge.

For 20 years after the missing girl's abduction at the age of 10, Nancy and other members of an organization called FLAME, cling to hope that the girl may still be alive. When Ralph (O'Bryne) is arrested for a later crime, the missing girl's remains are found buried beneath his shed—along with those of other girls he abused and killed. Nancy is then forced to face an unbearable nothingness: the finality of her loss. She describes joy returning when she and her surviving daughter caress and lay to rest her dead daughter's bones. Not long after, Nancy visits Ralph in prison and it is there that the play's climactic encounter occurs. In that scene, Kurtz and O'Byrne engaged in a delicate moral and emotional dance, surrounded by charged silence. Even in Broadway's Circle in the Square Theatre, where the play moved after its initial downtown run, the audience seemed to hold its collective breath until this heartstopping scene ended.

Nancy's ultimate forgiveness proves more torturous to the killer than revenge.

The third character in Lavery's terse drama is a research psychologist who announces a provocative thesis: "Serial Killing—a forgivable act?" This character, Agnetha (Robins), is the one Lavery was accused of appropriating from the work of psychiatrist Dorothy Otnow Lewis. In Lavery's play, Agnetha is an American whose Icelandic heritage becomes part of the work's symbolic freight. Her attitude toward Ralph remains constant and detached, even as she appears to develop sympathy for this monster.

In the New York production, Lavery's spare yet evocative language—including the unacknowledged, seamlessly interwoven borrowings that appear in some of Agnetha's speeches—was delivered with nuance by the actors. Director Doug Hughes, who guided the production with musical sensitivity, shaped the whole so meticulously that no false notes sounded. This truthfulness made the play's appalling emotional fallout compelling, its profound sorrow bearable. The production released its gathering tension in a bleak catharsis that allowed the audience to experience the play's core theme: How can we remain human while living with unbearable sorrow?

THE ACTION BEGINS with a dozen monologues that are clipped in their language, elusive in meaning and interconnected. In these early solos, each character is stuck, almost literally frozen. Agnetha grieves for David, her medical colleague of 10 years with whom—we later learn—she once had sex not long before his recent, sudden death. Nancy's loss has trapped her in an agony of uncertainty. Ralph is locked apart from human feeling; his only regret is that murdering little girls isn't legal. (A fourth actor, Sam Kitchin, silently stood guard in prison scenes.)

From these solos, the play moves into duets between Ralph and Agnetha. She measures his head. She proffers theories. She begins, stops, then resumes a lecture. Midway through the first act, Ralph is revealed as a serial killer and Nancy's missing daughter, Rhona, is identified as one of his victims. Nancy ricochets from despair to the joy of tenderly holding her daughter's bones to raging vindictiveness.

The second act brings Agnetha's attempt at resolving her own more tractable grief. Before the intense encounter between mother and murderer, Agnetha concludes her lecture. Calling herself an explorer navigating "the Arctic frozen sea of the criminal brain" she discounts the notion of evil as sufficient explanation of the serial murderers she has tested. They are grotesque life-destroying types driven "by forces beyond their control." (This section of Agnetha's speech and the following pithy conclusion—much quoted by reviewers of *Frozen*—derive from Gladwell's article on Lewis in *The New Yorker*.) Agnetha's central finding:

Sin or symptom? Brían F. O'Bryne and Laila Robins in Frozen. *Photo: Joan Marcus*

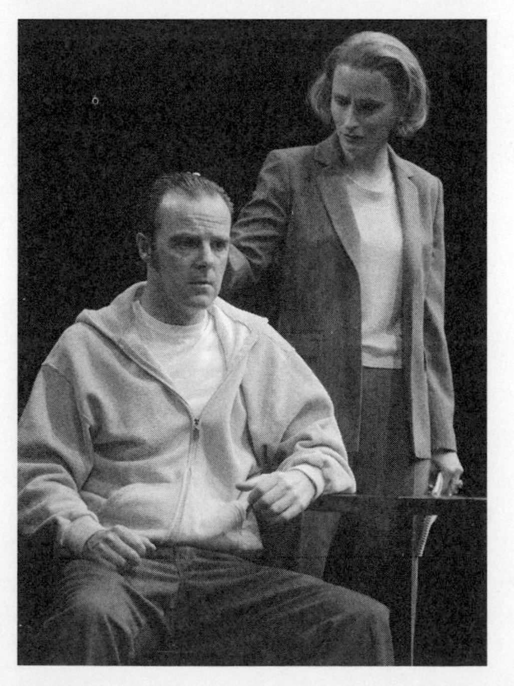

AGNETHA: [. . .] The difference between a crime of evil
and a crime of illness is the difference
between a sin and a symptom [. . . .]

Against Agnetha's wishes, Nancy makes her visit. With gentle persistence—and perhaps unconscious aggression—Nancy pierces Ralph's defenses. They are seated on opposite sides of a small table. She shows him snapshots of Rhona with her family. In a production with very few props, Kurtz proffered these carefully, her large eyes taking the measure of the man as her character slowly—stopping and starting—identified the people in the photos:

NANCY: [. . .] That's me holding her.
This is Ingrid, that's her sister, holding her.
This is them holding their pets.

O'Byrne's Ralph glanced sidelong at the images struggling not to focus until he commented upon the photo that most struck him—Rhona, alone, dressed as an octopus for a fancy-dress competition. "Did she win?" he asks. Nancy tells him she came in third, behind "Little Miss Muffet and a Loch Ness Monster." She tells Ralph that she made the springy octopus arms of the costume herself and he responds:

RALPH: I don't think I hurt her.
[. . .]
I don't think she was frightened at all . . .

Nancy rejects Ralph's self-deluding lies. She leads him on a harrowing journey back into his nightmare childhood. As he recalls his father's violence against him—the repeated blows, the cutting words—she quietly delivers the *coup de grâce*:

NANCY: [. . .] Can you see it hurt Rhona then?
Can you see it frightened her?
What you did.

Frustrated, his chest heaving, O'Byrne's hulking Ralph sheds messy, rusty tears for himself. O'Byrne brought this same awkward unfamiliarity with human pity to Ralph's subsequent attempts to write a letter of apology to Nancy. Furious that he's been touched, filled with what he thinks is cancer but we know is remorse, he returns to the stage in workout clothes. Saying he won't be "gnawed to death," he fashions a noose and hangs himself.

LAVERY, A YORKSHIRE veteran of fringe and gay theater companies, wrote *Frozen* soon after her long-married parents died, the mother from an accident during surgery, her father, not long after, from loneliness. Grief, death, sex and anger have been Lavery's self-proclaimed subjects since. *Frozen* opened at the Birmingham Repertory Theatre in 1998 and was followed by another "grown-up" play, *A Wedding Story* about a physician mother with Alzheimer's disease and her gay daughter.

In 2002, the Birmingham production of *Frozen* opened at the National Theatre, again directed by Bill Alexander, with Anita Dobson as Nancy, Tom Georgeson as Ralph and Josie Lawrence as Agnetha. Critic Kate Kellaway of *The Observer* echoed her British colleagues in naming Lavery one of England's best, most consistently underrated playwrights. "Her talent is lavish," Kellaway wrote. "She is a wonderful technician and always surprising: it is never possible to second-guess her." Lavery's career has resulted in television films, radio plays, children's books, youth drama and a praised biography of Tallulah Bankhead.

Lavery's craft is deft, almost invisible. She employs a double time-scheme in *Frozen*. Viewed from Nancy's perspective, more than 20 years pass from her opening scene to her valediction in the churchyard. She appears in monologues that are set hours, months, then several years after the abduction—and in two-handers set 20 years later. For Agnetha, the action occurs over a few weeks or months after Ralph has been arrested and tried. And it is Agnetha who opens the play. The time schemes align in Scene 12 (there are 32 in total); from then on, the action for all three characters moves tensely in sync.

Played on a thrust stage, backed in New York by designer Hugh Landwehr's glacier blue cyclorama, Hughes's fluid, straightforward presentation—one scene blending seamlessly into the next with no blackouts—eased audiences through shifts of time and place. His staging emphasized the spatial and musical qualities of the play, which is organized by thematic repetitions and counterpoints.

ONE OBVIOUS PATTERN of imagery in *Frozen* works variations upon the title and proves problematic. Lavery told interviewers that the play was partially inspired by television footage showing parents of children abducted and killed by England's Moors' Murderers during the 1960s. Years later these mothers and fathers still appeared frozen, trapped in time and grief.

Reviewers on both sides of the Atlantic rightly felt Lavery overused the icy images. Agnetha says several times that a criminal with "insufficiency

Tragic ties: Laila Robins and Swoosie Kurtz in Frozen. *Photo: Joan Marcus*

of suppression" is like a person who is icebound. The psychologist's riffs about her Icelandic background—her name is Gottmondsdottir—also feel forced. Agnetha lives in her head, and her chilly, pseudoscientific exactitude doesn't require added symbolic underscoring. In Scene 9 when Nancy recounts how she learned from policemen about the shed where young bodies have been found, Lavery calls for the sound of "ice floes cracking." Sound designer David Van Tieghem wisely did not emphasize that cue.

A more effective and less obvious store of images derives from myth and fairy tale. These embody the play's most moving themes and counter-themes, centering on Nancy's double loss: the abduction of Rhona and Nancy's estrangement from (and reconciliation with) the older daughter, Ingrid.

Nancy first appears waiting for Rhona to return after sending her off to her grandmother's house. Nancy and her demanding mother share a love of gardening—but do not see eye-to-eye on pruning (and quite a bit more). Similarly, Nancy and the adolescent Ingrid are having a bad patch themselves. That's why Nancy asked Rhona instead of the older girl to take the clippers to her grandmother's house.

Descriptions of Rhona, Ingrid and Bob—Nancy's wandering husband—are startlingly precise, if fragmentary. Nancy first describes her younger girl as a little panda, with dark smudges round her eyes from mascara taken from Ingrid. The feuding girls are in the midst of a cease-fire, says Nancy, who reports that she has had it with all of them. Rhona becomes a Little Red Riding Hood sauntering off in the late afternoon to grandmother's house; she's a miniature Beauty to Ralph's "mesmerizing rattlesnake" of a Beast.

Shrewdly creating familiarity and emotional resonance, Lavery names each of Rhona's most-loved objects twice. Her witch stone—described first on the girl's Nature Table and later, when Nancy places it with her bones—becomes iconic, fabulous. So, too, a bit of gorse with sheep's wool wrapped in it from an encounter with a lamb and its mother. There's her stuffed animal, Leo the Lion, with its bald patch where Rhona had cut his hair: "Rhona's Rough Cuts," Nancy jokes. Throughout these monologues, with no literal props, Nancy recounts Ingrid's comments: the teenager's insistence that Rhona is the favored daughter, the good girl. Later, though, we also learn of Ingrid's compassionate communion with her mother as they place Rhona's treasures in a small coffin with her bones.

Nancy is initially skeptical of Ingrid's New Age journey. The mother tells of resisting her adult daughter's ideas about "letting go," making "space" and the "Life Force." On a journey aimed at healing herself, Ingrid writes to her mother in truisms about forgiveness that Nancy instinctively rejects. Instead of Ingrid telling where and how she is:

> NANCY: [. . . T]hese mucky little parcels start arriving
> inside
> cloth squares about this big . . .
> Bright colours with foreign type writing on . . .
> Handkerchiefs?
> Head Squares?

Kurtz made the audience feel that Nancy both resented and deeply missed her surviving daughter. Reading Ingrid's message from Lhasa explaining the squares as Tibetan prayer flags, Kurtz's staccato delivery grew fluent, her tone curious:

> NANCY: [. . .] They are hung up each year
> to signify
> hope
> transformation
> and the spreading of compassion. As the year progresses
> the wind disperses the energy of the words,

which carry the power to pacify and heal
Everything they touch.

Nancy shoves them into her "bits and bobs drawer." But as Ralph's trial begins and the inspector refuses to allow her to see Rhona's remains, Nancy feels as close to being "not alive" as she has ever been. She unfurls the flags, like laundry on a line.

NANCY: [T]hey flap and flap and
The gate opens and
this thin, thin, brown thing head wrapped in a lot of cloth
[. . .]
Ingrid.
Ingrid.
Ingrid.

When the mother and her surviving daughter finally reunite, Ingrid's newly brown head echoes the color that they find so beautiful as each, in turn, holds Rhona's brown skull and gleaming bones close to her heart. An earthy mortician stands close, encouraging them. Hamlet and the Gravedigger seem near too, bringing the perspective born of touching mortality.

Even the shed that Ralph considers his headquarters sustains the gruesome archetypal resonance of the story. The Beast catalogued his kiddie-porn and buried his victims in a lock-up on Far Forest Lane.

Ralph's homicidal motives remain murky, ambiguous. He's feeling "offish": his landlady fed him meat he doesn't like. So he kills. O'Byrne bent down to re-enact the seductions, his voice falling almost to a whisper:

RALPH: Hello.
Hello.
Hello.
Hello.

Sweetly, as if calling to a kitten, he insinuated himself, getting each of seven girls to respond. "You make it work," he says, "she's in the van." Ralph also supplies a description of the evening when time stopped for Nancy. "Lovely evening," he recalls. "Sunny . . . but with a light southerly breeze." The offhand tone of O'Byrne's voice was devastating.

AGNETHA'S THEORIES ABOUT the criminal mind are ultimately unconvincing and unimportant. Neither she nor, to a lesser degree, Ralph is the emotional and thematic crux of the drama. Her neurological hypotheses—that childhood trauma causes frontal lobe dysfunction; that hormonal stress leads to an underdeveloped cortex and conscience—play as intellectual diversions beside the enormity of Ralph's crimes and Nancy's stark pain.

Given the charges of plagiarism made against Lavery, it's worth noting that the fictional psychologist might well have articulated a different set of theories. A year before the New York production, Lavery told an Australian interviewer that the key to the scientific side of her research was a different book, *The Murder of Childhood* by Ray Wyre and Tim Tate. Their theory that childhood sexual abuse causes profound and pathological changes in the structure of the brain is "hugely disputed," Lavery told the *Australian Weekend*, adding "A psychologist friend of mine came and said 'That's just a load of cobblers!'" Clearly, the scientific accuracy of psychological explanations for Ralph's behavior meant far less to the playwright than the dramatic use she would make of such theories.

MCC's beautifully acted production, saturated with grief and sadness, was steeped in the knowledge that life can be tragic and people ultimately unknowable. Harrowing emotions, expressed in Lavery's spare writing, exist in counterpoint to the mental and moral struggles of the brainy researcher. More than a plot device, yet less than a fully written character, Agnetha at least brings a final ironizing perspective to the play.

We discover in a brief coda that her affair with David has contaminated her grief at his death with precisely the shame, guilt and remorse that homicidal Ralph had been incapable of feeling. O'Byrne's Ralph—a finicky, porn-collecting lump of inhumanity in an undershirt and slick-backed hair, a banal criminal so fastidious and efficient, so proud of the tattoos that memorialize each murder—was a man whom Agnetha viewed as morally neutral. Yet she feels culpable for her lesser crime of sexual betrayal. In the church graveyard, she turns to Nancy for absolution. Agnetha wants to know if she should tell David's wife, her good friend, about the brief affair.

> NANCY: No.
>
> You just suffer.

Nancy offers the only comfort available—cold, perhaps, and bleak. But real.

> NANCY: [. . .] You knew what you were doing.
>
> Live with it.

2003–2004 Best Play
2004 ATCA/Steinberg Award

INTIMATE APPAREL

By Lynn Nottage

○○○○○

Essay by Lenora Inez Brown

> ESTHER: The other evening I was at my sewing machine and I stopped work and all this time had passed, gone. Years really. And I known right there that some things ain't meant to be. And that's all right, ain't it? And I wouldn't have thought no more about it, but then I got this . . .

IT STARTED WITH a photograph: a sepia-toned image of an unidentified negro woman positioned at her sewing machine, her fingers forever frozen in an act that will inspire a creative idea nearly a century later. Somewhere between the outline of the female form and the edge of the photo a story remained trapped, waiting to reveal the often stereotyped, if not ignored colored woman's existence. Throughout *Intimate Apparel*, Lynn Nottage's spare, eloquent drama, the imagined lives of an unnamed, forgotten seamstress and her companions—her intimates—unfold in 1905 New York.

In truth, though, it started with a story. "*Intimate Apparel* really began with my great-grandmother," Nottage wrote in an e-mail.

> She was a seamstress (she made intimate apparel) at the turn of the century. She corresponded with a man based in Panama and they subsequently married. It was a story that I had heard told by my grandmother, only once. I discovered the image of grandmother, while I was formulating the idea for the play. It was synchronicity.

Isn't that the way it is with history? There is the truth and the rumored truth. An event happens and it is either immortalized—through idealistic and poetic language, perhaps—or it disappears entirely until someone discovers it. As much as the style of Nottage's writing differs from play to play, what remains consistent is her dedication to exploring the histories of people whom the keepers of history often choose not to notice. More often

Under ware: Viola Davis and Lauren Velez in Intimate Apparel. *Photo: Joan Marcus*

than not these compositions for the stage are the stories of women of color, of African descent.

WRITERS OF HISTORICAL fiction often work toward verisimilitude. Life, it seems, cannot be explored unless mired in the accoutrements of the past. Such attention to detail suggests that modern audiences are not trusted to find the connections between bygone and modern eras. Nowhere in *Intimate Apparel*, though, does Nottage succumb to the traditional motifs that often give way to stereotypes. She opts to probe the vagaries of human friendship: the timeless ways people struggle to connect.

In *Las Meninas* (2002), *Intimate Apparel* (2003) and *Fabulation Or, the Re-Education of Undine*—a "companion piece" to *Intimate Apparel* that is set to premiere in the 2004–05 season—Nottage creates depictions of injustice, stereotype and prejudice without the common accompaniment of anger. The characters voice frustration and seek better lives, but they set anger aside. Injustice drives her characters but they also understand that they must accept the current world in order to change it—because hating would devour them and render them powerless to effect change.

Writers such as David Mamet and August Wilson shape emotional landscapes with similar language from play to play. Nottage, however, chooses a linguistic style and structure suited to each of her play's themes and characters. In *Intimate Apparel* that style consists of simple, direct dialogue laced with humor—much of it surfacing at unexpected moments. Instead of punctuating lines with scripted pauses that tell an actor or audience how to feel in response to a situation, in *Intimate Apparel* Nottage provides actors resting points that they can shape and fill: actors choose the silences. To refrain from writing where the pauses take place shows an amazing degree of confidence in her storytelling—and that of the actors.

Esther's confidence and ability to move between worlds diminishes.

It's interesting to follow the idea at the center of her plays: there is no singular way to think, feel or behave as a person of African descent. Many plays focusing on the African-American community highlight the lives of a particular socioeconomic world (working and lower class) and a single perspective on African culture. Nottage's dramatic worlds always revel in the diversity of color, opinion, spirit and financial success in an ethnic community that so many try to homogenize.

INTIMATE APPAREL ESSENTIALLY is a collection of snapshots. A slightly fragmentary style shapes this and other Nottage plays, particularly *Las Meninas* and *Fabulation*, plays that also focus on uncovering character through history. Her dramaturgy reminds us that history isn't always as neat as we'd like, and neither are people's lives.

The plot that connects these six lives is even simpler than the serendipitous photograph. Esther, a 35-year-old African-American seamstress—an old maid in those days—travels between Mrs. Van Buren's elegant boudoir and Mayme's seedy bedroom, bringing gorgeous hand-sewn corsets and other intimate apparel to the women. She often stops to purchase cloth from Mr. Marks, a Romanian Jew who lives in a garment district flat, before returning home to Mrs. Dickson's boarding house for colored girls. Between these visits she "hears" letters from George, a Barbadian laborer working on the Panama Canal who begins to write to Esther out of the blue. Without so much as a photograph or a pencil sketch, the two begin a romantic and somewhat clandestine correspondence. Neither can read nor write, so they depend on others to craft their missives. Bedazzled by each other's prose, the two marry.

Act II begins like Act I with Esther in her room—now shared with George—and with a bit of a confrontation. George encroaches on her space, but she doesn't mind much because she is now not alone. As a married woman, Esther now receives invitations to church teas. She exists. But we can tell things are wrong between them, as he physically withdraws from her. Suddenly, Esther's confidence and ability to move between worlds diminishes.

MANY PLAYS THAT focus on African-American women depict cultures in which the women work against one another or are isolated from one another. Often, either skin color or money divides the women. Alice Childress's *Wedding Band*, most similar to *Intimate Apparel*, maintains the boundaries between the uneducated and the financially challenged through literacy

Fancy "friend": Viola Davis and Arija Bareikis in Intimate Apparel. *Photo: Joan Marcus*

and skin color—light-skinned women are literate and achieve wealth, dark-skinned women are illiterate and subservient. Childress describes the negative impact that division has among black women in 1918—when her play is set—and 1966 (when it was written). Ntozake Shange's choreopoem, *For Colored Girls Who Have Considered Suicide When the Rainbow Is Enuf* (1974), celebrates the differences of color within the African-American community but rarely do the women appear together (in the writing) except to support and heal each other's wounded souls. Kia Corthron's *Breath, Boom* centers on girl gangs, and the power structures within them, providing a window into division among African-American women who have been discarded by society.

This season saw progress in the African-American canon of sisterhood depicted onstage. Kirsten Greenidge's *Sans-culottes in the Promised Land*—chosen for the 2004 Humana Festival of New American Plays at Actors Theatre of Louisville—and Nottage's play create more complex and realistic depictions of life among women of color. Greenidge focuses on women of African descent and of various economic levels who respond to the notion of being African. Unlike earlier plays, though, the women are not pitted against one another. They judge each other's choices negatively but do not actively engage in breaking one another down and neither do Nottage's African-American female characters.

As *Intimate Apparel* opens, Esther avoids the wedding celebration of another young woman in Mrs. Dickinson's home. After 18 years, Esther has seen 22 less talented, more beautiful (and sociable) women married. Her financial independence—she has saved $100 for each year at Mrs. Dickson's amassing $1800 in her crazy quilt to finance her dream of a beauty parlor for colored women—doesn't add to her attractiveness. In 1905 when African-American men cannot find work easily even in a Northern city like New York, a black woman's ability to negotiate the black and white worlds of business poses a threat to the black male ego.

Esther is a modern woman, but she is lonely. Her success, ambition and age separate her from many of the women in the boarding house—and her spinster status prevents her from socializing with the church ladies, a community with which she longs to connect.

> ESTHER: I sat up in Saint Martin's for years, and didn't none of them church ladies bother with me until I walked in on your arm, and suddenly they want Mrs. Armstrong over for tea.

The two African-American women Esther befriends are also financially independent, but even they are kept at a distance. Esther is shamed by her illiteracy before Mrs. Dickson, her landlady, and Mayme's work as a prostitute draws a line that's difficult to erase entirely. Binding them all, though, is a mutual lack of connection in a community of women (and men). Everything in their lives revolves around a business transaction. People connect with these women out of temporary necessity. Esther's presence is particularly valued, though, because her encounters transcend the transaction. With her, they unveil bits of themselves without the fear of being judged. Each considers Esther a friend.

> ESTHER: You didn't expect me to be here for the rest of my life?
>
> MRS. DICKSON: I guess I sort of did. I'm so used to hearing your sewing machine and foot tapping up here.
>
> ESTHER: Another gal will move into this room and by supper you'll be fussing about something new.
>
> MRS. DICKSON: You say that with such certainty. You hurt my feelings, Miss Esther Mills.

In truth, every scene in this play—a tale of love, loneliness and the inherent paradox of intimacy—is a transaction of some sort. Some of the characters forget this truth more quickly than others. Mrs. Van Buren experiences joy when Esther fits her for corsets and crosses the line when she kisses Esther passionately:

> ESTHER: Friends? How we friends? When I ain't never been through your front door. You love me? What of me do you love?
>
> MRS. VAN BUREN: Esther, you are the only one who's been in my room in all these months. And it's only in here with you, that I feel . . . happy. Please, I want us to be friends?

It is Esther's awareness of the contrived nature of her relationship with these intimates that gives the play its bittersweet tone and strong connection with today's women. Too often driven by a desire to have it all—career and family—we spend time attaining the necessary education and jobs to insure successful careers at the expense of having personal lives.

Esther's marriage to George is ill-fated from his first letter, but hope exists for her just as it may for many a successful African-American woman involved in a relationship that might make others think twice. Using the prism of history, Nottage taps the wellspring of the contemporary world often discussed on *20/20* and in the pages of *Essence* magazine: the black woman with a career, education and talent finds herself somewhat unwelcome in society—and finds connecting with a mate even more difficult. News stories and magazine articles focus on telling black women what they already know: that unlike other women, the pool of marriageable

Love starved: Viola Davis and Russell Hornsby in Intimate Apparel. *Photo: Joan Marcus*

black men has dwindled to the point where a PhD or CEO shouldn't be surprised if she marries a man with a GED. For a well-educated financially independent African-American woman the odds of marrying well are as slim in 2003 as they were in 1905.

ALTHOUGH MANY WOMEN responded favorably to the play, some men were less positive. African-American men took issue with Nottage's characterization of George, claiming he conforms to the stereotypical bad, black man. These detractors failed to see Nottage's depiction of George's strength. Yes, he squanders money on rum, women and dice; yes, he's uneducated and sees himself and his family as nothing more than chattel; but his speeches in Act II are some of the most impassioned arguments for the frustrations of racism. They provide insight to how the world came to be rather than excusing his behavior.

> GEORGE: Thursday last I stood all day, it cold too, waitin' for the chief, waiting to interview. Do yuh have tools, boy? Yes! Do yuh know how to operate a machine, boy? Yes. But 'e point just so to the Irishmen, the German and the tall Norwegian who's at least fifty

> years plus five. And I got more experience than the lot. I tell 'e so. Next time, 'e say. Next time, George.

George represents the black male's difficulty moving between two worlds, where his mere existence and physical strength threatens the world around him. George's plight focuses on the stress placed on a relationship in which a proud man has to ask his wife for money.

> GEORGE: [. . . H]ow it look to people. Me, sitting 'ere, waitin' on fortune, you out there courtin' it.

INTIMATE APPAREL WAS co-commissioned by Baltimore's Center Stage and Southern California's South Coast Repertory. South Coast's longtime dramaturg Jerry Patch shepherded the two-city premiere, and the accompanying rewrites, while Kate Whoriskey directed. But it wasn't until New York's Roundabout Theatre Company produced *Intimate Apparel*—at the Laura Pels Theatre in the newly opened Harold and Miriam Steinberg Center for Theatre—that Nottage fully realized her play. The earlier productions allowed her to see where to revise, an opportunity few playwrights get. August Wilson has that luxury, but most writers find themselves saddled with the burden of trying to perfect their plays with one production—and then praying for a second production some years later (if they're lucky). According to the Roundabout's online production history, Nottage's was the theater's third production by an African-American writer in its 37-year history—the first was *A Raisin in the Sun* by Lorraine Hansberry in the 1985–86 season, the second was *Blue* by Charles Randolph-Wright in 2000–01. Daniel Sullivan directed the Roundabout production with Viola Davis as Esther.

Davis is the ideal actor for the role. Her characteristic tomboyish gait was perfect here, for even though Esther worked with fine fabrics and frequented places of elegant or gawdy opulence, she never feels quite at home. As gifted a seamstress as Esther may be, Davis showed that Esther can never totally transform her life to become an insider. Her magnificent performance captured the spirit of a black woman unpracticed at social intercourse who, at times, actually enjoys her life. When her Esther smiled to embrace the world, her face contorted before bursting into something akin to a child's delighted grin.

The friendship inspiring the greatest smile from Esther is the one with Mr. Marks (Corey Stoll), the Jewish purveyor of cloth. Their shared passion for fine fabric barely masks a constantly growing attraction to one another. Throughout the depiction of their relationship, however, Nottage avoids the usual Jewish versus African American argument, a division typically fueled by misunderstanding and irrationality. What separates these star-crossed lovers is the knowledge that the world isn't quite ready for them—and they aren't yet strong enough to separate themselves from their pasts. Stoll brought a gentle warmth to Marks, giving a sensuality to their scenes more titillating than any physical encounter. Throughout his performance, Stoll's Marks softly and tentatively chooses his words—aware and in awe of Esther's fragility.

The design and direction of the Roundabout production, buoyed the actors as their characters found ways to circumvent society's rigid boundaries. To highlight their isolation, Sullivan set scenes in distinct areas of the stage with scene designer Derek McLane using bold strokes—and few set pieces—to indicate each private space. It doesn't seem possible that emphasizing the emptiness of the playing space can actually fashion a more intimate world, but it did here. The spare set focused attention on the actors, heightening their smallest attempt to connect. The visual void magnified the nuance, intensifying the longing and sense of loneliness. Allen Lee Hughes's lighting was similarly spare. Typically with such scene designs, light defines distinct areas with clean crisp lines, leaving an impenetrable visual wall of light. Here the lighting shielded the characters only somewhat from the outside world. It illuminated their sanctuaries but kept the remaining stage area subtly in shadow, consistently reminding audience and characters that the rules of engagement are differ wildly.

IN *INTIMATE APPAREL* the irony is that you can be surrounded by people, somewhat successful in your chosen path—whether you own a business or marry well—and lonely nevertheless. A still void surrounds each scene, yet an energy of possibility pulses beneath. Sullivan captured this with a tableau at the end of Act I. Esther in her wedding dress and George in an ill-fitting suit stand on either side of the bed, staring headlong into the future with frozen expressions. Given the circumstances of their courtship, it looks like terror tinged with a bit of excitement. Above them, a title appears: "Unidentified Negro Couple c. 1905," underlining the notion that an unnamed, unidentified photograph contains a story rich with meaning and nuance.

This play speaks of the unremembered who build history silently, without regard of making their mark—which they manage to do in their own ways.

In a final tableau, Esther sits smiling, bent over her sewing machine with her hand on her belly. Another title appears: "Unidentified Negro Woman c. 1905."

2003–2004 Best Play

LIVING OUT

By Lisa Loomer

○○○○○

Essay by Charles Wright

> ANA: How come you live in?
>
> ZOILA: Because she ask me. And when I said no, I got fired. So I said yes.
>
> ANA: [. . .] One day we should all stay home!

LISA LOOMER BECAME a *cause célèbre* when *The Waiting Room*, her powerfully grotesque comedy, appeared in a succession of nonprofit resident theaters around the United States between 1994 and 1996. Yet, oddly enough, none of Loomer's works has enjoyed a high-profile commercial engagement and, despite her prominence among current dramatists, she's hardly known to the public. Once writer-in-residence at Intar, the distinguished Off Off Broadway showcase for Latino drama, Loomer represents a melancholy phenomenon of contemporary American theater—an acclaimed playwright who resorts to work in film and television for the bulk of her living. Her most conspicuous credit to date is the screenplay of Susanna Kaysen's memoir, *Girl, Interrupted* (though hers wasn't the version ultimately filmed). Were it not for the national network of financially underwritten theaters, Loomer wouldn't have the visibility, however limited, she currently enjoys.

Living Out, the provocative problem play that inaugurated the 25th anniversary season of Second Stage Theatre, involves a Los Angeles couple who recruit an immigrant without a green card to care for their newborn daughter. A decade ago, this situation sparked a flurry of public discourse when news organizations discovered that Zoë Baird, President Bill Clinton's 1993 nominee for Attorney General, had failed to pay social security taxes for household employees who, also, lacked working papers.

The social background of *Living Out* is an urban world transformed by the "second wave" of feminist activism during the final third of the 20th century. In current American culture, with its child-centered perspective and labor-intensive standards for parenting, a multitude of women depend

Surrogate moms: Liza Colón-Zayas, Zilah Mendoza and Maria Elena Ramirez in Living Out. *Photo: Joan Marcus*

on immigrants—predominantly female, largely from Central America and the Caribbean—in order to leave home every morning and compete for professional advancement. The play's title refers, on its surface, to the status of nannies who toil in other people's homes but maintain residences of their own. That arrangement is viewed, at least within the work force, as preferable to "living in." "Living out" accords the caregiver an identity of her own; "living in" is the reviled, last-ditch alternative, tantamount to indentured servitude.

In writing about the parent-nanny relationship, Loomer tills ground that has had a thorough going-over, of late, by American novelists, such as Emma McLaughlin, Nicola Kraus and Benjamin Cheever. In their farcical 2002 novel, *The Nanny Diaries*, McLaughlin and Kraus offer the nanny's eye view of a pampered, selfish mother on Manhattan's Upper East Side and her inhumane treatment of the younger woman who looks after her child. In the 2004 novel *The Good Nanny*, Cheever creates an exemplary caregiver as foil to his protagonists, a pair of naïve, hyper-neurotic Baby Boomers fleeing the New York City literary scene for suburban domesticity.

Loomer, like Cheever, McLaughlin and Kraus, handles the subject with wit, as well as satire; but her satire is gentler, further removed from invective than theirs. *Living Out* opens as sprightly, carefully observed comedy, drawing humor primarily from the recognizable interaction of fully developed characters. It concludes, however, on a tragic plane, with the death of a child as the ultimate link in a chain of misunderstandings that begins with a lie—ostensibly a minor lie. Such shifts in style and mood aren't easy for dramatists to pull off; and plays of this sort demand intricate calibration in actors' performances. Even when competently acted, such tonal changes are likely to unnerve the audience. Loomer's success in this dramaturgical crapshoot is a tribute to the accomplished nature of her craft and a principal reason why *Living Out* elicited wide-reaching "word of mouth" among New York audiences during its run.

Loomer creates full-bodied characters, believable and sympathetic.

AT THE CENTER of *Living Out* is Salvadoran Ana Hernandez (Zilah Mendoza), a former dental student who has fled a homeland devastated by poverty, unemployment, earthquake, civil war and death squads, leaving behind a son to be raised, at least temporarily, by relatives. In Los Angeles, where she lives on the Eastside with husband Bobby (Gary Perez) and son Santiago (an offstage character), Ana's situation is improved but hardly ideal. Because her English skills are patchy, the employment most accessible to her is child care. As a candidate for nanny jobs, she's as competent as Mary Poppins but as put-upon as Jane Eyre. In the swift, cinematic scenes that open the play, Ana comes close to snagging two placements until her prospective employers—Wallace (Judith Hawking) and Linda (Kelly Coffield Park)—hear that she has a son living with her. "I need someone who can make my kids a priority," whines Linda. The less empathetic Wallace doesn't bother explaining:

> WALLACE: I specifically told the agency not to send me anyone with a young child. I don't know what's wrong with those people!

In her third interview, she foregoes the truth:

> ANA: I have two boys. [. . .] But they are both in El Salvador.

Ana gets the job. Her new employer, Nancy Robin (Kathryn Meisle), is an entertainment lawyer at a fancy firm who lives on the more affluent Westside. About to return to work after maternity leave, Nancy fears her employers may relegate her to the "mommy track."

LOOMER DIRECTS THAT the Eastside scenes in *Living Out* should be played in the same area of the stage as the Westside scenes, rather than being separated. What's more, the Hernandez and Robin households are to be represented with the same props and furnishings, sometimes simultaneously. For instance, in Act I,

> Ana's husband, Bobby, sits in the chair DSR reading the Sports Section of *La Opinion*. Nancy's husband, Richard, reads the Sports Section of the [*Los Angeles*] *Times* on the couch. The scenes on the Eastside and the Westside are simultaneous [. . .] but each woman clearly speaks to her own husband.

This is effective dramatic craft, well implemented in New York by Jo Bonney's direction and Neil Patel's efficient, eye-appealing stage design. In that production, scenes of the two families' lives overlapped and bled into each other, stressing the differences and, more importantly, the similarities of the two.

In Ana and Nancy, Loomer creates full-bodied characters, believable and sympathetic. What's striking—from the audience's perspective, at least—is how much the two have in common, though neither is conscious of the coincidence:

Guilt trip: Kathryn Meisle and Zilah Mendoza in Living Out. *Photo: Joan Marcus*

¶ Each woman feels compelled to work outside the home. Nancy's husband, Richard (Joseph Urla), a public defender, doesn't earn enough to supply the accoutrements of fine living—cars, restaurant meals, newfangled appliances, and a house in a good neighborhood with a hefty mortgage—to which the couple aspires.

¶ Each is pressed by her spouse to spend more time at home. Bobby considers it unmanly to have a working wife; Richard feels Nancy isn't giving their baby sufficient attention.

¶ Each is plagued with guilt about the limited time she spends with her offspring. Ana grieves about separation from her older son, who has lived apart from her for most of his life; she's anxious about relying on others to fetch Santi from school and soccer practice. Nancy stews about missing landmarks in Jenna's early development.

Periodically, throughout the play, Loomer interposes scenes on a park bench that alternate between a clique of nannies (Ana and two other women from Latin American countries) and a clique of "mommies" (Nancy and two affluent Westsiders, Wallace and Linda). These scenes are comparable to the antiphonal choruses of classical Greek drama. Both groups gossip and kvetch, each faction regarding the other as its principal irritation. In a brief monologue, for instance, Wallace—ostensibly a stay-at-home mom—discusses hiring a full-time nanny for her son, Jackson.

> WALLACE: Well, I just got a new nanny [. . . a]nd maybe for the first week or so, I'll just leave a little cash on the kitchen counter—like I've just—left it, you know . . . And when I get home I'll count it and see how much is gone. If it's just a little change, well, no bigee . . . [. . .] But the next time anything is missing, be it a dollar or a hand towel or a yogurt—I'll mention it. Casually. I'll just say "Gee, didn't I buy two cherry yogurts?" And if she doesn't say, "Oh—I took one for lunch"—then I have to fire her.

In a subsequent scene, Wallace's nanny, Zoila (Liza Colón-Zayas), offers another version of the same circumstances:

> ZOILA: Mrs. Breyer—she got so much money, she just leave it around all over the place. Anybody could come in and find it. These peoples got no respect for money. Gringos.

IN ACT I, Ana and Nancy become acquainted, their lives increasingly entangled. New to parenting, Nancy recognizes with alarm that Ana is more adept than she at handling an infant. When Ana confesses her immigration woes, Nancy puts her in touch with an appropriate lawyer and lends her a thousand dollars to cover his fee. To repay the loan, Ana makes herself available, as needed, for overtime child care.

In the second act, the women's relationship becomes increasingly complicated. Nancy, working hard and traveling constantly on business, is ever more dependent on Ana. Nancy's marriage suffers from her absences; and there's indication that, with diminished sexual activity between Nancy and Richard, his eye is roving in Ana's direction. The play's rising action spikes when Nancy, summoned to an after-hours business meeting, throws herself on Ana's mercy for emergency child care. It's the stuff of melodrama, but handled with reserve by the playwright.

> NANCY: Ana . . . do you think you could possibly do me a huge favor and work late tonight? [. . .]
>
> ANA: No—I already got plans.
>
> NANCY: Oh gee. I'm sorry . . . (*beat*) Ana, I know it's awful of me to ask—but could you possibly change them?
>
> [. . . .]
>
> ANA: No. (*beat*) It's a—a family thing.

The fiction that both her sons are back in El Salvador is too well established; Ana can't bring herself to confess her long-standing lie.

> ANA: (*feeling cornered*) I already worked off the overtime for the thousand dollars . . . [. . .]
>
> NANCY: I know that! But Richard's working late—there's really no one else I can call—
>
> [. . . .]
>
> NANCY: Well, could you possibly just do me a—favor? Just this one time? (*touches her hand*) As a . . . a friend?

Ana acquiesces, turning to Bobby's sister to retrieve Santiago from his soccer match. When Santiago suffers an asthma attack during the match, the sister doesn't get him to a hospital quickly enough. Alerted that Santiago is *in extremis*, Ana bundles the Robins' baby into her car and rushes to her own child's side.

Nancy and Richard return to find baby and nanny missing. When all is explained, they view Ana as a betrayer (despite twinges of middle-class liberal guilt).

> NANCY: She was doing me a *favor*—as a friend!
>
> RICHARD: No. Honey, you were working. Ana was working. [. . .] Everyone's working and paying someone else to take

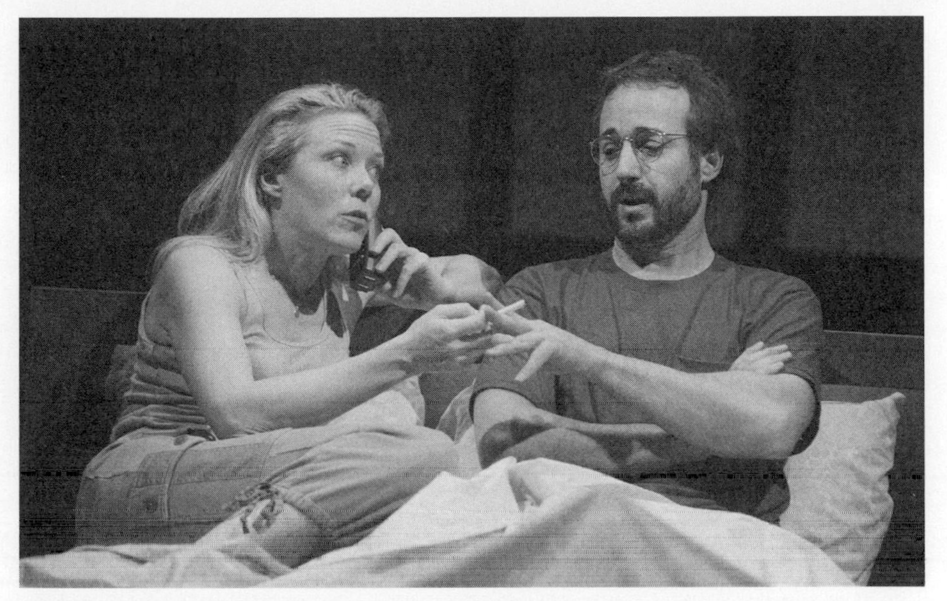

Liberal rationale: Kathryn Meisle and Joseph Urla in Living Out. *Photo: Joan Marcus*

> care of their child—it's insane! It's insane people even have to leave their families to come to this country—
>
> NANCY: (*feeling guilty*) Well, we funded the war in El Salvador—
>
> RICHARD: We personally?
>
> NANCY: We pay taxes—
>
> RICHARD: (*ironic*) So in a couple of years we can hire a nanny from Iraq.

Nancy and Ana are confronted with the fact that they neither are, nor ever can be, friends. Yet their connection isn't cleanly severed; and the play's conclusion is an excruciating telephone exchange that leaves them in emotional limbo.

> NANCY: (*With enormous difficulty*) Well, as I said in my note, we . . . we decided we're just going to take care of Jenna ourselves—for now . . .
>
> (*Ana nods, but doesn't reply.*)
>
> NANCY: (*con't*) But I just wanted to say how—badly I feel, Ana, about what happened . . . And to thank you for . . . everything. And if you need anything, a reference—anything . . . (*waits*) I hope you'll let me know.
>
> ANA: I'm fine. I got another job, Mrs. Robin.
>
> (*Nancy nods.*)

In an ironic *coup de grâce* Nancy, the conscientious liberal, is so distressed by Ana's lie (however self-protective it may have been) that she's blind to clues that Santiago's medical crisis has been fatal.

The misunderstandings and exposed lie bring the women face to face with the peculiar nature of the relationship that Loomer is writing about. It's an intimate relationship, yet, ultimately, a business contract. And, in the case of Nancy and Ana, it's a botched contract. Linda Winer, writing in *Newsday* on the morning after the opening, remarked that *Living Out* contains "no heroes or villains, just real-enough people trying not to be obnoxious while pretending to be more than bosses and employees and trying not to recognize the inequity of their lives."

The psychological inevitability of the play's conclusion is reflected in the deeper significance of its title, evoking as it does the way ordinary citizens "live out" unwittingly the agendas or "scripts" that society and government foist upon them. At its darkest, Loomer's play concerns the ways its characters, both the Central Americans and the United States citizens, are affected by official decisions in which they have no hand and of which they're often unaware. The characters' daily lives are profoundly influenced by the immigration policies their leaders implement and the wars they wage. Sixteen years after Reagan left office, for instance, both the Hernandez and Robin households feel the impact of that administration's involvement in El Salvador.

SECOND STAGE TREATED *Living Out* to a slick, fast-moving production that confirmed the company's place in the upper echelon of Manhattan theater. Patel's sleek, brightly colored set, complemented by David Weiner's lighting design, was as handsome and contemporary-looking as Second Stage's 296-seat, state-of-the-art theater—which opened five years ago.

Mendoza, making one of the noteworthy debuts of the New York season, was the only member of the cast who had also appeared in the play's premiere at the Mark Taper Forum in Los Angeles. As the sympathetic Ana, Mendoza gave an intelligent, nuanced performance, never capitulating to the melodrama of the play's plot. In the role of Nancy, the always reliable Meisle had a more difficult assignment. Nancy—educated, affluent, and ambitious—would be recognizable to most audience members at a nonethnic, subscription theater in Manhattan, such as Second Stage. But the character is also open to ridicule. To her credit, Meisle made Nancy understandable. Under the guidance of Bonney, one of the more adroit directors presently working in New York, the two actors maintained exquisite balance in a text that could readily tip in Ana's favor.

Writing in *New York*, the erudite John Simon exclaimed, "Finally, finally, a real play!" Simon characterized *Living Out* as "a marvelously witty comedy that seamlessly turns serious . . ." and described the Second Stage production as an event in which "writing, directing, acting and design come excitingly and memorably together" in a play "made special by the author's talent for understatement, suggestion, lacerating implication—leaving things eloquently unsaid yet shadowingly present." Margo Jefferson, covering *Living Out* for *The New York Times,* grudgingly acknowledged much that was worthy in both the script and its staging. But she opened her review with the unsubstantiated comment that Loomer "works hard to apply sitcom conventions to a two-hour play with serious intentions." Because producers consider plaudits from the *Times* essential to the success of a theatrical venture, Jefferson's wild-card assessment probably cost *Living Out* the chance of a commercial engagement or even a longer extension at Second Stage.

Though the *Times* couldn't recant Jefferson's assessment, its editors subsequently published a sympathetic profile of the playwright on the first page of the paper's Arts section. According to that piece, Loomer described her background to reporter Julie Salamon as "complicated," remarking that "she had spent a lot of time living in Mexico" but "refus[ing] to elaborate." The playwright wished aloud to Salamon that *Living Out* might "generate discussion between nannies and the mothers who hire them," then lamented the "paradox" of contemporary theater that, with the high cost of tickets, "[t]he airing of these matters is a luxury too expensive for most of those who care for others' children." Notwithstanding the economics of today's stage, in *Living Out,* Loomer achieves something remarkable—an evenhanded depiction of the dilemmas of all of her characters—Latino and Anglo, Gentile and Jew, and, not least, the offstage children.

2003–2004 Best Play

THE LONG CHRISTMAS RIDE HOME

By Paula Vogel

○○○○○

Essay by Tish Dace

> MINISTER: Buddha taught us that the world
> And all its joys are fleeting, too soon melted away.
> But rather than renounce the joys of this world [. . .]
> Why not embrace what will too soon be gone?

IMMEDIATELY AFTER SEPTEMBER 11, 2001, Paula Vogel poured out a bold new play. She wrote her first draft in not weeks but days. While other authors responding to that event might have produced works overtly political, Vogel delved into highly personal material in order to create her most universal play, which dramatizes the origins, in family dysfunction, of insecurities we share.

The Long Christmas Ride Home takes us on a journey back to a childhood holiday, one we least want to remember. A family of five—two parents in the front seat, three kids in back—drive to the grandparents' house for Christmas dinner. Vogel depicts not the Hallmark card version, but what often constitutes the real thing.

The play places us inside the memory of son Stephen. He enters as an adult, then waits a beat, keeping us expectant. His parents enter, and they sit. These three look at each other for another beat, and they "share a common breath." Although the parents will narrate hereafter, Vogel establishes we are experiencing Stephen's memories by giving him the opening line:

> STEPHEN: It was a very cold Christmas in a long and cold winter—decades and days ago.

Three Bunraku puppet children appear, manipulated by puppeteers, including the actors who also later play their adult versions. The puppets sit on a bench behind their parents, and the car starts towards the grandparents' apartment. Man and Woman—Father and Mother—argue about the temperature that day. Father insists she remember it his way, as "*fucking*

Christmas cheer: Randy Graff, Catherine Kellner, Will McCormack, Enid Graham and Mark Blum in The Long Christmas Ride Home. *Photo: Carol Rosegg*

freezing *frigid*." He describes inching along roads inside the Washington, DC, Beltway "in a filthy Rambler." Man and Woman perform the children's lines, too. Man, in a child's voice, cries "Mama, I'm going to be sick," and the Stephen puppet mimes opening a car window. Man then delivers Claire's line, "If you're gonna throw up, do it on your clothes this time," but Woman wails Rebecca's plea "Can I please sit up front?"

VOGEL PLANTS INFORMATION that Father doesn't drive well because he grew up in New York City. When he grows irritable because the children bicker, he throws the Rambler into a skid. We will remember later the way Father has translated anger into dangerous driving. The playwright also shows us Mother's indifference to Stephen's car sickness as she orders him to stick his head out the window. And we learn the typical nature of this holiday hectoring when Mother enjoins Father "We go through this every year. Please. It's Christmas." Momentarily, we observe Christmas joy in the children's dance on the back seat. As they celebrate, Claire, 7, dreams of turkey and gravy, cranberries and pie. Rebecca, 12, craves hot boys. Stephen, 9, also thinks of boys, but suffers pangs of conscience.

Soon Rebecca kicks her sister, restoring our anxieties at the familiar scene. The parents, self-absorbed, again ignore the squabbling children.

Mother considers having an affair. Father rhapsodizes—in his head—about the affair he's already having, then dismisses a gesture of affection from his wife by snapping "I can't *breathe* in this family."

Mother considers her husband's new lover more threatening than his previous womanizing and wonders if he has spent all their money on gifts for Sheila. (He has.) Why did she marry the only Jewish man in the world who does not adore his *shiksa* wife? Could she win him back by having another child?

Meanwhile Stephen anticipates disappointing gifts. However, he delights in recalling the Christmas Eve service from the previous night.

Vogel likewise enjoins us to live in the moment.

Because we're following Stephen's memories, this takes us to a Unitarian Universalist Church in Rock Springs, Maryland. There, in a rare moment of harmony, Father and Mother joke by muttering a Hebrew and a Catholic prayer respectively. Claire repeatedly demands "What do we believe," and Minister shares, on "the most spiritual Night of the West [. . . .] The beauty of Japan, the peace of the East." He believes the Great Spirit infuses the Japanese woodblock prints of Edo, so he shows slides.

Minister displays prints of Mt. Fuji encrusted with snow, cherry blossoms, even a courtesan, and urges his Western listeners to adopt the Eastern embrace of "what will too soon be gone." He speaks of our mortality, and he terms this ephemeral realm of sensual pleasure "Ukiyo-e: The Floating World." He endorses not only "Joy to the World" but also "Joy in the World!" He urges his congregation not to judge, but instead to embrace "the Here and Now." Minister, Man and Woman, chorally, tell us, "We are all in this Floating World together." Vogel celebrates the peaceful coexistence of the three religions she has placed in close and sometimes comic proximity.

After a visual feast of Japanese silks, crèche, and manger, the congregation sings and dances. As the family returns to the car, Claire inquires "Do we believe in Buddha?" Mother responds the children can decide for themselves when they're older because they're the product of intermarriage, which Father defines as "the mingling of blood from two cultures at war." When the play returns to Christmas day, we learn Minister has made a convert: Stephen has spent the trip to grandmother's house imagining swirling kimonos, cherry blossoms, lanterns and other icons of the Floating World.

The actor who played the Minister enacts Grandmother and Grandfather, who give the children presents found in their building's trash room. After presenting a stained scarf to Rebecca and mittens missing fingertips to Claire, Grandmother remarks "It's amazing what people throw away." When the children thank her for their gifts, for the first time the actors who portray them as adults—rather than Man and Woman—speak for the puppets and narrate for them. This episode has engraved itself on their adult hearts.

Father knows and respects his children so little that he gives his sissy son a soccer ball; his little tomboy, not the cowboy boots and guns she requested, but a feminine bracelet; and his third child a diary, which she knows the other two will read to humiliate her.

The two men, who have been drinking steadily, now quarrel. Grandfather rebukes Father for mismanaging money. Stephen tries to wear Claire's bracelet but breaks it when she twists away. Father orders the boy to get his "little Pansy Ass out to the car" and wait while the rest of the

Memory's filter: Catherine Kellner, Will McCormack and Enid Graham in The Long Christmas Ride Home. *Photo: Carol Rosegg*

family eat dinner. Father kicks "at his son," and Grandfather protests the banishment into the cold and the kick. Insults fly, then fists and kicks follow, and the two combatants crash onto the dinner no one will eat. Grandfather throws them out, and Father orders them into the car.

ON THE TRIP home, Rebecca plans to write in her new diary that she hates her sister, her family, her life. Claire puzzles over a name Grandfather has called Father: "kike." Not knowing the word, Claire visualizes "kite"—one of many comic touches in this often dark play. And Stephen, understanding that his Father does not love him, cries. The ominous silence resembles that on a pond "right before the dreadful cracking of ice." When Mother cannot resist complaining—"Well. what a lovely Christmas you've given me"—Father draws back his right hand to hit her, and the children freeze.

As Rebecca vows "I will never have children," the adult actor rips free of the puppet, and Rebecca leaps into a Christmas night 25 years in the future. Freezing and drunk, she pounds on the door, but her boyfriend Chester, played by a puppet, refuses to open it. He has read her mail, so he knows she's pregnant. He has read her diary, so he knows the baby isn't his. And he has changed the locks. The puppet "goes berserk," rages, weeps, then suddenly proposes. As she refuses to have the baby, we learn Stephen has died. Chester won't let her in, so she searches for her car until she gives up and falls asleep in a snow drift. Stephen's ghost breathes like a winter wind to wake her, sober her, save her. She leaves, determined to find her car or other shelter.

Stephen returns us to the moment when Father's hand was raised to strike Mother. This time adult Claire rushes from the car into a Christmas 24 years ahead, when she has tracked her lover Naomi to a tryst at another woman's apartment. Claire stands on the street, wanting to get in. She observes "Two naked lesbian law student puppets, one short, one tall [. . .] entwined." She takes out a revolver and laments "If I hadn't lost Naomi. If I'd kept Stephen alive." Her words echo the child Claire's thoughts when she blames herself for the family debacle. As she puts the gun in her mouth, Stephen's ghost stops her, gives her the will to live, and then returns us to the car. There Father again prepares to strike Mother.

Child Stephen vows he will never do such a thing, and his adult flees the car to a door in San Francisco's Castro 15 years ahead, where he too stands outside, pounding, begging Joe to let him in. As he cries, he poses a familiar question, asked earlier about his Father: "Why does he not love me?" Then he goes to a backroom at a gay bar. He hopes he can "forget how blue Joe's eyes are" while having anonymous unprotected sex with a man—i.e., a puppet—he can't see. "They simulate a sexual act," Vogel writes in her stage direction, "that means this play will never be performed in Texas."

Immediately, Stephen returns to the present. A ghost, he speaks of his act of self-destruction—with nobody to stop him as he stopped his sisters: "I could feel the virus entering my body. But I could not undo what had been done. [. . .] As my grandmother would say: It's amazing what people throw away." After death, he is granted a day each year to observe the Floating World. He returns on Christmas night and remains 24 hours until the night of the Feast of Stephen. He says of our ghosts who return, "We watch you for a day. We are with you in the twilight." He visits his sisters once a year, and he looks for a beautiful man. The actor who played Minister and the grandparents enters as the beautiful man whom Stephen seeks and finds. After performing a Noh dance, the beautiful man gives Stephen breath, the breath so important at key moments in this play.

Then Stephen returns us to the Rambler, where he breathes life into his child puppet and whispers "Ukiyo-E!" In a *coup de théâtre*, puppeteers manipulate Man and Woman, who no longer narrate, but only speak Father's and Mother's lines. For the fourth time, we watch the violent scene begin. For the first time, Father, guided by his puppeteers, completes striking her, "ritualistically," and wood blocks create the blow's sounds. The car spins off the road and teeters "at the brink of a steep precipice," metaphorical as well as real. Stephen's ghost narrates, "We held our breath." And then Mother cannot resist:

> MOTHER: You son of a bitch. You bastard. Go ahead. Kill us all.
>
> You reckless bastard. Throw us all away.

She taunts him further:

> MOTHER: You don't have the balls.

It's a line we have already heard Rebecca yell at Chester.

Claire wants to leave the car, which would kill them. Young Stephen stops her. Then Father prays to a god he does not believe in, "Let me take back this day." He safely maneuvers the car off the cliff, and, Stephen tells us, "We breathed as one."

MORE AMERICANS KILL themselves at Christmas than at any other time. We expect to feel joyful then, but many of us instead remember bad holidays. Christmas intensifies the depression of depressives. Each year the ghosts of Christmases past visit us.

Peace on earth: Will McCormack, Randy Graff and Catherine Kellner in The Long Christmas Ride Home. *Photo: Carol Rosegg*

Vogel's play taps into this national neurosis. She gets the national character just right too: self-obsessing. The family's narcissism runs too deep for them to care about and respect each other. Although parents should focus on their children at Christmas, these don't. Because she cannot control her bitterness, Mother dares Father to step on the gas and end their lives.

The children take their family legacies into adulthood, neatly symbolized by each using, years later, the secondhand gifts grandmother gave them. When Stephen courts death, he has internalized his father's homophobic contempt for him. When Stephen's ghost stops both of his sisters from killing themselves, they have been reenacting their parents' behavior.

When Rebecca cheats on her boyfriend, she behaves like Father. Also like Father, she has drunk too much, so she lies down in the snow to die. Like Stephen, Claire takes Mother's role, victim of a cheating spouse. In her despair at losing her partner's love, she prepares to shoot herself.

Stephen's ghost, however, rouses Rebecca and prompts Claire to put away the revolver. He also breathes life into his younger self, played by a puppet, and they embrace, which recalls a similarly touching moment in Caryl Churchill's *Cloud Nine*.

VOGEL FOUND A MODEL in another American dramatist who wrote about the reality of family life in a nonrealistic, presentational style. Inspired by Thornton Wilder's *Our Town*, *The Happy Journey to Trenton and Camden* and *The Long Christmas Dinner*, *Christmas Ride* substitutes a gay man who dies of AIDS for Emily Webb returning after death to her childhood home in Grover's Corners, where she laments the failure of people to appreciate life "every, every minute." Vogel's Stephen regrets the self-destructive despair with which he allowed himself to become infected. Unlike Emily, he doesn't abandon his opportunity to return to the Floating World, but instead during his visits breathes the will to live into his siblings and embraces life.

The playwright employs a mix of Asian forms to dramatize Buddhist philosophy. The church sermon articulates her notion of what we can take away from a practice that is usually more contemplative; perhaps we should term her interpretation pseudo-Buddhist. Vogel's script advocates staging the play using "one westerner's misunderstanding of Bunraku. The misunderstanding is key." She asks for a soundscape that employs a samisen player, Bunraku music, bells, wooden clappers, "Christmas music adapted to the tonal scales of Bunraku" and lots of singing. Vogel also requires that the Man and Woman use rich voices.

To her Asian auditory array she adds a visual Noh feast. Nothing high-tech, of course. But the minimalist staging—short bleachers serving as a Rambler in a setting "simple, elegant, bare"—does not make what we look at dull. She gives us luscious Japanese projections, a Buddhist Christmas pageant employing puppets and gorgeous silks. Basil Twist created puppets for Mark Brokaw's mounting at Vineyard Theatre (and Oskar Eustis's earlier Trinity Rep staging), which play eight roles. He designed three nearly lifesize Bunraku puppets with faces identical to childhood photos of the actors playing the children as adults. For the New York production, Twist chose pseudo-Indonesian shadow puppets to play Rebecca's Chester, Claire's Naomi and her "golden girl" Betty, and Stephen's fatal trick in the bar.

THE DRAMATIST'S SUBTITLE, *A Puppet Play With Actors*, emphasizes the puppets rather than the people. Apart from the aesthetic triumph of correlating form and content, employing puppets suits a memory play.

Stephen's Noh ghost recalls, not precisely the people who populated his home, but his childhood perception. He remembers himself and his siblings as not fully people, just puppets under Mother and Father's control. How appropriate, then, that the parents speak for the children—even their thoughts—in the early scenes. On another level, puppets and narrators impart the once-upon-a-time universality that Wilder's narrators and minimalist settings—themselves inspired by Noh dramas—achieve. That Vogel has written her Noh play in blank verse and free verse augments this effect.

Vogel has said regarding her script's form, "to feel emotion, one must have distance." Her puppets provide it. That's why the puppeteers turn Father and Mother into puppets as he finally lands his blow. Otherwise, he would traumatize us, which would deflect the hopefulness for the family's survival implied when he backs the Rambler off the cliff. Vogel also restores our focus on the children, not the parents. We perceive the effect of the older generation on the younger. We grieve our own damaged childhoods—and then move on. Redemption beckons.

Many plays dramatize marriage as a doomed institution and life for offspring as hell. Many plays portray domestic violence—physical and psychological. But Vogel depicts multigenerational domestic dysfunction with originality and power. Reviewers strove to capture this: Bill Gale of TheaterNewEngland.com called *Christmas Ride* "a great play." *Variety*'s Markland Taylor termed it "fiercely beautiful writing." Michael Kuchwara for the Associated Press judged it "haunting and stunning," while Michael Sommers, in *The Star-Ledger*, pronounced it "elegantly written and staged." Ben Brantley devoted many *New York Times* column inches to praising the play in a host of evocative ways, such as "shiver-making experience." Several critics called it "magical" and New Yorkers stood in line for hours in a blizzard hoping for tickets. The run was extended, but not for as long as the demand required, because Randy Graff (Woman) had to rehearse *Fiddler on the Roof*.

Could those clambering to see it have understood how vulnerable the play would make them feel, how its painful scenes would devastate? Watching this daring, puppet-version of *Long Day's Journey Into Night* hurts, despite its distancing devices. Yet the impact goes beyond pain.

Vogel reminds us "We are all in this Floating World together." She likewise enjoins us to live in the moment, to breathe, see, hear in the moment, to relish each second and each person. Paradoxically, her play filled with narcissistic anguish, death and near-death urges us to seize joy in this world which soon will vanish. Live and love! *The Long Christmas Ride Home* offers Vogel's life-affirming response to our 21st-century demons.

2003–2004 Best Play

OMNIUM GATHERUM

By Theresa Rebeck and Alexandra Gersten-Vassilaros

○○○○○

Essay by Chris Jones

> MOHAMMED. The world does not want to know the Arab. You only want to erase the Arab. You want to take our land, and steal our oil, to corrupt our women, demean our culture, and degrade our god. That is what you want.
>
> SUZIE: Oh, now don't be negative! It's a party!

THE FIRST REACTION of the American theater to September 11, 2001, was visceral, emotional and overcome by a need to dramatize overwhelming human pain. Critics and audiences implicitly understood the necessity for the catharsis found in such rapidly hatched works of the moment as *The Guys*. But during those trying months, there developed a general sense that a mature, complex, globally savvy, daring and smart play—directly about the terrorist attacks and our tough new world of homeland insecurity—had still to be written. *Omnium Gatherum* is the first of those plays. One could make a case that it's still the only one.

Therein a group of savvy but shell-shocked dinner-party guests chat and eat a gourmet meal onstage. The action manages to reveal the self-indulgent side of free discourse and to consume a terrorist by way of dessert. The play's counter-intuitive style is satirical. Ergo, this actually is a daring dark comedy about the American response to September 11, an event that many people thought would resist such treatment—in perpetuity.

When one added into the mix an otherwise weak slate of plays at the 2003 Humana Festival of New American Plays at the Actors Theatre of Louisville, *Omnium Gatherum* caused something of a sensation during its wildly successful Kentucky premiere in March 2003. Producers and agents were swooping around the creatives with more than their usual sense of urgency: *Omnium Gatherum* was hot.

In Louisville, it felt as though the people who had written this thing were all too aware that this was a play that did not want to wait. Although neither of them was well known for overtly political fare, authors Theresa

Who's hungry? Kristine Nielsen in the Off Broadway production of Omnium Gatherum. *Photo: Joan Marcus*

Rebeck and Alexandra Gersten-Vassilaros had reacted remarkably quickly. They responded boldly to the new global obsession with Arab-American relationships and the moral rectitude of killing terrorists first—lest they kill us—and asking questions about civil liberties later.

Written directly after September 11, *Omnium Gatherum* was first read at the Actors Studio in New York in March 2002. Further development took place that spring and summer at the New York Stage and Film Company and the Powerhouse Theatre at Vassar College. And there was yet another workshop at Naked Angels in New York City during January 2003.

Six months after Will Frears's Louisville production in spring 2003—probably too long for the political oven to hold the necessary heat—a partially re-cast (and thoroughly redesigned) incarnation of the play made it to New York. It opened September 25, 2003, at the Variety Arts Theatre under the auspices of producers Robert Cole and Joyce Johnson.

THE DELAY IN getting *Omnium* to New York raised concerns about timing and timeliness. It seemed that producers should have rushed the play into town because the complacency and sense of denial it so aptly attacked were shifting like sand on a beach. As it turned out, the Louisville excitement never was fully recreated in New York. A few stars (or even one) might have helped lift the Off Broadway production. Much of the problem in New York, however, was due to changing times, not changing performances.

The play's dramatic milieu was lively in both of Frears's productions, which featured lots of delicious food appearing and disappearing. Aside from the indisputable quality and timeliness of the writing, there was also a clever little gimmick. Most of the characters at this theatrical dinner party—chatting about current events as helicopters buzz ominously overhead—appear to be shrewd and carefully observed parodies of real people. But the majority of the parodied persons aren't the kind of mainstream celebrities that a general audience immediately would recognize.

The play's dramatic milieu was lively in both of Frears's productions.

They are members of the literary and journalistic cognoscenti. And thus audience members and critics who were members of—or aspired to be members of—that auspicious group immediately fell over each other in Louisville, trying to be the first to figure out who represented whom.

It's an interactive parlor game—and simultaneously a dig at our pervasive culture of diametrically opposed opining, talking heads babbling away on cable and achieving nothing. That little mystery—with its aura of good gossip—unquestionably increased the appeal of the play. By the end of the Louisville opening, it already had been widely discerned that the hostess of the party, Suzie, was based on Martha Stewart (ironically, the premiere of *Omnium Gatherum* preceded Stewart's very public legal troubles). Adding to that ambivalence, Kristine Nielsen played the role as a kind of Stewart on steroids, leaving no doubt as to the source of her character, but nonetheless stopping short of overt impersonation.

Around the table at this post-September 11 dinner thrown by the Suzie-Martha compote—with equal attention paid to the mixing and matching of both guests and side-dishes—are a number of other people whose conversational tropes and politics sound strangely familiar.

Take Roger, a windy, self-assured, no-nonsense purveyor of best sellers whose response to terrorism could be paraphrased as "fry the lot of 'em." He sure sounds like the novelist Tom Clancy.

> ROGER: What are we supposed to do? Spend all our time worrying about the complexities? Listen to me. We don't have time. So I'm not

> getting involved in all this hand wringing. We have to get a little crazy on everybody, is what we have to do.

The counterpoint to Roger at the table is the liberal Terence, a fey and pretentiously British-sounding intellectual who comes with all the elitist grace notes of a Christopher Hitchens:

> TERENCE: Cambridge, darling, you had to keep up. These men are madman, you'd say they were psychotic, if that wasn't an insult to psychotics everywhere. If you link all the critical analyses of the capitalist project to the destruction of the twin towers, you associate the horrific violence of one particular act with a more benign set of goals—social justice, say, or the diminishment of poverty worldwide.

Suzie also has invited an Arab-American—suave, savvy, well educated, sympathetic to Western mores and able to recognize a hint of spearmint in a meal from fifty paces. He has the distinct air of Edward Said, intoning on "paradox. Like America itself. Which is at once both the thing and its opposite."

The remaining guests—a black female literary type, Julia, and a standard-issue über-vegan self-destructive feminist, Lydia—are harder to relate directly to a real person, although a few people had their theories. Surely, though, we've had dinner with these types of people even if we don't recognize their "true" identities. Some of the guests at this dinner

Round table: The cast of Omnium Gatherum *in the 2003 Humana Festival production. Photo: John Fitzgerald*

party have more intentionally generic identities—including a working-class firefighter named Jeff, invited to join the soirée by Suzie in a fit of genuine gratitude. In Suzie's gesture, of course, there is also the overwhelming urge to patronize that is employed by urban liberals everywhere. While others argue over accompaniments, Jeff spends much of his evening looking for the Ranch salad dressing. We are expected to sympathize.

THE LAST CHARACTER arrives very late in the play. He is Suzie's surprise for dessert. He is—or, more accurately, was—an actual terrorist named, naturally enough, Mohammad. He flew one of the planes into the Twin Towers and spews hatred for America. Remarkably, in this play he actually gets a fair hearing, as in this debate with the conservative Roger:

> MOHAMMED: Three thousands of your people die in the World Trade Center, do you know how many you've killed in Afghanistan and Iraq, how many you've abandoned to die under your trade embargoes in Pakistan?
>
> ROGER: You tested nuclear weapons!
>
> MOHAMMED. You invented nuclear weapons! You come into our lands only to murder us, how many Iraqi children murdered in their homes, so you can have your oil—
>
> ROGER: Listen to me. Your leaders are conning you.
>
> MOHAMMED: (*Overlap*) You are the bully of the world—
>
> ROGER: Listen to me, will you just—
>
> JULIA: Stop, it's going nowhere—
>
> MOHAMMED: (*Overlap*) We suffer and die under your war machine everywhere, you only export war to our peoples in Palestine, in Afghanistan, in Iraq, everywhere, everywhere you kill us—
>
> ROGER: By making American the perpetual target of your troubles, you allow your leader to deceive you and steal from you . . . aah forget it!
>
> MOHAMMED: (*Overlap*) And your media distorts and lies about our world, and makes us look like simpleminded masses, so you can continue to murder us without feeling—
>
> ROGER: My blood pressure is soaring—I'm not listening!!
>
> MOHAMMED: You know this to be true!!!.

Since Mohammed must be as dead as the rest of the September 11 perpetrators, the play thus takes a rather different tack towards the end, beginning when fireman Jeff casually observes that he'll never get to see his kids again. So he's dead, too.

We never know for sure if the other characters are dead—which would make this a true dinner-party-from-hell—but the internal logic of the play implies that indeed is the case. The revelation of the dead fireman hits the audience between the teeth, switching the mood from satirical little soupçon to a theatrical experience of greater complexity.

Even if its allegories aren't precisely personal, it's quickly clear that *Omnium Gatherum* essentially fantasizes about bringing together a variety of thinkers and stakeholders in the American relationship with the world and encouraging engagement in rational discourse. But the playwrights construct an orgy of shared excess—the sort that even liberals enjoy—and let their characters discuss, debate and, eventually, destroy each other in a feast of intolerance. It's a theatrical subversion of the American spirit displayed onstage by characters who claim to be tolerant—until that ideal is severely tested.

The great strength of the play is its deft blending of political commentary and social satire. The dialogue at the party weaves political theorizing with talk of fingerling potatoes, and fights over the Arab world with the correct pronunciation of "Coush Coush." It's all done with the style and accuracy of people who have been at too many such arty dinner parties and know all that goes on.

> SUZIE: [. . .] The main course sont arrivez. You're really going to enjoy this one! This, my friends, is a dish from the south of Pakistan, a favorite among moderate Shiite's—(*To Roger*) Not one word! Which has been reimagined with a lively Southwestern flair. (*Continuing to the group*) Comprised of freshly blessed lamb [. . . .]

AT THE END of the intermissionless play, the fetishization of domestic entertaining epitomized by Stewart and her ilk is revealed as an absurd obsession in a world at crisis. The characters of this play stick their heads in the sand—or, at least, the braised lamb. And when they emerge, it's mainly to parrot generalities, received truths and otherwise display their ignorance. More than anything, the play functions as an indictment of the compliance of the American liberal—a creature lost in a good bottle of vintage red while soldiers take over the world.

The main weakness of the script lies with a finale that spends far too long on intra-Arab issues, when western attitudes should still be wriggling on the hook. Some critics wanted more didacticism, arguing that the play was silly and imprecise and woolly—although that might be the whole point of the work.

Liquor-ish: Dean Nolen, Kristine Nielsen and Jenny Bacon in the Off Broadway production of Omnium Gatherum. *Photo: Joan Marcus*

Writing in the *The New York Times*, Frank Rich complained:

> This glib play which congratulates a complacent audience on its own moral superiority to the nattering nabobs onstage, is part of the problem, not the solution, at a time when America, arguably, is waltzing into what the former CIA director James Woolsey has called the next world war.

That point taken, one could argue that *Ominun Gatherum* did not set out to be a polemic. Certainly, few other contemporary American plays have been willing to engage in such topics as, say, whether or not Israel has a right to exist, the views of terrorists and whether or not bourgeois liberals can be "liberals" in any meaningful sense of that word.

To date, only *Omnium Gatherum* has dared to evoke (and critique) the sheer panic that afflicted American political and social discourse after the events of September 11—a panic that haunts us to this day.

2003–2004 Best Play

SMALL TRAGEDY

By Craig Lucas

○○○○○

Essay by Charles Isherwood

> PAOLA: What human beings don't want to know, they just, literally, allow themselves not to know.

THERE'S REALLY NO such thing as a small tragedy, is there? The title of Craig Lucas's play is a small joke, an oxymoron that gently underscores the knotty complexities of this beguiling comedy about a ragged troupe of young actors wrestling with Sophocles and their own sorrows in a Cambridge, Massachusetts, rehearsal room.

The play came and went all too quickly at Playwrights Horizons, despite a miraculously good production from director Mark Wing-Davey and a fresh, appealing young cast led by up-and-comer Lee Pace. Some critics were befuddled by Lucas's meticulously naturalistic presentation of the trivial workings of a small-potatoes theatrical venture. In scenes that rarely build to any sort of artificially imposed dramatic point, Lucas affectionately depicts the desultory arguments over line readings, the petty rivalries and burgeoning affections of actors—supplied with all of the traditional insecurities and pretensions.

Although *Oedipus Rex* is the play earnestly mangled by these young performers, a quote from another Greek tragedy, *Ajax*, might serve as the play's epigraph: "Everything is brought by time itself from darkness into light." At first, there are few suggestions that shadows will play any part in the proceedings. We seem merely to be witnessing a funky, languidly paced comedy about a small theater troupe just getting started in Cambridge.

They're aiming preposterously high: Nathaniel, the genially pompous director who is returning to theater after his Hollywood career flamed out quickly, has provided his own adaptation of *Oedipus*, full of hilarious anachronisms: "He looks pretty happy," observes a priest of the title character. "I want this production to feel like a bullet going right into the wound," Nathaniel intones bombastically. As the play opens we watch him audition

Bearing witness: Masked members of the company in Small Tragedy. *Photo: Joan Marcus*

a handful of nervous young actors, while his sharp-witted wife, Paola, ostensibly also his co-director, keeps herself carefully in the background.

Jen, a baby-faced blonde who's come back to acting after a failed marriage, flees her audition in tears. Her ditzy, insecure roommate Fanny, chugging from a Thermos as she awaits her turn ("It's only wine"), babbles nervously at her neighbor, a swarthily handsome young man named Hakija. He distracts her with a gruesome story about his past that he later dismisses as a joke, leaving her unnerved.

The cast is completed by the eager, lanky young Chris, instantly nicknamed Christmas. Still in drama school, he is clearly new to the process: Even before his audition gets under way he begins peppering the director with earnest questions about the play's contemporary relevance. "I mean, I don't believe that, do you, that things are pre-determined?" he stammers. "Neither do they," replies Nathaniel, referring to the Greeks. "They thought they were *fated*, big difference." Such casual discussions of fate and free will become a recurring thread throughout the play, as the actors struggle, sometimes comically, to imagine their way into the remote world of the play, little realizing how painfully pertinent its themes will prove to be.

Once rehearsals begin, the exotic Hakija, cast in the title role, becomes the cynosure of attention, sexual and otherwise—thanks in no small measure to the magnetic intensity of Pace's performance in this, the play's key role. Hakija's casual suggestions on improving the text are quickly taken up by Nathaniel, who predicts stardom. (Paola, whose intelligent ideas are ignored, is outraged.) Jen, cast as Jocasta, flirts casually with her Oedipus, keeping it on the down-low since Fanny is still bruised by Hakija's cruel joke. And Christmas, thrilled to have his first real acting gig, is later moved to hysteria by the grim tale Hakija unfolds about his past: A Bosnian Muslim, he was the only survivor of a massacre that wiped out his entire village.

Can the horrors of contemporary history be domesticated?

THE PLAY IS loosely constructed around scenes that shift instantly and almost imperceptibly between rehearsals, where the actors fumble their way through Nathaniel's pothole-ridden version of Sophocles, and bars where cast and crew socialize. Characters are developed in limpid, offhand strokes, through dialogue that is so impeccably natural it seems unscripted.

Lucas, a former actor himself, beautifully conveys the sudden, sweet intimacy that springs up between aspiring artists engaged in a grandiose adventure on a $.99 budget. The play has the shaggy, artless artfulness of a great Robert Altman movie, and Lucas employs the classic Altman device of overlapping dialogue throughout. Sometimes three separate conversations will take place simultaneously, but the dialogue is so carefully structured that the result is not confusion but a deeper kind of clarity and concentration. The technique paradoxically lends a natural dramatic emphasis to moments of revelation, as when, while her husband plays pedagogue to the enraptured Christmas, and Jen and Hakija trade quietly flirtatious intimacies, Paola casually tells Fanny the reason that she and Nathaniel fled Hollywood: His about-to-explode career went off the rails when they discovered that Paola was HIV-positive.

Indeed, even as the intoxicating excitement of youthful enterprise spreads a happy glow over these variously troubled kids, little conflicts, and deeper griefs, begin to emerge. As they do, the playwright's more serious purposes emerge. Lucas is not merely setting out to write a modest comedy about the fears and foibles of struggling actors, lovable though the play is on just those terms. He also aims to explore how the ideas expressed in Greek tragedy can resonate in everyday lives a couple of millennia later. In this undistinguished rehearsal hall in a Boston suburb, small-fry actors squabble and flirt—clumsily but earnestly trying to tease out the meanings of the text at hand—even as they remain, touchingly, blind to its real implications in their lives.

Lucas playfully makes light of this idea even as he chases it down surprising byways. The characters muse earnestly on the possible contemporary relevance of *Oedipus*: "But if Oedipus is America?" Jen burbles excitedly. "And the chorus is the ongoing debate among the populace about what's the best course of action like we used to have before TV made everything one big opinion, and Jocasta is the conservative because she doesn't want Oedipus to ask any more questions."

Nathaniel claims to disdain cheap attempts to season the play with contemporary "relevance," but, being naturally pretentious, chimes in anyway: "If anything, Teiresias is the *Wall Street Journal* telling everybody what is completely obvious if they would get their heads out of their buttholes: America is fated to be an Empire."

The director even goes so far as to instruct his actors to search for—or imagine—themselves into tragedy: "Look into your own lives [. . .] and

Humanity's curse: Lee Pace (foreground) and Ana Reeder in Small Tragedy. *Photo: Joan Marcus*

change the narrative, but by only as much as you need to in order to place yourself at the center of a tragedy." But Lucas has already woven into the play's texture revelations suggesting how fate has played fast and loose with some of their lives. Nathaniel and Paola have struggled with both illness and alcoholism. And Jen makes light of her own unhappy past: a marriage that fell apart even as she became pregnant, an abortion. Hakija calls her on it:

> HAKIJA: Why did you make a joke about what happened to you?
>
> JEN: I don't know. Because it's sad.
>
> HAKIJA: It's not sad.
>
> JEN: No?
>
> HAKIJA: It's tragic.
>
> JEN: Oh, well, I knew who he was, even though, I mean, yes, I thought he hung the moon, but I was also probably making a bargain with myself: I could have a beautiful life, he'd make a lot of money and our children would be safe, but I wasn't, I mean, I don't think I was a victim. What? . . . And killing your father and fucking your mother is tragic, my story is . . . what's that?
>
> HAKIJA: Americans. You all think [. . .] mortal creatures can win.

Jen protests, but

> HAKIJA: You are—more than you think, yes . . . much more . . . like our Oedipus: Blind to your own tragedy, not to mention [. . .] anyone else's.

Paola echoes the idea in a separate discussion: "What human beings don't want to know, they just [. . .] literally, allow themselves to not know."

Ultimately it's the brooding, elusive Hakija who will come to seem a living symbol of fate's agency in human lives—and of the lengths to which men will go to escape its consequences. His cruel history seems to be strangely echoed in lines from Sophocles's play ("All killed, save one"). But, like Oedipus himself, Hakija is not who he seems to be. Enigmatic pronouncements to his friends—"You can't explain human beings"—will come to have unsettling significance in the play's last scene, which takes place long after the actors have embarked upon their various, sometimes surprising destinies.

SEVERAL YEARS HAVE passed. Paola and Fanny, who exchanged a furtive, surprising kiss during a boozy, festive party after the production's opening night, have become lovers and moved upstate. They're adopting a Chinese baby. Christmas likewise has given up his acting aspirations. He now works for their landscaping business and rents a room in their house. Nathaniel is directing a TV soap, and lives just down the hall from Jen and Hakija, who have just had a child.

While Hakija is filming a Robert De Niro picture—his big break—Paola, Fanny and Christmas arrive unannounced to pay a visit to Jen. But they have a more urgent purpose: Christmas has discovered, while on a charitable visit to Bosnia (he's become a Unitarian), that Hakija's story of his family being massacred is not true; he has stolen someone else's history. Worse still, the role he actually played in the atrocities that swept the Balkans was not that of victim but perpetrator: A videotape shows him participating in a brutal rape and murder.

Jen's confrontation with Hakija is the play's dramatic climax. In his remorseful, hysterical confession, Hakija casts himself as a victim of circumstance:

> HAKIJA: There was no choice for us. When the Serbs came through, it was clear that either we participated or we were killed [. . .] I promise you that I did not . . . *choose*.

Hakija may have been fated to enact monstrous deeds, but as a human being living in contemporary America—and not a figure in a tragedy—he has a chance to escape the brutal consequences of his acts. Jen can choose what to do with her knowledge—send her husband back to Serbia to face retribution for crimes he may have been forced to commit, or bury the knowledge forever. For her, the decision is clear. In the play's final speech, directly addressed to the audience, she announces:

> JEN: I don't believe in tragedy. Did you know that there is no other word for it in any other language, it is always a variant of the Greek word: Tragedy. It belongs to them . . . I choose to be happy [. . . .] You can do that. You really can. Hak still always says that Americans don't understand tragedy, and I hope that could always be true. Don't you?

The play ends with this ambivalent question hanging in the air, resonating alongside innumerable others. Can the horrors of contemporary history be domesticated, made "small" and somehow comprehensible, tamed as they are inevitably into the fabric of everyday life? Does the play's tragedy lie in Hakija's morally destructive encounter with the forces of history, or Jen's decision to make peace with it?

Although, like the Greek tragedies, Lucas's play does not propound any easy solutions to the problems it addresses, in the end it is not, itself, a tragedy—true tragedy really did end with the Greeks. The play is a genial,

Foul player: Lee Pace and Ana Reeder in Small Tragedy. *Photo: Joan Marcus*

wonderfully well-observed comedy that evolves gently into a disquieting examination of the ways in which the themes of guilt and fate and justice can bleed off the pages of an old script into actors' lives.

The mediating forum of art evaporates as the play's characters are left to confront grim truths about the potentially destructive interaction of circumstance and human psychology. In its unforced, deliberately casual way, Lucas's play illuminates the idea that while the gods who once doled out heinous destinies to kings and queens may no longer lay claim to the contemporary imagination, fate itself—the unseen web of happenstance that shapes human lives to their disparate ends—is as implacable as ever.

2003–2004 Best Play

THE VIOLET HOUR

By Richard Greenberg

○○○○○

Essay by Michael Feingold

JESSIE: I was asking: Why are you wrecked men all so damned happy? Is that too much to answer?

JOHN: No, I don't think it is.

JESSIE: Then tell me.

JOHN: I think it's because the century's still so young . . . and all the worst things have already happened in it.

JESSIE: *Have* they already happened?

JOHN: Oh, yes, of course.

Nothing could be worse than the war.

WHAT WOULDN'T WE give to know what tomorrow will bring? And the worst is, when tomorrow arrives, we always look back and see where it came from, how we ran unquestioningly along the winding path that brought us to where we are, and usually wish we weren't. "Everybody," as the old wisecrack reminds us, "has 20/20 hindsight." And a character in one of T.S. Eliot's late plays describes his life, seen in retrospect, as

the mistaken attempts to correct mistakes
By methods which proved to be equally mistaken.

Yes, indeed. If we knew what was going to happen tomorrow, we would know where to settle, what profession to take up, in which stocks to invest, which girl or boy to marry, how to protect ourselves from all the buffetings of chance. And maybe most important of all, we would be able to see whom we would become, how the choices we made in life would leave us when we looked back at the end. We would be safe. And when you don't know what tomorrow will bring, you're never safe. If you don't believe me, think back to where you were on September 10, 2001, and ponder what's happened, to you and the world, between then and now.

John Pace Seavering, the youthful central figure of Richard Greenberg's *The Violet Hour*, is a man standing at a crossroads, badly needing to know the outcome of the major choice he is about to make in life. He is a curious

Useful news: Dagmara Dominczyk, Scott Foley and Robert Sean Leonard in The Violet Hour. *Photo: Joan Marcus*

figure, at once supremely confident and hopelessly conflicted. The year is 1919, the moment when Modernism brought a new energy to a world that had seen the supposed truths of the 19th century collapse in the ruins of World War I. A recent graduate of Princeton, John is also a survivor of the war, simultaneously disillusioned and optimistic. ("I'm not young," he says, but later, reflecting on his war experiences, corrects himself: "Those who aren't dead are young.")

Heir to a modest trust fund that comes to him in trickles, John has just started a publishing business, with no capital, no list, and not even a fully furnished office. All he has, beyond "a sort of mission," are piles of unsolicited manuscripts, an inexplicable, noisily preposterous employee named Gidger—John can never remember whether that's the man's first or last name—and enough money, he believes, to publish one book. His dilemma is which of two books he will choose; the selection will affect not only the success of his publishing venture, but also his personal destiny and that of everyone else involved in his choice. One prospective book is a gigantic first novel by Seavering's closest friend (perhaps more than friend) from college, Denis ("Denny") McCleary, while the other is the utterly frank autobiography of Seavering's mistress (perhaps not so exclusively his as he thinks), the popular African-American vocalist Jessie Brewster.

For each of Seavering's prospective authors, publication is a matter of urgency. Denny has just discovered the love of his life—the Chicago meat-packing heiress, Rosamund Plinth—whose father is in the process of arranging her marriage to a brewery heir back in the Midwest ("steak and ale," Seavering comments sardonically). This makes penniless Denny desperate: Publishing is his only way to prove that he has "prospects" which might make him an acceptable son-in-law to Rosamund's money-minded father. Meanwhile, Jessie, some 20 years older than her lover, is fighting her own race against time. As she remarks tartly to John, "I haven't got as much century to go as you have."

When you don't know what tomorrow will bring, you're never safe.

Both Jessie and Denny expect publication to bring them future fame, to fix them in the public memory as part of American literary history. Set in a time when the renewal of hope, political as well as artistic, was widespread, Greenberg's play is a bittersweet love poem to the concept of posterity. It is a pointed rebuke to our own time, trapped as it is in the wash of corporate "planned obsolescence," mindlessly churning out new cultural "product," while draining the planet's natural resources, and giving next to no thought to the future. Poised on the brink of the 20th century, Seavering and his circle, for all their fears, are figures of hope. "I don't know what will *happen*," he says, "but I know that it will be *right*."

Seavering's idealism is Greenberg's salute to a moment in America when writing and publishing—even the writing and publishing of plays—had meaning. Not irrelevantly, the action takes place on a day when John and Jessie have planned to spend the evening at the theater, seeing a hit show with the improbably arch title, *Faintly My Heart*, for which "tickets are impossible to come by," despite Gidger's haughty assertion that it is utterly predictable from start to finish. (He hasn't seen it, of course; he explains loftily that, "Seeing it might get in the way of my opinion"—the first of the script's many meta-theatrical jokes on the nature of theatergoing and the theater's unsteady position in our cultural hierarchy.) John's search for his mislaid theater tickets, with which the play opens, is interrupted by the successive arrivals of Denny and Jessie—the latter walking in just as Denny, having leapt to the conclusion that John has agreed to publish his novel, is planting a passionate kiss on his former college roommate's mouth.

The successive scenes with Denny and with Jessie make John's dilemma clear: Whichever book he chooses to publish, he will lose either his lover or his friend, and may possibly wreck the life of the person he rejects, not to mention whatever contribution to cultural history that person might have made through him.

ENTER, WITH IMMACULATE timing, the machine. Not, as in pre-modern plays, a god that emerges from a machine, but fittingly for the era people called the Machine Age, a machine that itself constitutes a sort of god. Inexplicably delivered to Seavering's outer office and maniacally tended by Gidger, it's a mass of gears that magically starts to spew out pages just as Seavering finds himself impaled on the horns of his dilemma. And what's on those pages? Here, Greenberg makes an elegant alliance between nostalgia and science fiction—two genres that have more in common than one might casually assume. Both, after all, are the product of dissatisfaction with one's own time, and the present gives us plenty to be dissatisfied with.

The device of linking the past with the future has been used before: The great caricaturist and drama critic Max Beerbohm, in his much-anthologized 1919 short story "Enoch Soames," imagined a "decadent"

Bosom buds: Robert Sean Leonard and Scott Foley in The Violet Hour. *Photo: Joan Marcus*

fin de siècle poet who sells his soul to the Devil for a chance to verify his immortality in a library of the future (complete with computerized card catalogue and Shavian "modernized" spelling); the French director René Clair's 1944 Hollywood film, *It Happened Tomorrow* (released on video around the time Greenberg was developing *The Violet Hour*), featured Dick Powell as a young newspaper reporter, in the early 1900s, who under mysterious circumstances obtain's a copy of tomorrow's daily paper before it is printed, and tries to plan out his future life on the basis of it.

Greenberg's ingenuity links the two themes, creating a distinctively contemporary feeling from their merger. In Seavering, Enoch Soames's despair at seeing his great creative efforts—for which he has "given" his soul—reduced to a dismissive footnote in some future misreading of his era's history combines with the mounting terror of René Clair's hero as he watches the steps he's taken to secure tomorrow produce increasingly destructive unplanned consequences.

The second act of *The Violet Hour* is a near-surreal series of revelations and flashes forward that display the dangers of roads taken. In the unnerving present, Rosamund, thinking John has rejected Denny's novel, may be contemplating suicide. While the novice publisher frantically phones her known haunts, trying to avert this disaster, he has to fight off encroaching visions of another alternative—her survival to produce, with Denny, a worst-case nightmare marriage in which her increasing insanity is matched by the shriveling of his gifts into alcoholic sterility and self-loathing. (Though the circumstances are different, the real-life model for the relationship is manifestly that of Scott and Zelda Fitzgerald, and our awareness of its painful cost to American culture adds fuel to the intensity of Greenberg's play.)

SIMULTANEOUSLY, IN SWATCHES of events that alternate with his agonies over Rosamund and Denny, Seavering learns that much of the fascinating past commemorated in Jessie Brewster's book is a lie, built up to conceal more sordid and shabbier truths, with which he is forced to confront her—and which the machine's printouts reveal may ultimately destroy her. He even learns how and why his efforts to keep their illicit (and for the era, particularly scandalous) relationship secret will fail. In a parallel, Kafkaesque sidelight on John's increasing misery, Gidger, in running commentary, discovers an antithetical, perhaps even more painful revelation: He is a man forgotten by history, reduced to an anonymous employee of indeterminate gender, receiving a final crushing blow in the play's funniest line: "My *dog* becomes famous."

As an additional, comic, degradation, John is compelled to view his relationships, and the achievements of those he loves, from the perspectives of the 20th century's parade of successive fashions in literary criticism—Freudian, Marxist, feminist, Structuralist, postmodernist. While the emotions at the core of the action are grittingly painful, Greenberg has glorious fun parodying contemporary fashions in literary scholarship and critical theory. (Of one particularly jargon-laden specimen of today's academic prose, Seavering says, puzzled, "It appears to be written in patois.")

These satirical jabs at the thinking of our own time serve multiple functions. Apart from casting a nostalgic glow on the era in which we see the characters living—a time that for them appears fraught with tension and confusion—the literary jokes reinforce the play's bittersweet theme, its awareness that the present is all we have, that whatever we choose to do now will not only lead us into unwanted destinies, it will be read by generations to come in ways that we can never fully predict or comprehend. We are part of the fabric of each other's lives, and of life as a whole; our only recourse is to surrender to that knowledge while living as wisely as we reasonably can.

In this regard, our era—which spends its life scrutinizing the past for new "readings," instead of discovering how to live for itself—has no reason to feel superior to the more venturesome eras on which it obsesses, alternately glamorizing and debunking. The maniacal reading and reinterpreting of John Pace Seavering's life, in whatever terms the scholars choose, can never be anything but a shadow or a joke compared to the living of that life in its own natural measure. (It is probably not by accident that Denny's preferred way of addressing his friend is "Pace.")

The running joke on critical theory serves, as well, to fix the play's consciousness in our time rather than that of its characters. Though it comes to us disguised as a typical 1920s Broadway drama with comic relief, it is in fact a running commentary on such a play, its characters frequently calling attention to their own entrances, exits, and the expository information they supply. ("These aren't clothes we're wearing," John says, after the machine's output has made him self-conscious about becoming part of history, "they're *costumes*.") The script's final line, spoken as the curtain comes down, is, "We don't want to miss the curtain." All five of the characters are going off—the machine having unexpectedly printed out three additional tickets to see *Faintly My Heart*—the "entirely predictable" hit play to which John had been planning to escort Jessie. And it is perhaps "entirely predictable" that the horrible events adumbrated by the machine's outpouring of texts have not happened, and perhaps will not happen.

Secret caresses: Robin Miles and Robert Sean Leonard in The Violet Hour. *Photo: Joan Marcus*

John has made his decision about which book to publish, a decision that simultaneously embraces life and evades any strict definition of it. He has chosen both, risking financial disaster for the sake of values between which he finds it impossible to choose. This is not a "literal" decision, as it would have to be in a more realistic play. His decision is a way of reminding us that we are at the theater watching a play, that things arrange themselves differently on the stage than in our lives and that their ability to do so is one reason we take pleasure in theatergoing. As opposed to film, in which the point is most often to capture or to simulate reality, the stage's chief pleasure is to essentialize that reality, to take liberties with it for the sake of heightening our sense of it.

A PHOTOGRAPH PLAYS an important part in *The Violet Hour.* We never see it and it may not even exist. Like the imaginary play, *Faintly My Heart*, about which we learn nothing specific except through the biased opinion of Gidger, who hasn't seen it, the photograph is something on which the characters fixate, an object that is somehow ultimately meaningful for them. Its subject is a woman looking in a shop window.

> JOHN: Her chin is propped on her finger. She's trying to decide whether to buy a dress. Across the street from her—she doesn't see this—a man is taking her photograph. I know what the photograph will look like. All shades of gray and the light bunching behind her, that ghost look.

And he remarks, irrationally but prophetically,

> JOHN: This all happened ages ago.

In a sense, everything recorded by history has happened. Our modern propensity for keeping and archiving records of the past is central to our dislocation from the process—from the *action*—of living in the moment. This is what the play's characters are struggling to rediscover, just as their generation (Gertrude Stein's "lost generation") strove frantically to rediscover it after the death-in-life nightmare of World War I. The kinship with our own time—reeling from the scars of a century's worth of wars, and trapped in a technological web that can extend to record people's every move and thought (surveillance cameras, reality television, web "blogging")—is self-evident.

The Violet Hour, the play's title (which is also the title Denny has just invented for his mammoth novel), is the microcosm for this ephemeral yet permanently fixed state of indecision—the indeterminate hour when daylight is giving way to night, work to pleasure. (There is also a double pun buried inside it: "Violet" like "lavender" is an archaic euphemism for variant sexuality in men; further back in American slang usage it is also a euphemism for mixed-race ancestry of the kind that has enabled Jessie to "pass" at one point in her life.)

For John, the woman staring in the dress shop window is an image of his own indecision, but when we hear about her again, it is from Denny and Rosamund, late in the play's action, in a conciliatory mood and ready to face all obstacles. For them, the woman is not hesitating but

> ROSAMUND: [. . . P]lanning every sort of happiness . . . and it was such a lovely thing . . . to see a lovely young girl, in the hour before evening, pondering the figure she'd cut, on a splendid occasion, in a gorgeous frock, and knowing that happiness can be bought—
>
> DENNY: For a little while, at least.

And we duly learn that Denny and Rosamund are the cause of the photograph, the taking of which John has observed: The photographer had come there to get pictures of the new skyscraper going up nearby—another tribute to modern technology—but Denny and Rosamund have prevailed on him to photograph the woman instead, to focus on the human factor, instead of the mechanical.

> JOHN: Do you suppose she's still there?
>
> DENNY: Well, even if she isn't, the photographer gave me his address . . . We'll have the photograph we'll memorialize the moment.

And this, finally, is what *The Violet Hour* does for its characters, and reminds us always to do for ourselves. Because it is through Denny and Rosamund's return, and their link to the image that has preoccupied John, that he realizes he cannot make his choices as a defense against history, only as a way of adding to it.

> JOHN: It makes no difference what I do, it will happen as it happens. The century will take its course.
>
> GIDGER: That's all right, John—there'll be other centuries.

And on that bittersweet, optimistic note, they all go to the theater, where "we'll know everything that's going to happen . . . but we'll enjoy it anyway. We'll find a way." As, Greenberg implies, we must find a way to enjoy living our lives, despite all the awfulness that we and the world are likely to bring into them. No choice we make will ever wholly defend us from the caprices of life, its dangerous habit of turning everything into a disaster or a joke. For those who listen sharply, Greenberg has tucked in at several points in the text (including Rosamund's description of the woman gazing at the dress shop window), the date of the action: It takes place on April Fool's Day.

2003–2004 Best Play

WELL

By Lisa Kron

○○○○○

Essay by Michael Sommers

> LISA: See, don't bring your mother on stage with you. This is something I'm realizing. It's a very bad idea. [. . .] Wow, this avant-garde metatheatrical thing will just bite you in the ass.

A PLAY DISGUISED as an autobiographical performance piece, *Well* proves to be not nearly as straightforward as it initially seems. Soon, though, *Well* develops a delightful life of its own.

Apparently escaping the control of its writer and central figure, Lisa Kron, *Well* careens toward its own ends despite Kron's dogged efforts to keep her show on track. Scenes are disrupted, narrative is derailed, fourth walls fall and unbidden characters materialize. The author abandons the play in frustration, actors quit and the entire event skids to an embarrassed halt. Despite such disasters erupting onstage—or due to them, really—*Well* takes audiences into unexpected realizations that mirror the play's essential theme.

A funny, yet thoughtful piece regarding the importance of understanding other people and their situations in life, *Well* is adeptly crafted in an open, anything-goes style. Freewheeling though the play registers in actual performance—"some kind of fucked up downtown bullshit," one character calls it—*Well* actually possesses a tightly structured text.

Playwright Lisa Kron is expert at communicating directly with viewers. The Michigan-born, Manhattan-based monologue artist has created solo performances since the mid-1980s. As a member of The Five Lesbian Brothers, she collaborated on several satirical comedies. Kron's subsequent solo works reveal a lively gift for relating personal experiences to more universal themes as in *101 Humiliating Stories* (1994), and in *2.5 Minute Ride* (1999), both of which examine the ways we construct public and private identity.

The playwright herself originated the role of "Lisa Kron" in the Public Theater's Off Broadway production of *Well*. No doubt other actors

Discourse: Lisa Kron in Well. *Photo: Michal Daniel*

in future productions will also excel as this wry character described as a "performance artist writing a play NOT about herself." Out she comes in her New York-y black slacks and tailored black blouse, a smart, convivial woman who advises viewers to turn off their cell phones and open their candy wrappers.

Actually, another character is already onstage when the audience enters the theatre. The greater portion of designer Allen Moyer's airy environs is open space set against a watercolor-blue background. In contrast, one corner is devoted to a realistic slice of the Kron family's living room in Lansing, Michigan. For all of the minor clutter of stacked magazines and newspapers, the comfy spot boasts orderly shelves and cupboards arrayed with file folders and whimsical bric-a-brac. A long staircase leads upstairs. A well-worn recliner covered with a crocheted afghan is situated at its heart and upon it snoozes Lisa's mom, Ann Kron (Jayne Houdyshell). A housewife of ample size and frumpy appearance in her late 60s, Ann wears a drab housedress, a dark blue cardigan and slippers. Glasses hang from a chain about her neck.

Occasionally referring to a deck of index cards, Lisa brightly introduces the piece.

> LISA: This play is NOT about my mother and me. [. . .] It's not ABOUT these things but it does use these things as a vehicle for a (*Lisa reads*

> *directly from one of the cards)* "theatrical exploration of issues of health and illness both in the individual and in a community."

Perhaps echoing a dubious thought running through some viewers' minds at this remark, Ann groans "Oh, dear lord" in her sleep.

OF COURSE, *WELL* covers these matters and more. In a swift 100 minutes and over 30 scenes, two different though interconnecting stories are related and the play's greater theme concerning the difficulty of empathetic perception arises, even as the show itself apparently falls apart before viewers' eyes. But first Lisa brings her mother up to speed. Waking up, Ann

> *Well* takes audiences into unexpected realizations that mirror the play's theme.

briefly mentions the bad allergy day she's having and then is surprised by the sight of the audience. She affably greets them anyway, hospitably offering sodas and bags of chips. "Okay, listen up, people," Lisa warns the audience. "No drinks. We're not going to complicate this thing with drinks."

Suddenly a thought strikes Ann. "You're not writing a play about me, are you?" she asks Lisa, eyeing the audience. Lisa terms it more of "a solo show with other people in it" and explains that she's telling two stories regarding wellness.

> LISA: Okay. Look. It's not ABOUT either one of us. I work using autobiographical material but ultimately this is a theatrical exploration of a universal experience. [. . .] I mean, I certainly wouldn't be the first person to write a play about her mother. Boy, I'll tell you, I wish I was that original!

Lisa steps into a square of light that periodically isolates her from the action. She confides to the audience how Ann is "not a theater person" and doesn't share the same perceptions about Lisa's time spent in the allergy unit in a Chicago hospital. As it later turns out, Ann's truth about her efforts with a neighborhood group also differs considerably from Lisa's version.

While the play's four ensemble actors roll onstage a pair of hospital beds, Lisa anecdotally launches into her college-age experiences at the allergy-testing unit. As Ann watches the action from her recliner, Lisa and the actors evoke Lisa's first day there. Lisa learns about the nasty regimen of fasts and enemas preparatory to testing her tolerance of various foods and odors. Her fellow patients include a desperately cheerful Kay and morose Joy, who tries to be sunny but proves to be a big drag.

Stepping back into her special light, Lisa clarifies her themes.

> LISA: I would say the two main things we believe in as a family are allergies and racial integration. In the same way my mother believes that a host of symptoms often dismissed as psychosomatic [. . .] are really caused by allergies; she also believes in the positive effects of racial integration.

Now Lisa and the other actors flesh out Ann's seven-year crusade to resuscitate her Lansing neighborhood, which in 1968 appeared to be in a terminal decline. As black families moved in, the city gave up on the area, withdrawing its resources and closing schools. Ann, however, believed that an organization based upon social activities such as Fourth of July parades could create a strong sense of community that would foster future political efforts.

As Lisa and the ensemble make a set change to continue the allergy unit story, Ann mildly comments that the preceding scene "seemed awfully compressed." Before Lisa can completely respond, a black youngster barges onstage and harasses her. Startled, Lisa thinks she might be Lori Jones.

Up and at 'em: Lisa Kron and Jayne Houdyshell in Well. *Photo: Michal Daniel*

Recalling Lori as a little meanie who tortured Lisa all through grade school, Ann wonders whether she is part of the show. "Oh my God. I hope not," gasps Lisa, hurriedly returning to the allergy unit, where she, Kay and Joy competitively compare their symptoms.

SOON, HOWEVER, THE play shifts to Lansing for a scene involving seven-year-old Lisa's experiences with her black playmates. In the meantime, Ann, who left the stage for a bit—"Damn diuretic"—limps back to watch the proceedings and despite Lisa's impatience chats up the other actors, asking whether they're enjoying being in the play. Taken aback by Ann's warm interest, they variously reply that the play is interesting but seems a little confusing.

So the play swings between its parallel stories. Halfway through the intermissionless work, Ann is freely interjecting comments. Meanwhile, to Lisa's increasing dismay, the actors are getting chummy with her unexpectedly vibrant mother. Drawing copies of articles from files among her well-organized shelves—which she built herself—Ann offers the ensemble some information regarding allergies. Scarcely the dull housewife she initially seemed, Ann quotes the likes of Susan Sontag on illness to one actor before Lisa irritably beckons her back for more hospital business.

"I have to go," the actor who plays Joy reluctantly tells Ann, confidentially adding, "I like talking to you better, though." Ann generously says that Lisa is more used to doing one-woman shows and is still trying to figure out how to deal with other actors.

Back among the hospital beds, which Lisa has peevishly set up alone, she and Joy talk about the testing they've done that day. Joy was sniffing bottles of various chemicals. Lisa humorously describes her own messy testing of yeast, which frothed all over the place. Joy typically doesn't respond. "Oh, Joy," Lisa snaps. "Never mind. You want to be miserable be miserable." A few seconds later Lisa learns from a nurse how earlier that day Joy suffered an extreme reaction to something and plunged into anaphylactic shock. When Lisa tries to apologize, Joy simply says, "I know I'm no fun. I know I'm hard to be around. It's not what I want. I'm just so tired of being sick."

The other patient, Kay, further articulates Joy's frustration in a later scene.

> KAY: You know what the problem is with being sick? It's that you're sick. People who are healthy think they know how you could get better because when they imagine what your life is like they imagine having your sickness on top of their health.

Subsequent neighborhood scenes are amended by Ann, who notes that little racial tension marked its democratic processes, even though Lisa experienced problems of her own.

> ANN: Oh, it's true that you had some tension with some of the black kids but, honey, you didn't fit in particularly well with the white kids either. You were your own person, which is one of the things I really like about you. Did you tell them yet about how unusual you were?

Rather than suffer her mother's interpretation, Lisa relates several amusing, though embarrassing incidents. Like the time when she imaginatively dressed in rags as a grubby Poor Little Match Girl for a costume party and was chagrined to find all of the other girls dolled up as fairy princesses. Or that gruesome day when fifth-grader Lisa and two chums—wild for *Little House on the Prairie* heroine Laura Ingalls Wilder—decided to attend school clad in long calico prairie dresses and sunbonnets and were forevermore ostracized by their classmates.

This memory draws the rambunctious Lori Jones back onstage to wrestle an astounded Lisa to the ground, who can't believe she's getting beat up in her own play. Ann intervenes. Lori wanders off, muttering that—no matter what Lisa wants—she belongs in the play because she was part of Lisa's life.

An even more painful episode that Lisa reluctantly recalls is when her mother almost died because the family was so accustomed to Ann being ill that they scarcely noticed when she took a near-fatal turn for the worse.

THE "PLAY" ABRUPTLY melts down after Ann candidly questions the inaccuracies she's observed in Lisa's dramatization. Incensed and frustrated, Lisa stomps up the stairs and out of her play, abandoning the stage to Ann.

Leaning forward in her La-Z-Boy, Ann quietly chats to the audience about how her belief in integration probably evolved. Ann recalls when she visited racist Baltimore in the early 1950s to spend time with the family of her black roommate from college.

> ANN: I guess when I went there I had very strong feelings about the evils of segregation and the evils of discrimination [. . . .] But through the experience of living there I started to realize that you just don't imagine anyone else's situation is very different from yours unless you've been in a situation where you're different yourself.

Ann confirms how hard it was to fight chronic fatigue to lead the neighborhood association—or to accomplish anything else. "There's so much

Cast consciousness: Joel Van Liew, Lisa Kron, Kenajuan Bentley and Welker White. Photo: Michal Daniel

I would do if I had the energy," she sighs. "You can't imagine." Then she talks of Lisa—"she is like an amazing star to me"—and their bonds.

After Ann drifts into a doze, the appalled ensemble members unsuccessfully try to finesse the awkward situation. When Lisa finally returns to restart the play, the other actors have no sympathy with her irritated inability to accept Ann's state. They fondly say goodbye to Ann and go.

Alone with her mother, anxiously retreating in and out of her isolating square of light, Lisa makes several stuttering attempts to comprehend how she managed to get well but Ann could not. "I think that I have chosen to be healthy but how do I know, really, that I won't end up in that chair like that?," she worries.

Lisa is stunned when Ann tells her to get out of her silly spotlight and deal with it. But much as she tries, Lisa still cannot resolve their differences.

> LISA: Mom, I see your physical reality, I see you struggle. Oh my god, it's so painful. [. . .] You're so sick—and you're so well. Explain that to me. You don't make any sense as a character.

Now Ann's familiar manners vanish as the actor who portrays her decides to leave as well, saying that Lisa can best understand this dichotomy by reading one of Ann's old speeches to the neighborhood association. Looking the speech over, Lisa agrees that it's the perfect ending for the play. She recalls how her mother's magical ability to empathize could connect people of many different backgrounds.

> LISA: (*reading the final lines of Ann's speech*) This is what integration means. It means weaving into the whole even the parts that are uncomfortable or don't seem to fit. Even the parts that are complicated and painful. What is more worthy of our time and our love than this?

A SUBTLE, INSIGHTFUL play regarding perception, indirection and personal perspective, *Well* is written with effortless fluency. The chain of increasingly awkward onstage events that Kron forges leads viewers to revelations they never anticipated. The anecdotal nature of Kron's writing offers an abundance of colorful, often droll and always very human detail.

Director Leigh Silverman's production smoothly bridged the play's many transitions, making its metatheatrical dynamic look natural and unaffected. Backed by a versatile ensemble, Kron played a stage version of herself with humorous aplomb. In a lovely performance of warm verisimilitude as Ann, Houdyshell anchored the play deeply in viewers' hearts.

In an era when too many people judge others all too quickly and easily, *Well* yields unexpected wisdom about the value of compassion, gently reminding us that not everything is merely what it appears.

PLAYS PRODUCED IN NEW YORK

PLAYS PRODUCED ON BROADWAY

○○○○○

FIGURES IN PARENTHESES following a play's title give the number of performances. These figures do not include previews or extra nonprofit performances. In the case of a transfer, the Off Broadway run is noted but not added to the figure in parentheses.

Plays marked with an asterisk (*) were still in a projected run June 1, 2004. Their number of performances is figured through May 31, 2004.

In a listing of a show's numbers—dances, sketches, musical scenes, etc.—the titles of songs are identified wherever possible by their appearance in quotation marks (").

HOLDOVERS FROM PREVIOUS SEASONS

BROADWAY SHOWS THAT were running on June 1, 2003 are listed below. More detailed information about them appears in previous *Best Plays* volumes of the years in which they opened. Important cast changes since opening night are recorded in the Cast Replacements section in the volume.

***The Phantom of the Opera** (6,814). Musical with book by Richard Stilgoe and Andrew Lloyd Webber; music by Andrew Lloyd Webber; lyrics by Charles Hart; additional lyrics by Richard Stilgoe; adapted from the novel by Gaston Leroux. Opened January 26, 1988.

***Beauty and the Beast** (4,143). Musical with book by Linda Woolverton; music by Alan Menken; lyrics by Howard Ashman and Tim Rice. Opened April 18, 1994.

***Rent** (3,370). Transfer from Off Broadway of the musical with book, music and lyrics by Jonathan Larson. Opened Off Off Broadway January 26, 1996 and Off Broadway February 13, 1996 where it played 56 performances through March 31, 1996; transferred to Broadway April 29, 1996.

***Chicago** (3,138). Revival of the musical based on the play by Maurine Dallas Watkins; book by Fred Ebb and Bob Fosse; music by John Kander; lyrics by Fred Ebb; original production directed and choreographed by Bob Fosse. Opened November 14, 1996.

***The Lion King** (2,768). Musical adapted from the screenplay by Irene Mecchi, Jonathan Roberts and Linda Woolverton; book by Roger Allers and Irene Mecchi; music by Elton John; lyrics by Tim Rice; additional music and lyrics by Lebo M, Mark Mancina, Jay Rifkin, Julie Taymor and Hans Zimmer. Opened November 13, 1997.

Cabaret (2,377). Revival of the musical based on the play by John van Druten and stories by Christopher Isherwood; book by Joe Masteroff; music by John Kander; lyrics by Fred Ebb. Opened March 19, 1998. (Closed January 4, 2004)

***Aida** (1,740). Musical suggested by the Giuseppe Verdi opera; book by Linda Woolverton, Robert Falls and David Henry Hwang; music by Elton John; lyrics by Tim Rice. Opened March 23, 2000.

***The Producers** (1,294). Musical with book by Mel Brooks and Thomas Meehan; music and lyrics by Mel Brooks. Opened April 19, 2001.

***42nd Street** (1,268). Revival of the musical based on the novel by Bradford Ropes and the 1933 movie; book by Michael Stewart and Mark Bramble; music by Harry Warren; lyrics by Al Dubin. Opened May 2, 2001.

Urinetown (965). Transfer from Off Broadway of the musical with book and lyrics by Greg Kotis; music and lyrics by Mark Hollmann. Opened September 20, 2001. (Closed January 18, 2004)

***Mamma Mia!** (1,102). Musical with book by Catherine Johnson; music and lyrics by Benny Andersson and Björn Ulvaeus, some songs with Stig Anderson. Opened October 18, 2001.

***Thoroughly Modern Millie** (879). Musical with book by Richard Morris and Dick Scanlan; new music by Jeanine Tesori; new lyrics by Dick Scanlan; based on the story and screenplay by Richard Morris for the Universal Pictures film. Opened April 18, 2002.

***Hairspray** (743). Musical with book by Mark O'Donnell and Thomas Meehan; music by Marc Shaiman; lyrics by Marc Shaiman and Scott Wittman; based on the film by John Waters. Opened August 15, 2002.

Say Goodnight, Gracie (364). By Rupert Holmes. Opened October 10, 2002. (Closed August 24, 2003)

***Movin' Out** (664). Dance musical based on the songs of Billy Joel; with music and lyrics by Mr. Joel; conceived by Twyla Tharp. Opened October 24, 2002.

Man of La Mancha (304). Revival of the musical with book by Dale Wasserman; music by Mitch Leigh; lyrics by Joe Darion. Opened December 5, 2002. (Closed August 31, 2003)

La Bohème (228). Revival of the opera with libretto by Giuseppe Giacosa and Luigi Illica; music by Giacomo Puccini; based on stories from *Scènes de la Vie de Bohème* by Henri Mürger. Opened December 8, 2002. (Closed June 29, 2003)

Take Me Out (355). Transfer from Off Broadway of the play by Richard Greenberg. Opened February 27, 2003. (Closed January 4, 2004)

The Play What I Wrote (89). By Hamish McColl, Sean Foley and Eddie Braben. Opened March 30, 2003. (Closed June 15, 2003)

Life (x) 3 (104). By Yasmina Reza; translated by Christopher Hampton. Opened March 31, 2003. (Closed June 29, 2003)

Roundabout Theatre Company production of **A Day in the Death of Joe Egg** (69). Revival of the play by Peter Nichols. Opened April 3, 2003. (Closed June 1, 2003)

Roundabout Theatre Company production of **Nine** (285). Revival of the musical with book by Arthur Kopit; music and lyrics by Maury Yeston; adapted from the Italian by Mario Fratti. Opened April 10, 2003. (Closed December 14, 2003)

A Year With Frog and Toad (73). Musical with book and lyrics by Willie Reale; music by Robert Reale; based on the children's books by Arnold Lobel. Opened April 13, 2003. (Closed June 15, 2003)

Enchanted April (143). By Matthew Barber; from the novel by Elizabeth von Arnim. Opened April 29, 2003. (Closed August 31, 2003)

Salome (40) Revival of the play by Oscar Wilde. Opened April 30, 2003. (Closed June 12, 2003)

Gypsy (451). Revival of the musical with book by Arthur Laurents; music by Jule Styne; lyrics by Stephen Sondheim; suggested by the memoirs of Gypsy Rose Lee. Opened May 1, 2003. (Closed May 30, 2004)

Roundabout Theatre Company production of **The Look of Love** (49). Musical revue with music by Burt Bacharach; lyrics by Hal David; conceived by David Thompson, Scott Ellis, David Loud and Ann Reinking. Opened May 4, 2003. (Closed June 15, 2003)

Long Day's Journey Into Night (117). Revival of the play by Eugene O'Neill. Opened May 6, 2003. (Closed August 31, 2003)

PLAYS PRODUCED JUNE 1, 2003–MAY 31, 2004

Roundabout Theatre Company production of **Master Harold . . . and the Boys** (49). Revival of the play by Athol Fugard. Todd Haimes artistic director, Ellen Richard managing director, Julia C. Levy executive director of external relations, at the Royale Theatre. Opened June 1, 2003. (Closed July 13, 2003)

Sam .... Danny Glover
Hally .... Christopher Denham
Willie .... Michael Boatman

Understudies: Messrs. Glover, Boatman—Daryl Edwards; Mr. Denham—Bobby Steggert.

Directed by Lonny Price; scenery, John Lee Beatty; costumes, Jane Greenwood; lighting, Peter Kaczorowski; sound, Brian Ronan; casting, Jim Carnahan, Mele Nagler; production stage

Hally's friends: Michael Boatman and Danny Glover in Master Harold . . . and the Boys. *Photo: Joan Marcus*

manager, Jay Adler; stage manager, Debra Acquavella; press, Boneau/Bryan-Brown, Adrian Bryan-Brown, Matt Polk, Amy Dinnerman.

Time: 1950. Place: St. Georges Park Tea Room, Port Elizabeth, South Africa. Presented without intermission.

Oedipal and racial tensions erupt when a white South African teenager confronts two longtime black employees of his family's business. First presentation of record at Yale Repertory Theatre in New Haven (3/12–27/1982). A 1981–82 *Best Plays* choice, the original Broadway production opened at the Lyceum Theatre (5/4/1982–2/26/1983; 344 performances). Zakes Mokae received a 1982 Tony Award for best featured actor.

Roundabout Theatre Company presentation of the **Deaf West Theatre** production of **Big River: The Adventures of Huckleberry Finn** (67). Revival of the musical with book by William Hauptman; music and lyrics by Roger Miller; adapted from the novel by Mark Twain. Todd Haimes artistic director, Ellen Richard managing director, Julia C. Levy executive director of external affairs for Roundabout Theatre Company; Ed Waterstreet artistic director, Bill O'Brien producing director for Deaf West Theatre, in association with Center Theatre Group/Mark Taper Forum, at the American Airlines Theatre. Opened July 24, 2003. (Closed September 21, 2003)

Mark Twain; Voice of Huck .... Daniel Jenkins
Huckleberry Finn .... Tyrone Giordano
Jim .... Michael McElroy
Tom Sawyer; Ensemble .... Michael Arden
Widow Douglas; Voice of Sally; Ensemble .... Gina Ferrall
Miss Watson; Sally; Ensemble .... Phyllis Frelich
Mary Jane Wilkes; Voice of Miss Watson; Voice of Joanna Wilkes; Ensemble .... Melissa van der Schyff
Judge Thatcher; Harvey Wilkes; Silas; First Man; Ensemble .... Iosif Schneiderman
Ben Rogers; Puppeteer; Andy; Ronald Robinson; Voice of Young Fool; Voice of Sheriff Bell; Ensemble .... Scott Barnhardt
Jo Harper; Lafe; Donald Robinson; Ensemble .... Rod Keller
Dick Simon; Hank; Young Fool; Sheriff Bell; Ensemble .... Ryan Schlecht
Voice of Dick Simon; Voice of Harvey Wilkes; Voice of Hank; Second Man; Ensemble .... Drew McVety
Pap; Duke; Ensemble .... Troy Kotsur
Pap; King; Voice of Silas; Ensemble .... Lyle Kanouse
Joanna Wilkes; Ensemble .... Alexandria Wailes
Preacher; Doctor; Voice of Judge; Voice of Duke; Voice of First Man; Ensemble .... Walter Charles
Alice; Voice of Alice's Daughter; Slave; Ensemble .... Gwen Stewart
Alice's Daughter; Slave; Ensemble .... Christina Ellison Dunams

Orchestra: Steven Landau conductor, piano; Gordon Titcomb banjo, guitar, dobro, mandolin, harmonica; Greg Utzig guitar, dobro, banjo, mandolin; Cenovia Cummins fiddle, mandolin; Dave Phillips acoustic bass; Frank Pagano percussion, dulcimer.

Understudies: Mr. Jenkins—Drew McVety; Mr. Giordano—Guthrie Nutter; Mses. Ferrall, van der Schyff, Wailes—Catherine Brunell; Ms. Frelich—Alexandria Wailes; Mr. McElroy—David Aron Damane; Mr. Arden—Rod Keller; Messrs. Barnhardt, Keller—Kevin Massey; Messrs. Schlecht, Schneiderman—Guthrie Nutter; Mr. Kotsur—Ryan Schlecht; Messrs. Kanouse, McVety, Charles—George McDaniel.

Directed and choreographed by Jeff Calhoun; scenery, Ray Klausen; costumes, David R. Zyla; lighting, Michael Gilliam; sound, Peter Fitzgerald; music direction and special music arrangements, Mr. Landau; music coordinator, John Miller; associate director and choreographer, Coy Middlebrook;

Ol' muddy: Tyrone Girodano and Michael McElroy in Big River. *Photo: Joan Marcus*

casting, Jim Carnahan; production stage manager, Peter Hanson; press, Boneau/Bryan-Brown, Adrian Bryan-Brown, Matt Polk, Jessica Johnson.

Revival of a musical journey through the life of Mark Twain's famous character. In this version hearing and deaf actors signed and sang. First presentation of record at the American Repertory Theatre in Massachusetts (2/17/1984) before a run at La Jolla Playhouse (6/19–7/14/1984. First presented on Broadway at the Eugene O'Neill Theatre (4/25/1985–9/20/1987; 1005 performances) where it received seven 1985 Tony Awards.

ACT I

Overture

Scene 1: St. Petersburg, Missouri; the Illinois shore; Jackson's Island

"Do You Wanna Go To Heaven?" .... Company

"We Are the Boys" .... Tom, Gang

"Waitin' for the Light to Shine" .... Huck

"Guv'ment" .... Pap

"I, Huckleberry, Me" .... Huck

"Muddy Water" .... Jim, Huck

Scene 2: On the river, south of St. Louis

"The Crossing" .... Slaves

Scene 3: On the river, near Cairo, Illinois

"River in the Rain" .... Huck, Jim

Scene 4: On the Riverbank, in Kentucky

"When the Sun Goes Down in the South" .... King, Duke, Huck, Jim

ACT II

Entr'acte

Scene 5: In Bricktown, Tennessee

"The Royal Nonesuch" .... Duke, Huck, Hank, Andy, Lafe, Company

"Worlds Apart" .... Jim, Huck

Scene 6: .... In Hillsboro, Arkansas

"Arkansas" .... Young Fool

"How Blest We Are" .... Alice, Alice's Daughter, Company
"You Oughta Be Here With Me" .... Mary Jane, Joanna, Donald, Ronald
"How Blest We Are" (Reprise) .... Alice, Alice's Daughter
"Leavin's Not the Only Way to Go" .... Huck, Mary Jane, Jim

Scene 7: On a farm near Hillsboro

"Waitin' for the Light to Shine" (Reprise) .... Huck, Alice, Alice's Daughter, Jim, Company
"Free at Last" .... Jim and Company
"Muddy Water" (Reprise) .... Huck, Jim

***Avenue Q** (348). Transfer of the Off Off Broadway musical with book by Jeff Whitty; music and lyrics by Robert Lopez and Jeff Marx. Produced by Kevin McCollum, Robyn Goodman, Jeffrey Seller, Vineyard Theatre and The New Group at the Golden Theatre. Opened July 31, 2003.

Princeton; Rod .... John Tartaglia
Brian .... Jordan Gelber
Kate Monster; Lucy; Others .... Stephanie D'Abruzzo
Nicky; Trekkie Monster; Bear; Others .... Rick Lyon
Christmas Eve .... Ann Harada
Gary Coleman .... Natalie Venetia Belcon
Mrs. T.; Bear; Others .... Jennifer Barnhart
Ensemble .... Jodi Eichelberger, Peter Linz

Orchestra: Gary Adler conductor, keyboard; Mark Hartman associate conductor, keyboard; Maryann McSweeney bass; Brian Koonin guitar; Patience Higgins reeds; Michael Croiter drums.

Understudies: Mr. Tartaglia—Jodi Eichelberger, Peter Linz; Mr. Gelber—Peter Linz; Ms. D'Abruzzo—Jennifer Barnhart, Aymee Garcia; Mr. Lyon—Jodi Eichelberger, Peter Linz; Ms. Barnhart—Aymee Garcia; Ms. Harada—Erin Quill; Ms. Belcon—Carmen Ruby Floyd.

Directed by Jason Moore; choreography, Ken Roberson; scenery, Anna Louizos; costumes, Mirena Rada; lighting, Howell Binkley; sound, Acme Sound Partners; orchestrations, music supervision and arrangements, Stephen Oremus; music direction and incidental music, Mr. Adler; music coordinator, Michael Keller; associate producers, Sonny Everett, Walter Grossman, Morton Swinsky; casting, Cindy Tolan; production stage manager, Evan Ensign; press, Sam Rudy Media Relations, Sam Rudy, Robert Lasko.

Time: The present. Place: An outer borough of New York City. Presented in two parts.

Sesame Street-inspired musical celebration of urban angst in the overeducated under-35 set. Transferred from an Off Off Broadway run at Vineyard Theatre (3/19–5/11/2003; 47 performances). 2004 Tony Awards honoree for best book, best score and best musical.

ACT I

Avenue Q Theme .... Company
"What Do You Do With a BA in English?"/"It Sucks to be Me" .... Company
"If You Were Gay" .... Nicky, Rod
"Purpose" .... Princeton
"Everyone's a Little Bit Racist" .... Princeton, Kate, Gary, Brian, Christmas Eve
"The Internet Is for Porn" .... Kate, Trekkie Monster, Men
"Mix Tape" .... Kate, Princeton
""I'm Not Wearing Underwear Today" .... Brian
"Special" .... Lucy
"You Can Be as Loud as the Hell You Want (When You're Making Love)" .... Gary, Bad Idea Bears
"Fantasies Come True" .... Rod, Kate
"My Girlfriend, Who Lives in Canada" .... Rod
"There's a Fine, Fine Line" .... Kate

ACT II

"There Is Life Outside Your Apartment" .... Brian, Company
"The More You Ruv Someone" .... Christmas Eve, Kate
"Schadenfreude" .... Gary, Nicky

Kate monster: Stephanie D'Abruzzo and friend in Avenue Q. *Photo: Carol Rosegg*

"I Wish I Could Go Back to College" .... Kate, Nicky, Princeton
"The Money Song" .... Nicky, Princeton, Gary, Christmas Eve, Brian, Trekkie Monster
"For Now" .... Company

***Little Shop of Horrors** (276). Revival of the musical with book and lyrics by Howard Ashman; music by Alan Menken; based on the film by Roger Corman. Produced by Marc Routh, Richard Frankel, Thomas Viertel, Steven Baruch, James D. Stern, Douglas L. Meyer, Rick Steiner/John and Bonnie Osher, Simone Genatt Haft, in association with Frederic H. Mayerson, Amy Danis/Mark Johannes, at the Virginia Theatre. Opened October 2, 2003.

Chiffon .... DeQuina Moore
Crystal .... Trisha Jeffrey
Ronnette .... Carla J. Hargrove
Mushnik .... Rob Bartlett
Audrey .... Kerry Butler
Seymour .... Hunter Foster
Orin; Others .... Douglas Sills
Voice of Audrey II .... Michael-Leon Wooley
Prologue Voice .... Don Morrow

Audrey II Manipulation: Martin P. Robinson, Anthony Asbury, Bill Remington, Matt Vogel.

Ensemble: Anthony Asbury, Bill Remington, Martin P. Robinson, Douglas Sills, Michael-Leon Wooley, Matt Vogel.

Orchestra: Henry Aronson conductor, keyboard; John Samorian associate conductor, keyboard; John Benthal guitar, mandolin; Steve Gelfand bass; Tom Murray, Matt Hong woodwinds; Tony Kadleck, Dave Spier trumpet; David Yee percussion; Rich Mercurio drums.

Understudies: Mses. Moore, Jeffrey, Hargrove—Ta'Rea Campbell; Mr. Bartlett—Ray DeMattis; Mr. Wooley—Michael James Leslie; Messrs. Foster, Sills—Jonathan Rayson; Ms. Butler—Jessica-Snow Wilson.

Directed by Jerry Zaks; choreography, Kathleen Marshall; scenery, Scott Pask; costumes, William Ivey Long; lighting, Donald Holder; sound, T. Richard Fitzgerald; puppet design, The Jim Henson Company, Martin P. Robinson; orchestrations, Danny Troob; music direction, Mr. Aronson; vocal arrangements, Robert Billig; music supervision and arrangements, Michael Kosarin; music coordinator, John Miller; associate producers, HoriPro/Tokyo Broadcasting System, Clear Channel

Monster love: Kerry Butler and Hunter Foster in Little Shop of Horrors. *Photo: Paul Kolnik*

Entertainment, Endgame Entertainment, Zemiro, Morton Swinsky/Michael Fuchs, Judith Marinoff Cohn, Rhoda Mayerson; casting, Bernard Telsey Casting; production stage manager, Karen Armstrong, stage manager, Adam John Hunter; press, Barlow-Hartman Public Relations, John Barlow, Michael Hartman, Jeremy Shaffer.

Time: 1950s. Place: Greenwich Village, New York City. Presented in two parts.

A carnivorous plant transforms the life of its nebbish tender as it grows out of control. First presentation of record by the WPA Theatre (5/6/1982; 24 performances) before an Off Broadway run at the Orpheum Theatre (7/27/1982–11/1/1987; 2,209 performances).

ACT I

"Little Shop of Horrors" .... Chiffon, Crystal, Ronnette
"Downtown (Skid Row)" .... Company
"Da-Doo" .... Seymour, Chiffon, Crystal, Ronnette
"Grow for Me" .... Seymour
"Ya Never Know" .... Mushnik, Seymour, Chiffon, Crystal, Ronnette
"Somewhere That's Green" .... Audrey
"Closed for Renovation" .... Mushnik, Seymour, Audrey
"Dentist!" .... Orin, Chiffon, Crystal, Ronnette
"Mushnik and Son" .... Mushnik, Seymour
"Git It" .... Seymour, Audrey II, Chiffon, Crystal, Ronnette
"Now (It's Just the Gas)" .... Orin, Seymour

ACT II

"Call Back in the Morning" .... Audrey, Seymour
"Suddenly Seymour" .... Seymour, Audrey, Chiffon, Crystal, Ronnette
"Suppertime" .... Audrey II, Chiffon, Crystal, Ronnette
"The Meek Shall Inherit" .... Seymour, Chiffon, Crystal, Ronnette, Bernstein, Luce, Snip
"Sominex"/"Suppertime" (Reprise) .... Audrey, Audrey II
"Somewhere That's Green" (Reprise) .... Audrey
Finale: "Don't Feed the Plants" .... Company

Stern stuff: Tovah Feldshuh in Golda's Balcony. *Photo: Aaron Epstein*

***Golda's Balcony** (249). Transfer from Off Broadway of the solo performance piece by William Gibson. Produced by Manhattan Ensemble Theater, David Fishelson, Roy Gabay, Randall L. Wreghitt, Jerry and Cindy Benjamin, Cheryl and Philip Milstein, Jerome L. Stern, David and Sylvia Steiner at the Helen Hayes Theatre. Opened October 15, 2003.

Golda Meir .... Tovah Feldshuh

Directed by Scott Schwartz; scenery, Anna Louizos; costumes, Jess Goldstein; lighting, Howell Binkley; sound and music, Mark Bennett; projections, Batwin and Robin Productions; assistant director, Nell Balaban; dramaturg, Aaron Leichter; associate producers, Lynne Peyser, Stephen Herman, Zev Guber, Dede Harris/Ruth Hendel/Sharon Karmazin/Morton Swinsky, James E. Sparnon, Sandra Garner; production stage manager, Charles M. Turner III; press, Richard Kornberg and Associates, Richard Kornberg, Rick Miramontez, Don Summa, Tom D'Ambrosio, Carrie Friedman.

Presented without intermission.

Israeli prime minister charts her life as a Jewish patriot and worries over the future of her nation when threatened from without. First presented by Shakespeare and Company, Lenox, Massachusetts (5/18/2002). This production originated at the Manhattan Ensemble Theater (3/26–7/13/2003; 72 performances).

***The Boy From Oz** (248). Musical with book by Martin Sherman, original book by Nick Enright; book and lyrics by Peter Allen and others. Produced by Ben Gannon and Robert Fox at the Imperial Theatre. Opened October 16, 2003.

Peter Allen .... Hugh Jackman
Boy (Young Peter) ...... Mitchel David Federan
Marion Woolnough .... Beth Fowler
Dick Woolnough .... Michael Mulheren
Chris Bell .... Timothy A. Fitz-Gerald
Judy Garland .... Isabel Keating
Mark Herron .... John Hill
Liza Minnelli .... Stephanie J. Block
Trio .... Colleen Hawks, Tari Kelly, Stephanie Kurtzuba
Greg Connell .... Jarrod Emick
Dee Anthony .... Michael Mulheren

Ensemble: Leslie Alexander, Brad Anderson, Kelly Crandall, Naleah Dey, Nicholas Dromard, Timothy A. Fitz-Gerald, Christopher Freeman, Tyler Hanes, Colleen Hawks, John Hill, Pamela

Jordan, Tari Kelly, Stephanie Kurtzuba, Heather Laws, Brian J. Marcum, Jennifer Savelli, Matthew Stocke.

Orchestra: Patrick Vaccariello conductor; Jim Laev associate conductor, keyboard; Sylvia D'Avanzo concertmaster; Victor Heifets, Fritz Krakowski, Wende Namkung, Cecelia Hobbs Gardner, Nina Evtuhov violin; Mairi Dorman, Vivian Israel cello; Cary Potts bass; J McGeehan guitar; Ted Nash, Ben Kono, Ken Dybisz, Don McGeen reeds; Jeff Kievit lead trumpet; Tino Gagliardi, Earl Gardner trumpet; Clint Sharman, Randy Andros trombone; Mark Berman keyboard; Dan McMillan percussion; Brian Brake drums.

Standby for Mr. Jackman—Kevin Spirtas.

Understudies: Mr. Jackman—John Hill; Mr. Federan—P. J. Verhoest; Ms.Fowler—Leslie Alexander; Mr. Mulheren—Matthew Stocke; Ms. Keating—Stephanie Kurtzuba, Heather Laws; Ms. Block—Tari Kelly, Heather Laws; Mr. Emick—Brad Anderson, John Hill, Kevin Spirtas.

Swings: Todd Anderson, Jessica Hartman.

Directed by Philip Wm. McKinley; choreography, Joey McKneely; scenery, Robin Wagner; costumes, William Ivey Long; lighting, Donald Holder; sound, Acme Sound Partners; wig and hair, Paul Huntley; orchestrations, Michael Gibson; music coordinator, Michael Keller; dance music arrangements, Mark Hummel; music direction, incidental music and vocal arrangements, Mr. Vaccariello; casting, Dave Clemmons Casting, Joseph McConnell; production stage manager, Eileen F. Haggerty; stage manager, Richard C. Rauscher; press, Boneau/Bryan-Brown, Adrian Bryan-Brown, Jackie Green, Joe Perrotta.

Time: 1950s–1990s. Place: Australia, Hong Kong and New York. Presented in two parts.

Celebration of the life and music of showman Peter Allen. The original version opened at Her Majesty's Theatre in Sydney, Australia (3/5/1998) and toured the continent for more than two years.

Judy and fan: Isabel Keating and Hugh Jackman in The Boy From Oz. *Photo: Joan Marcus*

ACT I

Overture

Prologue: Peter in concert
"The Lives of Me" .... Peter

The 1950s
Scene 1: Various locations in Tenterfield, Australia
"When I Get My Name in Lights" .... Boy, Ensemble
"When I Get My Name in Lights" (Reprise) .... Peter

The 1960s
Scene 2: Australian Bandstand television performance
"Love Crazy" .... Chris, Peter, Ensemble
(Peter Allen, Adrienne Anderson)
Scene 3: Hong Kong Hilton Hotel
"Waltzing Matilda" .... Peter, Chris
(Marie Cowan, A.B. "Banjo" Paterson)
"All I Wanted Was the Dream" .... Judy
Scene 4: Hong Kong; New York City
"Only an Older Woman" .... Judy, Peter, Chris, Mark
"Best That You Can Do" .... Peter, Liza
(Burt Bacharach, Carole Bayer Sager, Peter Allen, Christopher Cross)
Scene 5: Peter and Liza's apartment
"Don't Wish Too Hard" .... Judy
(Carole Bayer Sager, Peter Allen)
"Come Save Me" .... Liza, Peter
Scene 6: Peter and Liza's apartment, months later
"Continental American" .... Peter, Ensemble
(Peter Allen and Carole Bayer Sager)
Scene 7: Liza's act
"She Loves to Hear the Music" .... Liza, Ensemble
(Peter Allen and Carole Bayer Sager)
Scene 8: Peter in concert
"Quiet Please, There's a Lady on Stage" .... Peter, Judy
(Peter Allen, Carole Bayer Sager)
The 1970s
Scene 9: Peter and Liza's apartment
"I'd Rather Leave While I'm in Love" .... Liza, Peter
(Peter Allen, Carole Bayer Sager)
Scene 10: Marion's Home
"Not the Boy Next Door" .... Peter, Marion
(Peter Allen, Dean Pitchford)

ACT II

The 1970s
Scene 1: Reno Sweeney
"Bi Coastal" .... Peter, Trio
(Peter Allen, David Foster, Tom Keane)
Scene 2: Peter's apartment
"If You Were Wondering' .... Peter, Greg
Scene 3: Dee's office; The Copacabana Club
"Sure Thing Baby" .... Dee, Greg, Peter, Trio, Male Ensemble

The 1980s
Scene 4: Radio City Music Hall, January 15, 1981
"Everything Old Is New Again" .... Peter, Rockettes
(Peter Allen, Carole Bayer Sager)
Scene 5: Peter's dressing room, Radio City Music Hall
"Everything Old Is New Again" (Reprise) .... Marion, Dee, Greg

Scene 6: Peter's apartment
"Love Don't Need a Reason" .... Peter, Greg
(Peter Allen, Marsha Malamet, Michael Callen)

The 1990s
Scene 7: Peter's apartment
"I Honestly Love You" .... Greg
(Peter Allen, Jeff Barry)
"You and Me" Liza, Peter
(Peter Allen, Carole Bayer Sager)
Scene 8: Marion's Home; The Australian Concert; Peter in concert
"I Still Call Australia Home" .... Peter, Ensemble
"Don't Cry Out Loud" .... Marion
(Peter Allen, Carole Bayer Sager)
"Once Before I Go" .... Peter
(Peter Allen, Dean Pitchford)
"I Go to Rio" .... Peter, Company
(Peter Allen, Adrienne Anderson)

Damaged goods: Eileen Atkins and John Lithgow in The Retreat From Moscow. *Photo: Joan Marcus*

The Retreat From Moscow (147). By William Nicholson. Produced by Susan Quint Gallin, Stuart Thompson, Ron Kastner, True Love Productions, Mary Lu Roffe and Jam Theatricals at the Booth Theatre. Opened October 23, 2003. (Closed February 29, 2004)

Edward .... John Lithgow
Alice .... Eileen Atkins
Jamie .... Ben Chaplin

Standbys: Mr. Lithgow—Edmond Genest; Mr. Chaplin—Mark Saturno; Ms. Atkins—Sandra Shipley.

Directed by Daniel Sullivan; scenery, John Lee Beatty; costumes, Jane Greenwood; lighting, Brian MacDevitt; music and sound, John Gromada; associate producer, McGhee Entertainment Inc.; casting, Daniel Swee; production stage manager, Roy Harris; stage manager, Denise Yaney; press, Barlow-Hartman Public Relations, John Barlow, Michael Hartman, Wayne Wolfe.

Time: Present. Place: England. Presented in two parts.

A husband escapes the emotional attrition of marriage late in middle age, leaving his wife unhinged and his son trapped amid the psychological debris. First presented at the Chichester Festival Theatre, UK (10/12/1999).

Six Dance Lessons in Six Weeks (30). By Richard Alfieri. Produced by Rodger Hess, Marcia Seligson, Entpro Plays Inc., Carolyn S. Chambers, Sight Sound and Action Ltd., Brantley M. Dunaway, Judy Arnold and Patricia Greenwald at the Belasco Theatre. Opened October 29, 2003. (Closed November 23, 2003)

Lily Harrison .... Polly Bergen
Michael Minetti .... Mark Hamill

Standbys: Ms. Bergen—Kathleen Doyle; Mr. Hamill—Joseph Kolinski.

Directed by Arthur Allan Seidelman; choreography, Kay Cole; scenery, Roy Christopher; costumes, Helen Butler; lighting, Tom Ruzika; sound, Philip G. Allen; associate producers, Marilyn Gilbert, Nathan Rundlett, Etelvina Hutchins, Scottie Held and Joseph M. Eastwood; casting, Cindi Rush Casting; production stage manager, Jim Semmelman; stage manager, Marci Glotzer; press, Boneau/Bryan-Brown, Adrian Bryan-Brown, Jackie Green, Susanne Tighe, Juliana Hannett.

Time: The present. Place: Lily Harrison's condo in St. Petersburg Beach, Florida. Presented in two parts.

An unlikely friendship blossoms between an older woman and her dance teacher. First presentation of record at the Geffen Playhouse in Los Angeles (6/7/2001) with Uta Hagen and David Hyde Pierce.

***Wicked** (244). Musical with book by Winnie Holzman; music and lyrics by Stephen Schwartz; based on a novel by Gregory Maguire. Produced by Marc Platt, Universal Pictures, The Araca Group, Jon B. Platt and David Stone at the Gershwin Theatre. Opened October 30, 2003.

Glinda .... Kristin Chenoweth
Witch's Father .... Sean McCourt
Witch's Mother .... Cristy Candler
Midwife .... Jan Neuberger
Elphaba .... Idina Menzel
Nessarose .... Michelle Federer
Boq .... Christopher Fitzgerald
Madame Morrible .... Carole Shelley
Doctor Dillamond .... William Youmans
Fiyero .... Norbert Leo Butz
Ozian Official .... Sean McCourt
The Wonderful Wizard of Oz .... Joel Grey
Chistery .... Manuel Herrera

Ensemble: Ioana Alfonso, Ben Cameron, Cristy Candler, Kristy Cates, Melissa Bell Chait, Marcus Choi, Kristoffer Cusick, Kathy Deitch, Melissa Fahn, Rhett G. George, Manuel Herrera, Kisha Howard, LJ Jellison, Sean McCourt, Corinne McFadden, Jan Neuberger, Walter Winston Oneil, Andrew Palermo, Andy Pellick, Michael Seelbach, Lorna Ventura, Derrick Williams.

Orchestra: Stephen Oremus conductor; Alex Lacamoire associate conductor, piano, synthesizer; Christian Hebel concertmaster; Victor Schultz violin; Kevin Roy viola; Dan Miller cello; Konrad Adderley bass; Greg Skaff guitar; John Moses clarinet, soprano sax; John Campo bassoon, baritone sax, clarinet; Tuck Lee oboe; Helen Campo flute; Jon Owens lead trumpet; Tom Hoyt trumpet; Dale Kirkland, Douglas Purviance trombone; Theo Primis, Kelly Dent, French horn; Paul Loesel, David Evans keyboard; Ric Molina, Andy Jones percussion; Gary Seligson drums; Laura Sherman harp.

Standby for Ms. Menzel—Eden Espinosa.

Understudies: Ms. Chenoweth—Melissa Bell Chait; Ms. Menzel—Kristy Cates; Mr. Butz—Kristoffer Cusick; Messrs. Grey, Youmans—Sean McCourt; Ms. Shelley—Jan Neuberger, Lorna Ventura; Mr. Fitzgerald—Andrew Palermo; Ms. Federer—Cristy Candler, Eden Espinosa.

Swings: Kristen Leigh Gorski, Mark Myars.

Directed by Joe Mantello; choreography, Wayne Cilento; scenery, Eugene Lee; costumes, Susan Hilferty; lighting, Kenneth Posner; sound, Tony Meola; projections, Elaine J. McCarthy; special

Ahhhhhz: Kristin Chenoweth and Idina Menzel in Wicked. *Photo: Joan Marcus*

effects, Chic Silber; flying sequences, Paul Rubin/ZFX Inc.; wigs and hair, Tom Watson; orchestrations, William David Brohn; music arrangements, Messrs. Lacamoire and Oremus; music direction, Mr. Oremus; music coordinator, Michael Keller; dance arrangements, James Lynn Abbott; executive producers, Marcia Goldberg and Nina Essman; casting, Bernard Telsey Casting; production stage manager, Steven Beckler; stage manager, Erica Schwartz; press, The Publicity Office, Bob Fennell, Marc Thibodeau, Michael S. Borowski.

Presented in two parts.

The unknown story of the Wicked Witch of the West. First presentation of record at San Francisco's Curran Theatre (6/10/2003).

ACT I

"No One Mourns the Wicked" .... Glinda, Citizens of Oz
"Dear Old Shiz" .... Students
"The Wizard and I" .... Morrible, Elphaba
"What Is This Feeling?" .... Galinda, Elphaba, Students
"Something Bad" .... Dr. Dillamond, Elphaba
"Dancing Through Life" .... Fiyero, Galinda, Boq, Nessarose, Elphaba, Students
"Popular" .... Galinda
"I'm Not That Girl" .... Elphaba
"One Short Day" .... Elphaba, Glinda, Denizens of the Emerald City
"A Sentimental Man" .... The Wizard
"Defying Gravity" .... Elphaba, Glinda, Guards, Citizens of Oz

ACT II

"No One Mourns the Wicked" (Reprise) .... Citizens of Oz
"Thank Goodness" .... Glinda, Morrible, Citizens of Oz
"The Wicked Witch of the East" .... Elphaba, Nessarose, Boq
"Wonderful" .... The Wizard, Elphaba
"I'm Not That Girl" (Reprise) .... Glinda
"As Long as You're Mine" .... Elphaba, Fiyero

"No Good Deed"	Elphaba
"March of the Witch Hunters"	Boq, Citizens of Oz
"For Good"	Glinda, Elphaba
"Finale"	All

Cat on a Hot Tin Roof (145). Revival of the play by Tennessee Williams. Produced by Bill Kenwright at the Music Box. Opened November 2, 2003. (Closed March 7, 2004)

Margaret	Ashley Judd	Lacey	Alvin Keith
Brick	Jason Patric	Brightie	Starla Benford
Mae	Amy Hohn	Nursemaid	Jo Twiss
Grooper	Michael Mastro	Buster	Charles Saxton
Big Mama	Margo Martindale	Dixie	Isabella Mehiel
Reverend Tooker	Patrick Collins	Trixie	Pamela Jane Henning
Big Daddy	Ned Beatty	Polly	Muireann Phelan
Doctor Baugh	Edwin C. Owens	Sonny	Zachary Ross

Standby: Mr. Patric—Ted Koch.

Understudies: Mses. Judd, Hohn—Kelly McAndrew; Mr. Beatty—Edwin C. Owens; Ms. Martindale—Jo Twiss; Messrs. Mastro, Collins—Ted Koch; Mr. Owens—Patrick Collins; Mr. Keith—Starla Benford.

Directed by Anthony Page; scenery, Maria Bjornson; costumes, Jane Greenwood; lighting, Howard Harrison; sound, Christopher Cronin; music, Neil McArthur; casting, Pat McCorkle; production stage manager, Susie Cordon; stage manager, Allison Sommers; press, Philip Rinaldi Publicity, Philip Rinaldi, Barbara Carroll.

Time: Mid-1950s. Place: A bed-sitting room and section of the gallery of a plantation home in the Mississippi Delta. Presented in three parts.

A family struggles over its legacy—and the meaning of "truth"—when the patriarch is ill with cancer. A 1954–55 *Best Plays* choice, the original Broadway production opened at the Morosco Theatre (3/24/1955–11/17/1956; 694 performances). There have been three Broadway revivals. This production was first presented at London's Lyric Theatre with Brendan Fraser and Frances O'Connor as Brick and Maggie (9/18/2001–1/12/2002).

Cat *fight? Ned Beatty and Ashley Judd in* Cat on a Hot Tin Roof. *Photo: Joan Marcus*

Manhattan Theatre Club production of **The Violet Hour** (54). By Richard Greenberg. Lynne Meadow artistic director, Barry Grove executive producer at the Biltmore Theatre. Opened November 6, 2003. (Closed December 21, 2003)

Gidger .... Mario Cantone
Rosamund Plinth .... Dagmara Dominczyk
Denis McCleary .... Scott Foley
John Pace Seavering ...... Robert Sean Leonard
Jessie Brewster .... Robin Miles

Understudies: Ms. Miles—Eisa Davis; Messrs. Leonard, Foley, Cantone—Robert L. Devaney; Ms. Dominczyk—Heather Mazur.

Directed by Evan Yionoulis; scenery, Christopher Barreca; costumes, Jane Greenwood; lighting, Donald Holder; sound, Scott Myers; special effects, Gregory Meeh; casting, Nancy Piccione, David Caparelliotis; production stage manager, Ed Fitzgerald; stage manager, James FitzSimmons; press, Boneau/Bryan-Brown, Chris Boneau, Jim Byk, Aaron Meier.

Time: April 1, 1919. Place: An office in a Manhattan tower. Presented in two parts.

It's morning in the Modern age when a mysterious machine delivers disheartening dispatches from the future. First presented at South Coast Repertory, Costa Mesa, California (11/8/2002). A 2003–04 *Best Plays* choice (see essay by Michael Feingold in this volume).

Roundabout Theatre Company production of **The Caretaker** (63). Revival of the play by Harold Pinter. Todd Haimes artistic director, Ellen Richard managing director, Julia C. Levy executive director of external relations, at the American Airlines Theatre. Opened November 9, 2003. (Closed January 4, 2004)

Mick .... Aidan Gillen
Aston .... Kyle MacLachlan
Davies .... Patrick Stewart

Standbys: Messrs. Gillen and MacLachlan—Karl Kenzler; Mr. Stewart—Julian Gamble.

Directed by David Jones; scenery, John Lee Beatty; costumes, Jane Greenwood; lighting, Peter Kaczorowski; sound, Scott Lehrer; casting, Jim Carnahan; production stage manager, Matthew Silver; stage manager, Leslie C. Lyter; press, Boneau/Bryan-Brown, Adrian Bryan-Brown, Matt Polk, Jessica Johnson.

Time: A winter night, the next morning and two weeks later. Place: A house in west London. Presented in three parts.

Three men locked in a triangle of emotional menace. First presentation of record was given at the Arts Theatre Club in London (4/27/1960) before a transfer to the West End's Dutchess Theatre (5/30/1960). A 1961–62 *Best Plays* choice, the original Broadway production opened at the Lyceum Theatre (10/4/1961–2/24/1962; 165 performances). There have been two Broadway revivals.

Sexaholix . . . a Love Story (28) Revival of the solo performance piece by John Leguizamo. Produced by Tate Entertainment Group at the Broadway Theatre. Opened November 11, 2003. (Closed December 7, 2003)

Performed by Mr. Leguizamo

Directed by Peter Askin; press, Bill Evans and Associates, Jim Randolph.

A return engagement of Mr. Leguizamo's musings on sex, love and parenthood. First presented on Broadway at the Royale Theatre (12/2/2001–2/10/2002; 67 performances).

Taboo (100). Musical with book by Charles Busch; adapted from the original book by Mark Davies; music and lyrics by Boy George. Produced by Rosie O'Donnell and Adam Kenwright at the Plymouth Theatre. Opened November 13, 2003. (Closed February 8, 2004)

Big Sue .... Liz McCartney
Philip Sallon .... Raúl Esparza
George .... Euan Morton
Nicola .... Sarah Uriarte Berry
Marilyn .... Jeffrey Carlson
Marcus .... Cary Shields
Leigh Bowery .... George O'Dowd

Ensemble: Jennifer Cody, Dioni Michelle Collins, Brooke Elliott, Felice B. Gajda, William Robert Gaynor, Curtis Holbrook, Jennifer K. Mrozik, Nathan Peck, Alexander Quiroga, Asa Somers, Denise Summerford, Gregory Treco.

Boy meets boy: Euan Morton and George O'Dowd in Taboo. *Photo: Joan Marcus*

Orchestra: Jason Howland conductor, keyboard; Daniel A. Weiss associate conductor, second keyboard, second guitar; Sean Carney violin; Arthur Dibble viola; Ted Mook cello; David Kuhn bass; Kevan Frost guitar; Charles Pillow reeds; Chris Jago drums.

Standbys: Messrs. Esparza, O'Dowd—Donnie R. Keshawarz.

Understudies: Ms. McCartney—Dioni Michelle Collins, Brooke Elliott; Mr. Morton—Asa Somers, Gregory Treco; Ms. Berry—Lori Holmes, Jennifer K. Mrozik, Denise Summerford; Mr. Carlson—Alexander Quiroga, Gregory Treco; Mr. Shields—William Robert Gaynor.

Directed by Christopher Renshaw; choreography, Mark Dendy; scenery, Tim Goodchild; costumes, Mike Nicholls, Bobby Pearce; lighting, Natasha Katz; sound, Jonathan Deans; hair and makeup, Christine Bateman; fight direction, Rick Sordelet; additional composition, Mr. Frost; orchestrations, Steve Margoshes; additional music, John Themis, Richie Stevens; music supervision and arrangements, John McDaniel; music direction, Mr. Howland; music coordinator, Michael Keller; associate producer, Daniel MacDonald, Lori E. Seid, Michael Fuchs; casting, Bernard Telsey Casting; production stage manager, Peter Wolf; stage manager, Karen Moore; press, Barlow-Hartman Public Relations, John Barlow, Michael Hartman, Bill Coyle, Rob Finn.

Time: 1980s. Place: An abandoned warehouse that housed the club Taboo, and other places in and around London. Presented in two parts.

Alienated youth in London's gay and transgender club scene see one of their own become a major star. An earlier version was presented in London at the Venue (1/29/2002–4/26/2003).

ACT I

"Freak"/"Ode to Attention Seekers" .... Philip, Ensemble
"Stranger in This World" .... George, Big Sue, Philip, Ensemble
"Safe in the City" .... Nicola, Ensemble
"Dress to Kill" .... Ensemble
"Genocide Peroxide" .... Marilyn, Ensemble
"I'll Have You All" .... Leigh, Men
"Sexual Confusion" .... Big Sue, Philip, George, Marcus
"Pretty Lies" .... George

"Guttersnipe" .... George, Marilyn, Ensemble
"Love Is a Question Mark" .... Marcus, George, Leigh, Nicola
"Do You Really Want to Hurt Me" .... George, Ensemble
"Church of the Poison Mind"/"Karma Chameleon" .... George, Ensemble

ACT II

"Everything Taboo" .... Leigh, Ensemble
"Talk Amongst Yourselves" .... Big Sue
"The Fame Game" .... George, Ensemble
"I See Through You" .... Marcus
"Ich Bin Kunst" .... Leigh
"Petrified" .... Philip
"Out of Fashion" .... George, Marilyn, Philip, Marcus, Leigh
"Il Adore" .... Nicola, Ensemble
"Come on in From the Outside" .... Company

Anna in the Tropics (113). By Nilo Cruz. Produced by Roger Berlind, Daryl Roth, Ray Larsen, in association with Robert G. Bartner, at the Royale Theatre. Opened November 16, 2003. (Closed February 22, 2004)

Eliades .... John Ortiz
Santiago .... Victor Argo
Cheché .... David Zayas
Marela .... Vanessa Aspillaga
Conchita .... Daphne Rubin-Vega
Ofelia .... Priscilla Lopez
Juan Julian .... Jimmy Smits
Palomo .... John Ortiz

Understudies: Messrs. Ortiz, Argo, Zayas, Smits—Jason Manuel Olazábal.

Directed by Emily Mann; scenery, Robert Brill; costumes, Anita Yavich; lighting, Peter Kaczorowski; sound, Dan Moses Schreier; casting, Bernard Telsey Casting; production stage manager, Cheryl Mintz; stage manager, Joshua Halperin; press, Barlow-Hartman Public Relations, John Barlow, Michael Hartman, Wayne Wolfe.

Time: 1929. Place: Ybor City in Tampa, Florida. Presented in two parts.

A *lector* brings literature, love and sadness to a family of Cuban cigarmakers in Florida. This production was first presented at the McCarter Theatre Center, Princeton, New Jersey (9/17/2003). First presentation of record was given at the New Theatre, Coral Gables, Florida (10/12/2002). Winner of the 2003 American Theatre Critics/Steinberg New Play Award and the 2003 Pulitzer Prize in drama. A 2003–04 *Best Plays* choice (see essay by Christine Dolen in this volume).

The Oldest Living Confederate Widow Tells All (1). Solo performance piece by Martin Tahse; based on the novel by Allan Gurganus. Produced by Elliot Martin, Jane Bergère, Morton Swinsky, Ruth Hendel and Everett King at the Longacre Theatre. Opened November 17, 2003. (Closed November 17, 2003)

Lucy Marsden .... Ellen Burstyn

Directed by Don Scardino; scenery, Allen Moyer; costumes, Jane Greenwood; lighting, Kenneth Posner; sound, Peter Fitzgerald; projections, Wendall K. Harrington; production stage manager, Dianne Trulock; press, Richard Kornberg and Associates, Tom D'Ambrosio.

Presented in two parts.

An elderly widow recounts tales (and characters) from a bygone era. First presented at the Old Globe Theatre in San Diego (2/1/2003).

Laughing Room Only (14). Musical revue with book by Dennis Blair and Digby Wolfe; music and lyrics by Doug Katsaros; additional material by Jackie Mason. Produced by Jyll Rosenfeld, Jon Stoll, James Scibelli, in association with Sidney Kimmel, John Morgan and The Helen Hayes Theatre Company, at the Brooks Atkinson Theatre. Opened November 19, 2003. (Closed November 30, 2003)

Performed by Mr. Mason, Darrin Baker, Robert Creighton, Ruth Gottschall, Cheryl Stern, Barry Finkel.

Short run: Ellen Burstyn in The Oldest Living Confederate Widow Tells All. *Photo: Joan Marcus*

Standbys: Michael Gruber, Danette Holden.

Directed by Robert Johanson; choreography, Michael Lichtefeld; scenery, Michael Anania; costumes, Thom Heyer; lighting, Paul D. Miller; sound, Peter Hylenski; orchestrations, Mr. Katsaros; music direction and vocal arrangements, Joseph Baker; dance arrangements, Ian Herman; assistant director, Jayme McDaniel; associate choregrapher, Joe Bowerman; casting, Norman Meranus; production stage manager, C. Randall White.

Presented in two parts.

Mr. Mason's ninth Broadway comedy. The first was *A Teaspoon Every Four Hours*, presented at the ANTA Playhouse–now the Virginia Theatre–for one performance (6/14/1969) following 97 previews.

Lincoln Center Theater production of **Henry IV** (58). Revival of the play by William Shakespeare; adapted by Dakin Matthews. André Bishop artistic director, Bernard Gersten executive producer at the Vivian Beaumont Theater. Opened November 20, 2003. (Closed January 18, 2004)

King Henry IV .... Richard Easton
Henry ("Hal"),
  Prince of Wales .... Michael Hayden
John of Lancaster .... Lorenzo Pisoni
Chief Justice Warwick .... Dakin Matthews
Earl of Westmoreland .... Tyrees Allen
Thomas Percy,
  Earl of Worcester .... Byron Jennings
Earl of Northumberland .... Terry Beaver
Lady Northumberland .... Dana Ivey
Henry Percy ("Hotspur") .... Ethan Hawke
Lady Percy .... Audra McDonald
Owen Glendower .... Dakin Matthews
Sir Richard Vernon .... Peter Jay Fernandez
Edmund Mortimer .... Scott Ferrara
Lady Mortimer .... Anastasia Barzee
Lord Hastings .... Stevie Ray Dallimore
Archbishop of York .... Tom Bloom
Earl of Douglas .... C.J. Wilson
Sir John Falstaff .... Kevin Kline

Princely jest: Michael Hayden, Kevin Kline and company in Henry IV. *Photo: Paul Kolnik*

Poins	Steve Rankin
Pistol	David Manis
Nym	Ty Jones
Bardolph	Stephen DeRosa
Mistress Quickly	Dana Ivey
Doll Tearsheet	Genevieve Elam
Francis	Aaron Krohn
Ralph	Jed Orlemann
Justice Shallow	Jeff Weiss
Justice Silence	Tom Bloom
Davy	Jed Orlemann

Ensemble: Christine Marie Brown, Albert Jones, Ty Jones, Lucas Caleb Rooney, Daniel Stewart Sherman, Corey Stoll, Baylen Thomas, Nance Williamson, Richard Ziman.

Understudies: Mr. Easton—Dakin Matthews; Mr. Hayden—Lorenzo Pisoni; Mr. Kline—David Manis; Mr. Hawke—Scott Ferrara; Messrs. Rankin, Jennings, Allen—Stevie Ray Dallimore; Messrs. Matthews (Glendower), Bloom (Archbishop of York)—Richard Ziman; Ms. Ivey—Nance Williamson; Messrs. Weiss (Shallow), Bloom (Silence)—Stephen DeRosa; Mr. Jones—Albert Jones; Mses. McDonald, Elam, Barzee, Mr. Orlemann (Davy)—Christine Marie Brown; Mr. Beaver—Peter Jay Fernandez; Mr. Pisoni—Jed Orlemann; Messrs. Ferrara, Dallimore—Baylen Thomas; Mr. DeRosa—Aaron Krohn; Mr. Manis—C.J. Wilson; Mr. Wilson—Lucas Caleb Rooney; Mr. Fernandez—Ty Jones.

Directed by Jack O'Brien; scenery, Ralph Funicello; costumes, Jess Goldstein; lighting, Brian MacDevitt; music and sound, Mark Bennett; special effects, Gregory Meeh; fight direction, Steve Rankin; associate director, Matt August; dramaturg, Mr. Matthews; stage manager, Michael Brunner; press, Philip Rinaldi Publicity, Philip Rinaldi, Barbara Carroll.

Time: 1403. Place: England. Presented in three parts.

Adaptation of the two parts of William Shakespeare's *Henry IV* into one play focusing on political struggle and Prince Hal's rejection of his wild ways. Although the two plays were probably performed in the late 1500s, the earliest accounts of performance derive from the diary of Samuel Pepys (for Part 1 in 1660) and from a 1700 adaptation of Part 2 by Thomas Betterton. First presentations of record in New York were at the Theatre in Chapel Street (Part 1: 12/18/1761) and the Park Theatre (Part 2: 2/4/1822). During the early 20th century, a popular version of Part 1 included an interpolation from Part 2 of the crowd-pleasing (and purist-annoying) recruiting scene. This version was used by the Players Club in its "Fifth Annual Revival" at the Knickerbocker Theatre (5/31/1926) and in a production featuring Maurice Evans as Falstaff at the St. James Theatre (1/30/1939).

***Wonderful Town** (217). Revival of the musical with book by Joseph Fields and Jerome Chodorov; music by Leonard Bernstein; lyrics by Betty Comden and Adolph Green; based on the play *My Sister Eileen* by Messrs. Fields and Chodorov, and on stories by Ruth McKenney. Produced by Roger Berlind and Barry and Fran Weissler, in association with Edwin W. Schloss, Allen Spivak, Clear Channel Entertainment and Harvey Weinstein, at the Al Hirschfeld Theatre. Opened November 23, 2003.

Tour Guide .... Ken Barnett
Appopolous .... David Margulies
Officer Lonigan .... Timothy Shew
Wreck .... Raymond Jaramillo McLeod
Helen .... Nancy Anderson
Violet .... Linda Mugleston
Speedy Valenti .... Stanley Wayne Mathis
Eileen Sherwood .... Jennifer Westfeldt
Ruth Sherwood .... Donna Murphy
Italian Chef .... Vince Pesce
Italian Waiter .... Rick Faugno
Drunks .... David Eggers, Devin Richards
Strange Man .... Ray Wills
Frank Lippencott .... Peter Benson
Robert Baker .... Gregg Edelman
Associate Editors .... Ken Barnett, Ray Wills
Mrs. Wade .... Randy Danson
Kid .... Mark Price
Chick Clark .... Michael McGrath
Shore Patrolman .... Ray Wills

Cadets: David Eggers, Rick Faugno, Vince Pesce, Mark Price, Devin Richards, J.D. Webster.

Policemen: Ken Barnett, David Eggers, Vince Pesce, Devin Richards, J.D. Webster, Ray Wills.

Greenwich Villagers: Ken Barnett, Joyce Chittick, Susan Derry, David Eggers, Rick Faugno, Lorin Latarro, Linda Mugleston, Tina Ou, Vince Pesce, Mark Price, Devin Richards, Angela Robinson, Megan Sikora, J.D. Webster, Ray Wills.

Orchestra: Rob Fisher conductor; Rob Berman alternate conductor; Leslie Stifelman associate conductor, piano; Marilyn Reynolds, Christoph Franzgrote, Rebekah Johnson, Lisa Matricardi, Masako Yanagita violin; Jill Jaffe, Crystal Garner viola; Diane Barere, Lanny Paykin cello; Lou Bruno bass; Steven Kenyon, Lino Gomez, Fred DeChristofaro, Edward Salkin, John Winder woodwinds; Stu Satalof, David Trigg, David Gale, Ron Tooley trumpet; Jack Gale, Jason Jackson, Jack Schatz trombone; David Ratajczak drums and percussion.

Drowsy dames: Donna Murphy and Jennifer Westfeldt in Wonderful Town. *Photo: Paul Kolnik*

Understudies: Mses. Murphy, Danson—Linda Mugleston; Ms. Westfeldt—Nancy Anderson, Susan Derry; Messrs. Edelman, McLeod, Shew—Matthew Shepard; Mr. Benson—David Eggers; Messrs. Margulies, McGrath—Ray Wills; Mr. Mathis—Randy Donaldson; Ms. Anderson—Joyce Chittick.

Swings: Randy Donaldson, Stephanie Fredricks, Lisa Mayer, Matthew Shepard.

Directed and choreographed by Kathleen Marshall; scenery, John Lee Beatty; costumes, Martin Pakledinaz; lighting, Peter Kaczorowski; sound, Lew Mead; orchestrations, Don Walker; music direction and vocal arrangements, Mr. Fisher; music coordinator, Seymour Red Press; assistant director, Marc Bruni; associate choreographer, Daniel H. Posener; executive producer, Alecia Parker; production stage manager, Peter Hanson; stage managers, Kimberly Russell, Maximo Torres; press, The Pete Sanders Group, Pete Sanders, Glenna Freedman, Jim Mannino.

Time: 1935. Place: New York City. Presented in two parts.

Sisters from Ohio move to the big city. A 1952–53 *Best Plays* choice, the original Broadway production opened at the Winter Garden Theatre (2/25/1953–7/3/1954; 559 performances) where it received five 1953 Tony Awards. The 2003–04 production received a Tony Award for best choreography.

ACT I

Overture .... Orchestra
"Christopher Street" .... Tour Guide, Tourists, Villagers
"Ohio" .... Ruth, Eileen
"Conquering New York" .... Ruth, Eileen, Frank, New Yorkers
"One Hundred Easy Ways" .... Ruth
"What a Waste" .... Baker, Associate Editors
"Ruth's Story Vignettes" .... Baker, Ruth, Associate Editors
"A Little Bit in Love" .... Eileen
"Pass the Football" .... Wreck, Villagers
"Conversation Piece" .... Eileen, Frank, Ruth, Chick, Baker
"A Quiet Girl" .... Baker
"A Quiet Girl" (Reprise) .... Ruth
"Conga!" .... Ruth, Cadets
"Conga!" (Reprise) .... Company

Karma chameleon: Jefferson Mays in I Am My Own Wife. *Photo: Joan Marcus*

ACT II

"My Darlin' Eileen" .... Officer Lonigan, Eileen, Policemen
"Swing" .... Ruth, Villagers
"Ohio" (Reprise) .... Ruth, Eileen
"It's Love" .... Eileen, Baker, Villagers
Ballet at the Village Vortex .... Villagers
"Wrong Note Rag" .... Ruth, Eileen, Villagers
Finale .... Company

***I Am My Own Wife** (199). Transfer of the Off Broadway solo performance piece by Doug Wright. Produced by Delphi Productions, in association with Playwrights Horizons, at the Lyceum Theatre. Opened December 3, 2003.

Charlotte von Mahlsdorf .... Jefferson Mays

Directed by Moisés Kaufman; scenery, Derek McLane; costumes, Janice Pytel; lighting, David Lander; sound, Andre J. Pluess and Ben Sussman; production stage manager, Nancy Harrington; press, Richard Kornberg and Associates, Richard Kornberg, Don Summa, Tom D'Ambrosio.

Time: The Nazi Years; the Communist Years. Place: Various locations in the US and Germany. Presented in two parts.

Solo performance centering on a man who lives as a woman under politically challenging circumstances in what was once known as East Germany. Commissioned by Playwrights Horizons, it was first presented at the La Jolla Playhouse (7/10/2001) after development at the Sundance Theatre Laboratory. A 2002–03 *Best Plays* choice, the original New York production opened at Playwrights Horizons (5/27/2003; 80 performances). This production received 2004 Tony Awards for best play and best actor in a play

Never Gonna Dance (84). Musical with book by Jeffrey Hatcher; music by Jerome Kern; lyrics by Dorothy Fields, Oscar Hammerstein II, Otto Harbach, Johnny Mercer, Ira Gershwin, Bernard Dougall, P.G. Wodehouse, Jimmy McHugh and Edward Laska; based on the RKO Pictures film *Swing Time* and a story by Erwin Gelsey. Produced by Weissberger Theater Group/Jay Harris, Edgar Bronfman Jr., James Walsh, Ted Hartley/RKO Pictures, Harvey Weinstein at the Broadhurst Theatre. Opened December 4, 2003. (Closed February 15, 2004)

The Charms .... Roxane Barlow, Sally Mae Dunn, Jennifer Frankel
Lucky Garnett .... Noah Racey
Mr. Chalfont .... Philip LeStrange
Margaret Chalfont .... Deborah Leamy
A Minister .... Kirby Ward
Mabel Pritt .... Karen Ziemba
Penny Carroll .... Nancy Lemenager
Alfred J. Morganthal .... Peter Gerety
Mr. Pangborn .... Peter Bartlett
Major Bowes .... Ron Orbach
Miss Tattersall .... Julie Connors
Ricardo Romero .... David Pittu
The Rome-Tones .... Julio Agustin, Jason Gillman, T. Oliver Reid
Spud .... Eugene Fleming
Velma .... Deidre Goodwin
Dice Raymond .... Timothy J. Alex
Waitresses .... Sally Mae Dunn, Jennifer Frankel, Ipsita Paul
A Construction Worker .... Kirby Ward

Ensemble: Julio Agustin, Timothy J. Alex, Roxane Barlow, Julie Connors, Sally Mae Dunn, Jennifer Frankel, Jason Gillman, Greg Graham, Kenya Unique Massey, Ipsita Paul, T. Oliver Reid, Kirby Ward, Tommar Wilson.

Orchestra: Robert Billig conductor; James Sampliner associate conductor, keyboard; Howard Joines assistant conductor, percussion; Mineko Yajima concertmaster, James Tsao, Jonathan Dinklage, Claire Chan violin; Sarah Carter cello; Benjamin Franklin Brown bass; Chuck Wilson, Rick Heckman, Mark Thrasher reeds; Don Downs, John Chudoba trumpet; Keith O'Quinn, Michael Boschen trombone; Russell Rizner, French horn; Zane Mark keyboard; Dean Sharenow drums.

Understudies: Mr. Racey—Jason Gillman, Greg Graham; Ms. Lemenager—Nili Bassman, Deborah Leamy; Ms. Ziemba—Sally Mae Dunn, Jennifer Frankel; Mr. Gerety—Ron Orbach, Kirby Ward; Mr. Bartlett—Julio Agustin, Philip LeStrange; Mr. Pittu—Julio Agustin, Timothy J. Alex; Ms.

Sea Gullah: Anthony Mackie and Aunjanue Ellis in Drowning Crow. *Photo: Joan Marcus*

Leamy—Julie Connors; Mr. LeStrange—Timothy J. Alex, Kirby Ward; Mr. Orbach—Timothy J. Alex, Kirby Ward; Mr. Fleming—T. Oliver Reid, Tommar Wilson; Ms. Goodwin—Kenya Unique Massey, Ipsita Paul.

Swings: Nili Bassman, Ashley Hull, Denis Jones, Tony Yazbeck.

Directed by Michael Greif; choreography, Jerry Mitchell; scenery, Robin Wagner; costumes, William Ivey Long; lighting, Paul Gallo; sound, Acme Sound Partners; orchestrations, Harold Wheeler; music direction and vocal arrangements, Mr. Billig; song arrangements, Mr. Sampliner; dance music arrangements, Mr. Mark; music coordinator, John Miller; associate director, Leigh Silverman; associate choreographer, Jodi Moccia; casting, Bernard Telsey Casting; production stage manager, Kristen Harris; stage manager, Michael John Egan; press, Boneau/Bryan-Brown, Adrian Bryan-Brown, Amy Jacobs, Juliana Hannett.

Time: 1936. Place: Punxsutawney, Pennsylvania; New York City. Presented in two parts.

Rags-to-riches tale of a guy who's dying to dance, but promises to refrain from exercising his terpsichorean talents.

ACT I

Punxsutawney, Pennsylvania

"Dearly Beloved" (Mercer) .... Lucky, Charms

"Put Me to the Test" (Gershwin) .... Lucky

New York City

"I Won't Dance" (Hammerstein, Fields, McHugh, Harbach) .... Lucky, Company

"Pick Yourself Up" (Fields) .... Penny, Lucky

"Pick Yourself Up" (Reprise) .... Mabel, Morganthal

"Who?" (Hammerstein, Harbach) .... Ricardo, Rome-Tones

"I'm Old Fashioned" (Mercer) .... Penny

Spud and Velma's Audition

"She Didn't Say Yes, She Didn't Say No" (Harbach) .... Spud, Velma

"The Song Is You" (Hammerstein) .... Mabel, Morganthal, Waitresses

"The Way You Look Tonight" (Fields) .... Lucky, Penny

ACT II

"Waltz in Swing Time" (Fields) .... Company
"Shimmy With Me" (Wodehouse) .... Mabel, Company
"A Fine Romance" (Fields) .... Penny, Lucky, Mabel, Morganthal
"I'll Be Hard to Handle" (Dougall) .... Spud, Velma
"I Got Love" (Fields) .... Mabel
"The Most Exciting Night" (Fields, Harbach) .... Ricardo, Rome-Tones
"Remind Me" (Fields) .... Penny, Lucky
"Never Gonna Dance" (Fields) .... Lucky, Penny
"Dearly Beloved"/"I Won't Dance" (Reprise) .... Company

Manhattan Theatre Club production of **Drowning Crow** (54). By Regina Taylor; adapted from *The Seagull* by Anton Chekhov. Lynne Meadow artistic director, Barry Grove executive producer at the Biltmore Theatre. Opened February 19, 2004. (Closed April 4, 2004)

Yak .... Peter Macon
Okra .... Baron Vaughn
Constantine Trip (C-Trip) .... Anthony Mackie
Simon .... Curtis McClarin
Mary Bow .... Tracie Thoms
Peter Nicholas .... Paul Butler
Hannah Jordan .... Aunjanue Ellis
Eugene Dawn .... Roger Robinson
Paula Andrea Bow .... Stephanie Berry
Sammy Bow .... Stephen McKinley Henderson
Josephine Nicholas Ark .... Alfre Woodard
Jackie .... Ebony Jo-Ann
Robert Alexander Trigor . Peter Francis James

Understudies: Mses. Woodard, Berry, Jo-Ann—Caroline Clay; Messrs. James, McClarin, Macon, Vaughn—Joseph Edward; Mr. Mackie—Peter Macon; Mses. Ellis, Thoms—Tiffany Thompson; Messrs. Butler, Henderson, Robinson—Ronald Wyche.

Directed by Marion McClinton; choreography, Ken Roberson; scenery, David Gallo; costumes, Paul Tazewell; lighting, Ken Billington; sound, Dan Moses Schreier; music, Daryl Waters; projections, Wendall K. Harrington; production stage manager, Diane DiVita; stage manager, Cynthia Kocher; press, Boneau/Bryan-Brown, Chris Boneau, Jim Byk, Aaron Meier.

Time: The present. Place: Gullah Islands, South Carolina. Presented in two parts.

Adaptation of Chekhov's classic play using contemporary language, imagery and music. First presented at the Goodman Theatre in Chicago (1/21/2002).

***Fiddler on the Roof** (109). Revival of the musical with book by Joseph Stein; music by Jerry Bock; lyrics by Sheldon Harnick; based on stories by Sholom Aleichem. Produced by James L. Nederlander, Stewart F. Lane/Bonnie Comley, Harbor Entertainment, Terry Allen Kramer, Bob Boyett/Lawrence Horowitz, Clear Channel Entertainment at the Minskoff Theatre. Opened February 26, 2004.

Tevye .... Alfred Molina
Golde .... Randy Graff
Tzeitel .... Sally Murphy
Hodel .... Laura Michelle Kelly
Chava .... Tricia Paoluccio
Shprintze .... Lea Michele
Bielke .... Molly Ephraim
Yente, the Matchmaker .... Nancy Opel
Lazar Wolf .... David Wohl
Rabbi .... Yusef Bulos
Mordcha .... Philip Hoffman
Avram .... Mark Lotito
Jakov .... David Rossmer
Chaim .... Bruce Winant
Shandel .... Barbara Tirrell
Mirala .... Marsha Waterbury
Fredel .... Rita Harvey
Rivka .... Joy Hermalyn
Motel .... John Cariani
Perchik .... Robert Petkoff
Mendel .... Chris Ghelfi
Yussel .... Enrique Brown
Yitzuk .... Randy Bobish
Label .... Jeff Lewis
Shloime .... Francis Toumbakaris
Anya .... Melissa Bohon
Surcha .... Haviland Stillwell
Nachum, the Beggar .... Tom Titone
Fiddler .... Nick Danielson
Boy .... Michael Tommer
Boy (alt.) .... Sean Curley
Constable .... Stephen Lee Anderson
Fyedka .... David Ayers
Sasha .... Jonathan Sharp
Vladek .... Stephen Ward Billeisen
Vladimir .... Keith K. Ühl

Little fiddle? Randy Graff, Alfred Molina and Nick Danielson (with fiddle) in Fiddler on the Roof. *Photo: Carol Rosegg*

Boris .... Craig Ramsay
Grandma Tzeitel .... Haviland Stillwell
Fruma Sarah .... Joy Hermalyn
Onstage clarinetist .... Andrew Sterman

Bottle dancers: Randy Bobish, Enrique Brown, Chris Ghelfi, Jeff Lewis, Francis Toumbakaris.

Orchestra: Kevin Stites conductor; Charles duChateau associate conductor, cello; Martin Agee concertmaster; Cenovia Cummins, Conrad Harris, Heidi Stubner, Antoine Silverman violin; Debra Shufelt, Maxine Roach viola; Peter Sachon cello; Peter Donovan bass; Greg Utzig guitar, mandolin, lute; Brian Miller flute; Mr. Sterman, Martha Hyde flute, clarinet; Matthew Dine oboe; Marc Goldberg bassoon; Wayne duMaine lead trumpet; Tim Schadt, Joseph Reardon trumpet; Lisa Albrecht trombone, euphonium; Larry DiBello, Peter Schoettler, French horn; Elaine Lord accordion, celeste; Billy Miller drums, percussion.

Understudies: Mr. Molina—Philip Hoffman, Mark Lotito; Ms. Graff—Barbara Tirrell, Marsha Waterbury; Ms. Opel—Joy Hermalyn, Barbara Tirrell; Ms. Murphy—Rita Harvey, Gina Lamparella; Ms. Kelly—Rita Harvey, Haviland Stillwell; Ms. Paoluccio—Melissa Bohon, Lea Michele; Mses. Michele, Ephraim—Melissa Bohon, Haviland Stillwell; Mr. Cariani—Jeff Lewis, David Rossmer; Mr. Petkoff—David Rossmer, Randy Bobish; Mr. Ayers—Stephen Ward Billeisen, Jonathan Sharp; Mr. Wohl—Philip Hoffman, Mark Lotito; Mr. Anderson—Mark Lotito, Bruce Winant; Mr. Danielson—Antoine Silverman, David Rossmer; Mr. Bulos—Tom Titone, Bruce Winant; Mr. Ghelfi—Randy Bobish, Roger Rosen; Mr. Hoffman—Tom Titone, Bruce Winant; Mr. Lotito—Tom Titone, Roger Rosen; Mses. Stillwell, Hermalyn—Gina Lamparella; Mr. Tommer—Sean Curley, David Best.

Swings: Gina Lamparella, Roger Rosen, Gustavo Wons.

Directed by David Leveaux; choreography, Jerome Robbins; scenery, Tom Pye; costumes, Vicki Mortimer; lighting, Brian MacDevitt; sound, Acme Sound Partners; flying sequences, ZFX Inc.; wigs and hair, David Brian Brown; orchestrations, Don Walker, Larry Hochman; music coordinator, Michael Keller; musical staging, Jonathan Butterell; music direction, Mr. Stites; production stage manager, David John O'Brien; stage manager, Jenny Dewar; press, Barlow-Hartman Public Relations, John Barlow, Michael Hartman, Wayne Wolfe.

Time: 1905. Place: Anatevka, Russia. Presented in two parts.

The life of a milkman and his family in czarist Russia. A 1964–65 *Best Plays* choice, the original Broadway production opened at the Imperial Theatre (9/22/1964–7/2/1972; 3242 performances).

Later in its first run, the musical moved to the Majestic Theatre and then to the Broadway Theatre. The first production received nine 1965 Tony Awards and a special 1972 Tony Award for its long run. There have been four Broadway revivals.

ACT I

"Tradition" .... Company
"Matchmaker" .... Tzeitel, Hodel, Chava, Shprintze, Bielke
"If I Were a Rich Man" .... Tevye
"Sabbath Prayer" .... Family, Villagers
"To Life" .... Tevye, Lazar, Village Men
"Miracle of Miracles" .... Motel
"Tevye's Dream" .... Company
"Sunrise, Sunset" .... Family, Villagers

ACT II

"Now I Have Everything" .... Perchik, Hodel
"Do You Love Me?" .... Tevye, Golde
"Topsy-Turvy" .... Yente, Rivka, Mirala
"Far From the Home I Love" .... Hodel
"Chavaleh" .... Tevye
"Anatevka" .... Family, Villagers

Lincoln Center Theater production of **King Lear** (33). By William Shakespeare. André Bishop artistic director, Bernard Gersten executive producer, in association with the Stratford Festival of Canada, at the Vivian Beaumont Theater. Opened March 4, 2004. (Closed April 18, 2004)

King Lear .... Christopher Plummer
Goneril .... Domini Blythe
Regan .... Lucy Peacock
Cordelia .... Claire Jullien
Duke of Albany .... Ian Deakin
Duke of Cornwall .... Stephen Russell
Earl of Kent .... Benedict Campbell
Earl of Gloucester .... James Blendick
Edgar .... Brent Carver
Edmund .... Geraint Wyn Davies
Fool .... Barry MacGregor
King of France .... Paul O'Brien

Kingdom cutter: Christopher Plummer in King Lear. *Photo: Joan Marcus*

Duke of Burgundy .... Guy Paul
Oswald .... Brian Tree
Curan .... Eric Sheffer Stevens
Cornwall's Servants .... David Furr,
Christopher McHale, Jay Edwards
Old Man .... Leo Leyden
Doctor .... William Cain
Captain .... David Furr
Herald .... Quentin Maré

Ensemble: Caroline Bootle, Jay Edwards, David Furr, Douglas Harmsen, Leo Leyden, Matt Loney, Quentin Maré, Christopher McHale, Andy Prosky, Christopher Randolph, Brian Sgambati, Eric Sheffer Stevens, Baylen Thomas, Susan Wilder.

Understudies: Mr. Plummer—Benedict Campbell; Mr. Campbell—Stephen Russell; Mr. MacGregor—Brian Tree; Messrs. Blendick, Leyden—William Cain; Mr. Deakin—Paul O'Brien; Mr. Russell—Guy Paul; Messrs. Cain, Furr—Christopher McHale; Mr. Davies—Quentin Maré; Ms. Jullien—Caroline Bootle; Mses. Blythe, Peacock—Susan Wilder; Mr. O'Brien—Christopher Randolph; Mr. Carver—Douglas Harmsen; Mr. Tree—Andy Prosky; Mr. Paul—Eric Sheffer Stevens; Messrs. Stevens, Maré—Matt Loney; Messrs. Furr, McHale, Edwards—Baylen Thomas.

Directed by Jonathan Miller; scenery, Ralph Funicello; costumes, Clare Mitchell; lighting, Robert Thomson; music, Berthold Carrière; sound, Scott Anderson; casting, Daniel Swee; stage manager, Brian Scott; press, Philip Rinaldi Publicity, Barbara Carroll.

Presented in two parts.

An aged king disrupts all of civilized society when he injudiciously divides his kingdom and sets in motion grave events. First presentation of record at the court of King James I (12/26/1606). First presentation of record in the US at New York's Theatre in Nassau Street (1/14/1754) was influenced by Nahum Tate's 1681 adaptation of *King Lear*. First US presentation of the Shakespeare version was given by William C. Macready at the Park Theatre (9/27/1844).

*__Roundabout Theatre Company__ production of **Twentieth Century** (76). Revival of the play by Ben Hecht and Charles MacArthur; based on a play by Charles Bruce Millholland; adapted by Ken Ludwig. Todd Haimes artistic director, Ellen Richard managing director, Julia C. Levy executive director of external relations, at the American Airlines Theatre. Opened March 25, 2004.

Comic turns: Alec Baldwin and Anne Heche in Twentieth Century. *Photo: Joan Marcus*

Anita Highland .... Kellie Overbey
Dr. Grover Lockwood .... Jonathan Walker
Porter .... Robert M. Jiménez
Matthew Clark .... Tom Aldredge
Owen O'Malley .... Dan Butler
Conductor .... Terry Beaver
Ida Webb .... Julie Halston
Oscar Jaffe .... Alec Baldwin
Lily Garland .... Anne Heche
George Smith .... Ryan Shively
Beard .... Stephen DeRosa
Detective .... Patrick Boll
Max Jacobs .... Stephen DeRosa

Ensemble: Patrick Boll, Todd Cerveris, Darian Dauchan, Bill English, Virginia Louise Smith.

Understudies: Mr. Baldwin—Patrick Boll; Mses. Heche, Halston, Overbey—Virginia Louise Smith; Messrs. Butler, Walker, DeRosa—Todd Cerveris; Messrs. Aldredge, Beaver—Robert M. Jiménez; Messrs. Shively, Boll—Bill English; Mr. Jiménez—Darian Dauchan.

Directed by Walter Bobbie; scenery, John Lee Beatty; costumes, William Ivey Long; lighting, Peter Kaczorowski; sound, Acme Sound Partners; casting, Jim Carnahan, Mele Nagler; production stage manager, James Harker; stage manager, Leslie C. Lyter; press, Boneau/Bryan-Brown, Adrian Bryan-Brown, Matt Polk, Jessica Johnson.

Time: October 1938. Place: Aboard the Twentieth Century Limited. Presented in two parts.

Comedy about a theater producer desperately trying to keep his business afloat and the complication that ensue when he boards a famous rail line. First presentation of record at Broadway's Broadhurst Theatre (12/29/1932–5/20/1933; 152 performances). There have been two Broadway revivals and a 1978 musical adaptation, *On the Twentieth Century*.

Lincoln Center Theater production of **Barbara Cook's Broadway!** (7). André Bishop artistic director, Bernard Gersten executive producer, at the Vivian Beaumont Theater. Opened March 28, 2004. (Closed April 18, 2004)

Performed by Ms. Cook, with Wally Harper (piano) and Richard Sarpola (bass).

Music direction and arrangement, Mr. Harper; stage manager, Mahlon Kruse; press, Philip Rinaldi, Barbara Carroll.

Presented without intermission.

Another in a series of solo performance pieces in which Ms. Cook sings and tells anecdotes about the songs and her career in the theater.

***Sly Fox** (69). Revival of the play by Larry Gelbart; based on *Volpone* by Ben Jonson. Produced by Julian Schlossberg, Roy Furman, Ben Sprecher, Michael Gardner, Jim Fantaci, Cheryl Lachowicz, Christine Duncan and Nelle Nugent, by arrangement with Andrew Braunsberg, at the Ethel Barrymore Theatre. Opened April 1, 2004.

Simon Able .... Eric Stoltz
Sly's servants .... Jeremy Hollingworth, Charles Antalosky, Linda Halaska
Foxwell J. Sly .... Richard Dreyfuss
Lawyer Craven .... Bronson Pinchot
Jethro Crouch .... René Auberjonois
Abner Truckle .... Bob Dishy
Miss Fancy .... Rachel York
Mrs. Truckle .... Elizabeth Berkley
Crouch's servant .... Jason Ma
Captain Crouch .... Nick Wyman
Chief of Police .... Peter Scolari
1st Policeman .... Robert LaVelle
2nd Policeman .... Gordon Joseph Weiss
3rd Policeman .... Jeff Talbott
Court Clerk .... Professor Irwin Corey
Judge .... Richard Dreyfuss

Understudies: Mr. Stoltz—Jeremy Hollingworth; Mr. Dishy—Peter Scolari, Gordon Joseph Weiss; Mr. Auberjonois—Professor Irwin Corey, Charles Antalosky; Mses. Berkley, York—Linda Halaska; Mr. Wyman—Robert LaVelle; Mr. Pinchot—Peter Scolari, Gordon Joseph Weiss; Mr. Scolari—Charles Antalosky, Gordon Joseph Weiss; Mr. Corey—Charles Antalosky; Messrs. LaVelle, Weiss, Talbott—Jeff Talbott, Jason Ma; Messrs. Weiss, Ma, Hollingworth, Antalosky, Ms. Halaska (Bailiff and Servants)—Jeff Talbott.

Directed by Arthur Penn; scenery, George Jenkins and Jesse Poleshuck; costumes, Albert Wolsky; lighting, Phil Monat; sound, T. Richard Fitzgerald and Carl Casella; fight direction, B.H. Barry; associate producers, Aaron Levy, Jill Furman, Debra Black, Peter May; casting, Stuart

Western justice: Professor Irwin Corey, Richard Dreyfuss and Eric Stoltz in Sly Fox. *Photo: Carol Rosegg*

Howard and Amy Schecter; production stage manager, Marybeth Abel; stage manager, Bryan Landrine; press, The Publicity Office, Bob Fennell, Marc Thibodeau, Michael S. Borowski.

Time: A day in the late 1800s. Place: San Francisco. Presented in two parts.

A lecherous miser and his clever servant fleece corrupt citizens. A 1976–77 *Best Plays* choice, the original Broadway production opened at the Broadhurst Theatre (12/14/1976–2/19/1978; 495 performances). There has been one Broadway revival. An earlier musical adaptation of *Volpone*, titled *Foxy*, was first presented on Broadway at the Ziegfeld Theatre (2/16–4/18/1964; 72 performances). Bert Lahr received a 1964 Tony Award for best actor in a musical as the title character in *Foxy*.

Match (53). By Stephen Belber. Produced by The Araca Group, East of Doheny Theatricals, Chase Mishkin, in association with Ray and Kit Sawyer, Carol Grose, at the Plymouth Theatre. Opened April 8, 2004. (Closed May 23, 2004)

Toby .... Frank Langella   Lisa .... Jane Adams
Mike .... Ray Liotta

Understudies: Mr. Langella—Malcolm Ingram; Mr. Liotta—Karl Bury; Ms. Adams—Alexandra Neil.

Directed by Nicholas Martin; scenery, James Noone; costumes, Michael Krass; lighting, Brian MacDevitt; sound, Kurt Kellenberger and Jerry Yager; fight direction, Rick Sordelet; associate producers, Clint Bond Jr., Edward Nelson; casting, Bernard Telsey Casting; production stage manager, Andrea "Spook" Testani; stage manager, Stephen M. Kaus; press, Boneau/Bryan-Brown, Adrian Bryan-Brown, Jackie Green, Joe Perrotta.

Time: The Present. Place: Upper Manhattan. Presented in two parts.

An eccentric former dancer in the autumn of his life discovers that he may have a long-lost relative.

Sixteen Wounded (12). By Eliam Kraiem. Produced by Jujamcyn Theaters, Producers Four and Robert G. Bartner, in association with Debra Black, Lisa Vioni, Michael Watt, at the Walter Kerr Theatre. Opened April 15, 2004. (Closed April 25, 2004)

Hans .... Judd Hirsch
Sonya .... Jan Maxwell
Mahmoud .... Omar Metwally
Nora .... Martha Plimpton
Ashraf .... Waleed F. Zuaiter

Understudies: Mr. Hirsch—Martin Rayner; Mses. Maxwell, Plimpton—Natacha Roi; Mr. Metwally—Waleed F. Zuaiter, Jonathan Hova; Mr. Zuaiter—Jonathan Hova.

Directed by Garry Hynes; scenery and costumes, Francis O'Connor; lighting, James F. Ingalls; music and sound, John Gromada; special effects, Gregory Meeh; fight direction, Thomas Schall; associate producers, Jerry Meyer, Patrick Catullo; casting, Jay Binder, Jack Bowdan; production stage manager, David Hyslop; stage manager, Deirdre McCrane; press, Barlow-Hartman Public Relations, John Barlow, Michael Hartman, Bill Coyle, Andrew Snyder.

Time: 1992–94. Place: A bakery in Amsterdam. Presented in two parts.

An Palestinian "sleeper" becomes friends with a Jewish baker and falls in love with a girl before he is confronted by the terrorist who controls him. First presented as part of the Cherry Lane Theatre's Mentor Project in New York (5/14/2002). Later presented at the Long Wharf Theatre in New Haven (2/12/2003).

*__Roundabout Theatre Company__ production of **Assassins** (45). Revival of the musical with book by John Weidman; music and lyrics by Stephen Sondheim. Todd Haimes artistic director, Ellen Richard managing director, Julia C. Levy executive director of external relations, at Studio 54. Opened April 22, 2004.

Proprietor .... Marc Kudisch
Leon Czolgosz .... James Barbour
John Hinckley .... Alexander Gemignani
Charles Guiteau .... Denis O'Hare

Family ties: Frank Langella, Ray Liotta and Jane Adams in Match. *Photo: Joan Marcus*

Terror track: Judd Hirsch and Omar Metwally in Sixteen Wounded. *Photo: Joan Marcus*

American carnival: The company of Assassins. *Photo: Joan Marcus*

Giuseppe Zangara .... Jeffrey Kuhn
Samuel Byck .... Mario Cantone
Lynette "Squeaky"
Fromme .... Mary Catherine Garrison
Sara Jane Moore .... Becky Ann Baker
John Wilkes Booth .... Michael Cerveris
Balladeer .... Neil Patrick Harris
David Herold .... Brandon Wardell
Emma Goldman .... Anne L. Nathan
James Blaine .... James Clow
President James Garfield .... Merwin Foard
Billy .... Eamon Foley
President Gerald Ford .... James Clow
Lee Harvey Oswald .... Neil Patrick Harris

Ensemble: James Clow, Merwin Foard, Eamon Foley, Kendra Kassebaum, Anne L. Nathan, Brandon Wardell

Orchestra: Paul Gemignani conductor; Nicholas Michael Archer associate conductor, keyboard; Paul Ford keyboard; Dennis Anderson flute, piccolo, clarinet, soprano sax, harmonica; Andrew Shreeves oboe, English horn, piccolo, clarinet, alto sax; Scott Schachter clarinet, flute, piccolo, bass clarinet, E-flat clarinet, tenor sax; Mark Thrasher bassoon, clarinet, baritone sax; Dominic Derasse trumpet, cornet; Phil Granger trumpet, flugelhorn; Ronald Sell, French horn; Bruce Eidem trombone, euphonium; Scott Kuney guitar, banjo, mandolin; John Beal bass, electric bass; Larry Lelli drums, percussion.

Understudies: Ms. Garrison—Kendra Kassebaum; Messrs. Cerveris, O'Hare—James Clow; Messrs. Barbour, Cantone, Kudisch—Merwin Foard; Messrs. Gemignani, Harris, Kuhn—Brandon Wardell.

Swings: Ken Krugman, Sally Wilfert, Chris Peluso.

Directed by Joe Mantello; choreography, Jonathan Butterell; scenery, Robert Brill; costumes, Susan Hilferty; lighting, Jules Fisher and Peggy Eisenhauer; sound, Dan Moses Schreier; orchestrations, Michael Starobin; musical director, Mr. Gemignani; casting, Jim Carnahan; production stage manager, William Joseph Barnes; stage manager, Jon Krause; press, Boneau/Bryan-Brown, Adrian Bryan-Brown, Matt Polk, Jessica Johnson.

Presented without intermission.

A motley collection of presidential assassins (and those who failed the task) examine the dark edges of the American dream. First presentation of record at Off Broadway's Playwrights Horizons (1/27–2/15/1991; 25 performances).

MUSICAL NUMBERS

"Everybody's Got the Right" .... Proprietor, Czolgosz, Guiteau, Fromme, Byck, Booth, Zangara, Hinckley, Moore
"The Ballad of Booth" .... Balladeeer, Booth
"How I Saved Roosevelt" .... Zangara, Ensemble
"Gun Song" .... Czolgosz, Booth, Guiteau, Moore
"The Ballad of Czolgosz" .... Balladeer, Ensemble
"Unworthy of Your Love" .... Hinckley, Fromme
"The Ballad of Guiteau" .... Guiteau, Balladeer
"Another National Anthem" .... Proprietor, Czolgosz, Booth, Hinckley, Fromme, Zangara, Moore, Guiteau, Byck, Balladeer
"Something Just Broke" .... Ensemble
"Everybody's Got the Right" .... Moore, Byck, Czolgosz, Zangara, Fromme, Hinckley, Oswald, Guiteau, Booth

***Jumpers** (41). Revival of the play by Tom Stoppard. Produced by Boyett Ostar Productions, Nederlander Presentations Inc., Freddy DeMann, Jean Doumanian, Stephanie McClelland, Arielle Tepper, in association with the National Theatre of Great Britain, at the Brooks Atkinson Theatre. Opened April 25, 2004.

Dorothy .... Essie Davis
Secretary .... Eliza Lumley
Crouch .... John Rogan
George .... Simon Russell Beale
Archie .... Nicky Henson
Bones .... Nicholas Woodeson
Greystoke; Jumper .... Michael Hollick
McFee; Jumper .... Hillel Meltzer

Jumpers: Michael Arnold, Andrew Asnes, Clark Scott Carmichael, Tom Hildebrand, Don Johanson, Joseph P. McDonnell.

Orchestra: Tim Weil conductor, keyboard; James Saporito drums; Richard Sarpola bass.

Like a melody: Essie Davis in Jumpers. *Photo: Hugo Glendinning*

Standbys: Mr. Beale—John Curless; Mses. Davis, Lumley—Crista Moore; Mr. Henson—Tony Carlin; Messrs. Woodeson, Rogan—Julian Gamble.

Swings: Karl Christian, Aaron Vexler.

Directed by David Leveaux; choreography, Aidan Treays; scenery, Vicki Mortimer; costumes, Nicky Gillibrand; lighting, Paule Constable; sound, John Leonard for Aura; music, Corin Buckeridge; music coordinator, Michael Keller; associate director, Matt Wilde; casting, Jim Carnahan; production stage manager, Arthur Gaffin; stage manager, Laurie Goldfeder; press, Boneau/Bryan-Brown, Adrian Bryan-Brown, Jim Byk, Juliana Hannett.

Presented in two parts.

Comic meditation on the befuddlement attendant to questions regarding the existence of God and the nature of being, as experienced by a hapless professor of philosophy. A 1973–74 *Best Plays* choice, the original Broadway production opened at the Billy Rose Theatre (4/22–6/1/1974; 48 performances). First US presentation of record was given at the Kennedy Center (2/18/1974). First presentation of record was given at the National Theatre's Old Vic in London (2/2/1972). The 2003–2004 production was first presented at the National Theatre in London (6/19–11/7/2003) before a run at the Piccadilly Theatre (11/20/2003–3/6/2004).

***A Raisin in the Sun** (40). Revival of the play by Lorraine Hansberry. Produced by David Binder, Vivek J. Tiwary, Susan Batson, Carl Rumbaugh, Ruth Hendel, Jayne Baron Sherman, Dede Harris, in association with Arielle Tepper, Barbara Whitman, Cynthia Stroum, at the Royale Theatre. Opened April 26, 2004.

Ruth Younger .... Audra McDonald   Travis Younger .... Alexander Mitchell

Walter Lee Younger .... Sean Combs
Beneatha Younger .... Sanaa Lathan
Lena Younger .... Phylicia Rashad
Joseph Asagai .... Teagle F. Bougere
George Murchison .... Frank Harts
Karl Lindner .... David Aaron Baker
Bobo .... Bill Nunn
Moving Men .... Lawrence Ballard,
Billy Eugene Jones

Directed by Kenny Leon; scenery, Thomas Lynch; costumes, Paul Tazewell; lighting, Brian MacDevitt; sound, T. Richard Fitzgerald; music, Dwight Andrews; associate producers, Brian Savelson, Hal Goldberg; casting, James Calleri; production stage manager, Michael Brunner; stage manager, Narda Alcorn; press, The Publicity Office, Bob Fennell, Marc Thibodeau, Michael S. Borowski.

Time: 1950s. Place: Chicago's Southside. Presented in two parts.

An African-American family awaits an insurance check that each member hopes will provide entry to the American dream. A 1958–59 *Best Plays* choice, the original Broadway production opened at the Ethel Barrymore Theatre (3/11/1959–6/25/1960; 530 performances). Seven months into its 15-month run, the first production moved to the Belasco Theatre. The 2003–2004 production was the first Broadway presentation of the play in 45 years; it received 2004 Tony Awards for best actress (Ms. Rashad) and best featured actress in a play (Ms. McDonald).

***Bombay Dreams** (36). Musical with book by Meera Syal and Thomas Meehan; music by A.R. Rahman; lyrics by Don Black; based on an idea by Shekhar Kapur and Andrew Lloyd Webber. Produced by Waxman Williams Entertainment and TGA Entertainment, in association with Denise Rich and Ralph Williams, Scott Prisand and Danny Seraphine, Harold Thau/Max Cooper/Judy Arnold and Brantley Dunaway, Independent Presenters Network, at the Broadway Theatre. Opened April 29, 2004.

Akaash .... Manu Narayan
Eunuchs (Hijira) .... Ron Nahass,
Bobby Pestka,
Darryl Semira, Kirk Torigoe
Ram .... Mueen Jahan Ahmad
Salim .... Aalok Mehta
Shanti .... Madhur Jaffrey
Sweetie .... Sriram Ganesan
Munna (Wed. mat., Thur., Sat. mat., Sun.)
.... Neil Jay Shastri
Munna (Tue., Wed., Fri., Sat. eves.)
.... Tanvir Gopal

Man to man: Sean Combs and Alexander Mitchell in A Raisin in the Sun. *Photo: Joan Marcus*

Hard Hats .... Suresh John, Gabriel Burrafato
Vikram .... Deep Katdare
Priya .... Anisha Nagarajan
Madan .... Marvin L. Ishmael
Pageant Announcer .... Zahf Paroo
Rani .... Ayesha Dharker
Policemen .... Zahf Paroo, Gabriel Burrafato
Shaheen .... Jolly Abraham
Kitty DaSouza .... Sarah Ripard
Movie Sweetie .... Darryl Semira
Movie Shanti .... Anjali Bhimani
Movie Akaash .... Zahf Paroo
Wedding Qawali Singers .... Gabriel Burrafato, Ian Jutsun, Zahf Paroo

Ensemble: Jolly Abraham, Mueen Jahan Ahmad, Aaron J. Albano, Celine Alwyn, Anjali Bhimani, Shane Bland, Gabriel Burrafato, Wendy Calio, Tiffany Michelle Cooper, Sheetal Gandhi, Krystal Kiran Garib, Tania Marie Hakkim, Dell Howlett, Suresh John, Ian Jutsun, Miriam Laube, Aalok Mehta, Ron Nahass, Michelle Nigalan, Zahf Paroo, Danny Pathan, Bobby Pestka, Kafi Pierre, Sarah Ripard, Darryl Semira, Kirk Torigoe.

Orchestra: James L. Abbott conductor; Dan Riddle associate conductor; Sylvia D'Avanzo concertmaster; Sean Carney, Nina Evtuhov, Pauline Kim, Ming Yeh violin; Liuh-Wen Ting, Arthur Dibble viola; Ted Mook, Roger Shall cello; Randy Landau bass; Anders Bostrom flute; Charles Pillow oboe, English horn; Adam Ben-David, Dan Riddle, Ann Gerschefski keyboard; Deep Singh, David Sharma percussion; Ray Grappone drums.

Understudies: Mr. Narayan—Aaron J. Albano, Zahf Paroo, Danny Pathan; Ms. Nagarajan—Krystal Kiran Garib, Sheetal Gandhi, Michelle Nigalan; Ms. Dharker—Jolly Abraham, Anjali Bhimani, Sarah Ripard; Mr. Ganesan—Shane Bland, Darryl Semira; Ms. Jaffrey—Anjali Bhimani, Sarah Ripard; Mr. Katdare—Gabriel Burrafato, Zahf Paroo; Mr. Ishmael—Mueen Jahan Ahmad, Suresh John, Ian Jutsun; Messrs. Shastri, Gopal—Tanvir Gopal, Neil Jay Shastri.

Swings: Rommy Sandhu, Lisa Stevens, James R. Whittington, Nicole Winhoffer.

Directed by Steven Pimlott; choreography, Anthony Van Laast and Farah Khan; scenery and costumes, Mark Thompson; lighting, Hugh Vanstone; sound, Mick Potter; fight direction, J. Steven White; music direction, dance music arrangement, Mr. Abbott; additional musical arrangements, Christopher Nightingale; music supervision, arrangements, orchestrations, Paul Bogaev; music coordinator, Michael Keller; associate directors, Lucy Skilbeck, Thomas Caruso; associate

Border crossings: The Hijira in Bombay Dreams. *Photo: Joan Marcus*

choreographers, Lisa Stevens, Nichola Treherne; executive producer, Waxwill Theatrical Divison; associate producers, Sudhir Vaishnav, The Entertainment Partnership, Alexander Fraser, Ken Denison; casting, Tara Rubin Casting; production stage manager, Bonnie L. Becker; press, Barlow-Hartman Public Relations, John Barlow, Michael Hartman, Jeremy Shaffer.

Presented in two parts.

Musical parody of "Bollywood" movies from India with a framework celebrating the possibility of attaining fame and fortune. First presentation of record was given at London's Apollo Victoria Theatre (6/19/2002–6/13/2004).

ACT I

Scene One: Paradise Slum
Overture: "Salaa'm Bombay" .... Akaash, Sweetie, Ensemble
"Bollywood" .... Akaash, Ensemble
Scene Two: Shanti and Akaash's Home
"Love's Never Easy" .... Sweetie, Priya, Ensemble
Scene Three: The Miss India Pageant, Backstage
Scene Four: The Miss India Pageant, Frontstage
"Lovely, Lovely Ladies" .... Rani, Ensemble
"Bhangra" .... Akaash, Rani, Ensemble
Scene Five: The Miss India Pageant, Backstage
Scene Six: Film set of *Diamond in the Rough*
"Shakalaka Baby" .... Rani, Akaash, Ensemble
"I Could Live Here" .... Akaash
"Is This Love?" .... Priya
Scene Seven: Akaash's New Apartment
"Famous" .... Madan, Rani, Akaash, Guests
Scene Eight: *Diamond in the Rough* Premiere
"Love's Never Easy" (Reprise) .... Priya, Sweetie

ACT II

Scene One: The Annual Indian Film Awards
"Chaiyya Chaiyya" .... Akaash, Rani, Ensemble
Scene Two: Akaash's Hilltop Mansion
"How Many Stars?" .... Akaash, Priya
Scene Three: Film Set of *Bombay Dreams*
"Salaa'm Bombay" (Reprise) .... Rani, Ensemble
"Hero" .... Sweetie, Priya
Scene Four: Paradise Slum
Scene Five: Outside theTaj Royale Beach Hotel
"Ganesh Procession" .... Company
Scene Six: Juhu Beach
"The Journey Home" .... Akaash
Scene Seven: Paradise Slum
Scene Eight: The Taj Royale Beach Hotel
"Wedding Qawali" .... Company

***Caroline, or Change** (32). Transfer from Off Broadway of the musical with book and lyrics by Tony Kushner; music by Jeanine Tesori. Produced by Carole Shorenstein Hays, HBO Films, Jujamcyn Theaters, Freddy DeMann, Scott Rudin, Ruth Hendel/ Elisabeth Morten/Cheryl Wiesenfeld, Fox Theatricals/Jennifer Manocherian/Jane Bergère, Roger Berlind, Clear Channel Entertainment, Joan Cullman, Greg Holland/Scott E. Nederlander, Margo Lion, Daryl Roth, Frederick Zollo, Jeffrey Sine, in association with The Public Theater, at the Eugene O'Neill Theatre. Opened May 2, 2004.

Caroline Thibodeaux .... Tonya Pinkins
The Washing Machine .... Capathia Jenkins
The Radio .... Tracy Nicole Chapman, Marva Hicks, Ramona Keller
Noah Gellman .... Harrison Chad
The Dryer .... Chuck Cooper
Grandma Gellman .... Alice Playten
Grandpa Gellman .... Reathel Bean

Constant change: Chandra Wilson, Tonya Pinkins and Anika Noni Rose in Caroline, or Change. *Photo: Michal Daniel*

Rose Stopnick Gellman .... Veanne Cox
Stuart Gellman .... David Costabile
Dotty Moffett .... Chandra Wilson
The Moon .... Aisha de Haas
The Bus .... Chuck Cooper
Emmie Thibodeaux .... Anika Noni Rose
Jackie Thibodeaux .... Leon G. Thomas III
Joe Thibodeaux .... Marcus Carl Franklin
Mr. Stopnick .... Larry Keith

Orchestra: Linda Twine conductor; Matthew Sklar associate conductor, keyboard; Paul Woodiel, Christopher Cardona violin; David Creswell viola; Anja Wood cello; Steve Bargonetti guitar; Benjamin Franklin Brown bass; Paul Garment, Stephen Wisner reeds; John Clancy, Shane Shanahan percussion.

Standbys: Ms. Pinkins—Adriane Lenox; Ms. Jenkins—Ledisi; Mses. Chapman, Hicks, Keller—Shannon Antalan, Vanessa A. Jones, Brandi Chavonne Massey, Ledisi; Mr. Chad—Sy Adamowsky; Mr. Cooper—Milton Craig Nealy; Ms. Playten—Sue Goodman; Mr. Bean—Donald Grody; Ms. Cox—Sue Goodman; Mr. Costabile—Adam Heller; Ms. Wilson—Vanessa A. Jones; Ms. De Haas—Vanessa A. Jones; Ms. Rose—Shannon Antalan; Messrs. Thomas, Franklin—Chevon Rutty; Mr. Keith—Donald Grody.

Directed by George C. Wolfe; choreography, Hope Clarke; scenery, Riccardo Hernández; costumes, Paul Tazewell; lighting, Jules Fisher and Peggy Eisenhauer; sound, Jon Weston; hair, Jeffrey Frank; orchestrations, Rick Bassett, Joseph Joubert, Buryl Red; music supervision, Kimberly Grigsby; music direction, Ms. Twine; music coordinator, John Miller; casting, Jordan Thaler, Heidi Griffiths; production stage manager, Rick Steiger; stage manager, Lisa Dawn Cave; press, Boneau/Bryan-Brown, Chris Boneau, Amy Jacobs, Juliana Hannett.

Time: November–December 1963. Place: Lake Charles, Louisiana. Presented in two parts.

Musical about a motherless young Jewish boy's relationship with his family's African-American maid in the Kennedy-era South. Transferred from The Public Theater's Newman Theater (11/30/

2003–2/1/2004; 106 performances). See Plays Produced Off Broadway section in the volume. A 2003–04 *Best Plays* choice (see essay by John Istel in this volume).

ACT I	ACT II
Scene 1: Washer/Dryer	Scene 7: Ironing
Scene 2: Cabbage	Scene 8: The Chanukah Party
Scene 3: Long Distance	Scene 9: The Twenty-Dollar Bill
Scene 4: Moon Change	Scene 10: Aftermath
Scene 5: Duets	Scene 11: Lot's Wife
Scene 6: The Bleach Cup	Scene 12: How Long Has This Been Going On?

Epilogue

Helping hand: Brían F. O'Bryne, Sam Kitchin and Swoosie Kurtz in Frozen. *Photo: Joan Marcus*

***Frozen** (32). Transfer from Off Off Broadway of the play by Bryony Lavery. Produced by MCC Theater (Robert LuPone, Bernard Telsey, William Cantler, John G. Schultz), Harold Newman, Frederick Zollo/Nicholas Paleologos and Jeffrey Sine, Roy Gabay, Lorie Cowen Levy and Beth Smith, Peggy Hill, Thompson H. Rogers, Morton Swinsky/ Michael Filerman/Ruth Hendel, Spring Sirkin/Marianne Mills/Jim Baldassare, Darren Bagert at the Circle in the Square. Opened May 4, 2004.

Agnetha	Laila Robins	Ralph	Brían F. O'Byrne
Nancy	Swoosie Kurtz	Guard	Sam Kitchin

Directed by Doug Hughes; scenery, Hugh Landwehr; costumes, Catherine Zuber; lighting, Clifton Taylor; music and sound, David Van Tieghem; fight direction, Rick Sordelet; associate producers, Edmund and Mary Fusco; production stage manager, James FitzSimmons; casting, Bernard Telsey Casting; press, Boneau/Bryan-Brown, Chris Boneau, Adriana Douzos.

Presented in two parts.

A serial murderer is inextricably linked to two women: one is the mother of a girl he killed, the other a researcher of psychopathology. First presentation of record was given in at Birmingham Repertory Theatre (5/1/1998) in the UK. A revised version of *Frozen* later ran in London at the

National Theatre's Cottesloe Theatre (7/3–8/24/2002). First US presentation of record was given Off Off Broadway by MCC Theater at the East 13th Street Theatre (3/18–4/11/2004; 27 performances). A 2003–04 *Best Plays* choice (see essay by Anne Marie Welsh in this volume).

Prymate (5). By Mark Medoff. Produced by Michael Parva, Chase Mishkin, Leonard Soloway, in association with Debra Black, at the Longacre Theatre. Opened May 5, 2004. (Closed May 8, 2004)

Graham	André De Shields	Avrum	James Naughton
Esther	Phyllis Frelich	Allison	Heather Tom

Understudies: Ms. Tom—Kathryn Finch; Ms. Frelich—Jackie Roth; Mr. De Shields—Ronald Wyche.

Directed by Edwin Sherin; choreography, Mr. De Shields; scenery, Robert Steinberg; costumes, Colleen Muscha; lighting, Jeff Nellis; sound, Michael Smith; fight direction, Paul Steger; associate producer, Steven W. Wallace; production stage manager, Peter Wolfe; stage manager, Andrea O. Saraffian; press, The Pete Sanders Group.

Presented without intermission.

An actor portrays a gorilla who is central to a battle between medical ethics and animal rights. First presentation of record was given at Florida State University in Tallahassee (2/20–2/29/2004).

***Marc Salem's Mind Games on Broadway** (2). Produced by Delphi Productions at the Lyceum Theatre. Opened May 24, 2004.

Performed by Mr. Salem.

Press, Richard Kornberg and Associates.

Presented without intermission.

Mentalist performing his work on nights when *I Am My Own Wife* is dark. Mr. Salem performed

Second love: Laura Linney and Byron Jennings in Sight Unseen. *Photo: Joan Marcus*

similar acts in *Marc Salem's Mind Games* (11/17/1997–5/31/1998; 237 performances) at the Westside Theatre Downstairs and *Marc Salem's Mind Games Too* 12/3/2001–1/13/2002; 48 performances) at the Duke on 42nd Street.

***Manhattan Theatre Club** production of **Sight Unseen** (8). Revival of the play by Donald Margulies. Lynne Meadow artistic director, Barry Grove executive producer at the Biltmore Theatre. Opened May 25, 2004.

Jonathan Waxman .... Ben Shenkman
Nick .... Byron Jennings
Patricia .... Laura Linney
Grete .... Ana Reeder

Understudies: Mr. Shenkman—J. Anthony Crane; Mr. Jennings—Paul DeBoy; Mses. Linney, Reeder—Kate Forbes.

Directed by Daniel Sullivan; scenery, Douglas W. Schmidt; costumes, Jess Goldstein; lighting, Pat Collins, music and sound, John Gromada; casting, Nancy Piccione and David Caparelliotis; production stage manager, Roy Harris; stage manager, Denise Yaney; press, Boneau/Bryan-Brown, Chris Boneau, Jim Byk, Aaron Meier.

Time: 1991; 1976; 1974. Place: Norfolk and London, England; Brooklyn and Upstate New York. Presented in two parts.

An artist's success does not exempt him from recriminations he experiences when confronting his past (and the present). First presentation of record was given at South Coast Repertory (9/21/1991) in Costa Mesa, California. A 1991–92 *Best Plays* choice, the original New York production opened at Manhattan Theatre Club's City Center Stage II (1/20–9/6/1992; 263 performances).

PLAYS PRODUCED OFF BROADWAY

○○○○○

FOR THE PURPOSES of *Best Plays* listing, the term "Off Broadway" signifies a show that opened for general audiences in a Manhattan theater seating 499 or fewer and 1) employed an Equity cast, 2) planned a regular schedule of 8 performances a week in an open-ended run (7 a week for solo shows and some other exceptions) and 3) offered itself to public comment by critics after a designated opening performance.

Figures in parentheses following a play's title give number of performances. These numbers do not include previews or extra non-profit performances. Performance interruptions for cast changes and other breaks have been taken into account. Performance numbers are figured in consultation with press representatives and company managements.

Plays marked with an asterisk (*) were still in a projected run on June 1, 2004. The number of performances is figured from press opening through May 31, 2004.

In a listing of a show's numbers—dances, sketches, musical scenes, etc.—the titles of songs are identified wherever possible by their appearance in quotation marks (").

HOLDOVERS FROM PREVIOUS SEASONS

OFF BROADWAY SHOWS that were running on June 1, 2003 are listed below. More detailed information about them appears in previous *Best Plays* volumes of appropriate date. Important cast changes since opening night are recorded in the Cast Replacements section in the volume.

***Perfect Crime** (7,089). By Warren Manzi. Opened October 16, 1987.

***Blue Man Group (Tubes)** (6,393). Performance piece by and with Blue Man Group. Opened November 17, 1991.

***Stomp** (4,298). Percussion performance piece created by Luke Cresswell and Steve McNicholas. Opened February 27, 1994.

***I Love You, You're Perfect, Now Change** (3,255). Musical revue with book and lyrics by Joe DiPietro; music by Jimmy Roberts. Opened August 1, 1996.

***De La Guarda** (2,356). Spectacle devised by De La Guarda (Pichon Baldinu, Diqui James, Gabriel Kerpel, Fabio D'Aquila, Tomas James, Alejandro Garcia, Gabriella Baldini). Opened June 16, 1998.

***Naked Boys Singing!** (2,031). Musical revue conceived by Robert Schrock; written by various authors. Opened July 22, 1999.

***The Donkey Show** (1,225). Musical conceived and created by Randy Weiner and Diane Paulus; adapted from William Shakespeare's *A Midsummer Night's Dream*. Opened August 12, 1999.

***Forbidden Broadway: 20th Anniversary Celebration** (944). Musical revue created and written by Gerard Alessandrini. Opened February 25, 2002.

***Menopause: The Musical** (927). Musical revue with book and lyrics by Jeanie Linders; music by various popular artists. Opened April 4, 2002.

The Exonerated (608). By Jessica Blank and Erik Jensen. Opened October 10, 2002. (Closed March 7, 2004)

Bartenders (228). Solo performance by Louis Mustillo. Opened November 22, 2002. (Closed July 6, 2003)

Barbra's Wedding (101). By Daniel Stern. Opened March 5, 2003. (Closed June 15, 2003)

Our Lady of 121st Street (166). By Stephen Adly Guirgis. Opened March 6, 2003. (Closed July 27, 2003)

Tea at Five (127). By Matthew Lombardo. Opened March 9, 2003. (Closed July 13, 2003)

Zanna, Don't! (112). Musical with book, music and lyrics by Tim Acito; additional book and lyrics by Alexander Dinelaris. Opened March 20, 2003. (Closed June 29, 2003)

Manhattan Ensemble Theater production of **Golda's Balcony** (116). By William Gibson. Opened March 26, 2003. (Closed July 13, 2003)

Hank Williams: Lost Highway (132). Transfer of the Off Off Broadway musical with book by Randal Myler and Mark Harelik; music and lyrics based on the work of Mr. Williams. Opened March 26, 2003. (Closed July 20, 2003)

Talking Heads (177). By Alan Bennett. Opened April 6, 2003. (Closed September 7, 2003)

The Last Sunday in June (103). Transfer of the Off Off Broadway play by Jonathan Tolins. Opened April 9, 2003. (Closed July 6, 2003)

New York Theatre Workshop production of **Cavedweller** (30). By Kate Moira Ryan; based on a novel by Dorothy Allison. Opened May 8, 2003. (Closed June 1, 2003)

Atlantic Theater Company production of **Writer's Block** (54). By Woody Allen. Opened May 15, 2003. (Closed June 29, 2003)

Manhattan Theatre Club production of **Humble Boy** (57). By Charlotte Jones. Opened May 18, 2003. (Closed July 6, 2003)

Boobs! The Musical (The World According to Ruth Wallis) (304). Musical revue with book by Steve Mackes and Michael Whaley; music and lyrics by Ruth Wallis. Opened May 19, 2003. (Closed February 8, 2004)

Playwrights Horizons production of ***I Am My Own Wife** (80). By Doug Wright. Opened May 27, 2003. (Closed August 3, 2003)

PLAYS PRODUCED JUNE 1, 2003–MAY 31, 2004

Manhattan Theatre Club production of **Last Dance** (40). By Marsha Norman. Lynne Meadow artistic director, Barry Grove executive producer, at City Center Stage II. Opened June 3, 2003. (Closed July 6, 2003)

Georgeanne .... Heather Goldenhersh
Cab .... Lorenzo Pisoni
Randall .... David Rasche
Charlotte .... JoBeth Williams

Directed by Ms. Meadow; scenery, Loy Arcenas; costumes, Ann Roth; lighting, Duane Schuler; sound, Bruce Ellman; music, Jason Robert Brown; casting, David Caparelliotis, Nancy Piccione; production stage manager, James FitzSimmons; press, Boneau/Bryan-Brown, Chris Boneau, Jim Byk, Aaron Meier.

Time: The present. Place: The southern coast of France. Presented without intermission.

A well-known woman novelist renounces love for the life of the aesthete.

The Prince and the Pauper (102). Revival of the musical with book by Bernie Garzia and Ray Roderick; music by Neil Berg; lyrics by Messrs. Berg, Garzia and Roderick; based on the novel by Mark Twain. Produced by Leftfield Productions, Marian Lerman Jacobs, at the Lamb's Theatre. Opened June 4, 2003. (Closed August 31, 2003)

Lady Edith; Karyn .... Leslie Castay
Tom Canty;
The Pauper .... Jimmy Dieffenbach
Miles; Charlie; Patch .... Robert Evan
Lady Jane; Jamie .... Allison Fischer
Annie; Floozy;
Baker's wife .... Amy Goldberger
Prince Edward .... Dennis Michael Hall
Father Andrew; Pike .... James Hindman
Hermit; Dresser .... Roland Rusinek
Hugh Hendon; Stache .... Wayne Schroder
John Canty; King Henry;
Castle Cook .... Dan Sharkey
Mary Canty; Maggie .... Sally Wilfert

Uncle Red? Kala Savage and Mark Feuerstein in A Bad Friend. *Photo: Joan Marcus*

Directed by Mr. Roderick; scenery, Dana Kenn; costumes, Samantha Fleming; lighting, Eric T. Haugen; sound, One Dream Sound; fight direction, Rick Sordelet; associate producer, Douglas N. Wall; casting, Dave Clemmons; press, Cromarty and Company, Peter Cromarty.

Presented in two parts.

Two boys exchange lives and learn important lessons about how others inhabit the world.

Abby Sage Richardson wrote the first theatrical adaptation of record—not a musical—which opened at the Broadway Theatre (1/20/1890) with Mark Twain in attendance. This production was first presented at the Lamb's Theatre (6/16/2002; 194 performances).

Lincoln Center Theater production of **A Bad Friend** (56). By Jules Feiffer. André Bishop artistic director, Bernard Gersten executive producer at the Mitzi E. Newhouse Theater. Opened June 9, 2003. (Closed July 27, 2003)

Uncle Morty .... Mark Feuerstein
Rose .... Kala Savage
Emil .... Larry Bryggman
Naomi .... Jan Maxwell
Shelly .... Jonathan Hadary
Fallon .... David Harbour
Radio Voice .... Peter Rini

Understudies: Messrs. Feuerstein, Harbour—Peter Rini; Messrs. Bryggman, Hadary—Terry Layman; Ms. Savage—Blythe Auffarth; Ms. Maxwell—Shelley Williams.

Directed by Jerry Zaks; scenery, Douglas Stein; costumes, William Ivey Long; lighting, Paul Gallo; sound, Aural Fixation; projections, Jan Hartley; casting, Daniel Swee; stage manager, Thom Widmann; press, Philip Rinaldi Publicity, Philip Rinaldi, Barbara Carroll.

Time: The McCarthy era. Place: New York. Presented in two parts.

Politics and betrayals—large and small—among a family of doctrinaire progressives.

National Actors Theatre production of **The Persians** (21). Revival of the play by Aeschylus; adapted by Ellen McLaughlin. Tony Randall artistic director, at Michael Schimmel Center for the Arts. Opened June 10, 2003. (Closed June 29, 2003)

Counsellors .... Jon DeVries, Ed Dixon, Herb Foster, Michael Potts, Henry Stram, Henry Strozier, Charles Turner
Attosa .... Roberta Maxwell
Herald .... Brennan Brown
Darius .... Len Cariou
Xerxes .... Michael Stuhlbarg

Directed by Ethan McSweeny; scenery, James Noone; costumes, Jess Goldstein; lighting, Kevin Adams, music and sound, Michael Roth; projections, Marilys Ernst; production stage manager, James Latus; press, Springer/Chicoine Public Relations, Gary Springer, Joe Trentacosta.

Presented without intermission.

Imperial hubris leads to devastation when the underdog Greeks are victorious over Persia at Salamis. First presented in 472 BCE, it is the earliest extant Greek drama and the only surviving Greek tragedy centering on a historical subject.

Brooklyn Academy of Music presentation of the **Royal Dramatic Theatre of Sweden** production of **Ghosts** (5). Revival of the play by Henrik Ibsen; translated and adapted by Ingmar Bergman. Alan H. Fishman chairman of the board, Karen Brooks Hopkins president, Joseph V. Melillo executive producer, at the Harvey Theater. Opened June 10, 2003. (Closed June 14, 2003)

Mrs. Helene Alving .... Pernilla August
Osvald Alving .... Jonas Malmsjö
Pastor Manders .... Jan Malmsjö
Jacob Engstrand .... Örjan Ramberg
Regine Engstrand .... Angela Kovacs

Directed by Mr. Bergman; scenery, Göran Wassberg; costumes, Anna Bergman; lighting, Pierre Leveau; press, Sandy Sawotka, Melissa Cusick, Fatima Kafele, Tamara McCaw, Kila Packett.

Presented in two parts.

Version of Ibsen's classic drama on parental corruption and its grip on the next generation as adapted—with cuts and additions—by the Swedish filmmaker. The original version was first

Charming aesthete: Jonas Malmsjö and Pernilla August in Ghosts. *Photo: Stephanie Berger*

presented in Chicago (in Norwegian) at Aurora Turner Hall (5/20/1882) after which it toured other communities in the Upper Midwest. Banned from public performance in England until 1914, *Ghosts* was first presented in English by the Independent Theatre Society (5/13/1891) in a "private" performance. The first presentation of record in New York was a German-language version (*Die Gespenster*) at the Amberg Theatre (3/27/1891). The first English-language presentation of record in New York was given at the Garden Theatre (1/5/1894) as a subscription performance.

Playwrights Horizons production of **Bad Dates** (33). Solo performance piece by Theresa Rebeck. Tim Sanford artistic director, Leslie Marcus managing director, William Russo general manager, in the Peter Jay Sharp Theater. Opened June 15, 2003. (Closed July 6, 2003)

Haley .... Julie White

Directed by John Benjamin Hickey; scenery, Derek McLane; costumes, Mattie Ullrich; lighting, Frances Aronson; sound, Bruce Ellman; casting, James Calleri; production stage manager, Megan Schneid; press, The Publicity Office, Bob Fennell, Marc Thibodeau, Michael S. Borowski, Candi Adams.

Time: Present. Place: New York City. Presented without intermission.

One woman comically wades in the shallow end of the dating pool.

Mack the Knife (56). Musical revue by Chaz Esposito and James Haddon. Produced by Splish Splash Productions at the Theatre at St. Peter's. Opened June 22, 2003. (Closed August 10, 2003)

Performed by Mr. Esposito, with music by Larry Frenock.

Directed by Mr. Esposito; scenery, Martin Machitto; lighting and sound, John Pappas; music direction and arrangements, James Haddon; press, KPM Associates, Kevin P. McAnarney, Grant Lindsey.

Raconteuse: Julie White in Bad Dates. *Photo: Carol Rosegg*

Presented in two parts.

Celebration of the life and work of Bobby Darin.

Musical numbers included: "Splish Splash," "Dream Lover," "Beyond the Sea," "Things," "You're the Reason I'm Living," "If I Were a Carpenter," "Mack theKnife."

The Aquila Theatre Company production of **The Importance of Being Earnest** (41). Revival of the play by Oscar Wilde. Peter Meineck producing artistic director, at the Baruch Performing Arts Center. Opened June 29, 2003. (Closed August 3, 2003)

Algernon Moncrieff .... Guy Oliver-Watts
John (Jack) Worthing .... Richard Willis
Lady Bracknell .... Alex Webb
Hon. Gwendolen Fairfax .... Cameron Blair
Miss Prism .... Renata Friedman
Cecily Cardew .... Lindsay Rae Taylor
Lane; Manservant;
Rev. Canon Chasuble .... Andrew Schwartz
Merriman; Butler .... Ryan Conarro

Directed by Robert Richmond; scenery, Mr. Richmond and Mr. Meineck; lighting, David Dunford; production stage manager, Allegra Libonati; press, The Pete Sanders Group.

Presented in two parts.

Cloaked identity, social standing and the institution of marriage are all in play in this classic comedy. First perfomance of record at London's St. James Theatre (2/14/1895). First presented in New York at the Empire Theatre (4/22/1895).

Second Stage Theatre production of **The Notebooks of Leonardo da Vinci** (41). By Mary Zimmerman; based on the work of Mr. da Vinci. Carole Rothman artistic director,

Carol Fishman managing director, in association with the Berkeley Repertory Theatre. Opened June 29, 2003. (Closed August 3, 2003)

Leonardo .... Anjali Bhimani
Leonardo .... Lucia Brawley
Leonardo .... Lizzy Cooper Davis
Leonardo .... Christopher Donahue
Leonardo .... Kyle Hall
Leonardo .... Doug Hara
Leonardo .... Louise Lamson
Leonardo .... Mariann Mayberry
Leonardo .... Paul Oakley Stovall

Directed by Ms. Zimmerman; scenery, Scott Bradley; costumes, Mara Blumenfeld, based on designs by Allison Reeds; lighting, T.J. Gerckens; sound, Michael Bodeen; music, Miriam Strum and Mr. Bodeen; production stage manager, Cynthia Cahill; stage manager, Bethany Ford; press, Richard Kornberg and Associates, Tom D'Ambrosio, Don Summa, Rick Miramontez, Carrie Friedman.

Presented without intermission.

Exploration of the ideas and consciousness of Leonardo da Vinci told from the perspective of nine energetic Leonardos. First presentation of record at the Goodman Studio Theatre in Chicago (11/9/1993) after development at Northwestern University and the Lookingglass Theatre Company.

The Public Theater production of **Henry V** (21). Revival of the play by William Shakespeare. George C. Wolfe producer, Mara Manus executive director, at the Delacorte Theater. Opened July 15, 2003. (Closed August 10, 2003)

Chorus .... Steven Rattazzi
King Henry, the Fifth .... Liev Schreiber
Duke of Clarence .... Ryan McCarthy
Duke of Gloucester .... David Flaherty
Duke of Exeter .... Daniel Oreskes
Earl of Westmoreland .... Tom Alan Robbins

The breech: Liev Schreiber and company in Henry V. *Photo: Michal Daniel*

Archbishop of Canterbury ..... David Costabile
Bishop of Ely ..... Peter Gerety
Earl of Cambridge ..... Mark Gerald Douglas
Lord Scroop ..... Gregory Derelian
Sir Thomas Grey ..... Steven Rattazzi
Bardolph ..... Tom Alan Robbins
Nym ..... Dan Moran
Pistol ..... Bronson Pinchot
Boy ..... Nicholas T. Rock
Nell Quickly ..... Mercedes Herrero
Captain Fluellen ..... Peter Gerety
Captain Gower ..... Martin Rayner
Captain Jamy ..... Orlando Pabotoy
Captain Morris ..... Mark Gerald Douglas
Charles the Sixth ..... Martin Rayner
Queen Isabel ..... Peter Gerety
Louis, the Dauphin ..... Ryan Shively
Princess Katherine ..... Nicole Leach
Alice ..... Mercedes Herrero
Charles Delabreth ..... Adam Dannheisser
Montjoy ..... David Costabile
Duke of Orleans ..... Mark Gerald Douglas
Duke of Bourbon ..... Colman Domingo
Earl of Grandpre ..... Dan Moran
Duke of Burgundy ..... Tom Alan Robbins
Monsieur Le Fer ..... Orlando Pabotoy
Governor of Harfleur ..... Jon Dolton
French Messenger ..... Gbenga Akinnagbe
John Bates ..... Steven Rattazzi
Alexander Court ..... Mike Strickland
Michael Williams ..... Adam Dannheisser
Queen Elizabeth ..... Arie Thompson

Directed by Mark Wing-Davey; choreography, David Neumann; scenery, Mark Wendland; costumes, Gabriel Berry; lighting, David Weiner; sound, Acme Sound Partners; music, John Gromada; casting, Jordan Thaler, Heidi Griffiths; production stage manager, Lisa Porter; press, Carol R. Fineman, Elizabeth Wehrle.

Presented in two parts.

The heroic ideal of patriotism is undermined by political machinations and the horrors of war when King Henry leads his country into battle. First presentation of record was given at the court of King James I (1/7/1605). First presentation of record in New York was given at the Park Theatre (12/17/1804), under the management of William Dunlap, with Thomas A. Cooper in the title role and Lewis Hallam Jr. as the King of France.

New York Theatre Workshop production of **Flesh and Blood** (45). By Peter Gaitens; adapted from the novel by Michael Cunningham. James C. Nicola artistic director, Lynn Moffat managing director. Opened July 16, 2003. (Closed August 24, 2003)

Zoe; Jamal's Daughter ..... Martha Plimpton
Jamal; Levon ..... Airrion Doss
Ben; Joel ..... Sean Dugan
Constantine Stassos ..... John Sierros
Billy ..... Peter Gaitens
Harry; Cody; Matt ..... Peter Frechette
Cassandra ..... Jeff Weiss
Magda; Rosemary;
Trancas; Charlotte ..... Patricia Buckley
Susan ..... Jessica Hecht
Mary Stassos ..... Cherry Jones
Todd; Mr. Fleming; Ted;
Nick; Foster; Officer ..... Chris McGarry

Directed by Doug Hughes; scenery, Christine Jones; costumes, Paul Tazewell; lighting, Scott Zielinski; sound and music, David Van Tieghem; production stage manager, Charles Means; press, Richard Kornberg and Associates, Richard Kornberg, Don Summa.

Time: 1930s to present day. Place: New York and vicinity. Presented in two parts.

Three generations of an American family deal with changing attitudes toward gender and sexuality through the decades. First presented at Portland Center Stage in Oregon (10/30–11/18/2001).

Capitol Steps: Between Iraq and a Hard Place (50). Musical revue by Bill Strauss, Elaina Newport and Mark Eaton. Produced by Eric Krebs and Capitol Steps at the John Houseman Theatre. Opened July 19, 2003. (Closed August 31, 2003)

Performed by Mr. Strauss, Ms. Newport, Mike Carruthers, Kevin Corbett, Morgan Duncan, Ann Johnson, Linda Rose Payne, Jack Rowles, Bari Sedar, Tracey Stephens, Mike Thornton, Mike Tilford, Jamie Zemarel.

Directed by Mr. Strauss, Ms. Newport and Mr. Eaton; scenery, R.J. Matson; costumes, Ms. Payne; lighting, Krista Martocci; sound, Jill B.C. DuBoff; music director, Ken Lundie; press, Jeffrey Richards Associates, Irene Gandy, Alana O'Brien, Eric Sanders.

Presented in two parts.

Musical lampoon of politics and politicians.

Edge (61). Solo performance piece by Paul Alexander. Produced by Daryl Roth at the DR2 Theatre. Opened July 21, 2003. (Closed September 20, 2003)

Sylvia Plath .... Angelica Torn

Directed by Mr. Alexander; costumes, Gabrielle Hammil; lighting, Joe Levasseur; sound, Dennis Michael Keefe; production stage manager, Leslie Anne Pinney; press, Barlow-Hartman Public Relations, John Barlow, Michael Hartman.

Time: February 11, 1963. Place: Sylvia Plath's London flat. Presented in two parts.

Sylvia Plath unburdens herself to an audience in the moments before she plans to commit suicide.

That Day in September (45). Solo performance piece by Artie Van Why. Produced by Carolyn Rossi Copeland Productions and Marie B Corporation, in association with The Lamb's Theatre Company, at the Lamb's Theatre. Opened July 23, 2003. (Closed August 31, 2003)

Performed by Mr. Van Why.

Directed by Richard Masur; scenery, Marjorie Bradley Kellogg; lighting, Ann G. Wrightson; sound, Jake Hall; stage manager, Robert Ross Parker.

Chronicle of one-man's life and how it is changed by the events surrounding September 11, 2001.

Irish Repertory Theatre production of **The Love-Hungry Farmer** (52). Revival of the solo performance piece by Des Keogh; based on the writings of John B. Keane. Charlotte Moore artistic director, Ciarán O'Reilly producing director. Opened August 7, 2003. (Closed September 28, 2003)

Performed by Mr. Keogh.

Directed by Ms. Moore; costumes, David Toser; lighting, Sean Farrell; production stage manager, Andrew Theodorou; press, Barlow-Hartman Public Relations, Joe Perrotta.

Forlorn farmer struggles with longing, love and loneliness. Return engagement from the 2002–2003 season.

The Thing About Men (199). Musical with book and lyrics by Joe DiPietro; music by Jimmy Roberts. Based on the screenplay *Men* by Doris Dörrie. Produced by Jonathan Pollard, Bernie Kukoff and Tony Converse, in association with James Hammerstein Productions, at the Promenade Theatre. Opened August 27, 2003. (Closed February 15, 2004)

Tom .... Marc Kudisch
Sebastian .... Ron Bohmer
Lucy .... Leah Hocking
Man .... Daniel Reichard
Woman .... Jennifer Simard

Orchestra: Lynne Shankel conductor, keyboard; Victoria Paterson violin; Peter Sachon cello, percussion; Christopher Miele reeds.

Understudies: Mses. Hocking, Simard—Carter Calvert; Messrs. Kudisch, Bohmer, Reichard—Daniel Cooney, Graham Rowat.

Directed by Mark Clements; choreography, Rob Ashford; scenery, Richard Hoover; costumes, Gregory Gale; lighting, Ken Billington; sound, Jon Weston; orchestrations, Bruce Coughlin; music director, Ms. Shankel; music coordinator, John Miller; associate producers, Gregory Taft Gerard, Karen Jason; casting, Cindi Rush; production stage manager, Debra Acquavella; press, Richard Kornberg and Associates, Richard Kornberg, Tom D'Ambrosio.

Presented in two parts.

Musical battle of the sexes from the authors of the long-running *I Love You, You're Perfect, Now Change.*

ACT I

"Oh, What a Man" .... Tom, Lucy, Man, Woman
"No Competition for Me" .... Tom, Taxi Driver

"Opportunity Knocking" .... Tom
"Free, Easy Guy" .... Sebastian, Lucy
"Take Me Into You, Lucy the Greatest Friend" .... Sebastian, Tom
"Downtown Bohemian Slum" .... Company

ACT II

"You Will Never Get Into This Restaurant" .... Maitre d'
"Me, Too" .... Sebastian, Cindy Waiter
"One-Woman Man" .... Sebastian, Waiter, Tom
"Take Me Into You" (Reprise) .... Lucy
"Highway of Your Heart" .... Country Singer
"The Road to Lucy" .... Tom, Sebastian, Lucy
"Make Me a Promise, Thomas" .... Tom, Lucy
"New, Beautiful Man" .... Tom, Sebastian, Stylists
"I Can't Have It All" (Finale) .... Company

Trumbo (157). By Christopher Trumbo; based on the letters of Dalton Trumbo. Produced by Claudia Catania and The Westside Theatre at the Westside Theatre Downstairs. Opened September 4, 2003. (Closed January 18, 2004)

Dalton Trumbo .... Nathan Lane   Christopher Trumbo .... Gordon MacDonald

Directed by Peter Askin; scenery, Loy Arcenas; lighting, Jeff Croiter, sound and music, John Gromada; video, Dennis Diamond; associate producer, Terry Byrne; casting, Margery Simkin; production stage manager, Arabella Powell; press, The Publicity Office, Bob Fennell.

Presented without intermission.

Epistolary drama centered on the challenges faced by screenwriter Dalton Trumbo and his family after he was blacklisted during red-baiting witchhunts of the late 1940s and early 1950s. Mr. Lane (9/4–21) was succeeded by F. Murray Abraham (9/23–10/12), Brian Dennehy (10/14–11/9), Gore Vidal (11/11–16), Richard Dreyfuss (11/18–23), Roger Rees (11/25–30), Robert Loggia (12/2–7), Christopher Lloyd (12/9–28), Michael Richards (12/29–1/4), Chris Cooper (1/6–11), Charles Durning (1/13–18).

Berkshire Village Idiot (30). Solo performance piece by Michael Isaac Connor. Produced by David S. Singer and Jennifer Manocherian at the Zipper Theatre. Opened September 4, 2003. (Closed September 28, 2003)

Performed by Mr. Connor.

Directed by Barry Edelstein; scenery, Derek McLane; lighting, Russell H. Champa; sound, John Gromada; press, Barlow-Hartman Public Relations, Michael Hartman, Jeremy Shaffer.

Time: 1970s. Place: Berkshire Village. Presented without intermission.

Stories of a young man's life growing up in the Berkshires. First presented at the Williamstown Theatre Festival in Massachusetts (7/30/2003).

New York Theatre Workshop production of **Flow** (33). Transfer from Off Off Broadway of the solo performance piece by Will Power. James C. Nicola artistic director, Lynn Moffat managing director. Opened September 5, 2003. (Closed October 5, 2003)

Performed by Mr. Power, with DJ Reborn.

Directed by Danny Hoch; scenery, David Ellis; costumes, Gabriel Berry; lighting, Sarah Sidman; music director, Ms. Reborn; production stage manager, Timothy R. Semon; press, Richard Kornberg and Associates, Richard Kornberg, Don Summa.

Presented without intermission.

Poetic tales of life in urban America set to a hip-hop beat. Transferred from Performance Space 122 (6/26–7/20/2003; 26 performances).

Portraits (17). By Jonathan Bell. Produced by Vincent Curcio at the Union Square Theatre. Opened September 21, 2003. (Closed October 5, 2003)

Andrew .... Christopher Coucill
Betty .... Darrie Lawrence
Daniel .... Victor Slezak
Arifa .... Anjali Bhimani
John .... Matte Osian
Ruth .... Roberta Maxwell
Nancy .... Dana Reeve

Understudies: Mses. Reeve, Bhimani—Erika LaVonn; Messrs. Coucill, Slezak, Osian—Matt Loney; Mses. Lawrence, Maxwell—Susanne Marley.

Directed by Mark Pinter; scenery, Andrew Knapp; costumes, Charles Schoonmaker; lighting, Aaron Meadow; sound, Raymond D. Schilke; music, Joshua Pearl; casting, Jay Binder Casting, Jack Bowdan; production stage manager, Kimothy Cruse; stage manager, Alden Fulcomer; press, The Pete Sanders Group, Pete Sanders, Glenna Freedman, Jim Mannino.

Time: Post-September 11, 2001. Place: New York and other locations. Presented without intermission.

Individual stories of grief, guilt, fear and the possibility of healing through art in the aftermath of terrorist attacks.

A Rooster in the Henhouse (25). Solo performance piece by John O'Hern. Produced by Ohoby Productions at the Lion and Kirk Theatres. Opened September 21, 2003 at the Lion Theatre. (Closed October 4, 2003) Reopened October 8, 2003 at the Kirk Theatre. (Closed October 25, 2003)

Performed by Mr. O'Hern.

Directed by Mark S. Graham; lighting, Greg MacPherson; production stage manager, Jennifer G. Birge; press, Origlio Public Relations, Tony Origlio.

Presented without intermission.

An actor becomes Mr. Mom and receives advice from an array of well-meaning characters in this comic monologue.

Picture this: (from top) Matte Osian, Roberta Maxwell and Dana Reeve in Portraits. *Photo: Joan Marcus*

Omnium Gatherum (77). By Theresa Rebeck and Alexandra Gersten-Vassilaros. Produced by Robert Cole, Joyce Johnson, in association with Jujamcyn Theaters, Charles Flateman/Kerrin Behrend, at the Variety Arts Theatre. Opened September 25, 2003. (Closed November 30, 2003)

Suzie	Kristine Nielsen	Khalid	Edward A. Hajj
Roger	Phillip Clark	Terence	Dean Nolen
Lydia	Jenny Bacon	Jeff	Joseph Lyle Taylor
Julia	Melanna Gray	Mohammed	Amir Arison

Directed by Will Frears; scenery, David Rockwell; costumes, Junghyun Georgia Lee; lighting, Jules Fisher and Peggy Eisenhauer; sound, Vincent Olivieri; casting, Bernard Telsey Casting; production stage manager, Jane Grey; stage manager, Sid King; press, Richard Kornberg and Associates, Richard Kornberg, Don Summa, Rick Miramontez, Carrie Friedman, Tom D'Ambrosio.

Time: The present, or somewhere around there. Place: An elegant dinner party. Presented without intermission.

A diverse group of postmodern, post-September 11 diners drink, feast and argue over politics, terrror and gastronomy. First presented at the 2003 Humana Festival of New American Plays by the Actors Theatre of Louisville. A 2003–04 *Best Plays* choice (see essay by Chris Jones in this volume).

Playwrights Horizons production of **Recent Tragic Events** (17). By Craig Wright. Tim Sanford artistic director, Leslie Marcus managing director, William Russo general manager. Opened September 28, 2003. (Closed October 12, 2003)

Waverly	Heather Graham	Nancy	Colleen Werthmann
Andrew	Hamish Linklater	Stage Manager	Kalimi Baxter
Ron	Jesse J. Perez		

Directed by Michael John Garcés; scenery, Adam Stockhausen; costumes, Elizabeth Hope Clancy; lighting, Kirk Bookman; sound and music, Scott Myers; casting, James Calleri; production stage manager, Shelli Aderman; press, The Publicity Office, Bob Fennell, Michael S. Borowski.

Quick study: Heather Graham, Hamish Linklater, Jesse J. Perez and Colleen Werthmann in Recent Tragic Events. *Photo: Joan Marcus*

American dreamers: Zilah Mendoza and Gary Perez in Living Out. *Photo: Joan Marcus*

Time: September 12, 2001. Place: An apartment in Minneapolis. Presented in two parts.

A blind date is made more awkward by its proximity to September 11, 2001, and by the woman's fear that something may have happened to her New York-based sister. First presented by Woolly Mammoth Theatre Company in Washington, DC (8/19/2002). A 2003 American Theatre Critics/Steinberg New Play Citation honoree.

Second Stage Theatre production of **Living Out** (40). By Lisa Loomer. Carole Rothman artistic director, Timothy J. McClimon executive director. Opened September 30, 2003. (Closed November 2, 2003)

Zoila Tezo .... Liza Colón-Zayas
Wallace Breyer .... Judith Hawking
Nancy Robin .... Kathryn Meisle
Ana Hernandez .... Zilah Mendoza
Linda Billings Farzam .... Kelly Coffield Park
Bobby Hernandez .... Gary Perez
Sandra Zavala .... Maria Elena Ramirez
Richard Robin .... Joseph Urla

Directed by Jo Bonney; scenery, Neil Patel; costumes, Emilio Sosa; lighting, David Weiner; sound, John Gromada; production stage manager, Pamela Edington; stage manager, Kelly Hance; casting, Tara Rubin Casting; press, Richard Kornberg and Associates, Richard Kornberg, Tom D'Ambrosio, Don Summa, Rick Miramontez, Carrie Friedman.

Time: The present. Place: Los Angeles, California. Presented in two parts.

The complexities of two-career families as experienced by well-to-do consumers and their immigrant child-care providers. First presented by the Center Theatre Group/Mark Taper Forum (1/29/2002). A 2003–04 *Best Plays* choice (see essay by Charles Wright in this volume).

Rounding Third (72). By Richard Dresser. Produced by Eric Krebs, Ted Tulchin, Robert G. Bartner, Chase Mishkin, Jerry Frankel, in association with M. Kilburg Reedy, at the John Houseman Theatre. Opened October 7, 2003. (Closed December 7, 2003)

Michael .... Matthew Arkin
Don .... Robert Clohessy

Directed by John Rando; scenery, Derek McLane; lighting, F. Mitchell Dana; sound, Jill B.C. DuBoff; music, Robert Reale; fight direction, Rick Sordelet; casting, Barry Moss; production stage manager, Jack Gianino; stage manager, Babette Roberts; press, Jeffrey Richards Associates.

Time: The present. Place: A baseball field. Presented in two parts.

Little League baseball coaches from opposite ends of the social spectrum discuss life as seen through the prism of baseball.

Beckett/Albee (102). Collection of one-acts by Samuel Beckett and Edward Albee. Produced by Elizabeth Ireland McCann, Daryl Roth, Roger Berlind, Terry Allen Kramer, Scott Rudin, Nick Simunek, in association with Robert G. Bartner, at Century Center for the Performing Arts. Opened October 9, 2003. (Closed January 4, 2004)

Not I by Samuel Beckett

Mouth .... Marian Seldes   Auditor .... Peter Kybart

A Piece of Monologue by Samuel Beckett

Speaker .... Brian Murray

Footfalls by Samuel Beckett

May .... Marian Seldes   Woman's Voice .... Delphi Harrington

Counting the Ways by Edward Albee

She .... Marian Seldes   He .... Brian Murray

Standby: Mr. Murray—Peter Kybart.

Directed by Lawrence Sacharow; scenery and costumes, Catherine Zuber; lighting, Michael Chybowski; sound, Mark Bennett and Ken Travis; casting, James Calleri; production stage manager, Charles Means; press, Shirley Herz Associates, Shirley Herz, Sam Rudy, Kevin P. McAnarney, Robert Lasko, Val Sherman.

Presented in two parts.

Works by Messrs. Beckett and Albee as interpreted by a pair of magisterial actors.

The Public Theater production of **The Two Noble Kinsmen** (22). Revival of the play by William Shakespeare and John Fletcher. George C. Wolfe producer, Mara Manus

Rosy picture? Marian Seldes and Brian Murray in Counting the Ways. *Photo: Carol Rosegg*

Theme emerges: Graham Hamilton, David Harbour and Doan Ly in The Two Noble Kinsmen. *Photo: Michal Daniel*

executive director, in Martinson Hall. Opened October 19, 2003. (Closed November 9, 2003)

Athenians
- Theseus .... Sam Tsoutsouvas
- Pirithous .... Tyrone Mitchell Henderson
- Hippolyta .... Opal Alladin
- Emilia .... Doan Ly
- Jailer .... Jonathan Fried
- Wooer .... Liam Craig
- Jailer's Daughter .... Jennifer Ikeda
- Waiting Woman .... Candy Buckley
- Countrymen .... Candy Buckley, Jonathan Fried, Liam Craig
- Doctor .... Candy Buckley

Thebans
- Arcite .... David Harbour
- Palamon .... Graham Hamilton
- Queens .... Candy Buckley, Jonathan Fried, Liam Craig
- Valerius .... Jonathan Fried

Gods
- Mars .... Sam Tsoutsouvas
- Venus .... Jennifer Ikeda
- Diana .... Opal Alladin

Directed by Darko Tresnjak; scenery, David P. Gordon; costumes, Linda Cho; lighting, Robert Wierzel; sound, Michael Creason; fight direction, DeeAnn Weir; associate producer, Steven Tabakin; casting, Jordan Thaler, Heidi Griffiths; production stage manager, Francesca Russell; press, Carol R. Fineman, Elizabeth Wehrle.

Presented in two parts.

Jailed cousins fall in love with a noble princess and duel for her hand but the winning combatant dies accidentally—the loser gains her hand. Although the play was probably written before 1614, there is no extant record of its performance before one noted by Samuel Pepys in 1664. First presentation of record in the US was given at the Antioch Area Theater's 1955 summer Shakespeare festival in Ohio, under the direction of Arthur Lithgow.

Manhattan Theatre Club production of **Iron** (80). By Rona Munro. Lynne Meadow artistic director, Barry Grove executive producer, at City Center Stage II. Opened October 21, 2003. (Closed December 28, 2003)

Guard 1 .... John Curless
Josie .... Jennifer Dundas
Fay .... Lisa Emery
Guard 2 .... Susan Pourfar

Directed by Anna D. Shapiro; scenery and costumes, Mark Wendland; lighting, Kevin Adams; sound, Bruce Ellman; casting, David Caparelliotis, Nancy Piccione; production stage manager, Alex Lyu Volckhausen; press, Boneau/Bryan-Brown, Chris Boneau, Jim Byk, Aaron Meier.

Presented in two parts.

Imprisoned mother confronted by her daughter 15 years after killing the girl's father. First presented by the Traverse Theatre Company (UK) at the Edinburgh Fringe Festival (8/2002) before a run at London's Royal Court Theatre Downstairs (1/27–3/1/2003).

Listen to My Heart: The Songs of David Friedman (52). Musical revue with music and lyrics by Mr. Friedman; additional lyrics by Scott Barnes, Robin Boudreau, Deborah Brevoort, Clarissa Dane, Kathie Lee Gifford, Peter Kellogg, Alix Korey, Portia Nelson, Muriel Robinson, Barbara Rothstein. Produced by Victoria Lang, Pier Paolo Piccoli and William P. Suter at Upstairs at Studio 54. Opened October 23, 2003. (Closed December 7, 2003)

Performed by Allison Briner, Joe Cassidy, Mr. Friedman, Michael Hunsaker, Ms. Korey, Anne Runolfsson.

Directed by Mark Waldrop; scenery, Michael Anania; costumes, Markas Henry; lighting and sound, Matt Berman; associate producer, Carol Cogan Savitsky; casting, Alan Filderman; production stage manager, Mr. Berman.

Presented in two parts.

Songs from the *oeuvre* of Mr. Friedman.

Fantasy girl: Lacey Kohl and John Cullum in Wilder. *Photo: Joan Marcus*

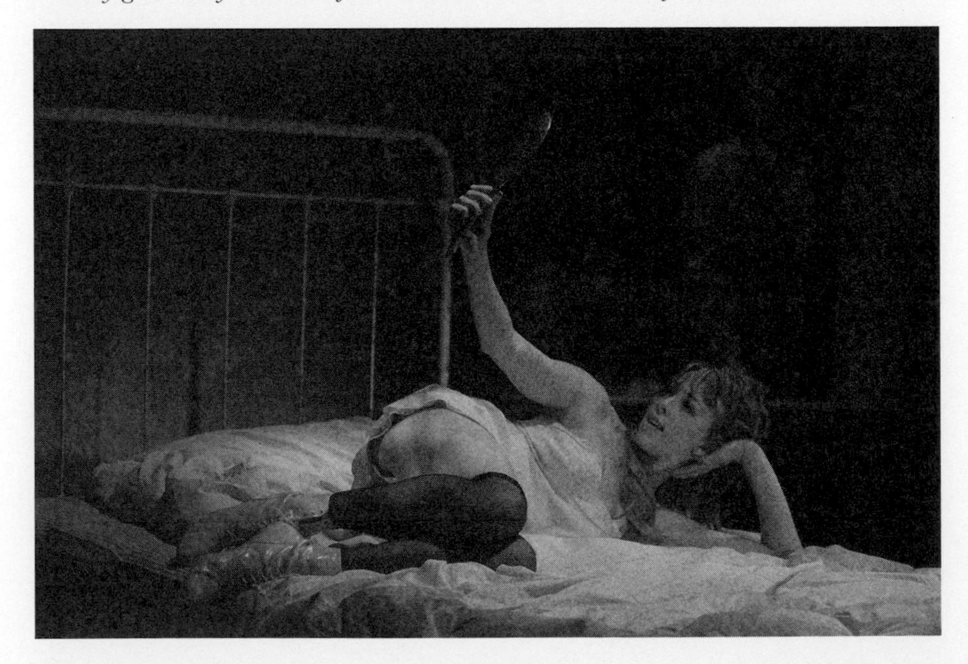

Just talkin': Ben Gazzara in Nobody Don't Like Yogi. *Photo: Alex Ottaviano*

Playwrights Horizons production of **Wilder** (21). Musical by Erin Cressida Wilson, Jack Herrick and Mike Craver. Tim Sanford artistic director, Leslie Marcus managing director, William Russo general manager, in the Peter Jay Sharp Theater. Opened October 26, 2003. (Closed November 14, 2003)

Mike .... Mike Craver
Old Wilder .... John Cullum
Jack .... Jack Herrick
Jessie; Melora .... Lacey Kohl
Wilder .... Jeremiah Miller

Directed by Lisa Portes; choreography, Jane Comfort; scenery and costumes, G.W. Mercier; lighting, Jane Cox; sound, Tom Morse; music direction, Mr. Herrick; associate producer, Ira Weitzman; casting, James Calleri, production stage manager, Renée Lutz; press, The Publicity Office, Bob Fennell, Marc Thibodeau, Michael S. Borowski.

Time: The Great Depression. Place: A dilapidated brothel in Denver. Presented without intermission.

Musical focusing on a young man's troubled rites-of-passage and his return (in memory) as an older man.

Nobody Don't Like Yogi (97). Solo performance piece by Thomas Lysaght. Produced by Don Gregory at the Lamb's Theatre. Opened October 26, 2003. (Closed January 18, 2004)

Yogi Berra .... Ben Gazzara

Directed by Paul Linke; scenery and costumes, Tony Walton; lighting, Ken Billington; sound, Tony Melfa; stage manager, John Handy; press, Bill Evans and Associates, Bill Evans, Jim Randolph.

Time: Opening day, 1999. Place: The players' clubhouse in Yankee Stadium. Presented without intermission.

The wit and wisdom of baseball's most-quoted malapropist. First presented at Bay Street Theatre in Sag Harbor, New York (5/2003), before a run at Syracuse Stage (8/20–9/7/2003).

The New 42nd Street presentation of the **Theatre de la Jeune Lune** production of **Hamlet** (12). Revival of the play by William Shakespeare; adapted by Paddy Hayter with Theatre de la Jeune Lune. Barbra Berlovitz, Steven Epp, Vincent Gracieux, Robert Rosen, Dominique Serrand artistic directors, at the New Victory Theater. Opened October 26, 2003. (Closed November 2, 2003)

Claudius .... Vincent Gracieux
Gertrude .... Barbra Berlovitz
Hamlet .... Steven Epp
Ghost .... Vincent Gracieux
Polonius .... Luverne Seifert
Laertes .... Stephen Cartmell
Ophelia .... Sarah Agnew
Horatio .... Jason Lambert
Osric .... Kevin Bitterman
Priest .... Kristopher Lencowski
Marcellus .... Joel Spence
Bernardo .... Kristopher Lencowski
Francisco .... Kevin Bitterman
Gravediggers .... Joel Spence, Luverne Seifert
Player King .... Joel Spence
Players and Chorus .... Company

Musicians: Eric Jensen keyboard; Elizabeth Karges cello.

Directed by Paddy Hayter; scenery, Fredericka Hayter; costumes, Sonya Berlovitz; lighting, Marcus Dilliard; music and music direction, Mr. Jensen; stage manager, Andrea C. Hendricks; press, Lauren Daniluk.

Presented in two parts.

Touring version of Shakespeare's play about a man confronting adulthood, familial treachery, mortality and responsibility. First presentation of record was in 1600 or 1601 by the Chamberlain's Men. First presentation of record in New York was by the American Company featuring Lewis Hallam Jr. as Hamlet, with David Douglass as Claudius and Mrs. David Douglass as Gertrude at the Theatre in Chapel Street (11/26/1761).

Private Jokes, Public Places (127). By Oren Safdie. Produced by Steven Chaikelson, Donny Epstein, Ergo Entertainment, Avram C. Freedberg, Yeeshai Gross, Elie Landau and Brannon Wiles at the Theater at the Center for Architecture. Opened November 5, 2003. (Closed February 22, 2004)

William .... Anthony Rapp
Margaret .... M.J. Kang
Colin .... Geoffrey Wade
Erhardt .... Sebastian Roché

Directed by Maria Mileaf; scenery, Neil Patel; costumes, Laurie Churba; lighting, Jeff Croiter; casting, Cindy Tolan; production stage manager, Tom Taylor; press, Sam Rudy Media Relations, Sam Rudy; Robert Lasko.

Presented without intermission.

A graduate student presents her thesis to a committee at an architecture school. First presentation of record was given at the Malibu Stage Company (10/11–28/2001) in California before a runs at the Elephant Theatre in Hollywood (12/2002) and at La MaMa E.T.C. (5/1–18/2003).

Lypsinka! As I Lay Lip-Synching (48). Solo performance piece by John Epperson. Produced by Phil Ciasullo Conard, Jeanette Finch-Walton, Tweed Theaterworks, in association with Margaret Cotter, at the Minetta Lane Theatre. Opened November 5, 2003. (Closed December 21, 2003)

Lypsinka .... Mr. Epperson

Directed by Kevin Malony; scenery and lighting, Mark T. Simpson; costumes, Bryant Hoven; sound, Brett Jarvis; wig design, Mitch Ely; press, The Publicity Office, Bob Fennell, Michael S. Borowski.

Presented without intermission.

Another in series of gendercrossing constructions performed to recorded text and music. First presentation of record was given at Show nightclub (8/13–9/14/2003).

***Fame on 42nd Street** (232). Musical with book by José Fernandez; music by Steve Margoshes; lyrics by Jacques Levy; based on the MGM Studios film developed by David De Silva. Produced by Richard Martini, Allen Spivak and Joop van den Ende/Dodger Stage Holding, by arrangement with the Father Fame Foundation, at the Little Shubert Theatre. Opened November 11, 2003.

Nick Piazza .... Christopher J. Hanke
Serena Katz .... Sara Schmidt
José (Joe) Vegas .... José Restrepo
Carmen Diaz .... Nicole Leach

Twisted sister: John Epperson in Lypsinka! As I Lay Lip-Synching. *Photo: Rosalie O'Connor*

Mabel Washington .... Q. Smith
Grace "Lambchops" Lamb .... Jenna Coker
Miss Ester Sherman .... Cheryl Freeman
Schlomo Metzenbaum .... Dennis Moench
Tyrone Jackson .... Shakiem Evans
Mr. Myers .... Peter Reardon
Ms. Greta Bell .... Nancy Hess
Mr. Sheinkopf .... Gannon McHale
Goodman "Goody" King .... Michael Kary
Iris Kelly .... Emily Corney

Ensemble: Angela Brydon, Alexis Carra, Ryan Christopher Chotto, David Finch, David Garcia, Jesse Nager, Jennifer Parsinen, Dawn Noel Pignuola, Eduardo Rioseco, Enrico Rodriguez, Danita Salamida, Erika Weber.

Orchestra: Eric Barnes conductor, first keyboard; Lynn Crigler associate conductor, second keyboard; Edward Hamilton guitar; Vincent Fay electric bass; Matthew Taylor reeds; Joseph Giorgianni trumpet; Bryan Johnson trombone; David Tancredi drums.

Understudies: Mr. Hanke—Eduardo Rioseco; Ms. Schmidt—Alexis Carra, Erika Weber; Mr. Restrepo—Enrico Rodriguez, David Finch; Ms. Leach—Erika Weber; Ms. Smith—Danita Salamida; Ms. Coker—Danita Salamida; Ms. Freeman—Nancy Hess; Mr. Moench—David Finch; Mr. Evans—Jesse Nager; Mr. Reardon—David Finch; Ms. Hess—Danita Salamida, Erika Weber; Mr. McHale—Peter Reardon; Mr. Kary—David Finch; Ms. Corney—Alexis Carra.

Swings: David Finch, Jesse Nager, Danita Salamida, Erika Weber.

Directed by Drew Scott Harris; choreography, Lars Bethke; scenery, Norbert U. Kolb; costumes, Paul Tazewell; lighting, Ken Billington; sound, Christopher K. Bond; music direction, Mr. Barnes; music coordinator, John Monaco; associate producers, Larry Magid, Adam Spivak, Lee Marshall, Joe Marsh; casting, Stuart Howard and Amy Schecter; production stage manager, Mr. Bond; stage manager, Inga Pedersen; press, Boneau/Bryan-Brown, Adrian Bryan-Brown; Susanne Tighe, Adriana Douzos.

Time: 1980–84. Place: New York's High School for the Performing Arts. Presented in two parts.

Teens struggle to form identities as young adults and as performing artists. First presentation of record at the Coconut Grove Playhouse in Coral Gables, Florida (1988).

New York Theatre Workshop production of **The Beard of Avon** (40). By Amy Freed. James C. Nicola artistic director, Lynn Moffat managing director. Opened November 18, 2003. (Closed December 21, 2003)

Minstrel; Walter Fitch;
Earl of Derby; Player .... Timothy Doyle
Richard Burbage;
Lord Walsingham .... James Gale
Anne Hathaway .... Kate Jennings Grant
Edward De Vere .... Mark Harelik
Old Colin; Lord Burleigh;
Lucy; Player .... Tom Lacy
Henry Condel;
Sir Francis Bacon .... Alan Mandell
William Shakspere .... Tim Blake Nelson
John Heminge .... David Schramm
Geoffrey Dunderbread;
Lady Lettice .... Justin Schultz
Henry Wriothesley; Player .... Jeff Whitty
Queen Elizabeth .... Mary Louise Wilson

Directed by Doug Hughes; scenery, Neil Patel; costumes, Catherine Zuber; lighting, Michael Chybowski, sound and music, David Van Tieghem; production stage manager, Judith Schoenfeld; press, Richard Kornberg and Associates, Richard Kornberg, Don Summa.

Time: Late 16th century. Place: London and rural areas. Presented in two parts.

Was Shakespeare really "Shakespeare" or was he the bumpkinous döppelganger of the idle rich? Or both? First presented at South Coast Repertory in Costa Mesa, California (6/1–7/1/2001) before productions in Seattle, San Francisco, Salt Lake City and Chicago.

Cherry Lane Theatre production of **Women on Fire** (59). Solo performance piece by Irene O'Garden. Angelina Fiordellisi artistic director. Opened November 19, 2003. (Closed December 21, 2003) Reopened January 7, 2004. (Closed February 8, 2004)

Performed by Judith Ivey.

Directed by Mary B. Robinson; scenery and costumes, Michael Krass; lighting, Pat Dignan; sound, Bart Fasbender; production stage manager, Misha Siegel-Rivers.

Presented without intermission.

The post-postmodern condition of women in a world of shifting gender roles and expectations.

Our Sinatra: A Musical Celebration (133). Revival of the musical revue by Eric Comstock, Hilary Kole and Christopher Gines. Produced by Jack Lewin at Birdland. Opened November 20, 2003. (Closed March 14, 2004)

Performed by Ms. Kole, Tony DeSare, Adam James.

Directed by Kurt Stamm, with Richard Maltby Jr.; lighting, Jeff Nellis; press, Origlio Public Relations, Tony Origlio, Martine Sainvil.

Performance of more than 50 songs made famous by Frank Sinatra over the span of his career. First presented in the Algonquin Hotel's Oak Room (8/1999). Transferred to Off Broadway's Blue Angel Theatre and later to the Reprise Room at Dillon's (12/19/1999; 1,096 performances).

The Public Theater production of **Caroline, or Change** (106). Musical with book and lyrics by Tony Kushner; music by Jeanine Tesori. George C. Wolfe producer, Mara Manus executive director, in the Newman Theater. Opened November 30, 2003. (Closed February 1, 2004)

Caroline Thibodeaux .... Tonya Pinkins
The Washing Machine .... Capathia Jenkins
The Radio .... Tracy Nicole Chapman,
Marva Hicks, Ramona Keller
Noah Gellman .... Harrison Chad
The Dryer .... Chuck Cooper
Grandma Gellman .... Alice Playten
Grandpa Gellman .... Reathel Bean
Rose Stopnick Gellman .... Veanne Cox
Stuart Gellman .... David Costabile
Dotty Moffett .... Chandra Wilson
The Moon .... Adriane Lenox
The Bus .... Chuck Cooper
Emmie Thibodeaux .... Anika Noni Rose
Jackie Thibodeaux .... Kevin Ricardo Tate
Joe Thibodeaux .... Marcus Carl Franklin
Mr. Stopnick .... Larry Keith

Kid stuff: Marcus Carl Franklin, Anika Noni Rose, Harrison Chad, Kevin Ricardo Tate in Caroline, or Change. *Photo: Michal Daniel*

Orchestra: Linda Twine conductor; Antoine Silverman, Chris Cardona violin; David Creswell viola; Anja Wood cello; Paul Garment first reed; Stephen Wisner second reed; Steve Bargonetti guitar; Peter Donovan bass; Ed Alstrom piano; John Clancy, Shane Shanahan percussion.

Directed by George C. Wolfe; choreography, Hope Clarke; scenery, Riccardo Hernández; costumes, Paul Tazewell; lighting, Jules Fisher and Peggy Eisenhauer; sound, Jon Weston; hair, Jeffrey Frank; orchestrations, Rick Bassett, Joseph Joubert, Buryl Red; music supervision, Kimberly Grigsby; music direction, Ms. Twine; associate producers, Peter DuBois, Steven Tabakin; casting, Jordan Thaler, Heidi Griffiths; production stage manager, Rick Steiger; stage manager, Lisa Dawn Cave; press, Carol R. Fineman, Elizabeth Wehrle.

Time: November–December 1963. Place: Lake Charles, Louisiana. Presented in two parts.

Musical about a motherless young Jewish boy's relationship with his family's African-American maid in the Kennedy-era South. Transferred to Broadway's Eugene O'Neill Theatre (5/2/2004; 32 performances through May 31). See Plays Produced on Broadway section in the volume. A 2003–04 *Best Plays* choice (see essay by John Istel in this volume).

ACT I

Scene 1: Washer/Dryer
Scene 2: Cabbage
Scene 3: Long Distance
Scene 4: Moon Change
Scene 5: Duets
Scene 6: The Bleach Cup

ACT II

Scene 7: Ironing
Scene 8: The Chanukah Party
Scene 9: The Twenty-Dollar Bill
Scene 10: Aftermath
Scene 11: Lot's Wife
Scene 12: How Long Has This Been Going On?

Epilogue

Playwrights Horizons production of **Juvenilia** (17). By Wendy MacLeod. Tim Sanford artistic director, Leslie Marcus managing director, William Russo general manager. Opened December 7, 2003. (Closed December 21, 2003)

Henry .... Ian Brennan
Meredith .... Aubrey Dollar
Brodie .... Luke MacFarlane
Angie .... Erica N. Tazel

Directed by David Petrarca; scenery, Michael Yeargan; costumes, Martin Pakledinaz; lighting, Mark McCullough; sound, Rob Milburn and Michael Bodeen; casting, James Calleri; production stage manager, David Sugarman; stage manager, Barclay Stiff; press, The Publicity Office, Bob Fennell, Michael S. Borowski.

Time: A Friday evening in the present. Place: A college dorm room. Presented in two parts.

College kids indulge in love, lust and loathing as they bare their souls.

Lincoln Center Theater production of **Nothing but the Truth** (48). By John Kani. André Bishop artistic director, Bernard Gersten executive producer, at the Mitzi E. Newhouse. Opened December 7, 2003. (Closed January 18, 2004)

Mandisa MacKay .... Esmeralda Bihl
Sipho Makhaya .... John Kani
Thando Makhaya .... Warona Seane

Directed by Janice Honeyman; scenery and cóstumes, Sarah Roberts; lighting, Mannie Manim; stage manager, Thom Widmann; press, Philip Rinaldi Publicity, Philip Rinaldi, Barbara Carroll.

Time: The post-apartheid era. Place: South Africa. Presented in two parts.

Family drama examining cultural tensions between those who lived through apartheid and those who escaped to live elsewhere. First presented at the Market Theatre in Johannesburg, South Africa (9/26/2002).

Teen spirit? Erica N. Tazel and Aubrey Dollar in Juvenilia. *Photo: Joan Marcus*

Blind ambition: Phylicia Rashad and Erika Alexander in The Story. *Photo: Michal Daniel*

The Public Theater production of **The Story** (15). By Tracey Scott Wilson. George C. Wolfe producer, Mara Manus executive director, in association with the Long Wharf Theatre (Gordon Edelstein artistic director, Michael Stotts managing director), in the Anspacher Theater. Opened December 10, 2003. (Closed December 21, 2003)

Yvonne .... Erika Alexander
Jeff; Tim Dunn .... Stephen Kunken
Pat .... Phylicia Rashad
Neil .... Damon Gupton
Jessica Dunn .... Sarah Grace Wilson
Detective; Ensemble .... Michelle Hurst
Carla; Ensemble .... Kalimi Baxter
Reporter; Ensemble ..... Susan Kelechi Watson
Latisha .... Tammi Clayton

Directed by Loretta Greco; scenery, Robert Brill; costumes, Emilio Sosa; lighting, James Vermeulen; sound and music, Robert Kaplowitz; associate producers, Peter DuBois, Steven Tabakin; casting, Jordan Thaler, Heidi Griffiths; production stage manager, Buzz Cohen; stage manager, Damon W. Arrington; press, Carol R. Fineman, Elizabeth Wehrle.

Time: The present. Place: The newsroom of a large daily paper and locations around a city. Presented in two parts.

A career-driven African-American woman stops at nothing to get (or make) a big story.

Sholom Aleichem–Now You're Talking! (50). Solo performance piece by Saul Reichlin; based on the stories of Mr. Aleichem. Produced by Lone Star Theatre LLC at the DR2 Theatre. Opened December 14, 2003. (Closed February 1, 2004)

Performed by Mr. Reichlin.

Ten stories, in a two-hour performance, about a long-lost Jewish culture.

Addicted . . . a Comedy of Substance (113). Solo performance piece by Mark Lundholm. Produced by Clear Channel Entertainment at the Zipper Theatre. December 14, 2003. (Closed March 21, 2004)

Performed by Mr. Lundholm.

Directed by Bob Balaban; scenery, Walt Spangler; lighting, Paul Miller; sound, Randy Hansen and Duncan Robert Edwards; executive producer, Jennifer Costello, Clint Mitchell; associate producer, Erin McMurrough; press, Barlow-Hartman Public Relations, Michael Hartman, Jeremy Shaffer, Dayle Gruet.

Presented without intermission.

One man's personal journey through drugs, alcohol and family dysfunction on the way to becoming a performer of dark comedy.

Second Stage Theatre production of **Dinner With Demons** (40). Solo performance piece by Jonathan Reynolds. Carole Rothman artistic director, Timothy J. McClimon executive director. Opened December 16, 2003. (January 18, 2004)

Performed by Mr. Reynolds.

Directed by Peter Askin; scenery, Heidi Ettinger; lighting, Kevin Adams; sound, John Gromada; production stage manager, Kelly Hance; press, Richard Kornberg and Associates, Richard Kornberg, Tom D'Ambrosio.

Presented without intermission.

The author tells personal stories as he prepares a sumptuous repast.

***The York Theatre Company** production of **The Musical of Musicals–The Musical** (54). Musical with book by Eric Rockwell and Joanne Bogart; music by Mr. Rockwell; lyrics by Ms. Bogart. James Morgan artistic director, in association with Musicals Tonight!, at the Theatre at St. Peter's. Opened December 16, 2003. (Closed January 25, 2004) Reopened May 24, 2004.

Performed by Craig Fols, Lovette George, Mr. Rockwell, Ms. Bogart.

Directed by Pamela Hunt; scenery, Mr. Morgan; costumes, John Carver Sullivan; lighting Mary Jo Dondlinger; press, Cohn Davis Bigar Communications, Helene Davis, Dan Dutcher.

Presented in two parts.

Five abbreviated musicals are presented as parody of five different Broadway musical styles including those of Richard Rodgers and Oscar Hammerstein II, Stephen Sondheim, Jerry Herman, Andrew Lloyd Webber and John Kander and Fred Ebb.

Manhattan Theatre Club production of **Rose's Dilemma** (54). By Neil Simon. Lynne Meadow artistic director, Barry Grove executive producer, at City Center Stage I. Opened December 18, 2003. (Closed February 1, 2004)

Rose Steiner .... Patricia Hodges
Gavin Clancy .... David Aaron Baker
Arlene Moss .... Geneva Carr
Walsh McLaren .... John Cullum

Directed by Ms. Meadow; scenery, Thomas Lynch; costumes, William Ivey Long; lighting, Pat Collins; sound, Bruce Ellman; wigs, Paul Huntley; production stage manager, Robert Witherow; press, Boneau/Bryan-Brown, Chris Boneau, Jim Byk, Aaron Meier.

Time: The present. Place: The Hamptons. Presented in two parts.

A woman writer retires to her beach house to mourn her dead lover and winds up trading quips with his ghost. First presented at the Geffen Playhouse as *Rose and Walsh* (2/5/2003).

Theatre for a New Audience production of **The Last Letter** (27). Solo performance piece by Frederick Wiseman; adapted from the novel *Life and Fate* by Vasily Grossman; translated by Robert Chandler. Jeffrey Horowitz artistic director, Dorothy Ryan managing director, at the Lucille Lortel Theatre. Opened December 18, 2003. (Closed January 11, 2004)

Performed by Kathleen Chalfant.

Directed by Mr. Wiseman; scenery, Douglas Stein; costumes, Miranda Hoffman; lighting, Donald Holder; casting, Deborah Brown; production stage manager, Jennifer Rae Moore; press, Bruce Cohen Group.

Presented without intermission.

Performance of the final communication from a mother—victim of the Holocaust—to her son.

New York Gilbert and Sullivan Players production of **Iolanthe** (4). Revival of the operetta with book by W.S. Gilbert; music by Arthur Sullivan. Albert Bergeret artistic director, at City Center. Opened January 9, 2004. (Closed January 11, 2004)

Lord Chancellor .... Stephen O'Brien
Fairy Queen .... Melissa Parks
Phyllis .... Kimilee Bryant
Lord Mountararat .... Richard Holmes
Private Willis .... Ross Crutchlow

Directed by Mr. Bergeret; scenery, Jack Garver; costumes, Gail J. Wofford; lighting, Sally Small; press, Cromarty and Company, Peter Cromarty.

Presented in two parts.

Fairies disrupt the House of Lords in this satire on love and class privilege. First presentation of record at London's Savoy Theatre (11/25/1882).

New York Gilbert and Sullivan Players production of **H.M.S Pinafore** (4). Revival of the operetta with book by W.S. Gilbert; music by Arthur Sullivan. Albert Bergeret artistic director, at City Center. Opened January 16, 2004. (Closed January 18, 2004)

Sir Joseph Porter .... Stephen Quint
Captain .... Keith Jurosko
Josephine .... Kimilee Bryant
Ralph Rackstraw .... Michael Harris

Direction and scenery, Mr. Bergeret; costumes, Gail J. Wofford; lighting, Sally Small; press, Cromarty and Company, Peter Cromarty.

Presented in two parts.

A sailor loves the captain's daughter, but nothing is simple where the upper class is concerned. First presentation of record was given at London's Opera Comique (5/28/1878).

New York Gilbert and Sullivan Players production of **The Mikado** (4). Revival of the operetta with book by W.S. Gilbert; music by Arthur Sullivan. Albert Bergeret artistic director, at City Center. Opened January 23, 2004. (Closed January 25, 2004)

Mikado .... Keith Jurosko
Yum-Yum .... Laurelyn Watson
Katisha .... Melissa Parks
Nanki-Poo .... Michael Harris
Ko-Ko .... Stephen Quint

Direction and scenery, Mr. Bergeret; costumes, Gail J. Wofford; lighting, Sally Small; press, Cromarty and Company, Peter Cromarty.

Presented in two parts.

Star-crossed love and mistaken identity played in a fantasy Japan. First presentation of record at London's Savoy Theatre (3/14/1885).

Irish Repertory Theatre production of **Eden** (57). By Eugene O'Brien. Charlotte Moore artistic director, Ciarán O'Reilly producing director. Opened February 1, 2004. (Closed March 21, 2004)

Breda .... Catherine Byrne
Billy .... Ciarán O'Reilly

Directed by John Tillinger; scenery and costumes, Klara Zieglerova; lighting, Howell Binkley; production stage manager, Colette Morris, press, Barlow-Hartman Public Relations, Jeremy Shaffer.

Presented in two parts.

An Irish marriage suffers the chill that sometimes arrives with the onset of middle age. First presentation of record at Dublin's Peacock Theatre (January 2001).

They Wrote That? (41). Musical revue with music by Barry Mann; lyrics by Cynthia Weil. Produced by CTM Productions and James B. Freydberg at the McGinn/Cazale Theatre. Opened February 5, 2004. (Closed March 14, 2004)

Hit meisters: Barry Mann and Cynthia Weil in They Wrote That? *Photo: Joan Marcus*

Performed by Mr. Mann and Ms. Weil, with Deb Lyons, Moeisha McGill, Jenelle Lynn Randall.

Orchestra: Fred Mollin conductor, guitar; Steve Tarshis electric guitar; Paul Ossola upright and electric bass; Charlie Giordano second keyboard; Denny McDermott drums, percussion.

Directed by Richard Maltby Jr.; scenery, Neil Patel; costumes, Laurie Churba; lighting, Heather Carson; sound, Peter Fitzgerald; musical staging, Kurt Stamm; casting, Dave Clemmons Casting; production stage manager, James Latus; press, Boneau/Bryan-Brown, Chris Boneau, Jackie Green.

Presented without intermission.

Songs and patter relating to the careers of Mr. Mann and Ms. Weil.

Musical numbers included: "You've Lost That Lovin' Feeling," "Sometimes When We Touch," "We've Gotta Get Out of this Place," "Here You Come Again," "Blame It on the Bossa Nova," "Make Your Own Kind of Music," "Who Put the Bomp," "On Broadway," "Just Once," "Don't Know Much," "He's So Shy," "Running With the Night," "Walkin' in the Rain," "Love How You Love Me."

New York Theatre Workshop production of **Valhalla** (54). By Paul Rudnick. James C. Nicola artistic director, Lynn Moffat managing director. Opened February 5, 2004. (Closed March 21, 2004)

Henry Lee Stafford,
  Helmut; Singer .... Scott Barrow
Queen Marie; Margaret Avery;
  Princess Enid;
  Natalie Kippelbaum .... Candy Buckley
James Avery .... Sean Dugan
King Ludwig .... Peter Frechette
Sally Mortimer; Princess Sophie;
  Princess Patricia; Marie Antoinette;
  Annie Avery .... Samantha Soule
Footman; Otto; Pfeiffer;
  Princess Ursula; Rev. Howesbury;
  Sergeant .... Jack Willis

Directed by Christopher Ashley; choreography, Daniel Pelzig; scenery, Thomas Lynch; costumes, William Ivey Long; lighting, Kenneth Posner; sound, Mark Bennett; production stage manager, Sarah Bittenbender; press, Richard Kornberg and Associates, Don Summa.

Presented in two parts.

Comedy centering on the peculiarities of two gay males: one a boy in Texas, the other a mad 19th-century royal in Bavaria.

The York Theatre Company production of **Max Morath: Ragtime and Again** (41). Solo performance piece by Mr. Morath. James Morgan artistic director at the Theatre at St. Peter's. Opened February 8, 2004. (Closed March 14, 2004)

Performed by Mr. Morath.

Directed by Robert Marks; scenery, Mr. Morgan; lighting, Mary Jo Dondlinger; production stage manager, Jay McLeod; press, Cohn Davis Bigar Communications, Helene Davis.

Presented in two parts.

Songs and stories from the early 20th century heyday of ragtime music.

City Center Encores! presentation of **Can-Can** (5). Concert version of the musical with book by Abe Burrows; music and lyrics by Cole Porter; concert adaptation by David Lee. Jack Viertel artistic director, Rob Fisher music director, Kathleen Marshall director-in-residence, at City Center. Opened February 12, 2004. (Closed February 15, 2004)

La Mome Pistache .... Patti LuPone
Judge Aristide Forestier .... Michael Nouri
Boris Adzinidzinadze .... Reg Rogers
Claudine .... Charlotte d'Amboise
Hilaire Jussac .... Paul Schoeffler
Celestine .... Caitlin Carter
Theophile .... David Costabile
Etienne .... Michael Goldstrom
Hercule ....David Hibbard
Marie ....Mary Ann Lamb
Gabrielle .... Solange Sandy
Apache Dancer .... Robert Wersinger
Judge Paul Barriere .... Eli Wallach

Mad royal: Jack Willis and Peter Frechette in Valhalla. *Photo: Joan Marcus*

Border buster: Sarah Jones in Bridge and Tunnel. *Photo: Brian Michael Thomas*

Directed by Lonny Price; choreography, Melinda Roy; scenery, John Lee Beatty; costumes, Toni-Leslie James; lighting, Kenneth Posner; sound, Scott Lehrer; music direction, Michael Kosarin; casting, Jay Binder, production stage manager, Jeffrey M. Markowitz; press, Barlow-Hartman Public Relations, John Barlow, Bill Coyle.

Time: Turn of the 20th century. Place: Paris. Presented in two parts.

The performance of a risqué dance kick-starts a legal battle over morality. First presented on Broadway at the Shubert Theatre (5/7/1953–6/25/1955; 892 performances). The original production received 1954 Tony Awards for best choreography (Michael Kidd) and best featured actress in a musical (Gwen Verdon). There was a Broadway revival at the Minskoff Theatre (4/30–5/3/1981; 5 performances).

Brooklyn Academy of Music presentation of the **Theatre for a New Audience** production of **Pericles** (10). Revival of the play by William Shakespeare. Alan H. Fishman chairman of the board, Karen Brooks Hopkins president, Joseph V. Melillo executive producer, at the Harvey Theater. Opened February 17, 2004. (Closed February 22, 2004)

Gower; Lychorida .... Brenda Wehle
Antiochus; Pericles .... Christopher McCann
Pericles; Lysimachus .... Tim Hopper
Daughter of Antiochus;
Marina .... Julyana Soelistyo
Thaliard; Leonine .... Graham Winton
Helicanus; Cerimon .... Philip Goodwin
Cleon; Pandar .... Robert LuPone
Dionyza; Bawd .... Kristine Nielsen
Simonides; Boult .... Andrew Weems
Thais .... Linda Powell

Ensemble: Glenn Fleshler, Bruce Turk, Albert Jones, Paul Niebanck.

Directed by Bartlett Sher; scenery and lighting, Christopher Akerlind; costumes, Elizabeth Caitlin Ward; sound and music, Peter John Still; dramaturg, Ben Nadler; production stage manager, Judith Schoenfeld; press, Sandy Sawotka, Fatima Kafele, Eva Chien, Tamara McCaw, Jennifer Lam.

Presented in two parts.

Early romance in which the title character suffers many reversals of fortune that ultimately lead to a happy ending. A production of Theatre for a New Audience (Jeffrey Horowitz artistic director, Dorothy Ryan managing director). First presented in 1607 or 1608 in London. First US presentation of record at California's Pasadena Community Playhouse (6/29/1936).

Ensemble Studio Theatre production of **Roulette** (31). By Paul Weitz. Curt Dempster artistic director, Susann Brinkley executive director, at the John Houseman Theatre. Opened February 18, 2004. (Closed March 14, 2004)

Jon .... Larry Bryggman
Virginia .... Ana Gasteyer
Jock .... Shawn Hatosy
Enid .... Leslie Lyles
Jenny .... Anna Paquin
Steve .... Mark Setlock

Directed by Trip Cullman; scenery, Takeshi Kata; costumes, Alejo Vietti; lighting, Greg MacPherson; sound, Aural Fixation; music, Michael Friedman; production stage manager, Lori Ann Zepp; press, David Gersten and Associates.

Presented in two parts.

Dysfunctional-family comedy driven by sex, drugs and a loaded gun. First presented at Vassar College's Powerhouse Theatre (August 2003).

***Bridge and Tunnel** (88). Solo performance piece by Sarah Jones. Produced by Meryl Streep and The Culture Project, in association with Robert Dragotta, Jayson Jackson, Michael Alden, Eric Falkenstein, Marcia Roberts, Jean Kennedy Smith, Tom Wirtshafter, at 45 Bleecker. Opened February 19, 2004.

Performed by Ms. Jones.

Directed by Tony Taccone; scenery, Blake Lethem; lighting, Alexander V. Nichols; sound, DJ Rekha and Chris Meade; assistant director, Steve Colman; stage manager, Annie Brown; press, Origlio Public Relations, Tony Origlio, Martine Sainvil.

Presented without intermission.

An actorly celebration of the multicultural nature of contemporary New York City set within the frame of a poetry slam.

Magic Hands Freddy (85). By Arje Shaw. Produced by Dana Matthow, Steve Alpert and Kenneth Greiner at the Soho Playhouse. Opened February 19, 2004. (Closed May 2, 2004)

Freddy .... Michael Rispoli
Calvin .... Ralph Macchio
Maria .... Antoinette LaVecchia
Sal; Others .... Ed Chemaly

Understudies: Mr. Macchio—Matthew Boston; Ms. LaVecchia—Michele Melland; Mr. Rispoli—Steve Scionti, Matt Servitto.

Directed by Rebecca Taylor; scenery and lighting, Jason Sturm; costumes, Yvonne De Moravia; stage manager, Adam Grosswirth.

Presented in two parts.

Title character, a masseur, learns he has been betrayed by his wife and his dead brother and that his daughter is not his own child.

Lincoln Center Theater production of **Big Bill** (97). By A.R. Gurney. André Bishop artistic director, Bernard Gersten executive producer, at the Mitzi E. Newhouse. Opened February 22, 2004. (Closed May 16, 2004)

William T. Tilden II .... John Michael Higgins
Umpire; Judge; Others .... David Cromwell
Herb; Maddox; Others .... Stephen Rowe
Mary Garden;
Suzanne Lenglen; Others .... Margaret Welsh
Student; Ball Boy; Others .... Alex Knold
Pete; Ball Boy; Others .... Michael Esper
Jimmy;
Ball Boy; Others .... Donal Thoms-Cappello
Arthur; Ball Boy; Others .... Jeremiah Miller

Understudies: Mr. Higgins—Jack Koenig; Messrs. Cromwell, Row—Michael Hammond; Ms. Welsh—Wendy Rich Stetson, Mercedes Herrero; Messrs. Knold, Esper, Thoms-Cappello, Miller—Gideon Banner; Mr. Knold (Student)—Donal Thoms-Cappello; Mr. Esper (Pete)—Jeremiah Miller; Mr. Thoms-Cappello (Jimmy)—Michael Esper; Mr. Miller (Arthur)—Alex Knold.

Directed by Mark Lamos; scenery, John Lee Beatty; costumes, Jess Goldstein; lighting, Rui Rita; sound, Scott Stauffer; stage manager, Fredric H. Orner; casting, Cindy Tolan and Daniel Swee; press, Philip Rinaldi, Barbara Carroll.

Time: Middle of the 20th century. Presented without intermission.

The penchant of a tennis great for young men overshadows his outstanding values as a sportsman and athlete. First presented at the Williamstown Theatre Festival (7/2–13/2003).

***Bug** (105). By Tracy Letts. Produced by Scott Morfee, Amy Danis and Mark Johannes, in association with Planetearth Partners, at the Barrow Street Theatre. Opened February 29, 2004.

Agnes White	Shannon Cochran
R.C.	Amy Landecker
Peter Evans	Michael Shannon
Jerry Goss	Michael Cullen
Dr. Sweet	Reed Birney

Understudies: Allyn Burrows, Dee Pelletier.

Directed by Dexter Bullard; scenery, Lauren Helpern; costumes, Kim Gill; lighting, Tyler Micoleau; sound, Brian Ronan; fight direction; J. David Brimmer; production stage manager, Richard A. Hodge; press, Publicity Outfitters, Timothy Haskell, Tanya Bershadsky.

Presented in two parts.

A former soldier, living at the margin of society, fears that the government is using him as a science project. First presentation of record at London's Gate Theatre (9/20/1996).

The Moonlight Room (72). Transfer of the Off Off Broadway play by Tristine Skyler. Produced by Arielle Tepper and Freddy DeMann, in association with Solecist Productions, at the Beckett Theatre. Opened March 1, 2004. (Closed May 2, 2004)

Sal	Laura Breckenridge
Joshua	Brendan Sexton III
Mrs. Kelly	Kathryn Layng
Mr. Wells	Lawrence James
Adam	Mark Rosenthal

Directed by Jeff Cohen; scenery, Marion Williams; costumes, Kim Gill; lighting, Scott Bolman; sound, Laura Grace Brown; production stage manager, Michael V. Mendelson; press, Carol Fineman Publicity, Carol R. Fineman, Leslie Baden.

Time: Present. Place: A New York hospital. Presented in two parts.

New York teens live wild, secretive lives alienated from their concerned, overextended parents. Transfer of the Worth Street Theater Company production first presented Off Off Broadway at the Tribeca Playhouse (11/3–12/14/2003; 30 performances).

Second Stage Theatre production of **Wintertime** (24). By Charles L. Mee. Carole Rothman artistic director, Timothy J. McClimon executive director. Opened March 2, 2004. (Closed March 21, 2004)

Jacqueline	Tina Benko
Ariel	Brienin Bryant
Hilda	Marylouise Burke
Francois	Michael Cerveris
Edmund	T. Scott Cunningham
Bertha	Carmen de Lavallade
Jonathan	Christopher Denham
Frank	Nicholas Hormann
Maria	Marsha Mason
Bob	Danny Mastrogiorgio

Directed by David Schweizer; choreography, Sean Curran; scenery, Andrew Lieberman; costumes, David Zinn; lighting, Kevin Adams; sound, Eric Shim; production stage manager, Christine Lemme; stage manager, Kelly Hance; press, Richard Kornberg and Associates, Richard Kornberg, Tom D'Ambrosio.

Presented in two parts.

Romantic chill: Michael Cerveris and Marsha Mason in Wintertime. *Photo: Joan Marcus*

A sex comedy tossing several pairs of lovers together to create a farcical salad. First presented at La Jolla Playhouse (8/13–9/15/2002). This production originated at the McCarter Theatre Center in Princeton (10/14–11/2/2003).

Ministry of Progress (30). Musical with book by Kim Hughes; music and songs by John Beltzer, Sara Carlson, Philip Dessinger, Ted Eyes, Alex Forbes, Kathy Hart, Ms. Hughes, Gary Levine, Christian Martirano, Jeremy Schonfeld, Tony Visconti; based on a radio play by Charles Morrow. Produced by Terry E. Schnuck at the Jane Street Theatre. Opened March 4, 2004. (Closed March 28, 2004)

Performed by Jason Scott Campbell, Brian J. Dorsey, Tyne Firmin, Gary Maricheck, Jennifer McCabe, Maia Moss, Julie Reiber, Stacey Sargeant, Richard E. Waits, Christian Whelan.

Directed by Ms. Hughes; scenery, Adriana Serrano; costumes, Fabio Toblini; lighting, Jason Kantrowitz; sound, Michael G. Ward; orchestrations and music direction, Christian Martirano; press, The Jacksina Company, Judy Jacksina, Debra Page.

Presented without intermission.

A musical journey through the chilly anonymity of modern bureaucracy.

***Cookin'** (97). Transfer of the Off Off Broadway performance piece by Seung Whan Song. Produced by PMC Production Company Ltd., Kwang Ho Lee, Mr. Song, The Broadway Asia Company, Simone Genatt Haft, Marc Routh, in association with Zemiro, Morton Swinsky/Michael Fuchs, Amy Danis/Mark Johannes, at the Minetta Lane Theatre. Opened March 7, 2004.

Chefs gone wild: Members of the company in Cookin'. *Photo: Joan Marcus*

Performed by Kang Il Kim, Won Hae Kim, Bum Chan Lee, Chu Ja Seo, Ho Yeoul Sul, Hyung Suk Jung, Ji Won Kang, Young Hoon Kim, Sung Min Lee.

Directed by Mr. Song; scenery, Dong Woo Park; costumes, Hee Joo Kim; lighting, Hak Young Kim; sound, Hyun Park; fight direction, Jamie Guan; assistant directors, Won Hae Kim, Seung Yong You; executive producer, Sunny Oh; associate producer, Jong Heon Kim; casting, Lynne Taylor-Corbett; production stage manger, Mark Willoughby; press, Barlow-Hartman Public Relations, John Barlow, Jeremy Shaffer, Dayle Gruet.

Presented without intermission.

Anxious chefs prepare a wedding feast in a hectic production that uses cookware to make its percussive points. Transfer of the Off Off Broadway production that opened at the New Victory Theater (9/25–10/19/2003; 24 performances).

New York City Opera production of **Sweeney Todd** (11). Revival of the musical with book by Hugh Wheeler; music and lyrics by Stephen Sondheim; from an adaptation by Christopher Bond. Paul Kellogg general and artistic director, Sherwin M. Goldman executive producer, George Manahan music director, at the New York State Theater. Opened March 9, 2004. (Closed March 28, 2004)

Anthony Hope .... Keith Phares
Sweeney Todd .... Mark Delavan
Timothy Nolen (alt.)
Beggar Woman .... Judith Blazer
Mrs. Lovett .... Elaine Paige
Myrna Paris (alt.)

Judge Turpin .... Walter Charles
The Beadle .... Roland Rusinek
Johanna .... Sarah Coburn
Tobias Ragg .... Keith Jameson
Pirelli .... Andrew Drost
Jonas Fogg; Birdseller .... William Ledbetter

Directed by Arthur Masella, based on Harold Prince's production; choreography, Larry Fuller; scenery, Eugene Lee; costumes, Franne Lee; lighting, Ken Billington; sound, Abe Jacob; orchestrations, Jonathan Tunick; music direction, Mr. Manahan; press, Richard Kornberg and Associates.

Presented in two parts.

Actors prepare: Mary Shultz, Ana Reeder and Rosemarie DeWitt in Small Tragedy. *Photo: Joan Marcus*

The Demon Barber of Fleet Street returns to fill Mrs. Lovett's meat pies. A 1978–79 *Best Plays* choice, the original Broadway production opened at the Uris Theatre (3/1/1979–6/29/1980; 557 performances) where it won nine 1979 Tony Awards.

Playwrights Horizons production of **Small Tragedy** (22). By Craig Lucas. Tim Sanford artistic director, Leslie Marcus managing director, William Russo general manager. Opened March 11, 2004. (Closed March 28, 2004)

Jen .... Ana Reeder
Paola .... Mary Shultz
Nathaniel .... Rob Campbell
Christmas .... Daniel Eric Gold
Hakija .... Lee Pace
Fanny .... Rosemarie DeWitt

Directed by Mark Wing-Davey; scenery, Douglas Stein; costumes, Marina Draghici; lighting, Jennifer Tipton; sound and music, John Gromada; casting, James Calleri; production stage manager, Thom Widmann; press, The Publicity Office, Bob Fennell, Marc Thibodeau, Michael S. Borowski, Jeremy Hooper.

Time: Mid-1990s; late 1990s. Place: Cambridge; Boston; New York City. Presented in two parts.

Lives in the theater are, by turns, satirized and valorized before one actor's past comes to light. A 2003–04 *Best Plays* choice (see essay by Charles Isherwood in this volume).

*__The Public Theater__ presentation of **The Actors' Gang** production of **Embedded** (78). By Tim Robbins; with reportage by John Simpson (BBC), Alan Feuer (*The New York Times*), Robert Fisk (*The Independent*), Martha Gellhorn. George C. Wolfe producer, Mara Manus executive director, at the Newman Theater. Opened March 14, 2004.

Sarge; Cove; Journalist .... Brian T. Finney
Maryanne; Gwen; Woof .... Kate Mulligan
June; Kitten Kattan .... Toni Torres
Monk; Journalist .... Ben Gain
Jen's Dad; Dick;
Buford T.; Journalist .... Steven M. Porter
Jen-Jen Ryan; Journalist .... Kaili Hollister
Jen's Mom; Amy; Woof .... Lolly Ward

Media maelstrom: Andrew Wheeler in Embedded. *Photo: Michal Daniel*

Gondola; Journalist .... Riki Lindhome
Rum-Rum; Chip Webb .... Brian Powell
Pearly White; Stringer .... Andrew Wheeler
Colonel; Announcer .... V.J. Foster
Perez; Camera Kid .... J.R. Martinez
Lieutenant; Journalist .... Mark Lewis

Directed by Mr. Robbins; scenery, Richard Hoover; costumes, Yasuko Takahara; lighting, Adam H. Greene; sound, David Robbins; masks, Erhard Stiefel; projections, Elaine J. McCarthy; associate producers, Peter DuBois, Steven Tabakin; casting, Jordan Thaler, Heidi Griffiths; production stage manager, Samantha Jane Robson; press, Carol R. Fineman, Elizabeth Wehrle.

Time: October 2002–June 2003. Place: Various locations in the US, Kuwait and Iraq. Presented without intermission.

A Brechtian exploration of the US action against Iraq, its impact on ordinary Americans and how war supports the designs of a political clique in Washington, DC. First presented by The Actors' Gang (Tim Robbins artistic director, Greg Reiner managing director, Samantha Jane Robson producer) at its theater in Hollywood, California (11/15–2/1/2004).

Brooklyn Academy of Music presentation of the **Watermill Theatre/Propeller** production **A Midsummer Night's Dream** (14). Revival of the play by William Shakespeare. Alan H. Fishman chairman of the board, Karen Brooks Hopkins president, Joseph V. Melillo executive producer, at the Harvey Theater. Opened March 16, 2004. (Closed March 28, 2004)

Bottom .... Tony Bell
Lysander .... Dugald Bruce-Lockhart
Titania .... Sam Callis
Moth/Fairy .... Alasdair Craig
Hippolyta .... Emilio Doorasingh
Theseus .... Matthew Flynn
Fairy .... Alexander Giles
Helena .... Robert Hands
Oberon .... Barnaby Kay
Demetrius; Snout .... Vincent Leigh
Hermia; Snug .... Jonathan McGuinness
Quince; Egeus .... Chris Myles
Puck; Starveling .... Simon Scardifield
Flute .... Jules Werner

Directed by Edward Hall; scenery and costumes, Michael Pavelka; lighting, Ben Ormerod; music, Tony Bell, Dugald Bruce-Lockhart, Jules Werner; dramaturg, Roger Warren; press, Sandy Sawotka, Fatima Kafele, Eva Chien, Tamara McCaw, Jennifer Lam.

All-male production of Shakespeare's comic take on the transformative power of love. First production of record was an adaptation titled *A Play of Robin Goodfellow* at the court of King James I in 1604. The play is believed to have been written for performance at an aristocrat's wedding, probably in 1596, but no record survives. First US production of record was given at New York's Park Theatre (11/9/1826 and 11/24/1826; 2 performances).

My Kitchen Wars (53). By Dorothy Lyman; adapted from Betty Fussell's memoir. Produced by Robin Strasser and Beverly Penberthy. Opened March 17, 2004. (Closed May 1, 2004)

Performed by Ms. Lyman and Melissa Sweeney.

Directed by Elinor Renfield; scenery, George H. Landry; lighting, Ji-youn Chang; sound, Ms. Sweeney; music direction, Bill Cunliffe; press, The Pete Sanders Group, Glenna Freedman, Jim Mannino.

Presented without intermission.

A frustrated housewife finds her true calling as a guru of gourmet cooking.

Silent Laughter (26). By Billy Van Zandt and Jane Milmore. Produced by Carolyn Rossi Copeland, in association with The Lamb's Theatre Company, at the Lamb's Theatre. Opened March 18, 2004. (Closed April 11, 2004)

Ruth .... Jane Milmore
Billy .... Billy Van Zandt
Billy's Pal .... Glenn Jones
Lionel Drippinwithit .... John Gregorio
Sarge .... Art Neill

Ensemble: James Darrah, Jim Fitzpatrick, Ken Jennings, Megan Byrne, Ed Carlo.

Directed by Mr. Van Zandt; scenery, Dana Kenn; costumes, Cynthia Nordstrom; lighting, Richard Winkler; production stage manager, Thom Schilling.

Time: 1917. Presented in two parts.

Silent slapstick comedy with music.

More (29). Solo performance piece by Yeardley Smith. Produced by Kevin Schon at the Union Square Theatre. Opened March 22, 2004. (Closed April 18, 2004)

Performed by Ms. Smith.

Directed by Judith Ivey; scenery, Loy Arcenas; costumes, John Schneeman; lighting, Beverly Emmons; sound, David Meschter; production stage manager, Neil Krasnow; press, Sam Rudy Media Relations.

Presented without intermission.

The woman who voices a significant character in an iconic American cartoon—Lisa on *The Simpsons*—shares her inner life.

Johnny Guitar (63). Musical with book by Nicholas van Hoogstraten; music by Joel Higgins and Martin Silvestri; lyrics by Mr. Higgins; based on the Republic Entertainment film and the novel by Roy Chanslor. Produced by A Definite Maybe Productions and Mark H. Kress, in association with Victoria Lang and Pier Paolo Piccoli and The Century Center for the Performing Arts, at the Century Center for the Performing Arts. Opened March 23, 2004. (Closed May 16, 2004)

Vienna; Title Singer .... Judy McLane
Johnny Guitar .... Steve Blanchard
Sam; Ned .... Grant Norman
Tom; Bart; Carl; David .... David Sinkus
Eddie; Hank, Jenks .... Jason Edwards
Emma Small .... Ann Crumb
Mr. McIvers .... Ed Sala
The Dancin' Kid .... Robert Evan
Turkey; Western Singer .... Robb Sapp

Understudies: Kevin Kraft, Kristie Dale Sanders.

Directed by Mr. Higgins; choreography, Jane Lanier; scenery, Van Santvoord; costumes, Kaye Voyce; lighting, Ed McCarthy; sound, Laura Grace Brown; arrangements, Steve Wright; music direction, James Mironchik; associate director, Ian Belton; associate producers, Sarah Brockus, Jeffrey Kent; casting, Stephanie Klapper; production stage manager, Matthew Lacey; press, The Karpel Group, Bridget Klapinski, Josh Rosenzweig.

Presented in two parts.

Musical spoof of a 1954 Joan Crawford film that toys with gender roles and hidden longings.

***From Door to Door** (78). By James Sherman. Produced by Morton Wolkowitz and Chase Mishkin at the Westside Theatre Downstairs. Opened March 24, 2004.

Bessie .... Anita Keal
Deborah .... Sarah McCafrey
Mary .... Suzanne Toren

Understudies: Ms. McCafrey—Kathryn Competatore; Mses. Keal, Toren—Susan Moses.

Directed by Joe Brancato; scenery, Tony Straiges; costumes, Ingrid Maurer; lighting, Jeff Nellis; sound, Johnna Doty; casting, Alan Filderman; production stage manager, Barclay Stiff; press, The Pete Sanders Group, Pete Sanders, Glenna Freedman.

Time: 1939 to the present. Presented without intermission.

Comedy about the challenges faced by three generations of Jewish women.

City Center Encores! presentation of **Pardon My English** (5). Concert version of the musical with book by Herbert Fields and Morrie Ryskind; music by George Gershwin; lyrics by Ira Gershwin; adapted by David Ives. Jack Viertel artistic director, Rob Fisher music director, Kathleen Marshall director-in-residence, at City Center. Opened March 25, 2004. (Closed March 28, 2004)

Golo Schmidt;
Michael Bramleigh .... Brian d'Arcy James
Gita Gobel .... Emily Skinner
Frieda Bauer .... Jennifer Laura Thompson
Herman Bauer .... Rob Bartlett
Dickie Carter .... Don Stephenson
Dr. Adolph Steiner .... Tom Alan Robbins
Magda .... Felicia Finley
Sergeant Schultz .... Kevin Carolan
Katz .... Lee Zarrett

Directed by Gary Griffin; choreography, Rob Ashford; scenery, John Lee Beatty; costumes, Martin Pakledinaz; lighting, Ken Billington; sound, Scott Lehrer; production stage manager, Karen Moore.

Presented in two parts.

Reconstruction of the 1933 musical madcap about an Englishman who becomes a German gangster when rapped on the head. In the bad timing department, the original ran during rising Nazi turmoil accompanying the ascent of Adolf Hitler: the notorious Reichstag fire was just days after the show's closing. First presented on Broadway at the Majestic Theatre (1/20/1933; 46 performances).

***Ears on a Beatle** (73). By Mark St. Germain. Produced by Daryl Roth, Debra Black and Leon Wildes at the DR2 Theatre. Opened March 28, 2004.

Howard Ballantine .... Dan Lauria
Daniel McClure .... Bill Dawes

Directed by Mr. St. Germain; scenery, Eric Renschler; costumes, David C. Woolard; lighting, Daniel Ordower; sound, Randy Hansen; projections, Carl Casella; production stage manager, Brian Maschka; press, Sam Rudy Media Relations, Sam Rudy.

Time: 1970s. Place: New York City. Presented without intermission.

Docudrama centered on the US government's surveillance of John Lennon. First presented at Barrington Stage Company in Massachusetts (7/9–23/2003).

The Public Theater production of **Well** (57). By Lisa Kron. George C. Wolfe producer, Mara Manus executive director, in Martinson Hall. Opened March 28, 2004. (Closed May 16, 2004)

Performed by Ms. Kron, Kenajuan Bentley, Saidah Arrika Ekulona, Jayne Houdyshell, Joel Van Liew, Welker White.

Directed by Leigh Silverman; scenery, Allen Moyer; costumes, Miranda Hoffman; lighting, Christopher Akerlind; sound, Jill B.C. DuBoff; associate producers, Peter DuBois, Steven Tabakin; casting, Jordan Thaler, Heidi Griffiths; production stage manager, Martha Donaldson; press, Carol R. Fineman, Elizabeth Wehrle.

Presented without intermission.

Woman examines the impact of emotional well-being on physical health in a performance piece that shifts between competing narratives. A 2003–04 *Best Plays* choice (see essay by Michael Sommers in this volume).

***The Marijuana-Logues** (71). By Arj Barker, Doug Benson and Tony Camin. Produced by Ideal Entertainment Group and Magic Arts and Entertainment at the Actors' Playhouse. Opened March 30, 2004.

Performed by Messrs. Barker, Benson, Camin.

Directed by Jim Millan; scenery and lighting, Gregory Allen Hirsch; sound, Michael G. Ward; press, The Karpel Group, Bridget Klapinski, Billy Zavelson.

Presented without intermission.

Discourses on the pleasures of pot.

***Manhattan Theatre Club** production of **Sarah, Sarah** (72). By Daniel Goldfarb. Lynne Meadow artistic director, Barry Grove executive producer, at City Center Stage II. Opened March 30, 2004.

Arthur "Artie" Grosberg;
Miles .... Andrew Katz
Vincent; Arthur Grosberg .... Richard Masur
Rochelle Bloom; Maggie .... Lori Prince
Sarah Grosberg;
Jeannie Grosberg .... J. Smith-Cameron

Immigrant's nightmare: J. Smith Cameron, Richard Masur and Andrew Katz in Sarah, Sarah. *Photo: Joan Marcus*

Understudies: Mr. Katz—Jason Jurman; Mr. Masur—Charles Stransky; Ms. Prince—Cameron Blair; Ms. Smith-Cameron—Suzanne Grodner.

Directed by Mark Nelson; scenery, James Noone, costumes, Michael Krass; lighting, Howell Binkley; sound and music, Scott Killian; production stage manager, Jennifer Rae Moore; stage manager, Julie C. Miller; press, Boneau/Bryan-Brown, Chris Boneau, Jim Byk, Aaron Meier.

Time: 1961; 2001. Place: Toronto; China. Presented in two parts.

A Jewish family confronts its identity in a domestic comedy that spans two generations.

***Roundabout Theatre Company** production of **Intimate Apparel** (57). By Lynn Nottage. Todd Haimes artistic director, Ellen Richard managing director, Julia C. Levy executive director of external affairs, in the Laura Pels Theatre at the Harold and Miriam Steinberg Center for Theatre. Opened April 11, 2004.

Esther .... Viola Davis
Mrs. Dickson .... Lynda Gravátt
George .... Russell Hornsby
Mrs. Van Buren .... Arija Bareikis
Mr. Marks .... Corey Stoll
Mayme .... Lauren Velez

Directed by Daniel Sullivan; scenery, Derek McLane; costumes, Catherine Zuber; lighting, Allen Lee Hughes; sound, Marc Gwinn; music, Harold Wheeler; casting, Mele Nagler; press, Boneau/Bryan-Brown, Joe Perrotta, Matt Polk, Jessica Johnson.

Understudies: Mses. Davis, Velez—Gwendolyn Mulamba; Ms. Gravátt—Edloe Blackwell; Mr. Hornsby—Charles Parnell; Ms. Bareikis—Nisi Sturgis; Mr. Stoll—Darren Goldstein.

Time: 1905. Place: Manhattan. Presented in two parts.

An African-American seamstress struggles for love and her place in society. First presented as a joint partnership by Baltimore's Center Stage (2/26/2003) and South Coast Repertory (4/18/2003) in Costa Mesa, California. A 2003–04 *Best Plays* choice (see essay by Lenora Inez Brown in this volume) and 2004 American Theatre Critics/Steinberg New Play Award honoree.

Forbidden fruit: Viola Davis and Corey Stoll in Intimate Apparel. *Photo: Joan Marcus*

Boy's life: Martin Moran in The Tricky Part.
Photo: Joan Marcus

The Tricky Part (56). Solo performance piece by Martin Moran. Produced by James B. Freydberg, CTM Productions, Wendy vanden Heuvel and Sharon Rosen, in association with True Love Productions, at the McGinn/Cazale Theatre. Opened April 12, 2004. (Closed May 30, 2004)

Performed by Mr. Moran

Directed by Seth Barrish; scenery, Paul Steinberg; costumes, Laurie Churba; lighting, Heather Carson; production stage manager, Tom Taylor; press, Boneau/Bryan-Brown, Chris Boneau, Susanne Tighe.

Presented without intermission.

A man of middle age sifts through memories accumulated when, as a 12-year-old boy, he was seduced by a 30-year-old pedophile. Developed at the Sundance Theatre Laboratory, Long Wharf Theatre, McCarter Theatre Center and The Barrow Group.

Chef's Theater: A Musical Feast (50). Musical revue with songs by Lynn Ahrens and Stephen Flaherty, Andrew Lippa, Marcy Heisler, Zina Goldrich. Produced by West Egg Entertainment, Marty Bell, Greg Smith and Stephen Fass at the Supper Club. Opened April 14, 2004. (Closed May 18, 2004)

Performed by Ms. Ahrens, Jason Robert Brown, Michael Cavanaugh, Mr. Flaherty, Ms. Heisler, Mylinda Hull, Lauren Kennedy, Shannon Lewis, Janine LaManna, Mr. Lippa, Julia Murney, Kelli O'Hara, Adam Pascal, Michele Pawk, Billy Porter, Paige Price, Alice Ripley, Daphne Rubin-Vega, Kate Shindle, Jim Walton, Ms. Goldrich.

Chefs: Todd English, Tom Valenti, Tyler Florence, Mary Sue Milliken, Susan Feniger, Michael Lomonaco, Michael Romano, Rick Moonen.

Sommeliers: Josh Wesson, Andrea Immer, Steve Olsen.

Directed by Stafford Arima; choreography, Casey Nicholaw; scenery, Beowulf Boritt; costumes, DKNY; lighting, Ben Stanton; executive producer, Joe Allegro.

A rotating repertory of well-known chefs create meals served to tunes of a musical revue. Performance number includes special dessert programs and family brunches on weekends.

The Public Theater production of **Biro** (22). Solo performance piece by Ntare Guma Mbaho Mwine. George C. Wolfe producer, Mara Manus executive director, in LuEsther Hall. Opened April 18, 2004. (Closed May 9, 2004)

Biro .... Mr. Mwine

Directed by Peter DuBois; scenery, Riccardo Hernández; lighting, Chad McArver; sound, Acme Sound Partners; projections, Peter Nigrini; casting, Jordan Thaler, Heidi Griffiths; production stage manager, Damon W. Arrington; press, Carol R. Fineman, Elizabeth Wehrle.

Presented without intermission.

An African's struggle for survival against the odds of war, disease and the vicissitudes of emigration. First presented at Uganda's National Theatre in Kampala (January 2003) before a run at London's Drill Hall (November 2003).

***Loudmouth** (49). By Toxic Audio. Produced by Eric Krebs and the John Houseman Theatre Center, in association with Castle Talent Inc. and M. Kilburg Reedy, at the John Houseman Theatre. Opened April 18, 2004.

Performed by Jeremy James, Shalisa James, René Ruiz, Paul Sperrazza, Michelle Mailhot-Valines.

Directed by Mr. Ruiz; scenery and lighting, Peter R. Feuchtwanger; costumes, David Brooks; sound, John A. Valines III; press, Terence Womble, Alan Miller.

Vocalists provide sonic accompaniment to a variety of compositions.

Bare: A Pop Opera (43). Musical with book by Jon Hartmere Jr. and Damon Intrabartolo; music by Mr. Intrabartolo; lyrics by Mr. Hartmere Jr. Produced by Dodger Stage Holding and Jack Grossbart/Marc Schwartz at the American Theatre of Actors. Opened April 19, 2004. (Closed May 27, 2004)

Performed by Sasha Allen, Scott Allgauer, Michael Arden, Romelda T. Benjamin, Isaac Calpito, Mike Cannon, Adam Fleming, Jenna Leigh Green, Kearran Giovanni, John Hill, Kaitlin Hopkins, Natalie Joy Johnson, Aaron Lohr, Jim Price, Lindsay Scott, Kay Trinidad.

Orchestra: Damon Intrabartolo conductor, keyboard; Jesse Vargas assistant conductor, keyboard; David Madden acoustic guitar, keyboard; Kyle Smith acoustic guitar, electric guitar; Adam Countryman bass; Kevin Rice drums, percussion.

Directed by Kristin Hanggi; choreography, Sergio Trujillo; scenery, David Gallo; costumes, David C. Woolard; lighting, Mike Baldassari; sound, Domonic Sack; associate producers, William M. Apfelbaum, Amanda DuBois; casting, Dave Clemmons Casting; production stage manager, Phyllis Schray; press, Boneau/Bryan-Brown, Adrian Bryan-Brown, Jim Byk, Aaron Meier.

Presented in two parts.

Coming-of-age musical set in a Catholic boarding school. First presented at Los Angeles's Hudson Theatre (10/14/2000–2/25/2001).

Musical numbers included: "Epiphany," "You and I," "Role of a Lifetime," "Auditions," "Love, Dad," "Wonderland," "A Quiet Night at Home," "Best Kept Secret," "Confession," "Portrait of a Girl," "Birthday, Bitch!," "One Kiss," "Are You There?," "911! Emergency!," "Reputation Stain'd," "Ever After," "Spring," "One," "Wedding Bells," "In the Hallway," "Touch My Soul," "See Me," "Warning," "Pilgrim's Hands," "God Don't Make No Trash," "All Grown Up," "Promise," "Cross," "Two Households," "Queen Mab," "Bare," "A Glooming Peace," "Absolution," "No Voice."

Best friends: Kate Jennings Grant, David Harbour, Bradley White and Daphne Rubin-Vega in Between Us. *Photo: Joan Marcus*

***Manhattan Theatre Club** production of **Between Us** (48). By Joe Hortua. Lynne Meadow artistic director, Barry Grove executive producer, at City Center Stage I. Opened April 20, 2004.

Sharyl .... Kate Jennings Grant
Joel .... David Harbour
Grace .... Daphne Rubin-Vega
Carlo .... Bradley White

Understudies: Mses. Grant, Rubin-Vega—Heather Lea Anderson; Messrs. Harbour, White—Wayne Maugans.

Directed by Christopher Ashley; scenery, Neil Patel; costumes, Jess Goldstein; lighting, Christopher Akerlind; sound, Darron L. West; casting, Nancy Piccione, David Caparelliotis; production stage manager, Kelley Kirkpatrick; stage manager, Robyn Henry; press, Boneau/Bryan-Brown, Chris Boneau, Jim Byk, Aaron Meier.

Time: 1999; 2002. Place: A fashionable midwestern home; a New York apartment. Presented in two parts.

Two couples confront their demons (and marriages) as they grow into middle age.

***The Public Theater** presentation of the **Worth Street Theater Company** production of **The Normal Heart** (46). Revival of the play by Larry Kramer. George C. Wolfe producer, Mara Manus executive director, in the Anspacher Theater. Opened April 21, 2004.

Ned Weeks .... Raúl Esparza
Craig Donner; Grady; Examining Doctor; Orderly .... Paul Whitthorne
Mickey Marcus .... Fred Berman
David; Hiram Keebler; Examining Doctor; Orderly .... Jay Russell
Dr. Emma Brookner .... Joanna Gleason
Bruce Niles .... Mark Dobies
Felix Turner .... Billy Warlock
Ben Weeks .... Richard Bekins
Tommy Boatwright .... McCaleb Burnett

Directed by David Esbjornson; scenery, Eugene Lee; costumes, Jess Goldstein; lighting, Ken Billington; sound, Tony Meola; casting, Stuart Howard, Amy Schecter, Mark Simon; production stage manager, Thom Gates; press, Carol Fineman Publicity, Carol R. Fineman, Leslie Baden, Meghan Zaneski.

Time: July 1981–May 1984. Place: Various locations in New York City. Presented in two parts.

Gay activist sounds alarm at the rising number of cases of AIDS and is frustrated by the indifference he meets. A production of the Worth Street Theater Company (Jeff Cohen artistic director, Carol R. Fineman executive producer, Vern T. Calhoun producer). First presented by Joseph Papp at the Public Theater (4/21/1985–5/5/1986; 294 performances).

City Center Encores! presentation of **Bye Bye Birdie** (5). Concert version of the musical with book by Michael Stewart; music by Charles Strouse; lyrics by Lee Adams. Jack Viertel artistic director, Rob Fisher music director, Kathleen Marshall director-in-residence, at City Center. Opened May 6, 2004. (Closed May 10, 2004)

Rosie Alvarez .... Karen Ziemba
Albert Peterson .... Daniel Jenkins
Conrad Birdie .... William Robert Gaynor
Mr. MacAfee .... Walter Bobbie
Mae Peterson .... Doris Roberts
Hugo Peabody .... Keith Nobbs
Kim MacAfee .... Jessica Grové
Mrs. MacAfee .... Victoria Clark
Randolph MacAfee .... William Ullrich

Directed by Jerry Zaks; choreography, Casey Nicholaw; scenery, John Lee Beatty; costumes, William Ivey Long, lighting, Ken Billington; sound, Peter Fitzgerald; casting, Jay Binder; production stage manager, Karen Moore; press, Barlow-Hartman Public Relations, John Barlow, Bill Coyle, Andrew Snyder.

A rock and roll star is drafted and his manager schemes to get his investment in the singer to pay off first. First presented on Broadway at the Martin Beck Theatre (4/14/1960–10/7/1961; 607 performances). The original production received 1961 Tony Awards for best musical, best director (Gower Champion), best choreographer (Mr. Champion), best supporting actor in a musical (Dick Van Dyke).

***The Public Theater** presentation of the **Labyrinth Theater Company** production of **Guinea Pig Solo** (22). By Brett C. Leonard; based on *Woyzeck* by Georg Büchner. George C. Wolfe producer, Mara Manus executive director, in the Shiva Theater. Opened May 9, 2004.

Linda .... Kim Director
Junior .... Alexander Flores
Doctor .... Robert Glaudini
Gary .... Stephen Adly Guirgis
John .... Jason Manuel Olazábal
José Solo .... John Ortiz
Charlie .... Richard Petrocelli
Nikki; Receptionist .... Portia
Vivian .... Judy Reyes

Directed by Ian Belton; scenery, Andromache Chalfant; costumes, Kaye Voyce; lighting, Paul Whitaker; sound, Fitz Patton; fight direction, David Anzuelo; production stage manager, Rachel N. Fachner; press; Carol R. Fineman, Elizabeth Wehrle.

Time: The present. Place: New York City. Presented in two parts.

A veteran returning from the Middle East battles his war-tortured psyche and attempts to stitch his life back together. First in a planned series of collaborations between the Public Theater and the Labyrinth Theater Company (Philip Seymour Hoffman artistic director, John Ortiz artistic director, Oliver Dow executive director).

Brooklyn Academy of Music presentation of the **Steppenwolf Theatre Company** and **Center Theatre Group/Mark Taper Forum** production of **Homebody/Kabul** (21). Revival of the play by Tony Kushner. Alan H. Fishman chairman of the board, Karen Brooks Hopkins president, Joseph V. Melillo executive producer, at the Harvey Theater. Opened May 11, 2004. (Closed May 30, 2004)

The Homebody .... Linda Emond
Dr. Qari Shah .... Ali Reza

Where's Mom? Firdous Bamji and Maggie Gyllenhaal in Homebody/Kabul. *Photo: Stephanie Berger*

Mullah Ali Aftar Durranni .... Aasif Mandvi
Milton Ceiling .... Reed Birney
Priscilla Ceiling .... Maggie Gyllenhaal
Quango Twistleton .... Bill Camp
Munkrat; Border Guard .... Rahul Gupta
Khwaja Aziz Mondanabosh ...... Firdous Bamji
Zai Garshi .... Dariush Kashani
Woman in Burqa; Mahala ....Rita Wolf

Ensemble: Rod Gnapp, Laura Kachergus, Kamal Maray, Arian Moayed, Michelle Morain, Diana Simonzadeh.

Directed by Frank Galati; scenery, James Schuette; costumes, Mara Blumenfeld; lighting, Christopher Akerlind; sound and music, Joe Cerqua; fight direction, Thomas Schall; assistant director, Kappy Kilburn; casting, Amy Lieberman, Erica Daniels; press, Sandy Sawotka, Fatima Kafele, Eva Chien, Tamara McCaw, Jennifer Lam.

Time: August 1998; spring 1999. Setting: London; Kabul. Presented in three parts.

Drama about an Englishwoman who "disappears" into her fantasies, which leads her family to Afghanistan and into confrontation with that culture's dangerous realities. A 2001–02 *Best Plays* choice, the original Off Broadway production opened at the New York Theatre Workshop (12/19/2001; 86 performances). The 2003–04 production was first presented by the Steppenwolf Theatre Company in Chicago (7/10–8/31/2003) and the Mark Taper Forum in Los Angeles (10/1–11/9/2003).

***The Joys of Sex** (23). Musical with book by Melissa Levis and David Weinstein; music by Mr. Weinstein; lyrics by Ms. Levis. Produced by Ben Sprecher, William P. Miller, Kenneth D. Greenblatt and Benjamin C. Singer at the Variety Arts Theatre. Opened May 12, 2004.

Howard Nolton; Irving .... Ron Bohmer
Brian Shapiro; Others .... David Josefsberg
Stephs Nolton; Others ..... Stephanie Kurtzuba
April Jones; Others ....Jenelle Lynn Randall

Directed by Jeremy Dobrish; choreography, Lisa Shriver; scenery, Neil Patel; costumes, David C. Woolard; lighting, Donald Holder; sound, T. Richard Fitzgerald; music direction, Steven Ray Watkins; orchestrations and arrangements, David Weinstein; production stage manager, Katherine Lee Boyer; press, The Publicity Office, Bob Fennell, Marc Thibodeau, Michael S. Borowski.

Presented without intermission.

A musical romp through contemporary sexuality and sexual relationships.

MUSICAL NUMBERS

"The Joy of Sex"	Company
"'O' No"	Stephs
"Cup of Sugar"	April, Howard
"Intercourse on the Internet"	Brian, Gladys
"The First Time"	Company
"One Night Stand"	April
"In the Parlor Be a Lady"	Granny, Stephs
"Twins"	Howard, Twins
"In Our Fantasy"	Company
"Kinks"	Brian
"The Vault"	Brian, Gladys, Irving, Pleasure Boy, Mistress Pain
"The Three-Way"	Howard
"Pandora's Box"	Stephs
"Free the Tiger"	Stephs, Howard, April
"I Need It Bad"	Company
"Fantasy Come True"	Howard
"Not Too Nice"	Brian, April
"Making Love With You"	Company
"The Joys of Sex" (Reprise)	Company

*__Atlantic Theater Company__ production of __The Two and Only__ (22). Solo performance piece by Jay Johnson. Neil Pepe artistic director, in association with Roger Alan Gindi, Stewart F. Lane and Bonnie Comley, Dan Whitten, Herbert Goldsmith Productions, WetRock Entertainment. Opened May 13, 2004.

Performed by Mr. Johnson.

Directed by Murphy Cross and Paul Kreppel; scenery, Beowulf Boritt; lighting, Clifton Taylor; sound, David Gotwald; music, Michael Andreas; production stage manager, Lori Ann Zepp; press, Bill Evans and Associates, Jim Randolph.

Presented without intermission.

Ventriloquist who achieved fame on the television program *Soap* recounts his fascination with his art form.

*__New York Theatre Workshop__ production of __Light Raise the Roof__ (13). By Kia Corthron. James C. Nicola artistic director, Lynn Moffat managing director. Opened May 20, 2004.

Em	Moe Moe Alston
Zekie	Robert Beitzel
Arnell; Others	Caroline Stefanie Clay
Toddo's Wife; Others	Romi Dias
Toddo; Others	Royce Johnson
Mai	Mia Katigbak
Free	J. Kyle Manzay
Cole	Chris McKinney
Boy; Others	Andres Munar
Bebbie	April Yvette Thompson
Marmalade; Others	Colleen Werthmann

Directed by Michael John Garcés; scenery, Narelle Sissons; costumes, Gabriel Berry; lighting, Ben Stanton; sound, Robert Kaplowitz; production stage manager, Shelli Aderman; press; Richard Kornberg and Associates, Richard Kornberg, Don Summa.

Presented in two parts.

A streetwise builder of homes from discarded materials battles to keep his community housed.

*__Playwrights Horizons__ production of __Chinese Friends__ (6). By Jon Robin Baitz. Tim Sanford artistic director, Leslie Marcus managing director, William Russo general manager. Opened May 27, 2004.

Family politics: Tyler Francavilla, Peter Strauss, Bess Wohl and Will McCormack in Chinese Friends. *Photo: Joan Marcus*

Arthur Brice .... Peter Strauss
Ajax .... Tyler Francavilla
Stephan .... Will McCormack
Alegra .... Bess Wohl

Directed by Robert Egan; scenery, Santo Loquasto; costumes, Laura Bauer; lighting, Donald Holder; sound and music, Obadiah Eaves; fight direction, Joseph Travers; casting, James Calleri; production stage manager, James Latus; press, The Publicity Office, Bob Fennell, Marc Thibodeau, Michael S. Borowski.

Time: Autumn, 2030. Place: A remote island somewhere in New England. Presented in two parts.

Younger set tortures an aging politician for his machinations in an earlier era.

CAST REPLACEMENTS AND TOURING COMPANIES

○○○○○

Compiled by Paul Hardt

THE FOLLOWING IS a list of the major cast replacements of record in productions that opened during the current and in previous seasons, and other New York shows that were on a first-class tour in 2003–04.

The name of each major role is listed in *italics* beneath the title of the play in the first column. In the second column directly opposite appears the name of the actor who created the role in the original New York production (whose opening date appears in *italics* at the top of the column). Indented immediately beneath the original actor's name are the names of subsequent New York replacements—with the date of replacement when available.

The third column gives information about first-class touring companies. When there is more than one roadshow company, #1, #2, etc., appear before the name of the performer who created the role in each company (and the city and date of each company's first performance appears in *italics* at the top of the column). Subsequent replacements are also listed beneath names in the same manner as the New York companies, with dates when available.

AIDA

	New York 3/23/00
Aida	Heather Headley Maya Days 9/13/01 Simone 1/29/02 Saycon Sengbloh 6/16/03 Toni Braxton 6/30/03 Michelle Williams 11/18/03 Deborah Cox 2/17/04
Radames	Adam Pascal Richard H. Blake 6/16/03 Will Chase 6/30/03
Amneris	Sherie René Scott Taylor Dayne Idina Menzel 9/13/01 Felicia Finley 1/29/02 Mandy Gonzales 6/30/03 Lisa Brescia

Mereb	Damian Perkins Delisco Eric LaJuan Summers 2/17/04
Zoser	John Hickok Donnie Kehr Micky Dolenz 1/6/04

BEAUTY AND THE BEAST

	New York 4/18/94
Beast	Terrence Mann Jeff McCarthy Chuck Wagner James Barbour Steve Blanchard Jeff McCarthy 2/17/04 Steve Blanchard 4/13/04
Belle	Susan Egan Sarah Uriarte Berry Christianne Tisdale Kerry Butler Deborah Gibson Kim Huber Toni Braxton Andrea McArdle Sarah Litzsinger Jamie-Lynn Sigler Sarah Litzsinger 2/11/03 Megan McGinnis 4/15/03 Christy Carlson Romano 2/17/04
Lefou	Kenny Raskin Harrison Beal Jamie Torcellini Jeffrey Howard Schecter Jay Brian Winnick 11/12/99 Gerard McIsaac Brad Aspel Steve Lavner Aldrin Gonzalez
Gaston	Burke Moses Marc Kudisch Steve Blanchard Patrick Ryan Sullivan Christopher Sieber Chris Hoch 12/10/02 Grant Norman
Maurice	Tom Bosley MacIntyre Dixon Tom Bosley Kurt Knudson Timothy Jerome J.B. Adams 11/12/99 Jamie Ross
Cogsworth	Heath Lamberts Peter Bartlett

	Robert Gibby Brand
	John Christopher Jones
	Jeff Brooks 11/12/99
Lumiere	Gary Beach
	Lee Roy Reams
	Patrick Quinn
	Gary Beach
	Meshach Taylor
	Patrick Page
	Paul Schoeffler
	Patrick Page
	Bryan Batt
	Rob Lorey 5/7/02
	David DeVries
Babette	Stacey Logan
	Pamela Winslow
	Leslie Castay
	Pam Klinger
	Louisa Kendrick
	Pam Klinger
Mrs. Potts	Beth Fowler
	Cass Morgan
	Beth Fowler
	Barbara Marineau 11/12/99
	Beth Fowler
	Cass Morgan
	Alma Cuervo 2/17/04

CABARET

	New York 3/19/98
	Closed 1/4/2004
Emcee	Alan Cumming
	Robert Sella 9/17/98
	Alan Cumming 12/1/98
	Michael C. Hall 6/8/99
	Matt McGrath10/17/01
	Raúl Esparza 10/26/01
	John Stamos 4/29/02
	Raúl Esparza
	Neil Patrick Harris 1/1/03
	Jon Secada 6/6/03
	Adam Pascal 10/17/03
Sally Bowles	Natasha Richardson
	Jennifer Jason Leigh 8/20/98
	Mary McCormack 3/2/99
	Susan Egan 6/17/99
	Joely Fisher 6/2/00
	Lea Thompson 8/2/00
	Katie Finneran 11/21/00
	Gina Gershon 1/19–6/17/01
	Kate Shindle 6/19/01
	Brooke Shields 7/3/01
	Molly Ringwald 12/18/01
	Jane Leeves 4/29/01

	Molly Ringwald Heather Laws 1/27/03 Deborah Gibson 2/18/03 Melina Kanakaredes 6/27/04 Susan Egan 9/1/03
Clifford Bradshaw	John Benjamin Hickey Boyd Gaines 3/2/99 Michael Hayden 8/3/99 Matthew Greer 1/19/01 Rick Holmes
Ernst Ludwig	Denis O'Hare Michael Stuhlbarg 5/4/99 Martin Moran 11/9/99 Peter Benson 1/19/01 Martin Moran 10/27/03
Fraulein Schneider	Mary Louise Wilson Blair Brown 8/20/98 Carole Shelley 5/4/99 Polly Bergen Carole Shelley Alma Cuervo 2/18/03 Mariette Hartley Blair Brown 9/22/03
Fraulein Kost	Michele Pawk Victoria Clark 5/4/99 Candy Buckley Penny Ayn Maas Jane Summerhays Liz McConahay
Herr Schultz	Ron Rifkin Laurence Luckinbill 5/4/99 Dick Latessa 11/9/99 Larry Keith Hal Linden Tom Bosley 12/12/02 Tony Roberts 9/22/03

CHICAGO

	New York 11/14/96	*Washington, DC 6/10/03*
Roxie Hart	Ann Reinking Marilu Henner Karen Ziemba Belle Calaway Charlotte d'Amboise Sandy Duncan 8/12/99 Belle Calaway 1/18/00 Charlotte d'Amboise 3/24/00 Belle Calaway Nana Visitor Petra Nielsen 10/8/01 Nana Visitor 11/19/01 Belle Calaway 1/13/02 Denise Van Outen 3/18/02 Belle Calaway 4/22/02	Bianca Marroquin

	Amy Spanger 8/6/02	
	Belle Calaway	
	Tracy Shayne 4/15/03	
	Melanie Griffith 7/11/03	
	Charlotte d'Amboise 10/7/03	
	Bianca Marroquin 12/15/03	
	Gretchen Mol 1/5/04	
	Charlotte d'Amboise 3/1/04	
Velma Kelly	Bebe Neuwirth	Brenda Braxton
	Nancy Hess	Reva Rice 12/30/03
	Ute Lemper	
	Bebe Neuwirth	
	Ruthie Henshall 5/25/99	
	Mamie Duncan-Gibbs 10/26/99	
	Bebe Neuwirth 1/18/00	
	Donna Marie Asbury 3/23/00	
	Sharon Lawrence 4/11/00	
	Vicki Lewis	
	Jasmine Guy	
	Bebe Neuwirth	
	Donna Marie Asbury	
	Deidre Goodwin	
	Vicki Lewis	
	Deidre Goodwin 6/29/01	
	Anna Montanaro 7/9/01	
	Deidre Goodwin 9/14/01	
	Donna Marie Asbury	
	Roxane Carrasco 1/13/02	
	Deidre Goodwin 3/18/02	
	Stephanie Pope	
	Roxane Carrasco	
	Caroline O'Connor 11/8/02	
	Brenda Braxton 3/3/03	
	Deidre Goodwin 6/24/03	
	Reva Rice 10/7/03	
	Brenda Braxton 1/1/04	
	Pia Dowes 4/8/04	
	Brenda Braxton 5/16/04	
Billy Flynn	James Naughton	Gregory Harrison
	Gregory Jbara	Patrick Swayze 12/30/03
	Hinton Battle	Tom Wopat 1/27/04
	Alan Thicke	
	Michael Berresse	
	Brent Barrett	
	Robert Urich 1/11/00	
	Clarke Peters 2/1/00	
	Brent Barrett 2/15/00	
	Chuck Cooper	
	Brent Barrett 7/2/01	
	Chuck Cooper 8/27/01	
	George Hamilton 11/12/01	
	Eric Jordan Young 1/18/02	
	Ron Raines 3/26/02	
	George Hamilton 5/21/02	
	Michael C. Hall 8/8/02	
	Destan Owens	
	Taye Diggs	

	Billy Zane 11/8/02	
	Kevin Richardson 1/20/03	
	Clarke Peters	
	Gregory Harrison	
	Brent Barrett 6/2/03	
	Patrick Swayze 12/15/03	
	James Naughton 01/05/04	
	Norm Lewis 2/2/04	
	Christopher Sieber 3/23/04	
	Tom Wopat 5/16/04	
Amos Hart	Joel Grey	Ray Bokhour
	Ernie Sabella	
	Tom McGowan	
	P.J. Benjamin	
	Ernie Sabella 11/23/99	
	P.J. Benjamin	
	Tom McGowan	
	P.J. Benjamin	
	Ray Bokhour 7/30/01	
	P.J. Benjamin 8/13/01	
	Rob Bartlett	
	P.J. Benjamin 3/3/03	
Matron	Marcia Lewis	Roz Ryan
	Roz Ryan	Marcia Lewis 8/4/03
	Marcia Lewis	Carol Woods 9/23/03
	Roz Ryan	
	Marcia Lewis	
	Roz Ryan	
	Marcia Lewis	
	Jennifer Holliday 6/18/01	
	Marcia Lewis 8/27/01	
	Roz Ryan 11/16/01	
	Michele Pawk 1/14/02	
	Alix Korey 3/4/02	

Ma and me: Shirley Jones and Patrick Cassidy in 42nd Street.
Photo: Joan Marcus

	B.J. Crosby 3/3/03 Angie Stone 4/15/03 Camille Saviola 6/10/03 Debbie Gravitte 12/15/03 Roz Ryan 3/15/04	
Mary Sunshine	D. Sabella J. Loeffelholz R. Bean A. Saunders J. Maldonado R. Bean A. Saunders 1/2/02 R. Bean 1/14/02 M. Agnes D. Sabella 3/24/03 D. Sabella 3/24/03 R. Bean 5/17/04	R. Bean

42ND STREET

	New York 5/2/01	*Kansas City 8/4/02*
Peggy Sawyer	Kate Levering Meredith Patterson Kate Levering 8/30/02 Nadine Isenegger	Catherine Wreford Shannon O'Bryan
Julian Marsh	Michael Cumpsty Michael Dantuono Tom Wopat 7/21/02 Patrick Ryan Sullivan Patrick Cassidy 5/7/04	Patrick Ryan Sullivan Darren Kelly
Billy Lawler	David Elder	Robert Spring
Dorothy Brock	Christine Ebersole Beth Leavel 6/9/02 Shirley Jones 5/7/04	Blair Ross Marcy McGuigan

HAIRSPRAY

	New York 8/15/02	*Baltimore 9/17/03*
Tracy Turnblad	Marissa Jaret Winokur Kathy Brier 8/12/03 Carly Jibson 5/4/04	Carly Jibson Keala Settle 4/13/04
Edna Turnblad	Harvey Fierstein Michael McKean 5/4/04	Bruce Vilanch
Wilbur Turnblad	Dick Latessa	Todd Susman
Amber Von Tussle	Laura Bell Bundy Tracy Jai Edwards 7/14/03	Jordan Ballard
Velma Von Tussle	Linda Hart Barbara Walsh 7/14/03	Susan Cella
Link Larkin	Matthew Morrison Richard H. Blake 1/13/04	Austin Miller
Motormouth Maybelle	Mary Bond Davis	Charlotte Crossley

Seaweed	Corey Reynolds Chester Gregory II 7/14/03	Terron Brooks
Penny Pingleton	Kerry Butler Jennifer Gambatese 6/15/04 Brooke Tansley 4/11/04 Jennifer Gambatese 6/15/04	Sandra DeNise
Corny Collins	Clarke Thorell Jonathan Dokuchitz 1/13/04	Troy Britton Johnson
Little Inez	Danelle Eugenia Wilson Aja Maria Johnson 7/19/03	Kianna Underwood

I LOVE YOU, YOU'RE PERFECT, NOW CHANGE

Man #1	Jordan Leeds Danny Burstein 10/01/96 Adam Grupper 8/22/97 Gary Imhoff 2/09/98 Adam Grupper 4/01/98 Jordan Leeds 3/17/99 Bob Walton 10/27/00 Jordan Leeds 1/30/01 Darrin Baker 1/29/02 Danny Burstein 4/12/02 Jordan Leeds 6/03/02
Man #2	Robert Roznowski Kevin Pariseau 5/25/98 Adam Hunter 4/20/01 Sean Arbuckle 9/23/02 Frank Baiocchi 2/17/03 Colin Stokes 10/10/03
Woman #1	Jennifer Simard Erin Leigh Peck 5/25/98 Kelly Anne Clark 1/10/00 Andrea Chamberlain 3/13/00 Lori Hammel 11/04/00 Andrea Chamberlain 1/29/01 Amanda Watkins 8/24/01 Karyn Quackenbush 1/02/02 Marissa Burgoyne 8/09/02 Andrea Chamberlain 12/17/02 Karyn Quackenbush 2/17/03 Sandy Rustin 6/13/03
Woman #2	Melissa Weil Cheryl Stern 2/16/98 Mylinda Hull 9/17/00 Melissa Weil 2/09/01 Evy O'Rourke 3/13/01 Marylee Graffeo 6/11/01 Cheryl Stern 1/18/02 Marylee Graffeo 3/11/02 Janet Metz 4/26/02 Anne Bobby 12/17/02 Janet Metz 3/03/03

THE LION KING

	New York 11/13/97	*#1 Gazelle Company*
		#2 Cheetah Company
Rafiki	Tsidii Le Loka	#1 Futhi Mhlongo
	Thuli Dumakude 11/11/98	#2 Thandazile A. Soni
	Sheila Gibbs	
	Nomvula Dlamini	
	Tshidi Manye	
Mufasa	Samuel E. Wright	#1 Alton Fitzgerald White
	Alton Fitzgerald White	Thomas Corey Robinson
		#2 Rufus Bonds Jr.
Sarabi	Gina Breedlove	#1 Jean Michelle Grier
	Meena T. Jahi 8/4/98	#2 Marvette Williams
	Denise Marie Williams	
	Meena T. Jahi	
	Robyn Payne	
Zazu	Geoff Hoyle	#1 Jeffrey Binder
	Bill Bowers 10/21/98	Mark Cameron Pow
	Robert Dorfman	#2 Derek Hasenstab
	Tony Freeman	
	Adam Stein	
	Jeffrey Binder	
Scar	John Vickery	#1 Patrick Page
	Tom Hewitt 10/21/98	Dan Donohue
	Derek Smith	#2 Larry Yando
	Patrick Page	
Banzai	Stanley Wayne Mathis	#1 James Brown-Orleans
	Keith Bennett 9/30/98	#2 Melvin Abston
	Leonard Joseph	
	Curtiss I' Cook	
	Rodrick Covington	
Shenzi	Tracy Nicole Chapman	#1 Jacquelyn Renae Hodges
	Vanessa S. Jones	#2 Shaullanda Lacombe
	Lana Gordon	
	Marlayna Sims	
Ed	Kevin Cahoon	#1 Wayne Pyle
	Jeff Skowron 10/21/98	#2 Brian Sills
	Jeff Gurner	
	Timothy Gulan	
	Thom Christopher Warren	
	Enrique Segura	
Timon	Max Casella	#1 John Plumpis
	Danny Rutigliano 6/16/98	#2 Benjamin Clost
	John E. Brady	Adam Hunter
	Danny Rutigliano	
Pumbaa	Tom Alan Robbins	#1 Ben Lipitz
		#2 Bob Amaral
		Phil Fiorini
Simba	Jason Raize	#1 Alan Mingo Jr.
	Christopher Jackson	#2 Brandon Victor Dixon
	Josh Tower	Brandon Louis
Nala	Heather Headley	#1 Kissy Simmons
	Mary Randle 7/7/98	Lisa Nicole Wilkerson

	Heather Headley 12/8/98 Bashirrah Creswell Sharon L. Young Rene Elise Goldsberry Kissy Simmons	#2 Adia Ginneh Dobbins

MAMMA MIA!

	New York 10/18/01	*#1 US Tour* *#2 2nd Tour* *#3 Las Vegas*
Donna Sheridan	Louise Pitre Dee Hoty 10/22/03	#1 Dee Hoty #2 Monique Lund #3 Tina Walsh
Sophie Sheridan	Tina Maddigan Jenny Fellner 10/22/03	#1 Chilina Kennedy #2 Kristie Marsden #3 Jill Paice
Tanya	Karen Mason Jeanine Morick Tamara Bernier	#1 Cynthia Sophiea #2 Ellen Harvey #3 Karole Foreman
Rosie	Judy Kaye Harriett D. Foy	#1 Rosalyn Rahn Kerins #2 Robin Baxter #3 Jennifer Perry
Sky	Joe Machota	#1 P.J. Griffith #2 Chris Bolan #3 Victor Wallace
Sam Carmichael	David W. Keeley John Hillner David W. Keeley John Hillner	#1 Gary Lynch #2 Don Noble #3 Nick Cokas
Harry Bright	Dean Nolen Richard Binsley Michael Winther	#1 Michael DeVries #2 James Kall #3 Michael Piontek
Bill Austin	Ken Marks Adam LeFevre	#1 Craig Bennett #2 Pearce Bunting #3 Mark Leydorf

MOVIN' OUT

	New York 10/24/02	*Detroit 1/26/04*
Brenda	Elizabeth Parkinson Nancy Lemenager 5/8/04	Holly Cruikshank Laurie Kanyok
Eddie	John Selya	Ron Todorowski Brendan King
Tony	Keith Roberts Ian Carney Keith Roberts	David Gomez Corbin Popp
James	Benjamin G. Bowman Kurt Froman	Matthew Dibble
Judy	Ashley Tuttle Mabel Modrono	Julieta Gros
Vocalist	Michael Cavanaugh	Matt Wilson Darren Holden

NINE

	New York 3/21/03 *Closed 12/14/03*
Guido	Antonio Banderas
	John Stamos 10/07/03
Louisa	Mary Stuart Masterson
Carla	Jane Krakowski
	Sara Gettelfinger 10/07/03
Liliane La Fleur	Chita Rivera
	Eartha Kitt 10/7/03
Claudia	Laura Benanti
	Rebecca Luker 9/2/03
Guido's Mother	Mary Beth Peil
	Marni Nixon 10/7/03
Lady of the Spa	Deidre Goodwin
	Jacqueline Hendy

THE PHANTOM OF THE OPERA

	New York 1/26/88	*National Tour*
The Phantom	Michael Crawford	Franc D'Ambrosio
	Thomas James O'Leary	Brad Little
	Hugh Panaro 2/1/99	Ted Keegan
	Howard McGillin 8/23/99	Brad Little
	Brad Little	Ted Keegan
	Howard McGillin	Brad Little
	Hugh Panaro 4/14/03	Gary Mauer
	Howard McGillin 12/22/03	
	Hugh Panaro 1/5/04	
Christine Daaé	Sarah Brightman	Tracy Shane
	Sandra Joseph 1/29/98	Kimilee Bryant
	Adrienne McEwan 8/2/99	Amy Jo Arrington
	Sarah Pfisterer 1/17/00	Rebecca Pitcher
	Sandra Joseph 10/30/00	Kathy Voytko
	Sarah Pfisterer 8/6/01	Julie Hanson
	Elizabeth Southard 3/25/02	Rebecca Pitcher
	Lisa Vroman 4/22/02	Lisa Vroman
	Sandra Joseph 6/10/03	Rebecca Pitcher
Christine Daaé (alt.)	Patti Cohenour	Tamra Hayden
	Adrienne McEwan	Marie Danvers
	Sarah Pfisterer	Megan Starr-Levitt
	Adrienne McEwan	Marni Raab
	Lisa Vroman 10/30/00	Elizabeth Southard
	Adrienne McEwan 7/9/01	
	Julie Hanson 9/20/03	
Raoul	Steve Barton	Ciaran Sheehan
	Gary Mauer 4/19/99	Jason Pebworth 1/29/97
	Jim Weitzer 4/23/01	Jim Weitzer
	Michael Shawn Lewis 11/2/01	Jason Pebworth 7/22/98
	John Cudia 4/7/03	Richard Todd Adams 3/31/99
	Jim Weitzer 10/3/03	Jim Weitzer 1/12/00
	John Cudia 12/21/03	John Cudia
		Tim Martin Gleason

THE PRODUCERS

	New York 4/19/01	*#1 Max Company* *#2 Leo Company*
Max Bialystock	Nathan Lane Henry Goodman 3/19/02 Brad Oscar 4/16/02 Lewis J. Stadlen Fred Applegate 10/7/03 Nathan Lane 12/31/03 Brad Oscar 4/6/04	#1 Lewis J. Stadlen Jason Alexander 4/21/03 Lewis J. Stadlen 1/6/04 #2 Bob Amaral
Leo Bloom	Matthew Broderick Steven Weber 3/19/02 Roger Bart 12/17/02 Don Stephenson 5/20/03 Matthew Broderick 12/31/03 Roger Bart 4/6/04	#1 Don Stephenson Martin Short 4/21/03 Alan Ruck 1/6/04 #2 Andy Taylor
Ulla	Cady Huffman Sarah Cornell 8/5/03 Angie L. Schworer 11/4/03	#1 Angie L. Schworer Charley Izabella King 1/6/04 #2 Ida Leigh Curtis
Roger De Bris	Gary Beach John Treacy Egan Gary Beach 10/7/03	#1 Lee Roy Reams Gary Beach Lee Roy Reams 1/6/04 #2 Stuart Marland
Carmen Ghia	Roger Bart Sam Harris 7/2/02 Brad Musgrove 12/17/02	#1 Jeff Hyslop Michael Paternostro Josh Prince Harry Bouvy #2 Rich Affanato
Franz Liebkind	Brad Oscar John Treacy Egan Peter Samuel John Treacy Egan	#1 Bill Nolte Fred Applegate #2 Bill Nolte

RENT

	New York 4/29/96
Roger Davis	Adam Pascal Norbert Leo Butz Richard H. Blake (alt.) Manley Pope 6/1/02 Sebastian Arcelus 12/30/02 Ryan Link 9/8/03 Jeremy Kushnier 11/14/03
Mark Cohen	Anthony Rapp Jim Poulos Trey Ellett 5/15/00 Matt Caplan 6/1/02 Joey Fatone 8/5/02 Matt Caplan 12/23/02
Tom Collins	Jesse L. Martin Michael McElroy Rufus Bonds Jr. 9/7/99 Alan Mingo Jr. 4/10/00

	Mark Leroy Jackson 1/15/01 Mark Richard Ford 2/3/02
Benjamin Coffin III	Taye Diggs Jacques C. Smith Stu James 3/13/00 D'Monroe
Joanne Jefferson	Fredi Walker Gwen Stewart Alia León Kenna J. Ramsey Danielle Lee Greaves 10/4/99 Natalie Venetia Belcon 10/2/00 Myiia Watson-Davis 6/1/02 Merle Dandridge 10/28/02 Kenna J. Ramsey 3/03/03 Merle Dandridge
Angel Schunard	Wilson Jermaine Heredia Wilson Cruz Shaun Earl Jose Llana Jai Rodriguez Andy Señor 1/31/00 Jai Rodriguez 3/10/02 Andy Señor 2/17/03
Mimi Marquez	Daphne Rubin-Vega Marcy Harriell 4/5/97 Krysten Cummings Maya Days Loraine Velez 2/28/00 Karmine Alers 6/1/02 Krystal L. Washington 5/15/03 Melanie Brown 4/19/04
Maureen Johnson	Idina Menzel Sherie René Scott Kristen Lee Kelly Tamara Podemski Cristina Fadale 10/4/99 Maggie Benjamin 6/1/02 Cristina Fadale 10/28/02 Maggie Benjamin

TAKE ME OUT

	New York *Closed 1/4/04*
Darren Lemming	Daniel Sunjata
Mason Marzac	Denis O'Hare
Kippy Sunderstrom	Neal Huff
Shane Mungitt	Frederick Weller Myk Watford 11/4/03
Rodriguez	Gene Gabriel Maximillian Alexander 11/4/03
Toddy Koovitz	David Eigenberg Anthony Joseph DeSantis 7/22/03

THOROUGHLY MODERN MILLIE

	New York 4/18/02	*Kansas City 6/15/03*
Millie	Sutton Foster Susan Egan 2/16/04	Darcie Roberts
Jimmy	Gavin Creel Christian Borle 4/29/03	Matt Cavenaugh Joey Sorge 1/12/04
Mrs. Meers	Harriet Harris Delta Burke 2/26/03 Terry Burrell 2/16/04 Dixie Carter 2/23/04	Hollis Resnik
Trevor Grayson	Marc Kudisch Christopher Sieber 1/28/03 Kevin Earley 4/29/03	Sean Krill
Muzzy	Sheryl Lee Ralph Leslie Uggams 4/22/03	Pamela Isaacs
Dorothy Brown	Angela Christian Emily Rozek 6/11/04 Jessica Grové 6/15/04	Diana Kaarina
Miss Flannery	Anne L. Nathan Liz McCartney 3/1/04	Janelle A. Robinson

URINETOWN

	New York 9/20/02 *Closed 1/18/04*	*San Francisco 6/24/03*
Caldwell B.Cladwell	John Cullum Don Richard 8/17/03 Charles Shaughnessy 9/9/03	Ron Holgate
Bobby Strong	Hunter Foster Charlie Pollack 4/1/03 Tom Cavanagh 5/20/03 Hunter Foster 7/8/03 Luther Creek 7/29/03	Charlie Pollack
Hope	Jennifer Laura Thompson Anastasia Barzee 12/20/02 Amy Spanger 7/8/03	Christiane Noll
Office Lockstock	Jeff McCarthy James Barbour 6/13/03 Jeff McCarthy 7/8/03	Tom Hewitt Jeff McCarthy
Mrs. Pennywise	Nancy Opel Victoria Clark Carolee Carmello 4/29/03	Beth McVey
Little Sally	Spencer Kayden Megan Lawrence 8/27/02 Spencer Kayden 3/25/03	Meghan Strange

FIRST-CLASS NATIONAL TOURS

JESUS CHRIST SUPERSTAR

	La Mirada, CA 11/11/02 *Closed 6/20/03 Nashville*
Jesus	Sebastian Bach Eric Kunze
Judas	Carl Anderson Lawrence Clayton
Mary Magdalene	Natalie Toro
Pontius Pilate	Stephen Breithaupt
Caiaphas	Lawson Skala
Herod	Peter Kevoian Barry Dennen
Simon	Todd Fournier
Peter	James Clow Johnny Hawkins

LES MISÉRABLES

	Atlanta 9/9/03
Jean Valjean	Randal Keith
Javert	James Clow Joseph Mahowald Stephen Tewksbury
Fantine	Tonya Dixon
Eponine	Ma-Anne Dionisio
Cosette	Amanda Huddleston
Marius	Josh Young
Enjolras	John-Andrew Clark
Thénardier	Michael Kostroff
Madame Thénardier	Cindy Benson

NUNSENSE

	Houston 12/9/03 *Closed 5/2/04 Greenville, SC*
Sr. Mary Regina	Kaye Ballard
Sr. Mary Leo	Georgia Engel
Sr. Amnesia	Mimi Hines
Sr. Robert Anne	Lee Meriwether
Sr. Hubert	Darlene Love

THE GRADUATE

	San Francisco 8/9/03 *Closed 6/27/04 Charlotte, NC*
Mrs. Robinson	Jerry Hall Linda Gray 11/11/03 Lorraine Bracco 1/6/04 Kelly McGillis 3/16/04
Benjamin Braddock	Ryder Strong Jonathan Kaplan 11/11/03
Elaine Robinson	Devon Sorvari
Mr. Braddock	William Hill

Mrs. Braddock	Kate Skinner
	Corinna May
Mr. Robinson	Dennis Parlato

THE KING AND I

	Pittsburgh 6/15/04
Anna	Sandy Duncan
King	Martin Vidnovic
Tuptim	Luz Lor
Lun Tha	Martin Sola
Lady Tiang	Catherine MiEun Choi

THE SEASON OFF OFF BROADWAY

THE SEASON OFF OFF BROADWAY

○○○○○ *By Mel Gussow* ○○○○○

THE LINE BETWEEN Off Off Broadway and the so-called commercial theater has become blurred. Increasingly, shows that have begun Off Off have moved not just to Off Broadway but also to Broadway, this season with *Avenue Q*, *Golda's Balcony* and *Frozen*, Bryony Lavery's powerful drama about a child killer. All three shows were nominated for Tony Awards, and *Avenue Q* won as best musical and Brían F. O'Byrne in *Frozen* was named best featured actor. (See the Plays Produced on Broadway section in this volume for more information.) *Frozen*, which was also chosen as a 2003–2004 Best Play, had an earlier production at London's National Theatre. Instead of being taken up by one of New York's major institutional theaters, it had its American premiere at MCC Theater, formerly Manhattan Class Company. For good reasons, producers—and theatergoers—keep their eye on Off Off, in particular on companies such as MCC Theater, Vineyard Theatre, the Flea Theater, the New Group and Signature Theatre Company. In contrast to Broadway, this was a highly rewarding season Off Off, with several challenging new plays, experimental productions and restorative revivals.

Under the direction of Jim Simpson, the Flea has become a downtown haven for adventurous theater by Mac Wellman, Len Jenkin and others. Because of its success, the Flea has been able to attract name actors for short runs—several seasons ago with a rotating cast in *The Guys*. One of the most intriguing events at the Flea has been the partial co-opting of A.R. Gurney, a quintessentially uptown playwright. At the Flea, Gurney has been able to flex his political inclinations, last season with *O Jerusalem*, this season with *Mrs. Farnsworth*. Meanwhile, Lincoln Center offered the Off Broadway premiere of the playwright's *Big Bill*, his contemplation of the story of the damaged life of tennis ace Bill Tilden.

An outstanding OOB production, *Mrs. Farnsworth*, nimbly directed by Simpson, was as disarming as it was provocative. A kind of classroom lecture, it is a three-character play in which a WASPish Connecticut woman enters a class in creative writing and expresses her wish to write a *roman à clef* about her troubling past affair with someone who closely resembles George W. Bush. Sigourney Weaver was ideally cast as Margery Farnsworth, who is perfectly aware of the snobbishness of her set. As she says:

> MRS. FARNSWORTH: In the summer we go to Fisher's Island. It's a kind of final fortress for WASPs. The Jews had Masada, we have Fisher's Island. We sail and play tennis. And play charades at parties. There are a lot of people in the world who'd like a life like that. That's what they hope to get when they move to Greenwich. But of course they don't. And they can't get near Fisher's Island.

Weaver's splendid performance was equaled by John Lithgow's as her husband Forrest, who as we gradually realized, was not as conservative as he might have seemed.

> MR. FARNSWORTH: We're stuck with a president who's way over his head. And why? Because he's been bailed out and propped up by his family all of his life. Which is why he is now so dependent on a bunch of ruthless Republicans who are manipulating him for their own fell purposes.

Before playing her role, Weaver must have studied all those upper class suburbanites who populate Gurney's other plays (and John Cheever stories). As for Lithgow, he merged himself with William F. Buckley. Danny Burstein ably completed the trio as the teacher, with several other actors playing other students in the class. There were many twists and turns before the play reached its inevitable resolution. Gurney had wicked fun at the expense of President Bush and other politicians, and the audience shared in that enjoyment. This sharpshooting comedy has a future life, star schedules permitting.

EXPERIMENTATION, THAT HALLMARK of Off Off Broadway, was best represented at 2003 Lincoln Center Festival and at the Next Wave Festival at the Brooklyn Academy of Music, the first with Deborah Warner's *The Angel Project* (the highlight of the Lincoln Center Festival), the second with Anne Bogart's *bobrauschenbergamerica*. On the strength of these two pieces, Warner and Bogart remain two of the deftest, most inventive conceptual directors on the international scene—both are outstanding OOB productions.

In *The Angel Project*, which, in a variant version played Perth, Australia, Warner harnessed New York City to her innovative directorial imagination. Scouting locations, she looked for spaces that would introduce New Yorkers to their own city—or at least to aspects of it that were unfamiliar. One by one, theatergoers were led through a journey that began on Roosevelt Island and spread over midtown Manhattan. In characteristic fashion, Warner furnished some of the sites with emblematic objects as well as actors playing silent angels. The 27th floor of an office building on the Avenue of the Americas was filled with feathers and had a sweeping view of Bryant Park, which from that height looked like a crosspatch quilt. One Times Square, where the ball drops on New Year's Eve, had a room deep in sand and lilies with a towering view of the Paramount building and Times Square itself.

Some of the sites were more evocative than others, and the project did not have the intense focus of Warner's *St. Pancras Project*, which she presented in 1995 at the London International Festival of Theatre. That

Sigourney Weaver's splendid performance was equaled by John Lithgow's.

earlier experience was confined to one location, the long-unused, palatial Midland Grand Hotel. But *The Angel Project* was an illuminating exploration, with its own sense of mystery, as we were introduced to elements of a city we thought we knew so well. All of this was enhanced by the fact that each journey was solitary. The ambulatory audience was expected to make its own contribution to the experience. The project, Warner said, was "like inviting somebody in, giving them a key to a house and then leaving them to it." An audience member's enthusiasm partly depended on his openness, on a willingness to let go and join this site-specific adventure.

Bobrauschenbergamerica, written by Charles L. Mee and directed by Bogart, was an inspired jaunt through the mind and metaphor of Robert Rauschenberg. The production was a colorful, crazy comic strip of symbols, signs and images endemic to the artist's work. It was the most vibrant in Bogart's series of biographical plays (others have dealt with Marshall McLuhan and Robert Wilson). In this freewheeling collage, Old Glory vied with chickens (and chicken jokes), a stuffed deer and a bathtub.

Rauschenberg is from Port Arthur, Texas and Robert Wilson is from Waco. A line from the play, "Art was not a part of our lives," could apply to both of them. There was a middle America, nonintellectual aura to the show, making it possible to trace the origins of the artist's work. Characters popped up in unlikely places, cavorting on a Rauschenbergian landscape. Full credit must go to the extraordinary design team: James Schuette who did the scenery and costumes, Brian Scott for the lighting, Darron L. West for the sound. But the genius behind the venture was the always venturesome Bogart.

Another innovative director, Lee Breuer offered his reinterpretation of *A Doll's House* at St. Ann's Warehouse in Brooklyn. Taking the title literally, he constructed a doll-house version of Ibsen, which he titled *Dollhouse*. The male characters, beginning with Torvald Helmer, were played by actors under five feet tall. The female actors, some six feet tall, towered over them, and the set consisted of tiny tables and chairs and a toy piano. The intention was not so much to cut the play down to size as to give a physical presence to symbolism within. On his Ontological stage, the perennial Richard Foreman delved into contemporary politics with *King Cowboy Rufus Rules the Universe*, which in a program note acknowledged that the play was a response to George W. Bush.

Theodora Skipitares, another stalwart of Off Off experimentation, and a regular at La MaMa, was given a Helen Merrill Award (named after and funded by the late play agent) for distinguished achievement at midcareer. I was one of five judges to vote her that prize—which she richly deserved. For 20 years she has been creating theatrical works of remarkable ingenuity. Skipitares is a puppeteer, sculptor, designer, playwright and performance artist who has enhanced Off Off Broadway—and the theater in general—with musical parables about science, history, mythology, art and politics. In her work, bunraku joins hands with tall totemic figures, and dioramas like those at the Museum of Natural History come life. With Skipitares, there are no limits to her curiosity—or her imagination. In common with Foreman, she has gone her own individual way, and, despite all economic pressures, has survived with her integrity intact.

SIGNATURE THEATRE COMPANY took a bold step into performance art by devoting a season to the work of Bill Irwin, following such esteemed playwriting predecessors as Arthur Miller, Edward Albee, Sam Shepard and Lanford Wilson. The Irwin season—three plays written by and starring the playwright—represents an outstanding OOB event. As a clown and actor, Irwin has generally been a creator of his work, beginning with *The Regard of Flight* in 1982. He opened his Signature year auspiciously with *The Harlequin Studies*, a delightful commentary on *commedia dell'arte*. Irwin and his frequent collaborator, Doug Skinner, played professors introducing the audience to the intricacies of the form, with Skinner tinkling on a toy piano. There were also quick takes, some solo, some with a company of actors and acrobats. In one sketch, Irwin played Harlequin in service to his master (Paxton Whitehead) and in love with his master's marriageable

Signature Theatre's Bill Irwin Season

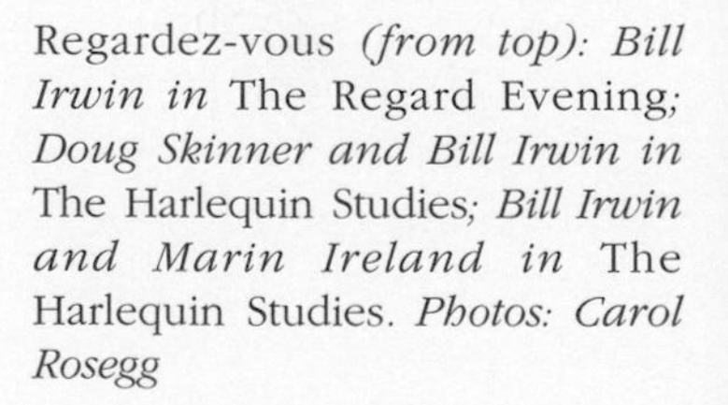

Regardez-vous *(from top): Bill Irwin in* The Regard Evening; *Doug Skinner and Bill Irwin in* The Harlequin Studies; *Bill Irwin and Marin Ireland in* The Harlequin Studies. *Photos: Carol Rosegg*

daughter (Marin Ireland). Foiling an evil rival (Rocco Sisto), Irwin performed many virtuosic turns, including a passionate pas de deux with a hatrack.

Next in line was *The Regard Evening*. The first act was an artful, mirthful abbreviated run-through of the original *Regard*, with Skinner once again at the piano and also as an academic analyzer of the "New Theater," the satiric subject of Irwin's comedic thrusts. In the second act, Irwin offered sardonic commentary on his earlier clownish forays, with Michael O'Connor acting as a pesky intruder from the audience. Irwin saved his most ambitious for last, *Mr. Fox: A Rumination*, a thoughtful, introspective look at George L. Fox, America's first celebrity clown. The play—and this really was a play—began with a *coup de théâtre*, Irwin sitting at a dressing table, putting on clown white and slowly transforming into Fox. Later there was a hilarious variation on Irwin's classic routine with a trunk, with heads popping out of a series of compartments in a chest of drawers. And still later, Geoff Hoyle, another longtime Irwin collaborator, did his own delirious routine as a three-legged man. But the heart of the play was the story of Fox, a self-defeatist who fell from his perch, as did his own signature character, Humpty Dumpty. The play was both historical and autobiographical, as aspects of Irwin merged with his protagonist. "I cry to be present," a line from an Irwin poem written many years ago, was repeated several times in *Mr. Fox*. More than anything, that line encapsulated the performer's dilemma. As Irwin once explained, "When you're onstage, part of you wants to be off as soon as possible. Once you're offstage, everything is in anticipation of the next time you're on."

Among the new plays, one of the most original was *The Flu Season* by Will Eno—an outstanding OOB production. A skillful, self-referential comedy, moving swiftly between reality and illusion, it evoked memories of Pirandello and Ionesco—as well as Albee—while bravely treading its own tightrope. The scene was a psychiatric sanatorium and the characters included two patients (Andrew Benator and Roxanna Hope) who are hopelessly in love, a doctor, a nurse and two supervisory figures named Prologue and Epilogue.

Prologue (Matthew Lawler), of course, introduces the play, welcoming the audience to "a chronicle of love and no love, of interiors and exteriors, of weather, change, entry-level psychology and time; but oh, lo—what chronicle isn't?" Then he repeatedly interrupts the action. Epilogue (David Fitzgerald), adds afterthoughts. As he confides, "I come later, after, more coldly and with a little less optimism." Both provide textual guidance to the playwright. On one level, the play was a blaze of language, but deep inside there was a sensitive story about love and death. A Rude Mechs production, the play was directed by Hal Brooks.

Brooke Berman's *Smashing*, an outstanding OOB production, was a sharp thrust of comedy about celebrity and fiction. Abby, short for Absinthe (Katharine Powell), is the daughter of a famous, egotistical novelist (Joseph Siravo). When she is 16, she has a brief, torrid affair with her father's protégé (David Barlow), himself a hopeful writer. Later, he writes a best-selling novel about this "dirty little girl," and she decides to track him down in London.

Accompanying her is her best friend (Merritt Wever), who has her own fixation on Madonna. So, in London, they have two targets: the tell-all novelist and the inapproachable pop star. In the play there were devastating portraits of the two writers and probing portraits of the two women—and of a third man, a quirky night clerk (Lucas Papaelias) who helps in the Madonna search. Charmingly told, *Smashing* was given a modest but sprightly production by Trip Cullman.

With *Suitcase* Melissa James Gibson returned to Soho Rep and to the territory of her earlier Best Play, *[sic]*—in other words, New York apartment dwellers. In this case, two friends sit in their lofty apartments, not finishing their dissertations, talking to each other on the phone and fending off their boyfriends. The evening was engaging—up to a point. Gibson has a screwball approach to theater, self-referential (in common with *The Flu Season*) and

Storyteller: T.R. Knight and Robert Hogan in Boy. *Photo: James Leynse*

somewhat self-indulgent. There were worthy performances by Christina Kirk (who was in *[sic]*), Jeremy Shamos and Thomas Jay Ryan.

In *Intrigue With Faye* (at MCC Theater), Kate Robin attempted a high-tech look at a couple who make a video record of themselves (and of others) in conflict. Benjamin Bratt and Julianna Margulies were an attractive pair, but their roles were one-dimensional. The most interesting part of the play was on tape, featuring scenes with Swoosie Kurtz and others.

IN ITS 19TH SEASON, Primary Stages opened a new theater at 59 East 59th Street, while retaining its other space on West 45th Street, where it presented A.R. Gurney's *Strictly Academic* and Julia Jordan's *Boy*. The new theater was inaugurated with *The Stendhal Syndrome*, two Terrence McNally one-acts on the interwoven subjects of art and sex. One of the plays, *Full Frontal Nudity*, was new; *Prelude and Liebestod* had been seen before. The new play, in which tourists had diverse reactions to Michelangelo's *David*, was slight and attenuated, but the older play was marked by its intensity. Playing an orchestral conductor clearly patterned after Leonard Bernstein, Richard Thomas captured the character's obsessiveness and magnetism. Isabella Rossellini and Michael Countryman offered helpful support as the conductor's wife and his concertmaster.

Ensemble Studio Theatre was forced to postpone its annual festival of new short plays, but did present the full-length *Roulette* by Paul Weitz, which seemed like a reaction to the film *American Beauty*. At the center was a severely dysfunctional family, in which the father (Larry Bryggman) had to bear most of the burdens. His response was to play Russian roulette, and the first act ended with him blowing his mind away—if not actually killing himself. The play was quixotic as well as intriguing, and Bryggman managed to humanize this outwardly calm lunatic.

George Grizzard's performance was the high point of Nicky Silver's strangely aberrant *Beautiful Child* (at Vineyard Theatre), a play about child abuse. Grizzard was the father in still another dysfunctional family. His son comes home and announces that he is in love with his 8-year-old student. How do the parents—Penny Fuller is the mother—react? Too few questions were asked, and none answered satisfactorily as the play sailed into neverneverland—and ended far out on a limb.

Vineyard Theatre, which co-produced *Avenue Q*, also presented Paula Vogel's *The Long Christmas Ride Home* (a 2003–2004 Best Play) and Christopher Shinn's *Where Do We Live?*, a sprawling play about a collision of New York neighbors. Gay white men are obsessed with sex while black

Family bliss? Mark Blum, Enid Graham, Will McCormack, Catherine Kellner, Randy Graff in The Long Christmas Ride Home. *Photo: Carol Rosegg*

men (in the apartment next door) deal drugs. There were some pertinent moments, as the play ambled from one room to another. But the two situations were never fully integrated (the black story was more interesting), and the play was awkwardly staged. Watching it, I was reminded of Kenneth Lonergan's *This Is Our Youth*, which was far more artful and revealing. Shinn, however, remains a very promising young writer.

ONE-PERSON SHOWS are always a tricky business. I remember Tony Kushner once expressing his reservations about the form: "A Volkswagen pulls up into the center ring of the circus—and one clown steps out. How much fun is that?" This is, I think, a very shrewd remark, but the validity of a one-person show certainly depends on who is playing the part. Performers are indefatigable, and one has only to think of Jefferson Mays in *I Am My Own Wife* to see how well it can be done. David Auburn adapted *The Journals of Mihail Sebastian*, (Auburn's first play since *Proof* won the Pulitzer Prize) from Sebastian's diary about his survival in Romania through successive dictatorships. The play was earnest (as was the actor Stephen Kunken), but it seemed endless, snippets that remained fixed to the page.

In an entirely different vein, there was *Namedropping*, David Rothenberg's entertaining memoir of his life as a Broadway press agent for Alexander Cohen, among others. The evening (at the Mint Theater) was informal and anecdotal, a rambling account of merry (and sometime rueful) escapades. His memories ranged from very bad (after he spent a summer escorting Joan Fontaine through her press obligations, she forgot who he was) to pleasurable Peggy Lee (who sang to him over the telephone), Richard Burton, Elizabeth Taylor and Bette Davis.

IRISH REPERTORY THEATRE had a success with its intimate revival of *Finian's Rainbow*, as did the New Group with its revival of Wallace Shawn's *Aunt Dan and Lemon*. Lili Taylor had an apt air of ingenuousness as Lemon, but Kristen Johnston was unconvincing as Dan—an Oxford don—and some of the others in the cast seemed amateurish. Even in this disappointing production by Scott Elliott, the play remained as startling and disturbing as it was in 1985—when Shawn first enveloped us in his story of insidious fascism.

Spring Storm is a Tennessee Williams play waiting to be discovered. Written in 1937 when Williams was 26, it was submitted the next year to his playwriting class at the University of Iowa. Williams read it aloud, and, he remembered, it was met by "a long and all but unendurable silence." His teacher was dismissive of it. After failing to get it produced, Williams put the play aside. It was never staged in his lifetime, but it is resonant with characters and situations that were to be fully developed in plays of his maturity.

The central character Heavenly Critchfield is an antecedent of Blanche and Alma. The young man whom she loves was later embodied by Stanley Kowalski, among others. With this all in mind, I looked forward with great anticipation to the New York premiere, directed by Coy Middlebrook at Theatre at St. Clement's. Unfortunately, neither the director nor the largely inexperienced cast seemed up to the challenging assignment, with the definite exception of Carlin Glynn, a very experienced actor, who was excellent in the role of Heavenly's aunt.

Meanwhile, other companies continued to explore classics, with Mint Theater Company bringing back its production of *Far and Wide*, a version of Arthur Schnitzler's *Das Weite Land*, and also offering two plays by A.A. Milne, *Mr. Pim Passes By* and *The Truth About Blayds*. Peccadillo Theater Company produces forgotten American classics, presenting plays by Sidney Howard, Philip Barry and Dawn Powell, among others. This season, it worked its magic with Elmer Rice's *Counsellor-at-Law*, a 1931 Broadway hit with Paul Muni and later a John Barrymore movie. What might have seemed dated on the page was brought resoundingly to life in Dan Wackerman's exhilarating production. A full three acts, the play is long, but glided smoothly by, without missing a beat.

Headlining the show was John Rubinstein delivering a superb performance in the title role as a son of the workingclass, who through ambition, charisma and deviousness, rises in the field of law. Even as he tackles the most sordid—and high-paying—cases, he never forgets his roots. Though hardboiled in his dealings with his foes, he remains a soft touch and—like a James Cagney character—devoted to his mother.

Rubinstein's energy and enthusiasm emboldened the rest of the cast and made his character seem completely relevant. He anchored the production, but the other actors were very much in character (and occasionally, as demanded, in caricature): the trophy wife (Beth Glover), the loyal secretary (Lanie MacEwan), the eager receptionist (Tara Sands) and the devoted mother (Mary Carver), to name a few of the 15 actors who inhabited this law office. Happily, they embraced the play not as an artifact but as living organism. Credit also goes to Chris Jones and Amy Bradshaw for their sets and costumes, which kept everything firmly but subtly in period.

WITHOUT QUESTION, THE saddest event of the season—and the greatest loss to the theater—was the suicide of Spalding Gray. In the early 1980s, he emerged from the ensemble of the Wooster Group to perform his monologues from life. Sitting at a table with a glass of water and a spiral notebook or a stack of file cards, he told the hilarious and moving tales of his days as a son, actor, husband and householder.

In plays like *Sex and Death to the Age 14* and *A Personal History of the American Theater*, he made a confessional seem eminently theatrical. He continued to do so as he expanded his vision in *Swimming to Cambodia*, a two-part rumination inspired by his experience as an actor in the movie, *The Killing Fields*. It did not matter if he was onstage at the minuscule Performing Garage or in the vast Vivian Beaumont Theater at Lincoln Center. What he did—even before a large audience—never wavered and remained true to his self-image while always retaining his ironic sense of humor. Gray was a true original—representing the best of Off Off Broadway. When his body was finally found, I thought, if only Spalding had lived, what an amazing story he would have to tell us.

PLAYS PRODUCED OFF OFF BROADWAY AND ADDITIONAL NYC PRESENTATIONS

○○○○○

Compiled by Vivian Cary Jenkins with Lara D. Nielsen

BELOW IS A comprehensive sampling of 2003–04 Off Off Broadway productions in New York. There is no definitive "Off Off Broadway" area or qualification. To try to define or regiment it would be untrue to its fluid, often exploratory purpose. This listing of hundreds of works produced by scores of OOB groups is as inclusive as reliable sources allow. This section pertains to professional theater in New York that is covered by neither Broadway nor full Off Broadway contracts.

The more active and established producing groups are identified in **bold face type**, in alphabetical order, with artistic policies and the names of its leaders given whenever possible. Each group's 2003–04 schedule, with emphasis on new plays, is listed with play titles in CAPITAL LETTERS. Often these are works-in-progress with changing scripts, casts and directors, sometimes without an engagement of record (but an opening or early performance date is included when available).

Many of these Off Off Broadway groups have long since outgrown a merely experimental status and offer programs that are the equal—and in many cases the superior—of anything in the New York theater. These listings include special contractual arrangements such as the showcase code, letters of agreement (allowing for longer runs and higher admission prices than usual) and, closer to the edge of commercial theater, so-called "mini-contracts." In the list below, available data has been compiled from press representatives, company managers and publications of record.

A large selection of developing groups and other shows that made appearances Off Off Broadway during the season under review appears under the "Miscellaneous" heading at the end of this listing.

Amas Musical Theatre. Dedicated to bringing people of all races, creeds, colors and national origins together through the performing arts. Donna Trinkoff producing director.

FROM MY HOMETOWN. Musical with book by Lee Summers, Ty Stephens and Herbert Rawlings Jr.; music by Messrs. Summers, Stephens, Will Barrow and others. June 19, 2003. Directed by Kevin Ramsey; choreography, Leslie Dockery, Kevin Ramsey; scenery, Matthew Myhrum; costumes, Deborah A. Cheretun; lighting, Aaron Spivey; sound, Ryan Powers; music direction and orchestrations, Jo Lynn Burks. With Kevin R. Free, André Garner, Rodney Hicks. Presented in association with Ben Blake and Mr. Summers.

Dark birds: Clark Gregg, Chris Bauer and Mary McCann in The Night Heron. *Photo: Carol Rosegg*

SEX! THE MUSICAL. Musical by David Coffman. October 27, 2003. Directed by Devanand Janki.

THE FUNKENTINE RAPTURE. Musical with book by Lee Summers and Ben Blake; music and lyrics by Mr. Summers. November 3, 2003.

SPIN. Musical with book, music and lyrics by M. Kilburg Reedy. November 17, 2003. Directed by Matt Morrow.

SIX WOMEN WITH BRAIN DEATH. Musical with book by Cheryl Benge, Christy Brandt, Rosanna E. Coppedge, Valerie Fagan, Ross Freese, Mark Houston, Sandee Johnson, Peggy Pharr Wilson; music and lyrics by Mr. Houston. December 8, 2003. Directed by Matt M. Morrow.

BLACKOUT. Musical with book and lyrics by Sharleen Cooper Cohen; music by Debra Barsha. December 4, 2003. Directed by Phillip George.

Atlantic Theater Company. Produces new plays and reinterpretations of classics that speak in a contemporary voice on issues reflecting today's society. Neil Pepe artistic director.

THE NIGHT HERON. By Jez Butterworth. October 7, 2003. Directed by Neil Pepe; scenery, Walt Spangler; costumes, Laura Bauer; lighting, Tyler Micoleau; sound, Scott Myers. With Chris Bauer, Clark Gregg, Mary McCann, Damian Young, Jordan Lage, Joe Stipek, Jim Frangione.

FRAME 312. By Keith Reddin. December 11, 2003. Directed by Karen Kohlhaas; scenery, Walt Spangler; costumes, Mimi O'Donnell; lighting, Robert Perry; sound, Scott Myers. With Mary Beth Peil, Larry Bryggman, Maggie Kiley, Ana Reeder, Mandy Siegfried, Greg Stuhr.

SEA OF TRANQUILITY. By Howard Korder. February 25, 2004. Directed by Neil Pepe; scenery, Santo Loquasto; costumes, Kaye Voyce; lighting, David Weiner; sound, Scott Myers;

music, David Yazbek. With Dylan Baker, Patricia Kalember, Jordan Lage, Todd Weeks, Betsy Aidem, Heidi Armbruster, Liz Elkins, Jason Fuchs, Lizbeth Mackay, Matthew Saldivar, Rafael Sardina.

Brooklyn Academy of Music Next Wave Festival. Since 1983, this annual three-month festival has presented hundreds of performing arts events, including dozens world premieres. Featuring leading international artists, it is one of the world's largest festivals of contemporary performing arts. Alan H. Fishman chairman of the board, Karen Brooks Hopkins president, Joseph V. Melillo executive producer.

HENRY IV, PART ONE. By William Shakespeare. September 30, 2003. Directed by Richard Maxwell; scenery, Stephanie Nelson; costumes, Kaye Voyce; lighting, Jane Cox. With the New York City Players.

THE SOUND OF OCEAN. By U Theatre. October 7, 2003. Directed and choreographed by Liu Ching-Ming; scenery, Liu Chung-Hsing; costumes, Yip Kam-Tim; lighting, Lin Keh-Hua, music, Wong Chee-Mun.

BOBRAUSCHENBERGAMERICA. By Charles L. Mee. October 14, 2003. Directed by Anne Bogart; costumes and scenery, James Schuette; lighting, Brian H. Scott; sound, Darron L. West. With the SITI Company. Presented in association with True Love Productions.

THE NEW YORKERS. By Michael Gordon, David Lang and Julia Wolfe; with texts by Lou Reed. October 22, 2003. Directed by Barry Edelstein; lighting, Jane Cox; sound, Andrew Cotton; projections, Jan Hartley, Michael Clark, Ben Katchor, Laurie Olinder; video, Doug Aitken, William Wegman. With Bang on a Can All-Stars, Ethel, Michael Gordon Band, Theo Bleckmann.

AINADAMAR. Opera with book by David Henry Hwang; music by Osvaldo Golijov. October 28, 2003. Directed by Chay Yew; scenery, Daniel Ostling; costumes, Anita Yavich; lighting, Kevin Adams; conductor, Miguel Harth-Bedoya. With Dawn Upshaw, Tanglewood Music Center Vocal Fellows and Orchestra.

THE HANGING MAN. By Phelim McDermott, Lee Simpson and Julian Crouch. November 4, 2003. Directed by Messrs. McDermott, Simpson and Crouch; scenery, Messrs. McDermott, Simpson, Crouch and Phil Eddolls; costumes, Stephen Snell; lighting, Colin Grenfell; sound, Darron L. West.

ALLADEEN. By Keith Khan, Marianne Weems and Ali Zaidi; with text by Martha Baer. December 2, 2003. Directed by Ms. Weems; scenery, Mr. Kahn and Mr. Zaidi; lighting, Jennifer Tipton; sound, Dan Dobson; video, Christopher Kondek; music; Shrikanth Sriram (Shri).

Classic Stage Company. Reinventing and revitalizing the classics for contemporary audiences. Barry Edelstein and Brian Kulick artistic directors, Anne Tanaka producing director.

SAVANNAH BAY. By Marguerite Duras; translated by Barbara Bray. June 10, 2003. Directed by Les Waters; scenery, Myung Hee Cho; costumes, Ilona Somogyi; lighting, Robert Wierzel; sound, Darron L. West. With Kathleen Chalfant, Marin Ireland.

THE FIRST LOOK FESTIVAL. October 1–12, 2003.

THE JEW OF MALTA. By Christopher Marlowe. Directed by Brian Kulick. With Ron Liebman.

ARDEN OF FAVERSHAM. By Anonymous. Directed by Erica Schmidt. With Frances McDormand.

VOLPONE. By Ben Jonson. Directed by Michael Sexton. With F. Murray Abraham.

RICHARD III. By William Shakespeare. Directed by Barry Edelstein. With John Turturro, Julianna Margulies, Lynn Cohen, Brian Keane, Ronald Guttman, Peter Jacobson, Daniel Oreskes, James Joseph O'Neill, Phyllis Somerville, Stephen Barker Turner.

THE MYSTERIES. Adapted by Dario Fo, Mikhail Bulgakov, Tony Harrison and Borislav Pekic from the Wakefield and York Cycles. January 8, 2004. Directed by Brian Kulick;

Lear-y look: Leroy Logan in Antigone. *Photo: Paula Court*

scenery, Mark Wendland; costumes, Mattie Ullrich; lighting, Kevin Adams; sound, Darron L. West. With Bill Buell, Mario Campanaro, Michael Potts, Carmen Roman, John Rothman, Jennifer Roszell, Michael Stuhlbarg, Sam Tsoutsouvas, Chandler Williams.

ANTIGONE. By Mac Wellman. April 27, 2004. Directed by Paul Lazar; choreography by Annie-B Parson; scenery, Joanne Howard; costumes, Claudia Stephens; lighting, Jay Ryan; sound, Jane Shaw and Ms. Parson; music, Cynthia Hopkins. With Nancy Ellis, Molly Hickok, Leroy Logan, Dierdre O'Connell, Rebecca Wisocky.

Ensemble Studio Theatre. Membership organization of playwrights, actors, directors and designers dedicated to supporting individual theater artists and developing new works. Stages more than 300 projects each season, ranging from readings to fully mounted productions. Curt Dempster artistic director.

MARATHON 2003 (SERIES B). June 1–21, 2003.

HI THERE, MR. MACHINE. By Leslie Ayvazian. Directed by Leigh Silverman. With Ms. Ayvazian.

THE CHANGING OF THE GUARD. By Amy Staats. Directed by Mark Roberts. With Julie Leedes, Diana Ruppe, Scotty Bloch.

WASHED UP ON THE POTOMAC. By Lynn Rosen. Directed by Eileen Myers. With Anne Torsiglieri, Sean Sutherland, Maria Thayer, Joan Rosenfels, William Franke.

WATER MUSIC. By Tina Howe. Directed by Pam MacKinnon. With Lizbeth Mackay, Juan Carlos Hernandez, Laura Heisler.

WOMAN AT A THRESHOLD, BECKONING. By John Guare. Directed by Will Pomerantz. With Andrew Weems, Miriam Laube, Chris Ceraso, Ted Neustadt, Michael Cullen, Michael Thomas Holmes, India Cooper, Jay Patterson.

THICKER THAN WATER: NEW ONE-ACT PLAYS. March 4–28, 2004.

WATER-BORN. By Edith L. Freni. Directed by Brian Roff. With Annie McNamara, Michael Szeles.

CHARLIE BLAKE'S BOAT. By Graeme Gillis. Directed by Jamie Richards. With Leo Lauer, Katie Barrett.

D.C. By Daria Polatin. Directed by R.J. Tolan. With Shana Dowdeswell, Gideon Glick, Joanna Parson.

WELCOME BACK, BUDDY COMBS. By Ben Rosenthal. Directed by Abigail Zealey Bess. With Denny Bess, Diana Ruppe, Johnny Giacalone.

FIRST LIGHT 2004. April 9–May 3, 2004.

TOOTH AND CLAW. By Michael Hollinger. Directed by Dave P. Moore. With Gloria Biegler, Steven Crossley, Flora Diaz, Jojo Gonzalez, Sebastian LaCause, Ruben Luque, Nathan Perez, Anthony Ruiz, Joaquin Torres, Noel Velez.

DAYS OF HAPPINESS. By Arthur Giron. Directed by David Shookhoff.

THE MONKEY ROOM. By Kevin Fisher. Directed by Mark Roberts.

L'ORNITOTERO: THE BIRD MACHINE. By Carlo Adinolfi and Renee Phillipi.

GUTENBERG: THE MUSICAL. By Scott Brown and Anthony King.

PARADISE OF EARTHWORMS. By David Valdes Greenwood. Directed by R.J. Tolan.

BLACKFOOT NOTES. By Rajendra Ramoon Maharaj. Directed by Kirsten Berkman.

GIRL SCIENCE. By Larry Loebell.

TWIN PRIMES. By Alex Lewin.

THE SEPARATION OF BLOOD. By Bridgette Wimberly.

THE BONES OF GIANTS. By Cheryl L. Davis.

PROGRESS IN FLYING. By Lynn Rosen.

Intar. Identifies, develops and presents the talents of gifted Hispanic-American theater artists and multicultural visual artists. Max Ferrá, Michael John Garcés producing artistic directors.

FAITH, HOPE AND CHARITY. By Alberto Pedro; translated by Caridad Svich. June 5, 2003. Directed by Max Ferrá; scenery Van Santvoord; costumes, Ali Turns; lighting, Chris Dallos; sound, David M. Lawson; music, Marc Anthony Thompson. With Maria Cellario, Judith Delgado, Dana Manno, Mizan Nunes. Presented in association with New Federal Theatre.

THE COOK. By Eduardo Machado. November 20, 2003. Directed by Michael John Garcés; scenery, Antje Ellermann; costumes, Elizabeth Hope Clancy; lighting, Kirk Bookman; sound, David M. Lawson; music, José Conde. With Maggie Bofill, Zabryna Guevara, Jason Madera, Jason Quarles, Nilaja Sun.

Irish Repertory Theatre. Brings works by Irish and Irish-American playwrights to a wider audience and develops new works focusing on a wide range of cultural experience. Charlotte Moore artistic director, Ciarán O'Reilly producing director.

PLAYING BURTON. By Mark Jenkins. August 14, 2003. Directed by Mr. Jenkins; scenery and lighting, Mark Hankla; costumes, David Toser; sound, Dan Donnelly. With Brian Mallon. Presented in association with Redbranch Productions.

THE COLLEEN BAWN. By Dion Boucicault. October 19, 2003. Directed by Charlotte Moore; scenery, James Morgan; costumes, Linda Fisher; lighting, Brian Nason; sound, Zachary Williamson. With Paul Vincent Black, James Cleveland, Terry Donnelly, Laura James Flynn,

George Heslin, John Keating, Colin Lane, Declan Mooney, Heather O'Neill, Ciarán O'Reilly, Caroline Winterson.

CHRISTMAS WITH TOMMY MAKEM. December 4, 2003. Directed by Charlotte Moore. With Tommy and Rory Makem.

FINIAN'S RAINBOW. Musical with book by E.Y. Harburg and Fred Saidy; music by Burton Lane; lyrics by Mr. Harburg; adapted by Charlotte Moore. April 15, 2004. Directed by Ms. Moore; choreography, Barry McNabb; scenery, James Morgan; costumes, David Toser; lighting, Mary Jo Dondlinger. With Mark Aldrich, Melissa Errico; Jonathan Freeman, Malcolm Gets, Jonathan Hadley, Eric Jackson, Jayne Ackley Lynch, Kimberly Dawn Neumann, Kerry O'Malley, John Sloman, David Staller, Joacquin Stevens, Max von Essen, Terri White.

Jean Cocteau Repertory. Founded by Eve Adamson in 1971, the company is dedicated to the production of classic theatre by a resident company of actors. David Fuller producing artistic director.

THE THREEPENNY OPERA. Musical with book and lyrics by Bertolt Brecht; music by Kurt Weill; adapted by Marc Blitzstein. September 7, 2003. Directed by David Fuller; scenery, Roman Tatarowicz; costumes, Joanne Haas; lighting, Giles Hogya. With Natalie Ballesteros, Harris Berlinsky, Danny Dempsey, Eileen Glenn, Abe Goldfarb, Angus Hepburn, Kate Holland, Brian Lee Huynh, Marlene May, Sara Mayer, Timothy McDonough, Joey Piscopo, Elise Stone, Amy Lee Williams, Chad A. Suitts.

LYSISTRATA. By Aristophanes; translated and adapted by David Lee Jiranek. November 2, 2003. Directed by David Fuller; scenery, James F. Wolk; costumes, Margaret McKowen; sound and music, Guy Sherman/Aural Fixation. With Elise Stone, Eileen Glenn, Amanda Jones, Marlene May, Carolyn Ratteray, Jolie Garrett, Brian Lee Huynh, Allen Hale, Angus Hepburn, Michael Surabian, Harris Berlinsky, Abe Goldfarb.

DOÑA ROSITA THE SPINSTER. By Federico Garcia Lorca; adapted by Gwynne Edwards. January 15, 2004. Directed by Ernest Johns; scenery, Roman Tatarowicz; costumes, Margaret McKowen; lighting, David Kniep; sound and music, Charles Berigan; With Natalie Ballesteros, Danaher Dempsey, Eileen Glenn, Amanda Jones, Marlene May, Sara Mayer, Timothy McDonough, Carolyn Rattaray, Craig Smith, Elise Stone, Michael Surabian, Amy Lee Williams.

THE WILD DUCK. By Henrik Ibsen; translated by Rolf Fjelde. February 29, 2004. Directed by Eve Adamson; scenery, Robert Klingelhoefer; costumes, Margaret McKowen, Joel Ebarb; lighting, Ms. Adamson; sound and music, Ellen Mandel. With Bill Fairbairn, Chad A. Suitts, Eileen Glenn, Harris Berlinsky, Tim Morton, Michael Surabian, Angela Madden, Erin Scanlon, Danaher Dempsey, Allen Hale, Sara Jeanne Asselin, Dan Zisson.

THE BOURGEOIS GENTLEMAN. By Molière; translated by Rod McLucas. April 25, 2004. Directed by Rod McLucas; scenery, Robert Martin; costumes, Robin I. Shane; lighting, Wendy Luedtke; music, Raphael Crystal. With Sara Jeanne Asselin, Natalie Ballesteros, Pascal Beauboeuf, Danaher Dempsey, Bill Fairbairn, Allen Hale, Kristina Klebe, Marlene May, Sara Mayer, Timothy McDonough, Ralph Petrarca, Carolyn Ratteray, Lindsey White, Angus Hepburn.

La MaMa Experimental Theatre Club (ETC). A workshop for experimental theater of all kinds. Ellen Stewart founder and director.

Schedule included:

CALENDAR OF STONE. By Denise Stoklos. June 12, 2003. Directed by Ms. Stoklos; scenery, Thais Stoklos Kignel and Leonardo Ceolin; costumes, Marie Toscano; lighting, Pedro Kroupa and Antonia Ratto; sound, Ms. Stoklos, Piata Stoklos Kignel, Thais Stoklos Kignel and Antonia Ratto. With Ms. Stoklos.

MARGA GOMEZ'S INTIMATE DETAILS. By Ms. Gomez. June 19, 2003. Directed by David Schweizer. With Ms. Gomez.

SWAN. By Oleh Lysheha; translated by Mr. Lysheha and James Brasfield. June 19, 2003. Directed by Virlana Tkacz; scenery, costumes and lighting, Watoku Ueno; video, Andrea Odezynska. With Andrew Coltreaux Soomi Kim.

TARGET AUDIENCE (THE CODE OF THE WESTERN). By Jim Neu. September 19, 2003. Directed by Keith McDermott; scenery, David Fritz; costumes, Angela Wendt; lighting, Arthur Adair, music, Harry Mann; projections, Charles Dennis. With Mr. Neu, Deborah Auer, Bill Rice.

THE BACCHAE: TORN TO PIECES. By Euripides. October 9, 2003. Directed by Susan Fenichell; scenery and costumes, David Zinn; lighting, Mary Louise Geiger; music, David Russell. With Ellen McLaughlin, Amy Lee Maguire, Matt Pepper, David Russell, Paul Savas.

THE MIDDLE BEAST. By Joe Kodeih, Elie Karam and Marc Kodeih. October 10, 2003. Directed by Mr. Kodeih; With Mr. Kodeih, Ms. Karam, Mario Bassil, Jacques Maroun, Taranahsa Wallace.

FOREIGN AIDS. By Pieter-Dirk Uys. October 23, 2003. With Mr. Uys.

PHILOKTETES. By John Jesurun. October 23, 2003. With Jeff Weiss.

HO'ICHI, THE EAR LESS. By Ryo Onodera; based on a Japanese ghost fable by Yakumo Koizumi. October 23, 2003. Directed by Kanako Hiyama; music, Yukio Tsuji. With Tom Lee, Lars Preece.

CHANG IN A VOID MOON. By John Jesurun. October 31, 2003. Directed by Mr. Jesurun. With John Hagan, Donna Herman, Ruth Gray, Helena White, Anna Kohler, Sanghi Wagner, Oscar de la Fe Colon, Lisa Herman, Nicky Paraiso, Rebecca Moore, Greg Mehrten, Mary Shultz, Black-Eyed Susan, Ching Valdes-Aran, David Cale.

HENRY 5. By William Shakespeare; adapted by Thaddeus Phillips. November 3, 2003. Directed by Tatiana Mallarino; scenery, Mr. Phillips. With Mr. Phillips.

WORLD WAR NOW OR HOW SEYMOUR GOT HIS GUN OFF. By Mark Eisenstein. November 11, 2003. Directed by Tom O'Horgan. With Edward Asner, Estelle Parsons, Brian Backer, Charles Balcer, Brian Dusseau, Joseph Del Giodice, Bobby Faust, Richard Hirschfeld, Peter Linari, Katarina Oost, Nick Taylor.

BUTT-CRACK BINGO. By Jack Bump. November 13, 2004. Directed by David Soul. With Brian Bickerstaff, Jeff Biehl, Danny Camiel, Alien Comic (Tom Murrin), Laura Flanagan, Gibson Frasier, Laura Kindred, April Sweeney, Conrad Rheims, Eve Udesky.

RAMAYANA 2K3. By Robert A. Prior. November 20, 2003. Directed by Mr. Prior; choreography, Stephen Hues; costumes, Mr. Prior, Lisa Leighton; lighting, Jerry Browning; sound, Scott Jennings; projections, Yo Suzuki. With Fabulous Monsters Performance Group.

THE GOOD FAITH: 1940–1990. Musical with book, music and lyrics by Harold Dean James. November 20, 2003. Directed by Mr. James; choreography, Guillermo Resto. With Paul Albe, Jamie Leigh Allen, Jason Blaine, Daniel Clymer, Erika Dioniso, Linus Gelber, Grant Machan, Joe Matheson, Gheree O'Bannon, Rachel Ponce, Christiane Szabo, Christa Victoria, Cezar Williams.

GLAMOUR, GLORY AND GOLD. By Jackie Curtis. December 4, 2003. Directed by Joe Preston. With D'Arcy Drollinger, Clayton Dean Smith, Janine Kyanko, John Patrick Kelly, Laverne Cox, Bryan Safi, Boris Kievsky, Christopher Ross.

WOZA ALBERT! By Percy Mtwa, Mbongeni Ngema, Barney Simon. December 16, 2003. Directed by Lucky Ngema; with Patrick Ssenjovu, Lucky Ngema.

THE BROTHERS KARAMAZOV. By Fyodor Dostoyevsky; adapted by Alexander Harrington. January 2, 2004. Directed by Mr. Harrington; scenery and lighting, Tony Penna; costumes, Rebecca J. Bernstein; fight direction, J. David Brimmer. With Gary Andrews, Steven L. Barron, Anthony Cataldo, Stafford Clark-Price, J. Anthony Crane, Alessio Franko, Antony Hagopian, Jim Iseman III, Danielle Langlois, Christopher Lukas, J.M. McDonough, Chris Meyer, Winslow Mohr, George Morafetis, Peter Oliver, Jennifer Opalcz, Margo Skinner, Yaakov Sullivan, Sorrel Tomlinson, Svetlana Yankovskaya.

OUT AT SEA and STRIPTEASE. By Slawomir Mrozek; *Out at Sea* translated by Amiel Melnick and Asha Oniszczuk; *Striptease* translated by Lola Gruenthal. January 4, 2004. Directed by Paul Bargetto; scenery, Young-ju Baik; costumes, Oana Botez-Ban; lighting, Paul Bargetto. With Cornel Gabara, Troy Lavalle, Paul Todaro, Nora Laudani.

LINAS IS KINSKI. By Linas Phillips. January 8, 2004. Directed by Mr. Phillips; scenery, Chris Skeens; sound and video, Mr. Phillips. With Mr. Phillips, Larissa Dooley, Jim Fletcher.

DEFENSES OF PRAGUE. By Sophia Murashkovsky. January 22, 2004. Directed by Leslie Lee; choreography, Stas Kmiec; scenery, Dara Wishingrad; costumes, Rosemary Ponzo; lighting, Russell Drapkin; sound, Nick Moore. With Walter Krochmal, Nicholas Mongiardo-Cooper, Angelica Ayala, Nina Savinsky, Julie Saad, Vina Less, Maria Hurdle, Chris Alonzo, Dan Kastoriano, Maya Levy, Gary Andrews, Malia Miller, Channie Waites, Robert Eggers, Meghan Andrews, Erin Lehy.

LAST SUPPER. By Lars Norén; translated by Marita Lindholm-Gochman. January 22, 2004. Directed by Zishan Ugurlu; scenery and lighting, Jeremy Morris; costumes, Kimberly Matela; sound and music, Paul Bothén; With Raïna von Waldenburg, Tullan Holmqvist, Dan Illian, Olle Agélii.

KLUB KA: THE BLUES LEGEND. By James V. Hatch and Suzanne Noguere. February 5, 2004. Directed by Tisch Jones; scenery and lighting, David Thayer; costumes, Jenny Nutting; sound, Anton Jones. With Kevin "B.F." Burt, Janice Bishop, Michael Kachingwe, Frankie Cordero, Emily Happe, Eric Forsythe, Cary Gant, Christa Victoria, Amy Olson, Dara Bengelsdorf, Yaritza Pizarro, Rod Bladel, Sean Christopher Lewis.

ODYSSEY: THE HOMECOMING. By Theodora Skipitares. February 12, 2004. Directed by Ms. Skipitares; lighting, Pat Dignan; music, Arnold Dreyblatt; with Michael Kelly, Chris Maresca, Alisa Mello, Bernadette Witzack, Bronwyn Bittetti, Amanda Villalobos.

EXPIRATION DATE. By Abla Khoury. February 12, 2004. Directed by Ms. Khoury; lighting, Federico Restrepo. With Zishan Ugurlu, Abla Khoury, Najla Said, Patrick Ssenjovu, Chris Wild, Sara Galassini, Denise Greber, Federico Restrepo.

THE WARRIOR'S SISTER. By Virlana Tkacz, Sayan Zhambalov and Erhena Zhambalov. March 6, 2004. Directed by Ms. Tkacz, Mr. Zhambalov, Ms. Zhambalov; scenery, costumes and lighting, Watoku Ueno; choreography, Shigeko Suga. With Mr. Zhambalov, Ms. Zhambalov, Victor Zhalsaov, Bayarto Endonov, Eunice Wong, Andrew Coltreaux, Hettiene Park, Meredith Wright.

Family plan: Anna Paquin, Josh Charles and Melissa Leo in The Distance From Here. *Photo: Dixie Sheridan*

ANCHORPECTORIS. By Gerald Thomas. March 6, 2004. Directed by Mr. Thomas; scenery, Mr. Thomas; sound, David Lawson. With Nikki Alikakos, George Bartenieff, Chantal Bushelle, Sonia Elaine Butler, Sean P. Doran, Fabiana Guglielmetti, Kate Holland, Josh Mann, Stephen Nisbet, Kila Packett, Stacey Raymond, Tom Walker.

HOUSE/BOY 2004. By Nicky Paraiso. April 22, 2004. Directed by Ralph B. Peña; choreography, Chris Yon; scenery, Donald Eastman; costumes, Gabriel Berry. With Mr. Paraiso.

THE LIFE AND DEATH OF TOM THUMB THE GREAT; adapted from the book by Henry Fielding; music by Brendan Connelly. May 13, 2004. Directed by Brooke O'Harra; choreography, Barbara Lanciers; costumes, Juliann Kroboth; lighting, Justin Townsend; video, Bilal Khan. With Brian Bickerstaff, Suli Holum, Matthew Stadelmann, Mary Regan, Cecile Evans, David B. Gould, Lula Graves, Lauren Brown, Tatiana Pavela, Matt Shapiro, Matt Berger, Juliana Sanderson.

THE CODE OF THE WESTERN RIDES AGAIN. By Jim Neu. May 13, 2004. Directed by Keith McDermott; scenery, David Fritz. With Mr. Neu, Deborah Auer, Bill Rice.

THE LIFE AND TIMES OF LEE HARVEY OSWALD. By Vít Horejš. May 27, 2004. Directed by Mr. Horejš; choreography, Martha Tornay; costumes, Theresa Linnihan. With Deborah Beshaw, Michelle Beshaw, David Friend, Mr. Horejš, Ron Jones, Sarah Lafferty, Theresa Linnihan, Emily Wilson, Benjamin Caron.

Lincoln Center Festival 2003. An annual international summer arts festival offering classic and contemporary work. Nigel Redden director.

THE ANGEL PROJECT. By Deborah Warner. July 8, 2003. Directed by Ms. Warner; scenery, Tom Pye; costumes, John Bright.

MYTHOS. By Rina Yerushalmi; translated by Aharon Shabtai and Shimon Buzaglo. July 8, 2003. Directed by Ms. Yerushami; scenery, Rafi Segal and Eyal Weizman; costumes, Anna Chrouscheva; lighting, Avi-Yona Bueno; projections, Idan Levy. With Titina K. Assefa, Noa Barkai, Gal Barzilay, Maya Ben Avraham, Ruthie Ben-Efrat, Avraham Cohen, Barak Gonen, Emmanuel Hannon, Michal Kalman, Yehuda Lazarovich, Noa Raban, Yousef Sweid, Karin Tepper, Yoav Yeffet. Presented in association with Itim Theatre Ensemble and the Cameri Theatre of Tel Aviv.

PANSORI. Five solo Korean epics. *Heungboga*. July 16, 2003. With Kim Soo-yeon. *Sugungga*. July 17, 2003. With Cho Tong-dal. *Simcheongga*. July 18, 2003. With Kim Young-ja. *Jeokbyeokga*. July 19, 2003. With Kim Il-goo. *Chunhyangga*. July 20, 2003. With Ahn Suk-sun.

THE ORPHAN OF ZHAO. Chinese epic presented in separate Chinese- and English-language productions; based on the play by Ji Juan-Xiang; English adaptation by David Greenspan. July 19, 2003. Directed by Chen Shi-Zheng; music by Stephin Merritt. With David Patrick Kelly, Rob Campbell, William Youmans, Jenny Bacon.

Mabou Mines. Mabou Mines, established in 1970, is a theater company that creates new works based on original and existing texts. The current artistic directorate includes Lee Breuer, Sharon Fogarty, Ruth Maleczech, Frederick Neumann and Terry O'Reilly.

DOLLHOUSE. By Henrik Ibsen; adapted by Lee Breuer. November 19, 2003. Directed by Mr. Breuer; choreography, Martha Clarke, Eamonn Farrel, Clove Galilee, Erik Liberman, Jane Catherine Shaw, Norman Snow; scenery, Narelle Sissons; costumes, Meganne George; lighting, Mary Louise Geiger; sound, Edward Cosla; puppetry, Jane Catherine Shaw. With Mark Povinelli, Maude Mitchell, Kristopher Medina, Honora Ferguson, Ricardo Gil, Lisa Harris, Tate Katie Mitchell, Zachary Houppert Nunns, Matthew Forker, Sophie Forker.

MCC Theater. Dedicated to the promotion of emerging writers, actors, directors and theatrical designers. Robert LuPone and Bernard Telsey artistic directors, William Cantler associate artistic director.

INTRIGUE WITH FAYE. By Kate Robin. June 11, 2003. Directed by Jim Simpson; scenery, Riccardo Hernández; costumes, Fabio Toblini; lighting, Robert Wierzel; music and sound, Fabian Obispo; video, Dennis Diamond. With Julianna Margulies, Benjamin Bratt; video appearances by Michael Gaston, Craig Bierko, Jenna Lamia, Gretchen Mol, Swoosie Kurtz, Tom Noonan.

BRIGHT IDEAS. By Eric Coble. November 12, 2003. Directed by John Rando; scenery, Rob Odorisio; costumes, Gregory Gale; lighting, James Vermeulen; sound, Fabian Obispo. With Orlagh Cassidy, Colman Domingo, Paul Fitzgerald, Seana Kofoed, Linda Marie Larson.

FROZEN. By Bryony Lavery. March 18, 2004. Directed by Doug Hughes; scenery, Hugh Landwehr; costumes, Catherine Zuber; lighting, Clifton Taylor; music and sound, David Van Tieghem. With Swoosie Kurtz, Brían F. O'Byrne, Laila Robins, Sam Kitchin. Transferred to a Broadway run at the Circle in the Square Theatre (5/4/2004; 32 performances as of 5/31/2004). See Plays Produced on Broadway section in this volume. A 2003–04 *Best Plays* choice (see essay by Anne Marie Welsh in this volume).

THE DISTANCE FROM HERE. By Neil LaBute. May 6, 2004. Directed by Michael Greif; scenery, Louisa Thompson; costumes, Angela Wendt; lighting, James Vermuelen; sound and music, Robert Kaplowitz; fight direction, Rick Sordelet. With Amelia Alvarez, Ian Brennan, Josh Charles, Melissa Leo, Logan Marshall-Green, Anna Paquin, Alison Pill, Mark Webber.

Mint Theater Company. Committed to bringing new vitality to worthy but neglected plays. Jonathan Bank artistic director.

THE DAUGHTER-IN-LAW. By D.H. Lawrence. June 15, 2003. Directed by Martin L. Platt; scenery, Bill Clarke; costumes, Holly Poe Durbin; lighting, Jeff Nellis. With Mikel Sarah Lambert, Jodie Lynne McClintock, Angela Reed, Peter Russo, Gareth Saxe.

FAR AND WIDE (DAS WEITE LAND). By Arthur Schnitzler; adapted by Jonathan Bank. September 18, 2003. Directed by Mr. Bank; scenery, Vicki R. Davis; costumes, Theresa Squire; lighting, Josh Bradford; sound, Stefan Jacobs. With Kate Arrington, Kelly AuCoin, Ezra Barnes, Lisa Bostnar, Lee Bryant, Anne-Marie Cusson, Joshua Decker, Kurt Everhart, Ken Kliban, Allen Lewis Rickman, Hans Tester, Matthew Wilkas, Pilar Witherspoon.

National Actors Theatre. Formed in 1991 to present fresh and illuminating productions of classic plays, as well as significant, lesser-known works. Now involved in a cultural and educational partnership with Pace University in downtown Manhattan. Tony Randall artistic director.

RIGHT YOU ARE. By Luigi Pirandello; translated by Eric Bentley. December 7, 2003. Directed by Fabrizio Melano; scenery, James Noone; costumes, Noel Taylor; lighting, Kirk Bookman; sound, Richard Fitzgerald. With Yolande Bavan, Brennan Brown, Fred Burrell, Edmund C. Davys, Mireille Enos, Herb Foster, Penny Fuller, Peter Ganim, Jurian Hughes, Addie Johnson, Florencia Lozano, Peter Maloney, Natalie Norwick, Tony Randall, Henry Strozier, Maria Tucci.

New Dramatists. An organization devoted to playwrights. Members may use the facilities for projects ranging from private readings of their material to public scripts-in-hand readings. Listed below are readings open to the public during the season under review. Todd London artistic director, Joel K. Ruark executive director.

TEATRO MARIA. By Lonnie Carter. June 23, 2003. Directed by Loy Arcenas. With Michael Stuhlbarg, Celia Howard, Bree Elrod, Charles Randall, Michael Matthis, April Matthis, John Wernke.

MOVE. By Brooke Berman. June 26, 2003. Directed by Randy White. With Dee Pelletier, Josh Hecht, Marin Ireland, Michael Chernus, Michael Stuhlbarg.

INFINITUDE. By Sung Rno. June 26, 2003. Directed by Linsay Firman. With Paul H. Juhn, Sue Jean Kim, Michi Barall, Tom Lee, Andy Pang, C.S. Lee.

SICK AGAIN. By Gordon Dahlquist. June 30, 2003. Directed by Randy White. With Scott Bryer, Laura Flanagan, Patrick McNulty, Melinda Wade.

New Resident Event. September 8, 2003. DARK YELLOW. By Julia Jordan. With Paul Sparks, Isaac Maddow-Zimet. A TEXAS CAROL. By Daniel Alexander Jones. With Cindy Creekmore, Gretchen Lee Krich, Ana Parea, Randolph Curtis Rand, T. Ryder Smith. CUSTOMS. By Michael John Garcés. Directed by Sturgis Warner. With Lourdes Martin, Andres Mudor, Matthew Maguire. APPARITION. By Anne Washburn. Directed by Linsay Firman. With T. Ryder Smith, Scott Blumenthal. A MONOLOGUE. By Gary Sunshine. Directed by Trip Cullman. With Glenn Fitzgerald. THE HOLY MOTHER OF HADLEY NEW YORK. By Barbara Wiechmann.With Gretchen Lee Krich, Matthew Macguire. PAINTED SNAKE IN A PAINTED CHAIR. By Ellen Maddow. With Diane Beckett, Lizzie Olesker, Ms. Maddow, Randolph Curtis Rand, Gary Brownlee.

PLACES PLEASE: ACT ONE. By Warren Kliewer. September 16, 2003. Directed by Cliff Goodwin. With Michèle LaRue.

BLASTED. By Sarah Kane. September 16, 2003. Directed by Jon Schumacher. With Marin Ireland, Michael Cumpsty, Gareth Saxe, Rachel Aronson.

LEAVING ITALY. By Sybil Patten. September 9, 2003. Directed by Randy White. With Jess Wexler, Charles H. Hyman, Johnny Giacalone, Dee Pelletier.

THREE CONTINENTS. By Catherine Filloux. September 22, 2003. Directed by Jean Randich. With Larissa Kiel, Annabel LaLonde, Kristin Griffith, Bruce MacVittie, Yusef Bulos, Michelle Rios.

ANATOMY 1968. By Karen Hartman. September 23, 2003. Directed by Randy White. With Larissa Kiel, Rich Canzano, Yusef Bulos, Taylor Mac Bowyer, Angel Desai.

The Barbara Barondess MacLean Festival. ANON. By Kate Robin. September 29, 2003. Directed by Melissa Kievman. With Katy Selverstone, Josh Hamilton, Beth Lincks, Charlotte Colavin, Bill Buell, Mia Barron, Lindsey Gates, Joanna Liao, Melinda Wade, Vanessa Aspillaga, Liz Douglas, Keli Garrett, Sarah Trelease, Eisa Davis. MESSALINA. By Gordon Dahlquist. September 30, 2003. Directed by David Levine. With John McAdams, Laura Flanagan, Daria Polatin, Lee Tergesen, Molly Powell, Bill Dawes. SIBERIA. By Diana Son. October 3, 2003. With Kevin Carroll, Rick Holmes, Geoffrey Molloy, Sonnie Brown, Jessica Hecht, KJ Sanchez. THE DEVIL'S PLAYGROUND. By Doug Wright. October 6, 2003. With Michael Tisdale, Jefferson Mays, Edward Hibbert, Kristine Nielsen, Stacie Morgain Lewis, Susan Lyons, Laura Heisler, Jack Ferver, Christopher Evan Welch. BOBBY M. By Edwin Sanchez. October 7, 2003. With Lorenzo Laboy, David Ayers, Mireille Enos, Roderick Hill, Julie Halston, Alvaro Mendoza, Michelle Rios, Jon Schumacher. SANDERMANIA. By Sander Hicks. October 8, 2003. Directed by Mahayana Landowne. With Jenny Weaver, Joey Liao, Dan O'Brien, Roderick Hill, Ron Riley, Nick Colt.

FALLING PETALS. By Ben Ellis. October 20, 2003. Directed by Steve Cosson. With Alicia Goranson, Ted Schneider, Mandy Siegfried, Lynne McCollough, Buzz Bovshow.

SLEEPER. By Justin Boyd. October 21, 2003. Directed by Hayley Nutt. With Charles Parnell, Dan O'Brien, Yvonne Woods, Yusef Bulos.

FROZEN. By Bryony Lavery. October 23, 2003. Directed by Anne Kauffman. With Ken Marks, Barbara eda-Young, Karen Young, Sergei Burbank.

PERDITA GRACIA. By Caridad Svich. October 27, 2003. Directed by Debbie Saivetz. With April Matthis, Ellen Lancaster, Nilaja Sun, Alfredo Narciso, Ed Vassallo, Chris Wells, Flaco Navaja, Olivia Oguma, Lorenzo Laboy, Andres Munar.

Playtime. MY FIRST RADICAL. By Rogelio Martinez. November 13, 2003. Directed by Michael Sexton. With Carlo Alban, Laura Jo Anderson, Chris De Oni, Ed DeSoto, Matthew Maguire, Joseph Goodrich. WELLSPRING. By Ruth Margraff. November 14, 2003. Directed by Jean Randich. With Piter Fattouche, Lanna Joffrey, Ed Vassallo, Dawn Saito, Jennifer Gibbs, Akili Prince. BREAKFAST, LUNCH AND DINNER. By Luis Alfaro. November 14, 2003. Directed by Kim Rubinstein. With Saidah Arrika Ekulona, Michael Potts, Yvette Ganier, Leslie Elliard.

THE STREET OF USEFUL THINGS. By Stephanie Fleischmann. November 17, 2003. Directed by Linsay Firman. With Jenny Sterlin, Patrick Husted, Molly Powell, Emily Donahoe, Franca Barchiesi, Judith Lightfoot Clarke.

SMOKE AND MIRRORS. By Joseph Goodrich. November 17, 2003. Directed by Nick Faust. With Andrew Guilarte, Graham Brown, Elzbieta Czyzewska, Matthew Morgan, John McAdams, Dale Soules, Angel Desai.

MOLOCH AND OTHER DEMONS. By Jason Grote. December 1, 2003. Directed by Alex Corriea. With Kate Benson, Jeff Biehl, Michael Chernus, Patch Darragh, Michael Milligan.

UNTILWEFINDEACHOTHER. By Brooke Berman. December 4, 2003. Directed by Carolyn Cantor. With Naama Potok, Michael Chernus, Josie Whittlesey, David Barlow, Seth Herzog, Dara Fisher, Blythe Zava.

Yale Playwrights Festival. December 12, 2003. BURIED HISTORY and A SPLASH OF NUTMEG IN MILK. By Sarah Fornia. Directed by Daniella Topol. With Mark Blum, Geraldine Librandi, Mia Barron, Heather Mazur, Michael Goldstrom, Nicole Lowrance, Ching Valdes-Aran, Ron Crawford. LAST OF THE CHATTERBOX WOLVES. By Rolin Jones. Directed by Kim Rubinstein. With Jeanine Serralles, Clark Middleton, Greg Steinbruner, Brad Heberlee, Judith Hawking, Mia Barron. BANDITOS. By Jami O'Brien. Directed by Trip Cullman. With Heather Mazur, Joanna P. Adler, Siobhan Mahoney, Ching Valdes-Aran, Michael Chernus, Matthew Humphreys, Mark Blum, Lucas Papaelias, Tim Acito. AND JESUS MOONWALKS ON THE MISSISSIPI and DANCE THE HOLY GHOST. By Marcus Gardley. Directed by Seret Scott. With Kevin Carroll, Cherise Boothe, Barbara Pitts, Rony Clanton, Graham Brown, Ebony Jo-Ann.

Playground Workshop. AMAZING. By Brooke Berman. December 18, 2003. Directed by Ethan McSweeny. With Lucas Papaelias, Mandy Siegfried, Michael Chernus, Marin Ireland. THE LOST BOYS OF SUDAN. By Lonnie Carter. December 19, 2003. Directed by Peter Brosius. With Akili Prince, Teagle F. Bougere, April Matthis, Michael Rogers, Forrest McClendon, Mike Hodge, Jill Kotler, Keith Davis. THE MIDNIGHT TEA, OR THE PUZZLING MAPS OF BESSEMER SHANKS. By Glen Berger. December 19, 2003. Directed by Allison Narver. With Ann Arvia, Elyas Khan, Michelle Federer, Maria Thayer, David Ranson, Shelly Watson, Timothy Reynolds, Jesse Pennington.

ROME. By Herman Farrell. January 8, 2004. Directed by Mr. Farrell. With Akili Prince, Alice Haining, Rob Campbell, Jen Ryan, Joseph Urla.

PLASTICINE. By Vassily Sigarev. January 20, 2004. Directed by Jon Schumacher. With Luke MacFarlane, John Gallagher, Susan Ferrara, Laura Marks, Ken Marks, Alex Napier, Laura Kindred, Jeff Biehl, Matt Kalman, Flora Diaz.

FIREFACE. By Marius von Mayenburg. February 10, 2004. Directed by Jon Schumacher. With Elise Santora, Jon Krupp, June Raphael, Thomas Sadoski, Aaron Stanford.

RAW BOYS. By Dael Orlandersmith. February 11, 2004. Directed by Blanka Zizka. With Paul Vincent Black, John Keating, Colin Lane, Kathleen Doyle.

MADAME KILLER. By Honour Kane and Diana Kane; music by Paul Loesel. February 23, 2004. Directed by Linsay Firman. With Aedin Moloney, Jill Gascoine, Jan Leslie Harding, Okwui Okpokwasili, Thomas Schall, Derek Lucci.

THE NAME. By Jon Fosse. February 24, 2004. Directed by Jon Schumacher. With Christy Meyer, Jeffrey Scott Green, Kate Wetherhead, Mia Katigbak, Keith Randolph Smith, Thomas Sadoski.

BELIZE. By Paul Zimet; music by Ellen Maddow. March 16, 2004. With Eisa Davis, John Keating, T. Ryder Smith, Tina Shepard, Marjorie Johnson, Will Badgett, Connie Winston, Steven Rosen, Scott Blumenthal, Steven Rattazzi, Carolyn Goelzer, Blue Gene Tyranny.

IN THE NAME OF BOB. By Jono Hustis. March 23, 2004. With Julien Schwab, Ali Walsh, Eric Miller.

MARY BETH. By Matthew Kirsch. April 2, 2004. Directed by Joanna P. Adler. With Carla Briscoe, Matthew Stadelmann, Jenna Stern, Steven Rattazzi, Greg Stuhr, John Seitz.

THRUSH. By Caridad Svich. April 5, 2004. With Jeffrey Frace, Kristi Casey, Alfredo Narciso, Heidi Schreck, Chris Wells, Alexandra Oliver.

AUTODELETE://BEGINNING DUMP OF PHYSICAL MEMORY//. By Honour Kane; music by Eve Beglarian. April 5, 2004. Directed by Leigh Silverman. With Ms. Kane, Paul Vincent Black, David Greenspan, Alejandro Morales, Andy Phelan, Warren Elgort, John C. Russell.

MARIA KIZITO. By Erik Ehn. April 7, 2004. With Djola Branner, Laurie Carlos, Sandra DeLuca, Robbie McCauley, Stacey Robinson, Rhonda Ross, Vinie Burrows, Eisa Davis.

BLURRING SHINE. By Zakiyyah Alexander. April 12, 2004. Directed by Daniel Banks. With Danny Johnson, Archie Ekong, Kevin Carroll, Charles Anthony Burks, Charles Parnell.

BELTED BLUE, BLEEDING YELLOW. By Qui Nguyen. April 12, 2004. Directed by Victor Maog. With Pun Bandhu, Ben Wang, Mary Kickel.

THINGS BEYOND OUR CONTROL. By Jesse Kellerman. April 19, 2004. Directed by Ted Sod. With Jan Leslie Harding, Elise Santora, Edward A. Hajj, Jonathan Hogan, George Oliphant, Ed Vassallo, Elizabeth Canavan, Michael Esper, Dan Domingues.

PHOTOGRAPHS OF A BLACK MAN ON DISPLAY. By Rogelio Martinez. April 20, 2004. Directed by Leigh Silverman. With Dylan Baker, Kenajuan Bentley, Greg Bratman, Laura Breckenridge, Airrion Doss, Steven Rattazzi.

MEASURE FOR PLEASURE OR THE HAPPINESS OF PURSUIT. By David Grimm. April 26, 2004. Directed by Mr. Grimm. With Michael Stuhlbarg, John Steitz, Michael Tisdale, Justin Schultz, Laura Esterman, Dale Soules, Tamsin Hollo, Jesse Bernstein.

MARY PEABODY IN CUBA. By Anne Garcia-Romero. April 27, 2004. Directed by Leah C. Gardiner. With Mia Barron, Felix Solis, Guy Boyd, Kate Wetherhead, Mateo Gomez.

MORNINGS AT MANGANO'S. By Stacie Vourakis. April 28, 2004. Directed by Randy White. With Kathryn Foster, Charlotte Colavin, Andrew Zimmerman, Lynn Cohen, Ronald Cohen, James Himelsbach, Bruce MacVittie.

WET. By Liz Duffy Adams; music by Cliff Caruthers. May 3, 2004. Directed by Ms. Adams. With Isabel Keating, Elisa Terrezas, Sarah Lord, Sean Owens, George De La Pena, Daniel Breaker, Lee Rosen, Linda Jones.

SILENT CONCERTO. By Alejandro Morales. April 28, 2004. Directed by Scott Ebersold. With Susan O'Connor, Ivan Quintanilla, Lee Rosen.

THE LONG SEASON. By Chay Yew; music by Fabian Obispo. May 4, 2004. Directed by Peter DuBois. With Orville Mendoza, Rona Figueroa, Jose Llana, Francis Jue.

GIBRALTAR. By Octavio Solis. May 17, 2004. Directed by Liz Diamond. With Adriana Sevan, Jason Manuel Olazábal, Charles Parnell, Brian Keane, June Ballinger, Lucia Brawley, Charles H. Hyman, Peggy Scott.

ROSE OF CORAZON. By Keith Glover. May 18, 2004. Directed by Ed Herendeen. With Caesar Samayoa, Michael Flanigan, Joey Collins, Anney Giobbe, Arielle Jacobs, Christianne Tisdale.

TONGUE-TIED AND DUTY FREE. By James Nicholson. May 20, 2004. Directed by Sturgis Warner. With Yetta Gottesman, Steven Boyer, Jason Pugatch, Danielle Quisenberry, Karl Herlinger, Mercedes Herrero, Sam Guncler.

New Federal Theatre. Dedicated to integrating minorities into the mainstream of American theater through the training of artists and the presentation of plays by minorities and women. Woodie King Jr. producing director.

DISS DISS AND DISS DAT. Musical with book by Rajendra Ramoon Maharaj and Woodie King Jr.; music and lyrics by Funke Natives. November 2, 2003. Directed and choreographed by Mr. Maharaj; scenery, John Pollard; costumes, Anita Ellis; lighting, Antoinette Tynes; sound, Jairous L. Parker Sr. With Du Kelly, Amber Efe, Hannibal, McKenzie Frye, Rodney Gilbert, Bryan Taronne Jones, Sharifa LaGuerre, Ayana Wiles-Bey, Jonathan Anderson.

GREAT MEN OF GOSPEL. By Elizabeth Van Dyke. March 10, 2004. Directed by Ms. Van Dyke; choreography, Dyane Harvey. With Richard Bellazzin, Jeff Bolding, Ralph Carter, Cliff Terry, Gary E. Vincent, Montroville C. Williams.

WAITIN' 2 END HELL. By William A. Parker. May 27, 2004. Directed by Woodie King Jr.; scenery, Roger Predmore; costumes, Stephanie Rafferty; lighting, Antoinette Tynes; sound, Anthony Dixon. With O.L. Duke, Trish McCall, Eric McLendon, Elica Funatsu, Marcus Naylor, Ron Scott, Thyais Walsh.

New Group. Launches fresh acting, writing and design talent. Committed to cultivating a young and diverse theater-going audience by providing accessible ticket prices. Scott Elliott artistic director, Geoffrey Rich executive director, Ian Morgan associate artistic director.

AUNT DAN AND LEMON. By Wallace Shawn. December 18, 2003. Directed by Scott Elliott; scenery, Derek McLane; costumes, Eric Becker; lighting, Jason Lyons; sound, Ken Travis. With Kristen Johnston, Lili Taylor, Marcia Stephanie Blake, Liam Craig, Idris Elba, Melissa Errico, Carlos Leon, Emily Cass McDonnell, Brooke Sunny Moriber, Maulik Pancholy, Stephen Park, Bill Sage.

ROAR. By Betty Shamieh. March 22, 2004. Directed by Marion McClinton; scenery, Beowulf Boritt; costumes, Mattie Ullrich; lighting, Jason Lyons; sound, Ken Travis. With Annabella Sciorra, Sarita Choudhury, Sherri Eldin, Joseph Kamal, Daniel Oreskes.

New York Theatre Workshop. Dedicated to nurturing artists at all stages of their careers and to developing provocative new works. James C. Nicola artistic director, Lynn Moffat managing director.

THE ARCHITECTURE OF LOSS. By Julia Cho. January 11, 2004. Directed by Chay Yew; scenery, Riccardo Hernández; costumes, Linda Cho; lighting, Mary Louise Geiger; sound, Jill B.C. DuBoff. With Angel Desai, Mia Katigbak, Jason Lew, Will Marchetti, Matthew Saldivar, Victor Slezak, Eric Wippo.

Pan Asian Repertory Theatre. Introducing Asian-American theater to the general public with the aim of deepening appreciation and understanding of Asian-American cultural heritage. Tisa Chang artistic producing director.

LEGACY CODES. By Cherylene Lee. November 5, 2003. Directed by Ron Nakahara; scenery, Eric Renschler; costumes, Ingrid Maurer; lighting, Victor En Yu Tan. With Bonnie Black, Lindsey Gates, Wai Ching Ho, Scott Klavan, Jackson Loo, Les J.N. Mau.

KWATZ! By Ernest Abuba. March 24, 2004. Directed by Tisa Chang; scenery, Kaori Akazawa; costumes, Carol Pelletier; music and sound, Michael Mittelsdorf. With Arthur T. Acuña, John Baray, John Chou, Tran T. Thuc Hanh, Rosanne Ma, Tom Matsusaka, Shigeko Suga.

Performance Space 122. Provides artists of a wide range of experience a chance to develop work and find an audience. Mark Russell artistic director.

TRAGEDY IN 9 LIVES. Musical by Karen Houppert; music by Aaron Maxwell and Alexander MacSween. July 13, 2003. Directed by Stephen Nunns; choreography, Schellie Archbold; scenery, Ben Keightley; costumes, Nancy Brous; lighting, Shaun Fillion; sound, Eric Shim. With Juliana Francis, T. Ryder Smith, James "Tigger" Ferguson, Laura Flanagan, Chris Mirto, Chris Spencer Wells.

LIFE INTERRUPTED. By Spalding Gray. October 5, 2003. With Mr. Gray.

MATT AND BEN. By Mindy Kaling and Brenda Withers. August 7, 2003. Directed by David Warren; scenery, James Youmans; costumes, Anne Sung; lighting, Jeff Croiter; sound, Fitz Patton. With Mses. Kaling, Withers.

TO MY CHAGRIN. By Peggy Shaw. October 2, 2003. Directed by Lois Weaver. With Ms. Shaw, Vivian Stoll.

WHAT EVER: AN AMERICAN ODYSSEY IN EIGHT ACTS. By Heather Woodbury. September 4, 2003. Directed by Dudley Saunders; lighting, David Robkin. With Ms. Woodbury.

HOUSE OF NO MORE. By Caden Manson and Jemma Nelson. January 8, 2004. Directed by Mr. Manson; scenery, Mr. Manson; costumes, Machine; lighting, Jared Klein; sound, Ms. Nelson. With Rebecca Sumner Burgos, Ebony Hatchett, Heather Litter, Amy Miley, Ned Stresen-Reuter.

INSTRUCTIONS FOR FORGETTING. By Tim Echells. January 8, 2004. Directed by Mr. Echells; scenery, Richard Lowdon; video, Hugo Glendinning. With Mr. Echells.

Primary Stages. Dedicated to new American plays. Casey Childs executive producer, Andrew Leynse artistic director.

STRICTLY ACADEMIC. By A.R. Gurney. October 21, 2003. Directed by Paul Benedict; scenery, James Noone; costumes, Laura Crow; lighting, Deborah Constantine. With Remy Auberjonois, Susan Greenhill, Keith Reddin.

THE STENDHAL SYNDROME. By Terrence McNally. February 16, 2004. Directed by Leonard Foglia; scenery, Michael McGarty; costumes, David C. Woolard; lighting, Russell H. Champa; sound, David Van Tieghem; projections, Elaine J. McCarthy. With Richard Thomas, Isabella Rossellini, Michael Countryman, Jennifer Mudge, Yul Vasquez.

BOY. By Julia Jordan. May 18, 2004. Directed by Joe Calarco; scenery, Michael Fagin; costumes, Anne Kennedy; lighting, Chris Lee, sound and music, Lindsay Jones. With Kelly AuCoin, Robert Hogan, T.R. Knight, Caitlin O'Connel, Miriam Shor.

The Public Theater. Schedule of special projects, in addition to its regular Off Broadway productions. George C. Wolfe producer, Mara Manus executive director.

NEW WORK NOW! FESTIVAL OF NEW PLAY READINGS.

DIRTY TRICKS. By John Jeter. April 19, 2004. Directed by Margaret Whitton.

THE ANTIGONE PROJECT. By Amy Brenneman, Karen Hartman, Chiori Miyagawa, Lynn Nottage, Sabrina Peck, Caridad Svich. April 26, 2004. Directed by Ms. Peck.

Too late: Miriam Shor and Kelly AuCoin in Boy. *Photo: James Leynse*

WELLSPRING. By Ruth Margraff. May 3, 2004. Directed by Elyse Singer.

NINE PARTS OF DESIRE. May 10, 2004. By Heather Raffo.

SURFING DNA. May 17, 2004. By Jodi Long.

OUTLYING ISLANDS. By David Grieg. May 24, 2004. Directed by Jo Bonney.

Puerto Rican Traveling Theater. Professional company presenting English and Spanish productions of Puerto Rican and Hispanic playwrights, emphasizing subjects of relevance today. Miriam Colón Valle founder and producer.

BESSIE, THE BUTCHER OF PALM BEACH. By Allen Davis III. March 31, 2004. Directed by William Koch; scenery, Carlos Doria; costumes, Sandra King; lighting, Aaron J. Mason. With Miriam Cruz, Denia Brache, Alicia Kaplan, Fred Valle.

2003 FESTIVAL OF NEW PLAY READINGS. June 2-30, 2003.

POWER HOUSE. By Fred Crecca.

CONFESSIONS OF A P.K. By Henry Guzmán.

THE COURTSHIP OF DIDEROT. By María Elena Torres.

GONE FISHIN'–WON'T BE BACK. By Harding Robert de los Reyes.

SIN PARADISE. By George Joshua.

WELCOME TO MARGARET'S WORLD. By Oscar A. Colón.

A SIMPLE GIFT. By T. Cat Ford.

WHEN JOHNNY COMES MARCHING HOME. By Noemi Martínez.

LATE BLOOMING ROSES. By Allen Davis III.

Signature Theatre Company. Dedicated to the exploration of a playwright's body of work over the course of a single season. James Houghton artistic director.

THE HARLEQUIN STUDIES. By Bill Irwin. September 3, 2003. Directed by Mr. Irwin; scenery, Douglas Stein; costumes, Catherine Zuber; lighting, James Vermeulen; sound, Brett R. Jarvis. With Mr. Irwin, Marin Ireland, John Oyzon, Andrew Pacho, Rocco Sisto, Paxton Whitehead, Steven T. Williams, Doug Skinner, David Gold, Sean McMorris.

THE REGARD EVENING. By Bill Irwin; in collaboration with Doug Skinner, Michael O'Conner and Nancy Harrington. December 16, 2003. Directed by Mr. Irwin; scenery, Douglas Stein; costumes, Catherine Zuber; lighting, Nancy Schertler; sound, Brett R. Jarvis; video, Dennis Diamond. With Mr. Irwin, Doug Skinner, Michael O'Connor.

MR. FOX: A RUMINATION. By Bill Irwin. March 10, 2004. Directed by Mr. Irwin; scenery, Christine Jones; costumes, Elizabeth Caitlin Ward; lighting, James Vermeulen, sound, Brett R. Jarvis. With Mr. Irwin, Bianca Amato, Jason Butler Harner, Geoff Hoyle, Marc Damon Johnson, Peter Maloney, Richard Poe.

Soho Rep. Dedicated to new and cutting edge US playwrights. Daniel Aukin artistic director, Alexandra Conley executive director.

SUITCASE. By Melissa James Gibson. January 24, 2004. Directed by Daniel Aukin, scenery, Louisa Thompson; costumes, Maiko Matsushima; lighting, Matthew Frey; sound, Shane Rettig; music, Michael Friedman; projections, Elaine J. McCarthy. With Christina Kirk, Thomas Jay Ryan, Jeremy Shamos, Colleen Werthmann.

THE APPEAL. By Young Jean Lee. April 9, 2004. Directed by Ms. Lee; music, Matmos. With Maggie Hoffman, Michael Portnoy, Pete Simpson, James Stanley.

Theater for the New City. Developmental theater and new experimental works. Crystal Field executive director.

TULIPS AND CADAVERS. By Jimmy Camicia. March 18, 2004. Directed by Mr. Camicia; scenery, Vivian Lacorte; costumes, Lavinia Co-op; lighting, Alexander Bartenieff. With Mr. Camicia, Crystal Field, Craig Meade.

THE FIST. By Misha Shulman. March 25, 2004. Directed by Michael E. Rutenberg; scenery and costumes, Maiko Chii; lighting, Tamiko Komatsu. With Mr. Shulman, Bob Adrian, Judith Jablonka, Mark Brill, Anna Tsiriotakis, Don Lauer, Guy Yanay, Reed Young.

ELAINA VANCE'S LAST DANCE. By Stacy Presha. April 2, 2004. Directed by Carmen Matthis; scenery, Laurie Flynn-Redmond; costumes, Elgie C. Johnson; lighting, Ernest Baxter; sound, Joy Linscheid. With Dorothi Fox, Arthur French, Johnnie Mae, Bershan Shaw.

NOSSIG'S ANTICS. By Lazarre Seymour Simckes. April 25, 2004. Directed by Crystal Field; scenery, Donald L. Brooks; lighting, Alexander Bartenieff; sound, Joy Linscheid and David Nolan. With Stuart Rudin, Mira Rivera, Robert Fizsimmons, Robert Vaquero, Aesha Waks, Lei Zhou.

RITE OF RETURN. By Victoria Linchon. April 29, 2004. Directed by Ms. Linchon; scenery, Ryan Scott; sound, Allon Beausoleil. With Sanaz Mozafarian, Vittoria Setta, Jana Zenadeen, Mohamed Djellouli, A. Michael Elian, Anity Wlody, Frank Shkreli.

Theatre for a New Audience. Founded in 1979, the company's mission is to help develop the performance and study of Shakespeare and classic drama. Jeffrey Horowitz founding artistic director, Dorothy Ryan managing director.

ENGAGED. By W.S. Gilbert. April 29, 2004. Directed by Doug Hughes; scenery, John Lee Beatty; costumes, Catherine Zuber; lighting, Rui Rita; sound, Aural Fixation. With Danielle Ferland, James Gale, John Horton, John Christopher Jones, Maggie Lacey, Nicole Lowrance, David Don Miller, Caitlin Muelder, Jeremy Shamos, Sloane Shelton.

Vineyard Theatre. Multiart chamber theater dedicated to the development of new plays and musicals, music-theater collaborations and innovative revivals. Douglas Aibel artistic director, Jennifer Garvey-Blackwell executive director, Bardo S. Ramirez managing director.

EIGHT DAYS (BACKWARDS). By Jeremy Dobrish. June 16, 2003. Directed by Mark Brokaw; scenery, Mark Wendland; costumes, Michael Krass; lighting, Mary Louise Geiger; sound, Janet Kalas; music, Lewis Flinn. With Josh Radnor, David Garrison, Randy Danson, Bill Buell, Daniella Alonso.

THE LONG CHRISTMAS RIDE HOME. By Paula Vogel. November 4, 2003. Directed by Mark Brokaw; choreography, John Carrafa; scenery, Neil Patel; costumes, Jess Goldstein; lighting, Mark McCullough; music and sound, David Van Tieghem. With Mark Blum, Randy Graff, Sean Palmer, Catherine Kellner, Enid Graham, Will McCormack, Marc Petrosini, Sarah Provost, Lake Simons. A 2003–04 *Best Plays* choice (see essay by Tish Dace in this volume).

BEAUTIFUL CHILD. By Nicky Silver. February 24, 2004. Directed by Terry Kinney; scenery, Richard Hoover; costumes, Michael Krass; lighting, David Lander; music and sound, Obadiah Eaves. With George Grizzard, Penny Fuller, Steven Pasquale, Alexandra Gersten-Vassilaros, Kaitlin Hopkins.

WHERE DO WE LIVE? By Christopher Shinn. May 11, 2004. Directed by Mr. Shinn; scenery, Rachel Hauck; costumes, Mattie Ullrich; lighting, David Weiner; sound, Jill B.C. DuBoff; music, Storm P. With Burl Moseley, Luke MacFarlane, Emily Bergl, Aaron Stanford, Jesse Tyler Ferguson, Liz Stauber, Daryl Edwards, Aaron Yoo, Jacob Pitts.

Women's Project and Productions. Nurtures, develops and produces plays written and directed by women. Julia Miles founder, Loretta Greco producing artistic director, Jane Ann Crum managing director.

TOUCH. By Toni Press-Coffman. October 9, 2003. Directed by Loretta Greco; scenery, Michael Brown; costumes, Jeff Mahshie; lighting, James Vermeulen; sound and music, Robert Kaplowitz. With Tom Everett Scott, Michele Ammon, Matthew Del Negro, Yetta Gottesman.

BIRDY. By Naomi Wallace; adapted from the novel by William Wharton. December 2, 2003. Directed by Lisa Peterson; scenery, Riccardo Hernández; costumes, Gabriel Berry;

lighting, Scott Zielinski; sound, Jill B.C. DuBoff, music, David Van Tieghem. With Richard Bekins, Teagle F. Bougere, Zachary Knighton, Adam Rothenberg, Ted Schneider, Peter Stadlen.

MISCELLANEOUS

In the additional listing of 2003–04 Off Off Broadway productions below, the names of the producing groups or theaters appear in CAPITAL LETTERS and the titles of the works in *italics*.

ABINGDON THEATRE COMPANY. *Bruno Hauptmann Kissed My Forehead* by John Yearley. June 5, 2003. Directed by James F. Wolk; with Pun Bandhu, Lori Gardner, Joel Leffert, Joseph J. Menino, Pamela Paul, Michael Puzzo. *Beyond Recognition* by John Petrick. October 23, 2003. Directed by Kate Bushmann; with Christopher Burns, Michael Goduti, Michael Marisi Orenstein, Grant James Vargas. *The Pagans* by Ann Noble. March 3, 2004. Directed by Stephen Hollis; with Victoria Adams, Mark Alhadeff, Frank Anderson, Nora Chester, Christopher Drescher, Rachel Fowler, Susanne Marley, Steven Rishard. *Graduation Day* by Barton Bishop. May 14, 2004. Directed by Alex Dmitriev; with Alice Barden, Stephen Benson, David Holmes, Jacob Lavin, Rachel Alexa Norman.

ABINGDON THEATRE COMPLEX. *The Attic* by Stephen Gaydos. October 25, 2003. Directed by Paul Zablocki; with Michael Szeles, Josh Heine, Meg Howrey, Megan McNulty, Stephanie Weldon. *The Killer News*. Musical with book, music and lyrics by Steven P. Reed. December 3, 2003. Directed by Mr. Reed; with Linnea Redfern, Pete Stickel, Alexander Meltsin, Brigitte Beniquez, L.H. "Starborn" Bryant, Shelly Rudolph, Andrew Kletjian, Joseph Emil, W.B. Riggins, Steve Penser, G. Curtis Smith, John Lee, Gillian Fallon, Leighbarry Harvard, Christine Mogle, Miriam Lopez, Michele Burnett, Chris Cotten, George Grauer. *A Reed in the Wind* by Joseph P. McDonald. January 15, 2004. Directed by Ernie Martin; with Jack Walsh, Aubyn Philabaum, Phil Burke, Kevin Hagan. *States of Shock* by Sam Shepard. February 13, 2004. Directed by Cyndy Marion; with Richard Leighton, Diane Shilling, Dee Spencer, Rod Sweitzer, Bill Weeden. *Italian-American Cantos* by Anthony P. Pennino. April 18, 2004. Directed by Gregory Simmons; with Lisa Barnes, Joseph Camardella, Kathleen DeFouw, Suzanne DiDonna, Richard Kohn, Anita Michaels, Jarrod Pistilli, Paul Romanello, Christina Romanello, Joseph Schommer, Tom Walker. *Home Again* by Troy Hill. May 16, 2004. Directed by Mr. Hill; with Cynthia Barnett, Michael Fegley, Rachelle Guiragossian, Gerry Hildebrandt, Bryan Michael McGuire, Thomas James O'Leary, Kara Payne.

ACCESS THEATER. *The Journey of the Fifth Horse* by Ronald Ribman. August 14, 2003. Directed by Lise McDermott; with Dan Patrick Brady, Denise Dimirjian, Jonas Wadler, Duke York, Kim Clay, Eric Dente, Ledger Free, Fran Barkan, Lou Tally, Michael Boothroyd, Diedre Brennan, Jennifer J. Katz, Daniel Hicks, Robin Goldsmith. *Faster* by Jessica Almasy, Rachel Chavkin, Brian Hastert, Tiffany May, Kristen Sieh, Ryan West; inspired by James Gleick's book. November 20, 2003. Directed by Ms. Chavkin; with Ms. Almasy, Mr. Hastert, Ms. May, Ms. Sieh, Mr. West. *600 Days of Pain* by Gene Perelson and Jamil Ellis. March 11, 2004. Directed by Messrs. Perelson and Ellis; with Messrs. Perelson, Ellis.

THE ACTORS COMPANY THEATRE (TACT). *The Marriage of Bette and Boo* by Christopher Durang. October 18, 2003. Directed by Scott Alan Evans; with Cynthia Darlow, Cynthia Harris, Greg McFadden, Eve Michelson, James Murtaugh, James Prendergast, Kate Ross, Gregory Salata, Scott Schafer, Jenn Thompson. *Fathers and Sons* by Brian Friel; based on the novel by Ivan Turgenev. November 22, 2003. Directed by Stephen Hollis; with Sean Arbuckle, Mary Bacon, Lucas Beck, Jamie Bennett, Lynn Cohen, Francesca Di Mauro, Richard Ferrone, Sam Gregory, John Horton, Kelly Hutchinson, Elizabeth Shepard, David Staller, Ashley West. *The Good Soup (La Bonne Soupe)* by Felicien Marceau; adapted by Garson Kanin. January 24, 2004. Directed by Kyle Fabel; with Delphi Harrington, Margaret Nichols, Gregory Salata, Sean Arbuckle, Nora Chester, Francesca Di Mauro, Simon Jones, Jack Koenig, Darrie Lawrence, Greg McFadden, James Prendergast, Scott Schafer, Kelly Hutchinson, Joel Jones. *The Chalk Garden* by Enid Bagnold. March 13, 2004. Directed by John Christopher Jones; with Mary Bacon, Cynthia Darlow, Francesca Di Mauro, Cynthia Harris, Simon Jones, Darrie Lawrence, Gloria Moore, Nicholas Kepros. *The Triangle Factory Fire Project* by Christopher Piehler. May 14, 2004. Directed by Scott Alan Evans; with Jamie Bennett, Nora

Chester, Francesca Di Mauro, Kyle Fabel, James Murtaugh, Margaret Nichols, Scott Schafer, Kelly Hutchinson, Timothy McCracken.

ALTERED STAGES. *An Enola Gay Christmas* by Doug Field. December 4, 2003. Directed by Dana Snyder; with Nan Schmid.

AMERICAN THEATER OF ACTORS. *And Then There Was Nin* by Jennifer Ewing Pierce. June 27, 2003. Directed by Ms. Pierce; with Joshua Longo, Kalle Macrides, Mikeah Jennings, Khoa Nguyen, Tito Ruiz, Melanie Julian, Ryan Tavlin. *Confessions of a Wonderbabe* by Jennifer Ewing Pierce. July 1, 2003. Directed by Ms. Pierce; with Ryan Tavlin, Allison McAtee, Laura Winsor Attanasio. *The Wood Demon* by Anton Chekhov; translated by Carol Rocamora. August 8, 2003. Directed by Cynthia Dillon; with John Jamiel, Tashya Valdevit, Jeff Winter. *Dalliance in Vienna* by Douglas Braverman. December 4, 2003. Directed by Thomas Morrissey; with Glenn Kalison, Thomas James O'Leary, Christine Pedi, Lucas Steele, Emily Strang, Melinda Tanner, Ian Tomaschik. *Oresteia* by Aeschylus. January 19, 2004. *Agamemnon*, adapted by Erik Nelson. Directed by Mr. Nelson; with Saori Tsukada, Chris Oden. *The Mourners*, adapted by Yuval Sharon from *The Libation Bearers*. Directed by Mr. Sharon; with Constance Tarbox, Laura Knight, Sarah Fraunfelder, Tia Shearer, Layna Fisher, Jonathan Day, Caroline Worra, Jeanne Lehman, Cara Consilvio. *Eumenides*, adapted by David Johnston. Directed by Kevin Lee Newbury; with Cortney Keim, Beau Allulli, Kath Lichter, Michael Bell, Vivian Manning, Nell Gwynn, Heidi McAllister, Lori Lane Jefferson. *Promised Land* by Harvey Huddleston. January 30, 2004. Directed by Tom Dybeck; with David Mazzeo, Lynne McCollough, Matthew Faber, Danny Rose, Bruce McKinnon, Emily Sproch, Jasmine Goldman.

ATLANTIC 453. *The Hiding Place* by Jeff Whitty. January 19, 2004. Directed by Christian Parker; with Kate Blumberg. *The Bald Soprano* and *The Lesson* by Eugene Ionesco; translated by Tina Howe. April 13, 2004. Directed by Carl Forsman. NEW WORKS: CHANCE. Festival of short plays by Michael Dowling, Jerome Hairston, Jordan Lage, Scott Organ, Kate Moira Ryan. May 17, 2004. Directed by Ian Morgan, Mr. Organ, Anya Saffir, Gary Upton Schwartz, Sarah Stern; with Kate Blumberg, Jason Cornwell, Gretchen Egolf, Susan Finch, Christopher Innvar, Maggie Kiley, DeAnna Lenhart, Adam Lustick, Jenny Maguire, Greg Stuhr, Ray Anthony Thomas, Charles Tucker.

AQUILA THEATRE COMPANY. *The Importance of Being Earnest* by Oscar Wilde. June 29, 2003. Directed by Robert Richmond; with Guy Oliver-Watts, Andrew Schwartz, Richard Willis, Alex Webb, Cameron Blair, Renata Friedman, Lindsay Rae Taylor, Ryan Conarro. *Agamemnon* by Aeschylus. February 3, 2004. Directed by Robert Richmond; with Olympia Dukakis, Louis Zorich, David Adkins, Marco Barricelli, Louis Butelli, Gillian Claire Chadsey, Carissa Guild, Nicholas Kepros, Miriam Laube, Matthew Lewis, Toni Melaas, Thomas Schall, Magin Schantz, John Sierros, Alex Webb.

ARS NOVA. *Judy Speaks* by Mary Birdsong. August 11, 2003. Directed by Gregory Wolfe; with Ms. Birdsong. *The Wau Wau Sisters* by Tanya Gagné and Adrienne Truscott. May 20, 2004. Directed by Trip Cullman; with Mses. Gagné, Truscott.

AXIS COMPANY. *A Glance at New York* by Benjamin A. Baker. June 7, 2003. Directed by Randy Sharp; with Wren Arthur, Brian Barnhart, David Crabb, Joe Fuer, Laurie Kilmartin, Sue Ann Molinell, Edgar Oliver, Margo Passalaqua, Jim Sterling, Christopher Swift. *USS Frankenstein* by Axis Company. October 30, 2003. Directed by Randy Sharp, Brian Barnhart, Christopher Swift, Jim Sterling, David Crabb, Edgar Oliver. *In Token of My Admiration* by Axis Company. April 22, 2004. Directed by Randy Sharp; with Brian Barnhart, Joe Fuer.

BANK STREET THEATRE. *The Fishermen of Beaudrais* by Kathleen Rowlands and Joseph Rinaldi; adapted from the screenplay by Ring Lardner Jr. and Dalton Trumbo. July 3, 2003. Directed by Keith Oncale; with Matt Conley, Jennifer Lindsey, Richard Simon, Sherry Nehmer, Jennifer Chudy. *Jane* by S.N. Behrman. October 5, 2003. Directed by Dan Wackerman; with Susan Jeffries, Leila Martin, Richard Bekins, Roland Johnson, Chris Kipiniak, Kristina Bell, Matthew DeCapua. *Josh Kornbluth's Love and Taxes* by Mr. Kornbluth. December 8, 2003. Directed by David Dower; with Mr. Kornbluth. *Right as Ron* by Judd Bloch. February 2, 2004. Directed by Max Williams; with Thomas Guiry, Mark Auerbach, John Dohrman, Kathryn Ekblad, Susan-Kate Heaney, Jono Hustis, Carolyn Ladd, Yvonne Lin, Ben Lizza, Seth Michael May, John McAdams, Mike Mosley, Erica Rhodes, Jas Robertson. *Hannah and Martin* by Kate Fodor. March 31, 2004. Directed by Ron Russell; with David Strathairn, Melissa Friedman, Todd Cerveris, Laura Hicks, Teri Lamm, James Wallert, Brandon Miller, George Morfogen, Sandra Shipley. *Counsellor-at-Law* by Elmer Rice.

May 9, 2004. Directed by Dan Wackerman; with John Rubinstein, Madeleine Martin, Joseph Martin, D. Michael Berkowitz, Dennis Burke, Beth Glover, Nell Gwynn, James M. Larmer, David Lavine, Mark Light-Orr, Lanie MacEwan, Racheline Maltese, Sal Mistretta, Robert O'Gorman, Ginger Rich, Tara Sands, Letty Serra, Brian Taylor, Ashley West.

THE BARROW GROUP. *Sonnets for an Old Century* by José Rivera. October 3, 2003. Directed by Emory Van Cleve; with Tricia Alexandro, Rozie Bacchi, Dawn Bennett, Georgi Cerruti, Corinne Chandler, Monique Gabriela Curnen, Pietro Gonzalez, Kate McCauley, Myles O'Connor, Eric Paeper, Ron Piretti, Michael Cruz Sullivan, Hope Singsen, Martin Van Treuren, Kevin Craig West. *Lobby Hero* by Kenneth Lonergan. January 23, 2004. Directed by Donna Jean Fogel; with Jacob White, K. Lorrel Manning, Rozie Bacchi, Larry Mitchell.

BARUCH PERFORMING ARTS CENTER. TALES OF UNREST: JOSEPH CONRAD ON STAGE. October 6, 2003. *Arsat* by Christine Simpson; adapted from "The Lagoon." Directed by Ms. Simpson; with Jojo Gonzalez, Kevin Bartlett, Lydia Gaston, Tim Kang. *One Day More* by Mr. Conrad; adapted from "Tomorrow." Directed by Jonathan Bank; with Mel Gionson, Jojo Gonzalez, Maile Holck, Robert Wu. *Constellations* by Julie Book. December 14, 2003. Directed by Thomas G. Waites; with Stephanie Schweitzer, Ernest Mingione, James Riordan, Charlie Moss, Annie McGovern. *Kalighat* by Paul Knox. January 25, 2004. Directed by Mr. Knox; with Samir Ajmera, Susham Bedi, Omar Botros, Grainne de Buitlear, Anna Ewing Bull, Geeta Citygirl, Simon Deonarian, Prashant Kumar Gupta, Ranjit Gupte, Poorna Jagannathan, G.R. Johnson, Naheed Khan, Mami Kimura, Rizwan Manji, David Mason, Suneel Mubayi, Nitika Nadgar, Tyler Pierce, Karam Puri, Eliyas Qureshi, Shawn Rajguru, Giuliana Santini, Chandon Donny Sethi, Mukesh Sethi, Reena Shah, Usman Shaukat. *The Roaring Girle* by Thomas Middleton and Thomas Dekker; adapted by Alice Tuan and Melanie Joseph. February 20, 2004. Directed by Ms. Joseph; with Okwui Okpokwasili, Harry Hogan, Marissa Copeland, Douglas Rees, John Epperson, Rebecka Ray, Michael Urie, Clove Galilee, Michael Huston, Jodi Lin, Steven Rattazzi, Andrew McGinn, Steve Cuiffo, Mike Caban. *Three Seconds in the Key* by Deb Margolin. Directed by Loretta Greco; with Ms. Margolin. April 14, 2004. Directed by Alexandra Aron; with Catherine Curtin, Samuel R. Gates, Malcolm Morano, Ato Essandoh, Avery Glymph, David S. Shaw, Jeffrey Evan Thomas. *True West* by Sam Shepard. March 3, 2004. Directed by Thomas G. Waites; with Marlene Wallace, Sarah Jackson, Charlie Moss, Mary A. Sarno.

BECKETT THEATRE. *For Pete's Sake!* Musical with book by Randy Conti; music by Jeffrey Stein; lyrics by Douglas Farrell. October 14, 2003. Directed by Mr. Conti; with Kayla Mason, Chrystal Verdichizzi, Ron Carlos, Danny Carroll, Tatyana de Muns, Emily Gildea, Max Edmands, Ryan Crimmins, Jaime Gruber, Rebekah Rubenstein, Ashley Kilbride, Joanna Stein, Jade Elkind, Maddie Smith-Spanier, Frank Sansone, Ashlee Bakey, Amy Joscelyn, Ariel Azoff, Elise Tarantina, Dov Rubenstein, Lindsay Michaels, Hillary Goldfarb, Kaela Teilhaber, Tommy Joscelyn, Chenier Lewis, Sean Whiteford, Noah DeBiase, Alix Josefski. *Our Fathers* by Luigi Lunari. November 10, 2003. Directed by Stephen Jobes; with Mica Begnasco, John Wojda.

BELT THEATER. *The Nuclear Family* by John Gregorio, Stephen Guarino and Jimmy Bennett. September 10, 2003. Directed by Messrs. Gregorio, Guarino and Bennett; with Messrs. Gregorio, Guarino, Bennett. *Maggie May* by Tom O'Brien. February 16, 2004. Directed by Jocelyn Szabo; with Christiane Szabo, Ean Sheehy, Ethan Duff, Stephen Bradbury. *Too Much Light Makes the Baby Go Blind* by Greg Allen. April 2, 2004. Directed by the Neo-Futurists; with Katrina Toshiko, Desiree Burch, Michael Cyril Creighton, Rob Neill, Justin Tolley, Lindsay Brandon Hunter, Chris Dippel, Sarah Levy, Regie Cabico, Molly Flynn.

BLUE HERON ARTS CENTER. *The Flu Season* by Will Eno. Jannuary 29, 2004. Directed by Hal Brooks; with Matthew Lawler, David Fitzgerald, Andrew Benator, Roxanna Hope, Elizabeth Sherman, Scott Bowman, James Urbaniak. *Bee-Luther-Hatchee* by Thomas Gibbons. March 14, 2004. Directed by Jim Pelegano; with Perri Gaffney, Thomas James O'Leary, Gha'il Rhodes Benjamin, Catherine Eaton, Lance Spellerberg.

BOOMERANG THEATRE COMPANY. *The Hot Month* by Taylor Mac Bowyer. September 3, 2003. Directed by Marc Parees; with Ken Bolden, Paul Caiola, Samantha Desz, Pamela Dunlap, Vince Gatton. *The Substance of John* by Francis Kuzler. September 5, 2003. Directed by Cailin Heffernan; with David Arthur Bachrach, Ronald Cohen, Jason Field, Bram Heidiger, Jennifer Larkin, Aaron Lisman, Ben Masur, Susan Moses, Heather Paradise, Ian Pfister, Stu Richel, Sarah Sutel. *Keely and*

Du by Jane Martin. September 10, 2003. Directed by Rachel Wood; with Ken Bolden, Catherine Dowling, Peter O'Connor, Karen Sternberg. *Days of Wine and Roses* by J.P. Miller. October 3, 2003. Directed by Rachel Wood; with Mac Brydon, Wally Carroll, Ronald Cohen, Philip Emeott, John Flaherty, Margaret A. Flanagan, Andrea Judge, Montgomery Maguire, Victoria Rosen, Paul Schnee, Laura Siner.

CAFÉ A GO GO THEATRE. *Café A Go Go*. Musical by Joe Corcoran and Dan Corcoran. June 5, 2003. Directed by John Hadden; with Vin Adinolfi, Jessica Aquino, Jessica Cannon, Wade Fisher, Zachary Gilman, Stacie May Hassler, Matthew Knowland, John-Mark McGaha, Jasika Nicole Pruitt, Stephanie St. Hilaire.

CAP 21. THE BARBARA WOLFF MONDAY NIGHT READING SERIES. *Touch of Rapture* by Mary Fenger Gail. October 27, 2003. Directed by Rasa Allan Kazlas. *Brain Children* by Liza Lentini. November 3, 2003. Directed by Melanie Sutherland. *The Siege of Ennis* by Eileen O'Leary. November 10, 2003. Directed by Lawrence Arancio. *Legacies* by Susan Cameron. November 17, 2003. Directed by David Grillo. *The Whispers of Saints* by Mark Scharf. March 22, 2004. Directed by Eliza Ventura. *An Untitled New Musical*. Musical with book and lyrics by Diane Seymour; music by Steven Schoenberg. March 29, 2004. Directed by Robert Billig. *Six of One*. Musical with book and lyrics by Scott Burkell; music by Paul Loesel. April 12, 2004. Directed by Frank Ventura.

CENTER STAGE. *The Chalk Garden* by Enid Bagnold. September 24, 2003. Directed by Terese Hayden; with Jacqueline Brookes, Charles Cissel, Emi Fujinami Jones, Robin Long, Roberta MacIvor, Caitlin McDonough-Thayer, Elizabeth Nafpaktitis, Mary Round, James Stevenson. *Waiting for Godot* by Samuel Beckett. October 10, 2003. Directed by Keith Teller; with Jeffrey M. Bender, Paul Molnar, Michael Rhodes, Greg Skura, Noah Longo. *Square One* by Steve Tesich. December 3, 2003. Directed by Allison Eve Zell; with Huda Bordeaux, Ethan Perry. *Mao on Line One* by Kimberly Megna. January 16, 2004. Directed by Kelly Gillespie; with Jeffrey M. Bender, Christy Collier, Natalie Gold, Eric Loscheider, Ellen Shanman, Michael Warner. *The Eliots* by Lear deBessonet. April 29, 2004. Directed by Ms. deBessonet; with Julie Kline, Christopher Logan Healy, Lethia Nall, Nate Schenkkan, Ryan West.

CHASHAMA. FIRST LIGHT: A FESTIVAL OF NEW SHORT PLAYS. June 12–29, 2003. PROGRAM A. *Your Call Is Important* by Craig Lucas. Directed by Marie-Louise Miller. *This Will Be the Death of Him* by David Dewitt. Directed by Vernice Miller. *The Long Shot* by Richard Cottrell. Directed by Elaine Morinaro. *Mermaids on the Hudson* by Anastasia Traina. Directed by Mary Monroe. *Lily of the Valley* by Lisa Humbertson. Directed by Erma Duricko. PROGRAM B. *Climate* by Joe Pintauro. Directed by Jude Schanzer. *Love* by Betty Shamieh. Directed by Janice Goldberg. *Informed Consent* by Paul Knox. Directed by Keith Greer. *Soooo Sad* by Ty Adams. Directed by Barbara Bosch. *The Fuqua, Slone, Reisenglass Appraisal* by Lawrence Harvey Schulman. Directed by Guy Giarrizzo. *Vert-Galant* by Jon Fraser. Directed by Mr. Fraser. *Sleeping in Tomorrow* by Duncan Pflaster. October 7, 2003. Directed by Clara Barton Green; with Lauren Adler, Sue Berch, Elizabeth Boskey, Wael Haggiagi, Dawn Pollock Jones, Paul Martin Kovic, Ehud Segev, Jason Specland, Sami Zetts. *As I Lay Dying* by William Faulkner; adapted by Andrew Grosso. November 11, 2003. Directed by Mr. Grosso; with Arthur Aulisi, Lynne Bolton, Drew Cortese, Meg Defoe, Jordan Gelber, Hillary Keegin, Susan O'Connor, Thomas Piper, Lorenzo Pisoni, Tommy Schrider, John Thomas Waite. *We're All Dead*. Musical with book and lyrics by Francis Heaney and James Evans; music by Mr. Heaney. November 15, 2003. Directed by Mr. Evans; with Jedidiah Cohen, Tom Bartos, Michelle Bialeck, Trisha Gorman, Tate Henderson, Sean P. Doran, Jason St. Sauver, Vanessa Longley-Cook. *High Heels and Red Noses* by Keith Nelson and Stephanie Monseu. January 12, 2004. Directed by Michael Preston and Barbara Karger; with the Bindlestiff Family Cirkus. *Madama Fortuna!* by Antonio Rodriguez. January 15, 2004. Directed by Mr. Rodriguez and Lisa Marie Black-Meller; with Drew Cortese, Aundre Chin, Jenny Penny Curry, Fred Gunsch, Luke Miller, Dalia Farmer, Erel Pilo. *The Ladies* by Anne Washburn. February 8, 2004. Directed by Anne Kauffman; with Quincy Tyler Bernstine, Jennifer Dundas, Nina Hellman, Jennifer R. Morris, Maria Striar, Alison Weller.

CHERRY LANE THEATRE. *Grasmere* by Kristina Leach. June 8, 2003. Directed by Joseph Arnold; with Darcy Blakesley, Annie Di Martino, Aaron Gordon, Logan Sledge. *Three Weeks After Paradise* by Israel Horovitz. September 11, 2003. Directed by Jill André; with Mel England. *Luscious Music* by Matthew Maguire. September 14, 2003. With Veronica Kehoe, Lourdes Martin, Eric Stoltz, Marisa Echeverria, Ray Anthony Thomas, Richard Petrocelli. *Moomtaj* by Michael Weller. September 15, 2003. Directed by Mr. Weller; with Jane Burd, Michael Emerson, Lisa Emery, Teresa L. Goding,

Jonathan Press, Jay O. Sanders. OLD VIC/NEW VOICES. September 17–24, 2003. *The Mentalists* by Richard Bean. Directed by Ari Edelson; with Bill Buell, David Cale. *The Drowned World* by Gary Owen. Directed by Tyler Marchant; with Chris Diamantopoulos, Jennifer Mudge, Michael Stuhlbarg, Mary Bacon. *A Listening Heaven* by Torben Betts. Directed by Erica Schmidt; with Marylouise Burke, Kathleen Chalfant, Allan Corduner, Daniel Gerroll, Deborah Rush, Heather Goldenhersh. *Port* by Simon Stephens. Directed by Dave Mowers; with Jen Albano, Keith Nobbs, Brennan Brown, Henry Woronicz, Greg McFadden, Kate Blumberg. TONGUES: A READING SERIES. November 5–December 3, 2003. *Days on Earth* by Richard Caliban. *Planet Eyes* by Erica Schmidt. *Bulrusher* by Eisa Davis. *Kindred Strangers* by David Batan. *Subways and Bedrooms* by Tasha Ross. *Please Stop Talking* by Sam Forman. *Luscious Music* by Matthew Maguire. *Cappy's Field* by Glyn O'Malley. *Heaven Hill, Nova Scotia* by Graeme Gillis. *800 Words: The Transmigration of Philip K. Dick* by Victoria Stewart. *Wordsworth* by Alexandra Bullen. YOUNG PLAYWRIGHTS FESTIVAL. January 6–February 20, 2004. *Thick* by Travis Baker. *Easter Candy* by Halley Feiffer. *The View From Tall* by Caitlin Montanye Parrish. MENTOR PROJECT: PUBLIC READINGS. January 12–26, 2004. *Double Sophia* by Kendra Levin; mentored by Michael Weller. Directed by Hayley Finn. *Wordsworth* by Alexandra Bullen; mentored by Ed Bullins. January 19, 2004. Directed by Richard Caliban. *Thunderbird* by Joseph Fisher; mentored by A.R. Gurney. January 26, 2004. Directed by Randy White. MENTOR PROJECT: SHOWCASES. March 10–May 22, 2004. *Double Sophia* by Kendra Levin; mentored by Michael Weller. Directed by Hayley Finn; with Janine Barris, Flora Diaz, Justin Grace, Kathryn Grody, Scott Klavan, Anna McCarthy, Peter Scanavino. *Wordsworth* by Alexandra Bullen; mentored by Ed Bullins. Directed by Richard Caliban; with Richard Hughes, Michael Reid, chandra thomas, Anne Louise Zachry. *Thunderbird* by Joseph Fisher; mentored by A.R. Gurney. Directed by Randy White; with Michael Chernus, Tonya Cornelisse, Laura Flanagan, Michael Rudko, Thomas Sadoski, Tamilla Woodard. *Open Heart*. Musical by Robby Benson. March 17, 2004. Directed by Matt Williams; with Mr. Benson, Karla DeVito, Stan Brown. TONGUES: READING SERIES. *Forest City* by Bridgette Wimberly. April 5, 2004. Directed by Marion McClinton; with Cecilia Antoinette, Caroline Clay, Wiley Moore, Charles Turner.

CHINA CLUB. *The Karaoke Show* by Randy Weiner. November 8, 2003. Directed by Diane Paulus; with Rachel Benbow Murdy, Julie Danao, David Diangelo, Aaron Fuksa, Emily Hellstrom, Charles King, Anderson Lim, Derek Mitchell-Giganti, Robert Orosco, Steve Park, Jordin Ruderman, Marc Santa Maria, Jenny Lee Stern, Erin Stutland, Anna Wilson, Welly Yang.

CLASSICAL THEATRE OF HARLEM. *Macbeth* by William Shakespeare. July 11, 2003. Directed by Alfred Preisser; with Ty Jones, April Yvette Thompson, Arthur French, Leopold Lowe, Lawrence Winslow, De'adre Aziza, Quonta Beasley, Onyemaechi Aharanwa. *Dream on Monkey Mountain* by Derek Walcott. October 3, 2003. Directed by Alfred Preisser; with André De Shields, Kim Sullivan, Benton Greene, Jerry Clicquot, Michael Early, Arthur James Solomon, Neil Dawson, Dele, Celli Pitt, De'adre Aziza, Jaime Carrillo, Tracy Jack, Adenrele Ojo, Catherine Jean-Charles, Melanie J-B Charles. *Mother Courage and Her Children* by Bertolt Brecht. February 6, 2004. Directed by Christopher McElroen; with Gwendolyn Mulamba, Oberon K.A. Adjepong, Onyemaechi Aharanwa, Jaime Carrillo, Michael Early, Rolando Garcia, Stephen Hansen, Devin Haqq, Leopold Lowe, James Miles, Michael C. O'Day, Parris Wittingham, James Rana, Anna Zastrow. *Trojan Women* by Euripides; adapted by Alfred Preisser. April 2, 2004. Directed by Mr. Preisser; with Onyemaechi Aharanwa, Tamela Aldridge, Brie Eley, Phyre Hawkins, Zora Howard, Kerisse Hutchinson, Rain Jack, Tracy Jack, Aman Re-Jack, Zainab Jah, Giselle Jones, Ty Jones, Anthony Lalor, Tonya Latrice, Lizan Mitchell, Folake Olowofoyeku, Ron Simons, Damani Varnado, Channie Waites, Robyne Landiss Walker.

CLEMENTE SOTO VELEZ CULTURAL CENTER. *Bald Diva!* by David Koteles. July 16, 2003. Directed by Jason Jacobs and Jamee Freedus. *Karoake Stories* by Euijoon Kim. August 8, 2003. Directed by Alan Muraoka; with Sekiya Billman, Cindy Cheung, Deborah S. Craig, Siho Ellsmore, Mel Gionson, Marcus Ho, Paul H. Juhn, David Jung, Tim Kang, Peter Kim, Evan Lai, Hoon Lee, Marissa Lichwick, Brian Nishii, Eileen Rivera, James Saito, Jonathan Salkin, Jason Schuchman, Kaipo Schwab, Rodney To, Keo Woolford, Aaron Yoo. *Road House: The Stage Play*. October 30, 2003. Directed by Timothy Haskell; with Taimak Guarriello, Jamie Benge, Christopher Joy, Harry Listig, Lucia Burns, Kellie Montanio, Nick Ahrens, Laura Baggett, Ago the Magichef, Rolando Zuniga, Rachael Roberts, Brian Kantrowitz. SONGS FROM COCONUT HILL: A FESTIVAL OF NEW WORKS BY LATINO PLAYWRIGHTS. March 22–April 4, 2004. *Adoration of the Old Woman* by José Rivera. *The Outside Man* by Robert Dominguez. *The Women of Nine* by Angie Cruz, Cyn Cañel Rossi and Karen

Torres. *Ley of the Land* by Fernando Mañon. *All Sides* by Michael J. Narvaez. *To the Baggage Claim* by Tanya Saracho. *Chained Dog* by Robert Santana. *Transplantations* by Janis Astor del Valle. *Fuego* by Juan Shamsul Alam. BLURRING THE LINES. November 3, 2003. *Sharkey's Night* by Brian Snapp. Directed by Mr. Snapp. *Blackstocking Jenkins* by Eric Michael Kochmer. Directed by Emanuel Bocchieri. *I Dreamed of Dogs* by Eric Michael Kochmer. Directed by Ross Peabody. *Troilus and Cressida* by William Shakespeare. March 4, 2004. Directed by Marc Fajer; with Kate Benson, Fernando Betancourt, Pascal Beauboeuf, Jennifer Boggs, Damian Buzzerio, Kiebpoli Calnek, Michelle Kovacs, Emily Mitchell, Michael Moore, Andrew Zimmerman.

CONNELLY THEATRE. *Can't Let Go* by Keith Reddin. June 1, 2003. Directed by Carl Forsman; with Rebecca Luker, Cheyenne Casebier, Glenn Fleshler, Brian Hutchison, Greg Stuhr. *Lost*. Musical with book by Kirk Wood Bromley; music by Jessica Grace Wing; lyrics by Mr. Bromley. September 5, 2003. Directed by Rob Urbinati; with Anni Bruno, Youssif Eid, Annemieke Marie Farrow, Molly Karlin, Adam Kemmerer, Ted Malawer, Janell O'Rourke, Timothy Reynolds, Ed Roggenkamp, Jenna Rose, Karin Lili Ruhe, Michael Ruby, John Schumacher, Kelly Spitco, April Vidal, Chanelle Wilson. *Good Morning, Bill* by P.G. Wodehouse. September 25, 2003. Directed by Carl Forsman; with Jeremiah Wiggins, Heidi Armbruster, Nick Toren, Bridget Ann White, Jenny Mercein, John Vennema, David Standish. *Julius Caesar* by William Shakespeare. November 9, 2003. Directed by Gregory Wolfe; with Mary Birdsong, Gabriel Edelman, Jay Gaussoin, Gail Giovaniello, Tatiana Gomberg, Bill Gorman, Christopher Haas, Kelly Kinsella, Sarah Knowlton, Ax Norman, Kim Patton, Mason Pettit, John Roque, Dan Snow, Justin Steeve, Paula Stevens, Christopher Yates. THE ORWELL PROJECT. February 8, 2004. *1984*; adapted by Alan Lyddiard. Directed by Ginevra Bull. *Animal Farm*. Musical adaptation with book by Peter Hall; music by Richard Peaslee; lyrics by Adrian Mitchell. Directed by David Travis. *First Lady Suite* by Michael John LaChiusa. April 4, 2004. Directed by Jack Cummings III; with Sherry D. Boone, Donna Lynne Champlin, Ruth Gottschall, James Hindman, Robyn Hussa, Julia Murney, Mary Beth Peil, Cheryl Stern, Diane Sutherland, Mary Testa. *School for Scandal* by Richard Brinsley Sheridan. April 24, 2003. Directed by Rebecca Patterson; with Lauren Jill Ahrold, Virginia Baeta, Cynthia Brown, Eliza Ladd, Valentina McKenzie, Maureen Porter, Shanti Elise Prasad, Gisele Richardson, Ami Shukla, DeeAnn Weir.

DR2 THEATRE. *The Last Resort or Farblondjet* by Jeremy Kareken. October 16, 2003. Directed by Michael Montel; with Ann Talman, Peter Rini, Robert Heller, Polly Lee, David Staller. *Antigone* by Jean Anouilh; adapted by Lewis Galantiere. October 29, 2003. Directed by Richard Kuranda; with Alicia Regan, David Gideon, Rufus Collins, Elle Zalejski, Carolyn Craig, Daryl Stokes.

DANCE THEATER WORKSHOP. *O, Say a Sunset* by Robin Holcomb; based on the writings of Rachel Carson. September 24, 2003. Directed by Nikki Appino; with Ms. Holcomb, Julie Rawley, Susanna Burney. *Abundance* by Marty Pottenger. January 8, 2004. Directed by Ms. Pottenger and Steve Bailey; with Cary Barker, Herb Downer, Joe Gioco, Thom Rivera, Nikki E. Walker.

DILLON'S. *Cratchett Farm*. Musical with book and lyrics by Al Pailet; music by Marshall Pailet. September 5, 2003. Directed and choreographed by Jay Duffer; with Dennis Moench, Justis Bolding, Hale Appleman, Eric Briarley, Richard True, Dan Vissers, Joanna Young. *The Show Might Go On* by David Kosh. November 3, 2003. Directed by Ann Bowen; with Frederic J. Bender, Ross Bechsler, Michael Bullrich, Ali Costine, Katherine Dillingham, Aramand Gabriel, Asta Hansen, Raymond Hill, Carl Maguire, Audrey Moore, Cameron Stevens, Dan Stowell. *Minimum Wage*. Musical by Charlie LaGreca and Jeff LaGreca; with Sean Altman. May 7, 2004. Directed by David G. Armstrong; with Messrs. LaGreca, Paul Ashley, Chris Carlisle, Brian Depetris, Harold Lieman, Elena Meulener, Paul Romero, Suzanne Slade, Leah Sprecher.

THE DIRECTORS COMPANY. *Once Upon a Time in New Jersey*. Musical with book and lyrics by Susan DiLallo, music by Stephen Weiner. June 25, 2003. Directed by Pat Birch; with Erin Annarella, Todd Buonopane, Nick Cavarra, Funda Duval, Alayna Gallo, Brian Munn, Robert Neary, Orfeh, Ginette Rhodes, Melanie Vaughan, Richard Vida, Wayne Wilcox. *Bad Girls* by Joyce Carol Oates. November 10, 2003. Directed by Susana Tubert; with Sarah Hyland, Merritt Wever, Anastasia Webb, Deborah LeCoy, David Sims Bishins. *The Pavilion* by Craig Wright. February 19, 2004. Directed by Lucie Tiberghien; with Jennifer Mudge, Lee Sellars, Paul Sparks.

EDGE THEATER COMPANY. *Blackbird* by Adam Rapp. April 15, 2004. Directed by Mr. Rapp; with Mandy Siegfried, Paul Sparks. *Now That's What I Call a Storm* by Ann Marie Healy. April 26, 2004. Directed by Carolyn Cantor; with Marylouise Burke, Daniel Ahearn, Guy Boyd, Rebecca Nelson, Ted Schneider, Daniel Talbott.

EMERGING ARTISTS THEATRE COMPANY. EATFEST 2003. November 5–23, 2003. *Bum Steer* by Justin Warner. Directed by Jason Bowcutt; with Kim Crooks, Nick Battiste. *Sum Touching* by Eric Kaiser. Directed by Lauren Jacobs; with Mike Boland, Jeff Branson. *'Til Death Do Us Part* by Jay C. Rehak. Directed by Julie Jensen; with Amy Bizjak, Tom Greenman, John Misselwitz, Kara Taitz. *Unfinished Work* by Edgar Chisholm. Directed by Chris Wojyltko; with Jeanine Abraham, Peter Levine. *Job Strikes Back* by Matt Casarino. Directed by JoEllen Notte; with Wynne Anders, Christopher Borg, Ashley Green, Bill Reinking, Christopher Yustin. *L-O-V-E* by Joan Ross Sorkin. Directed by Amy Fiore; with Eric Christie, Ellen Reilly. *Freshly Killed Doves* by Jonathan Reuning. Directed by Wes Apfel; with Erin Hadley, Bryan McKinley, Vivian Meisner. *True Love* by Chris Wojyltko. Directed by Derek Roche; with Aimee Howard, Richard Ezra Zekaria. *Prelude to the First Day* by Ted LoRusso. Directed by Sturgis Warner; with Erin Gann, Danielle Quisenberry, Mark Farnsworth, Matt Behan, Jim Ferris. *Cosmic Goofs* by Barbara Lindsay. Directed by Ian Marshall; with Peter Herrick, Dayna Steinfeld, Casey Weaver. *Claymont* by Kevin Brofsky. February 1, 2004. Directed by Derek Jamison; with Wynne Anders, Jacqueline Barsh, Glory Gallo, Jason Hare, Aimee Howard, Jason O'Connell, Stephen Sherman. EATFEST 2004. March 16–April 4, 2004. *The One About the Rabbi* by Mark Lambeck. Directed by Troy Miller; with Lavette Gleis, Wayne Henry, Geany Masai. *A Message for Angela* by Jack Rushen. Directed by Pamela Rosenberger; with Laura Fois, Tom Greenman, Christopher Michael Todd. *A Curtain Call to Arms* by Matt Casarino. Directed by Deb Guston; with Amy Bizjak, Ryan Duncan, Erin Hadley, Peter Herrick, Bryan McKinley, Vivian Meisner, Kim Reed, Bill Reinking, Wayne Temple, Tracee Chimo, Lela Frechette. *Markie7722* by Alex Lewin. Directed by Rebecca Kendall; with Desmond Dutcher, Jason O'Connell, J. Michael Zally. *Lights Out* by Cassie Angley. Directed by Amy Fiore; with Jessica Calvello, Stephanie Ila Silver; Rochele Tillman, Wynne Anders. *3 Women* by Michael Edwin Stuart. Directed by Dawn Copeland; with Valerie David, Glory Gallo, Robyn Ganeles. *Peaches En Regalia* by Steven Lyons. Directed by Andrew Ronan; with Matt Boethin, Carter Inskeep, Yvonne Roen, Casey Weaver.

FEZ. *Make Love* by Karen Finley. July 13, 2003. Directed by Lance Cruce; with Ms. Finley, Chris Tanner, Mr. Cruce. *Art, Life and Show-Biz* by Ain Gordon. April 18, 2004. Directed by Mr. Gordon; with Helen Gallagher, Lola Pashalinski, Valda Setterfield.

59E59. BRITS OFF BROADWAY. April 7–July 4, 2004. *My Arm* by Tim Crouch; with Mr. Crouch. *Sun Is Shining* by Matt Wilkinson. Directed by Mr. Wilkinson. *The Woman Destroyed* by Simone de Beauvoir; translated by Diana Quick; with Ms. Quick. *Heavenly* by Frantic Assembly. *Cooking for Kings* by Ian Kelly. Directed by Simon Green; with Mr. Kelly. *Absolutely Fascinating* by Fascinating Aida. *Ghost City* by Gary Owen. Directed by Simon Harris. *Berkoff's Women* and *No Fear!*; with Linda Marlowe. *Hurricane* by Richard Dormer. Directed by Rachel O'Riordan; with Mr. Dormer. *The Straits* by Gregory Burke. Directed by John Tiffany.

THE FLEA THEATER. *Getting Into Heaven* by Polly Draper. July 2, 2003. Directed by Claire Lundberg; with Ms. Draper, James Badge Dale, Gretchen Egolf, Barbara eda-Young, Cooper Pillot. *Like I Say* by Len Jenkin. October 30, 2003. Directed by Mr. Jenkin; with Oberon K.A. Adjepong, Matthew Dellapina, Paula Ehrenberg, Fernando Gambaroni, Shari Hellman, Lanna Joffrey, Carolinne Messihi, Melissa Miller, Jeffrey Nauman, Jack O'Neill, John Peterson, Jonathan Kells Phillips, Sayra Player, Jerry Zellers. *Cellophane* by Mac Wellman. September 17, 2003. Directed by Jim Simpson; with Oberon K.A. Adjepong, Katie Apicella, Matthew Dellapina, Paula Ehrenberg, Ayse Eldek, Fernando Gambaroni, Lindy Gomez, Sarah Hayon, Lanna Joffrey, Josh Mann, Holly McLean, Jace McLean, Carolinne Messihi, Jeffrey Nauman, John Peterson, Jonathan Kells Phillips, Monica Stith, Sakura Sugihara, Gilbert Vela, Aaron Yoo, Jerry Zellers. *Powder Keg* by Dejan Dukovski; translated by Philip Philipovich. November 10, 2003. Directed by Michelle Malavet; with Rafael De Mussa, Randy Ryan, James Nardella, Stacy Rock, Jace McLean. *The Parrot* by Paul Zimet and Ellen Maddow. January 21, 2004. Directed by Mr. Zimet; with Scott Blumenthal, Elizabeth Daniels, Matthew Dellapina, Autumn Dornfeld, Kimberly Gambino, Carolyn Goelzer, Paul Iacono, Steven Rosen, Renoly Santiago. *The Wanderer* by Dmitry Lipkin. March 2, 2004. Directed by Adam Melnick; with Anthony Arkin, Larry Block, Amelia Campbell, Matthew Dellapina, Brian Gottesman, Irma St. Paule, David Warshofsky. *Mrs. Farnsworth* by A.R. Gurney. April 7, 2004. Directed by Jim Simpson; with Sigourney Weaver, John Lithgow, Danny Burstein, Kate Benson, Fernando Gambaroni, Tarajia Morrell. *Design Your Kitchen* by Kate Ryan. April 14, 2004. Directed by Ms. Ryan and Jim Simpson. *The Lake* by Gary Winter. April 21, 2004. Directed by Hayley Finn; with Jennifer Boggs, Lanna Joffrey, Dan O'Brien, Sayra Player.

45 BLEECKER. *Don Jonny* by Anton Dudley and Jonathan Spottiswoode. November 3, 2003. Directed by Jesse Berger. *A Mad World, My Masters* by Thomas Middleton. November 4, 2003. Directed by Michael Barakiva. *The Witch of Edmonton* by Thomas Dekker, John Ford and William Rowley. November 9, 2003. Directed by David Grimm; with Morgan Jenness. *Danton's Death* by Georg Büchner. November 11, 2003. Directed by Christopher McCann. *Phaedra* by Elizabeth Egloff. November 16, 2003. Directed by Jesse Berger; with Amy Irving, Ruth Maleczech. *Kean* by Jean-Paul Sartre. November 18, 2003. Directed by Eleanor Holdridge. *The Tragedy of Hamlet, Prince of Denmark* by Rob Grace. November 21, 2003. Directed by Devon Berkshire; with Bradford Louryk, Michael Cyril Creighton, Hannah Bos, Paul Thureen, Phoebe Ventouras, Alexa Scott-Flaherty. *The Life of Spiders* by Kelly Stuart. March 19, 2004. Directed by Rebecca Holderness; with Tuomas Hil, Kathryn Foster, Kevin Kuhlke, Jessma Evans, Christopher Burns, Raïna von Waldenburg, Malinda Walford, Robert Airhart, Kate Kohler Amory, Brendan McCall, Mark Wilson. *The Internationalist* by Anne Washburn. April 19, 2004. Directed by Ken Rus Schmoll; with Mark Shanahan, Heidi Schreck, Gibson Frazier, Kristen Kosmas, Travis York.

45TH STREET THEATRE. *Anticipating Heat* by Charlotte Winters. January 6, 2004. Directed by Ria Cooper; with Devon Berkshire, Erin Logemann, Blake Longacre, Jen Wineman. *un becoming* by Rick Schweikert. February 11, 2004. Directed by Mr. Schweikert and Jeffrey Edward Carpenter; with Laura Flanagan, Tami Dixon, Benjamin Moore, David McCamish, Mr. Carpenter, Sage Fitzgerald, Naomi Barr. *The Journals of Mihail Sebastian* by Mr. Sebastian; adapted by David Auburn. March 23, 2004. Directed by Carl Forsman; with Stephen Kunken.

GREENWICH STREET THEATRE. *The Pitchfork Disney* by Philip Ridley. June 18, 2003. Directed by Kevin Kittle; with Victor Villar-Hauser, Tara Denby, James M. Larmer, Aidan Redmond. *Chekhov's Rifle* by Alex Ladd. September 23, 2003. Directed by Nolan Haims; with Austin Pendleton, Jess Osuna, Craig Bachmann, Veronica Bero, Bridget Flanery, Dawn McGee, George Morafetis. *Duet* by Otho Eskin. December 4, 2003. Directed by Ludovica Villar-Hauser; with Laura Esterman, Pamela Payton-Wright, Robert Emmet Lunney.

HAROLD CLURMAN THEATRE. *The Trials of MS Katherine* by Chuck McMahon. November 8, 2003. Directed by George Allison; with Janet Dunson, Ruth Miller, Jimmy Dean, Monica Bailey, Cecelia Riddett, Samantha Bilinkas, Stephen Benson, Darren Capozzi, Wilbur Edwin Henry, Joel Nagle. *Roar* by Betty Shamieh. April 7, 2004. Directed by Marion McClinton; with Annabella Sciorra, Sarita Choudhury, Sherri Eldin, Joseph Kamal, Daniel Oreskes.

HERE ARTS CENTER. FUSE: THE NYC CELEBRATION OF QUEER CULTURE. June 16–July 5, 2003. Schedule included: *Lesbian Pulp-O-Rama!* by Heather de Michele, Anna Fitzwater, Gretchen M. Michelfeld, Beatrice Terry. *Holly's Folly* by Brandon Olson and Chris Tanner. *Weekends at Ped Club* by Peter Morris. Directed by Joseph Rosswog. *Andy Horowitz's B.F.D.* by Mr. Horowitz. *Bad Girls!* by Greg Wolloch and Allison Castillo. *Gravity Always Wins* by Marc Spitz. July 11, 2003. Directed by Jonathan Lisecki; with Mr. Lisecki, Zeke Farrow, Andersen Gabrych, Philip Littell, Brian Reilly, Alexandra Oliver, Valerie Clift. RANDOM SEXUAL ACTS. Short Plays by John Lee and Derek Paul Narendra. August 4–20, 2003. Directed by Ava Clade; with Natalie Arkus, Kelly Ann Heaney, Brian Parks, Nick Paglino. *The Parisian Love Story* by Mr. Narendra. *Honesty* by Mr. Lee. *The Proposal* by Mr. Narendra. *Spam, Inc.* by Mr. Lee. *Lights, Camera, Action* by Mr. Narendra. *Mr. Gallico* by Sam Carter. August 8, 2003. Directed by Henry Caplan; with Jason Howard, Karl Herlinger, Tate Henderson. *belly: three shorts* by Alva Rogers. September 9, 2003. Directed by Julia Whitworth; with Sherry D. Boone, Myorah B. Middleton, Barbara Pitts, Margi Sharp, Sophia Skiles, Meredith Wright. *Anna Bella Eema* by Lisa D'Amour and Chris Sidorfsky. September 15, 2003. Directed by Katie Pearl; with Monica Appleby, April Matthis. Dale Soules. *Lesbian Pulp-O-Rama in A Very Pulpy Christmas* by Heather de Michele, Anna Fitzwater, Gretchen M. Michelfeld, Beatrice Terry. December 8, 2003. *These Very Serious Jokes* by Douglas Langworthy; adapted from Goethe's *Faust*. January 8, 2004. Directed by David Herskovits; with David Greenspan, Will Badgett, George Hannah, E.C. Kelly, Pun Bandhu, Yuri Skujins, Wayne Scott. *The Viy* by Nikolai Gogol; adapted by Richard Harland Smith. March 20, 2004. Directed by Mr. Smith; with Stephen Aloi, Jamie Askew, Roy Bacon, Jeff Buckner, Tom Cappadona, Michael Cuomo, Julie Hera, Karl Jacob, Leo Jenicek, Lou Kylis, Suzanne Levinson, Michelle Maryk, John McDermott, Misha Pogul, Jeremy Schwartz, Jarrod Spector, Julie Whitney. *The Mystery of the Charity of Joan of Arc* by Charles Pèguy; translated by Julian Green. May 12, 2004. Directed by David Herskovits; with Daphne Gaines, Jerusha Klemperer, Sophia Skiles.

THE IMMIGRANTS' THEATRE PROJECT. *Little Pitfall* by Markéta Bláhová; translated by Jiri Topel. January 21, 2004. Directed by Marcy Arlin; with Mayura Baweja, Oscar de la Fe Colon, Nannette Deasy, Adriana Gaviria, Eileen Rivera, Tzahi Moskovitz. NEW INDIGENOUS VOICES FROM AUSTRALIA. March 17–May 18, 2004. *Crowfire* by Jadah Milroy. Directed by Kaipo Schwab; with Bryan Andy. *Yanagai! Yanagai!* by Andrea James. Directed by Marcy Arlin; with Louise Bennett. *Box the Pony* by Scott Rankin and Leah Purcell. *Stolen* by Jane Harrison. Directed by Karen Oughtred; with Kylie Belling. *Conversations With the Dead* by Richard Frankland. Directed by Muriel Miguel; with Aaron Pederson.

INTAR 53. *Smashing* by Brooke Berman. October 12, 2003. Directed by Trip Cullman; with David Barlow, Lucas Papaelias, Katharine Powell, Joseph Siravo, Katherine Waterston, Merritt Wever.

THE IRONDALE ENSEMBLE PROJECT. *Outside the Law* by Jim Niesen and the company. May 11, 2004. Directed by Mr. Niesen; with Danny Bacher, Josh Bacher, Erin Biernard, Terry Greiss, Michael-David Gordon, Jack Lush, Barbara Mackenzie-Wood, Celli Pitt, Damen Scranton, Laura Wickens.

JOHN HOUSEMAN THEATRE CENTER. *Serenade the World: The Music and Words of Oscar Brown Jr.* Musical revue by Eric Krebs. July 29, 2003. Directed by Stephen Henderson; with Genovis Albright, Oscar Brown Trio. *Cupid and Psyche*. Musical with book and lyrics by Sean Hartley; music by Jihwan Kim. September 24, 2003. Directed by Timothy Childs; choreographed by Devanand Janki; with Laura Marie Duncan, Barrett Foa, Deborah Lew, Logan Lipton. *Golf.* Musical revue by Michael Roberts. October 8, 2003. Directed and choreographed by Christopher Scott; with Joel Blum, Trisha Rapier, Christopher Sutton, Sal Viviano.

JOHN MONTGOMERY THEATRE COMPANY. *Same Train* by Levy Lee Simon; music and lyrics by Mark Bruckner. February 7, 2004. Directed by Nicki H.J. Stadm; with Henry Afro-Bradley, Tamela Aldridge, Nicoye Banks, Thaddeus Daniels, Chris Evans, Indigo Melendez, LaRee Reese, Norman Small Jr.

JOSÉ QUINTERO THEATRE. *Safe* by Anthony Ruivivar and Tony Glazer. June 14, 2003. Directed by Mr. Ruivivar; with Jason Wiles, Henry Afro-Bradley, Carlin Glynn, Yvonne Jung, Coby Bell.

KIRK THEATRE. *American Storage* by Edward Allan Baker. November 3, 2003. Directed by Drew DeCorleto; with Stephen Brumble Jr., Teresa L. Goding, Andrew J. Hoff, Leo Lauer. *Trust* by Gary Mitchell. May 9, 2004. Directed by Erica Schmidt; with Ritchie Coster, Fiona Gallagher, Kevin Isola, Colin Lane, Dan McCabe, Declan Mooney, Meredith Zinner.

KRAINE THEATER. *Day of Reckoning* by Melody Cooper. April 14, 2004. Directed by Lorca Peress; with Freedome Bailey, Parris Nicole Cisco, Ms. Cooper, Michael Kennealy, Alima Lindsey.

LABYRINTH THEATER COMPANY. *Dutch Heart of Man* by Robert Glaudini. September 16, 2003. Directed by Charles Goforth; with Maggie Bofill, Maggie Burke, David Deblinger, Wilemina Olivia Garcia, Scott Hudson, Salvatore Inzerillo, Portia.

LARK PLAY DEVELOPMENT CENTER. ANNUAL PLAYWRIGHTS WEEK. June 4–7, 2003. *Mr. and Mrs. G* by Jeff Barow. Directed by Jim Ashcraft. *I'm Breathing the Water Now* by Bash Halow. Directed by May Adrales. *Humans Remain* by Robin Rice Lichtig. Directed by Daniella Topol. *Suspects* by Joe DiMiceli. Directed by Angel David. *Lingua* by Roger Williams. Directed by Michael Johnson-Chase. *The Motherline* by Chantal Bilodeau. Directed by Steven Williford. *Three Christs Live* by Dan O'Brien. Directed by Leah C. Gardiner. *The Grandmama Tree: A Folkfable* by Benard Cummings. Directed by Jack Cummings III. *Waxing West* by Saviana Stanescu. September 25, 2003. Directed by Michael Johnson-Chase; with Michael Bakkensen, Glynis Bell, Celia Howard, Tom Ligon, Connie Nelson, George Pappas, Wayne Schroder, Jennifer Dorr White. *Undone* by Andrea Thome. October 30, 2003. Directed by Victor Maog; with Denia Brache, Victoria Cartagena, Carlo D'Amore, Mateo Gomez, Ernesto Rodriguez, Teresa Yenque. *Sex in Other People's Houses* by Sonia Pabley. April 23, 2004. Directed by Ashok Sinha; with Rizwan Manji, Pooja Kumar, Nandita Shenoy, Samir Younis. *Jaz* and *Big Shoot* by Koffi Kwahulé; translated by Chantal Bilodeau. May 18, 2004. Directed by Michael Johnson-Chase; with Zabryna Guevara, Wayne Schroder, Sorab Wadia.

LION THEATRE. *White Widow*. Musical by Paul Dick; based on Mario Fratti's *Mafia*. June 7, 2003. Directed by Cara Reichel; with Patrick Spencer Bodd, Larry Brustofski, Sarah Corey, Michael Day, James Donegan, Dennis D. Driskill, Al Gordon, Matthew Allen Hardy, Gloria Hodes, Ronald Roy

Johnson Jr., Elizabeth Kinglsey, Rachel Styne, Marina Torres. *Unidentified Human Remains and the True Nature of Love* by Brad Fraser. March 27, 2004. Directed by Robert Bella; with Diana Ascher, Caroline Cagney, Lauren Castellano, Andrew Frost, Greg Jackson, Joe Stipek, Brandon Thompson. *The End of You* by Michael D. Cohen. May 14, 2004. Directed by Sarah Gurfield; with PJ Sosko, Poorna Jagannathan.

MANHATTAN ENSEMBLE THEATER. *The Hunger Waltz* by Sheila Callaghan. January 10, 2004. Directed by Olivia Honegger; with Susan O'Connor, Kittson O'Neill, Michael Connors, Brent Popolizio, Susan O'Connor.

MANHATTAN THEATRE SOURCE. *Three Sisters* by Anton Chekhov; translated by Boris Kievsky. January 7, 2004. Directed by Andrew Frank; with Daryl Boling, Ato Essandoh, Joe Ganem, Hope Garland, Carla Hayes, Jason Howard, Fiona Jones, Clyde Kelley, Mr. Kievsky, Neil Maffin, Mitchell Riggs, Carla Tassara, Ben Thomas, Catherine Zambri. *That Woman: Rebecca West Remembers* by Carl Rollyson, Anne Bobby and Helen Macleod. March 6, 2004. Directed by David Drake; with Anne Bobby. *Shrinkage* by Manuel Igrejas. March 31, 2004. Directed by Lory Henning-Dyson; with Susan Blackwell, Laura Camien, Jeffrey Doornbos.

MA-YI THEATRE COMPANY. *Wave* by Sung Rno. March 21, 2004. Directed by Will Pomerantz; with Michi Barall, Deborah S. Craig, Ron Domingo, Paul H. Juhn, Patrick McNulty, Aaron Yoo.

MAZER THEATER. *A Stoop on Orchard Street.* Musical by Jay Kholos. August 7, 2003. Directed by Lon Gary; with Edward Anthony, Selby Brown, Lili Corn, Valerie David, Eleni Delopoulos, Daniel Fischer, Mr. Gary, Deborah Grausman, Joel Halsted, Kristian Hunter Lazzaro, Stuart Marshall, Sarah Matteucci, David Mendell, Shad Olsen, Jonathan Schneidman, Joseph Spiotta, Scott Steven, Antonia Garza Szilagi, Sharon Taylor, Anne Tonelson, Marla Weiner, Stephanie Wilberding.

MELTING POT THEATER COMPANY. *Vanishing Point.* Musical with book by Liv Cummins and Robert Hartmann; music by Mr. Hartmann; lyrics by Ms. Cummins, Mr. Hartman and Scott Keys. April 26, 2004. Directed by Michelle Tattenbaum; with Alison Fraser, Emily Skinner, Barbara Walsh.

MIDTOWN INTERNATIONAL THEATRE FESTIVAL. July 14–August 3, 2003. Schedule included: *The Colonel's Wife* by Mario Fratti. Directed by Roi Escudero; with Mr. Escudero, Alex McCord, Michael Earle, Francisco Cantilo, Julio Soler, Paula Wilson. *The Remarkable Journey of Prince Jen.* Musical with book and lyrics by Brian Vinero; music by Seth Weinstein; based on the novel by Lloyd Alexander. Directed by Joel Froomkin; with Arthur Delos Santos, Timothy Huang. *Favorite Colors* by Scott R. Ritter. Directed by Ernest Abuba. *Companions* by Denis McKeown. Directed by Jason Grant. *Nice Guys Finish . . .* by Eric Alter. Directed by Rob Sullivan. *The Overdevelopment of Scott* by Sharon Fogarty. Directed by Ms. Fogarty. *Stained Glass Ugly* by Qui Nguyen. Directed by Robert Ross Parker. *Waiting for the Glaciers to Melt* by Brian Lane Green. *Who Am I* by Rodney E. Reyes. Directed by Mr. Reyes. *Walking Through the Night* by Haerry Kim. Directed by Christopher Petit. *Thrill Me: The Leopold and Loeb Story.* Musical with book, music and lyrics by Stephen Dolginoff. Directed by Martin Charnin. *Criminal* by Javier Daulte. Directed by Gwynn MacDonald. *The $25,000 Pyramid* by Nick Vigorito Jr. Directed by Morgan Doninger; with Damian Vanore, Anthony Vitrano, Tim Cinnante, Pete Mele, Michael Bullrich. *American Treacle.* Musical with book by Bricken Sparacino and Natalie Wilder; music by Ms. Sparacino, Eric Chercover, Michael Birch and Richard Homan; lyrics by Ms. Sparacino, Messrs. Chercover, Homan, Michael Birch; lyrics by Mses. Sparacino, Wilder, Messrs. Chercover, Birch, Homan. *BKC* by Matt Schapiro and Brad Webb. Directed by Messrs. Schapiro and Webb. *LiLiA!* By Libby Skala. Directed by Gabriel Barre; with Ms. Skala. *(Gone With) Miss Julie* by Shela Xoregos; based on a Michael Meyer translation of August Strindberg's *Miss Julie.* Directed and choreographed by Ms. Xoregos; with Keith Carter, Kim Gainer, Erin Hunter, Talie Melnyk, Carin Murphy, Gregory Ward. *Just Us Boys* by Frank Stancati. Directed by Catherine Lamm. *The Winner: A Brooklyn Fable.* Musical with book by Inez Basso Glick and Annmarie Fabricatore; music and lyrics by Stanley Glick. Directed by Ron Nakahara; with Michael Ricciardone, Marnie Baumer, Jeremy Ellison Gladstone. *That Play: A One Person Macbeth* by William Shakespeare; adapted by Tom Gualtieri and Heather Hill. Directed by Ms. Hill; with Mr. Gualtieri.

MINT SPACE. *The Heiress* by Henry James; adapted by Ruth and Augustus Goetz. January 14, 2004. Directed by Mahayana Landowne; with Michael Balsley, Sarah Dandridge, David Gochfeld, Rebecca Hoodwin, James Jacobson, Kelly Ann Moore, Jean Morgan, Dee Pelletier, Michele Tauber.

NEIGHBORHOOD PLAYHOUSE. *Handy Dandy* by William Gibson. December 9, 2003. Directed by Don Amendolia; with Helen Gallagher, Nicolas Surovy. *Tasting Memories* by Michael Fischetti and Emily Mitchell. May 21, 2004. Directed by Don Amendolia; with Messrs. Fischetti, Amendolia, Ms. Mitchell and a rotating cast including Rosemary Harris, Kitty Carlisle Hart, Philip Bosco, Tammy Grimes, Alvin Epstein, Richard Easton, Joy Franz, Kathleen Noone, Mel Cobb.

NEW VICTORY THEATER. *Cookin'* by Seung Whan Song. September 25, 2003. Directed Mr. Song; with Kang Il Kim, Won Hae Kim, Bum Chan Lee, Choo Ja Seo, Ho Yeoul Sul, Hyung Suk Jung, Ji Won Kang, Young Hoon Kim, Sung Min Lee. Transferred to an Off Broadway run at the Minetta Lane Theatre (3/7/2004; 97 performances as of 5/31/2004). See Plays Produced Off Broadway section in this volume. *Bug Music* by Don Byron. April 26, 2004. With Mr. Byron. *Idiots Adios: The Flaming Idiots*. With Rob Williams, Jon O'Connor, Kevin Hunt. May 26, 2004.

THE NEW YORK CITY HIP-HOP THEATER FESTIVAL. June 3-14, 2003. Schedule included: *Flow* by Will Power. Directed by Danny Hoch; with Mr. Power. *Till the Break of Dawn* by Danny Hoch. *Jack Ya Body Part 1: Storm's Solo for Two* by the Rubberband Dance Company. *Open Street Hydrant* by Jen Sabel. *Jack Ya Body Part 2: Olive* by the Rubberband Dance Company. *Beatbox: A Rapperetta* by Tommy Shepherd and Dan Wolf. *Word Becomes Flesh* by Marc Bamuthi. *bloodclaat* by D'bi Young. *Melic Composed* by Lisa Biggs and Tanisha Christie. *In the Heights* by Lin Manuel-Miranda. *Slick Rhymes* by Claudia Alick. *My Starship* by Zvi Rosenfeld. *Tea* by Ben Snyder. *Soundtrack City* by Yuri Lane. *Slice* by Kerri Kochanski. *Culture Bandit* by Vanessa Hidary. *Black Folks Guide to Black Folks* by Hanifah Walidah. *Bulletproof Deli* by Sabela. *Stakes Is High* by Pattydukes. *Angela's Mix Tape* by Eisa Davis. *In the Last Car* by MUMs. *Rough Draft of My Life* by tigerlily. *Rewind* by Greg Beuthin. *Giving Up the Gun* by David Rodriguez.

NEW YORK INTERNATIONAL FRINGE FESTIVAL. August 8–24, 2003. Schedule included: *Acts of Contrition* by Timothy Nolan. Directed by Vincent Marano. *American Fabulous* by Jeffrey Strouth; adapted by Troy Carson. Directed by Jonathan Warman; with Mr. Carson. *ASHIRA69 (Episode #1: Cult to the Chase!)* by Paul Sapp. Directed by Tina Polzin. *Berserker* by Paul Outlaw. Directed by Tanya Kane-Parry. *Caresses* by Sergei Belbel. Directed by Adam C. Eisenstein. *God Bless Americana: The Retro Vacation Slide Show* by Charles Phoenix. *Dear Charlotte* by Joy Gregory. Directed by Ms. Gregory and Anthony Byrnes. *"Buddy" Cianci: The Musical* by Jonathan Van Gieson and Mike Tarantino. Directed by Dean Strober. *A Life in Her Day* by Hilary Chaplain. Directed by Patricia Buckley. *Panic Is Not a Disorder* by Pat Candaras. With Ms. Candaras. *Faint* by Eric Sanders. Directed by Mr. Sanders. *Staggering Toward America* by Rik Reppe. Directed by Jack Rowe. *Big Girl, Little World* by Jay Duffer. Directed by Mr. Duffer. *Scalpel.* Musical with book, music and lyrics by D'Arcy Drollinger. Directed by John Ficarra. *The Irreplaceable Commodity* by Michael Minn. Directed and choreographed by Gary Slavin. *Mo(u)rning* by Adrian Rodriguez. Directed by Arian Blanco. *Freedom of Speech* by Eliza Jane Schneider. Directed by Sal Romeo. *Pale Idiot* by Kirk Lynn. Directed by Laramie Dennis.

92ND STREET Y. *Return Journey* by Bob Kingdom. November 9, 2003. Directed by Anthony Hopkins; with Mr. Kingdom.

OHIO THEATRE. ICE FACTORY 2003 SUMMER THEATER FESTIVAL. July 9–August 16, 2003. Schedule included: *Mother's Little Helper* by Lenora Champagne. Directed by Robert Lyons; with Ms. Champagne. *Conquest of the Universe* by Charles Ludlam. Directed by Emma Griffin. *Flop* created by Pig Iron Theatre. *The Myopia* by David Greenspan; with Mr. Greenspan. *Hatched* created by SaBooge Theatre. *Deception* by Jeremy Dobrish. Directed by Mr. Dobrish. *Moby Dick* by Herman Melville; adapted by Julian Rad. September 6, 2003. Directed by Hilary Adams; with Christopher Kelly, Michael Berry, Michael Shawn Montgomery, Mr. Rad, Antony Ferguson, Joseph Melendez, Eirik Gislason, William Metzo. *no meat no irony* by Robert Lyons. September 29, 2003. Directed by Mr. Lyons; with Celia Schaeffer, Jeremy Brisiel. *Terrotica* by Wade Bowen. October 23, 2003. Directed by Brad Krumholz; with Mr. Bowen, Rosaruby Glaberman, Sarah Dey Hirshan, Patricia Skarbinski. *Demon Baby* by Erin Courtney. January 9, 2004. Directed by Ken Rus Schmoll; with Heidi Schreck, Patrick McNulty, Nina Hellman, Gibson Frazier, Leo Kittay, Polly Lee, Mark Shanahan, Glenn Fleshler. *Superpowers* by Jeremy Dobrish. May 1, 2004. Directed by Jessica Davis-Irons; with Arthur Aulisi, Jeremy Brisiel, Ryan Bronz, Nina Hellman, Dana Croll Smith, Stan Lachow, Christy Meyer, Margie Stokley. *As I Lay Dying* by William Faulkner; adapted by Andrew Grosso. May 2, 2004. Directed by Mr. Grosso; with Arthur Aulisi, Sarah Bellows, Eric Martin

Brown, Drew Cortese, Aimee McCormick, Thomas Piper, Tommy Schrider, John Thomas Waite, Amy Laird Webb.

ONTOLOGICAL THEATRE. *Non-D* by Andrew Irons. August 20, 2003. Directed by Jessica Davis-Irons; with Emanuele Ancornini, Arthur Aulisi, Sarah Bellows, Jeremy Brisiel, Richard Hamilton Dibella, Jeremy Ellison-Gladstone, Margie Stokley. *King Cowboy Rufus Rules the Universe* by Richard Foreman. January 15, 2004. Directed by Mr. Foreman; with Juliana Francis, Jay Smith, T. Ryder Smith. *My Renaissance Faire Lady* by Evan Cabnet. May 8, 2004. Directed by Mr. Cabnet; with John Forest, Eris V. Migliorini, Corey Patrick, Caleb Scott, Noah Trepanier, Ted Welch.

PANTHEON THEATER. *New Anatomies* by Timberlake Wertenbaker. September 10, 2003. Directed by James Marshall; with Anna Hopkins, Shawn Kane, Mireya Lucio, Melanie Levy, Lilly Medville. *Sacrifice to Eros* by Frederick Timm. October 22, 2004. Directed by Marc Parees; with Pamela Dunlap, Jaime Sanchez, Caesar Samayoa, Don Clark Williams, Eric Jordan Young, Maria Helan Checa. *Seascape With Sharks and Dancer* by Don Nigro. November 5, 2003. Directed by Jason Eiland; with April Dawn Brown, Jef Cozza. *Metropolitan Operas* by Joe Pintauro. April 15, 2004. Directed by Lisa Melita French, Michael LoPorto, Francisco Solorzano; with Jeremy Brena, Gabriel Buentello, AnaMaria Correa, Kendra Leigh Landon, Victoria Malvagno, Keri Meoni, Chiara Montalto, Jay Rivera, Gilberto Ron, Mr. Solorzano, Dedra McCord-Ware. *Necropolis* by Don Nigro. May 13, 2004. Directed by John DiFusco; with Francesca Nina O'Keefe, Jim Thalman.

PARADISE THEATER. *People Die That Way* by Lisa Ebersole. February 22, 2004. Directed by Ms. Ebersole; with Dahl Colson, Ms. Ebersole, Ken Forman, Rhonda Keyser, Monique Vukovic.

PEARL THEATRE COMPANY. *The Rivals* by Richard Brinsley Sheridan. September 21, 2003. Directed by Robert Neff Williams; with Celeste Ciulla, Dominic Cuskern, Dan Daily, Robert Hock, Sean McNall, Christopher Moore, Edward Seamon, Carol Schultz, Rachel Botchan, Eunice Wong, Patrick Toon. *The Merchant of Venice* by William Shakespeare. November 2, 2003. Directed by Shepard Sobel; with Dan Daily, Cornell Womack, Jason Ma, Scott Whitehurst, Sean McNall, Christopher Moore, Celeste Ciulla, Rachel Botchan, Patrick Toon, Dominic Cuskern, Calli Sarkesh, Andy Prosky, Edward Seamon, Edward Griffin, Eunice Wong. *Persians* by Aeschylus. January 11, 2004. Directed by Shepard Sobel; with Joanne Camp, Robert Hock, Sean McNall, Scott Whitehurst. *Double Infidelity* by Marivaux; adapted by Oscar Mandel. February 22, 2003. Directed by Beatrice Terry; with Rachel Botchan, Scott Whitehurst, Christopher Moore, Celeste Ciulla, Dominic Cuskern, Sean McNall, Allison Nichols. *When We Dead Awaken* by Henrik Ibsen; translated by Rolf Fjelde. April 4, 2004. Directed by Benno Haenel; with Rachel Botchan, Joanne Camp, Robert Hock, Scott Whitehurst.

PELICAN STUDIO THEATER. *The Curate Shakespeare As You Like It* by Don Nigro. April 16, 2004. Directed by Christopher Thomasson; with Christopher Yeatts, Candice Holdorf, Sarah Sutel, Brian J. Carter, Josephine Cashman, Todd Butera, Timothy Roselle.

PETER JAY SHARP THEATER. *Fighting Words* by Sunil Kuruvilla. February 15, 2004. Directed by Liz Diamond; with Marin Ireland, Jayne Houdyshell, Pilar Witherspoon.

PHIL BOSAKOWSKI THEATRE. *The Tempest* and *Richard III* by William Shakespeare. October 23, 2003. Directed by Jason Alan Carvell. *Orestes* by Charles L. Mee. January 8, 2004. Directed by Ellen Beckerman; with Margot Ebling, Shawn Fagan, James Saidy.

PROSPECT THEATER COMPANY. *The Belle's Stratagem* by Hannah Cowley. September 27, 2003. Directed by Davis McCallum; with Dorothy Abraham, Robert Bowen Jr., Aysan Çelik, R. Paul Hamilton, Leo Kittay, Damian Long, Kate MacKenzie, Ian Oldaker, Saxon Palmer, Christian Roulleau, Wendy Rich Stetson, Ed Vassallo, Susan Wands. *The House of Bernarda Alba* by Federico Garcia Lorca. January 17, 2004. Directed by Cara Reichel; with Betty Hudson, Giovanna Zaccaro, Jennifer Michele Brown, Danielle Melanie Brown, Sandy York, Roxann Kraemer, Amy Hutchins, Juliet O'Brien, Anna Bullard, Susan Maris, Karen Sternberg, Jennifer Herzog, Jennifer Blood, Suzy Kaye, Arlene Love, Dara Seitzman, Jennifer McGeorge, Dolores Kenan. *The Afghanistan Project* by William Mastrosimone. February 3, 2004. With Christina Gelsone. *Man Is Man* by Bertolt Brecht, translated by Marcella Nowak. April 17, 2004. Directed by Jackson Gay; with Brad Heberlee, Dara Seitzman, Jennifer Bruno, Sarah Elliot, Robyn Ganeles, Matthew Humphreys, Austin Jones, Frank Liotti, Lisa Louttit, Mark Mattek, Nathaniel Nicco-Annan, Paul Paglia, Patricia Spahn, Joe Vena, Marnye Young. *Lonely Rhymes*. Musical revue by Peter Mills. April 22, 2004. Directed by Cara Reichel; with Jason Mills, Tracey Moore, Liz Power, Noah Weisberg.

RATTLESTICK THEATER. *An Evening With Burton and Russell* by Arnie Burton and Jay Russell. June 16, 2003. Directed by Shelley Delaney; with Messrs. Burton and Russell. *St. Crispin's Day* by Matt Pepper. June 22, 2003. Directed by Simon Hammerstein; with David Wilson Barnes, Lauren Berst, Lee Blair, Denis Butkus, Alex Draper, Mayhill Fowler, Michael Gladis, Darren Goldstein, Richard Liccardo, Tommy Schrider. *Four Beers* by David Van Vleck. September 29, 2003. Directed by Roger Danforth; with Robert LuPone, Peter Maloney, Lee Wilkof, Guy Boyd, Michael Cullen. *Five Flights* by Adam Bock. January 19, 2004. Directed by Kent Nicholson; with Joanna P. Adler, Jason Butler Harner, Kevin Karrick, Matthew Montelongo, Alice Ripley, Lisa Steindler.

RED ROOM. *Specter* by Don Nigro. September 12, 2003. Directed by Michael Kimmel. *Rabbithead* by Leora Barish. November 20, 2003. Directed by Nina V. Kerova. *Bald Diva!* by David Koteles. February 14, 2004. Directed by Jason Jacobs; with Tim Cusack, Gerald Marsini, Matthew Pritchard, Terrence Michael McCrossan, Jeffrey James Keyes, Nathan Blew.

ST. ANN'S WAREHOUSE. *Hiroshima Maiden* by Dan Hurlin. January 14, 2004. Directed by Mr. Hurlin; with Matthew Acheson, Nami Yamamoto, Dawn Akemi Seito, Lake Simons, Deana Headley, Tom Lee, Kazu Nakamura, Chris Green, Eric Wright, Yoko Myoi, Jeff Berman, Robert Een, Bill Ruyle. *Accidental Nostalgia* by Cynthia Hopkins. March 26, 2004. Directed by DJ Mendel; with Ms. Hopkins, Jim Findlay, Jeff Sugg.

SANDE SHURIN THEATRE. *Bitter Homes and Gardens* by John Benjamin Martin. July 24, 2003. Directed by Donna Castellano; with Jordan Auslander, Simcha Borenstein, Barbara Kidd Calvano, Ms. Castellano, Carlo Fiorletta, Brian James Grace, Alexis Iacono, Pierre Farrell, Stephen Wheeler. *The Sea* by Olafur Haukur Simonarson. June 13, 2003. Directed by Kristina O'Neal; with Richard Kohn, Evelyn Page, Simone Lutz, Elizabeth Flynn Jones, Liam Mitchell, Annette Fama Jarred, Brett Michael Dykes, Josh Stein Sapir, Christos Klapsis, Kristina O'Neal, T.J. Zale, Suzanne Levinson, Briana Trautman-Maier. *Riff-Raff* by Laurence Fishburne. December 11, 2003. Directed by Jason Summers; with Damien D. Smith, Sean Slater, Ben Rivers.

SANFORD MEISNER THEATER. *The Lark* by Jean Anouilh; adapted by Vanya Cassel Pawson. November 29, 2003. Directed by Ms. Pawson; with Lindsay Halladay, Clay Cockrell, Matt Semrick, Michael Boothroyd, David McCamish, Carlyle Lincoln, Ron Hirt, Peter Whalen, Patrick Mahoney, Silviane Chebance, Max Goldberg, Lino Alvarez, Gloria Garayua.

78TH STREET THEATRE LAB. *Notes to the Motherland* by Paul Rajeckas and George L. Chieffet. September 21, 2003. Directed by Mr. Chieffet; with Mr. Rajeckas. *All Is Almost Still* by Adam Seelig. May 8, 2004. Directed by Mr. Seelig; with Billie James, Craig Evans, Lawrence Merritt.

SHOW WORLD THEATER CENTER. *Lypsinka! As I Lay Lip-Synching* by John Epperson. August 14, 2003. Directed by Kevin Malony; with Mr. Epperson.

SOHO PLAYHOUSE. *Carnival Knowledge* by Todd Robbins. August 17, 2003. Directed by Kirsten Sanderson; with Mr. Robbins, Shannon Morrow, Little Jimmy.

STORM THEATRE. *The Rogueries of Scapin* by Molière; translated by Jack Clay. October 1, 2003. Directed by Stephen Logan Day; with Shay Ansari, Julisa Banbanaste, Dan Berkey, Ashton Crosby, Simon Deonarian, Adriane Erdos, Hugh Brandon Kelly, Kelleigh Miller, Maury Miller, Tim Roberts. *Noah* by Andre Obey, translated by Judith Suther and Earl Clowney. October 1, 2003. Directed by Peter Dobbins and Arin Arbus; with Jennifer Curfman, Bernardo De Paula, Sharon Freedman, Stacey Gladstone, David Huber, Marisa Lee, Peter Mantia, Damon Noland, Viviana L. Rodriquez, Timothy Rosselle, Matt Schuneman, Rolando J. Vargas. *Spokesong*. Musical with book and lyrics by Stewart Parker; music by Jimmy Kennedy. February 12, 2004. Directed by Peter Dobbins; with Jill Anderson, Colleen Crawford, Ethan Flower, Robin Haynes, Paul Jackel, Michael Mendiola. *A Midsummer Night's Dream* by William Shakespeare. May 24, 2004. Directed by Peter Dobbins; with John Riggins, Kate Shindle, Joshua Vasquez, Ethan Flower, Jo Benincasa, Adriane Erdos, Bernardo De Paula, Hugh Brandon Kelly, Geoffrey Warren Barnes II, Jose Sanchez, Eamon Montgomery, Joel C. Roman, Kelleigh Miller.

THE TANK. *Chocolate in Heat: Growing Up Arab in America* by Betty Shamieh. September 6, 2003. Directed by Sam Gold; with Ms. Shamieh, Piter Fattouche.

THEATRE AT ST. CLEMENT'S. *Spring Storm* by Tennessee Williams. May 9, 2004. Directed by Coy Middlebrook; with Kristen Cerelli, John Gazzale, David Gideon, Carlin Glynn, Elizabeth Kemp,

Krista Lambden, Joe B. McCarthy, Gabe Fazio, Patricia Marie Kelly, Marianne Matthews, Drew McVety, Sylvia Norman, Summer Serafin.

THEATRE 80. FAIRY TALES OF THE ABSURD. June 12, 2003. *Tales for Children* by Eugene Ionesco; translated by Karen Ott. *To Prepare a Hard Boiled Egg* by Eugene Ionesco; translated by Edward Einhorn. *One Head Too Many* by Edward Einhorn. Festival directed by Mr. Einhorn; with John Blaylock, Peter B. Brown, Ian W. Hill, Uma Incrocci, Celia Montgomery.

THEATRE 54. *MasterBulder: REBUILT* by Henrik Ibsen; adapted by Victoria Pero. November 8, 2003. Directed by Ms. Pero; with Chris Clavelli, Grant Neale, Emera Felice Krauss, Okwui Okpokwasili, Hilary Spector. *Little Pitfall* by Markéta Bláhová. January 21, 2004. Directed by Marcy Arlin; with Eileen Rivera, Nannette Deasy, Tzahi Moskovitz, Adriana Gaviria, Mayura Baweja, Oscar de la Fe Colon. *Orchidelirium* by Dave Carley. March 25, 2004. Directed by Stephen Wargo; with Margaret Norwood, Michael Poignand, Fred Arsenault, Navida Stein.

THEATRE 3. *Under Milk Wood* by Dylan Thomas. December 3, 2003. Directed by Moni Yakim; with Jeff Broitman, Phannie Davis, Olivia Goode, John Grimball, Emily Gunyou, Anna Guttormsgard, Jody Hegarty, Nina Millin, Brad Seal, Dan Truman.

THE THEATRE-STUDIO. *Clash by Night* by Clifford Odets. January 14, 2004. Directed by Ann Raychel; with Jack Fitz, Bob Gallagher, Hilary Howard, Abby Fox, Astrit Ibroci, Douglas Clark Johnson, Joshua Kauffman.

TRIAD THEATRE. *Who Killed Woody Allen?* by Dan Callahan, Brendan Connor and Tom Dunn. December 4, 2003. Directed by Messrs. Callahan, Connor, Dunn; with Peter Loureiro, Mr. Connor, Jillan Dugan, John Mooney, John Shaver, Christopher Wisner. *Mercury: The Afterlife and Times of a Rock God* by Charles Messina. January 14, 2004. Directed by Mr. Messina; with Amir Darvish. *Cirque Jacqueline* by Andrea Reese. March 17, 2004. Directed by Charles Messina; with Ms. Reese. *Love in Great Neck*. Musical with book by Tuvia Tenenbom and Maria Lowy; music and lyrics by Phil Rubin. May 15, 2004. Directed by Mr. Tenenbom; with Joan Fishman, Johnnie Mae, Mario Golden, Diane Quinn, Amitai Kedar.

TRILOGY THEATRE. *7 Blow Jobs* by Mac Wellman. June 19, 2003. Directed by Phillip Cruise; with Mr. Cruise, Robert Lincourt, Madeleine Maby, Edward Miller, Elizabeth Neptune, Billy Steel, Michael Whitney, Travis York. *Eat Your Heart Out* by Nick Hall. October 3, 2003. Directed by Nancy S. Chu; with Marc Diraison, Katie Honaker, David Brainard, Marlene Hamerling, Jim Kane. *Styrofoam* by Kevin Doyle. January 9, 2004. Directed by Brian Snapp; with Keri Meoni, Dan Roach, Varick Boyd, Patrick Shelfski.

T. SCHREIBER STUDIO. *Eastern Standard* by Richard Greenberg. October 11, 2004. Directed by Glenn Krutoff; with Michelle Bagwell, Shane Jacobsen, Debbie Jaffe, Andrea Marshall-Money, Jack Reiling, Jason Salmon, Conor T. McNamara, Diane Varisco. *Bedroom Farce* by Alan Ayckbourn. November 22, 2003. Directed by Janis Powell; with Donna Abraham, Gwendolyn Brown, Morgan Foxworth, Ed Franklin, Hillary Parker, Todd Reichart, Allyson Ryan, David Shoup. *Landscape of the Body* by John Guare. January 29, 2004. Directed by Terry Schreiber; with Kimilee Bryant, Albert Insinnia, Joseph Rodriguez, Jessica Allen, Loren Bidner, Francesco Brazzini, Pamela Crofton, Cristina Doikos, James Dunigan, Ian Campbell Dunn, Chris Lococo, Fred Tumas, Erica Wendal.

29TH STREET REP. *Bold Girls* by Rona Munro. September 18, 2003. Directed by Ludovica Villar-Hauser; with Paula Ewin, Heidi James, Moira MacDonald, Susan Barrett. *In the Belly of the Beast Revisited* by Jack Henry Abbott; adapted by Adrian Hall. March 8, 2004. Directed by Leo Farley; with David Mogentale, Heidi James, James E. Smith, Gordon Holmes.

URBAN STAGES. *More Than This* by Edmund De Santis. June 15, 2003. Directed by Marc Geller; with Eric Frandsen, Tracey Gilbert, Christopher H. Matthews, Lucy McMichael, Wendy Walker, Charlotte Hampden, Glenn Kalison, Abby Royle. *In Spite of Myself* by Antoinette LaVecchia. September 3, 2003. Directed by Jesse Berger; with Ms. LaVecchia. *Origins of Happiness* by Felix Pire. September 6, 2003. Directed by Angel David; with Mr. Pire. *Much Ado About Nothing* by William Shakespeare. October 4, 2003. Directed by Rebecca Patterson; with Lauren Jill Ahrold, Virginia Baeta, Jacqueline Gregg, Gretchen S. Hall, Zainab Jah, Shanti Elise Prasad, Ami Shukla, Carey Urban, DeeAnn Weir. *Ah, My Dear Andersen*. Fairy tales by Hans Christian Andersen; adapted by Aleksey Burago. December 5, 2003. Directed by Mr. Burago; with Snejana Chernova, Marissa Lichwick, Erica Newhouse, Nysheva-Starr. *Weights* by Lynn Manning. January 11, 2004.

Directed by Robert Egan; with Mr. Manning. *Summit Conference* by Robert David MacDonald. February 7, 2004. Directed by Kit Thacker; with Eric Altheide, Rita Pietropinto, Sarah Megan Thomas. *Seven Rabbits on a Pole* by John C. Picardi. April 6, 2004. Directed by Frances Hill; with Bob Ari, Stephanie Cozart, Linda Cook, Brian Hutchison, Kahan James, Anthony Veneziale.

VITAL THEATRE COMPANY. VITAL SIGNS: NEW WORKS FESTIVAL. October 30–November 20, 2003. *Progress* by Al Sjoerdsma. Directed by Jeff Griffin. *On the Edge* by Craig Pospisil. Directed by Tom Rowan. *World's Longest Kiss* by Peter Morris. Directed by Michael Scheman. *Gladiators or Kamikazes* by Peter Hardy. Directed by Randy Baruh. *The Recipe* by D. Lee Miller. Directed by Ken Lowstetter. *The Gallery* by Loretta Novick. Directed by Cynthia A. Thomas. *Arms and the Man* by Eric R. Pfeffinger. Directed by David Hilder. *An Actor Prepares* by Mark Young. Directed by Ari Kreith. *First One Down* by Blair Singer. Directed by Jesse Berger. *Young Sistas* by Lorna Littleway. Directed by Sue Lawless. *My Wife's Coat* by Kellie Overbey. Directed by Linda Ames Key. *One Sunday Morning* by Dennis Jones. Directed by Mark Hayes. *Dar and Barb* by Catherine Allen. Directed by Emily Tetzlaff. *Bliss* by Stefanie Zadravec. Directed by Georgi Cerruti. *Medusa* by Steven Christopher Yockey. Directed by Bob Cline. *Plastic* by Robert Shaffron. Directed by Mary Catherine Burke. *Milk in China* by Lisa Rosenthal. Directed by Derek Jamison. *Superhero* by Mark Harvey Levine. Directed by Gregory Thorson. *A Family Manual for Kwanzaa* by Aurin Squire. Directed by Kim Kefgen. *The Keepsake* by Andrew McCaldon. Directed by Claire M. Hewitt. *Ursa Minor* by Gary Giovannetti. Directed by Eric Parness. *Hijab* by Monica Raymond. Directed by Mahayana Landowne. *Natural History* by Jennifer Camp. Directed by Anton Dudley.

WALKERSPACE. *The Flid Show* by Richard Willett. November 2, 2003. Directed by Eliza Beckwith; with Alison Adams, Harley Adams, Katherine Heasley Clarvoe, Kim Donovan, Kate Downing, Suzanna Hay, Laurence Lau, Amy Staats, James Thomas, Chris Wight. *Ashes to Ashes* by Harold Pinter. December 3, 2003. Directed by Robert Mann; with Gloria Mann Craft, Warren Kelder. *So Close* by Marin Gazzaniga. May 15, 2004. Directed by Michael Sexton; with John Ellison Conlee, Perri Gaffney, Ms. Gazzaniga, Julia Gibson, Daniel Freedom Stewart, Cristine McMurdo-Wallis.

WHERE EAGLES DARE THEATRE. *LiLiA!* by Libby Skala. November 3, 2003. Directed by Ms. Skala; with Ms. Skala. *A Rockette's Tail* by JoAnna Rush. November 8, 2003. Directed by Walter Willison; with Ms. Rush.

WHITE BIRD PRODUCTIONS. *Cooking With Lard* by Cindy D. Hanson and Cheryl Norris. March 19, 2004. Directed by Paul Mullins; with Mses. Hanson, Norris, Lorrie Harrison, Bijou Clinger, Kathryn Dickinson.

WINGS THEATRE COMPANY. *Uncovering Eden* by George Barthel. June 2, 3004. Directed by L.J. Kleeman and Richard Bacon; with James A. Walsh, Raymond O. Wagner, Gabriel Rivas, Josh Mertz. *Jane Eyre: The Musical*. Musical with book and lyrics by Rebecca Thompson-Duvall and Kari Skousen; music by Bill Kilpatrick. June 27, 2003. Directed by Craig Duke; with Lilly Kershaw, Gabriel Rivera, Breton Frazier, Edward Harding, Kristin Carter, Maureen Griffin, Alicia Sable, Sydney Sahr, Anna Budinger, Leslie Klug, Leah Landau, Jenny Long, Paul Malamphy, Jay Gould, Peter Previti, Greg Horton, Daniel Hughes, Jason Adamo, Jackson Budinger. *Tales From the Manhattan Woods*. Musical based on *Die Fledermaus* by Johann Strauss Jr.; adapted by Frederick Stroppel; book and lyrics by Mr. Stroppel. November 13, 2003. Directed by Judith Fredricks; with Sarah Miller, Shawna Stone, Elizabeth Hillebrand, Ms. Fredricks, Elena Heimur, Jeffrey Reynolds, Steven Snow, David Gary, Walter Harman, Melanie Melcher, Kyle Bradford, Linsey Jager, Brian Costello, Frances Jones, Karen Coker, Gideon Dabi, Kevin Kash. *Vincent*. Musical with book, music and lyrics by Robert Mitchell. February 27, 2004. Directed by Judith Fredricks; with Paul Woodson, Mark Campbell, Sarah Marvel Bleasdale, Charles Karel, John Wilmes, Erik Schark, Cristin J. Hubbard, James Gilchrist, Daniel Gurvich, Walter Hartman, Lynne Henderson, Mara Kelly, James LaRosa, Sarah Lilley, James Murphy, Ian Rhodes, Nathan Lee Scherich, Jodie Trappe, Martin Vasquez, Kathleen Devine. *Six Degrees of Separation* by John Guare. April 8, 2004. Directed by Louis Reyes Cardenas and Sarah Rosenberg; with Ree Davis, Edmond Wilkinson, Bashir Solebo, Brian Tracy, Frank Tamez, Henry Garrett, Amy Johnson, Burke Adams, Peter Monro, Joe Moran, Rocco Lapenna, Valerie Garduno, Mr. Cardenas, Robert Berlin, Daphne Crosby, Marcelo DeOliveira, Lou Mastantuono. *African Nights* by Clint Jefferies. May 17, 2004. Directed by Jeffery Corrick; with Antwan Ward, Bekka Lindstrom, Joel Halpern, Sheri Delaine, Karen Stanion, Nick Marcotti, JoHary Ramos, Ed Roggenkamp.

THE WOOSTER GROUP. *Poor Theater*. Based on the work of Jerzy Grotowski, William Forsythe and Max Ernst. February 18, 2004. Directed by Elizabeth LeCompte; with Geoff Abbas, J. Reid

Farrington, Iver Findlay, Ari Fliakos, Sam Gold, Bozkurt Karasu, Ken Kobland, Christopher Kondek, Margaret Mann, Gabe Maxson, Sheena See, Scott Shepherd, Jennifer Tipton, Kate Valk, Ruud van den Akker.

WORKSHOP THEATER COMPANY. *5 O'Clock* by Richard Brockman. October 7, 2003. Directed by Mirra Bank; with Bob Adrian, Liz Amberly, Christopher Graham, Dena Tyler, Jake Robards. *Conversation With a Kleagle* by Rudy Gray. July 31, 2003. Directed by Stacy Waring; with Steve Aronson, Mark A. Daly, Willie Ann Gissendanner, Antonio D. Charity.

WORTH STREET THEATER COMPANY. *The Moonlight Room* by Tristine Skyler. November 3, 2003. Directed by Jeff Cohen; with Laura Breckenridge, Brendan Sexton III, Kathryn Layng, Lawrence James, Mark Rosenthal. Transferred to an Off Broadway run at the Beckett Theatre (3/1/2004; 72 performances as of 5/31/2004). See Plays Produced Off Broadway section in this volume. *The Mystery of Attraction* by Marlane Gomard Meyer. January 12, 2004. Directed by Jeff Cohen; with Richard Bekins, Deirdre O'Connell, Barry Del Sherman.

ZIPPER THEATER. *Here Lies Jenny*. Musical revue by Roger Rees; music by Kurt Weill; lyrics by Bertolt Brecht, Roger Fernay, Ira Gershwin, Jehuda Halevi, Langston Hughes, Alan Jay Lerner, Maurice Margre, Ogden Nash, Franz Werfel, Kurt Weill. May 27, 2004. Directed by Leslie Stifelman; with Bebe Neuwirth, Greg Butler, Shawn Emamjomeh, Ed Dixon.

THE SEASON AROUND THE UNITED STATES

AMERICAN THEATRE CRITICS/STEINBERG NEW PLAY AWARD AND CITATIONS

○○○○○

A DIRECTORY OF NEW UNITED STATES PRODUCTIONS

THE AMERICAN THEATRE CRITICS ASSOCIATION (ATCA) is the organization of drama critics in all media throughout the United States. One of the group's stated purposes is "To increase public awareness of the theater as a national resource." To this end, ATCA has annually cited outstanding new plays produced around the US, which were excerpted in our series beginning with the 1976–77 volume. As we continue our policy of celebrating playwrights and playwriting in *Best Plays*, we offer essays on the recipients of the 2004 American Theatre Critics/Steinberg New Play Award and Citations. The ATCA/Steinberg New Play Award of $15,000 was awarded to Lynn Nottage for her play *Intimate Apparel*—which was also named a Best Play for its Off Broadway run. ATCA/Steinberg New Play Citations were given to August Wilson for *Gem of the Ocean* and to Carson Kreitzer for *The Love Song of J. Robert Oppenheimer*. Citation honorees receive prizes of $5,000 each.

The ATCA awards are funded by the Harold and Mimi Steinberg Charitable Trust, which supports theater throughout the United States with its charitable giving. The ATCA/Steinberg New Play Award and Citations are given in a ceremony at Actors Theatre of Louisville. Essays in the next section—by Christopher Rawson (*Pittsburgh Post-Gazette*) and Rick Pender (Cincinnati *City Beat*)—celebrate the ATCA/Steinberg Citation honorees. An essay by Lenora Inez Brown on *Intimate Apparel* appears in The Best Plays of 2003–2004 section of this volume.

ATCA's 11th annual M. Elizabeth Osborn Award for a new playwright was voted to Rolin Jones for *The Intelligent Design of Jenny Chow*, produced by South Coast Repertory in Costa Mesa, California. Mr. Jones, a former student of ATCA/Steinberg honoree Nottage, received his award during the Steinberg ceremony at the Humana Festival of New American Plays in Louisville, Kentucky.

The process of selecting these outstanding plays is as follows: any American Theatre Critics Association member may nominate the first full professional production of a finished play (not a reading or an airing as a play-in-progress) that premieres outside New York City during the calendar year under consideration.

Nominated 2003 scripts were studied and discussed by the New Plays Committee chaired by Alec Harvey (*Birmingham News*). The committee included ATCA members Misha Berson (*Seattle Times*) Jackie Demaline (*Cincinnati Enquirer*), Michael Elkin (*Jewish Exponent,* Abington, Pennsylvania), Marianne Evett (Cleveland *Plain Dealer*, retired), Bill Gale (Theatre New England), Barbara Gross (freelance, Rockville, Maryland), Claudia W. Harris (freelance, *Back Stage*), Dick Kerekes (freelance, Jacksonville, Florida), Elizabeth Maupin (*Orlando Sentinel*), Nancy Melich (*Salt Lake Tribune*, retired), Kevin Nance (*The Tennessean*) and Herb Simpson (Rochester *City Newspaper*).

Committee members made their choices on the basis of script rather than production. If the timing of nominations and openings prevents some works from being considered in any given year, they may be eligible for consideration the following year if they haven't since moved to New York City.

2004 ATCA/Steinberg New Play Citation

GEM OF THE OCEAN

By August Wilson

○○○○○

Essay by Christopher Rawson

> AUNT ESTER: Miss Tyler passed it on to me. If you ever make up your mind I'm gonna pass it on to you. People say it's too much to carry. But I told myself somebody got to carry it. [. . .] I picked it up and walked with it. I got a strong memory. I got a long memory. People say you crazy to remember. But I ain't afraid to remember. I try to remember out loud. I keep my memories alive. I feed them. I got to feed them otherwise they'd eat me up. I got memories go way back. I'm carrying them for a lot of folk.

THAT'S AUNT ESTER talking, recruiting Black Mary to be her successor as prophet, shaman and healer of souls for the black community. But, of course, it is also August Wilson talking about his own long theatrical journey, in which he, too, has been carrying memories from way back for a lot of folk. That journey has now wound back to its beginning. Wilson's cycle of plays, one set in each decade of the 20th century, has arrived back at 1904 with *Gem of the Ocean*, set in an echoing house in the Hill District of Pittsburgh, the archetypal urban crossroads of his expansive American epic.

Gem is a rich addition to the grand Wilson design. In nine scenes broken into two acts, it takes us back to the living survivors of chattel slavery and then explores slavery's legacy in the post-Reconstruction migration from Southern farms to Northern cities, where new arrivals face economic slavery to the mills and to the law that supports their exploitation. Most affectingly, these arrivals also make a Joseph Campbell-like spiritual journey back into their own history and forward into self-definition and responsibility. Among the play's distinctions are Wilson's first black villain, his most sympathetic white character and the actual appearance of Aunt Ester, the mysterious, ancient healer spoken of in *Two Trains Running* (set in 1969) who then dies in *King Hedley II* (set in 1985).

Gem had its premiere production at Chicago's Goodman Theatre in April 2003, then was reworked and staged at Los Angeles's Mark Taper

Really old friends: Greta Oglesby and Anthony Chisholm in Gem of the Ocean *at the Goodman Theatre. Photo: Michael Brosilow*

Forum that July. The director was Wilson's frequent collaborator, Marion McClinton. As this is written, *Gem* is due to be reworked again at Boston's Huntington Theatre in September 2004, and move immediately to Broadway. This is the same developmental journey that has led the cycle's other eight plays (all but one also set in Pittsburgh) to the nation's stages. Only the 1990s play, the cycle's end, is yet to be seen, and it is already in draft form under the name *Radio Golf*.

For all its layers of history and myth—and its thematic riches—when it premiered in Chicago, *Gem* sometimes felt like a historical pageant, erratically springing to dramatic life. However admirable, Aunt Ester, its idealized central character, did not stir the audience as she should. Some of the wonderful Wilson monologues seemed less spontaneous and more illustrations of predetermined ideas. And the staging was static. But Wilson was pleased with the rewriting he did for Los Angeles. "It changed a lot," he said in August 2003. "Honed in, clarified. It's pretty much there, with a few more things to tackle." He thought the chief problem in Chicago was the casting. What made the most difference in Los Angeles, he said, was giving Aunt Ester to Phylicia Rashad, who was expected to go with the play to Broadway.

AMONG *GEM*'S SEVEN characters, Aunt Ester, Solly Two Kings and Eli were born as slaves. In 1857, at age 20, Solly took the Underground Railroad to Canada, then returned again and again to liberate 62 others before the Emancipation Proclamation. Called Uncle Alfred under slavery, he was later called David and Solomon—Two Kings—but Solly is the name that stuck. The Biblical Solomon, his namesake's actions remind us, provided leadership in addition to proverbial wisdom. There's nothing sentimental or nostalgic about Solly's memories of the Underground Railroad, because, now 67, he knows the fight continues. In response to northward migration, Southern communities are closing ranks to keep blacks in the new peonage of tenant

Gem of the Ocean vividly dramatizes a potent cultural legacy.

farming, company stores and chain gangs. A new Underground Railroad is needed to set them free. But Northern cities don't greet them with open arms: economic freedom remains a distant dream in the face of 1904 Pittsburgh's employers, cops and courts.

Although we meet at least one former slave in *Joe Turner's Come and Gone*, set in 1911, *Gem* is able to reach further back to make slavery vivid, as when Aunt Ester dramatically produces her own bill of sale. Now, the chief oppressor is Caesar, the black policeman who keeps order on the Hill for his white bosses downtown. A plantation overseer in modern guise, he is thoroughly corrupt, though Wilson sees beneath that corruption in a powerful monologue that gives Caesar context, if not moral justification.

What should be rendered unto Caesar? The problem is that he knows no boundaries, claiming universal jurisdiction. Aunt Ester stands for the opposing realms of history and spirit. Now 285, she must have been born (as we learned in the other plays) in 1619, the year a Dutch ship brought the first load of black slaves to Virginia. But for those who prefer a more literal life story, *Gem* makes it clear that this Ester is the latest manifestation of a long line of folk priestesses. We hear of her own apprenticeship to Miss Tyler and see her train Black Mary. (By this reckoning, the Aunt Ester who dies in *King Hedley II* is either Black Mary herself, well past 100, or her successor; perhaps the final play in the cycle will tell us whether that Aunt Ester anointed her own successor.)

The deadly standoff that eventually drives the plot is between Caesar, the energetic black entrepreneur who fronts for the mill owners, and Solly, a revolutionary who is as American as Tom Paine or Joe Hill. Solly weighs the biblical dichotomy: Smite the enemy or turn the other cheek? Caesar has no doubts: His rule book is not the Bible but the Pennsylvania Penal Code. "Fry the little fish," the mayor told him, "send the big fish to me." Caesar makes money running flop houses and other scams. Black Mary is his younger sister. He wants her to help run his growing empire. But Black Mary follows Ester, whose guiding stars are truth, self-discipline and commitment, wrapped in a stern but loving Christianity.

ESTER IS A visionary able to summon the City of Bones, the mid-Atlantic grave of thousands of enslaved Africans who perished during the middle passage. In the play's set-piece highlight, she, Black Mary, Eli and Solly conduct a seance-like visit to that ghostly, sacred city for the young initiate, Citizen Barlow.

> AUNT ESTER: I can take you there if you want to go. That's the center of the world. All this and everything else you can see is built on that City. It all come from there.

Trouble brewing: Yvette Ganier, Paul Butler, Kenny Leon and Peter Jay Fernandez in Gem of the Ocean *at the Goodman Theatre. Photo: Michael Brosilow*

Coming in the long first scene of Act II, this mystical journey provides a powerful spiritual climax, reminiscent of the Juba scene in *Joe Turner*. It is lessened only because we've been told to expect it all along. There is also a parallel political climax: in emulation of Solly, who set fire to the mill—emblem of oppression—Citizen Barlow sets out at the end of the play to burn down the jail. Barlow thereby accepts his role as Solly's successor just as surely as Black Mary will be Aunt Ester's. That "Solomon" gives way to "Citizen" suggests a secularization of the struggle, but that struggle continues.

The larger parallel is between the journey to freedom represented by the Underground Railway, both during slavery and in the northward migration of the 20th century, and the journey to spiritual freedom conducted by Aunt Ester in sustaining the lessons of the City of Bones with which she repairs the spiritual "hole" in Barlow. The characters in *Gem* have two lives—Solly collects dog droppings for fertilizer but also guides people to freedom; Ester is an old woman but also a priestess—and a third life in Biblical parallel. Ester's 285 years are few enough compared to those of the Biblical patriarchs.

The play is shot through with both explicit and implicit Christian parallels: Jesus in the Temple, Judas, Peter denying Christ, and even the bodies and blood that provided sustenance on a terrible voyage. *Gem* is organized around funerals and initiations, especially Barlow's apocalyptic vision, dressed in the language of the folk song, "12 Gates to the City." The City of Bones gleams with the shine and grandeur of marble, paying tribute to a terrible past, allowing enlightened movement toward what Ester calls redemption. But Barlow has a debt to pay in this world, too. In frustration at not being paid for his stint in the mill, he stole a bucket of nails (one of the play's many references to the crucifixion), for which another man is blamed and then martyred. Out of his guilt, Barlow learns to move forward and oppose Caesar in service to his own and his people's spirit.

This being Wilson, the play is also rich in side stories, many of them funny:

> SOLLY: I'm still wild about women. I had a couple of them try and poison me. With this one gal the doctor told me I was lucky. Say if I had eaten another bite I would have died. Good thing she couldn't cook. I was just eating to be polite.

We get glimpses, too, of the life of the community beyond Aunt Ester's sanctuary. We learn about the power and limitations of money. We get an unusual take on the Civil War. The sympathetic white character, by the way, is Rutherford Selig, the same peddler and "people finder" from *Joe Turner*. Here, he's just a helpful peddler, with no mention of his family's history as slave traders and trackers, although you can see how he himself might take up people finding in a few years.

IN CHICAGO, DAVID Gallo's set was impressive but, as wide as the Goodman's stage, it forced flatness on director McClinton's staging. The one huge room had a kitchen on one side, a giant door dead center and Ester's armchair (and a long staircase) on the other. The textured walls and two-story high, tiled ceiling were ornate, painted deep blue-green, with just a few purposeful dilapidations revealing lath beneath, like bones. Two soaring windows showed blue beyond. It was all emblematic: We could have been under water, approaching that gleaming City. Donald Holder's lights could also invoke the hold of a slave ship. Bracelets and beads set up a rhythmic soundscape and the City's iconography was spelled out on a colorful quilt.

Each of the pauses between scenes included snippets of solo violin, harmonica, penny whistle or clap and shout, sometimes creating a reductive Ken Burns feel more documentary than dramatic. Constanza Romero's costumes were realistic, except perhaps for Aunt Ester, who looked so much like historic images of Sojourner Truth that she might have been a museum display. In Los Angeles, the staging reportedly began to find more life, freeing itself from static passages when it seemed to take itself too seriously.

For the record, the Chicago cast was Greta Oglesby (Ester), Kenny Leon (Citizen Barlow), Peter Jay Fernandez (Caesar), Anthony Chisholm (Solly), Paul Butler (Eli), Yvette Ganier (Black Mary), and Raynor Scheine (Rutherford Selig). Besides Rashad, new casting in Los Angeles included Peter James Francis (Caesar), John Earl Jelks (Barlow) and Al White (Eli).

> O Columbia! the gem of the ocean,
> The home of the brave and the free,
> The shrine of each patriot's devotion,
> A world offers homage to thee.

So begins the famous secular hymn. Although it is never mentioned, the play's title recalls it, setting up an obvious ironic disjunction between America's promise of freedom and the reality for African Americans. But the Gem of the Ocean in the play is also that City of Bones, a talisman of a tragic history polished by observance into a sacred gem that honors the past and inspires the future. *Gem of the Ocean* is also said to be the name

City's gates: Greta Oglesby and Kenny Leon in Gem of the Ocean *at the Goodman Theatre. Photo: Michael Brosilow*

of a slave ship that slaves themselves brought to port after its masters abandoned it—another irony. The play also swims in water images—"God moved on the water, once," Aunt Ester says—and as water flows so must blood, symbol of tragedy but also life. Whatever further development it may undergo, *Gem of the Ocean* vividly dramatizes a potent cultural legacy. It provides a strange and compelling portal to Wilson's epic confrontation with the tragedy and hopes of the 20th century.

2004 ATCA/Steinberg New Play Citation

THE LOVE SONG OF J. ROBERT OPPENHEIMER

By Carson Kreitzer

○○○○○

Essay by Rick Pender

> OPPIE: We knew the world would not be the same.
> A few people laughed. A few people cried. Most people were silent.
> I remembered a line from the Hindu scriptures, the Bhagavad Gita.
> Vishnu is trying to persuade the prince that he should do his duty, and to impress him, takes on his multi-armed form and says Now I am become Death, the Destroyer of Worlds.

AS THE FATHER of the atomic bomb in 1945, J. Robert Oppenheimer unwillingly assumed a new persona, the "Destroyer of Worlds." He spent the balance of his life trying to overcome misunderstandings of his actions and intentions. Carson Kreitzer's *The Love Song of J. Robert Oppenheimer* explores his scientific work and his later efforts to compensate for the terrible devastation he unleashed on the world, telling Oppenheimer's story in a nonlinear fashion.

Kreitzer's script moves between events and scenes from Oppenheimer's life: domestic scenes with his wife, vignettes with his mistress, moments of scientific brainstorming with Manhattan Project colleagues in the 1940s, a 1950s hearing when his security clearance was revoked during the Communist witch-hunt. There are also scenes located in a timeless, tortured mental landscape where he wrestles with guilt and responsibility. Oppenheimer's muse (and fury) in these confrontations is Lilith, a character from Jewish mythology, created by God as Adam's mate, but set aside when she refused to be subservient. Lilith suffered for her pride, as did Oppenheimer.

The play's setting is the tormented mind of the gifted scientist. From start to finish, the audience roams through Oppenheimer's mental landscape, exploring his intellect, his religion, his rivalries, his relationships, his scruples, his doubts, his arrogance and his integrity. Rather than create an interminable monologue, Kreitzer haunts the physicist with Lilith, a dark doppelgänger.

Destroyer? Curzon Dobell in The Love Song of J. Robert Oppenheimer at the Cincinnati Playhouse in the Park. *Photo: Sandy Underwood*

> OPPIE: An apple falls and hits a man on the head.
> Thus begins Newtonian Physics. Which begat Theoretical Physics.
> A discipline that ends, with great violence, July 16, 1945. Trinity.
>
> I think this story is a metaphor. And it is knowledge which strikes Sir Isaac on the head.
>
> The Apple of course its time-honored stand-in since Eve, the first woman, plucked one from the Tree of Knowledge. And that first sweet bite led to enlightenment. Banishment from the Garden. And eventual death.
>
> LILITH: Sssssssshhhheeee wass not the firsst.
>
> OPPIE: (*smiles*) The early Hebrew tradition holds that there was another woman, before Eve. Made from earth, like Adam. Lilith.

In listing the play's characters, Kreitzer notes, "Lilith lives in the walls and ceiling, crawling up and across the chain link fence, perching, seething, lunging, curling up to sleep but never touching the floor. She is only visible to Oppenheimer." In the play's spring 2003 premiere production at the Cincinnati Playhouse in the Park, which awarded it the Lois and Richard Rosenthal New Play Prize, director Mark Wing-Davey delivered Lilith to audiences largely through video monitors hung throughout the intimate Thompson Shelterhouse Theatre.

FOR MOST OF the first act, Lilith (Judith Hawking) appeared only on the monitors, the camera tight on her face, her features frequently distorted and exaggerated as she shrieked and railed at "Oppie" (Curzon Dobell). When she finally rolled onstage in a wheelchair, bound in braces holding together her deteriorating body, Lilith's face continued to be projected from a tiny camera mounted on a bracket around her neck. She embodied the rage that Oppenheimer—an erudite, refined man—constantly suppressed.

Their tangled tales linger in the viewer's subconscious.

The play opens in the early 1950s, with Oppenheimer alone onstage, speaking quietly, smoking. We soon understand he is testifying before a board considering his security clearance for classified scientific work. His first words directly allude to T.S. Eliot's "The Love Song of J. Alfred Prufrock": "And how should I presume? And how should I begin?" Kreitzer wants audiences to grasp the common ground between her play and Eliot's iconic poem of desire and doubt.

In a March 2003 interview, Kreitzer told me,

> Eliot's poem is also a funny kind of love song, about regret and that which did not happen. It's the tender melancholy of the poem that I am referencing with Oppenheimer's life. What I love about it is the antithesis: Prufrock is a man who said, "Do I dare disturb the universe?" For Prufrock that was a metaphor, to disturb the universe in a very tiny way. Oppenheimer was a man who really disturbed the universe.

Citing another line — "I am not Prince Hamlet, nor was I meant to be" — Kreitzer added:

> Oppenheimer *is* Prince Hamlet. This is a looking back by a man who did change things and did not hesitate at certain moments, when perhaps he should have.

Oppenheimer disavows his alleged Communist sympathies; he's instantly challenged by the omnipresent Lilith, whose first word is a hissing, serpent-like exclamation, "sssssubversssive." Later in the play Oppenheimer objects to her constant barrage of insidious questions. She replies:

> LILITH: They could never get inside your head. Understand what made you tick tick tick tick tick tick tick tick tick. Their inquiry stopped at the ice blue eyes. While I. Have been inside your head a long, long time.

A series of opening vignettes present Oppenheimer's friend and ill-fated mistress, Jean, whose suicide—by drowning in a bathtub—is later represented; his scientific colleagues, including his rival Edward Teller; and his funny, frank, pragmatic wife, Kitty, who tries to keep him grounded despite his intellectual and scientific preoccupations. Kreitzer's non-chronological approach wastes no time before recreating the detonation of the first test of the atomic bomb in 1945. Following a tremendous explosion, Oppenheimer is asked if it's the end of the world.

> OPPIE: Maybe.
>
> (*Lilith laughs. She appears, teeth first, like the Cheshire Cat.*)
>
> That was the first time I saw your face.
>
> LILITH: You must admit. It would have been funny.
>
> OPPIE: What?

Temptresssss: Judith Hawking in The Love Song of J. Robert Oppenheimer *at the Cincinnati Playhouse in the Park. Photo: Sandy Underwood*

> LILITH: If you had
> ignited the atmosphere.
>
> Consumed the world in a fiery ball.
>
> OPPIE: (*Smiles.*) We were a little bit afraid.
>
> LILITH: Shows what you know.

Sliding earlier in time to Los Alamos laboratory, Oppenheimer and his scientific colleagues, mostly Jewish theoretical physicists, debate how best to create the deadly explosion that could end the war and stop Hitler's persecution of the Jews. As Germany's surrender becomes imminent, Oppenheimer and his team are pushed by military overseers to finish their work to create a weapon that will result in world dominance.

KREITZER USES BITING humor to convey several memorable characters. The first act concludes with the vivid image of a woman caught in the Hiroshima blast whose embroidered kimono pattern was burned into her flesh. The second act opens with Oppenheimer's aggressive competitor, the physicist Teller, "with a kimono as a dressing gown, over his clothes," delivering a ranting, self-centered monologue while shaving with a straight razor. Later in the second act, as Oppenheimer's security clearance continues to be scrutinized, FBI director J. Edgar Hoover weighs the charges of subversion that might be made against the scientist. Hoover is "swathed in scarves. He does the dance of the seven veils, removing one for each charge read. In the end, he is revealed in a sober gray suit and tie."

> HOOVER: Erect a Blank Wall between this man and any top-secret documents currently in his purview. Confiscate his filing cabinets. And subpoena that mistress!
>
> STRAUSS: We can't, sir. She's dead.
>
> HOOVER: A dead red?
>
> STRAUSS: Yes, sir.
>
> HOOVER: (*sighs*) I never thought I'd be sorry to hear those words.

Such leaps from low comedy to stark tragedy (the first act features a graphic rendition of Jean's suicide) are further evidence that Kreitzer's play is as poetic as it is dramatic. Rather than simply narrate Oppenheimer's life, the young writer—she was 33 when her play premiered in Cincinnati—uses symbols, allusions, metaphors and other rhetorical devices to knit the fabric of her script more tightly.

In our interview, Kreitzer said,

> I had wanted to write this play about Oppenheimer, but I didn't know why I, as opposed to any other competent playwright, should

> do it. I didn't know what would make it particularly my take. I knew I could do a good historical documentary-type play, but I wasn't interested.
>
> I tend to do plays that are fictions but based on real people and real events. I hear something or I read something and I go, "Wow, how could that have happened?" I'd been fascinated with Oppenheimer since high school. He struck me as a brilliant, tragic figure who created this very destructive bomb and spent the rest of his life trying to make it stop, trying to stop the spread of nuclear weapons.

KREITZER SKILLFULLY WEAVES episodes from Oppenheimer's life into her script, while mining their metaphorical value. For instance, early in the second act Oppenheimer recalls an episode from his college days.

> OPPIE: My first year at Cambridge I . . . was under a great deal of strain. Over summer's break, I went on holiday with friends to Corsica. We were to continue on to Sardinia, but I felt much refreshed and told my companions that I had to return to school immediately, as I'd left a poisoned apple on Professor Blackett's desk. It was a metaphor. Rotten scholarship, not a nice gift for a teacher. A bad paper. I discovered that my companions had missed the metaphor and worried that I'd cracked up for good.
>
> LILITH: And now. Did you return?
> Dare disturb the University?
>
> OPPIE: (*sits, beaten*) How could I? How could I?

Kreitzer's humorous echo of another question asked by Eliot's Prufrock ("Do I dare disturb the universe") sends symbolic sparks in many directions. The reference to the "poisoned apple" (also a reminder of the Garden of Eden and the banishment resulting from fearful knowledge) returns near the play's conclusion:

> OPPIE: I have left a poisoned apple on the desk.
> I must go back.
> I must go back.
>
> LILITH: There is no back.
> Little man. But you know that.
>
> OPPIE: *I should have been a pair of claws*
> *scuttling the ragged seas.*

The play's final lines again conjure Prufrock. Riddled with cancer and full of doubt about the Pandora's box he has opened, Oppenheimer tells Lilith:

> OPPIE: I have heard the mermaids singing
> in great howling sandstorms of desert winds and a fireball burst high above the earth.

Soul on fire: Judith Hawking and Curzon Dobell in The Love Song of J. Robert Oppenheimer *at the Cincinnati Playhouse in the Park. Photo: Sandy Underwood*

> For a moment there was just the unbearable brightness. As the sound raced across the desert to catch up.
> (*Lilith waits.*)
> For a moment, in utter silence.
> It had the light
> of a thousand suns.

An appreciation of *The Love Song of J. Robert Oppenheimer* is enhanced by a close reading of its allusive poetry, which links and contrasts the central character's existential dilemma with that of Eliot's Prufrock. Kreitzer's metaphoric writing, her symbolic characters and their tangled tales linger in the viewer's subconscious—much as Lilith inhabits Oppie's thoughts.

As with the forbidden fruit in the Garden of Eden—from the Tree of Knowledge—these theatrical elements are simultaneously tempting, threatening, disconcerting. Kreitzer's play puts its audience (and its readers) in a position analogous to Oppenheimer's. As we confront ideas that make us more aware of the dilemma of existence, our quandary is similar to his: we are exhilarated by knowledge, frightened by its implications.

A DIRECTORY OF NEW UNITED STATES PRODUCTIONS

○○○○○

Compiled by Rue E. Canvin

THIS LISTING INCLUDES professional productions that opened during the June 1, 2003–May 31, 2004 season. Its focus is on new plays—and other productions of note—by a variety of resident companies around the United States. Information on casts and credits, which are listed here in alphabetical order, by state, were supplied by the 92 producing organizations included. Resident theaters producing new plays and operating under contracts with Actors' Equity were queried for this comprehensive directory. Active US theater companies not included in this list may not have presented new (or newly revised) scripts during the year under review or had not responded to our query by July 1, 2004. Productions listed below are world premieres, US premieres, regional premieres, substantial revisions or otherwise worthy of note. Theaters in the US are encouraged to submit proposed listings of new works and new adaptations, in addition to the premieres indicated above, to the editor of *The Best Plays Theater Yearbook* series.

ALABAMA

Alabama Shakespeare Festival, Montgomery

Kent Thompson artistic director, Alan Harrison managing director

IAGO. By James McLure. June 20, 2003 (world premiere). Director, Kent Thompson; scenery, Emily Beck; costumes, Elizabeth Novak; lighting, Liz Lee; sound, Robert Harsch; music, Patric Byers; dramaturg , Gwen Orel; fight direction, Scot J. Mann.

Tony .... J. Paul Boehmer
Vivacity .... Kathleen McCall
Basil .... Philip Pleasants
Finney .... David Furr

Time: In the 1950s. Place: The backstage world of London theater.

DISGUISES. By Craig Warner. May 27, 2004 (world premiere). Director, Kent Thompson; scenery, Peter Harrison; costumes, Beth Novak; lighting, Rachel Budin; sound, Don Tindall; music, Gregg Coffin; dramaturg, Susan Willis.

Pierre-Augustin Caron .... Sam Gregory
Andre-Charles Caron .... Philip Pleasants
Madeleine Franquet; Marie-Antoinette .... Kathleen McCall
Adelaide .... Julia Watt
Henri Lepaute; Councillor Goezman; Jean-Paul Marat .... Rodney Clark
Marcel Vignon; Chevalier d'Eon; Doctor Benjamin .... Chris Mixon

Madame de Pompadour;
Emma .... Greta Lambert
Louis XV; Silas Dean .... Paul Hebron
Stewards .... James Denvil, Christian Rummel
Sophie .... Suzanne Curtis
Monsieur Paris-Duverney .... Philip Pleasants
Footman; Louis XVI .... Michael Bakkensen
Comte de la Blanche;
Soldier .... Harry Carnahan
Comte d'Artois;
Lord Stormont .... Thomas Ward
Duchesse de Polignac;
Simone .... Libby George
President Dupaty;
Jules; Barber .... Chris Qualls
Jacques .... Frederick Snyder
Beggar; President .... Antony Hagopian

Time: Late 18th-century France. Place: Paris, Versailles and environs.

ARIZONA

Arizona Theatre Company, Tucson

David Ira Goldstein artistic director

OVER THE MOON. By Steven Dietz; adapted from *The Small Bachelor* by P.G. Wodehouse. September 19, 2003 (world premiere). Director, David Ira Goldstein; scenery, Scott Weldin; costumes, David Kay Mickelsen; lighting, John McLain; sound, Brian Jerome Peterson; music, Roberta Carlson; production stage manager, Glenn Bruner. Presented in association with Seattle Repertory Theatre. (See Seattle Repertory Theatre listing for details.)

George Finch .... R. Hamilton Wright
Hamilton Beamish .... Bob Sorenson
Sigsbee Waddington .... Ken Ruta
Mrs. Waddington .... Suzy Hunt
Molly .... Liz McCarthy
Officer Garroway .... Jeff Steitzer
Madame Eulalie .... Kirsten Potter
Ferris .... David Pichette
Mullet .... Roberto Guajardo
Fanny .... Julie Briskman

Presented in two parts.

CALIFORNIA

The Actors' Gang Theatre, Hollywood

Tim Robbins founding artistic director

EMBEDDED. By Tim Robbins. November 15, 2003 (world premiere). Director, Mr. Robbins; scenery, Richard Hoover, costumes, Yasuko Takahara; lighting, Adam H. Greene; sound, David Robbins; stage manager, Samantha Jane Robson.

Sarge; Cove .... Brian T. Finney
June; Kitten Kattan .... Toni Torres
Jen's dad; Dick; Buford T. ... Steven M. Porter
Jen-Jen Ryan .... Kaili Hollister
Pearly White; Stringer .... Andrew Wheeler
Col. Hardchannel; Announcer .... V.J. Foster
Lieutenant .... Kirk Pynchon
Maryanne; Gwen; Woof .... Kate Mulligan
Monk .... Ben Cain
Jen's Mom; Amy Constant; Woof ... Lolly Ward
Rum-Rum; Chip Webb .... Brian Powell
Gondola .... Riki Lindhome
Perez; Camera Kid .... J.R. Martinez

Presented without intermission.

American Conservatory Theater, San Francisco

Carey Perloff artistic director, Heather Kitchen executive director

LES LIAISONS DANGEREUSES. By Giles Havergal; adapted from the novel by Choderlos de Laclos. September 17, 2003 (world premiere). Director, Mr. Havergal; choreography,

Francine Landes; scenery, Kate Edmunds; costumes, Deborah M. Dryden; lighting, Rui Rita; sound, Garth Hemphill; music, PeterD; dramaturg, Paul Walsh.

Madame .... Joan MacIntosh	Madame de Tourvel .... Libby West
Marquise de Merteuil .... Lise Bruneau	Cecile de Volanges .... Elizabeth Raetz
Viconte de Valmont .... Marco Barricelli	Chevalier Danceny .... Neil Hopkins

Ensemble: Anthony Fusco, Lauren Grace, Michelle Leavy, Scott Nordquist, Patrick Sieler, Taylor Valentine.

Presented in two parts.

LEVEE JAMES. By S.M. Shephard-Massat. February 25, 2004 (world premiere). Director, Israel Hicks; scenery, Loy Arcenas; costumes, Michael J. Cesario; lighting, Nancy Schertler; sound, Garth Hemphill.

Lily Grace Hoterfield .... Rosalyn Coleman	Fitzhugh Marvin .... Gregory Wallace
Wesley Slaton .... Steven Anthony Jones	

Presented in two parts.

A MOTHER. By Constance Congdon; adapted from the play *Vassa Zheleznova* by Maxim Gorky. May 19, 2004 (world premiere). Director, Carey Perloff; scenery, Ralph Funicello; costumes, Beaver Bauer; lighting, James F. Ingalls; sound, Garth Hemphill.

Vassa .... Olympia Dukakis	Liudmilla .... René Augesen
Mikhail .... Louis Zorich	Natalia .... Margaret Schenck
Anna .... Marcia Pizzo	Prokhor .... Tom Mardirosian
Semyon .... Reg Rogers	Lipa .... Jeri Lynn Cohen
Pavel .... John Keating	Anisia .... Lauren Grace

Presented in two parts.

Ahmanson Theatre, Los Angeles

Gordon Davidson artistic director, Charles Dillingham managing director

THE ROYAL FAMILY. By George S. Kaufman and Edna Ferber. March 27, 2004. Director, Tom Moore; scenery, Douglas W. Schmidt; costumes, Robert Blackman; lighting, Duane Schuler; sound, Jon Gottlieb; music, Corey Hirsch; fight direction, Steve Rankin; production stage manager, Elsbeth M. Collins.

Della .... Ellia English	Fanny Cavendish .... Marian Seldes
Jo .... Alan Mandell	Oscar Wolfe .... George S. Irving
Hallboy .... Charlie Kimball	Julie Cavendish .... Kate Mulgrew
McDermott .... Bobby C. King	Anthony Cavendish .... Daniel Gerroll
Western Union Messenger .... S. Marc Jordan	Chauffeur .... Bill Ferrell
Herbert Dean .... Charles Kimbrough	Gilbert Marshall .... Richard Cox
Kitty Dean .... Barbara Dirickson	Another Hallboy .... Arthur Hanket
Gwen .... Melinda Page Hamilton	Gunga .... Aflamu
Perry Stewart .... Robert L. Devaney	Miss Peake .... Eve Roberts

Time: November 1927 and a year later. Place: Duplex apartment of the Cavendish's on Fifth Avenue, New York City. Presented in two parts.

Berkeley Repertory Theatre

Tony Taccone artistic director, Susan Medak managing director

THE NOTEBOOKS OF LEONARDO DA VINCI. By Mary Zimmerman; based on the work of Mr. da Vinci. September 10, 2003. Director, Ms. Zimmerman; scenery, Scott

La Grande Dame: *Marian Seldes in* The Royal Family *at the Ahmanson Theatre, Los Angeles. Photo: Craig Schwartz*

Bradley; costumes, Mara Blumenfeld; lighting, T.J. Gerckens; sound, Michael Bodeen; music by Mr. Bodeen and Miriam Sturm; stage manager, Cynthia Cahill.

Leonardo .... Lucia Brawley
Leonardo .... Jane Cho
Leonardo .... Lizzy Cooper Davis
Leonardo .... Christopher Donahue
Leonardo .... Kyle Hall
Leonardo .... Doug Hara
Leonardo .... Mariann Mayberry
Leonardo .... Paul Oakley Stovall

YELLOWMAN. By Dael Orlandersmith. January 28, 2004. Director, Les Waters; scenery and costumes, Annie Smart; lighting, James F. Ingalls; dramaturg, Nicole Galland; stage manager, Cynthia Soffer.

Alma .... Deidrie N. Henry
Eugene .... Clark Jackson

CONTINENTAL DIVIDE: DAUGHTERS OF THE REVOLUTION and MOTHERS AGAINST. By David Edgar. November 16, 2003. Director, Tony Taccone; scenery, William Bloodgood; costumes, Deborah M. Dryden; lighting and video, Alexander V. Nichols; sound, Jeremy J. Lee; dramaturgs, Lue Morgan Douthit, Douglas Langworthy, Luan Schooler. Presented in association with Oregon Shakespeare Festival.

MOTHERS AGAINST

Caryl Marquez .... Vilma Silva
Don D'Avanzo .... Michael Elich
Connie Vine .... Robynn Rodriguez
Vincent Baptiste .... Derrick Lee Weeden
Deborah Vine .... Christine Williams
Mitchell Vine .... Tony DeBruno
Sheldon Vine .... Bill Geisslinger
Lorianne Weiner .... Susannah Schulman

DAUGHTERS OF THE REVOLUTION

Michael Bern .... Terry Layman
Abby; Beth; Branflake .... Michelle Duffy
Ryan; Pat; Snowbird .... Christine Williams
Jools; J.C.; Rainbow;
Bob LeJeune .... Jacob Ming-Trent
Elaine; Ash; Connie .... Robynn Rodriguez
Ted; Jimmy;
Nighthawk; Sheldon .... Bill Geisslinger
Arnie; Ira;
Eddie; Mitchell .... Tony DeBruno
Bill; Troy; Zee;
Don D'Avanzo .... Michael Elich
Kate; Therese;
Yolande; Hoola Hoop .... Vilma Silva
Dana; Nancy;
Trina; Aquarius .... Marielle Heller
Rebecca McKeene .... Melissa Smith
Blair Lowe .... Lorri Holt
Kwesi Ntuli .... Derrick Lee Weeden
Lorianne Weiner;
Firefly .... Susannah Schulman
Jack; Darren;
Sam; No Shit .... Craig W. Marker

Each play presented in two parts.

Curran Theatre, San Francisco

Carole Shorenstein Hays proprietor

WICKED. Musical with book by Winnie Holzman; music and lyrics by Stephen Schwartz; based on the novel by Gregory Maguire. June 10, 2003 (world premiere). Director, Joe Mantello; scenery, Eugene Lee; choreography, Wayne Cilento; costumes, Susan Hilferty; lighting, Kenneth Posner; sound, Tony Meola, music direction, Stephen Oremus. Presented by Marc Platt, Universal Pictures, The Araca Group, Jon B. Platt.

Glinda .... Kristin Chenoweth
Melena .... Cristy Candler
Frex; Nikidik .... Sean McCourt
Midwife .... Jan Neuberger
Boq .... Kirk McDonald
Elphaba .... Idina Menzel
Nessarose .... Michelle Federer
Madame Morrible .... Carole Shelley
Dr. Dillamond .... John Horton
Fiyero .... Norbert Leo Butz
The Wizard .... Robert Morse
Chistery .... Manuel Herrera

Ensemble: Ioana Alfonso, Stephanie J. Block, Ben Cameron, Melissa Bell Chait, Marcus Choi, Kristoffer Cusick, Kathy Deitch, Melissa Fahn, Rhett G. George, Kisha Howard, LJ Jellison, Corinne McFadden, Walter Winston Oneil, Andrew Palermo, Andy Pellick, Michael Seelbach.

Musical numbers included: "No One Mourns the Wicked," "Dear Old Shiz," "The Wizard and I," "What Is This Feeling?," "Something Bad," "Which Way's the Party?"/"We Deserve Each Other," "Popular," "I'm Not That Girl," "One Short Day," "A Sentimental Man?"/"The Chance to Fly,"

"Defying Gravity," "Thank Goodness"/"I Couldn't Be Happier," Wonderful," "As Long as You're Mine," "No Good Deed," "March of the Witch Hunters," "For Good."

Presented in two parts.

East West Players, Los Angeles

Tim Dang producing artistic director

PASSION. Musical with book by James Lapine; music and lyrics by Stephen Sondheim; based on the film *Passione D'Amore*. September 10, 2003. Director, Tim Dang; scenery, Victoria Petrovich; costumes, Naomi Yoshida Rodriguez; lighting, Jose Lopez; sound, Kaname Morishita; music direction, Scott Nagatani; production stage manager, Ricardo Figueroa.

Fosca's mother;
Attendant .... Kerry K. Carnahan
Mistress; Attendant .... Louise Marie Cornillez
Giorgio .... Michael Dalager
Lieutenant Barri .... Bonifacio Deoso Jr.
Major Rizzolli .... Dexter Echiverri
Private Augenti; Ludovic .... Randy Guiaya
Doctor Tambourri .... Michael Hagiwara
Clara .... Linda Igarashi
Fosca .... Jacqueline Kim
Colonel Ricci .... Orville Mendoza
Lieutenant Torasso .... Lito Villareal
Sergeant Lombardi;
Fosca's father .... Paul Wong

Musical numbers included: "Happiness," "After Happiness, Part I," "Happiness—Part II," "First Letter," "Second Letter," "Third Letter," "Fourth Letter," "Fosca's Entrance—Part I," "Fosca's Entrance—Part II," "Scene 3—Part I," "Scene 3—Part II," "Scene 3—Part III," "Three Days," "Fifth Letter," "Three Weeks," "Scene 7—Part I," "Scene 7—Part II," "Scene 8," "Flashback—Part I," "Flashback—Part II," "Flashback—Part III, "Flashback—Part IV," "Sunrise Letter," "Scene 9," "Scene 10," "Nightmare," "Forty Days," "Loving You," "Scene 11," "Scene 12," "Christmas Music," "Scene 13," "Scene 14," "Finale."

Time: 1863. Place: Italy. Presented without intermission.

MASHA NO HOME. By Lloyd Suh. November 12, 2003. Director, Henry Chan; scenery, Evan A. Bartoletti; costumes, Dori Quan; lighting, Rand Ryan; sound, Dennis Yen; stage manager, Victoria A. Gathe.

Annabell .... Esther K. Chae
Felix .... Teddy Chen Culver
Father .... Dennis Dun
Masha .... Julia Morizawa
Whitman .... Eddie Shin

Time: Present. Place: Outside New York City. Presented without intermission.

THE WIND CRIES MARY. By Philip Kan Gotanda. February 4, 2004. Director, Lisa Peterson; scenery, Rachel Hauck; costumes, Christopher Acebo; lighting, Rand Ryan; sound, Robbin E. Broad; stage manager, Victoria A. Gathe.

Rachel .... Jamile Abdullayeva
Aunt Gladys .... Diana Kay Cameron
Raymond .... Thomas Vincent Kelly
Eiko .... Jodi Long
Dr. Nakada .... Sab Shimono
Miles .... Kelvin Han Yee

Time: 1968. Place: San Francisco.

Intersection for the Arts, San Francisco

Deborah Cullinan executive director, Sean San Jose program director

PSYCHOS NEVER DREAM. By Denis Johnson. January 24, 2004. Director, Darrell Larson; scenery, James Faerron; costumes, Suzanna Castillo; lighting, Jim Cave; sound, Drew Yerys; stage manager, Michael G. Cano.

Critter	John Diehl	Red	Alexis Lezin
Floyd	Cully Fredricksen	Sarah	Catherine Castellanos

Presented in two parts.

WHEEL OF FORTUNE. By John Steppling. October 23, 2003 (world premiere). Director, Hector Correa; scenery, Lisa Dent; costumes, Christopher Verodosci; lighting, Christopher Studley; sound, Drew Yerys; music, Marcus Shelby; stage manager, Michael G. Cano.

Marie Bendix	Alexis Lezin	Det. Jermayne; Fr. Albert	Paul Santiago
Nella; Nurse	Nora El Samahy	Det. Hodges; Dr. Alcar	Michael Cheng
Jackie; Nurse 2	Dawn-Elin Fraser	Bendix	Donald E. Lacy Jr.

Presented in two parts.

Laguna Playhouse, Laguna Beach

Andrew Barnicle artistic director, Richard Stein executive director

HARVEY. By Mary Chase. July 13, 2003. Director, Charles Nelson Reilly; scenery, James Noone; lighting, Ken Billington; costumes, Noel Taylor; sound, David Edwards, production stage manager, David Mingrino. Presented in association with Don Gregory.

Myrtle Mae Simmons	Jill Van Velzer	Duane Wilson	James Van Patten
Veta Louise Simmons	Joyce Van Patten	Lyman Sanderson, MD	Stephen O'Mahoney
Elwood P. Dowd	Charles Durning	William R. Chumley, MD	Dick Van Patten
Harvey	Himself	Betty Chumley	Leslie Easterbrook
Mrs. Ethel Chauvenet	Pamela Gordon	Judge Omar Gaffney	Jack Betts
Ruth Kelly, RN	Erica Shaffer	E.J. Lofgren	William H. Bassett

Presented in three parts.

La Jolla Playhouse

Des McAnuff artistic director, Terrence Dwyer managing director

FRÄULEIN ELSE. By Francesca Faridany; based on the novella by Arthur Schnitzler. June 10, 2003. Director, Stephen Wadsworth; scenery, Thomas Lynch; costumes, Anna Oliver; lighting, Joan Arhelger; sound, Bill Williams; stage manager, Michael Suenkel. Presented in association with Berkeley Repertory Theatre.

Fräulein Else	Francesca Faridany	Mother	Mary Baird
Paul	Michael Tisdale	Herr Von Dorsday	Julian López-Morillas
Cissy	Lauren Lovett	Porter	Garrett Neergaard

Presented without intermission.

THE COUNTRY. By Martin Crimp. August 3, 2003. Director, Lisa Peterson; scenery, Rachel Hauck; costumes, Joyce Kim Lee; lighting, Christopher Akerlind; sound, Mark Bennett; dramaturg, Carrie Ryan; stage manager, Lori J. Weaver.

Richard	Gary Cole	Rebecca	Emily Bergl
Corinne	Catherine Dent		

Time: The present. Place: The country. Presented without intermission.

EDEN LANE. By Tom Donaghy. August 17, 2003 (world premiere). Director, Des McAnuff; scenery, John Arnone; costumes, David C. Woolard; lighting, Howell Binkley; sound, Robbin E. Broad; music, Michael Roth; dramaturg, Shirley Fishman; stage manager, Mark Tynan.

May	Roxanne Hart	Philip	François Giroday

Alberta	Rachel Jacobs	Ruby	Sara Avery
Timothy	Peter Paige	Eileen Marie	Kate McGregor-Stewart

Presented without intermission.

BEAUTY. By Tina Landau; based on the Grimm fairy tale. September 21, 2003. Director, Ms. Landau; scenery, Riccardo Hernández; costumes, Melina Root; lighting, Scott Zielinski; sound and music, Rob Milburn and Michael Bodeen; stage manager, Nevin Hedley.

Prince	David Ari	Rose	Kelli O'Hara
King Bertrand	Corey Brill	Prince	Adam Smith
James	Jason Danieley	Queen Marguerite	Amy Stewart
Constance	Lisa Harrow	Musician	Richard Tibbitts
Madeleine	Simone Vicari Moore		

Presented without intermission.

The Page to Stage Workshop. April 20–May 2, 2004.

700 SUNDAYS... BILLY CRYSTAL... A LIFE IN PROGRESS. By Mr. Crystal; additional material by Alan Zweibel. April 20, 2004. Director, Des McAnuff; scenery, David Weiner; lighting, David Lee Cuthbert; sound and projection designer, Chris Luessmann.

Performed by Mr. Crystal.

Lamb's Players Theatre, Coronado

Robert Smyth producing artistic director

THE GREAT DIVORCE. By Robert Smyth; adapted from the drama by C.S. Lewis. March 26, 2004. Director, Mr. Smyth; scenery, Mike Buckley; lighting, Nathan Peirson; costumes, Jeanne Reith; music, Deborah Gilmour Smyth; stage manager, Maria Mangiavellano.

Traveler .... Cynthia Gerber

Ensemble: Nick Cordileone, Paul Eggington, David Cochran Heath, Kerry Meads, Deborah Gilmour Smyth, Robert Smyth, Tom Stephenson.

Magic Theatre, San Francisco

Chris Smith artistic director, David Gluck managing director

THE SEX HABITS OF AMERICAN WOMEN. By Julie Marie Myatt. October 12, 2003 (world premiere). Director, Michael Bigelow Dixon; scenery and lighting, Kate Boyd; costumes, Todd Roehrman; sound, Michael Woody.

Fritz	Jarion Monroe	Ruby	Rebecca Noon
Agnes	Frances Lee McCain	Joy	Anne Darragh
Daisy	Deborah Fink	Dan	Mark Routhier
Edgar	Kevin Rolston	Katie	Stephanie Champion

Presented in two parts.

TRIPTYCH. By Edna O'Brien. December 12, 2003 (world premiere). Director, Paul Whitworth; scenery, Kate Edmunds; lighting, Kurt Landisman, costumes, B. Modern; sound, Michael Woody; stage manager, Sabrina Kniffin.

Mistress, aka Clarissa	Lise Bruneau	Daughter, aka Brandy	Tro M. Shaw
Wife, aka Pauline	Julia Brothers		

Presented without intermission.

DR. FAUSTUS. By David Mamet. February 28, 2004 (world premiere). Director, Mr. Mamet; scenery, Peter Larkin; costumes, Fumiko Bielefeldt; lighting, Russell H. Champa; magic design, Michael Weber and Ricky Jay; production stage manager, Dick Daley.

Dr. Faustus .... David Rasche
Wife .... Sandra Lindquist
Friend .... Colin Stinton
Magus .... Dominic Hoffman
Son .... Benjamin Beecroft; Nathan Wexler

Presented in two parts.

DRIFTING ELEGANT. By Stephen Belber. May 1, 2004 (world premiere). Director, Amy Glazer; scenery, Jeff Rowlings; costumes, Fumiko Bielefeldt; lighting, Jim Cave; sound, Steve Romanko; stage manager, Sarah Ellen Joynt.

Nate Jamison .... Darren Bridgett
Victor Saad .... Harry Dillon
Renny Lyles .... Michael Gene Sullivan
Kate Driscoll .... Barbara Pitts

Marin Theatre Company, Mill Valley

Lee Sankowich artistic director, Gabriella Calicchio managing director

THE LAST SCHWARTZ. By Deborah Zoe Laufer. January 13, 2004 (world premiere). Director, Lee Sankowich; scenery, Steve Coleman; costumes, Cassandra Carpenter; lighting, York Kennedy; sound; Norman Kern; stage manager, Dick Daley.

Gene .... Darren Bridgett
Bonnie .... Jill Eikenberry
Norma .... Sharon Lockwood
Simon .... Mark Phillips
Kia .... Megan Towle
Herb .... Michael Tucker

Presented in two parts.

Mark Taper Forum, Los Angeles

Gordon Davidson artistic director, Charles Dillingham managing director

GEM OF THE OCEAN. By August Wilson. July 30, 2003. Director, Marion McClinton; scenery, David Gallo; costumes, Constanza Romero; lighting, Donald Holder; sound, Dan Moses Schreier; music, Kathryn Bostic; fight direction, Steve Rankin; production stage manager, Narda Alcorn.

Solly Two Kings .... Anthony Chisholm
Black Mary .... Yvette Ganier
Caesar .... Peter Francis James
Citizen Barlow .... John Earl Jelks
Aunt Ester .... Phylicia Rashad
Rutherford Selig .... Raynor Scheine
Eli .... Al White

Time: 1904. Place: Aunt Ester's home in the Hill District of Pittsburgh, Pennsylvania. Presented in two parts.

HOMEBODY/KABUL. By Tony Kushner. October 1, 2003. Director, Frank Galati; scenery, James Schuette; costumes, Mara Blumenfeld; lighting, Christopher Akerlind; sound and music, Joe Cerqua; production stage manager, James T. McDermott. Presented in association with Steppenwolf Theatre Company, Chicago. (See Steppenwolf Theatre Company listing for details.)

The Homebody .... Linda Emond
Dr. Qari Shah .... Maz Jobrani
Mullah Ali Aftar Durranni .... Aasif Mandvi
Milton Ceiling .... Reed Birney
Quango Twistleton .... Bill Camp
Priscilla Ceiling .... Maggie Gyllenhaal
A Munkrat; Border Guard .... Rahul Gupta
Khwaja Aziz Mondanabosh ...... Firdous Bamji
Zai Garshi .... Dariush Kashani
Woman in Burqa; Mahala .... Rita Wolf

Ensemble: Mueen Jahan Ahmad, Gillian Doyle, Laura Kachergus, John Rafter Lee, Kamal Maray, Shaheen Vaaz.

Mark Taper Forum
2003–2004
Season

Lost girl: Maggie Gyllenhaal (top) in Homebody/Kabul. *Photo: Craig Schwartz.*

Ancient tears: Phylicia Rashad (center) in Gem of the Ocean. *Photo: Craig Schwartz.*

Forbidden lust: Abby Brammell and Sam Robards (bottom) in The Talking Cure. *Photo: Craig Schwartz.*

Time: August 1998; spring 1999. Place: London, England; Kabul, Afghanistan. Presented in three parts.

LIKE JAZZ. Musical with book by Larry Gelbart; music by Cy Coleman; lyrics by Alan and Marilyn Bergman. December 3, 2003 (world premiere). Director, Gordon Davidson; choreography, Patricia Birch; scenery and lighting, D. Martyn Bookwalter; costumes, Judith Dolan; sound, Jon Gottlieb and Philip G. Allen; music direction, Tom Kubis; production stage manager, Mary Michele Miner.

Performed by Patti Austin, Bill Cantos, Jennifer Chada, Cleavant Derricks, Katy Durham, Harry Groener, Dameka Hayes, Rick Jarrett, Greg Poland, Margo Reymundo, Nicki Richards, Jack Sheldon, Timothy Ware, Lillias White, Carlton Wilborn, Natalie Willes.

Musical numbers included: "Intro," "Biography," "He Was Cool," "In Miami," "Don't Touch My Horn," "Quality Time," "59th & 3rd," "Another Night, Another Song," "An Autumn Afternoon," "Those Hands," "Scattitude," "Music That You Know By Heart," "The Double Life of Billy T.," "A Little Trav'lin' Music," "Being Without You," "Cheatin', " "Before We Lose the Light," "Makin' Music."

THE TALKING CURE. By Christopher Hampton. April 14, 2004. Director, Gordon Davidson; scenery and projections, Peter Wexler; costumes, Durinda Wood; lighting, Paulie Jenkins; sound, Philip G. Allen; music, Karl Fredrik Lundeberg; fight direction, Steve Rankin; production stage manager, Mary Michele Miner.

Sabina Spielrein .... Abby Brammell
Carl Gustav Jung .... Sam Robards
Emma Jung .... Sue Cremin
Sigmund Freud .... Harris Yulin
Otto Gross .... Henri Lubatti
Agatha Jung .... Taylor Daubens
Nurse .... Shiva Rose McDermott
Nurse .... Libby West
Orderly .... P.J. Marino
Orderly .... John Hansen
S.S. Officer .... Bruce Katzman
Russian Girl; Gret Jung ...... Emily Rose Morris

Time: Between 1904 and 1913. Place: Zürich, Switzerland, Vienna, Austria. Presented in two parts.

New Conservatory Theater Center, San Francisco

Ed Decker artistic director

SEDUCTION. By Jack Heifner; based on *La Ronde* by Arthur Schnitzler. January 31, 2004 (world premiere). Director, Christopher Jenkins; scenery, Pedro Murteira; costumes, Keri Kitch; lighting, Jim Gross; sound, Jeremy Stone.

Performed by Christopher Maikish, Bradford J. Shreve, Scott Smith, Matthew Socha, Jason Wong.

Presented without intermission.

The Old Globe, San Diego

Jack O'Brien artistic director, Craig Noel artistic director, Louis G. Spisto executive director

TIME FLIES. By David Ives. August 2, 2003. Director, Matt August; scenery, David Ledsinger; costumes, Holly Poe Durbin; lighting, Chris Rynne; sound, Paul Peterson; stage manager, Julie Baldauff.

TIME FLIES

Horace .... Mark Setlock
May .... Mia Barron
David Attenborough .... David Adkins
Frog .... Jeffrey Brick

BABEL'S IN ARMS

Gorph .... Mark Setlock
Cannaphilt .... David Adkins
Businesswoman .... Nancy Bell
High Priestess .... Mia Barron
Eunuch .... Jeffrey Brick

THE GREEN HILL

Jake .... David Adkins
Sandy .... Nancy Bell
Ensemble .... Mia Barron, Jeffrey Brick, Mark Setlock

THE MYSTERY AT TWICKNAM VICARAGE

Roger .... David Adkins
Sarah .... Nancy Bell
Dexter .... Mark Setlock
Mona .... Mia Barron
Jeremy .... Jeffrey Brick

BOLERO

Man .... Mark Setlock
Woman .... Nancy Bell

LIVES OF THE SAINTS

Flo .... Mia Barron
Edna .... Nancy Bell
Ensemble .... Jeffrey Brick, David Adkins, Mark Setlock

RESURRECTION BLUES. By Arthur Miller. March 25, 2004 (West Coast premiere). Director, Mark Lamos; scenery, Riccardo Hernández; costumes, Lewis Brown; lighting, York Kennedy; sound, Paul Peterson; stage manager, Leila Knox.

Stanley .... Bruce Bohne
Skip L. Cheeseboro .... Chris Henry Coffey
Henry Schultz .... Daniel Davis
General Felix Barriaux .... John de Lancie
Phil .... Michael Doyle
Sarah .... Jennie-Lynn McMillin
Soldier .... Mike Newman
Emily Shapiro .... Jennifer Regan
Police Captain .... Neil Shah
Jeanine .... Dana Slamp
Nurse .... Jennifer Stewart
Soldier .... Karen Zippler

San Diego Repertory Theatre

Sam Woodhouse artistic director, Karen Wood managing director

THREE MO' DIVAS. Musical revue by Marion J. Caffey. March 19, 2004 (world premiere). Directed and choreographed by Ms. Caffey; scenery and lighting, Dale Jordan; costumes, Melanie Watnick, sound, Derek Brener; music direction and arrangements, Joseph Joubert; stage manager, Diana Moser.

Performed by Hope Briggs, Janinah Burnett, Henrietta Davis, Jamet Pittman, Vivian Reed, N'Kenge Simpson-Hoffman.

EARTHQUAKE SUN. By Luis Valdez. April 17, 2004 (world premiere). Director, Mr. Valdez; scenery and costumes, Giulio Cesare Perrone; lighting, Jennifer Setlow; sound, Paul Peterson; stage manager, Dana Anderson.

Performed by Linda Castro, Daniel Rangel, Lucinda Serrano, Kinan Valdez, Janel DuGuzman, Jeremiah M. Maestas, Arturo Medina, Sandra Ruiz, Melanie Anne Marsh.

San Jose Repertory Theatre

Timothy Near artistic director, Alexandra Urbanowski managing director

MARY'S WEDDING. By Stephen Massicotte. October 24, 2003. Director, Michael Butler; scenery and lighting, Alexander V. Nichols; costumes, B. Modern; lighting and sound, Jeff Mockus; stage manager, Jenny R. Friend.

Mary; Sgt. Flowerdew	Julie Jesneck	Charlie	Cody Nickell

WINTERTIME. By Charles L. Mee. December 5, 2003. Director, Timothy Near; scenery, Giulio Cesare Perrone; costumes, Shigeru Yaji; lighting, Lap Chi Chu; sound, Steve Schoenbeck; stage manager, Jenny R. Friend.

Jonathan	Joseph J. Parks	Edmund	Perry Ojeda
Ariel	Soraya Broukhim	Bertha	Wilma Bonet
Maria	Suzan Hanson	Hilda	Catherine E. Coulson
Francois	Michael Butler	Bob	Charles Dean
Frank	James Carpenter	Jacqueline	Mari-Esther Magaloni

South Coast Repertory, Costa Mesa

David Emmes producing artistic director, Martin Benson artistic director

SAFE IN HELL. By Amy Freed. April 9, 2004 (world premiere). Director, David Emmes, choreography, Sylvia C. Turner; scenery, Ralph Funicello; costumes, Nephelie Andonyadis; lighting, Peter Maradudin; sound, David Budries; dramaturgs, Jennifer Kiger and Jerry Patch; production stage manager, Jeff Gifford.

Increase Mather	Graeme Malcolm	Judge; Townsman; Ensemble	Don Took
Cotton Mather	Robert Sella	Abigail; Ensemble	Madison Dunaway
Mrs. Doakes; Ensemble	Colette Kilroy	Little Mary; Ensemble	Elisa Richardson
Reverend Doakes	Simon Billig	Tituba; Ensemble	Tracey A. Leigh
Indian Roger	Hal Landon Jr.	Maggie Smurt; Ensemble	Suzanne Jamieson

Time: 1691 and later. Place: Boston; Salem and vicinity. Presented in two parts.

MR. MARMALADE. By Noah Haidle. April 30, 2004 (world premiere). Director, Ethan McSweeny; scenery, Rachel Hauck; costumes, Angela Balogh Calin; lighting, Scott Zielinski; sound, Michael Roth; dramaturg, Jerry Patch; stage manager, Jamie A. Tucker.

Lucy	Eliza Pryor Nagel	Bradley	Marc Vietor
Mr. Marmalade	Glenn Fleshler	George; Cactus; Man	Larry Bates
Sookie; Emily; Sunflower	Heidi Dippold	Larry	Guilford Adams

Presented in two parts.

2003-04 NewSCRipts Season of Play Readings.

LINCOLNESQUE. By John Strand. November 10, 2003. Director, Warner Shook.
Performed by JD Cullum, Heidi Dippold, Gregory Itzin, James Waterston.

HAPPY VALLEY. By Aurorae Khoo. January 12, 2004. Director, Loy Arcenas.
Performed by Esther K. Chae, Jennifer Chu, Emily Kuroda, Ming Lo.

ANON. By Kate Robin. February 23, 2004. Director, Mark Rucker.
Performed by Emily Bergl, Matt Letscher, Sarah Rafferty, Elizabeth Ruscio, Kimberly Scott, Katy Selverstone, Carl Weintraub.

TWENTY SHADOWS. By Cusi Cram. April 12, 2004. Director, Mark Rucker.
Performed by Bridget Flanery, Nicholas Gonzalez; Norma Maldonado, Barbara Tarbuck.

7th Annual Pacific Playwights Festival. Four staged readings. May 7–9, 2004.

VESUVIUS. By Lucinda Coxon. Director, David Emmes; dramaturg, Jennifer Kiger.
Performed by Daniel Blinkoff, David Paul Francis, Anna Gunn, Jennifer Hinds, Kevin Sifuentes.

THE CLEAN HOUSE. By Sarah Ruhl. Director, Bill Rauch; dramaturg, Juliette Carrillo.
Performed by Ivonne Coll, François Giroday, Joan MacIntosh, Zilah Mendoza, Mary Lou Rosato.

THE SINGING FOREST. By Craig Lucas. Director, Bartlett Sher; dramaturg, John Glore.

South Coast Repertory 2003–2004 Season

Daddy's Boy? Robert Sella in Safe in Hell. *Photo: Ken Howard.*

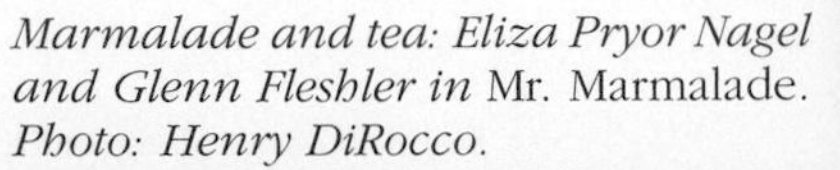

Marmalade and tea: Eliza Pryor Nagel and Glenn Fleshler in Mr. Marmalade. *Photo: Henry DiRocco.*

Performed by Robin Bartlett, George Coe, Fionnula Flanagan, Kristin Flanders, Nathanael Johnson, Matt Letscher, Lorenzo Pisoni, Stephen Spinella, John Vickery.

SAFE AS HOUSES. By Richard Greenberg. Director, Ethan McSweeny; dramaturg, Jerry Patch.

Performed by Nathan Baesel, Blair Brown, Robert Foxworth, Mary Joy, Valerie Mahaffey, Adam Scott.

Taper, Too at Ivy Substation, Culver City

Gordon Davidson artistic director

SEX PARASITE. By Jessica Goldberg. April 4, 2004 (world premiere). Director, Chay Yew; scenery and costumes, Yevgenia Nayberg; lighting, Jose Lopez; sound, John Zalewski; stage manager, Winnie Y. Yok.

Sir Bryan Donkin .... John Apicella
Elizabeth Cobb .... Shannon Holt
Havelock Ellis .... Liam Christopher O'Brien
Olive Schreiner .... Kirsten Potter
Maria Sharpe; Alice .... Jennifer Rau
Professor Karl Pearson .... Erik Sorenson

Presented in two parts.

TheatreWorks, Palo Alto

Robert Kelley artistic director, Randy Adams managing director

MEMPHIS. Musical with book and lyrics by Joe DiPietro; music and additional lyrics by David Bryan; based on a concept by George W. George. January 24, 2004. Director, Gabriel Barre; choreography, Todd L. Underwood; scenery, Bill Stabile; costumes, Pamela Scofield; lighting, Phil Monat; sound, Cliff Caruthers; dramaturg, Vicki Rozell. Presented in association with North Shore Music Theatre, Beverly, Massachusetts at the Mountain View Center for the Performing Arts. (See North Shore Music Theatre listing for details.)

Performed by Chad Kimball, Montego Glover, J. Bernard Calloway, Bob Greene, James Monroe Inglehart, Susan Mansur, Derrick B. Baskin, Molly Bell, Cyril Jamal Cooper, Valerie Rose Curiel, David Curley, Khalia Davis, Darrin Glasser, Sheila Howerton, John-elliott Kirk, Jeff Leibow, Melody McArtor, Rob Robinson, Brian Yates Sharber, Dawn L. Troupe, C. Kelly Wright.

Presented in two parts.

MY ANTONIA. By Scott Schwartz; adapted from the novel by Willa Cather. April 3, 2004 (world premiere). Director, Mr. Schwartz; choreography, Richard Powers; scenery, Joey Ragey and Daniela Nelke; costumes, Clare Henkel; lighting, Pamila Gray; sound, Cliff Caruthers; music, Stephen Schwartz; music direction, William Liberatore; fight direction, Richard Lane; dramaturg, Vicki Rozell.

Performed by Kurt Gravenhorst, Michael Butler, Ian Leonard, Jordan Lund, Joseph Ribeiro, Nancy Sauder, Richard C. Bolster, Nick Tagas, Jessica Meyers, Cass Morgan, J. Hayden Williams, Louis Parnell, Lianne Marie Dobbs, Anne Buelteman, Woody Taft, Julia Hornik, Ryan Lee.

COLORADO

Denver Center Theatre Company

Donovan Marley artistic director, Barbara E. Sellars producing director

JOHN BROWN'S BODY. By Laird Williamson; adapted from the play by Stephen Vincent Benét. (February 5, 2004). Director, Mr. Williamson; scenery and costumes, Andrew V.

Yelusich; lighting, Don Darnutzer; sound, David R. White; music, Larry Delinger; music direction, Lee Stametz.

Performed by Jacqueline Antaramian, Velina Brown, Bill Christ, Daniel Flick, Judd Frazier, Mike Hartman, Keith L. Hatten, Annette Helde, Jamie Horton, John Hutton, Johanna Jackson, Robert Libetti, Daniel Loeser, Randy Moore, Robin Moseley, Mark Rubald, Brett Scott, Michael Gene Sullivan, Allison Watrous, Kathleen White.

Place: America. Presented in two parts.

NAT "KING" COLE & ME: A Musical Healing. By Gregory Porter with Randal Myler. May 20, 2004 (world premiere). Director, Mr. Myler; scenery, Michael Brown; costumes, Kevin Copenhaver; lighting, Don Darnutzer; sound, Matthew C. Swartz; music, Gregory Porter; music direction, Kamau Kenyatta.

Gregory .... Gregory Porter
Mother .... Eloise Laws
Father .... Lloyd C. Porter
Young Gregory .... Tyriq J. Swingler

Presented in two parts.

CONNECTICUT

Eugene O'Neill Theater Center, Waterford

James Houghton artistic director, Howard Sherman executive director
Thomas Viertel chairman of the board, George C. White founder
Paulette Haupt artistic director of the Music Theater Conference

O'Neill Playwrights Conference. June 30–July 20, 2003

DARK MATTERS. By Roberto Aguirre-Sacasa.

A SMALL MELODRAMATIC STORY. By Stephen Belber.

BARKING GIRL. By Susan Bernfield.

FUENTE. By Cusi Cram.

ROCK SHORE. By Lisa Dillman.

AFTER ASHLEY. By Gina Gionfriddo.

MR. FOX: A RUMINATION. By Bill Irwin.

SMOKING KILLS. By Dominic Leggett.

CASCARONES. By Irma Mayorga.

DEEDS. By S.M. Shephard-Massat.

FATHER JOY. By Sheri Wilner.

THREE ITALIAN WOMEN. By Laura Maria Censabella.

THEATRE FOR ONE. By Christine Jones.

GOMPERS. By Adam Rapp.

Directors: Melia Bensussen, Carolyn Cantor, Laura Maria Censabella, Loretta Greco, James Houghton, Moisés Kaufman, Darrell Larson, Pam MacKinnon, Maria Mileaf, Erica Schmidt, Seret Scott, Rebecca Taichman.

Featured artists: Betsy Aidem, Jacqueline Antaramian, Matthew Arkin, Vanessa Aspillaga, Tina Benko, Rachel Matthews Black, Lillo Brancato Jr., Leon Addison Brown, Yusef Bulos, Paul Butler, Michael Chernus, Veronica Cruz, Mia Dillon, Beth Dixon, America Ferrer, Pamela J. Gray, Sean Haberle, Jason Butler Harner, Roderick Hill, Keith L. Hatten, Juan Carlos Hernandez, Bill Irwin, Sanjiv Jhaveri, E. Katherine Kerr, Ted Koch, Seana Kofoed, John Bedford Lloyd, Florencia Lozano, Peter Maloney, Jodie Markell, Chris McKinney, James Martinez, Tuck Milligan, Hasan Munem,

Julia Murney, Kevin O'Rourke, Jesse J. Perez, Lazaro Perez, Larry Pine, Katherine Pine, Linda Powell, Elizabeth Reaser, Alice Ripley, Dallas Roberts, Sebastian Roché, Nick Roesler, Reno Roop, Diana Ruppe, Jeanine Serralles, Socorro Santiago, Armand Schultz, John Seitz, Matthew Stadelmann; Josh Stamberg, Jaime Roman Tirelli, Jim True-Frost, Stephen Barker Turner, William Vatkin.

Goodspeed Musicals, Chester

Michael P. Price executive director, Sue Frost associate producer

CAMILLE CLAUDEL. Musical with book and lyrics by Nan Knighton; music by Frank Wildhorn. August 14, 2003. Director, Gabriel Barre; choreography, Mark Dendy; scenery, Walt Spangler; costumes, Constance Hoffman; lighting, Howell Binkley; sound, Mark Menard; music direction, Jeremy Roberts.

Paul Claudel .... Matt Bogart
Madame Claudel .... Rita Gardner
Camille Claudel .... Linda Eder
Auguste Rodin .... Michael Nouri
Monsieur Claudel .... Milo O'Shea

Ensemble: John Paul Almon, Timothy W. Bish, Nick Cavarra, Margaret Ann Gates, Natalie Hill, Antonia Kitsopoulos, Mayumi Miguel, Tracy Miller, Tricia Paoluccio, Darren Ritchie, Shonn Wiley.

A TREE GROWS IN BROOKLYN. Revision of the musical with book by George Abbott and Betty Smith; music by Arthur Schwartz; lyrics by Dorothy Fields; book revision by Elinor Renfield; based on the novel by Ms. Smith. October 10, 2003. Director, Ms. Renfield; choreography, Jennifer Paulson Lee; scenery, James Noone; costumes, Pamela Scofield; lighting, Jeff Croiter; music direction, Michael O'Flaherty; orchestrations, Dan DeLange; production stage manager, Donna Cooper Hilton.

Francie Nolan .... Remy Zaken
Miss McShane .... Mary Jo McConnell
Hildy .... Megan Walker
Della .... Leslie Marie Collins
Petey .... Zachary Halley
Willie .... Todd Buonopane
Allie .... Kevin Loreque
Johnny Nolan .... Deven May
Aloysius Moran .... Tom Souhrada
Katie .... Kerry O'Malley
Harry .... Adam Heller
Cissy .... Sari Wagner
Max; Mr. Swanson .... Steve Routman
Nellie .... Amber Stone
Mr. Moriarty .... Frank Stancati
Neighborhood Woman .... Leslie Klug
Maudie .... Katy Lin Persutti

Ensemble: Michael Buchanan, Zachary Halley, Danny Rothman, Adam Shonkwiler.

O. HENRY'S LOVERS. Musical with book and lyrics by Joe DiPietro; music by Michael Valenti; based on three short stories by Mr. Henry. November 13, 2003. Director, Gordon Greenberg; choreography, Christopher Gattelli; scenery, Neil Patel; costumes, Catherine Zuber; lighting, Jeff Croiter; music direction, Vadim Feichtner.

Porter; Dance teacher ....John Braden
Johnsy .... Emily Rabon Hall
Nevada Ross .... Celia Keenan-Bolger
Sue .... Megan Lawrence
Barbara Ross .... Amanda Naughton
Gilbert .... Richard Roland
Dr. Jerome Ross .... Joe Vincent

ALL SHOOK UP. Musical with book by Joe DiPietro; inspired by and featuring the songs of Elvis Presley. May 13, 2004. Director, Christopher Ashley; choreography, Jodi Moccia; scenery, David Rockwell; costumes, David C. Woolard; lighting, Donald Holder; sound, Brian Ronan; music direction, August Eriksmoen.

Natalie Haller ....Jennifer Gambatese
Jim Haller .... Jonathan Hadary
Miss Sandra .... Leah Hocking
Dean Hyde .... Ashton Holmes

Lorraine Hart .... Nikki M. James
Sheriff Earl .... John Jellison
Matilda Hyde .... Alix Korey
Dennis .... Mark Price
Chad .... Manley Pope
Sylvia Hart .... Sharon Wilkins

Ensemble: Paul Castree, Cara Cooper, Tyce Diorio, Katy Grenfell, Anika Larsen, John Eric Parker, Justin Patterson, Chryssie Whitehead, Virginia Woodruff.

Hartford Stage

Michael Wilson artistic director, Janet S. Suisman artistic director, Jim Ireland managing director

THE DEVIL'S MUSIC: THE LIFE AND BLUES OF BESSIE SMITH. By Angelo Parra. July 9, 2003. Director, Joe Brancato; scenery, Bill Stabile; costumes, Curtis Hay; lighting, Jeff Nellis; sound, Michael Miceli; production stage manager, Carmelita Becnel.

Bessie Smith .... Miche Braden
Pickle .... Jimmy Hankins
Musicians .... Pierre Andre, Chuk Fowler

Time: October 4, 1937. Place: Buffet flat in Tennessee.

HEDWIG AND THE ANGRY INCH. Musical with book by John Cameron Mitchell; music and lyrics by Stephen Trask. August 5, 2003. Director, Brad Rouse; scenery, Michael Olich; costumes, Miguel Angel Huidor; lighting, Howell Binkley; sound, Keith Bates and Elizabeth Atkinson; production stage manager, Patti Kelly.

Hedwig .... Anthony Rapp
Yitzhak .... Sara Siplak
Skszp; keyboard; guitar .... Brandon Lowry
Krzysztof; guitar .... John Purse
Jacek; bass .... Daniel Tomoko
Schlatko .... A.T. Vish

SAY GOODNIGHT, GRACIE. By Rupert Holmes. September 3, 2003. Director, John Tillinger; scenic consultant, John Lee Beatty; lighting, Howard Werner; sound, Kevin Lacy; music, Mr. Holmes; production stage manager, Marian DeWitt.

George Burns .... Frank Gorshin
Voice of Grace Allen .... Didi Conn

EIGHT BY TENN. By Tennessee Williams. October 8–November 2, 2003. Director, Michael Wilson; choreography, Peter Pucci; scenery, Jeff Cowie; costumes, David C. Woolard; lighting, John Ambrosone; music and sound, Fitz Patton; music direction, Rick Hipp-Flores; dramaturg, Christopher Baker; production stage manager, Carmelita Becnel.

Rose Program

THE PALOOKA (Edited by David Roessel and Nick Moschovakis)

The Palooka .... Kevin Geer
Trainer .... Remo Airaldi
Kid .... Curtis Billings

Place: Dressing room of a boxing arena.

PORTRAIT OF A MADONNA

Miss Lucretia Collins .... Annalee Jefferies
The Porter .... Helmar Augustus Cooper
The Elevator Boy .... Curtis Billings
The Doctor .... Kevin Geer
The Nurse .... Denny Dillon
Mr. Abrams .... Remo Airaldi

Place: The living room of a moderate-priced St. Louis apartment.

THE ONE EXCEPTION (Edited by Robert Bray)

Viola .... Annalee Jefferies
May .... Jennifer Harmon
Kyra .... Amanda Plummer

Time: The present.

NOW THE CATS WITH JEWELLED CLAWS

Manager .... Helmar Augustus Cooper
Madge .... Annalee Jefferies
Bea .... Jennifer Harmon
Waitress .... Denny Dillon
Hunched Man .... Kevin Geer
First Young Man .... Curtis Billings
Second Young Man .... Remo Airaldi

Place: A restaurant at lunch time in a major metropolis.

Blue Program

THE LADY OF LARKSPUR LOTION

Mrs. Hardwicke-Moore .... Elizabeth Ashley
Mrs. Wire .... Denny Dillon
The Writer .... Kevin Geer

Place: A rented room in the French Quarter of New Orleans.

SOMETHING UNSPOKEN

Miss Cornelia Scott .... Jennifer Harmon
Miss Grace Lancaster .... Annalee Jefferies

Place:The home of Cornelia Scott in Meridian, Mississippi.

THE CHALKY WHITE SUBSTANCE

Mark .... Helmar Augustus Cooper
Luke .... Curtis Billings

Place: One hundred years after a thermonuclear war.

THE GNÄDIGES FRÄULEIN

Polly .... Amanda Plummer
Molly .... Elizabeth Ashley
Permanent
Transient .... Helmar Augustus Cooper
The Gnädiges Fräulein .... Denny Dillon
Cocaloony .... Remo Airaldi
Indian Joe .... Kevin Geer

Place: A cottage on Cocaloony Key.

THE MYSTERY OF IRMA VEP. By Charles Ludlam. January 14, 2004. Director, Michael Wilson; scenery, Jeff Cowie; costumes, Alejo Vietti; lighting, Rui Rita; sound, Joe Pino; production stage manager, Carmelita Becnel.

Jane Twisden;
Lord Edgar Hillcrest;
An Intruder .... James Lecesne
Nicodemus Underwood;
Lady Enid Hillcrest;
Alcazar; Pev Amri .... Jeffery Roberson

Place: In library drawing room of Mandacrest, near Hampstead Heath; various places in Egypt. Presented in two parts.

METAMORPHOSES. By Mary Zimmerman; based on the work of Ovid. March 3, 2004. Presented in association with Missouri Repertory Theatre, Kansas City. (See Missouri Repertory Theatre listing for details.)

TOPDOG/UNDERDOG. By Suzan-Lori Parks. April 14, 2004. Director, Amy Morton; scenery, Loy Arcenas; costumes, Nan Cibula-Jenkins; lighting, Kevin Rigdon; sound, Rob Milburn and Michael Bodeen; fight direction, Bryan Bynes; production stage manager, Robert H. Satterlee. Presented in association with Steppenwolf Theatre Company, Chicago, and Alley Theatre, Houston. (See those listings for details.)

Booth .... K. Todd Freeman
Lincoln .... David Rainey

Time: Now. Place: Here. Presented in two parts.

PETER AND JERRY: A PLAY. By Edward Albee. May 28, 2004 (world premiere). Director, Pam MacKinnon; scenery, Jeff Cowie; lighting, Howell Binkley; costumes, Jess Goldstein; production stage manager, Carmelita Becnel.

HOMELIFE

Peter .... Frank Wood
Ann .... Johanna Day

THE ZOO STORY

Peter .... Frank Wood
Jerry .... Frederick Weller

Long Wharf Theatre, New Haven

Gordon Edelstein artistic director

FRAN'S BED. By James Lapine. October 30, 2003 (world premiere). Director, Mr. Lapine; scenery, Douglas Stein; costumes, Susan Hilferty; lighting, David Lander; sound, Fitz Patton; production stage manager, Lori J. Weaver.

Fran .... Mia Farrow
Vicky .... Carrie Preston
Dolly .... Brenda Pressley
Hank .... Harris Yulin
Birdie .... Kellie Overbey
Lynne .... Marcia DeBonis
Eddie .... Christopher Innvar

Presented without intermission.

Seven Angels Theatre, Waterbury

Semina De Laurentis artistic director

OSCAR AND FELIX: A NEW LOOK AT *THE ODD COUPLE*. By Neil Simon. November 8, 2003. Director, Julia Kiley; scenery, Sebastien Grouard; costumes, Renee Purdy; lighting, Susan Kinkade; sound, Asa F. Wember; production stage manager, Jean Marie Tickell.

Felix Ungar .... R. Bruce Connelly
Oscar Madison .... Sam Kitchin
Inez Costazuela .... Jean Tafler
Julia Costazuela .... Marissa Burgoyne
Murray .... Josh Bevans
Vinnie .... Johny Varricchione
Speed .... Tom Cochrane
Roy .... Brian Feinberg

Time: Warm summer nights. Place: Oscar Madison's apartment in New York City. Presented in two parts.

THE SWEEPERS. By John C. Picardi. February 21, 2004. Director, Semina De Laurentis; scenery, Erin Kiernan; costumes, Renee Purdy; lighting, Dana Sterling; sound, Asa F. Wember; production stage manager, Jean Marie Tickell.

Bella Cichinelli (McCarthy) .... Marina Re
Mary DeGrazia .... Cary Barker
Dotty Larnino .... Andrea Gallo
Sonny McCarthy-Cichinelli .... John Hayden
Karen Foletti .... Cristin Boyle

Time: June–August, 1945. Place: North End, Boston.

THE MATCHMAKER. By Phyllis Ryan; adapted from the novella *Letters of a Matchmaker* by John B. Keane. March 25, 2004. Director, Michael Scott; scenery, Michael McCaffey; costumes, Renee Purdy; lighting, Susan Kinkade; production stage manager, Jean Marie Tickell.

Performed by R. Bruce Connelly and Julia Kiley.

ROUTE 66. By Roger Bean. May 8, 2004. Director, Keith Andrews, scenery, Erin Kiernan; costumes, Renee Purdy; lighting, Susan Kinkade; sound, Asa F. Wember; music direction, Richard Derosa; production stage manager, Jean Marie Tickell.

Tenor I .... John Gardiner
Tenor II .... Paul Woodson
Baritone .... James Sasser
Bass .... Daniel Keeling

Yale Repertory Theatre, New Haven

James Bundy artistic director, Victoria Nolan managing director
Mark Bly associate artistic director

CULTURE CLASH IN AMERICCA. By Culture Clash. November 14, 2003. Director, Tony Taccone; scenery and lighting, Alexander V. Nichols; costumes, Donna Marie; dramaturg, Roweena Mackay; stage manager, Sterling Michols.

Performed by Richard Montoya, Ric Salinas, Herbert Sigüenza.

THE BLACK DAHLIA. By Mike Alfreds; adapted from the novel by James Ellroy. October 23, 2003. Director, Mr. Alfreds; scenery, Peter McKintosh; costumes, Anne Kenney; lighting, Stephen Strawbridge; sound, Daniel Baker; fight direction, B.H. Barry; dramaturgs, Mark Bly and Rachel Rusch.

Club Satan Owner; Conventioneer .... David Bardeen
Kay Lake; Marjorie Graham .... Amanda Cobb
Emmett Sprague; Sergeant Bill Koenig; Chief Green; Others .... Frank Deal
Officer Dwight "Bucky" Bleichert .... Mike Dooly
Sergeant Leland "Lee" Blanchard; Bobby DeWitt .... Marcus Dean Fuller
Ramona Sprague; Jane Chambers; Barmaid at LaVerne's; Aggie Underwood .... Mercedes Herrero
Ellis Loew; Johnny Vogel; Robert Manley .... Matt Hoverman
Sailor in Motel; Sid Man .... Allen E. Read
Madeleine Sprague; Betty Short .... Christina Rouner
Sheryl Saddon; Linda Martin; Sally Stinson; Others .... Sara Surrey
Sergeant Fritz Vogel; Milton Dolphine .... Graham Winton
Charles Issler; Parole Clerk .... Jeffrey Withers
Lt. Russ Millar; Cleo Short; Bevo Means; Others .... Mark Zeisler

Time: 1946–49. Place: Los Angeles. Presented in two parts.

ROTHSCHILD'S FIDDLE. By Kama Ginkas; adapted from the story by Anton Chekhov; supertitle translation by John Freedman. January 15, 2004 (world premiere). Director, Mr. Ginkas; scenery, Sergey Barkhin; costumes, Tatiana Barkhina; lighting, Gleb Filshtinsky; sound, Maria Bacharnikova; dramaturg, Yana Ross; stage manager, Alexandre Tsvetaev. Presented in association with the Moscow New Generation Theatre.

Yakov (Bronza) .... Valerii Barinov
Rothschild .... Igor Yasulovich
Marfa .... Arina Nesterova
Doctor's Assistant .... Alexei Dubrovsky

THE KING STAG. By Evan Yionoulis, Mike Yionoulis and Catherine Sheehy; adapted from the play by Carlo Gozzi. April 1, 2004. Director and choreographer, Ms. Yionoulis; scenery, Sergio Villegas; costumes, Camille Assaf; lighting, Stephen Strawbridge; sound, Sabrina McGuigan; music direction, Mike Yionoulis; dramaturgs, Emmy Grinwis and Catherine Sheehy; fight direction, Rick Sordelet; production stage manager, Stephanie L. Pearlman.

Cigolotti .... Matthew Cowles
Brighella .... Timothy Gulan
Smeraldina .... Lisa Jolley
A Harried Mother .... Daina Schatz
Her Difficult Son .... Alexander K. Sfakianos
Tartaglia .... Mark Zeisler
Clarice .... Jeanine Serralles
Pantalone .... Les J.N. Mau
Angela .... Opal Alladin
Leandro .... David Matranga
Truffaldino .... Jeremy Rabb
Deramo .... Bill Thompson
An Enchanted Statue .... Chad Callaghan
Durandarte .... B.J. Crosby
The Dapper Rappers
Li'l Moo Moo .... Ryan Quinn
Dr.Phat .... Bryan Terrell Clark
Mos'ly Deaf .... Jim Noonan

Time: An investment climate suspiciously like our own. Place: The enchanting Empire, theme park branch of multi-billion dollar entertainment conglomerate, Serendippo Worldwide, Inc.

THE MYSTERY PLAYS. By Roberto Aguirre-Sacasa. May 6, 2004 (world premiere). Director, Connie Grappo; scenery, Sandra Goldmark; costumes, Amanda Walker; lighting, S. Ryan Schmidt; sound, Keith Townsend Obadike; dramaturgs, Scott French and Rachel Rusch; stage manger, Elizabeth McCarter. Presented in association with Second Stage Theatre, New York.

Performed by Gavin Creel, Scott Ferrara, Leslie Lyles, Mark Margolis, Heather Mazur, Peter Stadlen.

Westport Country Playhouse

Joanne Woodward artistic director, Anne Keefe associate artistic director, Alison Harris executive director

THE GOOD GERMAN. By David Wiltse. June 27, 2003 (world premiere). Director, James Naughton; scenery, Hugh Landwehr; costumes, David Murin; lighting, Clifton Taylor; sound, Jerry Yager; fight direction, B.H. Barry.

Greta (Graeti) Vogel .... Kathleen McNenny
Wilhelm Braun .... Victor Slezak
Siemi Tauber .... Boyd Gaines
Karl Vogel .... Casey Biggs

DISTRICT OF COLUMBIA

Arena Stage, Washington

Molly Smith artistic director, Stephen Richard executive director

SHAKESPEARE IN HOLLYWOOD. By Ken Ludwig. September 12, 2003 (world premiere). Director, Kyle Donnelly; choreography, Karma Camp; scenery, Thomas Lynch; costumes, Jess Goldstein; lighting, Nancy Schertler; sound, Susan R. White; dramaturg, Michael Kinghorn; stage manager, Brady Ellen Poole.

Louella Parsons .... Ellen Karas
Max Reinhardt .... Robert Prosky
Dick Powell .... David Fendig
Jack Warner .... Rick Foucheux
Daryl .... Michael Skinner
Lydia Lansing .... Alice Ripley
Oberon .... Casey Biggs
Puck .... Emily Donahoe
Olivia Darnell .... Maggie Lacey
Will Hayes .... Everett Quinton
Joe E. Brown .... Hugh Nees
Jimmy Cagney .... Adam Richman

Ensemble: Bethany Caputo, Scott Graham, Eric Jorgensen, Robert McClure.

PROOF. By David Auburn. October 9, 2003. Director, Wendy C. Goldberg; scenery, Michael Brown; costumes, Anne Kennedy; lighting, Allen Lee Hughes; sound, Timothy M. Thompson.

Catherine .... Keira Naughton
Hal .... Barnaby Carpenter
Claire .... Susan Lynskey
Robert .... Michael Rudko

CAMELOT. Musical with book and lyrics by Alan Jay Lerner; music by Frederick Loewe; based on *The Once and Future King* by T.H. White. November 21, 2003. Director, Molly Smith; choreography, Baayork Lee; scenery, Kate Edmunds; costumes, Paul Tazewell; lighting, John Ambrosone; music direction, George Fulginiti-Shakar.

King Arthur .... Steven Skybell
Lancelot du Lac .... Matt Bogart
Queen Guenevere .... Kate Suber
Merlyn; Pellinore .... J. Fred Shiffman

Morgan Le Fey; Nimue ..... Christianne Tisdale
Mordred ..... Jack Ferver

The Knights of the Round Table

Sir Dinadan ..... Stephen Schmidt
Sir Lionel ..... Kevin Burrows
Sir Sagramore ..... Michael L. Forrest
Sir Bliant ..... Lawrence Brimmer
Sir Castor ..... Vic Dimonda
Sir Olatungi ..... John Lucas
Sir Tong Wi ..... Jeffrey Luke

Lords and Ladies of Camelot

Lady Sybil ..... Jennifer Andersen
Sir Colgrevance ..... Park Esse
Lady Catherine ..... Deanna Harris
Lady Anaya ..... Zoie Morris
Clarius ..... Eduardo Placer
Squire Dap ..... Bev Appleton
Tom of Warwick ..... James Soller, Brian Thane Wilson

Ensemble: Herald Anthony Aloise, Debra Buonaccorsi, Gabriel Veneziano.

CROWNS. By Regina Taylor; based on the book *Crowns: Portraits of Black Women in Church Hats* by Michael Cunningham and Craig Marberry. December 18, 2003. Director, Ms. Taylor; choreography, Dianne McIntyre; scenery, Riccardo Hernández; costumes, Emilio Sosa; lighting, Scott Zielinski; sound, Darron L. West; music direction, William Hubbard. Presented in association with Alliance Theatre Company, Atlanta, and the Goodman Theatre, Chicago. (See Alliance Theatre Company and the Goodman Theatre listings for details.)

Preacher; Man ..... John Steven Crowley
Yolanda ..... Desiré DuBose
Mother Shaw ..... Tina Fabrique
Wanda ..... Gail Grate
Mabel ..... Lynda Gravátt
Jeanette ..... Karan Kendrick
Velma ..... Bernadine Mitchell

YELLOWMAN. By Dael Orlandersmith. March 11, 2004. Director, Tazewell Thompson; scenery, Donald Eastman; costumes, LeVonne Lindsay; lighting, Robert Wierzel; sound, Fabian Obispo.

Alma ..... Laiona Michelle
Eugene ..... Howard W. Overshown

SEÑOR DISCRETION HIMSELF. Musical with book by Frank Loesser and Culture Clash; music and lyrics by Mr. Loesser; based on a short story by Budd Schulberg. April 15, 2004 (world premiere). Director, Charles Randolph-Wright; choreography, Doriana Sanchez; scenery, Thomas Lynch; costumes, Emilio Sosa; lighting, Michael Gilliam; sound, Timothy M. Thompson; music direction, Brian Cimmet; dramaturg, Michael Kinghorn.

Curandera ..... Doreen Montalvo
Pancito ..... Shawn Elliott
Father Francisco ..... Tony Chiroldes
Father Manuel ..... Carlos Lopez
Father Orlando ..... Robert Almodovar
Hilario ..... John Bolton
Carolina ..... Margo Reymundo
Lupita ..... Elena Shaddow
Martin ..... Ivan Hernandez

Ensemble: Venny Carranza, Steven Cupo, Rayanne Gonzales, Deanna Harris, Laura-Lisa, Lynnette Marrero, Eduardo Placer, Diego Prieto.

Musical numbers included: "Padre, I Have Sinned," "To See Her," "Pan, Pan, Pan," "Papa, Come Home," "I Dream," "I Got to Have a Somebody," "Nightmare," "The Real Curse of Drink," "You Understand Me," "Heaven Smiles on Tepancingo," "Companeros," "I Love Him, I Think," "Fifteen to Eighteen," "Hasta La Vista," "I Cannot Let You Go," "What Is Life?," "Pancito," "The Wisdom of the Heart."

Presented in two parts.

ORPHEUS DESCENDING. By Tennessee Williams. May 20, 2004. Director, Molly Smith; scenery; Bill C. Ray; costumes, Linda Cho; lighting, Michael Gilliam; sound and music,

Eric Shim; original songs, Jack Cannon; dramaturg, Michael Kinghorn; stage manager, Brady Ellen Poole.

Val Xavier .... Matt Bogart
Lady Torrance .... Chandler Vinton
Carol Cutrere .... Kate Goehring
Jabe Torrance .... J. Fred Shiffman
Dolly Hamma .... Rena Cherry Brown
Vee Talbott .... Janice Duclos
Eva Temple; Nurse .... Linda High
Pee Wee; Man .... Bruce M. Holmes
Beulah Binnings .... Kate Kiley
Dog Hamma; David Cutere .... Paul Morella
Sister Temple; Woman .... Anne Stone
Uncle Pleasant .... Frederick Strother
Sheriff Talbott .... Delaney Williams

Presented in two parts.

Downstairs Readings.

THE CRADLE OF MAN. By Melanie Marnich. October 23, 2003. Director, Howard Shalwitz.

SPIN MOVES. By Ken Weitzman. October 24, 2003. Director, Wendy C. Goldberg.

STORIES FROM JONESTOWN AND THE PEOPLES' TEMPLE. By Leigh Fondakowski. October 25, 2003. Director, Ms. Fondakowski.

PASSION PLAY, PART 3. By Sarah Ruhl. March 18, 2004. Director, Howard Shalwitz.

HURACÁN. By Nilo Cruz. March 19, 2004. Director, Molly Smith.

THE WINNING STREAK. By Lee Blessing. March 20, 2004. Director, Wendy C. Goldberg.

FALSE START. By Peter Hanrahan. March 21, 2004. Director, Tom Prewitt.

Folger Theatre, Washington

Janet Griffin artistic director

MELISSA ARCTIC. By Craig Wright; adapted from William Shakespeare's *The Winter's Tale*. January 28, 2004. Director, Aaron Posner; scenery, Tony Cisek; costumes, Kate Turner-Walker; lighting, Dan Covey; sound and music direction, James Sugg.

Time .... Kiah Victoria
Paul Anderson .... Kelly AuCoin
Leonard Mattson .... Ian Merrill Peakes
Mina Mattson .... Holly Twyford
Carl Kuchenmeister .... Kyle Thomas
Cindy Linda .... Dori Legg
"Lindy" Linda .... Michael Willis
Mike Goebel .... James Sugg
Alec Willoughby .... David Marks
Melissa Willoughby .... Miriam Liora Ganz
Ferris Anderson .... Mark Sullivan

The Kennedy Center, Washington

Eric Schaeffer artistic director, Max Woodward producer

BOUNCE. Musical with book by John Weidman, music and lyrics by Stephen Sondheim. October 30, 2003. A Kennedy Center presentation of the Goodman Theatre, Chicago, production. (See the Goodman Theatre listing for details.)

FIVE BY TENN. By Tennessee Williams. April 22, 2004. Director, Michael Kahn; scenery, Andrew Jackness; costumes, Catherine Zuber; lighting, Howell Binkley; sound; Martin Desjardins; music, Adam Wernick; stage manager, Daniel S. Rosokoff. Presented in association with Shakespeare Theatre, Washington. (See Shakespeare Theatre listing for details.)

The Writer .... Jeremy Lawrence

THESE ARE THE STAIRS YOU GOT TO WATCH

Policeman .... Edward Boroevich
Young Patron .... Joshua Drew
Mr. Kroger .... John Joseph Gallagher
Boy .... Hunter Gilmore
Older Patron .... Brian McMonagle
Young Patron .... Janet Patton
Carl .... Thomas Jay Ryan
Gladys .... Carrie Specksgoor
Cashier .... Joan van Ark
Policeman .... Myk Watford

ESCAPE

Anna .... Kathleen Chalfant
Donald Fenway .... Cameron Folmar
Mrs. Fenway .... Joan van Ark

AND TELL SAD STORIES OF THE DEATHS OF QUEENS

Candy Delaney .... Cameron Folmar
Alvin Krenning .... Hunter Gilmore
Jerry Johnson .... Brian McMonagle
Karl .... Myk Watford

THE MUNICIPAL ABATTOIR

Boy .... Cameron Folmar
Clerk .... Thomas Jay Ryan
Girl .... Carrie Specksgoor

I CAN'T IMAGINE TOMORROW

One .... Kathleen Chalfant
Two .... Thomas Jay Ryan

Presented in five parts.

A STREETCAR NAMED DESIRE. By Tennessee Williams. May 13, 2004. Director, Garry Hynes; scenery, John Lee Beatty; costumes, Jane Greenwood; lighting, Howell Binkley; sound, Scott Lehrer; stage manager, Paul-Douglas Michnewicz.

Stella Kowalski .... Amy Ryan
Stanley Kowalski .... Adam Rothenberg
Eunice Hubbell .... Amy McWilliams
Blanche DuBois .... Patricia Clarkson
Harold Mitchell .... Noah Emmerich
Steve Hubbell .... Michael John Casey
Pablo Gonzalez .... Tony Simione
A Young Collector .... Joshua Skidmore
Mexican Woman .... Cynthia Benjamin
Doctor .... Robert Michael McClure
Nurse .... Catherine Weidner

Time: 1947. Place: New Orleans. Presented in two parts.

Shakespeare Theatre, Washington

Michael Kahn artistic director, Nicholas T. Goldsborough managing director

GHOSTS. By Henrik Ibsen; adapted by Edwin Sherin. June 9, 2003. Director, Mr. Sherin; scenery, Walt Spangler; costumes, Jane Greenwood; lighting, Tyler Micoleau.

Mrs. Helen Alving .... Jane Alexander
Oswald Alving .... Alexander Pascal
Franklin Manders .... Ted Van Griethuysen
Jacob Strand .... André De Shields
Gina Strand .... Noel True

Time: 1981. Place: An island of the coast of Maine. Presented in two parts.

FIVE BY TENN. By Tennessee Williams. April 22, 2004. Presented in association with the Kennedy Center, Washington. (See the Kennedy Center listing for details.)

FLORIDA

Caldwell Theatre Company, Boca Raton

Michael Hall artistic director

THE LAST SUNDAY IN JUNE. By Jonathan Tolins. June 20, 2003. Director, Michael Hall; scenery, Tim Bennett; costumes, Patricia Burdett; lighting, Thomas Salzman; sound, Steve Shapiro; stage manager, Heather Loney.

Tom .... Jeff Meacham
Michael .... Nate Clark
Joe .... John Bixler
Brad .... Jack Garrity
Charles .... Steve Hayes
James .... Tim Burke
Scott .... Dean Strange
Susan .... Beth Bailey

Time: The last Sunday in June. Place: Tom and Michael's apartment on Christopher Street in Greenwich Village.

SHOWTUNE: THE WORDS AND MUSIC OF JERRY HERMAN. By Paul Gilger; adapted from the work of Mr. Herman. November 12, 2003. Director, Michael Hall; choreography, Barbara Flaten; scenery, Tim Bennett; costumes, Estela Vrancovich; lighting, Thomas Salzman; sound, Steve Shapiro; music direction, Bobby Peaco.

Man 1 .... Martin Vidnovic
Woman 1 .... Lourelene Snedeker
Man 2 .... Steve Wilson
Woman 2 .... Connie SaLoutos
Man 3 .... Benjamin Schrader
Woman 3 .... Stephanie Lynge
Man 4; Piano .... Bobby Peaco

Musical numbers included: "It's Today," "Big Time," "We Need a Little Christmas," "Put on Your Sunday Clothes," "A Little More Mascara," "The Man in the Moon," "I Am What I Am," "Song on the Sand," ""I Won't Send Roses," "Ribbons Down My Back," "Dancing," "It Takes a Woman," "Wherever He Ain't," "Hundreds of Girls," "So Long, Dearie," "And I Was Beautiful," "Kiss Her Now," "Time Heals Everything," "Before the Parade Passes By," "One Person," "Open a New Window," "Movies Were Movies," "Look What Happened to Mabel," "That's How Young I Feel," "My Best Girl," "Nelson," "Just Go to the Movies," "It Only Takes a Moment," "What Do I Do Now?," "Tap Your Troubles Away," "Bosom Buddies," "I Don't Want to Know," " Song on the Sand," "Shalom," "I'll Be Here Tomorrow,""If He Walked Into My Life," "I Promise You a Happy Ending," "Mame," "The Best of Times," "Hello Dolly!"

Presented in two parts.

DÉJÀ VU. By Jean-Jacques Bricaire and Maurice Lasaygues; English adaptation by John MacNicholas. January 9, 2004. Director, Bruce Lecure; scenery, Tim Bennett; costumes, Patricia Burdett; lighting, Thomas Salzman; sound, Steve Shapiro, stage manager, Heather Loney.

Petra .... Regan Thompson
Louis Lamart .... Yuval David
Albert Lamart .... Bob Rogerson
Frank J. Bromfield III .... Michael McKenzie
Mathilde Lasbry .... Lisa Bansavage

Place: Living room of Albert Lamart's townhouse in Paris. Presented in two parts.

IAGO. By James McLure. February 27, 2004. Director, Michael Hall; scenery, Tim Bennett; costumes, Patricia Burdett and Linda Shorrock; music, M. Anthony Reimer; stage manager, Jeffry George.

Tony .... Bob Rogerson
Vivacity .... Lisa Bansavage
Finney .... Neil Stewart
Basil .... Dennis Creaghan

Place: Various locations in England and Cyprus. Presented in two parts.

Coconut Grove Playhouse, Coral Gables

Arnold Mittelman producing artistic director, Laura Calzolari executive director

HALPERN AND JOHNSON. By Lionel Goldstein. March 20, 2004. Director, David Ellenstein; scenery, Paul Wonsek; costumes, Ellis Tillman; lighting, Kirk Bookman; sound, Steve Shapiro; production stage manager, Naomi Littman.

Joe Halpern .... Hal Linden
Dennis Johnson .... Brian Murray

Presented in two parts.

Hippodrome State Theatre, Gainesville

Lauren Caldwell artistic director

THE WAR OF THE WORLDS. By H.G. Wells; adapted by Lauren Caldwell. February 27, 2004. Director, Ms. Caldwell; scenery, Mihai Ciupe; costumes, Marilyn A. Wall and Lorelei Esser; lighting, Robert P. Robins; sound, Graham Johnson; dramaturg, Tammy Dygert.

Performed by Stephen Blackwell, Cameron Francis, Charlie Kevin, J. Salome Martinez Jr., Sara Morsey, Robin Thomas, James E. Webb Jr.

New Theatre, Coral Gables

Rafael de Acha artistic director, Eileen Suarez managing director

BEAUTY OF THE FATHER. By Nilo Cruz. January 3, 2004 (world premiere). Director, Rafael de Acha; scenery, Adrian W. Jones; costumes, Caron Grant; lighting, Travis Neff; sound, Ozzie Quintana. Presented in association with Seattle Repertory Theatre. (See Seattle Repertory Theatre listing for details.)

Emiliano .... Roberto Escobar
Mariana .... Ursula Freundlich
Paquita .... Teresa Maria Rojas
Karim .... Euramis Losada
Federico García Lorca .... Carlos Orizondo

Time: Summer of 1999. Place: A small town called Salobreña near Granada, Spain. Presented in two parts.

GEORGIA

Alliance Theatre Company, Atlanta

Susan V. Booth artistic director, Thomas Pechar managing director

KING HEDLEY II. By August Wilson. September 26, 2003. Director, Kent Gash; scenery, Emily Beck; costumes, Alvin B. Perry; lighting, Liz Lee; sound, Clay Benning; music, Justin Ellington; fight direction, Jason Armit and Scot J. Mann; dramaturg, Freddie Ashley.

Ruby .... Pat Bowie
Elmore .... Thomas Jefferson Byrd
Tonya .... Quincy Tyler Bernstine
Stool Pigeon .... Don Griffin
King Hedley II .... Keith Randolph Smith
Mister .... Geoffrey D. Williams

CROWNS. By Regina Taylor; adapted from the book by Michael Cunningham and Craig Marberry. October 8, 2003. Presented in association with Arena Stage, Washington, DC, and the Goodman Theatre, Chicago, Illinois. (See Arena Stage listing for details.)

THE SUBJECT TONIGHT IS LOVE. By Sandra Deer. November 19, 2003 (world premiere). Director, Kenny Leon; scenery, Robert Mark Morgan; costumes, Susan E. Mickey; lighting, Mary Louise Geiger; sound, Clay Benning; music, Dwight Andrews; dramaturg, Megan Monaghan.

Joshua Gold .... Mitchell Anderson
Ruby Land Parker .... Brenda Bynum
Diana Park Gold .... Linda Thorson

LEAP. By Jim Grimsley; with Susan V. Booth, Bill Nigut, Adam McNight, Megan Monaghan, Rosemary Newcott, Tom Key, Carol Mitchell-Leon and M. Michael Fauss. March 10, 200 (world premiere). Director, Ms. Booth; scenery, Roger Foster, costumes, Susan E. Mickey; lighting, Ken Yunker; music, Mr. Fauss; dramaturg, Ms. Monaghan.

Himself .... Tom Key
Himself .... Adam McKnight
Herself .... Carol Mitchell-Leon
Herself .... Rosemary Newcott
Himself .... Bill Nigut

A DEATH IN THE HOUSE NEXT DOOR TO KATHLEEN TURNER'S HOUSE ON LONG ISLAND. By William Ludel. May 5, 2004 (world premiere). Director, Jeff Steitzer; scenery, William S. Clarke; costumes, Laura Crow; lighting, Mary Louise Geiger; sound, Clay Benning; fight direction, Jason Armit; dramaturg, Freddie Ashley.

Walter Glass .... Walter Charles
Desi .... Brandon Dirden
Karen Glass (I) .... Beth Dixon
Lucy .... Morgan Hallett
Harvey Morton .... Bart Hansard
Karen Glass (II) .... Felicity LaFortune
Dr. Eddie Jerome .... Keith Reddin
Jason Glass .... David Marshall Silverman

7 Stages Theater, Atlanta

Del Hamilton artistic director, Faye Allen producing director, Raye Varney managing director

IPHIGENIA CRASH LAND FALLS ON THE NEON SHELL THAT WAS ONCE HER HEART (A RAVE-FABLE). By Caridad Svich. January 22, 2004 (world premiere). Director, Melissa Foulger; scenery, Ashlee A. White; costumes, Emily Gill; lighting, Rich Dunham; sound, Brian Ginn; video, Sabina Maja Angel; dramaturg, Steven Yockey; production stage manager, Heidi S. Howard.

Iphigenia .... Heather Starkel
Achilles; Fresa Girl .... Adam Fristoe
Adolfo; Fresa Girl;
Virtual MC; Soldier X;
General's Ass .... Ismail ibn Connor
Camilla,
Violeta Imperial;
Hermaphrodite Prince .... Kristi Casey
Orestes; News Anchor;
Virgin Puta; Fresa Girl .... Justin Welborn

Presented without intermission.

ILLINOIS

The Goodman Theatre, Chicago

Robert Falls artistic director, Roche Schulfer executive direrctor

BOUNCE. Musical with book by John Weidman, music and lyrics by Stephen Sondheim. June 30, 2003 (world premiere). Director, Harold Prince; choreography, Michael Arnold; scenery, Eugene Lee; costumes, Miguel Angel Huidor; lighting, Howell Binkley; sound, Duncan Robert Edwards; music direction, David Caddick; production stage manager, Alden Vasquez.

Con art: Richard Kind and Howard McGillin in Bounce *at the Goodman Theatre. Photo: Liz Lauren.*

Wilson Mizner	Howard McGillin	Mama Mizner	Jane Powell
Addison Mizner	Richard Kind	Hollis Bessemer	Gavin Creel
Nellie	Michele Pawk	Papa Mizner	Herndon Lackey

Ensemble: Sean Blake, Marilyn Bogetich, Tom Daugherty, Jeff Dumas, Deanna Dunagan, Nicole Grothues, Rick Hilsabeck, Jeff Parker, Harriet Nzinga Plumpp, Jenny Powers, Craig Ramsay, Jacquelyn Ritz, Fred Zimmerman.

Musical numbers included: "Bounce," "Opportunity," Gold!," "What's Your Rush?," "Next to You," "Addison's Trip Around the World," "Alaska," "New York Sequence," "The Best Thing That Ever Happened to Me," "Isn't He Something?," "The Game," "Talent," "You," "Addison's City," "Boca Raton," "Last Fight."

Time: 1896–1933. Place: America and elsewhere. Presented in two parts.

Edward Albee Festival

THE PLAY ABOUT THE BABY. By Edward Albee. September 30, 2003. Director, Pam MacKinnon; scenery, Todd Rosenthal; costumes, Birgit Rattenborg Wise; lighting, Robert Christen; sound, Andre Pluess and Ben Sussman; fight direction, Nick Sandys; production dramaturg, Rick DesRochers.

Boy	Scott Antonucci	The Man	Matt DeCaro
Girl	Julie Granata	The Woman	Linda Kimbrough

Presented in two parts.

THE GOAT, OR WHO IS SYLVIA? By Edward Albee. October 7, 2003. Director, Robert Falls; scenery and lighting, Michael Philippi; costumes, Nan Cibula-Jenkins; sound, Richard Woodbury; production dramaturg, Tom Creamer; production stage manager, Joseph Drummond.

Martin	Patrick Clear	Stevie	Barbara Robertson
Ross	William Dick	Billy	Michael Stahl-David

Edward Albee One-Act Plays. Three programs played in repertory with The Play About the Baby.

Program One

THE ZOO STORY. Director, Lynn Ann Bernatowicz; scenery, Todd Rosenthal; costumes, Rachel Anne Healy; lighting, Robert Christen; sound, Andre Pluess and Ben Sussman.

Peter .... Bradley Armacost
Jerry .... Steve Key

THE DEATH OF BESSIE SMITH. Director, Chuck Smith; scenery, Todd Rosenthal; costumes, Rachel Anne Healy; lighting, Robert Christen; sound, Andre Pluess and Ben Sussman.

Nurse .... Kati Brazda
Intern .... Scott Duff
Father .... Bill McGough
Jack .... Senuwell Smith
Bernie .... Michael Torrey
Second Nurse .... Jamie Virostko
Orderly .... Terrance Watts

Program Two

BOX. Director, Eric Rosen; scenery, Todd Rosenthal; costumes, Birgit Rattenborg Wise; lighting, Robert Christen; sound, Andre Pluess and Ben Sussman.

The Voice .... Linda Kimbrough

THE SANDBOX. Director, Eric Rosen; scenery, Todd Rosenthal; costumes, Birgit Rattenborg Wise; lighting, Robert Christen; sound, Andre Pluess and Ben Sussman.

Young Man .... Brad Burton
Daddy .... Ted Hoerl
The Musician .... Jason McDermott
Mommy .... Rondi Reed
Grandma .... Mary Seibel

FINDING THE SUN. Director, Eric Rosen; scenery, Todd Rosenthal; costumes, Birgit Rattenborg Wise; lighting, Robert Christen; sound, Andre Pluess and Ben Sussman.

Abigail .... Tiffany Scott
Benjamin .... Benjamin Newton
Cordelia .... Kati Brazda
Daniel .... Scott Duff
Edmee .... Patricia Kane
Fergus .... James Immekus
Gertrude .... Caitlin Hart
Henden .... Gary Wingert

Program Three

MARRIAGE PLAY. Director, Lou Contey; scenery, Todd Rosenthal; costumes, Rachel Anne Healy; lighting, Robert Christen; sound, Andre Pluess and Ben Sussman.

Gillian .... Linda Reiter
Jack .... Scott Rowe

THE LIGHT IN THE PIAZZA. Musical with book by Craig Lucas; music and lyrics by Adam Guettel; based on the novella by Elizabeth Spencer. January 20, 2004. Director, Bartlett Sher; choreography, Marcela Lorca; scenery, Michael Yeargan; costumes, Catherine Zuber; lighting, Christopher Akerlind; sound, Acme Sound Partners; music direction, Ted Sperling and Mr. Guettel; production dramaturg, Rick DesRochers. Presented in association with Intiman Theatre Company, Seattle, Washington. (See Intiman Theatre Company listing for details.)

Margaret Johnson .... Victoria Clark
Clara Johnson .... Celia Keenan-Bolger
Fabrizio Naccarelli .... Wayne Wilcox
Signor Naccarelli .... Mark Harelik
Signora Naccarelli .... Patti Cohenour
Giuseppe Naccarelli .... Glenn Seven Allen
Franca .... Kelli O'Hara
Roy Johnson .... Andrew Rothenberg

Ensemble: Amy Arbizzani, Stephen Rader, Jonathan Raviv, Brooke Sherrod.

Musical numbers included: "Statues and Stories," "The Beauty Is," "Passeggiata," "The Joy You Feel," "Dividing Day," "Savonarola," "Appuntamento," "Margaret," "Say It Somehow," "Aiutami," "The Light in the Piazza," "Octet," "Tirade," "Let's Walk," "Love to Me," "Fable."

Time: Summer 1953. Place: Florence; occasional side trips to America. Presented in two parts.

New Stages Series. January 21–January 25, 2004.

FLOYD AND CLEA UNDER THE WESTERN SKY. Musical with book and lyrics by David Cale; music by Jonathan Kreisberg and Mr. Cale. January 21, 2004. Director, Rick DesRochers.

Performed by Mr. Cale, Mr. DesRochers, Kalena Dickerson, James Gittins; Amy Jenkins; Eliki Kogiones; Jonathan Kreisberg; Kim Osgood, Tempe Thomas.

BFE (BUM FUCK EGYPT). By Julia Cho. January 22, 2004. Director, Lynn Ann Bernatowicz.

Performed by Ms. Bernatowicz, Christine Bunuan, Joe Dempsey, Rick DesRochers, Joseph Foronda, James Gittins, Cheryl Hamada, Amy Jensen, Ora Jones, Seung-Hee Kyung-Lee, Ian Nowak, Kim Osgood, Brian Plocharczyk, Melissa Sienicki, Jennifer Shin, Aprill Winney.

Time: Late 1990s. Place: BFE. Presented in two parts.

MARIELA IN THE DESERT. By Karen Zacarías. January 23, 2004. Director: Chris Garcia Peak.

Performed by Desmond Borges, Sandra Delgado, Joe Dempsey, Rick DesRochers, James Gittins, Amy Jensen, Sandra Marquez, Kim Osgood, Mr. Peak, Carmen Severino, Edward Torres, Marisol Velez.

Time: 1950. Place: Small ranch in the northern desert of Mexico. Presented in two parts.

SOFTLY BLUE. By Shepsu Aakhu. January 24, 2004. Director, Mignon McPherson Nance.

Performed by Glenda Zahra Baker, Daniel Bryant, Rick DesRochers, Mignon McPherson Nance, Kim Osgood, Rodney Stapleton, Carla Stillwell, LaRonika Thomas, Michelle Wilson.

CHEECH, OR THE CHRYSLER GUYS ARE IN TOWN. By François Létoureau; translated by Rick DesRochers. January 25, 2004. Director, Sean Graney.

Performed by Ryan Bolletino, Mr. DesRochers, Kurt Ehrmann, James Gittins, Jennifer Grace, Sean Graney, Amy Jensen, Rob Kauzaularic, Mechelle Moe, Kim Osgood, Vanessa Stalling, Steve Wilson.

Time: The present. Place: A day in disorder.

HERITAGE. By Brett Neveu. January 25, 2004. Director, Geoffrey Scott.

Performed by Tom Creamer, Rick DesRochers, Kristen Fitzgerald, James Gittins, Larry Grimm, Curtis Jackson, Amy Jensen, Kim Osgood, Geoffrey Scott, Will Simms II, Troy West, Cedric Young.

Time: The present. Place: Dining room of a home on a Louisiana plantation. Presented in two parts.

PROOF. By David Auburn. April 7, 2004. Director, Chuck Smith; costumes, Birgit Rattenborg Wise; lighting, Robert Christen; music and sound, Ray Nardelli and Joshua Horvath; dramaturg, Rick DesRochers.

Catherine .... Karen Aldridge
Claire .... Ora Jones
Hal .... Dwain A. Perry
Robert .... Phillip Edward VanLear

Time: The present. Place: Hyde Park, Chicago.

CROWNS. By Regina Taylor; adapted from the book by Michael Cunningham and Craig Marberry. March 16, 2004. Presented in association with Arena Stage, Washington, DC, and the Alliance Theatre Company, Atlanta, Georgia. (See Arena listing for details.)

MOONLIGHT AND MAGNOLIAS. By Ron Hutchinson. May 25, 2004 (world premiere). Director, Steve Robman; scenery and lighting, Michael Philippi; costumes, Birgit Rattenborg Wise; sound, Richard Woodbury; production dramaturg, Tom Creamer.

David O. Selznick	Ron Orbach	Victor Fleming	Rob Riley
Ben Hecht	William Dick	Selznick's assistant	Mary Seibel

Lookingglass Theatre Company, Chicago

Laura Eason artistic director, Jacqueline Russell executive director

RACE: HOW BLACK AND WHITES THINK ABOUT THE AMERICAN OBSESSION. By Joy Gregory and David Schwimmer; adapted from the book by Studs Terkel. June 13, 2003 (world premiere). Director, Mr. Schwimmer; scenery, Daniel Ostling; costumes, Mara Blumenfeld; lighting, Chris Binder; sound, Andre Pluess and Ben Sussman; production stage manager, Sara Gmitter.

Performed by DeAnna N.J. Brooks, Cheryl Lynn Bruce, Corryn Cummins, Tony Fitzpatrick, Anthony Fleming III, Ricardo Gutierrez, Cheryl Hamada, Reginald Nelson, Rusty Schwimmer, Joe Sikora, Andrew White, Cedric Young.

THE SECRET IN THE WINGS. By Mary Zimmerman. September 29, 2003. Director, Ms. Zimmerman; scenery, Daniel Ostling; costumes, Mara Blumenfeld; lighting, T.J. Gerckens; sound and music, Andre Pluess and Ben Sussman; production stage manager, Sara Gmitter.

Performed by Laura Eason, Tony Fitzpatrick; Raymond Fox; David Kersnar, Louise Lamson, Philip R. Smith, Heidi Stillman, Tracy Walsh, Andrew White.

Northlight Theatre, Skokie

BJ Jones artistic director, Philip J. Santora managing director

TUESDAYS WITH MORRIE. By Jeffrey Hatcher and Mitch Albom. October 15, 2003. Director, BJ Jones; scenery, Richard and Jacqueline Penrod; costumes, Rachel Anne Healy; lighting, Todd Hensley; music and sound, Andre Pluess; dramaturg, Rosanna Forrest.

Mitch Albom	Tracy Letts	Morrie Schwartz	Mike Nussbaum

Time: 1985; other times in Mitch's life. Place: Morrie Schwartz's study, West Newton, Massachusetts and other locations.

STUDS TERKEL'S "THE GOOD WAR." Musical by David H. Bell and Craig Carnelia. May 19, 2004 (world premiere). Director and choreographer, Mr. Bell; scenery, Tom Burch; lighting, Todd Hensley; costumes, Nan Zabriskie; sound, Robert Neuhaus; stage manager, Deya Friedman.

Man 4	Joshua Campbell	Man 1	Ron Rains
Man 2	Jeremy Cohen	Woman	Jacquelyn Ritz
Man 3	Patrick Gagnon	Man 7	Jeff Still
Man 6	George Keating	Man 5	Stef Tovar

Musical numbers included: "We Did It Before and We Can Do It Again," "Goodbye Mama, I'm Off to Yokahama," "I'll Be With You in Apple Blossom Time," "Uncle Sam Blues," "Till Then," "Comin' in on a Wing and a Prayer," "You Can't Get That No More," "Dear Mom," "Gute Nacht Mutter," "GI Jive," "Straighten Up and Fly Right," "This Is Worth Fighting For," "The Fox," "Stalin Wasn't Stallin'," "I'll Be Seeing You," "Moonlight Serenade."

Steppenwolf Theatre Company, Chicago

Martha Lavey artistic director, David Hawkanson executive director

HOMEBODY/KABUL. By Tony Kushner. July 20, 2003. Director, Frank Galati; scenery, James Schuette; costumes, Mara Blumenfeld; lighting, Christopher Akerlind; production stage manager, Robert H. Satterlee. Presented in association with the Mark Taper Forum, Los Angeles. (See Mark Taper Forum listing for details.)

The Homebody .... Amy Morton
Mullah Ali Aftar Durranni .... Aasif Mandvi
Milton Ceiling .... Reed Birney
Quango Twistleton ....Tracy Letts
Priscilla Ceiling ....Elizabeth Ledo
Khwaja Aziz Mondanabosh ...... Firdous Bamji
Mahala .... Diana Simonzadeh

Ensemble: Jeremy Beiler, Ali Farahnakian, Diana M. Konopka, Raymond Kurut, Omar Metwally, Arian Moayed, Christopher Yonan.

Presented in three parts.

TOPDOG/UNDERDOG. By Suzan-Lori Parks. September 21, 2003. Director, Amy Morton; scenery, Loy Arcenas; costumes, Nan Cibula-Jenkins; lighting, Kevin Rigdon; music and sound, Michael Bodeen and Rob Milburn; dramaturg, Nadine Warner; production stage manager, Robert H. Satterlee. Presented in association with Alley Theatre, Houston, and Dallas Theater Center. (See Alley Theatre and Dallas Theater Center listings for details.)

Booth .... K. Todd Freeman
Lincoln .... David Rainey

Time: Now. Place: Here.

ORANGE FLOWER WATER. By Craig Wright. November 23, 2003. Director, Rick Snyder; scenery, Robert G. Smith; costumes, Alison Heryer; lighting, Andrew Meyers; sound, Michael Kraskin, stage manager, Lara Maerz.

Performed by Darrell W. Cox, Molly Glynn, Whitney Sneed, Christian Stolte.

MAN FROM NEBRASKA. By Tracy Letts. November 30, 2003 (world premiere). Director, Anna D. Shapiro; scenery, Todd Rosenthal; costumes, Mara Blumenfeld; lighting, Ann G. Wrightson; sound, Rob Milburn and Michael Bodeen; music, Shawn Letts; dramaturg, Edward Sobel; stage manager, Malcolm Ewen.

Performed by Karen Aldridge, Richard Bull, Shannon Cochran, Barbara Ann Grimes, Beth Lacke, Rondi Reed, Michael Shannon, Rick Snyder, Thomas White.

OUR LADY OF 121ST STREET. By Stephen Adly Guirgis. February 15, 2004. Director, Will Frears; scenery, Thomas Lynch; costumes, Janice Pytel; lighting, Chris Binder; sound, Andre Pluess and Ben Sussman; dramaturg, Sarah Gubbins; stage manager, Alden Vasquez.

Performed by Robert Breuler, Keith Davis, Matt DeCaro, Kevin Christopher Fox, Ricardo Gutierrez, Eddie Martinez, Sammy A. Publes, Krissy Shields, Rebecca Spence, Marisabel Suarez, E. Milton Wheeler, Shané Williams.

A TALE OF TWO CITIES. By Laura Eason; adapted from the novel by Charles Dickens. March 6, 2004. Director, Jessica Thebus; scenery, John Dalton; costumes, Jennifer Roberts; lighting, JR Lederle; sound, Josh Schmidt; dramaturg, Fabrizio Almeida; stage manager, Kerry Epstein.

Performed by Wayne Brown, Brian McCaskill, Mark L. Montgomery, Derrick Nelson, Nigel Patterson, Niki Prugh, Elizabeth Rich, Dale Rivera.

THE FALL TO EARTH. By Joel Drake Johnson. April 3, 2004 (world premiere). Director, Rick Snyder; scenery, Jack Magaw; costumes, Alison Heryer; lighting, JR Lederle; sound, Joe Cerqua; stage manager, Michelle Medvin.

Fay .... Rondi Reed
Rachel .... Cheryl Graeff
Terry .... Sarah Charipar

Presented without intermission.

Victory Gardens Theater, Chicago

Dennis Zacek artistic director, Marcelle McVay managing director

THE END OF THE TOUR. By Joel Drake Johnson. June 2, 2003 (world premiere). Director, Sandy Shinner; scenery, Jeff Bauer; costumes, Judith Lundberg; lighting, Rita Pietraszek; sound, Andre Pluess and Ben Sussman; production stage manager, Tina M. Jach.

Jan Morris Williamson .... Annabel Armour
Andrew Morris .... Timothy Hendrickson
Chuck Williamson .... Rob Riley
David Sabin .... Andrew Rothenberg
Tommy Johns .... Marc Silvia
Norma Brown .... Kitty Taber
Mae Anne Pierce .... Mary Ann Thebus

Time: The present. Place: Primarily in Dixon, Illinois, "The Petunia City."

ANNA IN THE TROPICS. By Nilo Cruz. September 24, 2003. Director, Henry Godinez; scenery, Mary Griswold; costumes, Judith Lundberg; lighting, Jaymi Lee Smith; sound, Gustavo Leone; production stage manager, Tina M. Jach.

Conchita .... Charin Alvarez
Marela .... Sandra Delgado
Cheché .... Ricardo Gutierrez
Ofelia .... Sandra Marquez
Santiago .... Gustavo Mellado
Juan Julian .... Dale Rivera
Palomo .... Edward Torres

Time: 1929. Place: Tampa, Florida. A place called Ybor City. Presented in two parts.

HOMELAND SECURITY. By Stuart Flack. October 22, 2003 (world premiere). Director, Sandy Shinner; scenery, Jeff Bauer; costumes, Michelle Tesdall; lighting, Jaymi Lee Smith; sound, Chris Johnson; music, Fareed Haque and Kalyan Pathak; production stage manager, Ellyn Costello.

Raj Gupta .... Anish Jethmalani
Paul Gordon .... James Krag
Susan Freeman .... Julia Neary
Thomas Benjamin .... Kenn E. Head

Time: The present. Place: Chicago. Presented in two parts.

AFFLUENZA! By James Sherman. November 24, 2003 (world premiere). Director, Dennis Zacek; scenery, Mary Griswold; costumes, Judith Lundberg; lighting, Chris Phillips; sound, Andre Pluess and Ben Sussman; production stage manager, Tina M. Jach.

Ruth .... Roslyn Alexander
William .... Richard Henzel
Jerome .... David New
Dawn .... Kim Wade
Eugene .... Ian Westerfer
Bernard .... Cedric Young

Time: Today. Place: Chicago.

FREE MAN OF COLOR. By Charles Smith. January 26, 2004 (world premiere). Director, Andrea J. Dymond; scenery, Tim Morrison; costumes, Michelle Tesdall; lighting, Mary McDonald Badger; sound and music, Joe Cerqua; production stage manager, Rita Vreeland.

Jane Wilson .... Shelley Delaney
John N. Templeton .... Anthony Fleming III
Robert Wilson .... Gary Houston

Time: 1828. Place: Ohio University. Presented in two parts.

TRYING. By Joanna McClelland Glass. March 29, 2004 (world premiere). Director, Sandy Shinner; scenery, Jeff Bauer; costumes, Carolyn Cristofani; lighting, Jacqueline Reid; sound and music, Andrew Hopson; production stage manager, Tina M. Jach.

Judge Biddle .... Fritz Weaver
Sarah Schorr .... Kati Brazda

Time: November 1967–June 1968. Place: Judge Biddle's office over a garage in Georgetown. Presented in two parts.

KENTUCKY

Actors Theatre of Louisville

Marc Masterson artistic director, Alexander Speer executive director

I WORRY. By Sandra Tsing Loh. September 9, 2003. Director, David Schweizer; scenery, Andrew Lieberman; lighting, Paul Werner; sound, Benjamin Marcum; stage manager, Andrew Scheer.

Performed by Ms. Tsing Loh.

Presented in two parts.

TWO PIANOS, FOUR HANDS. By Ted Dykstra and Richard Greenblatt. February 6, 2004. Director, Mr. Greenblatt; scenery and lighting, Steve Lucas; sound, Benjamin Marcum; stage manager, Debra A. Freeman.

Richard .... Richard Carsey
Ted .... Tom Frey

Presented in two parts.

28th Annual Humana Festival of New American Plays. February 29–April 4, 2004.

KID-SIMPLE: A RADIO PLAY IN THE FLESH. By Jordan Harrison. February 29, 2004. Director, Darron L. West; scenery, Paul Owen; costumes, Lorraine Venberg; lighting, Tony Penna; sound, Bray Poor and Mr. West; dramaturg, Tanya Palmer; production stage manager, Paul Mills Holmes.

Moll .... Maria Dizzia
Oliver .... Max Ferguson
The Narrator .... Glynis Bell
The Mercenary .... Michael Ray Escamilla
Father;
Mr. Wachtel; Voice One .... Jason Pugatch
Mother;
Miss Kendrick; Voice Two .... Carla Harting
Foley Artist .... Clifford Endo Gulibert

Presented without intermission.

SANS-CULOTTES IN THE PROMISED LAND. By Kirsten Greenidge. March 6, 2004. Director, Randy White; scenery, Paul Owen; costumes, Junghyun Georgia Lee; lighting, Tony Penna; sound, Vincent Olivieri; fight direction, Drew Fracher; dramaturg, Sarah Gubbins; stage manager, Cat Domiano.

Carol .... Angela Bullock
Greg .... Leon Addison Brown
Lena .... April Matthis
Greta .... Kibibi Dillon
Carmel .... Sharon Hope
Charlotte .... Tamilla Woodard

Presented without intermission.

TALLGRASS GOTHIC. By Melanie Marnich. March 11, 2004. Director, Marc Masterson; scenery, Paul Owen; costumes, Lorraine Venberg; lighting, Deb Sullivan; sound, Vincent Olivieri; fight direction, Drew Fracher; dramaturg, Mead Hunter; stage manager, Debra A. Freeman.

2004 Humana Festival of New American Plays

Hay ride: Asa Somers and Lia Aprile in Tallgrass Gothic *(top). Photo: Harlan Taylor.*

Earplay: Jason Pugatch, Carla Harting and Maria Dizzia in Kid Simple. *Photo: Harlan Taylor.*

Big planner: Angela Bullock and Leon Addison Brown in Sans-culottes in the Promised Land. *Photo: Harlan Taylor.*

Laura .... Lia Aprile
Tin .... Michael A. Newcomer
Daniel .... Asa Somers
Mary .... Tonya Cornelisse
Scotto .... David Wagner
Filene .... Jesse Lenat

Time: The present. Place: Laura and Tin's porch and bed among the grasses of the American plains; an old church; a corner of a dilapidated barn; the junked back seat of a car.

Presented without intermission.

AT THE VANISHING POINT. By Naomi Iizuka. March 14, 2004. Director, Les Waters; scenery, Paul Owen; costumes, Connie Furr-Solomon; lighting, Tony Penna; sound, John Zalewski; music, Tara Jane O'Neil; dramaturg, Tanya Palmer; stage manager, Nancy Pittelman.

The Photographer .... Bruce McKenzie
Pete Henzel; Martin Kinflein; Jimmy Marston .... Trey Lyford
Ronnie Marston; Ida Miller; Maudie Totten .... Claudia Fielding
Nora Holtz; Tessa Rheingold .... Suli Holum
Mike Totten; Frank Henzel .... Lou Sumrall
School Children; Children's Chorus at St. Joe's .... A. Glaser, Luke Craven Glaser, Madeline Marchal

Time: Past and present. Place: Butchertown in Louisville, Kentucky. Presented without intermission.

THE RUBY SUNRISE. By Rinne Groff. March 20, 2004. Director, Oskar Eustis; scenery, Eugene Lee; costumes, Deborah Newhall; lighting, Deb Sullivan; sound, Bray Poor; dramaturg, Adrien-Alice Hansel; stage manager, Allison Tkac. Presented in association with Trinity Repertory Company, Providence, Rhode Island. (See Trinity Repertory Company listing for details.)

Ruby; Elizabeth Hunter .... Julie Jesneck
Henry; Paul Benjamin .... Stephen Thorne
Lois; Ethel Reed .... Anne Scurria
Lulu .... Jessica Wortham
Tad Rose .... Mauro Hantman
Martin Marcus .... Fred Sullivan Jr.
Suzie Tyrone .... Russell Arden Koplin

Time: 1927; 1952. Place: A boarding house in Indiana; a television network in New York City. Presented in two parts.

AFTER ASHLEY. By Gina Gionfriddo. March 21, 2004. Director, Marc Masterson; scenery, Paul Owen; costumes, Connie Furr-Solomon; lighting, Tony Penna; sound, Vincent Olivieri; dramaturg, Liz Engelman; stage manager, Andrew Scheer.

Justin Hammond .... Jesse Hooker
Ashley Hammond .... Carla Harting
Alden Hammond .... Stephen Barker Turner
David Gavin .... Frank X
Julie Bell .... Sabrina Veroczi
Roderick Lord .... Jason Pugatch

Time: 1999; 2002. Place: Bethesda, Maryland; New York City; central Florida. Presented in two parts.

FAST AND LOOSE. By José Cruz González, Kirsten Greenidge, Julie Marie Myatt and John Walch. March 26, 2004. Director, Wendy McClellan; scenery, Brenda Ellis; costumes, John P. White; lighting, Paul Werner; sound, Benjamin Marcum; fight direction, Drew Fracher; dramaturg, Steve Moulds; stage manager, Abigail Wright.

IN THIS HOUSE

Kathy .... Lisa Benner
Lynne; Claire .... Jody Christopherson
Kayla .... Wendy Gaunt
Robert; Cook .... Matthew Goldsborough
Bill .... David Wagner

2004 Humana Festival of New American Plays

Pre-mortem: Jesse Hooker and Carla Harting in After Ashley. *Photo: Harlan Taylor.*

Bird hunting: Sasha Andreev in Fast and Loose. *Photo: Harlan Taylor.*

Inside the box: Anna Scurria and Stephen Thorne in The Ruby Sunrise. *Photo: Harlan Taylor.*

UNION

Simon .... Ryan Barret
Camille .... Kibibi Dillon
Les .... Jesse Hooker
Margaret .... Emily Ruddock
Harry .... Adam Suritz
Jane .... Mary Tuomanen

THE MATING HABITS OF THE SAGE GROUSE

Adrian .... Sasha Andreev
Charley .... Gabel Eiben
Haley .... Marianna Frendo
Doug .... Patrick Hogan
Danielle .... Pirronne Yousefzadeh

WAKE GOD'S MAN

Sarah .... Natalie Arnold
Brian .... Max Ferguson
Ricardo .... Clifford Endo Gulibert
Man .... Tom Kelley
Annie .... Sarah Ann Kinsey
Beth .... Laura Riley

Presented without intermission.

Ten-Minute Plays. April 3–4, 2004. Presented without intermission.

KUWAIT. By Vincent Delaney. Director, Meredith McDonough; scenery, Paul Owen; costumes, Shana Lincoln, Andrea Scott and John P. White; lighting, Paul Werner; sound, Benjamin Marcum; dramaturg, Steve Moulds; stage manager, Debra A. Freeman.

Rachel .... Julie Jesneck
Kelsey .... Asa Somers
Miles .... Stephen Thorne

Time: The present. Place: A hotel room in the Middle East.

THE SPOT. By Steven Dietz. Director, William McNulty; scenery, Paul Owen; costumes, Shana Lincoln, Andrea Scott and John P. White; lighting, Paul Werner; sound, Benjamin Marcum; dramaturg, Steve Moulds; stage manager, Debra A. Freeman.

Chumley .... Mary Tuomanen
Wagner .... Mauro Hantman
Roger .... Fred Sullivan Jr.
Nelson .... Tom Kelley
Gloria .... Jody Christopherson
Betsy .... Emily Ruddock

Time: The present. Place: A soundstage.

A BONE CLOSE TO MY BRAIN. By Dan Dietz. Director, Meredith McDonough; scenery, Paul Owen; costumes, Shana Lincoln, Andrea Scott and John P. White; lighting, Paul Werner; sound, Benjamin Marcum; dramaturg, Steve Moulds; stage manager, Debra A. Freeman.

Man .... Michael A. Newcomer

FOUL TERRITORY. By Craig Wright. Director, Sturgis Warner; scenery, Paul Owen; costumes, Shana Lincoln, Andrea Scott, John P. White; lighting, Paul Werner; sound, Benjamin Marcum; dramaturg, Steve Moulds; stage manager, Debra A. Freeman.

Ruth .... Russell Arden Koplin
Owen .... Jesse Lenat

Time: The present. Place: A row of far-left field seats at Yankee Stadium.

BLUES FOR THE ALABAMA SKY. By Pearl Cleage. April 22, 2004. Director, Timothy Douglas; scenery, Tony Cisek; costumes, Lorraine Venberg; lighting, Tony Penna; sound, Vincent Olivieri; dramaturgs, Adrien-Alice Hansel and Erin Detrick; fight direction, Drew Fracher; production stage manager, Paul Mills Holmes.

Angel Allen .... Rachel Leslie
Guy Jacobs .... Darryl Theirse
Delia Patterson .... Cherise Boothe
Sam Thomas .... David Alan Anderson
Leland Cunningham .... Shane Taylor

Time: Summer 1930. Place: An apartment building in Harlem. Presented in two parts.

MAINE

Portland Stage Company

Anita Stewart artistic director

WOMEN AND THE SEA. By Shelley Berc and Anita Stewart. April 30, 2003 (world premiere). Director, Ms. Stewart; scenery, Michelle Gaston; costumes, Helen Rasmussen; sound, Christopher Fitze; lighting, Bryon Winn; music, George Andoniadis; stage manager, Marjorie Hanneld.

Maggie; Anna .... Nora Daly; Rebecca Stevens
Judith; Shirley; Linda; Gail .... Moira Driscoll
Susan; Jane .... Molly Powell
Marianne; Evelyn; Terri; Lori .... Amy Staats
Connie; Debbie; Carol; Pat .... Nicola Sheara
Mary Jo; Linda; Yuberquis; Norah .... Brigitte Viellieu-Davis

Place: Different locations at the water's edge in Maine. Presented in two parts.

MARYLAND

Center Stage, Baltimore

Irene Lewis artistic director, Michael Ross managing director

A.M. SUNDAY. By Jerome Hairston. November 19, 2003. Director, Marion McClinton; scenery, David Gallo; costumes, David Burdick; lighting, Donald Holder, sound, Shane Rettig; dramaturg, James Magruder; stage manager, Debra Acquavella.

Helen .... Johanna Day
Lorie .... Robyn Simpson
R.P. .... Ray Anthony Thomas
Jay .... JD Williams
Denny .... Massimo Delogu Jr.; Sylk

Time: Sunday morning to Thursday morning in early November. Place: The home of R.P. and Helen; a bus stop; the woods.

THE MISER. By Molière; translated and adapted by James Magruder. January 18, 2004. Director, David Schweizer; scenery, Riccardo Hernández; costumes, David Zinn; lighting, Russell H. Champa; sound and music, Mark Bennett; fight direction, J. Allen Suddeth; dramaturg, Gavin Witt; stage manager, Mike Schleifer.

La Flèche; Commissioner .... Dan Cordle
Mariane .... Christian Corp
Valère .... Trent Dawson
Frosine .... June Gable
Brindavoine .... Ian Gould
Elise .... Kate Guyton
Maître Jacques .... Jonathan Hammond
Harpagon .... Tom Mardirosian
Anselme; Maître Simon; Dame Claude .... John Ramsey
La Merluche .... Jake Riggs
Clèante .... Charles Daniel Sandoval
Violinist .... José Miguel Cueto

Place: Harpagon's house in Paris.

MASSACHUSETTS

American Repertory Theatre, Cambridge

Robert Woodruff artistic director, Robert J. Orchard executive director

LADY WITH A LAPDOG. By Kama Ginkas; adapted from a story by Anton Chekhov; translated by Ryan McKittrick and Julia Smeliansky. September 13, 2003. Director, Mr.

Ginkas; scenery, Sergey Barkhin; costumes, Tatiana Barkhina and Mr. Barkhin; lighting, Michael Chybowski; sound, David Remedios; stage manager, Chris De Camillis.

Dmitry Gurov .... Stephen Pelinski
Anna Sergeyevna .... Elisabeth Waterston
Gentleman Sunbather .... Trey Burvant
Gentleman Sunbather .... Robert Olinger

Time: Late 19th century. Place: By the sea at Yalta and other locations.

SNOW IN JUNE. By Charles L. Mee; adapted by Chen Shi-Zheng; music by Paul Dresher. November 29, 2003 (world premiere). Director, Mr. Chen; scenery, Yi Li Ming; costumes, Anita Yavich; lighting, Rick Fisher; sound, David Remedios; music direction, Evan Harlan; dramaturg, Ryan McKittrick; stage manager, Lisa Iacucci.

Girl .... Qian Yi
Widow; Doctor .... David Patrick Kelly
Old Man; Judge .... Rob Campbell
Boy .... Thomas Derrah

Ensemble: Kaolin Bass, Eliza Bell; Francesca Carlin, Tug Coker, Jodi Dick, Torsten Hillhouse, Patrick McCaffrey, Laura Nordin, William Peebles, Adam Peña, Nicole Shalhoub, Kathryn Weill.

Presented without intermission.

A MIDSUMMER NIGHT'S DREAM. By William Shakespeare. January 10, 2004. Director, Martha Clarke; scenery and costumes, Robert Israel; lighting, James F. Ingalls; sound, David Remedios; music, Richard Peaslee; flying, Flying by Foy; stage manager, Chris De Camillis.

Athens
Theseus .... John Campion
Hippolyta .... Karen MacDonald
Egeus .... Will LeBow
Hermia .... Michi Barall
Lysander .... Tug Coker
Demetrius .... Daniel Talbott
Helena .... Katharine Powell

Mechanicals
Peter Quince .... Will LeBow
Nick Bottom .... Thomas Derrah
Francis Flute .... Remo Airaldi
Tom Snout .... Will Peebles
Snug the Joiner .... Jeremy Geidt
Robin Starveling .... Jonathan Broke

Fairyland
Oberon .... John Campion
Titania .... Karen MacDonald
Puck .... Jesse J. Perez
Fairy .... Erica Berg
Fairy .... Olivia Grant
Fairy .... Lisa Giobbi
Fairy .... Paola Styron
Indian Boy .... Snow Guilfoyle

THE BIRTHDAY PARTY. By Harold Pinter. March 6, 2004. Director, JoAnne Akalaitis; scenery, Paul Steinberg; costumes, Gabriel Berry; lighting, Jennifer Tipton; sound and music, Bruce Odland; stage manager, M. Pat Hodge.

Meg .... Karen MacDonald
Petey .... Terence Rigby
Stanley .... Thomas Derrah
McCann .... Remo Airaldi
Lulu .... Elizabeth Laidlaw
Goldberg .... Will LeBow

OEDIPUS. By Sophocles; translated by Stephen Berg and Diskin Clay; music by Evan Ziporyn. May 15, 2004. Director, Robert Woodruff; scenery, Douglas Stein; costumes, Kasia Walicka Maimone; lighting, Christopher Akerlind; sound, David Remedios; dramaturg, Gideon Lester; stage manager, Chris De Camillis.

Oedipus .... John Campion
Chorus Leader .... Thomas Derrah
Kreon/Messenger .... Michael Potts
Teiresias/Shepherd .... Novella Nelson
Jocasta/Servant .... Stephanie Roth Haberle
Antigone .... Eliza Rose Fichter
Ismene .... Olivia Beckett Wise

Ensemble: Timur Bekbusunov, I Nyoman Catra, Jodi Dick, Suzanne Ehly, Paul Guttry, Anne Harley, Paul Shafer, Kasia Sokalla.

Barrington Stage Company, Sheffield

Julianne Boyd artistic director, Mitch Weiss managing director

EARS ON A BEATLE. By Mark St. Germain. July 6, 2003 (world premiere). Director, Mr. St.Germain; scenery, Eric Renschler; costumes, Melissa Parnzarello; lighting, Jim Milkey; sound, Randy Hansen; production stage manager, Brian Maschka.

Howard Ballantine .... Dan Lauria
Daniel McClure .... Bill Dawes

Voices: Dick Cavett, Geraldine Ferraro, Arlo Guthrie, Fred Savage, Robert Vaughn, Leon Wildes.

THE GAME. Musical with book and lyrics by Amy Powers and David Topchik; music by Megan Cavallari; Based on the novel *Les Liaisons Dangereuses* by Choderlos de Laclos. August 10, 2003 (world premiere). Director, Julianne Boyd; choreography, Jan Leys; scenery, Michael Anania; costumes, Fabio Toblini; lighting, Jeff Croiter; sound, Randy Hansen; music direction, Michael Morris; fight direction, Michael Burnet.

Cecile .... Cristin Boyle
Madame de Volanges .... Griffin Gardner
Marquise de Merteuil .... Sara Ramirez
Viconte de Valmont .... Christopher Innvar
Chevalier Danceny .... Greg Mills
Madame de Tourvel .... Heather Ayers
Madame de Rosemonde .... Joy Franz
Opera Diva .... Kelly Ellen Miller
Opera Tenor .... Jason Watkins
Emilie .... Chrysten Peddie
Azolan .... Lee Rosen
Servant .... Jesse Sullivan

Berkshire Theatre Festival, Stockbridge

Kate Maguire executive director

THE STILLBORN LOVER. By Timothy Findley. July 9, 2003. Director, Martin Rabbett; scenery, Michael Downs; costumes, David Murin; lighting, Fabrice Kebour; sound, Jason Tratta; stage manager, Linda Harris.

Harry Raymond .... Richard Chamberlain
Michael Riordan .... Keir Dullea
Corporal Mahavolitch .... Kaleo Griffith
Supt. Jackman .... Robert Emmet Lunney
Marion Raymond .... Lois Nettleton
Diana Marsden .... Jennifer Van Dyck
Juliet Riordan .... Jessica Walter

Presented in two parts.

Huntington Theatre Company, Boston

Nicholas Martin artistic director, Michael Maso managing director

BUTLEY. By Simon Gray. October 29, 2003. Director, Nicholas Martin; scenery, Alexander Dodge; costumes, Michael Krass; lighting, David Weiner; sound, Kurt Kellenberger; production stage manager; Stephen M. Kaus.

Ben Butley .... Nathan Lane
Joseph Keyston .... Benedick Bates
Miss Heasman .... Marguerite Stimpson
Edna Shaft .... Angela Thornton
Anne Butley .... Pamela J. Gray
Reg Nuttall .... Jake Weber
Mr. Gardner .... Austin Lysy
Students .... Allison Clear, Joe Lanza

Presented in two parts.

North Shore Music Theatre, Beverly

Jon Kimbell artistic director

MEMPHIS. Musical with book by Joe DiPietro; music by David Bryan; lyrics by Messrs. DiPietro and Bryan. September 23, 2003 (world premiere). Director, Gabriel Barre;

choreography, Todd L. Underwood; scenery, Bill Stabile; costumes, Pamela Scofield; lighting, Phil Monat; sound, John A. Stone; music direction, Gabriel Butler, production stage manager, Erik E. Hedblom. Presented in association with TheatreWorks, Palo Alto, California. (See TheatreWorks listing for details.)

Huey Calhoun .... Chad Kimball
Felicia Farrell .... Montego Glover
Delray Jones .... J. Bernard Calloway
Bobby .... Wayne W. Pretlow
Gladys Calhoun .... Susan Mansur
Mr. Simmons .... David Piel
Gator .... Derrick B. Baskin
Honey Malone .... Cynthia Thomas
Gordon Grant .... Neal Mayer
Perry Como .... Stephan Stubbins
Patti Page .... Catherine Carpenter
Roy Rogers .... Kevin Duda
Reverend Fletcher .... Kevin Covert
Florence .... Breanna Bradlee

Ensemble: Randy Aaron, Edward M. Barker, Anika Bobb, Frank Lawson, Jenelle Lynn Randall, Sarah Stiles, Neal Teare.

Presented in two parts.

Shakespeare and Company, Lenox

Tina Packer artistic director

MUCH ADO ABOUT NOTHING. By William Shakespeare. June 7, 2003. Director, Daniela Varon; choreography, Susan Dibble; scenery, Cameron Anderson; costumes, Jacqueline Firkins; lighting, Matthew E. Adelson; sound, Jason Fitzgerald and Daniela Varon; music, Sherrill Reynolds; fight direction, Kevin G. Coleman; production stage manager, Brenda J. Lillie.

Leonato .... Malcolm Ingram
Beatrice .... Paula Langton
Hero .... Stephanie Dodd
Antonio .... Mel Cobb
Ursula .... Lane Whittemore
Margaret .... Elizabeth Aspenlieder
Messenger; Watchman .... Lon Troland Bull
Don Pedro .... Jonathan Croy
Benedick .... Allyn Burrows
Claudio; .... Mark Saturno
Don John; Sexton .... Jason Asprey
Borachio .... Johnny Lee Davenport
Conrade .... Gabriel Vaughan
Balthasar;
Watchman; Friar .... Daniel J. Sherman
Musician;
Watchman .... Nathan Wolfe Coleman
Dogberry .... Jonathan Epstein
Verges .... Charlie Ravioli

Time: 1950s. Place: Sicily. Presented in two parts.

KING LEAR. By William Shakespeare. August 2, 2003. Director, Tina Packer; scenery, Kris Stone; costumes, Arthur Oliver; lighting, Matthew E. Adelson; sound, Jason Fitzgerald; fight direction, Michael F. Toomey; dramaturg, Stanley Richardson.

Kent; Others .... Malcolm Ingram
Gloucester .... Johnny Lee Davenport
Edgar .... Jason Asprey
Regan .... Elizabeth Aspenlieder
Goneril .... Ariel Bock
Cornwall; Others .... Mark Saturno
Albany; Others .... Daniel J. Sherman
Cordelia .... Kristin Wold
Burgundy; Others .... Lon Troland Bull
France; Others .... Michael F. Toomey
Oswald; Others .... Mel Cobb
King Lear .... Jonathan Epstein
Fool .... Kevin G. Coleman
Edmond .... John Douglas Thompson

Time: An ancient era. Place: Britain.

Studio Festival. August 26–31, 2003.

THE ACCIDENTAL ACTIVIST. By Kathryn Blume. Director, Michaela Hall.

AMELIA'S LIFE'S RIVER. By Amelia Broome.

PRESENT TENSE. By Michael Rubenfeld. Director, Allyn Burrows.

INTERPLAY. By Ron Goldman and Marjorie Zohn. Director, Ms. Zohn.

Williamstown Theatre Festival

Michael Ritchie producer, Deborah Fehr general manager, Jenny C. Gersten associate producer

AN ENEMY OF THE PEOPLE. By Henrik Ibsen; adapted by Christopher Hampton. August 20, 2003. Director, Gerald Freedman; scenery, John Ezell; costumes, Willa Kim; lighting, Mary Jo Dondlinger; sound, Otts Munderloh; stage manager, Grayson Meritt.

Doctor Tomas Stockmann ..... Mandy Patinkin
Mrs. Stockman ..... Annalee Jefferies
Petra ..... Dana Powers Acheson
Peter Stockman ..... Larry Pine
Morten Kiil ..... John LaGioia
Hovstad ..... T. Scott Cunningham
Billing ..... Bruce MacVittie
Captain Horster ..... Andrew May
Aslaksen ..... Peter Maloney
Ejlif ..... Henry Fuore
Morten ..... Tyler Stanton
Maid ..... Nancy McNulty

Townspeople: Kelly Brady, Mort Broch, Gus Danowski, Jordan Dean, Frank Faucette, Nancy McNulty, Michael Ouellete, Gary Tharp, Nick Thomas, Ted Wilson Welch, Liz Wisan.

Time: 2003. Place: A technical rehearsal of Henrik Ibsen's *An Enemy of the People*.

BIG BILL. By A.R. Gurney; based on *Big Bill Tilden* by Frank Deford, *Tilden and Tennis in the Twenties* by Arthur Voss and writings by Bill Tilden. July 2, 2003 (world premiere). Director, Mark Lamos; scenery, John Lee Beatty; costumes, Jess Goldstein; lighting, Rui Rita; sound, David Wallingford; stage manager, Fredric H. Orner.

William T. Tilden II ..... John Michael Higgins
Umpire; Judge; Others ..... David Cromwell
Maddox; Herb; Others ..... Stephen Rowe
Mary; Suzanne; Others ..... Margaret Welsh
Young man;
Arthur Anderson; Others ..... Gideon Banner

Ball Boys: Michael Cicetti, Jordan Coughtry, Andrew Fisher, Fisher K. Neal.

Time: Middle of the 20th century.

MOTHER OF INVENTION. By Alexandra Gersten-Vassilaros. July 16, 2003. Director, Nicholas Martin; scenery, Adam Stockhausen; costumes, Michael Krass; lighting, Jeff Croiter; sound, Matthew Burton; music, Loren Toolajian; stage manager, Stephen M. Kaus.

Miriam Buddwing ..... Estelle Parsons
Sannie ..... Diane Davis
Will ..... Matt McGrath
Serita ..... Lisa Benavides
Doug ..... Adam Rothenberg
Mr. Burger ..... Bob Dishy
Mitchell Buddwing ..... Andre Tremblay

Time: Late afternoon; next morning; noon, three days later. Place: Buddwing house in a New York City suburb. Presented in two parts

BERKSHIRE VILLAGE IDIOT. By Michael Isaac Connor. July 30, 2003. Director, Barry Edelstein; scenery, Derek McLane; lighting, Russell H. Champa; sound, John Gromada; stage manager, Megan Smith.

Performed by Mr. Connor.

Fridays @ 3. New Play Readings.

MOTHERHOUSE. By Victor Lodato. June 27, 2003. Director, Mark Brokaw.

MY DEATH. By John Epperson. July 11, 2003. Director, Nick Philippou.

THE WATER'S EDGE. By Theresa Rebeck. July 18, 2003. Director, Will Frears.

SEARCHING FOR CERTAINTY. By Mike O'Malley. July 25, 2003. Director, Peter Askin.

Staged readings of Anton Chekhov's works. August 12–16, 2003.

UNCLE VANYA. Adapted by Nikos Psacharopoulos. August 12, 2003. Director, Olympia Dukakis; scenery, Michael Carnahan; costumes, Jen Caprio; lighting, Ben Stanton; sound, Drew Levy; stage manager, Stephen M. Kaus.

Performed by Kate Burton, Ms. Dukakis, John Forest, Jennifer Harmon, George Morfogen, James Naughton, Austin Pendleton, Maria Tucci, Louis Zorich.

THE THREE SISTERS. Adapted by Nikos Psacharopoulos. August 13, 2003. Director, Austin Pendleton; scenery, Michael Carnahan; costumes, Jen Caprio; lighting, Ben Stanton; sound, Drew Levy; stage manager, Stephen M. Kaus.

Performed by George Bartenieff, Tom Brennan, Kate Burton, Michael Crane, Olympia Dukakis, Jennifer Harmon, Abby Huston, Austin Lysy, James McMenamin, James Naughton, Mr. Pendleton, Reg Rogers, Maria Tucci, Christina Zorich, Louis Zorich.

THE CHERRY ORCHARD. Adapted by Nikos Psacharopoulos. August 14, 2003. Director, Louis Zorich; scenery, Michael Carnahan; costumes, Jen Caprio; lighting, Ben Stanton; sound, Drew Levy; stage manager, Stephen M. Kaus.

Performed by George Bartenieff, Tom Brennan, Kate Burton, Olympia Dukakis, John Forest, Jennifer Harmon, Peter Hunt, Austin Lysy, James McMenamin, George Morfogen, Austin Pendleton, Reg Rogers, Maria Tucci, Christina Zorich, Mr. Zorich.

THE SEAGULL. Adapted by Nikos Psacharopoulos. August 15, 2003. Director, Peter Hunt; scenery, Michael Carnahan; costumes, Jen Caprio; lighting, Ben Stanton; sound, Drew Levy; stage manager, Stephen M. Kaus.

Performed by Tom Brennan, Kate Burton, Michael Crane, Jennifer Harmon, Abby Huston, Austin Lysy, George Morfogen, James Naughton, Reg Rogers, Rachel Siegel, Maria Tucci, Christina Zorich, Louis Zorich.

I TAKE YOUR HAND IN MINE. By Carol Rocamora; adapted from the letters of Anton Chekhov and Olga Knipper. August 16, 2003. Director, Peter Hunt; scenery, Michael Carnahan; costumes, Jen Caprio; lighting, Ben Stanton; sound, Drew Levy; stage manager, Stephen M. Kaus.

Performed by Olympia Dukakis and Louis Zorich.

MINNESOTA

The Guthrie Theater, Minneapolis

Joe Dowling artistic director, Thomas C. Proehl managing director

PRIDE AND PREJUDICE. By Jane Austen; adapted by James Maxwell; revised by Alan Stanford. August 1, 2003. Director, Joe Dowling; scenery, John Lee Beatty; costumes, Mathew J. LeFebvre; lighting, Kenneth Posner, sound, Scott Edwards; music, Tom Linker; dramaturg, Carla Steen.

Mr. Bennet .... Raye Birk
Mrs. Bennet .... Sally Wingert
Jane Bennet .... Cheyenne Casebier
Elizabeth Bennet .... Bianca Amato
Mary Bennet .... Tracey Maloney
Kitty Bennet .... Summer Hagen
Lydia Bennet .... Erin Anderson
Sir Wiliam Lucas .... Julian Bailey
Charlotte Lucas .... Laura Esping
Mr. Collins .... Richard S. Iglewski
Mr. Charles Bingley .... Lee Mark Nelson
Miss Caroline Bingley .... Jennifer Blagen
Mr. Darcy .... Matthew Greer
Colonel Fitzwilliam .... Robert O. Berdahl
Mr. Wickham .... Bard Goodrich
Captain Carter; Denny .... Alex Podulke
Lady Catherine De Bourgh .... Barbara Bryne
Miss Anne De Bourgh .... Virginia S. Burke
Mrs. Jenkinson .... Heather Kendzierski

Time: During the regency. Place: Rural Hertfordshire, the Bennets' home, Kent and Derbyshire, England. Presented in two parts.

NICKEL AND DIMED. By Joan Holden; based on the book *Nickel and Dimed: On (Not) Getting by in America* by Barbara Ehrenreich. August 13, 2003. Director, Bill Rauch; scenery, Christopher Acebo; costumes, Lynn Jeffries; lighting, Marcus Dilliard; sound, C. Andrew Mayer; dramaturg, Michael Bigelow Dixon.

Joan; Others .... Sarah Agnew
Hector; Others .... Natasha Arroyo
George; Others .... Christopher Liam Moore
Gail; Others .... Peggy O'Connell
Carlie; Others .... Isabell Monk O'Connor
Barbara .... Robynn Rodriguez
Musician .... Amy Van Patten

Time: 1998; 2000; 2003. Place: Florida; Maine; Minnesota. Presented in two parts.

CROWNS. By Regina Taylor. January 10, 2004. Director, Timothy Bond; choreography, Patdro Harris; scenery, Christine Jones; costumes, Reggie Ray; lighting, Allen Lee Hughes; sound, Scott Edwards; music direction, Sanford Moore; dramaturg, Faye M. Price.

Yolanda .... chandra thomas
Mother Shaw .... Greta Oglesby
Velma .... Jevetta Steele
Deaconess Mabel .... Barbara D. Mills
Jeanette .... Austene Van Williams-Clark
Wanda .... Regina Marie Williams
Preacher; Others .... T. Mychael Rambo

BOSTON MARRIAGE. By David Mamet. February 4, 2004. Director, Douglas Mercer; scenery, James Noone; costumes, Valerie Marcus Ramshur; lighting, Matthew Reinert; sound, Reid Rejsa; dramaturg, Jo Holcomb.

Claire .... Nadia Bower
Anna .... Sally Wingert
Catherine .... Summer Hagen

Time: End of 19th century. Place: Drawing room in Boston.

MISSOURI

Missouri Repertory Theatre, Kansas City

Peter Altman producing artistic director, William Prenevost managing director

METAMORPHOSES. By Mary Zimmerman; based on the work of Ovid. January 28, 2004. Director, Ms. Zimmerman; scenery, Daniel Ostling; costumes, Mara Blumenfeld; lighting, T.J. Gerckens; sound, Andre Pluess and Ben Sussman; music, Willy Schwarz; production stage manager, Chad Zodrow. Presented in association with Hartford Stage, Connecticut. (See Hartford Stage listing for details.)

Aphrodite; Others .... Antoinette Broderick
Myrrha; Others .... Sun Mee Chomet
Eurydice; Others .... Anne Fogarty
Midas; Others .... Raymond Fox
Orpheus; Others .... Kyle Hall
Erysichthon; Others .... Chris Kipiniak
Alcyone; Others .... Erika LaVonn
Phaeton; Others .... James McKay
Hermes; Others .... Paul Oakley Stovall
Therapist; Others .... Gabra Zackman

The Repertory Theatre of St. Louis

Steven Woolf artistic director, Mark D. Bernstein, managing director

METAMORPHOSES. By Mary Zimmerman; based on the work of Ovid. September 12, 2003. Director, Ms. Zimmerman; scenery, Daniel Ostling; costumes, Mara Blumenfeld; lighting, T.J. Gerckens; sound, Andre Pluess and Ben Sussman; music, Willy Schwarz; production stage manager, Glenn Dunn. Presented in association with Cincinnati Playhouse in the Park. (See the Cincinnati Playhouse in the Park listing for details.)

Alcyone; Others .... Cherise Boothe
Myrrha; Others .... Sun Mee Chomet
Erysichthon; Others ....Joe Dempsey
Eurydice; Others .... Anne Fogarty
Hermes; Others ....Antony Hagopian
Midas; Others ....Anthony Long
Phaeton; Others ....James McKay
Orpheus; Others .... Manu Narayan
Therapist; Others .... Lisa Tejero
Aphrodite; Others ....Tamilla Woodard

THE GOAT, OR WHO IS SYLVIA? By Edward Albee. October 24, 2003. Director, Steven Woolf; scenery, John Ezell; costumes, Garth Dunbar; lighting, Peter Sargent; stage manager, Champe Leary.

Martin ....Anderson Matthews
Stevie .... Carolyn Swift
Ross .... Bruce Longworth
Billy .... Clint Zugel

BLUE/ORANGE. By Joe Penhall. February 13, 2004. Director, Steven Woolf; costumes, Marie Anne Chiment; lighting, Mary Jo Dondlinger; stage manager, Glenn Dunn.

Christopher ....Rashaad Ernesto Green
Bruce ....Jeremy Webb
Roberts ....Anderson Matthews

Time: More than 24 hours. Place: National Health Service (NHS) psychiatric hospital, UK.

LIFE (X) 3. By Yasmina Reza. Translated by Christopher Hampton. January 23, 2004. Director, Thom Sesma; scenery, John Roslevich Jr.; costumes, Elizabeth Eisloeffel; lighting, Glenn Dunn; fight direction, Kim Bozark; stage manager, Champe Leary.

Henry ....Mark Jacoby
Sonia .... Bridget Ann White
Inez .... Mary Gordon Murray
Hubert .... Michael Rupert

Time: Evening. Place: A living room.

THE LAST 5 YEARS. Song cycle by Jason Robert Brown. March 26, 2004. Director, John Ruocco; scenery, Narelle Sissons; costumes, Curtis Hay; lighting, Mary Jo Dondlinger; music direction, David Geist; stage manager, Champe Leary.

Kathy .... Kate Baldwin
Jamie .... Anthony Holds

Musical numbers included: "Still Hurting," "Shiksa Goddess," "See I'm Smiling," "Moving Too Fast," "A Part of That," "The Schmuel Song," "A Summer in Ohio," "The Next Ten Minutes," A Miracle Would Happen/When You Come Home to Me," "Climbing Uphill," "If I Didn't Believe in You," "I Can Do Better Than That," "Nobody Needs to Know," "Goodbye Until Tomorrow/I Could Never Rescue You."

NEW JERSEY

Centenary Stage Company, Hackettstown

Carl Wallnau producing director, Catherine Rust associate producer

THE STRANGE MISADVENTURES OF PATTY, PATTY'S DAD, PATTY'S FRIEND JEN AND A BUNCH OF OTHER PEOPLE. By Allison Moore. February 27, 2004 (world premiere). Director, Margo Whitcomb; choreography, Carolyn Coulson-Grisby; scenery, Will Rothfuss; costumes, Julia Sharp; lighting, Jeffrey E. Salzberg; sound, Alden Fulcomer; stage manager, David A. Vandervliet.

Patty .... Clare O'Sheeran
Patty's Dad .... Michael Schelle
Jen ....Dana Halsted
Jack; Ashby .... Steven L. Barron
Mrs. Downs; Kate ....Jennifer Huntington
Rhonda; Vanessa .... Laura Quackenbush
Jim; Clark; Cassidy .... Chris Barber
Sue .... Desiree Fitzgerald
Clerk .... Greg Selm-Orr

Women Playwrights Series: Workshop Presentation. April 14, 2004

THE SIX THAT FELL. By Laura Henry. April 14, 2004. Director, Bobbie Besiack.

Jane .... Anne Connolly
Ermine .... Mari Green
Susan .... Merry LaRue
Jobeth .... Maria Brodeur
Constance .... Lea Antoline
Mitzi .... Kristin Hammond
Narrator .... Desiree Fitzgerald

Time: The present. Place: Jane's Living Room.

THE DEW POINT. By Neena Beber. April 21, 2004. Director, Kate Lyn Reiter.

Mimi .... Helen Coxe
Kai .... Jim Ireland
Jack .... Steven L. Barron
Phyllis .... Clare O'Sheeran
Greta .... Dawn Swearingen
Narrator .... Laura Quackenbush

Time: The present. Place: Mimi and Kai's apartment

REMEMBER ME. By Ruth Kirschner. April 28, 2004. Director, Margo Whitcomb.

Max .... J.C. Hoyt
Gray Kirby .... Wendy Scharfman
Violet .... Colleen Smith Wallnau
Elizabeth; Zeiring .... Catherine Rust
Bobby .... Galway McCullough
Narrator .... April Dunlop

Time: Christmas, 1998. Place: A residential brain injury rehabilitation clinic in the high desert.

George Street Playhouse, New Jersey

David Saint artistic director, Mitchell Krieger managing director

ATTACKS ON THE HEART. By Arthur Laurents. October 17, 2003 (world premiere). Director, David Saint; scenery, James Youmans; costumes, Theoni V. Aldredge; lighting, Joe Saint; sound, Christopher J. Bailey; stage manager, Thomas Clewell.

Leyla .... Cigdem Onat
Beecher .... Alan Rachins

Presented without intermission.

Luna Stage, Montclair

Jane Mandel artistic director

DRAGONS. Musical with book, music and lyrics by Sheldon Harnick; based on a Russian play by Yevgeny Schwarz. November 13, 2003 (world premiere). Director, James Glossman; choreography, Susan Ancheta; scenery, Fred Kinney; costumes, Bettina Bierly; lighting, Richard Curie; sound, Vin Scelsa; music direction, Stephen Randoy; stage manager, Barbara T. Dente.

The Cat .... Susan Ancheta
Miller .... Michael Aquino
Mrs. Weber .... Nellie Beavers
Charlemagne .... Kenneth Boys
Elsa .... Cecily Ellis
Mrs. Engel .... Seleena Harkness
Henry .... Garth Kravits
Lancelot .... Kirk Mouser
The Dragon .... Paul Murphy
Donkey .... Catherine Rogers
Weaver; Notary .... Anita Rundles
Blacksmith; Peddler; Notary .... Jake Speck
The Mayor .... Paul Whelihan

Musical numbers included: "A Mighty Race," "It Isn't Fair," "I Can't Stand Dragons," "What a Pretty Girl," "We're a Family," "War's Child," "If I Die Young," "No Profit in That," "No Profit in That," "Suddenly," "Set Us Free," "The Battle," "Passacaglia for Three," "Severed Heads,' "Remember Me," "Glory to the Dragon Slayer," "You Could Say That I Miss Him," "I Love Power," "The Wedding," "Take Care of One Another."

Presented in two parts.

McCarter Theatre Center, Princeton

Emily Mann artistic director, Jeffrey Woodward managing director

ANNA IN THE TROPICS. By Nilo Cruz. September 17, 2003. Director, Emily Mann; scenery, Robert Brill; costumes, Anita Yavich; lighting, Peter Kaczorowski; sound, Dan Moses Schreier; dramaturg, Janice Paran.

Eliades	John Ortiz	Conchita	Daphne Rubin-Vega
Santiago	Victor Argo	Ofelia	Priscilla Lopez
Cheché	David Zayas	Juan Julian	Jimmy Smits
Marela	Vanessa Aspillaga	Palomo	John Ortiz

Time: 1929. Place: Tampa, Florida. A place called Ybor City. Presented in two parts.

WINTERTIME. By Charles L. Mee. October 17, 2003. Director, David Schweizer; choreography, Sean Curran; scenery, Andrew Lieberman; costumes, David Zinn; lighting, Kevin Adams. Presented in association with Second Stage Theatre, New York. (See listing in Plays Produced Off Broadway section of this volume.)

Jonathan	McCaleb Burnett	Edmund	T. Scott Cunningham
Ariel	Brienin Bryant	Bertha	Carmen de Lavallade
Maria	Marsha Mason	Hilda	Lola Pashalinski
Francois	Michael Cerveris	Bob	Danny Mastrogiorgio
Frank	Nicholas Hormann	Jacqueline	Tina Benko

Time: Winter. Place: A summer house. Presented in two parts.

FRÄULEIN ELSE. By Francesca Faridany; adapted from the novella by Arthur Schnitzler. January 15, 2004. Director, Stephen Wadsworth; scenery, Thomas Lynch; costumes, Anna Oliver; lighting, Joan Arhelger; sound, Bill Williams; production stage manager, Alison Cote. Presented in association with Long Wharf Theatre, New Haven, Connecticut.

Else	Francesca Faridany	Mother	Mary Baird
Paul	Michael Tisdale	Herr van Dorsday	Julian López-Morillas
Cissy	Lauren Lovett	Porter	Omid Abtahi

Time: 1912. Place: A luxurious spa hotel, northern Italy.

Readings. September 29–March 15, 2004.

A FIRST CLASS MAN. By David Freeman. September 29, 2003.

Performed by Yolande Bavan, Robin Chadwick, Jonathan Fried, Edward A. Hajj, Chris Kipiniak, Miriam Laube, Graeme Malcolm, Amir Arison, David Sajadi, Samantha Soule.

THE SAME SEA. By Paul Binnerts; adapted from the novel by Amos Oz. November 24, 2003. Director, Mr. Binnerts.

Performed by Franca Barchiesi, Jeff Biehl, Jon DeVries, Shawn Fagan, Juliana Francis, Nancy Gabor, Teri Lamm, Erica Nagel, Daniel Oreskes, Peter Ratray.

RIDICULOUS FRAUD. By Beth Henley. December 8, 2003.

Performed by Leo Burmester, Cameron Folmar, Mary Catherine Garrison, Mark Linn-Baker, Laila Robins, Reg Rogers, Maria Thayer, Christopher Evan Welch.

THE BELLS. By Theresa Rebeck. December 15, 2003.

Performed by Fiona Gallagher, Peter Gerety, Marin Ireland, Craig Mathers, Mandy Patinkin, Thom Sesma, Isiah Whitlock Jr.

THE TRICKY PART. By Martin Moran. February 17, 2004. Director, Seth Barrish.

Performed by Mr. Moran.

LAST OF THE BOYS. By Steven Boyer. March 15, 2004. Director, Mr. Boyer.

Performed by Mr. Boyer, Kemati Porter, Lee Sellars, Joseph Siravo, Phyllis Somerville, Laurie Williams.

Paper Mill Playhouse, Millburn

Michael Gennaro president, Roy Miller associate producer, Mark S. Hoebee associate director

THE CHOSEN. By Aaron Posner and Chaim Potok; adapted from the novel by Mr. Potok. February 22, 2004. Director, David Ellenstein; scenery, Michael Anania; costumes, Ellis Tillman; lighting, Michael J. Eddy; sound, David R. Paterson and Steve Shapiro; production stage manager, Gail P. Luna.

Reb Saunders .... Theodore Bikel
David Malter .... Mitchell Greenberg
Young Reuven Malter .... Paul Kropfl
Reuven Malter .... Richard Topol
Danny Saunders .... John Lloyd Young

Time: 1944–48. Place: Various locations in Williamsburg, Brooklyn.

BABY. Musical with book by Sybille Pearson; music by David Shire; lyrics by Richard Maltby Jr. March 31, 2004. Director and choreographer, Mark S. Hoebee; scenery, Michael Anania, costumes, Thom Heyer; lighting, F. Mitchell Dana; sound, Duncan Robert Edwards; orchestrations, Jonathan Tunick; music direction, Eugene Gwozdz; production stage manager, Gail P. Luna.

Opening narration .... Allison Briner
Danny Hooper .... Chad Kimball
Lizzie Fields .... Moeisha McGill
Alan McNally .... Michael Rupert
Arlene McNally .... Carolee Carmello
Pam Sakarian .... LaChanze
Nick Sakarian .... Norm Lewis
Nurse; Voice of Mrs. Fields ...... Rosena M. Hill
Doctor .... Lenny Wolpe
Professor Weiss;
Bus Announcer .... Bill E. Dietrich
Dean Webber;
Exercise Instructor .... Erick Pinnick
Mrs. Hart .... Lois Sonnier Hart
Voice of operator .... Kelly Ellenwood

Ensemble: Allison Briner, Bill E. Dietrich, Kelly Ellenwood, Lois Sonnier Hart, Rosena M. Hill, Erick Pinnick, Brynn O'Malley, Julian Reyes.

Musical numbers included: "We Start Today," "What Could Be Better?," "The Plaza," "Baby, Baby, Baby," "I Want It All," "At Night She Comes Home to Me," "Fatherhood Blues," "Romance I," "I Chose Right," "The Story Goes On," "The Ladies Singing Their Song," "Patterns," "Romance II & III," "Easier to Love," "End of Summer," "Two People in Love," "And What If We Loved Like That," "With You."

Presented in two parts.

NEW YORK

Arena Players Repertory Company, East Farmingdale

Frederic DeFeis producer

COWBIRDS. By D.T. Arcieri. January 30, 2004 (world premiere). Director, Frederic DeFeis; scenery, Fred Sprauer; costumes, Lois Lockwood; lighting, Al Davis; stage manager, Evan Donnellan.

Tommy .... Jon French
Mother .... Annette Triquere
Candy .... Sarah Moore
Dad .... Rob Rosin

Time: Now. Place: Tommy's home; Candy's apartment and other locations.

PLACE SETTING. By Jack Canfora. February 5, 2004 (world premiere). Director, Frederic DeFeis; scenery, Fred Sprauer; costumes, Lois Lockwood; lighting, Al Davis; stage manager, Steve Grivas.

Andrea .... Christine Sullivan
Greg .... Skeeter Boxberger
Laura .... Adrianna Gitelle
Richard .... Eric Clavell
Lenny .... Spence Cohen
Charlotte .... Allyson Mantello

Time: New Year's Eve, 1999; New Year's Day, 2000. Place: The dining room of Greg and Andrea's suburban home. Presented in two parts.

Studio Arena Theatre, Buffalo

Gavin Cameron-Webb artistic director

WHILE WE WERE BOWLING. By Carter W. Lewis. March 26, 2004 (world premiere). Director, Gavin Cameron-Webb; scenery, Russell Metheny; costumes, Deborah L. Shippee; lighting, Phil Monat; sound, Ray Nardelli; production stage manager; Jessica Berlin.

Melvin; John .... Robert Rutland
Lydia McGlauphlin .... Lauren Bone
Frances McGlauphlin .... Carolyn Swift
Brent McGlauphlin .... James Nardella
Jeremy Reed .... James Miles
Stickpin Padowski .... Lucas Papaelias

Time: 1957–58. Place: The McGlauphlin home; Voelker's Bowling Alley, Buffalo. Presented in two parts.

Syracuse Stage

Robert Moss artistic director, Jim Clark producing director

NOBODY DON'T LIKE YOGI. By Thomas Lysaght. August 20, 2003 (world premiere). Director, Paul Linke; scenery and costumes, Tony Walton; lighting, Ken Billington; sound, Tony Melfa; stage manager, John Handy.

Performed by Ben Gazzara.

CONSTANT STAR. By Tazewell Thompson. October 24, 2003. Director, Mr. Thompson; scenery, Donald Eastman; costumes, Merrily Murray-Walsh; lighting, Robert Wierzel; sound, Fabian Obispo; vocal arrangement and music direction, Dianne Adams McDowell; stage manager, Katie Ahern.

Ida #1 .... Nadiyah S. Dorsey
Ida #4 .... Quanda Johnson
Ida #3 .... Tracey Conyer Lee
Ida #2 .... Laiona Michelle
Ida #5 .... Gayle Turner

HEDWIG AND THE ANGRY INCH. Musical with book by John Cameron Mitchell; music and lyrics by Stephen Trask. January 23, 2004. Director, Michael Donald Edwards; scenery, David Lawrence Meyer; costumes, Jacqueline Corcoran; lighting, R. Allen Babcock; sound, Jonathan Herter; music direction, S.J. Pickett; stage manager, Katie Ahern.

Hedwig .... Aaron Berk
Yitzhak .... S.J. Pickett

OHIO

Cincinnati Playhouse in the Park

Edward Stern producing artistic director, Buzz Ward executive director

ONE. By Joseph McDonough. October 2, 2003 (world premiere). Director, Edward Stern; scenery, Joseph P. Tilford; costumes, Elizabeth Covey; lighting, Thomas C. Hase; music, Douglas Lowry; stage manager, Andrea L. Shell.

Emily .... Anney Giobbe
Kyle .... Tim Altmeyer
Jill .... Henry Russell

METAMORPHOSES. By Mary Zimmerman; based on the work of Ovid. October 23, 2003. Presented in association with the Repertory Theatre of St. Louis. (See the Repertory Theatre of St. Louis listing for details.)

GOING GONE. By Karen Hartman. January 15, 2004 (world premiere). Director, Michael Bloom; scenery, Klara Zieglerova; costumes, Susan E. Mickey; lighting, Nancy Schertler; sound, Geoff Zink; stage manager, Jenifer Morrow.

Harry Hartman .... Tony Hoty
Mama .... Maureen Silliman
Maidle .... Laura Heisler
Hank the Hero; Voiceover .... Todd Gearhart
Hanky .... Jared Gertner

Attendants: David Ian Dahlman, Jeff DeMaria, Jeffrey Groh, Michael Joseph Thomas Ward.

Time: 1928–40; 1941. Place: A family's apartment in Cincinnati. Presented in two parts.

BLUE. By Charles Randolph-Wright. March 4, 2004. Director, Kenny Leon; scenery, Marjorie Bradley Kellogg; costumes, Susan E. Mickey; lighting, Tom Sturge; sound, Marc Gwinn; music by Nona Hendryx; lyrics, Ms. Hendryx and Mr. Randolph-Wright; music direction, Dwight Andrews; production stage manager, Bruce E. Coyle.

Reuben Clark .... Yusef Miller
Peggy Clark .... Denise Burse
Young Reuben;
Baby Blue .... Darnell Smith Jr.
Blue Williams .... Kevyn Morrow
Samuel Clark III .... Rashad J. Anthony
LaTonya Dinkins .... Tinashe Kajese
Samuel Clark,Jr. .... Peter Jay Fernandez
Tillie Clark .... Brenda Thomas

Time: 1978; 1993; 1996; 1999. Place: Kent, South Carolina. Presented in two parts.

HIDING BEHIND COMETS. By Brian Dykstra. March 25, 2004 (world premiere). Director, Michael Evan Haney; scenery, Kevin Rigdon; costumes, Gordon DeVinney; lighting, David Lander; sound, Chuck Hatcher; fight direction, Drew Fracher; production stage manager, Suann Pollock.

Troy .... Christine Conn
Honey .... Jacqueline van Biene
Erin .... Erica Schroeder
Cole .... Dan Moran

Time: Late summer. Place: A bar in a small northern California town.

OREGON

Oregon Shakespeare Festival, Ashland

Libby Appel artistic director, Paul Nicholson executive director

LORCA IN A GREEN DRESS. By Nilo Cruz. July 8, 2003 (world premiere). Director, Penny Metropulos; choreography, La Conja; scenery, William Bloodgood; costumes; Deborah M. Dryden; lighting, Michael Chybowski; sound, Jeremy J. Lee; music direction, La Conja; fight direction, John Sipes; dramaturg, Douglas Langworthy.

Lorca with Blood .... Armando Durán
Lorca as a Woman .... Heather Robison
Lorca in a White Suit .... Jonathan Haugen
Lorca in a Green Dress .... Cristofer Jean
Lorca in Bicycle Pants .... Juan Rivera LeBron
Guard .... Terri McMahon
General .... Ray Porter
Dancer .... La Conja
Guitarist .... Grant Ruiz

Place: The Lorca room. Presented in two parts.

THE VISIT. By Friedrich Dürrenmatt; adapted by Kenneth Albers; translated by Douglas Langworthy. February 21, 2004 (world premiere). Director, Mr. Albers, scenery, Michael Ganio; costumes, Susan E. Mickey; lighting, Robert Jared; sound and music, John Tanner; fight direction, John Sipes; dramaturg, Douglas Langworthy; stage manager, Gwen Turos.

The People of Güllen
Josef Schell .... Richard Elmore
Mayor .... John Pribyl
Teacher .... Linda Alper
Pastor .... Barry Kraft
Doctor .... Sandy McCallum
Painter .... Juan Rivera LeBron
Stationmaster;
Director; Bank President .... Tyrone Wilson
Rose Schell .... Catherine E. Coulson
Helmut Schell .... Matthew Brown
Liesl Schell .... Nell Geisslinger
Hofbauer .... U. Jonathan Toppo
Engel .... Brad Whitmore
Gertrude "Trude" Schmidt .... Suzanne Irving
Helga Müller .... Terri McMahon
Gymnast .... Dane Bowman
Policeman .... Shad Willingham

The Visitors
Claire Zachanassian .... Demetra Pittman
Bobby .... Clive Rosengren
Kobby .... Matt McTighe
Lobby .... Benjamin Reigel
Husbands; Anchorman .... Dane Bowman
Conductor; First Gangster .... James J. Peck
Second gangster .... Kyle Haden

Reporters: Dane Bowman, Matthew Brown, Kyle Haden, Juan Rivera LeBron; Brad Whitmore; Tyrone Wilson.

Place: In and around the city of Güllen. Presented in three parts.

HENRY VI. PART ONE: TALBOT AND JOAN. By William Shakespeare; adapted by Scott Kaiser. April 3, 2004 (world premiere). Directors, Libby Appel and Mr. Kaiser; scenery, William Bloodgood; costumes, Deborah M. Dryden; lighting, Robert Peterson; music, Todd Barton; fight direction, John Sipes; dramaturg, Lue Morgan Douthit.

The English
King Henry VI;
Duke of Bedford .... Cristofer Jean
Duke of Gloucester .... Mark Murphey
Duke of Exeter .... Robert Sicular
Bishop of Winchester .... Richard Farrell
Duke of Somerset .... Christopher DuVal
Earl of Suffolk .... Jeff Cummings
Richard Plantagenet .... William Langan
Earl of Warwick .... Armando Durán
Edmund Mortimer .... Richard Farrell
Sir John Talbot .... Jonathan Haugen
Young John Talbot;
Basset .... Laura Morache
Sir William Lucy;
Vernon .... Robin Goodrin Nordli

The French
Charles .... Christopher DuVal
Bastard of Orleans .... Jeff Cummings
Reignier .... Robert Sicular
Joan La Pucelle .... Tyler Layton
Duke of Burgundy .... Mark Murphey
Vision .... Laura Morache
Margaret .... Robin Goodrin Nordli
Shepherd .... Richard Farrell

Ensemble: Jeff Cummings, Armando Durán, Christopher DuVal, Richard Farrell, Jonathan Haugen, Cristofer Jean, William Langan, Tyler Layton, Laura Morache, Mark Murphey, Robin Goodrin Nordli, Robert Sicular.

Place: England and France. Presented in two parts.

PENNSYLVANIA

Arden Theatre Company, Philadelphia

Terrence J. Nolen producing artistic director, Amy L. Murphy managing director

CAFE PUTTANESCA. Musical with book by Michael Ogborn and Terrence J. Nolen; music and lyrics by Mr. Ogborn. September 13, 2003. Director, Mr. Nolen; scenery, Bob

Phillips; costumes, K.J. Gilmer; lighting, James Leitner; sound, Nick Rye; music direction, Vince DiMura; stage manager, Rachel R. Bush.

The Owner .... Tony Braithwaite
The Duchess .... Tracie Higgins
The Marquesa .... Jilline Ringle
The Baroness .... Mary Martello
The Piano Player .... Vince DiMura
The Cook .... Elisa Matthews

TOOTH AND CLAW. By Michael Hollinger. March 16, 2004 (world premiere). Director, Terrence J. Nolen; scenery, James Kronzer; costumes, Anne Kennedy; lighting, Michael Philippi; sound, Jorge Cousineau; music, John Stovicek; stage manager, Patricia G. Sabato.

Carlos .... David Grillo
Malcolm .... Donald Grody
Schuyler Baines .... Susan McKey
Ana .... Shirley Roeca

Ensemble: Alvaro Mendoza, Marcos Muiz, Elvis O. Nolasco, Tlaloc Anthony Rivas, Al D. Rodriguez, Paco Tolson.

City Theatre Company, Pittsburgh

Tracy Brigden artistic director, David Jobin managing director

GOMPERS. By Adam Rapp. May 12, 2004 (world premiere). Director, Tracy Brigden; scenery, David Korins; costumes, Angela M. Vesco; lighting, Jeff Croiter; production stage manager, Patti Kelly.

Performed by Jeffrey Carpenter, Garbie Dukes, John Magaro, Danny Mastrogiorgio, Bingo O'Malley, Anthony Rapp, Demond Robertson, Molly Simpson, Kiff vanden Heuvel, Robin Walsh.

InterAct Theatre, Philadelphia

Seth Rozin producing artistic director, Melissa Amster general manager

PERMANENT COLLECTION. By Thomas Gibbons. October 29, 2003 (world premiere). Director, Seth Rozin; scenery, Nick Embree; costumes, Andre Harrington; lighting, Peter Whinnery; sound, Kevin Francis; dramaturg, Larry Loebell.

Sterling North .... Frank X
Ella Franklin .... Sheila Stewart
Paul Barrow .... Tim Moyer
Kanika Weaver .... Ayoka Dorsey
Gillian Crane .... Maureen Torsney-Weir
Dr. Alfred Morris .... Tom McCarthy

Time: Present. Place: An art foundation in a suburb of a Northeastern city.

IN THE HEART OF AMERICA. By Naomi Wallace. February 18, 2004. Director, Seth Rozin; scenery, Dirk Durossette; costumes, Karen Ann Ledger, lighting, Peter Jakubowski; sound, Kevin Francis; dramaturg, Larry Loebell.

Craver Perry .... Davey White
Fairouz Saboura .... Soraya Broukhim
Lue Ming .... Jennifer Kato
Remzi Saboura .... Kevin Prowse
Boxler .... Buck Schirner

Time: Present and past. Place: The Saudi Desert and various locations in the US.

GOD OF DESIRE. By Dick Goldberg. May 12, 2004 (world premiere). Director, Seth Rozin; scenery, Tim Dugan; costumes, Karen Ann Ledger; lighting, Peter Whinnery; stage manager, Scott P. McNulty.

Edward Levitsky .... Jason Liebman
Mira Levitsky .... Susan Moses
Ben .... Michael Nathanson
Zayde .... Harry Philibosian
Rosenberg .... Seth Reichgott

The People's Light and Theatre Company, Malvern

Abigail Adams artistic director, Grace Grillet managing director

MIDONS, OR THE OBJECT OF DESIRE. By Lillian Groag. September 21, 2003. Director, Ms. Groag; scenery, John Conklin; costumes, Tracy Dorman; lighting, Russell H. Champa; sound, Charles T. Brastow.

The Lady; Moon; Falcon .... Susan McKey
The Knight; Falconer .... David Ingram
The Lord; Archbishop; Others .... Tom Teti
Troubadour; Others .... Kevin Bergen
The Countess; Pigboy .... Marcia Saunders
Duchess; Fanette .... Kathryn Petersen
Abbott; Others .... Stephen Novelli
Visored Knight; Others .... Scott Boulware

Presented in two parts.

Philadelphia Theatre Company, Philadelphia

Sara Garonzik producing artistic director, Ada G. Coppock general manager

TOPDOG/UNDERDOG. By Suzan-Lori Parks. October 15, 2003. Director, Leah C. Gardiner, scenery, Louisa Thompson; costumes, Andre Harrington; lighting, Traci Klainer; sound, Matthew Callahan; music, Darrin M. Rose; dramaturg, Michele Volansky.

Booth .... Billöah Greene
Lincoln .... Seth Gilliam

Time: The present. Place: A seedily furnished room.

NICKEL AND DIMED. By Joan Holden; based on the book *Nickel and Dimed: On (Not) Getting by in America* by Barbara Ehrenreich. January 28, 2004. Director, Maria Mileaf; scenery, Neil Patel; costumes, Janus Stefanowicz; lighting, David Lander; sound, Eileen Tague; music, Robert Maggio; dramaturg, Michele Volansky. Presented in association with Delaware Theatre Company, Wilmington.

Gail; Marge, Others .... Janis Dardaris
Barbara .... Elizabeth Norment
Nita; Philip, Others .... Karen Vicks
George; Editor, Others .... Paul Meshejian
Hector; Maddy, Others .... Michele Vazquez
Joan; Holly, Others .... Mollie Hall

Time: 1998–2000; 2004. Place: Florida; Maine; Minnesota. Presented in two parts.

ACCORDING TO GOLDMAN. By Bruce Graham. March 27, 2004 (world premiere). Director, Pamela Berlin; choreography, Liz Curtis; scenery, Michael Schweikardt; costumes, Amela Baksic, lighting, Ann G. Wrightson; sound, Nick Rye; dramaturg, Michele Volansky.

Gavin Miller .... Bruce McCarty
Melanie Miller .... Carmen Roman
Jeremiah Collins ....Tobias Segal

Time: The present. Place: The Miller home, a university classroom and various other suggested areas. Presented in two parts.

THE GOAT, OR WHO IS SYLVIA? By Edward Albee. May 26, 2004. Director, Tim Vasen; scenery, Todd Rosenthal; costumes, Murell Horton; lighting, Ann G. Wrightson; dramaturg, Michele Volansky.

Stevie Gray .... Elizabeth Norment
Martin Gray .... John Glover
Ross Tuttle .... Tom Teti
Billy Gray .... Bradford William Anderson

Spring Stages Festival of New Plays and Playwrights.

WOMEN AND NOOSE. By Bruce Walsh. May 3, 2004. Director, Daniel Kutner.

AT RISK. By Mary L. Hagy. May 4, 2004. Director, Jan Silverman.

GIRL SCIENCE. By Larry Loebell. May 6, 2004. Director, Nancy Kiracofe.

APPOINTMENT WITH A HIGH WIRE LADY. By Russell Davis. May 7, 2004. Director, Paul Meshejian.

Prince Music Theater, Philadelphia

Marjorie Samoff producing artistic director

THE GREAT OSTROVSKY. Musical with book by Avery Corman; music by Cy Coleman; lyrics by Messrs. Corman and Coleman. March 24, 2004. Director, Douglas C. Wager; choreography, Patricia Birch; scenery, Zach Brown; costumes, Miguel Angel Huidor; lighting, Troy A. Martin-O'Shia; sound, Matthew Callahan; music direction, Steven Gross; production stage manager, Lloyd Davis Jr.

David Ostrovsky .... Bob Gunton
Rose .... Louise Pitre
Jenny .... Rachel Ulanet
B.D. Kotlow .... Jeff Edgerton

Ensemble: Nick Corley, Jeffry Denman, Deanna L. Dys, Jonathan Hadary, Paul Kandel, Logan Lipton, Daniel Marcus, Edward Staudenmayer, Kirsten Wyatt.

Walnut Street Theatre, Philadelphia

Bernard Havard producing artistic director, Mark D. Sylvester managing director

LA VIE EN BLEU. Musical with book and lyrics by Jean-Michel Beriat and Raymond Jeannot; music by Pascal Stive; adapted by Bruce Lumpkin, Bill Van Horn and Elaine Rowan; translated by C.H. Popesco. September 10, 2003. Director, Mr. Lumpkin; choreography, Richard Stafford; scenery, John Farrell; costumes, Colleen McMillan; lighting, Jack Jacobs; sound, Matthew Callahan; production stage manager, Frank Anzalone.

Eva Humbert .... Jessica Boevers
Picasso .... Jeffrey Coon
Pablito .... David Corenswet
Marta O'Dette-Bregmer .... Natalie Cortez
Azul .... Gregory Daniels
Andre Breton .... Christopher DeAngelis
Marie-Therese Walter .... Christina DeCicco
Casegamus .... Ben Dibble
Georges Braque;
Jean Cocteau .... Michael Brian Dunn
Rosa .... Michelle Gaudette
Ambrose Vollard .... Laurent Giroux
Mother Picasso .... Mollie Hall
Fernande Olivier .... Joan Hess
Pablito .... Mark Indelicato
Frede .... David Jackson
Alice Derain .... Katie O'Shaughnessey
Olga Koklova .... Rebecca Robbins
Guillame Apollinaire .... Jonathan Stahl
Old Man .... Bill Van Horn
Germaine Pichot;
Gertrude Stein .... Denise Whelan
Daniel Khanveiller; Erik Satie .. Bruce Winant

Musical numbers included: "Le Commencement," "Studio," "Dear Minister," "Someone For Me," "Can-Can," "Come With Me," "Suicide," "Life in Blue," "Storm," "Fernande's Confession," "Meeting Pablo Picasso," "Compassion," "Trip to Spain," "Twilight," "Le Cirque Rose" "Eva, Ma Jolie," "L'Opera Des Cubes," "Failure," "Dark Times," "Up In Arms, " "Believe Succeed," "A Friendship Lost," "Separated Lovers," "The Message of Persuasion," "Roaring Twenties," "Super Reality," "Is It Right or Wrong?," "The Confrontation," "Loving You Both," "I Stand Alone," "Guernica."

Time: 1880–1943. Place: Europe. Presented in two parts.

HERE ON THE FLIGHT PATH. By Norm Foster. February 12, 2004. Director, Marcia Tratt; scenery, Glen Sears; costumes, K.J. Gilmer; lighting, Shelley Hicklin; sound, John Mock; production stage manager, Frank Anzalone.

John .... Russ Widdall
Faye; Angel; Gwen .... Therese Walden

Time: The present. Presented in two parts.

MOLL. By John B. Keane. April 22, 2004. Director, Donald Ewer; scenery, Robert Kramer; costumes, Melissa Black; lighting, Shelley Hicklin; sound, Matthew Callahan; production stage manager, Frank Anzalone.

Father Brest .... Benjamin Lloyd
Bridgie Andover .... Moira Rankin
Cannon Pratt .... Tom McCarthy
Father Loran .... David Volin
Moll Kettle .... Drucie McDaniel
Ulick .... George Spelvin
The Bishop .... Donald Ewer

Time: 1971. Place: Ballast, a village in western Ireland. Presented in two parts.

Wilma Theater, Philadelphia

Blanka Zizka and Jiri Zizka artistic directors, Lynn Landis managing director

RESURRECTION BLUES. By Arthur Miller. September 24, 2003. Director, Jiri Zizka; scenery, David P. Gordon; costumes, Janus Stefanowicz; lighting, Jerold R. Forsyth; sound, Bill Moriarty; dramaturg, Nakissa Etemad; stage manager, Patreshettarlini Adams.

General Felix Barriaux .... Munson Hicks
Henry Schultz .... Patrick Husted
Police Captain .... Lindsay Smiling
Emily Shapiro .... Gretchen Egolf
Skip L. Cheesboro .... Doug Wert
Phil .... William Zielinski
Sarah .... Miriam Ameena Hyman
Jeanine .... Patricia Ageheim
Stanley .... Douglas Rees

Ensemble: Jennifer Ann Brown, David Dallas, Patrick Doran, Ralph Edmonds, Karen MacArthur, Lindsay Smiling, William Zielinski.

Time: Present. Place: South American country. Presented in two parts.

EMBARRASSMENTS. Musical with book, music and lyrics by Laurence Klavan and Polly Pen; additional text by Ms. Pen. December 3, 2003 (world premiere). Director, Blanka Zizka; choreography, Andrew Simonet; scenery, Christine Jones; costumes, Janus Stefanowicz; lighting, Russell H. Champa; sound, Bill Moriarty; music direction, Mary Mitchell Campbell; dramaturg, Nakissa Etemad; stage manager, Patreshettarlini Adams.

Henry James .... Henry Stram
Alan Wayworth .... James Sugg
Violet Grey .... Jennifer Lyon
Mrs. Alsager .... Ann Morrison

Ensemble: Michael X. Martin, Jennie Eisenhower, Jesse Tyler Ferguson, Mary Martello.

WINTERTIME. By Charles L. Mee. March 17, 2004. Director, Jiri Zizka; scenery, Jerry Rojo; costumes, Janus Stefanowicz; lighting, Jerold R. Forsyth; sound, Bill Moriarty; dramaturg, Nakissa Etemad.

Jonathan .... Michael J. Ewing
Maria .... Elizabeth Hess
Bertha .... Prudence Wright Holmes
Bob .... Michael Laurence
Edmund .... Seth Reichgott
Hilda .... Dale Soules
Jacqueline .... Danielle Skraastad
Francois .... John Wojda
Frank .... Greg Wood
Ariel .... Julianna Zinkel

JESUS HOPPED THE "A" TRAIN. By Stephen Adly Guirgis. May 26, 2004. Director, Blanka Zizka; scenery, Anne Paterson; costumes, Janus Stefanowicz; lighting, Russell H. Champa; sound, Bill Moriarty; dramaturg, Nakissa Etemad.

Angel .... Vaneik Echeverria
Mary Jane .... Danielle Skraastad
D'Amico .... Salvatore Inzerillo
Lucius Jenkins .... John Douglas Thompson
Valdez .... Lindsay Smiling

Pittsburgh Public Theater

Ted Pappas artistic and executive director

THE CHIEF. By Rob Zellers and Gene Collier. November 6, 2003 (world premiere). Director, Ted Pappas; scenery and costumes, Anne Mundell; lighting, Phil Monat; sound, Zach Moore; production stage manager, Fred Noel.

Art Rooney .... Tom Atkins

ACCIDENTAL DEATH OF AN ANARCHIST. By Dario Fo; translated by Ron Jenkins. March 12, 2004. Presented in association with Dallas Theater Center. (See Dallas Theater Center listing for details.)

THINGS OF DRY HOURS. By Naomi Wallace. April 23, 2004 (world premiere). Director, Israel Hicks; scenery, James Noone; costumes, Gabriel Berry; lighting, Phil Monat; sound and music, Fitz Patton; dramaturg, Kyle Brenton; production stage manager, Nevin Hedley.

Cali Hogan .... Rosalyn Coleman
Tice Hogan .... Roger Robinson
Corbin Teel .... Robert Sedgwick

RHODE ISLAND

Trinity Repertory Company, Providence

Oskar Eustis artistic director, Edgar Dobie managing director

SONGS OF INNOCENCE, SONGS OF EXPERIENCE. Musical revue by Rachael Warren and Amanda Dehnert. December 12, 2003. Director, Ms. Dehnert; scenery, David Jenkins; costumes, William Lane; lighting, John Ambrosone; sound, Peter Sasha Hurowitz.

Singer .... Rachael Warren
Singer; Bass .... Drew Battles
Singer; Guitar .... Justin Blanchard
Singer .... Miriam Silverman
Guitar; Fiddle;
Banjo; Lap Steel .... Kevin Fallon
Drums; percussion .... Mike Sartini
Piano .... Amanda Dehnert

Presented in two parts.

THE RUBY SUNRISE. By Rinne Groff. May 19, 2004. Presented in association with Actors Theatre of Louisville. (See Actors Theatre of Louisville listing for details.)

TEXAS

Alley Theatre, Houston

Gregory Boyd artistic director, Paul R. Tetreault managing director

¡CANTINFLAS! By Herbert Sigüenza. September 24, 2003 (world premiere). Director, Max Ferrá; scenery and lighting, Alexander V. Nichols; stage manager, Lori Lundquist.

Cantinflas .... Herbert Sigüenza
Ana Williams .... Ann Candler Harlan
Ramon; Others .... Ezequiel Guerra Jr.
Maid; Others .... Vivis
Carpa Owner; Others .... Pablo Bracho

TOPDOG/UNDERDOG. By Suzan-Lori Parks. February 25, 2004. Presented in association with Steppenwolf Theatre Company, Chicago, and Dallas Theater Center. (See Steppenwolf Theatre Company and Dallas Theater Center listings for details.)

OUR LADY OF 121ST STREET. March 24, 2004. By Stephen Adly Guirgis. Director, James Black; scenery, Todd Rosenthal; costumes, Mara Blumenfeld; lighting, Michael Lincoln; dramaturg, Amy Steele.

Victor	James Belcher	Inez	Alice Gatling
Balthazar	Pablo Bracho	Norca	Patricia Duran
Rooftop	Alex Morris	Edwin	Luis Galindo
Father Lux	Charles Krohn	Pinky	Ezequiel Guerra Jr.
Flip	Adrian Porter	Marcia	Shelley Calene-Black
Gail	Philip Lehl	Sonia	Michelle Edwards

Place: In and around the Ortiz Funeral Home, Harlem. Presented in two parts.

LIFE (X) 3. By Yasmina Reza; translated by Christopher Hampton. March 31, 2004. Director, Pam MacKinnon; scenery, Kevin Rigdon; costumes, Linda Ross; lighting, John Ambrosone, sound, Joe Pino; stage manager, Elizabeth M. Berther.

Henry	Jeffrey Bean	Inez	Kimberly King
Sonia	Elizabeth Heflin	Hubert	Todd Waite
Child	Loren Thornton		

Dallas Theater Center

Richard Hamburger artistic director, Mark Hadley managing director

ACCIDENTAL DEATH OF AN ANARCHIST. By Dario Fo, translated by Ron Jenkins, revisions by Gloria Pastorino. January 20, 2004. Director, Richard Hamburger; scenery, Leiko Fuseya; costumes, Linda Cho; lighting, Stephen Strawbridge; sound, David Budries; fight direction, Bill Lengfelder; music direction, Terry Dobson; dramaturg, Kyle Brenton. Presented in association with Pittsburgh Public Theater. (See Pittsburgh Public Theater listing for details.)

The Maniac	Robert Dorfman	Deputy Police Chief	Craig Bockhorn
Inspector Bertozzo	Sean Runnette	Commissioner	Jerry Russell
Police Officer	Marcus Neely	Journalist	Mary Bacon
Police Officer	Doug Jackson		

Time: 1970. Place: Milan, a police station. Presented in two parts.

TOPDOG/UNDERDOG. By Suzan-Lori Parks. March 2, 2004. Presented in association with Steppenwolf Theatre Company, Chicago, and Alley Theatre, Houston. (See Steppenwolf Theatre Company and Alley Theatre listings for details.)

Kitchen Dog Theater, Dallas

Dan Day artistic director

HEDWIG AND THE ANGRY INCH. Musical with book by John Cameron Mitchell; music and lyrics by Stephen Trask. September 6, 2003. Director, Tina Parker, scenery, Suzanne Lavender and Ms. Parker; costumes, Patrick Johnson; lighting, Ms. Lavender; sound, Mark Griffin; music direction, Stephen Shelton Kirkham.

Hedwig; Tommy Gnosis	Joe Steakley	Lead Guitar	Keenan Wayne Nichols
Yitzhak	Laurie McNair	Drums	Clint Phillips
Keyboard; Guitar	Stephen Shelton Kirkham	Bass Guitar	Jacob Weber

THE DANUBE. By Maria Irene Fornes. November 8, 2003. Director, Dan Day; scenery and costumes, Marketa Fantova; lighting, J. Morgan Rowe-Morris; sound; Mark Griffin.

Paul Green .... Ian Leson
Mr. Sandor .... Joss Levine
Eve Sandor .... Kelly Abbott
Mr. Kovacs; Others .... Christopher Carlos

THE MERCY SEAT. By Neil LaBute. April 17, 2004. Director, Cecil O'Neal; scenery and costumes, Rhonda R. Gorman, lighting, Russell K. Dyer; sound, T.A. Dodson.

Ben Harcourt .... Max Hartman
Abby Prescott .... Michelle Michael

PERMANENT COLLECTION. By Thomas Gibbons. May 29, 2004 (world premiere). Director, Dan Day; costumes, Tina Parker; lighting, Russell K. Dyer; sound, Stephen Shelton Kirkham, dramaturg, Mallory E. Harwod.

Sterling North .... Clarence Gilyard
Ella Franklin .... Tippi Hunter
Paul Barrow .... Christopher Carlos
Alfred Morris .... Barry Nash
Kanika Weaver .... Jaquai Wade
Gillian Crane .... Leah Spillman

Rude Mechanicals, Austin

Madge Darlington, Lana Lesley, Kirk Lynn, Sarah Richardson, Shawn Sides
producing artistic directors

HOW LATE IT WAS, HOW LATE. By Kirk Lynn; adapted from the book by James Kelman. (September 5, 2003). Director, Sarah Richardson; production design, Brian H. Scott; scenery, Madge Darlington; costumes, Holly Francis; sound, Robert S. Fisher; video, Colin Lowry; production stage manager, José Angel Hernandez.

Sammy .... Dikran Utidjian
Woman .... Lana Lesley
Boy .... Ben Grimes
Man .... Robert Newell

STADIUM DEVILDARE. By Ruth Margraff. April 23, 2004 (world premiere). Director, Shawn Sides; scenery, Stephen Pruitt; costumes, Leslie Bonnell; lighting, Brian H. Scott; sound, Robert S. Fisher; music, Graham Reynolds, production stage manager, José Angel Hernandez.

Performed by Lana Lesley, Joey Hood, Jason Liebrecht, Robert S. Fisher.

Stage West, Fort Worth

Jerry Russell general manager, Jim Covault associate director

THE SHAPE OF THINGS. By Neil LaBute. February 12, 2004. Director, Jim Covault; scenery, Nelson Robinson; costumes, Mr. Covault and Peggy Kruger-O'Brien; lighting, Michael O'Brien.

Evelyn .... Dana Schultes
Phillip .... Cody Perret
Adam .... Lee Trull
Jenny .... Lynn Blackburn

Theatre Three, Dallas

Jac Alder executive producer and director

THE WILD PARTY. Musical with book by Michael John LaChiusa and George C. Wolfe; music and lyrics by Mr. LaChiusa; based on the poem by Joseph Moncure March. January 26, 2004. Director, Jac Alder; choreography, Jack Degelia; scenery, Harland Wright and Juan DiNero; costumes, Patty Korbelic Williams; lighting, Carl Munoz; production stage manager, Mr. Degelia.

Queenie .... Stephanie Riggs
Burrs .... Sonny Franks
Jackie .... Ric Leal
Madelaine True .... Melissa Renuka Kamath
Sally .... Kylah Magee
Eddie Mackrel .... Marcus M. Mauldin
Mae .... Reneé Smith
Nadine .... Carrie Slaughter
Phil D'Armano .... John Garcia
Oscar D'Armano .... Sergio Antonio Garcia
Dolores Montoya .... Janis Roeton
Gold .... Charles Ryan Roach
Goldberg .... Ricky Pope
Black .... Skie Ocasio
Kate .... Lisa-Gabrielle Green

Musical numbers included: "Queenie Wazza Blonde," "Marie is Tricky," "The Wild Party," "Dry," "My Beautiful Blonde," "Welcome to My Party," "Like Sally," "Breezin' Through Another Day," "Uptown," "Eddie and Mae," "Gold and Goldberg," "Moving Uptown," "Black Bottom," "Best Friend," "A Little M-m-m," "The Lights of Broadway," "Tabu," "Takin' Care of the Ladies," "Tabu Dance," "Wouldn't It Be Nice?," "Lowdown-Down," "Gin," "Wild, "Need," "Black is a Moocher," "People Like Us," "After Midnight Dies," "Golden Boy," "The Movin' Uptown Blues," "More, "Love Ain't Nothin'," "Welcome to Her Party," "What I Need," "How Many Women in the World?," "When It Ends," "This Is What It Is," "Finale."

Time: The 1920s. Place: Queenie and Burrs' apartment.

FIRST LADY SUITE. By Michael John LaChiusa. February 9, 2004. Director, Terry Dobson; scenery, Harland Wright; costumes, Patty Korbelic Williams; lighting, Jonas Houston; music direction, Mr. Dobson; production stage manager, Jac Alder.

Mary Gallagher;
Amelia Earhart .... Amy Mills
Evelyn Lincoln;
Lorena Hickok .... Sally Soldo
Jackie Kennedy;
Eleanor Roosevelt .... Lisa J. Miller
Lady Bird Johnson;
Margaret Truman .... Laura Yancey
Presidential Aide;
Ike Eisenhower .... Jeffrey Kinman
Mamie Eisenhower;
Bess Truman .... Connie Coit
Marian Anderson .... Jamelia Davis

Theatre Under the Stars, Houston

Frank M. Young president, John C. Breckenridge producer

BRIGADOON. Musical with book and lyrics by Alan Jay Lerner; music by Frederick Loewe. March 11, 2004. Director, Roy Hamlin; choreography, Susan McCarter Olson; scenery and costumes, Desmond Heeley; lighting, David Neville; sound, Christopher K. Bond; music direction, Steven Smith; production stage manager, Roger Allan Raby.

Tommy .... George Dvorsky
Jeff Douglas .... Mark Zimmerman
Piper Sloan .... Lars Sloan
Fiddler Jess .... Jessica Wright
Angus MacGuffie .... Kit Fordyce
Meg Brockie .... Ruth Gottschall
Sandy Dean .... Robert Leeds
Archie Beaton .... Rutherford Cravens
Harry Beaton .... Angelo Fraboni
Andrew MacLaren .... William Hardy
Fiona MacLaren .... Rachel deBenedet
Jean MacLaren .... Laura Scott
Maggie Anderson .... Ilene Bergelson
Charlie Dalyrymple .... Adam Lambert
Lundie .... Bettye Fitzpatrick
Reverend Forsythe .... Jim Shaffer
Stuart Dalyrmple .... Tye Blue
MacGregor .... Greg Dulcie
MacGavin .... Solomon
Frank .... Kit Fordyce
Jane Ashton .... Jessica Wright

Musical numbers included: "Down on MacConnachy Square," "Waitin' For My Dearie," "I'll Go Home with Bonnie Jean," "The Heather on the Hill," "The Love of My Life," "Jeannie's Packin' Up," "Come to Me, Bend to Me," "Almost Like Being in Love," "The Chase," "There But for You Go I." "My Mother's Wedding Day," "From This Day On."

UTAH

Utah Shakespeare Festival, Cedar City

Fred C. Adams executive director, Cameron Harvey producing artistic director

THE SERVANT OF TWO MASTERS. By Carlo Goldoni; adapted by Fred C. Adams. June 28, 2003. Director, Russell Treyz; scenery, R. Eric Stone; costumes, Alex Jaeger; lighting, Lonnie Alcaraz; sound, Lindsay Jones; music direction, Darryl W. Archibald; fight direction, Robin McFarquhar; dramaturg, Michael Flachmann.

Clarice .... Melinda Pfundstein
Florindo .... Chris Hatch
Dr. Lombardi .... Richard Kinter
Pantalone .... A. Bryan Humphrey
Smerldina .... Molly Rhode
Beatrice .... Sara Kathryn Bakker
Brighella .... John-Patrick Driscoll
Silvio .... Scott Haden
Truffaldino .... David Ivers
Guisseppe .... Mick Hilgers
Giacomo .... Martin Swoverland
Pinocchio .... R. Brian Normoyle

Place: Pantalone's house in Venice; Brighella's inn and the street outside. Presented in two parts.

Plays-in-Progress. July 21–August 29, 2003.

THE QUEEN'S TWO BODIES. By Jeanne Murray Walker. July 31, 2003. Director, J.R. Sullivan.

INDEPENDENCY. By Mark Steven Jensen. August 7, 2003. Director, George Judy.

DIGGING IN THE MARGINS. By Mark Rigney. August 14, 2003. Director, Bruce K. Sevy.

SUMMER EVER. By Riley Steiner. August 21, 2003. Director, Davey Marlin-Jones.

VIRGINIA

Signature Theatre, Arlington

Eric Schaeffer artistic director, Sam Sweet managing director

ALLEGRO. Musical with book and lyrics by Oscar Hammerstein II; music by Richard Rodgers; adapted by Joe DiPietro. January 11, 2004. Director, Eric Schaeffer; scenery, Eric Grims; costumes, Gregg Barnes; lighting, Ken Billington; orchestrations, Jonathan Tunick. Presented in association with James Hammerstein Productions.

Muriel Taylor .... Dana Krueger
Joseph Taylor Sr. .... Harry A. Winter
Marjorie Taylor .... April Harr Blandin
Jenny Brinker .... Laurie Saylor
Joseph Taylor Jr. .... Will Gartshore
Ned Brinker .... Dan Manning
Mitzi .... Lauren Williams
Charlie .... Stephen Gregory Smith
Hazel .... Jenna Sokolowski
Sally .... Tracey Lynn Olivera
Jacques .... Evan Casey
Ethel Brinker .... Donna Migliaccio
Dr. Lansdale .... Carl Randolph
Ethan .... Eric Thompson

TWENTIETH CENTURY. By Ben Hecht and Charles MacArthur; adapted by Ken Ludwig. August 24, 2003. Director, Eric Schaeffer; scenery, James Kronzer; costumes, Anne Kennedy; lighting, Jonathan Blandin.

Oscar Jaffe .... James Barbour
Lily Garland .... Holly Twyford
Max Jacobs .... Rick Hammerly
Dr. Lockwood .... Thomas Adrian Simpson
Anita Highland .... Rachel Gardner
Oliver Webb .... Harry A. Winter

Myrtle Clark .... Donna Migliaccio
Conductor .... Frederick Strother
Owen O'Malley .... Christopher Bloch
George Smith .... Will Gartshore

WASHINGTON

ACT Theatre, Seattle

Kurt Beattie artistic director, Susan Trapnell managing director

THE GOAT, OR WHO IS SYLVIA? By Edward Albee. July 31, 2003. Director, Warner Shook; scenery, Michael Olich; costumes, Frances Kenny; lighting, Mary Louise Geiger; sound, Eric Chappelle; dramaturg, Tom Bryant.

Stevie .... Cynthia Mace
Martin .... Brian Kerwin
Ross .... Frank Corrado
Billy .... Ian Fraser

Time: Midafternoon; a day or two later. Place: Martin and Stevie's living room.

OMNIUM GATHERUM. By Theresa Rebeck and Alexandra Gersten-Vassilaros. October 16, 2003. Director, Jon Jory; scenery, Robert Dahlstrom; costumes, Marcia Dixcy Jory; lighting, Greg Sullivan; sound, Eric Chappelle; stage manager, Anne Kearson.

Terence .... Kent Broadhurst
Jeff .... David Drummond
Server .... Timothy Evans
Julia .... Cynthia Jones
Khalid .... Joseph Kamal
Roger .... Eddie Levi Lee
Server .... Jane May
Mohammed .... Dennis Mosley
Lydia .... Mari Nelson
Suzie .... Marianne Owen

Empty Space Theatre, Seattle

Allison Narver artistic director

MING THE RUDE. Musical with book and lyrics by John Engerman, Rex McDowell, Phil Shallat, Bob Wright; music by Mr. Engerman. October 3, 2003 (world premiere). Director, Lori Larsen; choreography, Jayne Muirhead; scenery, Jenny Anderson; costumes, Melanie Burgess; lighting, Jeff Robbins; sound, Nathan Anderson; music direction, Rob Jones; stage manager, Katherine Coffman.

Eddie; Merle .... Bob Borwick
Queen Bess .... Sarah Rudinoff
Sir Pendulous Dewlaps .... Kevin C. Loomis
Vern; Popo .... Mike Meyer
Larry .... Troy Fischnaller
Betty; Sky Diver .... Nicole Boote
Sid Pensicola; Minion .... Jon Martin
John Monsignor Jr.;
Conrad; Minion .... Shawn Law
Parsec Princess;
Waiter; Minion .... Margot Bordelon
Drums .... Dan Tierney
Keyboards; Charm Glo .... Rob Jones

TWISTED OLIVIA. Solo performance piece by Everett Quinton. December 3, 2003. Director, Eureka; scenery, Heyd Fontenot; costumes, Brian C. Hemesath; lighting, Brian H. Scott; sound, Nathan Anderson; stage manager, Susan Lynn Rubin.

Performed by Mr. Quinton.

1984. By Wayne Rawley; adapted from a concept by Allison Narver. January 28, 2004 (world premiere). Director, Ms. Narver; scenery, Jay McAleer; costumes, Heather Shannon Moore; lighting, Connie Yun; sound and music, Nathan Anderson; stage manager, Suzie Haufle.

Julia .... Tessa Auberjonois
Winston Smith .... Adrian LaTourelle
O'Brien .... David Pichette

Ensemble: Marty Dinn, Troy Fischnaller, Phil Giesey, Sarah Harlett, Anna Henare, Christina Martin, Stacey Plum, Sarah Rudinoff, Erin Stewart, Dusty Warren, Jake Garrison, Grace Garrison, Joy Brooke Fairfield, Mallery MacKay-Brook.

(L)IMITATIONS OF LIFE. By Marcus Gardley; adapted from Fannie Hurst's 1933 novel and the 1959 film *Imitation of Life*; based on a concept by Susan Finque. March 17, 2004. Directors, Mr. Gardley and Ms. Finque; scenery, Karen Gjelsteen; costumes, Ron Erickson; lighting, Jon Harmon; sound, Nathan Anderson; music, Richard Gray; stage manager, Alison Perris.

Steve .... Nick Garrison
Lora .... Gretchen Lee Krich
Annie .... Tawnya Pettiford-Wates
Susie .... Bhama Roget
Stage Manager .... Sarah Rudinoff
Edwards .... Lathrop Walker
Sarah Jane .... Amber Wolfe

UBU. By Ki Gottberg; adapted from the works of Alfred Jarry. May 5, 2004. Director, Ms. Gottberg; scenery, Carol Clay; costumes, Melanie Burgess; lighting, Chris Reay; sound, Nathan Anderson; music, David Russell; stage manager, Sarah Mixon.

Ubu .... Sarah Rudinoff
Ma 2 .... Elizabeth Kenny
Ma 1 .... Sarah Harlett
Ma 3 .... Keiko Ichinose
Captain B; Ensemble .... Tim Hyland
Kingpin; Ensemble .... Erik Maahs
Boogerslaw; Ensemble .... Jon Martin
Ensemble .... Victoria Dicce, Erin Stewart, David Perez

Intiman Theatre Company, Seattle

Bartlett Sher artistic director, Laura Penn managing director

THE LIGHT IN THE PIAZZA. Musical with book by Craig Lucas; music and lyrics by Adam Guettel; based on the novella by Elizabeth Spencer. June 11, 2003 (world premiere). Director, Mr. Lucas; choreography, Pat Graney; scenery, Loy Arcenas; costumes, Catherine Zuber; lighting, Christopher Akerlind; sound, Acme Sound Partners; music direction, Ted Sperling. Presented in association with the Goodman Theatre, Chicago. (See the Goodman Theatre listing for details.)

Margaret Johnson .... Victoria Clark
Clara Johnson .... Celia Keenan-Bolger
Fabrizio Naccarelli .... Steven Pasquale
Signor Naccarelli .... Mark Harelik
Signora Naccarelli .... Patti Cohenour
Giuseppe Naccarelli .... Glenn Seven Allen
Franca .... Kelli O'Hara
Roy Johnson .... Robert Shampain
Shadow Couple ... Jeffrey Froome, Fae Phalen

Musical numbers included: "Statues and Stories," "The Beauty Is," "Passeggiata, "The Joy You Feel," "Dividing Day," "Hysteria," "Margaret," "Say It Somehow," "Aiutami," "The Light in the Piazza," "Octet," "Clara's Trade," "Love To Me," "Fable."

Time: Summer 1953. Place: Florence; occasional side trips to America. Presented in two parts.

Seattle Repertory Theatre

Sharon Ott artistic director, Benjamin Moore managing director

TOPDOG/UNDERDOG. By Suzan-Lori Parks. September 8, 2003. Director, George C. Wolfe; scenery, Riccardo Hernández; costumes, Emilio Sosa; lighting, Scott Zielinski; sound, Dan Moses Schreier; stage manager, Bret Torbeck.

Booth .... Larry Gilliard Jr.
Lincoln .... Harold Perrineau

OVER THE MOON. By Steven Dietz; adapted from *The Small Bachelor* by P.G. Wodehouse. November 17, 2003. Presented in association with Arizona Theatre Company. (See Arizona Theatre Company listing for details.)

LIVING OUT. By Lisa Loomer. January 12, 2004. Director, Sharon Ott; scenery, Matthew Smucker; costumes, Frances Kenny; lighting, Rick Paulsen; sound, Steve LeGrand; stage manager, JR Welden. Presented in association with Missouri Repertory Theatre, Kansas City.

Ana Hernandez .... Stephanie Diaz
Wallace Breyer .... Liz McCarthy
Linda Billings Farzam .... Leslie Law
Nancy Robin .... Julie Briskman
Richard Robin .... Paul Morgan Stetler
Bobby Hernandez ... Ricardo Antonio Chavira
Sandra Zavala .... Minerva Garcia
Zoila Tezo .... Maria Elena Ramirez

Time: The present. Place: Los Angeles.

THE O'CONNER GIRLS. By Katie Forgette. March 17, 2004 (world premiere). Director, Christine Sumption; scenery, Scott Weldin; costumes, Tesse Crocker; lighting, Peter Maradudin; sound, Eric Chappelle; stage manager, Stephanie Toste.

Sarah O'Conner .... Zoaunne LeRoy
Liz O'Conner .... Cynthia Lauren Tewes
Martha O'Conner .... Kate Purwin
Aunt Margie .... Laura Kenny
Dr. David Stevens .... Hans Altwies

Time: 1997. Place: Somewhere in Minnesota. Presented in two parts.

BEAUTY OF THE FATHER. By Nilo Cruz. April 28, 2004. Director, Sharon Ott; scenery, Etta Lilienthal; costumes, Deborah Trout; lighting, Peter Maradudin; sound, Steve LeGrand; dramaturg, Mame Hunt; stage manager, JR Welden. Presented in association with New Theatre, Coral Gables, Florida. (See New Theatre listing for details.)

Federico García Lorca .... Jonathan Nichols
Emiliano .... Tom Ramirez
Marina .... Onahoua Rodriguez
Paquita .... Karmin Murcelo
Karim .... Paul Nicholas

Time: Summer of 1999. Place: A small town called Salobreña near Granada, Spain. Presented in two parts.

New Play Workshop.

THE GOOD BODY. Solo performance piece by Eve Ensler. April 15, 2004. Director, Peter Askin; lighting, L.B. Morse, stage manager, Arabella Powell.

Performed by Ms. Ensler.

Women Playwrights Festival.

BFE (BUM FUCK EGYPT). By Julia Cho. June 4, 2003. Director, Sharon Ott.

THE CLEAN HOUSE. By Sarah Ruhl. June 5, 2003. Director, Kristin Newbom.

MARIELA IN THE DESERT. By Karen Zacarías. June 6, 2003. Director, Leslie Swackhamer.

DREAM OF HOME. By Kathleen Tolan. June 7, 2003. Director, Kurt Beattie.

AUTODELETE://BEGINNING DUMP OF PHYSICAL MEMORY//. By Honour Kane. May 5, 2004. Director, Jerry Manning.

SIX MINUTES. By Eisa Davis. May 6, 2004. Director, Kathleen Collins.

121° WEST. By Tanya Barfield. May 7, 2004. Director, Valerie Curtis-Newton.

ADA. By Rosanna Staffa. May 8, 2004. Director, Richard E.T. White.

WISCONSIN

Milwaukee Repertory Theater

Joseph Henreddy artistic director, Timothy J. Shields, managing director

NAPOLI MILIONARIA. By Eduardo De Filippo; translated by Maria Tucci. January 14, 2004. Director, Lillian Groag; scenery, Michael Ganio; costumes, Martha Hally; lighting, Robert Wierzel; sound, Michael Keck; stage manager, Mark Sahba.

Peppe the Jack .... Mark Corkins
Riccardo .... Jonathan Gillard Daly
Adelaide .... Laura Gordon
Ciappa .... Jim Pickering
Donna Peppeneia .... Rose Pickering
Gennaro .... Peter Silbert
Doctor .... Richard Halverson
Federico .... Michael Herold
Amalia .... Angela Iannone
Maria .... Colleen Madden
Enrico .... John Preston
Amadeo .... Triney Sandoval

THE CRIPPLE OF INISHMAAN. By Martin McDonagh. April 9, 2004. Director, Marshall W. Mason; scenery, David Potts; costumes, Jennifer von Mayrhauser; lighting, Phil Monat; sound, Lindsay Jones; music, Peter Kater; fight direction, Lee E. Ernst; stage manager, Judy Berdan.

Johnnypateenmike .... Jim Baker
Eileen .... Laurie Birmingham
Doctor McSharry .... Jonathan Gillard Daly
Kate .... Laura Gordon
Mammy .... Rose Pickering
Helen .... Elizabeth Ledo
Babbybobby .... Reese Madigan
Cripple Billy .... Sean Meehan
Bartley .... Bobby Steggert

FACTS AND FIGURES

LONG RUNS ON BROADWAY

○○○○○

THE FOLLOWING SHOWS have run 500 or more continuous performances in a single production, usually the first, not including previews or extra non-profit performances, allowing for vacation layoffs and special one-booking engagements, but not including return engagements after a show has gone on tour. In all cases, the numbers were obtained directly from the show's production offices. Where there are title similarities, the production is identified as follows: (p) straight play version, (m) musical version, (r) revival, (tr) transfer.

THROUGH MAY 31, 2004

PLAYS MARKED WITH ASTERISK WERE STILL PLAYING JUNE 1, 2004

Plays	*Performances*
Cats	7,485
*The Phantom of the Opera	6,814
Les Misérables	6,680
A Chorus Line	6,137
Oh! Calcutta! (r)	5,959
*Beauty and the Beast	4,143
Miss Saigon	4,097
42nd Street	3,486
Grease	3,388
*Rent	3,370
Fiddler on the Roof	3,242
Life With Father	3,224
Tobacco Road	3,182
*Chicago (m)(r)	3,138
Hello, Dolly!	2,844
*The Lion King	2,768
My Fair Lady	2,717
Annie	2,377
Cabaret (r)	2,377
Man of La Mancha	2,328
Abie's Irish Rose	2,327
Oklahoma!	2,212
Smokey Joe's Cafe	2,036
Pippin	1,944
South Pacific	1,925
The Magic Show	1,920
Deathtrap	1,793
Gemini	1,788
Harvey	1,775
Dancin'	1,774
La Cage aux Folles	1,761
Hair	1,750
*Aida	1,740

Plays	*Performances*
The Wiz	1,672
Born Yesterday	1,642
The Best Little Whorehouse in Texas	1,639
Crazy for You	1,622
Ain't Misbehavin'	1,604
Mary, Mary	1,572
Evita	1,567
The Voice of the Turtle	1,557
Jekyll & Hyde	1,543
Barefoot in the Park	1,530
Brighton Beach Memoirs	1,530
Dreamgirls	1,522
Mame (m)	1,508
Grease (r)	1,503
Same Time, Next Year	1,453
Arsenic and Old Lace	1,444
The Sound of Music	1,443
Me and My Girl	1,420
How to Succeed in Business Without Really Trying	1,417
Hellzapoppin'	1,404
The Music Man	1,375
Funny Girl	1,348
Mummenschanz	1,326
Angel Street	1,295
*The Producers	1,294
Lightnin'	1,291
Promises, Promises	1,281
*42nd Street (r)	1,268
The King and I	1,246
Cactus Flower	1,234
Sleuth	1,222
Torch Song Trilogy	1,222

Plays	*Performances*
1776	1,217
Equus	1,209
Sugar Babies	1,208
Guys and Dolls	1,200
Amadeus	1,181
Cabaret	1,165
Mister Roberts	1,157
Annie Get Your Gun	1,147
Guys and Dolls (r)	1,144
The Seven Year Itch	1,141
Bring in 'da Noise, Bring in 'da Funk	1,130
Butterflies Are Free	1,128
Pins and Needles	1,108
Mamma Mia!	1,102
Plaza Suite	1,097
Fosse	1,092
They're Playing Our Song	1,082
Grand Hotel (m)	1,077
Kiss Me, Kate	1,070
Don't Bother Me, I Can't Cope	1,065
The Pajama Game	1,063
Shenandoah	1,050
Annie Get Your Gun (r)	1,046
The Teahouse of the August Moon	1,027
Damn Yankees	1,019
Contact	1,010
Never Too Late	1,007
Big River	1,005
The Will Rogers Follies	983
Any Wednesday	982
Sunset Boulevard	977
Urinetown	965
A Funny Thing Happened on the Way to the Forum	964
The Odd Couple	964
Anna Lucasta	957
Kiss and Tell	956
Show Boat (r)	949
Dracula (r)	925
Bells Are Ringing	924
The Moon Is Blue	924
Beatlemania	920
Proof	917
The Elephant Man	916
Kiss of the Spider Woman	906
Luv	901
The Who's Tommy	900
Chicago (m)	898
Applause	896
Can-Can	892
Carousel	890
I'm Not Rappaport	890
Hats Off to Ice	889
Fanny	888
Children of a Lesser God	887
Follow the Girls	882
Kiss Me, Kate (m)(r)	881

Plays	*Performances*
*Thoroughly Modern Millie	879
City of Angels	878
Camelot	873
I Love My Wife	872
The Bat	867
My Sister Eileen	864
No, No, Nanette (r)	861
Ragtime	861
Song of Norway	860
Chapter Two	857
A Streetcar Named Desire	855
Barnum	854
Comedy in Music	849
Raisin	847
Blood Brothers	839
You Can't Take It With You	837
La Plume de Ma Tante	835
Three Men on a Horse	835
The Subject Was Roses	832
Black and Blue	824
The King and I (r)	807
Inherit the Wind	806
Anything Goes (r)	804
Titanic	804
No Time for Sergeants	796
Fiorello!	795
Where's Charley?	792
The Ladder	789
Forty Carats	780
Lost in Yonkers	780
The Prisoner of Second Avenue	780
M. Butterfly	777
The Tale of the Allergist's Wife	777
Oliver!	774
The Pirates of Penzance (1980 r)	772
The Full Monty	770
Woman of the Year	770
My One and Only	767
Sophisticated Ladies	767
Bubbling Brown Sugar	766
Into the Woods	765
State of the Union	765
Starlight Express	761
The First Year	760
Broadway Bound	756
You Know I Can't Hear You When the Water's Running	755
Two for the Seesaw	750
Joseph and the Amazing Technicolor Dreamcoat (r)	747
*Hairspray	743
Death of a Salesman	742
For Colored Girls . . .	742
Sons o' Fun	742
Candide (m, r)	740
Gentlemen Prefer Blondes	740
The Man Who Came to Dinner	739

Plays	*Performances*
Nine	739
Call Me Mister	734
Victor/Victoria	734
West Side Story	732
High Button Shoes	727
Finian's Rainbow	725
Claudia	722
The Gold Diggers	720
Jesus Christ Superstar	720
Carnival	719
The Diary of Anne Frank	717
A Funny Thing Happened on the Way to the Forum (r)	715
I Remember Mama	714
Tea and Sympathy	712
Junior Miss	710
Footloose	708
Last of the Red Hot Lovers	706
The Secret Garden	706
Company	705
Seventh Heaven	704
Gypsy (m)	702
The Miracle Worker	700
That Championship Season	700
The Music Man (m)(r)	698
Da	697
Cat on a Hot Tin Roof	694
Li'l Abner	693
The Children's Hour	691
Purlie	688
Dead End	687
The Lion and the Mouse	686
White Cargo	686
Dear Ruth	683
East Is West	680
Come Blow Your Horn	677
The Most Happy Fella	676
Defending the Caveman	671
The Doughgirls	671
The Impossible Years	670
Irene	670
Boy Meets Girl	669
The Tap Dance Kid	669
Beyond the Fringe	667
*Movin' Out	664
Who's Afraid of Virginia Woolf?	664
Blithe Spirit	657
A Trip to Chinatown	657
The Women	657
Bloomer Girl	654
The Fifth Season	654
Rain	648
Witness for the Prosecution	645
Call Me Madam	644
Janie	642
The Green Pastures	640
Auntie Mame (p)	639

Plays	*Performances*
A Man for All Seasons	637
The Music Master	635
Jerome Robbins' Broadway	634
The Fourposter	632
The Music Master	627
Two Gentlemen of Verona (m)	627
The Tenth Man	623
The Heidi Chronicles	621
Is Zat So?	618
Anniversary Waltz	615
The Happy Time (p)	614
Separate Rooms	613
Affairs of State	610
Oh! Calcutta! (tr)	610
Star and Garter	609
The Mystery of Edwin Drood	608
The Student Prince	608
Sweet Charity	608
Bye Bye Birdie	607
Riverdance on Broadway	605
Irene (r)	604
Sunday in the Park With George	604
Adonis	603
Broadway	603
Peg o' My Heart	603
Master Class	601
Street Scene (p)	601
Flower Drum Song	600
Kiki	600
A Little Night Music	600
Art	600
Agnes of God	599
Don't Drink the Water	598
Wish You Were Here	598
Sarafina!	597
A Society Circus	596
Absurd Person Singular	592
A Day in Hollywood/ A Night in the Ukraine	588
The Me Nobody Knows	586
The Two Mrs. Carrolls	585
Kismet (m)	583
Gypsy (m, r)	582
Brigadoon	581
Detective Story	581
No Strings	580
Brother Rat	577
Blossom Time	576
Pump Boys and Dinettes	573
Show Boat	572
The Show-Off	571
Sally	570
Jelly's Last Jam	569
Golden Boy (m)	568
One Touch of Venus	567
The Real Thing	566
Happy Birthday	564

Plays	*Performances*
Look Homeward, Angel	564
Morning's at Seven (r)	564
The Glass Menagerie	561
I Do! I Do!	560
Wonderful Town	559
The Last Night of Ballyhoo	557
Rose Marie	557
Strictly Dishonorable	557
Sweeney Todd	557
The Great White Hope	556
A Majority of One	556
The Sisters Rosensweig	556
Sunrise at Campobello	556
Toys in the Attic	556
Jamaica	555
Stop the World—I Want to Get Off	555
Florodora	553
Noises Off	553
Ziegfeld Follies (1943)	553
Dial "M" for Murder	552
Good News	551
Peter Pan (r)	551
How to Succeed in Business Without Really Trying (r)	548
Let's Face It	547
Milk and Honey	543
Within the Law	541
Pal Joey (r)	540
The Sound of Music (r)	540
What Makes Sammy Run?	540
The Sunshine Boys	538
What a Life	538
Crimes of the Heart	535
Damn Yankees (r)	533
The Unsinkable Molly Brown	532
The Red Mill (r)	531

Plays	*Performances*
Rumors	531
A Raisin in the Sun	530
Godspell (tr)	527
Fences	526
The Solid Gold Cadillac	526
Biloxi Blues	524
Irma La Douce	524
The Boomerang	522
Follies	521
Rosalinda	521
The Best Man	520
Chauve-Souris	520
Blackbirds of 1928	518
The Gin Game	517
Side Man	517
Sunny	517
Victoria Regina	517
Fifth of July	511
Half a Sixpence	511
The Vagabond King	511
The New Moon	509
The World of Suzie Wong	508
The Rothschilds	507
On Your Toes (r)	505
Sugar	505
Shuffle Along	504
Up in Central Park	504
Carmen Jones	503
Saturday Night Fever	502
The Member of the Wedding	501
Panama Hattie	501
Personal Appearance	501
Bird in Hand	500
Room Service	500
Sailor, Beware!	500
Tomorrow the World	500

LONG RUNS OFF BROADWAY

Plays	*Performances*
The Fantasticks	17,162
*Perfect Crime	7,089
*Tubes	6,393
Tony 'n' Tina's Wedding	4,914
*Stomp	4,298
Nunsense	3,672
*I Love You, You're Perfect, Now Change	3,255
The Threepenny Opera	2,611
Forbidden Broadway 1982–87	2,332
Little Shop of Horrors	2,209
Godspell	2,124
*Naked Boys Singing!	2,031
Vampire Lesbians of Sodom	2,024
*De La Guarda	2,356

Plays	*Performances*
Jacques Brel	1,847
Forever Plaid	1,811
Vanities	1,785
You're a Good Man, Charlie Brown	1,597
The Blacks	1,408
The Vagina Monologues	1,381
One Mo' Time	1,372
Grandma Sylvia's Funeral	1,360
Let My People Come	1,327
Late Nite Catechism	1,268
*The Donkey Show	1,225
Driving Miss Daisy	1,195
The Hot l Baltimore	1,166
I'm Getting My Act Together and Taking It on the Road	1,165

Plays	*Performances*
Little Mary Sunshine	1,143
Steel Magnolias	1,126
El Grande de Coca-Cola	1,114
The Proposition	1,109
Our Sinatra	1,096
Beau Jest	1,069
Tamara	1,036
One Flew Over the Cuckoo's Nest (r)	1,025
The Boys in the Band	1,000
Fool for Love	1,000
Other People's Money	990
Cloud 9	971
Secrets Every Smart Traveler Should Know	953
Sister Mary Ignatius Explains It All for You & The Actor's Nightmare	947
*Forbidden Broadway: 20th Anniversary Celebration	944
Your Own Thing	933
Curley McDimple	931
Leave It to Jane (r)	928
*Menopause: The Musical	927
Hedwig and the Angry Inch	857
Forbidden Broadway Strikes Back	850
When Pigs Fly	840
The Mad Show	871
Scrambled Feet	831
The Effect of Gamma Rays on Man-in-the-Moon Marigolds	819
Over the River and Through the Woods	800
A View From the Bridge (r)	780
The Boy Friend (r)	763
True West	762
Forbidden Broadway Cleans Up Its Act!	754
Isn't It Romantic	733
Dime a Dozen	728
The Pocket Watch	725
The Connection	722
The Passion of Dracula	714
Love, Janis	713
Adaptation & Next	707
Oh! Calcutta!	704
Scuba Duba	692

Plays	*Performances*
The Foreigner	686
The Knack	685
Fully Committed	675
The Club	674
The Balcony	672
Penn & Teller	666
Dinner With Friends	654
America Hurrah	634
Oil City Symphony	626
The Countess	618
The Exonerated	608
Hogan's Goat	607
Beehive	600
Criss Angel Mindfreak	600
The Trojan Women	600
The Syringa Tree	586
The Dining Room	583
Krapp's Last Tape & The Zoo Story	582
Three Tall Women	582
The Dumbwaiter & The Collection	578
Forbidden Broadway 1990	576
Dames at Sea	575
The Crucible (r)	571
The Iceman Cometh (r)	565
Forbidden Broadway 2001: A Spoof Odyssey	552
The Hostage (r)	545
Wit	545
What's a Nice Country Like You Doing in a State Like This?	543
Forbidden Broadway 1988	534
Gross Indecency: The Three Trials of Oscar Wilde	534
Frankie and Johnny in the Clair de Lune	533
Six Characters in Search of an Author (r)	529
All in the Timing	526
Oleanna	513
Making Porn	511
The Dirtiest Show in Town	509
Happy Ending & Day of Absence	504
Greater Tuna	501
A Shayna Maidel	501
The Boys From Syracuse (r)	500

NEW YORK DRAMA CRITICS' CIRCLE 1935–1936 TO 2003–2004

○○○○○

LISTED BELOW ARE the New York Drama Critics' Circle Awards from 1935–1936 through 2003–2004 classified as follows: (1) Best American Play, (2) Best Foreign Play, (3) Best Musical, (4) Best, Regardless of Category (this category was established by new voting rules in 1962–63 and did not exist prior to that year).

1935–36 (1) *Winterset*
1936–37 (1) *High Tor*
1937–38 (1) *Of Mice and Men*, (2) *Shadow and Substance*
1938–39 (1) No award, (2) *The White Steed*
1939–40 (1) *The Time of Your Life*
1940–41 (1) *Watch on the Rhine*, (2) *The Corn Is Green*
1941–42 (1) No award, (2) *Blithe Spirit*
1942–43 (1) *The Patriots*
1943–44 (2) *Jacobowsky and the Colonel*
1944–45 (1) *The Glass Menagerie*
1945–46 (3) *Carousel*
1946–47 (1) *All My Sons*, (2) *No Exit*, (3) *Brigadoon*
1947–48 (1) *A Streetcar Named Desire*, (2) *The Winslow Boy*
1948–49 (1) *Death of a Salesman*, (2) *The Madwoman of Chaillot*, (3) *South Pacific*
1949–50 (1) *The Member of the Wedding*, (2) *The Cocktail Party*, (3) *The Consul*
1950–51 (1) *Darkness at Noon*, (2) *The Lady's Not for Burning*, (3) *Guys and Dolls*
1951–52 (1) *I Am a Camera*, (2) *Venus Observed*, (3) *Pal Joey* (Special citation to *Don Juan in Hell*)
1952–53 (1) *Picnic*, (2) *The Love of Four Colonels*, (3) *Wonderful Town*
1953–54 (1) *The Teahouse of the August Moon*, (2) *Ondine*, (3) *The Golden Apple*
1954–55 (1) *Cat on a Hot Tin Roof*, (2) *Witness for the Prosecution*, (3) *The Saint of Bleecker Street*
1955–56 (1) *The Diary of Anne Frank*, (2) *Tiger at the Gates*, (3) *My Fair Lady*
1956–57 (1) *Long Day's Journey Into Night*, (2) *The Waltz of the Toreadors*, (3) *The Most Happy Fella*
1957–58 (1) *Look Homeward, Angel*, (2) *Look Back in Anger*, (3) *The Music Man*
1958–59 (1) *A Raisin in the Sun*, (2) *The Visit*, (3) *La Plume de Ma Tante*
1959–60 (1) *Toys in the Attic*, (2) *Five Finger Exercise*, (3) *Fiorello!*
1960–61 (1) *All the Way Home*, (2) *A Taste of Honey*, (3) *Carnival*
1961–62 (1) *The Night of the Iguana*, (2) *A Man for All Seasons*, (3) *How to Succeed in Business Without Really Trying*
1962–63 (4) *Who's Afraid of Virginia Woolf?* (Special citation to *Beyond the Fringe*)
1963–64 (4) *Luther*, (3) *Hello, Dolly!* (Special citation to *The Trojan Women*)
1964–65 (4) *The Subject Was Roses*, (3) *Fiddler on the Roof*
1965–66 (4) *The Persecution and Assassination of Marat as Performed by the Inmates of the Asylum of Charenton Under the Direction of the Marquis de Sade*, (3) *Man of La Mancha*
1966–67 (4) *The Homecoming*, (3) *Cabaret*
1967–68 (4) *Rosencrantz and Guildenstern Are Dead*, (3) *Your Own Thing*
1968–69 (4) *The Great White Hope*, (3) *1776*
1969–70 (4) *Borstal Boy*, (1) *The Effect of Gamma Rays on Man-in-the-Moon Marigolds*, (3) *Company*
1970–71 (4) *Home*, (1) *The House of Blue Leaves*, (3) *Follies*
1971–72 (4) *That Championship Season*, (2) *The Screens* (3) *Two Gentlemen of Verona* (Special citations to *Sticks and Bones* and *Old Times*)
1972–73 (4) *The Changing Room*, (1) *The Hot l Baltimore*, (3) *A Little Night Music*
1973–74 (4) *The Contractor*, (1) *Short Eyes*, (3) *Candide*
1974–75 (4) *Equus* (1) *The Taking of Miss Janie*, (3) *A Chorus Line*
1975–76 (4) *Travesties*, (1) *Streamers*, (3) *Pacific Overtures*

1976–77 (4) *Otherwise Engaged*, (1) *American Buffalo*, (3) *Annie*
1977–78 (4) *Da*, (3) *Ain't Misbehavin'*
1978–79 (4) *The Elephant Man*, (3) *Sweeney Todd, the Demon Barber of Fleet Street*
1979–80 (4) *Talley's Folly*, (2) *Betrayal*, (3) *Evita* (Special citation to Peter Brook's Le Centre International de Créations Théâtrales for its repertory)
1980–81 (4) *A Lesson From Aloes*, (1) *Crimes of the Heart* (Special citations to *Lena Horne: The Lady and Her Music* and the New York Shakespeare Festival production of *The Pirates of Penzance*)
1981–82 (4) *The Life & Adventures of Nicholas Nickleby*, (1) *A Soldier's Play*
1982–83 (4) *Brighton Beach Memoirs*, (2) *Plenty*, (3) *Little Shop of Horrors* (Special citation to Young Playwrights Festival)
1983–84 (4) *The Real Thing*, (1) *Glengarry Glen Ross*, (3) *Sunday in the Park With George* (Special citation to Samuel Beckett for the body of his work)
1984–85 (4) *Ma Rainey's Black Bottom*
1985–86 (4) *A Lie of the Mind*, (2) *Benefactors* (Special citation to *The Search for Signs of Intelligent Life in the Universe*)
1986–87 (4) *Fences*, (2) *Les Liaisons Dangereuses*, (3) *Les Misérables*
1987–88 (4) *Joe Turner's Come and Gone*, (2) *The Road to Mecca*, (3) *Into the Woods*
1988–89 (4) *The Heidi Chronicles*, (2) *Aristocrats* (Special citation to Bill Irwin for *Largely New York*)
1989–90 (4) *The Piano Lesson*, (2) *Privates on Parade*, (3) *City of Angels*
1990–91 (4) *Six Degrees of Separation*, (2) *Our Country's Good*, (3) *The Will Rogers Follies* (Special citation to Eileen Atkins for her portrayal of Virginia Woolf in *A Room of One's Own*)
1991–92 (4) *Dancing at Lughnasa*, (1) *Two Trains Running*
1992–93 (4) *Angels in America: Millennium Approaches*, (2) *Someone Who'll Watch Over Me*, (3) *Kiss of the Spider Woman*
1993–94 (4) *Three Tall Women* (Special citation to Anna Deavere Smith for her unique contribution to theatrical form)
1994–95 (4) *Arcadia*, (1) *Love! Valour! Compassion!* (Special citation to Signature Theatre Company for outstanding artistic achievement)
1995–96 (4) *Seven Guitars*, (2) *Molly Sweeney*, (3) *Rent*
1996–97 (4) *How I Learned to Drive*, (2) *Skylight*, (3) *Violet* (Special citation to *Chicago*)
1997–98 (4) *Art*, (1) *Pride's Crossing*, (3) *The Lion King* (Special citation to the revival production of *Cabaret*)
1998–99 (4) *Wit*, (3) *Parade*, (2) *Closer* (Special citation to David Hare for his contributions to the 1998–99 theater season: *Amy's View*, *Via Dolorosa* and *The Blue Room*)
1999–00 (4) *Jitney*, (3) *James Joyce's The Dead*, (2) *Copenhagen*
2000–01 (4) *The Invention of Love*, (1) *Proof*, (3) *The Producers*
2001–02 (4) *Edward Albee's The Goat, or Who is Sylvia?* (Special citation to Elaine Stritch for *Elaine Stritch at Liberty*)
2002–03 (4) *Take Me Out*, (2) *Talking Heads*, (3) *Hairspray*
2003–04 (4) *Intimate Apparel* (Special citation to Barbara Cook for her contribution to the musical theater)

NEW YORK DRAMA CRITICS' CIRCLE VOTING 2003–2004

Charles Isherwood (*Variety*), President

AT ITS MAY 11, 2004 meeting the New York Drama Critics' Circle declined to honor any musical foreign-play productions of the 2003–04 season. The group voted a best-of-bests award to Lynn Nottage's *Intimate Apparel* on a second, weighted ballot.

Of the 20 members of the Circle, only Elysa Gardner of *USA Today* was absent—she voted by proxy on the first ballot. The first round was tallied as follows: *Intimate Apparel* 6 (Gordon Cox, *Newsday*; Robert Feldberg, *The Bergen*

Record; John Heilpern, *The New York Observer*; Howard Kissel, *Daily News*; Donald Lyons, *New York Post*; Ken Mandelbaum, Broadway.com), *The Retreat From Moscow* 3 (Jacques le Sourd, Gannett/*Journal News*; Frank Scheck, *The Hollywood Reporter*; John Simon, *New York*), *The Beard of Avon* 2 (Clive Barnes, *New York Post*; David Cote, *Time Out New York*), *I Am My Own Wife* 2 (Michael Feingold, *The Village Voice*; Linda Winer, *Newsday*), *Well* 2 (David Sheward, *Back Stage*; Michael Sommers, *The Star-Ledger*/Newhouse Newspapers), *Frozen* 1 (Elysa Gardner, *USA Today*), *Small Tragedy* 1 (Charles Isherwood, *Variety*), *Bug* 1 (Michael Kuchwara, *The Associated Press*), *Living Out* 1 (Jeremy McCarter, *The New York Sun*), *Sea of Tranquility* 1 (Richard Zoglin, *Time*).

No play garnered a majority of votes on the first ballot—10 plays received affirmation in that round—so the group went to a weighted system for the next round, which allowed voters to select first, second and third choices. *Intimate Apparel* emerged as the winner in the second round—during which 12 plays received some combination of votes (*Match* and *Matt and Ben* were added to the mix following the first round). With 19 members present, *Intimate Apparel* appeared on 14 ballots. Honorees received their accolades at a Sardi's cocktail party May 18, 2004.

PULITZER PRIZE WINNERS 1916–1917 TO 2003–2004

1916–17 No award
1917–18 *Why Marry?* by Jesse Lynch Williams
1918–19 No award
1919–20 *Beyond the Horizon* by Eugene O'Neill
1920–21 *Miss Lulu Bett* by Zona Gale
1921–22 *Anna Christie* by Eugene O'Neill
1922–23 *Icebound* by Owen Davis
1923–24 *Hell-Bent fer Heaven* by Hatcher Hughes
1924–25 *They Knew What They Wanted* by Sidney Howard
1925–26 *Craig's Wife* by George Kelly
1926–27 *In Abraham's Bosom* by Paul Green
1927–28 *Strange Interlude* by Eugene O'Neill
1928–29 *Street Scene* by Elmer Rice
1929–30 *The Green Pastures* by Marc Connelly
1930–31 *Alison's House* by Susan Glaspell
1931–32 *Of Thee I Sing* by George S. Kaufman, Morrie Ryskind, Ira and George Gershwin
1932–33 *Both Your Houses* by Maxwell Anderson
1933–34 *Men in White* by Sidney Kingsley
1934–35 *The Old Maid* by Zoe Akins
1935–36 *Idiot's Delight* by Robert E. Sherwood
1936–37 *You Can't Take It With You* by Moss Hart and George S. Kaufman
1937–38 *Our Town* by Thornton Wilder
1938–39 *Abe Lincoln in Illinois* by Robert E. Sherwood
1939–40 *The Time of Your Life* by William Saroyan
1940–41 *There Shall Be No Night* by Robert E. Sherwood
1941–42 No award
1942–43 *The Skin of Our Teeth* by Thornton Wilder
1943–44 No award
1944–45 *Harvey* by Mary Chase
1945–46 *State of the Union* by Howard Lindsay and Russel Crouse
1946–47 No award
1947–48 *A Streetcar Named Desire* by Tennessee Williams
1948–49 *Death of a Salesman* by Arthur Miller
1949–50 *South Pacific* by Richard Rodgers, Oscar Hammerstein II and Joshua Logan
1950–51 No award
1951–52 *The Shrike* by Joseph Kramm
1952–53 *Picnic* by William Inge
1953–54 *The Teahouse of the August Moon* by John Patrick
1954–55 *Cat on a Hot Tin Roof* by Tennessee Williams
1955–56 *The Diary of Anne Frank* by Frances Goodrich and Albert Hackett
1956–57 *Long Day's Journey Into Night* by Eugene O'Neill
1957–58 *Look Homeward, Angel* by Ketti Frings
1958–59 *J.B.* by Archibald MacLeish
1959–60 *Fiorello!* by Jerome Weidman, George Abbott, Sheldon Harnick and Jerry Bock
1960–61 *All the Way Home* by Tad Mosel
1961–62 *How to Succeed in Business Without Really Trying* by Abe Burrows, Willie Gilbert, Jack Weinstock and Frank Loesser
1962–63 No award
1963–64 No award
1964–65 *The Subject Was Roses* by Frank D. Gilroy
1965–66 No award
1966–67 *A Delicate Balance* by Edward Albee
1967–68 No award
1968–69 *The Great White Hope* by Howard Sackler
1969–70 *No Place To Be Somebody* by Charles Gordone
1970–71 *The Effect of Gamma Rays on Man-in-the-Moon Marigolds* by Paul Zindel
1971–72 No award
1972–73 *That Championship Season* by Jason Miller
1973–74 No award
1974–75 *Seascape* by Edward Albee
1975–76 *A Chorus Line* by Michael Bennett, James Kirkwood, Nicholas Dante, Marvin Hamlisch and Edward Kleban
1976–77 *The Shadow Box* by Michael Cristofer
1977–78 *The Gin Game* by D.L. Coburn
1978–79 *Buried Child* by Sam Shepard
1979–80 *Talley's Folly* by Lanford Wilson
1980–81 *Crimes of the Heart* by Beth Henley
1981–82 *A Soldier's Play* by Charles Fuller
1982–83 *'night, Mother* by Marsha Norman
1983–84 *Glengarry Glen Ross* by David Mamet
1984–85 *Sunday in the Park With George* by James Lapine and Stephen Sondheim
1985–86 No award
1986–87 *Fences* by August Wilson

1987–88 *Driving Miss Daisy* by Alfred Uhry
1988–89 *The Heidi Chronicles* by Wendy Wasserstein
1989–90 *The Piano Lesson* by August Wilson
1990–91 *Lost in Yonkers* by Neil Simon
1991–92 *The Kentucky Cycle* by Robert Schenkkan
1992–93 *Angels in America: Millennium Approaches* by Tony Kushner
1993–94 *Three Tall Women* by Edward Albee
1994–95 *The Young Man From Atlanta* by Horton Foote
1995–96 *Rent* by Jonathan Larson
1996–97 No award
1997–98 *How I Learned to Drive* by Paula Vogel
1998–99 *Wit* by Margaret Edson
1999–00 *Dinner With Friends* by Donald Margulies
2000–01 *Proof* by David Auburn
2001–02 *Topdog/Underdog* by Suzan-Lori Parks
2002–03 *Anna in the Tropics* by Nilo Cruz
2003–04 *I Am My Own Wife* by Doug Wright

2004 TONY AWARDS

○○○○○

THE AMERICAN THEATRE WING'S 58th annual Tony Awards, named for Antoinette Perry, are presented in recognition of distinguished achievement in the Broadway theater. The League of American Theatres and Producers and the American Theatre Wing present these awards, founded by the Wing in 1947. Legitimate theater productions opening in 40 eligible Broadway theaters during the present Tony season—May 8, 2003 to May 5, 2004—were considered by the Tony Awards Nominating Committee (appointed by the Tony Awards Administration Committee) for the awards in 21 competitive categories. The 2003–2004 Nominating Committee included Maureen Anderman, actor; Ira Bernstein, manager; Stephen Bogardus, actor; Schulyer G. Chapin, executive; Kristen Childs, musical theater writer; Veronica Claypool, manager; Betty Corwin, archivist; Gretchen Cryer, composer; Jacqueline Z. Davis, executive; Merle Debuskey, press; Edgar Dobie, manager; Nancy Ford, composer; David Marshall Grant, actor; Micki Grant, composer; Julie Hughes, casting; Betty Jacobs, consultant; Geoffrey Johnson, casting; David Lindsay-Abaire, playwright; Enid Nemy, journalist; Gilbert Parker, agent; Shirley Rich, casting; Judith O. Rubin, executive; Bill Schelble, press; Rosemarie Tichler, casting; William Tynan, journalist; Jon Wilner, producer.

The Tony Awards are voted from the list of nominees by members of the theater and journalism professions: the governing boards of the five theater artists' organizations—Actors' Equity Association, the Dramatists' Guild, the Society of Stage Directors and Choreographers, United Scenic Artists and Casting Society of America—the members of the designated first night theater press, the board of directors of the American Theatre Wing and the membership of the League of American Theatres and Producers. Because of fluctuation in these groups, the size of the Tony electorate varies from year to year. For the 2003–2004 season there were 735 qualified Tony voters.

The 2003–2004 nominees follow, with winners in each category listed in **bold face type**.

BEST PLAY (award goes to both author and producer). *Anna in the Tropics* by Nilo Cruz, produced by Roger Berlind, Daryl Roth, Ray Larsen, Robert G. Bartner, The McCarter Theatre Center. *Frozen* by Bryony Lavery, produced by MCC Theater, Robert LuPone, Bernard Telsey, William Cantler, John G. Schultz, Hal Newman, Frederick Zollo/Nicholas Paleologos and Jeffrey Sine, Roy Gabay, Lorie Cowen Levy and Beth Smith, Peggy Hill, Thompson H. Rogers, Morton Swinsky/Michael Filerman/Ruth Hendel, Spring Sirkin/Marianne Mills/Jim Baldassare, Darren Bagert. ***I Am My Own Wife* by Doug Wright, produced by Delphi Productions, Playwrights Horizons**. *The Retreat From Moscow* by William Nicholson, produced by Susan Quint Gallin, Stuart Thompson, Ron Kastner, True Love Productions, Mary Lu Roffe, Jam Theatricals.

BEST MUSICAL (award goes to the producer). ***Avenue Q* produced by Kevin McCollum, Robyn Goodman, Jeffrey Seller, Vineyard Theatre, The New Group. *The Boy From Oz* produced by Ben Gannon, Robert Fox**. *Caroline, or Change* produced by Carole Shorenstein Hays, HBO Films, Jujamcyn Theaters, Freddy DeMann, Scott Rudin, Ruth Hendel/ Elisabeth Morten / Cheryl Wiesenfeld, Jane Bergère / Fox Theatricals / Jennifer Manocherian, Roger Berlind, Clear Channel Entertainment, Joan Cullman, Greg Holland/Scott E. Nederlander, Margo Lion, Daryl Roth, Frederick Zollo/Jeffrey Sine, The Public Theater. *Wicked* produced by Marc Platt, Universal Pictures, The Araca Group, Jon B. Platt, David Stone.

BEST BOOK OF A MUSICAL. Winnie Holzman for *Wicked*. Tony Kushner for *Caroline, or Change*. Martin Sherman for *The Boy From Oz*, original book by Nick Enright. **Jeff Whitty** for ***Avenue Q***.

BEST ORIGINAL SCORE (music and/or lyrics). Boy George (music) for *Taboo*. **Robert Lopez and Jeff Marx (music)** for ***Avenue Q***. Stephen Schwartz (music) for *Wicked*. Jeanine Tesori (music) and Tony Kushner (lyrics) for *Caroline, or Change*.

BEST REVIVAL OF A PLAY (award goes to the producer). ***Henry IV* produced by Lincoln Center Theater, André Bishop, Bernard Gersten**. *Jumpers* produced by Boyett Ostar Productions, Nederlander Presentations Inc., Freddy DeMann, Jean Doumanian, Stephanie McClelland, Arielle Tepper, The National Theatre of Great Britain. *King Lear* produced by Lincoln Center Theater, André Bishop, Bernard Gersten, Stratford Festival of Canada. *A Raisin in the Sun* produced by David Binder, Vivek J. Tiwary, Susan Batson, Carl Rumbaugh, Ruth Hendel, Arielle Tepper, Jayne Baron Sherman, Dede Harris, Barbara Whitman, Cynthia Stroum.

BEST REVIVAL OF A MUSICAL (award goes to the producer). ***Assassins* produced by Roundabout Theatre Company, Todd Haimes, Ellen Richard, Julia C. Levy**. *Big River* produced by Roundabout Theatre Company, Todd Haimes, Ellen Richard, Julia C. Levy, Deaf West Theatre, Ed Waterstreet, Bill O'Brien, Center Theatre Group/Mark Taper Forum. *Fiddler on the Roof* produced by James L. Nederlander, Stewart F. Lane/Bonnie Comley, Harbor Entertainment, Terry Allen Kramer, Bob Boyett/Lawrence Horowitz, Clear Channel Entertainment. *Wonderful Town* produced by Roger Berlind, Barry and Fran Weissler, Edwin W. Schloss, Allen Spivak, Clear Channel Entertainment, Harvey Weinstein.

BEST PERFORMANCE BY A LEADING ACTOR IN A PLAY. Simon Russell Beale in *Jumpers*, Kevin Kline in *Henry IV*, Frank Langella in *Match*, **Jefferson Mays** in ***I Am My Own Wife***, Christopher Plummer in *King Lear*.

BEST PERFORMANCE BY A LEADING ACTRESS IN A PLAY. Eileen Atkins in *The Retreat From Moscow*, Tovah Feldshuh in *Golda's Balcony*, Anne Heche in *Twentieth Century*, Swoosie Kurtz in *Frozen*, **Phylicia Rashad** in ***A Raisin in the Sun***.

BEST PERFORMANCE BY A LEADING ACTOR IN A MUSICAL. Hunter Foster in *Little Shop of Horrors*, **Hugh Jackman** in ***The Boy From Oz***, Alfred Molina in *Fiddler on the Roof*, Euan Morton in *Taboo*, John Tartaglia, *Avenue Q*.

BEST PERFORMANCE BY A LEADING ACTRESS IN A MUSICAL. Kristin Chenoweth in *Wicked*, Stephanie D'Abruzzo in *Avenue Q*, **Idina Menzel** in ***Wicked***, Donna Murphy in *Wonderful Town*, Tonya Pinkins in *Caroline, or Change*.

BEST PERFORMANCE BY A FEATURED ACTOR IN A PLAY. Tom Aldredge in *Twentieth Century*, Ben Chaplin in *The Retreat From Moscow*, Aidan Gillen in *The Caretaker*, Omar Metwally in *Sixteen Wounded*, **Brian F. O'Byrne** in ***Frozen***.

BEST PERFORMANCE BY A FEATURED ACTRESS IN A PLAY. Essie Davis in *Jumpers*, Sanaa Lathan in *A Raisin in the Sun*, Margo Martindale in *Cat on a Hot Tin Roof*, **Audra McDonald** in ***A Raisin in the Sun***, Daphne Rubin-Vega in *Anna in the Tropics*.

BEST PERFORMANCE BY A FEATURED ACTOR IN A MUSICAL. John Cariani in *Fiddler on the Roof*, **Michael Cerveris** in ***Assassins***, Raúl Esparza in *Taboo*, Michael McElroy in *Big River*, Denis O'Hare in *Assassins*.

BEST PERFORMANCE BY A FEATURED ACTRESS IN A MUSICAL. Beth Fowler in *The Boy From Oz*, Isabel Keating in *The Boy From Oz*, **Anika Noni Rose** in ***Caroline, or Change***, Jennifer Westfeldt in *Wonderful Town*, Karen Ziemba in *Never Gonna Dance*.

BEST SCENIC DESIGN. Robert Brill for *Assassins*, Ralph Funicello for *Henry IV*, **Eugene Lee** for ***Wicked***, Tom Pye for *Fiddler on the Roof*.

BEST COSTUME DESIGN. Jess Goldstein for *Henry IV*, **Susan Hilferty** for ***Wicked***, Mike Nicholls and Bobby Pearce for *Taboo*, Mark Thompson for *Bombay Dreams*.

BEST LIGHTING DESIGN. **Jules Fisher and Peggy Eisenhauer** for ***Assassins***, Brian MacDevitt for *Fiddler on the Roof*, Brian MacDevitt for *Henry IV*, Kenneth Posner for *Wicked*.

BEST CHOREOGRAPHY. Wayne Cilento for *Wicked*, **Kathleen Marshall** for ***Wonderful Town***, Jerry Mitchell for *Never Gonna Dance*, Anthony Van Laast and Farah Khan for *Bombay Dreams*.

BEST DIRECTION OF A PLAY. Doug Hughes for *Frozen*, Moisés Kaufman for *I Am My Own Wife*, David Leveaux for *Jumpers*, **Jack O'Brien** for ***Henry IV***.

BEST DIRECTION OF A MUSICAL. **Joe Mantello** for ***Assassins***, Kathleen Marshall for *Wonderful Town*, Jason Moore for *Avenue Q*, George C. Wolfe for *Caroline, or Change*.

BEST ORCHESTRATIONS. Paul Bogaev for *Bombay Dreams*, William David Brohn for *Wicked*, Larry Hochman for *Fiddler on the Roof*, **Michael Starobin** for ***Assassins***.

LIFETIME ACHIEVEMENT. **James M. Nederlander**.

REGIONAL THEATRE TONY AWARD. **Cincinnati Playhouse in the Park**, Cincinnati, Ohio.

TONY AWARD WINNERS, 1947–2004

LISTED BELOW ARE the Antoinette Perry (Tony) Award winners in the catgories of Best Play and Best Musical from the time these awards were established in 1947 until the present.

1947—No play or musical award
1948—*Mister Roberts*; no musical award
1949—*Death of a Salesman*; *Kiss Me, Kate*
1950—*The Cocktail Party*; *South Pacific*
1951—*The Rose Tattoo*; *Guys and Dolls*
1952—*The Fourposter*; *The King and I*
1953—*The Crucible*; *Wonderful Town*
1954—*The Teahouse of the August Moon*; *Kismet*
1955—*The Desperate Hours*; *The Pajama Game*
1956—*The Diary of Anne Frank*; *Damn Yankees*
1957—*Long Day's Journey Into Night*; *My Fair Lady*
1958—*Sunrise at Campobello*; *The Music Man*
1959—*J.B.*; *Redhead*
1960—*The Miracle Worker*; *Fiorello!* and *The Sound of Music* (tie)
1961—*Becket*; *Bye Bye Birdie*
1962—*A Man for All Seasons*; *How to Succeed in Business Without Really Trying*
1963—*Who's Afraid of Virginia Woolf?*; *A Funny Thing Happened on the Way to the Forum*
1964—*Luther*; *Hello, Dolly!*
1965—*The Subject Was Roses*; *Fiddler on the Roof*
1966—*The Persecution and Assassination of Marat as Performed by the Inmates of the Asylum of Charenton Under the Direction of the Marquis de Sade*; *Man of La Mancha*
1967—*The Homecoming*; *Cabaret*
1968—*Rosencrantz and Guildenstern Are Dead*; *Hallelujah, Baby!*
1969—*The Great White Hope*; *1776*
1970—*Borstal Boy*; *Applause*
1971—*Sleuth*; *Company*
1972—*Sticks and Bones*; *Two Gentlemen of Verona*
1973—*That Championship Season*; *A Little Night Music*
1974—*The River Niger*; *Raisin*
1975—*Equus*; *The Wiz*
1976—*Travesties*; *A Chorus Line*
1977—*The Shadow Box*; *Annie*
1978—*Da*; *Ain't Misbehavin'*
1979—*The Elephant Man*; *Sweeney Todd, the Demon Barber of Fleet Street*
1980—*Children of a Lesser God*; *Evita*
1981—*Amadeus*; *42nd Street*
1982—*The Life & Adventures of Nicholas Nickleby*; *Nine*
1983—*Torch Song Trilogy*; *Cats*
1984—*The Real Thing*; *La Cage aux Folles*
1985—*Biloxi Blues*; *Big River*
1986—*I'm Not Rappaport*; *The Mystery of Edwin Drood*
1987—*Fences*; *Les Misérables*
1988—*M. Butterfly*; *The Phantom of the Opera*
1989—*The Heidi Chronicles*; *Jerome Robbins' Broadway*
1990—*The Grapes of Wrath*; *City of Angels*
1991—*Lost in Yonkers*; *The Will Rogers Follies*
1992—*Dancing at Lughnasa*; *Crazy for You*
1993—*Angels in America, Part I: Millennium Approaches*; *Kiss of the Spider Woman*
1994—*Angels in America, Part II: Perestroika*; *Passion*
1995—*Love! Valour! Compassion!*; *Sunset Boulevard*
1996—*Master Class*; *Rent*
1997—*The Last Night of Ballyhoo*; *Titanic*
1998—*Art*; *The Lion King*
1999—*Side Man*; *Fosse*
2000—*Copenhagen*; *Contact*
2001—*Proof*; *The Producers*
2002—*The Goat, or Who is Sylvia*; *Thoroughly Modern Millie*
2003—*Take Me Out*; *Hairspray*
2004—*I Am My Own Wife*; *Avenue Q*

2004 LUCILLE LORTEL AWARDS

THE LUCILLE LORTEL AWARDS for outstanding Off Broadway achievement were established in 1985 by a resolution of the League of Off Broadway Theatres and Producers, which administers them and has presented them annually since 1986. Eligible for the 19th annual awards in 2004 were all Off Broadway productions that opened between April 1, 2003 and March 31, 2004. Winners were selected by a committee comprising Mark Dickerman, Susan Einhorn, Adam Feldman, George Forbes, Charles Isherwood, Walt Kiskaddon, Gerald Rabkin, Mark Rossier, Marc Routh, Donald Saddler, Tom Smedes, Anna Strasberg, Barbara Wolkoff.

PLAY. ***Bug*** by Tracy Letts.

MUSICAL. ***Caroline, or Change***. Book and lyrics by Tony Kushner, music by Jeanine Tesori.

OUTSTANDING SOLO SHOW. ***I Am My Own Wife*** by Doug Wright, starring Jefferson Mays.

ACTOR. **Brían F. O'Byrne** in *Frozen*.

ACTRESS. **Tonya Pinkins** in *Caroline, or Change*.

FEATURED ACTOR. **Will McCormack** in *The Long Christmas Ride Home*.

FEATURED ACTRESS. **Anika Noni Rose** in *Caroline, or Change*.

DIRECTION. **Dexter Bullard** for *Bug*.

CHOREOGRAPHY. **Hope Clarke** for *Caroline, or Change*.

SCENERY. **Derek McLane** for *I Am My Own Wife*.

COSTUMES. **Catherine Zuber** for *The Beard of Avon*.

LIGHTING. **Tyler Micoleau** for *Bug*.

SOUND. **Brian Ronan** for *Bug*.

BODY OF WORK. **The Public Theater**.

PLAYWRIGHTS' SIDEWALK. **Tony Kushner**.

EDITH OLIVER AWARD. **Kathleen Chalfant**.

UNIQUE THEATRICAL EXPERIENCE. ***Noche Flamenca***.

LORTEL AWARD WINNERS 1986–2004

LISTED BELOW ARE the Lucille Lortel Award winners in the categories of Outstanding Play and Outstanding Musical from the time these awards were established until the present.

1986—*Woza Africa!*; no musical award
1987—*The Common Pursuit*; no musical award
1988—No play or musical award
1989—*The Cocktail Hour*; no musical award
1990—No play or musical award
1991—*Aristocrats*; *Falsettoland*
1992—*Lips Together, Teeth Apart*; *And the World Goes 'Round*
1993—*The Destiny of Me*; *Forbidden Broadway*
1994—*Three Tall Women*; *Wings*
1995—*Camping With Henry & Tom*; *Jelly Roll!*
1996—*Molly Sweeney*; *Floyd Collins*
1997—*How I Learned to Drive*; *Violet*
1998—*Gross Indecency*, and *The Beauty Queen of Leenane* (tie); no musical award
1999—*Wit*; no musical award

2000—*Dinner With Friends*; *James Joyce's The Dead*
2001—*Proof*; *Bat Boy: The Musical*
2002—*Metamorphoses*; *Urinetown*
2003—*Take Me Out*; *Avenue Q*
2004—*Bug*; *Caroline, or Change*

AMERICAN THEATRE CRITICS/STEINBERG NEW PLAY AWARDS AND CITATIONS

○○○○○

INCLUDING PRINCIPAL CITATIONS AND NEW PLAY AWARD WINNERS, 1977–2004

BEGINNING WITH THE season of 1976–77, the American Theatre Critics Association (ATCA) has cited one or more outstanding new plays in United States theater. The principal honorees have been included in *Best Plays* since the first year. In 1986 the ATCA New Play Award was given for the first time, along with a $1,000 prize. The award and citations were renamed the **American Theatre Critics/Steinberg New Play Award and Citations** in 2000 (see essays on the 2004 ATCA/Steinberg honorees in the Season Around the United States section of this volume). The award dates were renumbered beginning with the 2000–2001 volume to correctly reflect the year in which ATCA conferred the honor.

NEW PLAY CITATIONS (1977–1985)

1977—*And the Soul Shall Dance* by Wakako Yamauchi
1978—*Getting Out* by Marsha Norman
1979—*Loose Ends* by Michael Weller
1980—*Custer* by Robert E. Ingham
1981—*Chekhov in Yalta* by John Driver and Jeffrey Haddow
1982—*Talking With* by Jane Martin
1983—*Closely Related* by Bruce MacDonald
1984—*Wasted* by Fred Gamel
1985—*Scheherazade* by Marisha Chamberlain

NEW PLAY AWARD (1986–1999)

1986—*Fences* by August Wilson
1987—*A Walk in the Woods* by Lee Blessing
1988—*Heathen Valley* by Romulus Linney
1989—*The Piano Lesson* by August Wilson
1990—*2* by Romulus Linney
1991—*Two Trains Running* by August Wilson
1992—*Could I Have This Dance?* by Doug Haverty
1993—*Children of Paradise: Shooting a Dream* by Steven Epp, Felicity Jones, Dominique Serrand and Paul Walsh
1994—*Keely and Du* by Jane Martin
1995—*The Nanjing Race* by Reggie Cheong-Leen
1996—*Amazing Grace* by Michael Cristofer

1997—*Jack and Jill* by Jane Martin
1998—*The Cider House Rules, Part II* by Peter Parnell
1999—*Book of Days* by Lanford Wilson.

ATCA/Steinberg New Play Award and Citations

2000—*Oo-Bla-Dee* by Regina Taylor
Citation: *Compleat Female Stage Beauty* by Jeffrey Hatcher
Citation: *Syncopation* by Allan Knee
2001—*Anton in Show Business* by Jane Martin
Citation: *Big Love* by Charles L. Mee
Citation: *King Hedley II* by August Wilson
2002—*The Carpetbagger's Children* by Horton Foote
Citation: *The Action Against Sol Schumann* by Jeffrey Sweet
Citation: *Joe and Betty* by Murray Mednick
2003—*Anna in the Tropics* by Nilo Cruz
Citation: *Recent Tragic Events* by Craig Wright
Citation: *Resurrection Blues* by Arthur Miller
2004—*Intimate Apparel* by Lynn Nottage
Citation: *Gem of the Ocean* by August Wilson
Citation: *The Love Song of J. Robert Oppenheimer* by Carson Kreitzer

ADDITIONAL PRIZES AND AWARDS 2003–2004

THE FOLLOWING IS a list of major awards for achievement in the theater this season. The names of honorees appear in **bold type**.

2002–2003 GEORGE JEAN NATHAN AWARD. For dramatic criticism. **Hilton Als**.

23ND ANNUAL WILLIAM INGE THEATRE FESTIVAL AWARD. For distinguished achievement in American theater. **Arthur Laurents**. Otis Guernsey New Voices Award: **Mary Portser**.

2004 M. ELIZABETH OSBORN AWARD. Presented by the American Theatre Critics Association to an emerging playwright. **Rolin Jones** for *The Intelligent Design of Jenny Chow*.

26TH ANNUAL KENNEDY CENTER HONORS. For distinguished achievement by individuals who have made significant contributions to American culture through the arts. **James Brown**, **Carol Burnett**, **Loretta Lynn**, **Mike Nichols**, **Itzhak Perlman**.

7TH ANNUAL KENNEDY CENTER–MARK TWAIN PRIZE. For American humor. **Lorne Michaels**.

2002 NATIONAL MEDALS OF THE ARTS. For individuals and organizations who have made outstanding contributions to the excellence, growth, support and availability of the arts in the United States, selected by the President from nominees presented by the National Endowment. ***Austin City Limits***, **Beverly Cleary**, **Rafe Esquith**, **Suzanne Farrell**, **Buddy Guy**, **Ron Howard**, **Mormon Tabernacle Choir**, **Leonard Slatkin**, **George Strait**, **Tommy Tune**.

2004 DRAMATISTS GUILD AWARDS. 2003 Elizabeth Hull–Kate Warriner Award to the playwright whose work deals with social, political or religious mores of the time, selected by the Dramatists Guild Council.

Doug Wright for *I Am My Own Wife*. Frederick Loewe Award for Dramatic Composition: **Jerry Bock**. Flora Roberts Award: **William Finn**. Lifetime Achievement: **John Kander** and **Fred Ebb**.

2004 HENRY HEWES DESIGN AWARDS (formerly American Theatre Wing Design Awards). For design originating in the US, selected by a committee comprising Jeffrey Eric Jenkins (chairman), Tish Dace, Glenda Frank, Mario Fratti, Randy Gener, Mel Gussow, Henry Hewes and Joan Ungaro. Scenic design: **David Korins** for *Blackbird*. Costume design: **Catherine Zuber** for *Intimate Apparel*. Lighting design: **Jules Fisher** and **Peggy Eisenhauer** for *Assassins*. Notable effects: **James Schuette** (scenery and costumes), **Brian H. Scott** (lighting) and **Darron L. West** (sound) for their design work in *bobrauschenbergamerica*.

26TH ANNUAL SUSAN SMITH BLACKBURN PRIZE. For women who have written works of outstanding quality for the English-speaking theater. **Sarah Ruhl** for *The Clean House*.

2003 GEORGE FREEDLEY MEMORIAL AWARD. For the best book about live theater published in the United States the previous year. ***A History of African American Theatre*** by **Errol G. Hill and James V. Hatch**. Special Jury prize: ***Everything Was Beautiful: The Birth of the Musical* Follies** by **Ted Chapin**.

23rd ANNUAL ASTAIRE AWARDS. For excellence in dance and choreography, administered by the Theatre Development Fund and selected by a committee comprising Douglas Watt (chairman), Clive Barnes, Howard Kissel, Michael Kuchwara, Donald McDonagh, Richard Philp, Charles L. Reinhart and Linda Winer. Choreography: **Kathleen Marshall** for *Wonderful Town*. Female dancer: **Donna Murphy** in *Wonderful Town*. Male dancer: **Hugh Jackman** in *The Boy From Oz*.

59TH ANNUAL CLARENCE DERWENT AWARDS. Given to a female and a male performer by Actors' Equity Association based on New York work that demonstrates promise. **Anika Noni Rose** and **John Tartaglia**.

2004 RICHARD RODGERS AWARDS. For staged readings of musicals in nonprofit theaters, administered by the American Academy of Arts and Letters and selected by a jury including Stephen Sondheim (chairman), Lynn Ahrens, Jack Beeson, John Guare, Sheldon Harnick, and Richard Maltby Jr., Jeanine Tesori and Francis Thorne. Richard Rodgers Production Award: ***The Tutor*** by **Maryrose Wood** and **Andrew Gerle**. Richard Rodgers Awards for Staged Readings: ***To Paint the Earth*** by Daniel Frederick Levin and Jonathan Portera; *Unlocked* by **Sam Carner** and **Derek Gregor**.

70TH ANNUAL DRAMA LEAGUE AWARDS. For distinguished achievement in the American theater. Play: ***I Am My Own Wife***. Musical: ***Wicked***. Revival of a play: ***Henry IV***. Revival of a musical: ***Assassins***. Performance: **Hugh Jackman** in *The Boy From Oz*. Julia Hansen Award for excellence in directing: **George C. Wolfe**. Achievement in Musical Theatre: **Donna Murphy**. Unique contribution to theater: **City Center Encores!: Jack Viertel**, **Arlene Shuler** and **Rob Fisher**.

2004 GEORGE OPPENHEIMER AWARD. To the best new American playwright, presented by *Newsday*. **Will Eno** for *The Flu Season*.

2004 NEW DRAMATISTS LIFETIME ACHIEVEMENT AWARD. To an individual who has made an outstanding artistic contribution to the American theater. **Meryl Streep**.

2004 *THEATRE WORLD* AWARDS. For outstanding debut performers in Broadway or Off Broadway theater during the 2003–2004 season, selected by a committee including Peter Filichia, Harry Haun, Ben Hodges, Frank Scheck, Matthew Murray, Michael Sommers, John Willis, and Linda Winer. **Shannon Cochran** in *Bug*,

Stephanie D'Abruzzo in *Avenue Q*, **Mitchel David Federan** in *The Boy From Oz*, **Alexander Gemignani** in *Assassins*, **Hugh Jackman** in *The Boy From Oz*, **Isabel Keating** in *The Boy From Oz*, **Sanaa Lathan** in *A Raisin in the Sun*, **Jefferson Mays** in *I Am My Own Wife*, **Euan Morton** in *Taboo*, **Anika Noni Rose** in *Caroline, or Change*, **John Tartaglia** in *Avenue Q*, **Jennifer Westfeldt** in *Wonderful Town* and **Sarah Jones** in *Bridge and Tunnel*.

49TH ANNUAL DRAMA DESK AWARDS. For outstanding achievement in the 2003–2004 season, voted by an association of New York drama reporters, editors and critics from nominations made by a committee. New play: ***I Am My Own Wife***. New musical: ***Wicked***. Revival of a play: ***Henry IV***. Revival of a musical: ***Assassins***. Book of a musical: **Winnie Holzman** for ***Wicked***. Music: **Jeanine Tesori** for ***Caroline, or Change***. Lyrics: **Stephen Schwartz** for ***Wicked***. Actor in a play: **Kevin Kline** in *Henry IV*. Actress in a play (tie): **Viola Davis** in *Intimate Apparel* and **Phylicia Rashad** in *A Raisin in the Sun*. Featured actor in a play: **Ned Beatty** in *Cat on a Hot Tin Roof*. Featured actress in a play: **Audra McDonald** in *A Raisin in the Sun*. Actor in a musical: **Hugh Jackman** in *The Boy From Oz*. Actress in a musical: **Donna Murphy** in *Wonderful Town*. Featured actor in a musical: **Raúl Esparza** in *Taboo*. Featured actress in a musical: **Isabel Keating** in *The Boy From Oz*. Solo performance: **Jefferson Mays** in *I Am My Own Wife*. Director of a play: **Jack O'Brien** for *Henry IV*. Director of a musical: **Joe Mantello** for *Wicked*. Choreography: **Kathleen Marshall** for *Wonderful Town*. Orchestrations: **Michael Starobin** for *Assassins*. Set design of a play: **John Lee Beatty** for *Twentieth Century*. Set design of a musical: **Eugene Lee** for *Wicked*. Costume design: **Susan Hilferty** for *Wicked*. Lighting design: **Jules Fisher** and **Peggy Eisenhauer** for *Assassins*. Sound design: **Dan Moses Schreier** for *Assassins*. Unique Theatrical Experience: **Toxic Audio** in *Loudmouth*. Distinguished Achievement: **Dakin Matthews** for his adaptation of William Shakespeare's Henry IV, parts 1 and 2; **The Flea Theater**; **The Classical Theatre of Harlem**.

54TH ANNUAL OUTER CRITICS' CIRCLE AWARDS. For outstanding achievement in the 2003–2004 season, voted by critics on out-of-town periodicals and media. Broadway play: ***I Am My Own Wife***. Off-Broadway play: ***Intimate Apparel***. Revival of a play: ***Henry IV***. Actor in a play: **Frank Langella** in ***Match***. Actress in a play: **Eileen Atkins** in ***The Retreat From Moscow***. Featured actor in a play: **Ned Beatty** in *Cat on a Hot Tin Roof*. Featured actress in a play: **Audra McDonald** in *A Raisin in the Sun*. Director of a play: **Jack O'Brien** for *Henry IV*. Broadway musical: ***Wicked***. Off-Broadway musical (tie): ***Johnny Guitar*** and ***The Thing About Men***. Revival of a musical: ***Wonderful Town***. Actor in a musical: **Hugh Jackman** in *The Boy From Oz*. Actress in a musical: **Donna Murphy** in *Wonderful Town*. Featured actor in a musical (tie): **John Cariani** in *Fiddler on the Roof* and **Michael Cerveris** in *Assassins*. Featured actress in a musical: **Karen Ziemba** in *Never Gonna Dance*. Director of a musical: **Joe Mantello** for *Wicked*. Choreography: **Kathleen Marshall** for *Wonderful Town*. Scenic design: **Eugene Lee** for *Wicked*. Costume design: **Susan Hilferty** for *Wicked*. Lighting design: **Jules Fisher** and **Peggy Eisenhauer** for *Assassins*. Solo performance: **Jefferson Mays** in *I Am My Own Wife*. John Gassner Playwriting Award: **Lynn Nottage** for *Intimate Apparel*. Special Achievement Award: **Ensemble performance and puppet artistry, the cast of *Avenue Q***.

49TH ANNUAL *VILLAGE VOICE* OBIE AWARDS. For outstanding achievement in Off and Off Off Broadway theater. Performance: **Viola Davis** in *Intimate Apparel*; **Lisa Emery** in *Iron*; **Jayne Houdyshell** in *Well*; **Sarah Jones** in *Bridge and Tunnel*; **Jefferson Mays** in *I Am My Own Wife*; **Zilah Mendoza** in *Living Out*; **Maude Mitchell** in *Mabou Mines's Dollhouse*; **Brían F. O'Byrne** in *Frozen*; **Tonya Pinkins** in *Caroline, or Change*; **Lili Taylor** in *Aunt Dan and Lemon*; **Shannon Cochran**, **Michael**

Shannon, **Michael Cullen**, **Amy Landecker** and **Reed Birney** in *Bug*; **Ana Reeder**, **Mary Shultz**, **Rob Campbell**, **Daniel Eric Gold**, **Lee Pace** and **Rosemarie DeWitt** in *Small Tragedy*. Direction: **Lee Breuer** for *Mabou Mines's Dollhouse*; **Moisés Kaufman** for *I Am My Own Wife*. Best American Play: ***Small Tragedy*** by **Craig Lucas**. Design: **Lauren Helpern** (scenery), **Tyler Micoleau** (lighting), **Brian Ronan** (sound), **Kim Gill** (costumes) and **Faye Armon** (props) for *Bug*; **Derek McLane** (scenery) for *I Am My Own Wife*, *Aunt Dan and Lemon* and *Intimate Apparel*. Music: **Robert Een** for *Hiroshima Maiden*.

Special Citations: **Pieter-Dirk Uys** for *Foreign AIDS*; **Tony Kushner** and **Jeanine Tesori** for *Caroline, or Change*; **Soho Rep** for *Molly's Dream*; **The Builders Association** and **motiroti** for *Alladeen*; **Kyle Jarrow** and **Alex Timbers** for *A Very Merry Unauthorized Children's Scientology Pageant*; **George C. Wolfe** for his stewardship of the Public Theater; **Martin Moran** for *The Tricky Part*; **Terry Nemeth** for play publishing at Theatre Communications Group. Grants: **The Civilians**, **Musicals Tonight**, **THAW (Theaters Against War)**. Ross Wetzsteon Award: **St. Ann's Warehouse** (**Susan Feldman**, artistic director). Lifetime Achievement: **Mark Russell**.

14TH ANNUAL CONNECTICUT CRITICS' CIRCLE AWARDS. For outstanding achievement in Connecticut theater during the 2002–2003 season. Production of a play: **Yale Repertory Theatre** for *The Mystery Plays*. Production of a musical: **Goodspeed Musicals** for *Very Good Eddie*. Actress in a play: **Jill Clayburgh** in *All My Sons*. Actor in a play (tie): **Hamish Linklater** in *Hamlet*; **Cody Nickell** in *Visiting Mr. Green*. Actress in a musical: **Julia Kiley** in *Follies*. Actor in a musical: **Randy Rogel** in *Very Good Eddie*. Direction of a play: **Oskar Eustis** for *The Long Christmas Ride Home*. Direction of a musical: **Gary John LaRosa** for *La Cage aux Folles*. Choreography: **Dan Siretta** for *Very Good Eddie*. Set design: **Adrian W. Jones** for *The Dazzle*. Lighting design (tie): **T.J. Gerckens** for *Metamorphoses*; **S. Ryan Schmidt** for *The Mystery Plays*. Costume design: **Suzy Benzinger** for *Very Good Eddie*. Sound design (tie): **Keith Townsend Obadike** for *The Mystery Plays*; Asa F. Wember for *Route 66*. Ensemble performance: **Antoinette Broderick**, **Sun Mee Chomet**, **Anne Fogarty**, **Raymond Fox**, **Kyle Hall**, **Chris Kipiniak**, **Erika LaVonn**, **James McKay**, **Paul Oakley Stovall**, **Gabra Zackman** in *Metamorphoses*.

Roadshow: **Hartford Stage** for *Hedwig and the Angry Inch*. Debut award (tie): **Zack Griffiths** in *The Goat, or Who Is Sylvia?*; **Remy Zaken** in *A Tree Grows in Brooklyn*. Tom Killen Memorial Award: **Bert Bernardi**, artistic director of Downtown Cabaret Children's Company. Special award: **Donald Margulies**.

22ND ANNUAL ELLIOT NORTON AWARDS. For outstanding contribution to the theater in Boston, voted by a Boston Theater Critics Association Selection Committee comprising Terry Byrne, Carolyn Clay, Iris Fanger, Joyce Kulhawik, Jon L. Lehman, Bill Marx, Ed Siegel and Caldwell Titcomb. Sustained Excellence: **Paula Plum**. Productions—Visiting company: ***As You Like It*** produced by Theatre Royal Bath, Sir Peter Hall Company, Broadway in Boston and Huntington Theatre Company at the Wilbur Theatre; Large resident company: ***The Long Christmas Ride Home*** produced by Trinity Repertory Company; Small resident company: ***Collected Stories*** produced by Gloucester Stage Company; Local fringe company (two awards): ***Jesus Hopped the "A" Train*** produced by Company One; ***Pussy on the House*** produced by The Gold Dust Orphans. Musical productions—Large resident company: ***Pacific Overtures*** produced by North Shore Music Theatre; Small resident company: **Sweeney Todd** produced by New Repertory Theatre. Actor—Large company: **Paxton Whitehead** in *What the Butler Saw*, Huntington Theatre Company. Actor—Small company: **Vincent E. Siders** in *Jesus Hopped the "A" Train*, Company One;

Monticel, Boston Playwrights' Theatre; and *Our Lady of 121st Street*, SpeakEasy Stage Company. Actress—Large company: **Julie White** in *Bad Dates*. Actress—Small company: **Leigh Barrett** in *Jacques Brel*, Gloucester Stage Company; *Sweeney Todd* and *The Threepenny Opera*, New Repertory Theatre; and *Follies*, Overture Productions. Director—Large company: **Kevin Moriarty** for *The Merry Wives of Windsor*, Trinity Repertory Company. Director—Small company: **Rick Lombardo** for *Sweeney Todd*, New Repertory Theatre. Scene design: **Yi Li Ming** for *Snow in June*, American Repertory Theatre. Special citations: **Overture Productions** for *Follies* concert; **Puppet Showplace Theatre** for 30 years of dedication to the ancient art of puppetry. Guest of Honor: **Edward Albee**.

20TH ANNUAL HELEN HAYES AWARDS. In recognition of excellence in Washington, D.C., theater, presented by the Washington Theatre Awards Society.

Resident productions—Play: ***The Drawer Boy*** produced by Round House Theatre. Musical: ***Crowns*** produced by Arena Stage. Lead actress, musical: **Jacquelyn Piro** in *110 in the Shade*, Signature Theatre. Lead actor, musical: **Tom McKenzie** in *Ragtime*, Toby's Dinner Theatre. Lead actress, play: **Nancy Robinette** in *The Rivals*, The Shakespeare Theatre. Lead actor, play (tie): **Ted van Griethuysen** in *The Life of Galileo*, The Studio Theatre; **Bruce Nelson** in *The Dazzle,* Rep Stage. Supporting actress, musical: **Lynda Gravátt** in *Crowns*, Arena Stage. Supporting actor, musical: **Stephen Gregory Smith** in *110 in the Shade*, Signature Theatre. Supporting actress, play: **Emily Donahoe** in *Shakespeare in Hollywood*, Arena Stage. Supporting actor, play: **Everett Quinton** in *Shakespeare in Hollywood*, Arena Stage. Director, play: **Kasi Campbell** for *The Dazzle*, Rep Stage. Director, musical: **Regina Taylor** for *Crowns*, Arena Stage. Scenic design, play or musical: **James Kronzer** for *The Drawer Boy*, Round House Theatre. Costume design, play or musical: **Paul Tazewell** for *Camelot*, Arena Stage. Lighting design, play or musical: **Daniel MacLean Wagner** for *The Drawer Boy*, Round House Theatre. Sound design, play or musical: **Martin Desjardins** for *A Midsummer Night's Dream*, The Shakespeare Theatre. Choreography: **Ilona Kessell** for *Ragtime*, Toby's Dinner Theatre. Musical direction: **William F. Hubbard** for *Crowns*, Arena Stage.

Non-resident productions—Production (tie): ***Chicago*** produced by the National Theatre; **Lackawanna Blues** produced by the Studio Theatre. Lead actress: **Bianca Marroquin** in *Chicago,* The National Theatre. Lead actor: **Ruben Santiago-Hudson** in *Lackawanna Blues,* The Studio Theatre. Supporting performer: **Patti Mariano** in *42nd Street*, The National Theatre.

Charles MacArthur Award for outstanding new play: ***Shakespeare in Hollywood*** by **Ken Ludwig**, Arena Stage.

35TH ANNUAL JOSEPH JEFFERSON AWARDS. For achievement in Chicago theater during the 2002–2003 season, given by the Jefferson Awards Committee in 26 competitive categories. Thirty-six producing organizations were nominated for various awards; 13 different companies were honored. Famous Door Theatre, topped all other companies by winning six awards for its production of *The Cider House Rules: Parts I and II.* The Second City e.t.c. followed closely with five awards; Drury Lane Theatre in Evergreen Park and Seanachaí Theatre Company were each thrice honored. The awards ceremony was held November 3, 2003 at the North Shore Center for the Performing Arts in Skokie, Illinois.

Resident productions—New work (three-way tie): *Theatre District* by **Richard Kramer**, About Face Theatre; *Only the Sound* by **Jenny Laird**, Chicago Dramatists; *We All Went Down to Amsterdam* by Bruce Norris, Steppenwolf Theatre Company. New Adaptation: *Crime and Punishment* by Marilyn Campbell and Curt Columbus, Writers' Theatre.

Production of a play: **Famous Door Theatre** for *The Cider House Rules: Parts I and II*. Production of a musical: **Drury Lane Theatre** for *Singin' in the Rain*. Production of a revue (tie): **The Second City e.t.c.** for *Curious George Goes to War* and *Pants on Fire*. Director of a play (Michael Maggio Award): **David Cromer** and **Marc Grapey** for *The Cider House Rules: Parts I and II*, Famous Door Theatre. Director of a musical: **Marc Robin** for *Singin' in the Rain*, Drury Lane Theatre. Director of a revue: **Ron West** for *Curious George Goes to War*, The Second City e.t.c. Actor in a principal role, play: **Larry Neumann Jr.** in *The Cider House Rules: Parts I and II*, Famous Door Theatre. Actress in a principal role, play: **Kymberly Mellen** in *Rocket to the Moon*, Writers' Theatre. Actor in a supporting role, play: **Maury Cooper** in *Judgment at Nuremberg*, Shattered Globe Theatre. Actress in a supporting role, play: **Jennifer Pompa** in *The Cider House Rules: Parts I and II*, Famous Door Theatre. Actor in a principal role, musical: **Richard Kind** in *Bounce*, The Goodman Theatre. Actress in a principal role, musical: **Joyce Faison** in *Lady Day at Emerson's Bar and Grill*, The Chicago Theatre Company. Actor in a supporting role, musical: **Richard Strimer** in *Singin' in the Rain*, Drury Lane Theatre. Actress in a supporting role, musical: **Deanna Dunagan** in *James Joyce's The Dead*, Court Theatre. Actor in a revue: **Keegan-Michael Key** in *Curious George Goes to War*, The Second City e.t.c. Actress in a revue: **Nyima Funk** in *Curious George Goes to War*, The Second City e.t.c. Ensemble: ***The Cider House Rules: Parts I and II*** produced by Famous Door Theatre. Scenic design: **Elizabeth E. Schuch** for *Journey's End*, Seanachaí Theatre Company. Costume design: **Nancy Missimi** for *Cats*, Marriott Theatre. Lighting design: **A. Cameron Zetty** for *Journey's End*, Seanachaí Theatre Company. Sound design: **Josh Schmidt** for *Journey's End*, Seanachaí Theatre Company. Choreography: **Marc Robin** for *Cats*, Marriott Theatre. Original music: **Joseph Fosco** for *The Cider House Rules: Parts I and II*, Famous Door Theatre. Musical direction: **Jeff Lewis** for *James Joyce's The Dead*, Court Theatre.

31ST ANNUAL JOSEPH JEFFERSON CITATIONS WING AWARDS. For outstanding achievement in professional productions during the 2003–2004 season of Chicago area theaters not operating under union contracts. Production (play): *Detective Story* produced by **Strawdog Theatre Company**; *Hannah and Martin* produced by **TimeLine Theatre Company**. Production (musical): *Dr. Sex* produced by **Bailiwick Repertory**. Ensembles: ***Angus, Thongs and Full Frontal Snogging***, Griffin Theatre Company; ***Detective Story***, Strawdog Theatre Company. Director (play): **Jeremy B. Cohen** for *Hannah and Martin*, TimeLine Theatre Company; **Shade Murray** for *Detective Story*, Strawdog Theatre Company. Director (musical): **David Zak** for *Dr. Sex*. New work: **Larry Bortniker** and **Sally Deering** for *Dr. Sex*, Bailiwick Repertory; **Sharon Evans** for *Blind Tasting*, Live Bait Theater; **Kate Fodor** for *Hannah and Martin*, TimeLine Theatre Company. New adaptation: **Christina Calvit** for *Angus, Thongs and Full Frontal Snogging*, Griffin Theatre Company; **Michael Murphy** for *Sin: A Cardinal Deposed*, Bailiwick Repertory. Actress in a principal role (play): **Kate Harris** in *Misery*, Pyewacket; **Donna McGough** in *Happy Days*, The Hypocrites; **Katherine Nawocki** in *Angus, Thongs and Full Frontal Snogging*, Griffin Theatre Company; **Elizabeth Rich** in *Hannah and Martin*, TimeLine Theatre Company. Actress in a principal role (musical): Sarah Laue in *Dr. Sex*, Bailiwick Repertory. Actor in a principal role (play): **Darrell W. Cox** in *Blackbird*, Profiles Theatre; **Jim Sherman** in *Sin: A Cardinal Deposed*, Bailiwick Repertory. Actor in a principal role (musical): **Jamie Axtell** in *Dr. Sex*. Actress in a supporting role (play): **Danica Ivancevic** in *Hannah and Martin*, TimeLine Theatre Company; **Kelly Schumann** in *Steel Magnolias*, Circle Theatre. Actress in a supporting role (musical): **Rebecca Finnegan** in *A Kurt Weill Review: Songs of Darkness and Light*, Theo Ubique Theatre Company. Actor in a supporting role (play): **Scott Aiello** in *Broadway Bound*, Pegasus Players; **Marco Verna** in *Blind Tasting*, Live Bait Theater. Actor in a supporting role (musical): **David Heimann** in *A Kurt Weill Review: Songs of Darkness and Light*, Theo Ubique Theatre Company; **Scott O'Brien** in *Pinafore!*, Bailiwick Repertory. Scenic design: **Tom Burch** for *Misery*, Pyewacket; **Robert A. Knuth** for *Steel Magnolias*, Circle Theatre; **Ray Vlcek** for *Detective Story*, Strawdog Theatre Company. Costume design: **Carol J. Blanchard** for *Amadeus*, Porchlight Music Theatre Chicago. Lighting design: **Brian Sidney Bembridge** for *Hannah and Martin*, TimeLine Theatre Company; **Jared Moore** for *Misery*, Pyewacket. Sound design: **Victoria DeIorio** for *The Shadow*, Lifeline Theatre. Choreography: **Brigitte Ditmars** for *Pinafore!*, Bailiwick Repertory; **Kristen Folzenlogen** for *Dr. Sex*, Bailiwick Repertory. Original music: **Poh'ro** for *Kiwi Black*, MPAACT. Musical direction: **Alan Bukowiecki** for *Dr. Sex*, Bailiwick Repertory; **Eugene Dizon** for *Amadeus*, Porchlight Music Theatre Chicago.

THE THEATER HALL OF FAME

○○○○○

THE THEATER HALL OF FAME was created in 1971 to honor those who have made outstanding contributions to the American theater in a career spanning at least 25 years. Honorees are elected annually by members of the American Theatre Critics Association, members of the Theater Hall of Fame and theater historians. Names of those elected in 2003 and inducted January 26, 2004 appear in ***bold italics***.

George Abbott
Maude Adams
Viola Adams
Jacob Adler
Stella Adler
Edward Albee
Theoni V. Aldredge
Ira Aldridge
Jane Alexander
Mary Alice
Winthrop Ames
Judith Anderson
Maxwell Anderson
Robert Anderson
Julie Andrews
Margaret Anglin
Jean Anouilh
Harold Arlen
George Arliss
Boris Aronson
Adele Astaire
Fred Astaire
Eileen Atkins
Brooks Atkinson
Lauren Bacall
Pearl Bailey
George Balanchine
William Ball
Anne Bancroft
Tallulah Bankhead
Richard Barr
Philip Barry
Ethel Barrymore
John Barrymore
Lionel Barrymore
Howard Bay
Nora Bayes
John Lee Beatty
Julian Beck
Samuel Beckett
Brian Bedford
S.N. Behrman
Norman Bel Geddes
David Belasco
Michael Bennett
Richard Bennett
Robert Russell Bennett
Eric Bentley
Irving Berlin
Sarah Bernhardt
Leonard Bernstein
Earl Blackwell
Kermit Bloomgarden
Jerry Bock
Ray Bolger
Edwin Booth
Junius Brutus Booth
Shirley Booth
Philip Bosco
Dion Boucicault
Alice Brady
Bertolt Brecht
Fannie Brice
Peter Brook
John Mason Brown
Robert Brustein
Billie Burke
Abe Burrows
Richard Burton
Mrs. Patrick Campbell
Zoe Caldwell
Eddie Cantor
Morris Carnovsky
Mrs. Leslie Carter
Gower Champion
Frank Chanfrau
Carol Channing
Stockard Channing
Ruth Chatterton
Paddy Chayefsky
Anton Chekhov
Ina Claire
Bobby Clark
Harold Clurman
Lee J. Cobb
Richard L. Coe
George M. Cohan
Alexander H. Cohen
Jack Cole
Cy Coleman
Constance Collier
Alvin Colt
Betty Comden
Marc Connelly
Barbara Cook
Katharine Cornell

Noel Coward
Jane Cowl
Lotta Crabtree
Cheryl Crawford
Hume Cronyn
Russel Crouse
Charlotte Cushman
Jean Dalrymple
Augustin Daly
E.L. Davenport
Gordon Davidson
Ossie Davis
Ruby Dee
Alfred de Liagre Jr.
Agnes DeMille
Colleen Dewhurst
Howard Dietz
Dudley Digges
Melvyn Douglas
Eddie Dowling
Alfred Drake
Marie Dressler
John Drew
Mrs. John Drew
William Dunlap
Mildred Dunnock
Charles Durning
Eleanora Duse
Jeanne Eagels
Fred Ebb
Florence Eldridge
Lehman Engel
Maurice Evans
Abe Feder
Jose Ferrer
Cy Feuer
Zelda Fichandler
Dorothy Fields
Herbert Fields
Lewis Fields
W.C. Fields
Jules Fisher
Minnie Maddern Fiske
Clyde Fitch
Geraldine Fitzgerald
Henry Fonda
Lynn Fontanne
Horton Foote
Edwin Forrest
Bob Fosse
Rudolf Friml
Charles Frohman
Robert Fryer
Athol Fugard
John Gassner
Larry Gelbart
Peter Gennaro
Grace George
George Gershwin
Ira Gershwin
Bernard Gersten
John Gielgud
W.S. Gilbert
Jack Gilford
William Gillette
Charles Gilpin
Lillian Gish
John Golden
Max Gordon
Ruth Gordon
Adolph Green
Paul Green
Charlotte Greenwood
Jane Greenwood
Joel Grey
Tammy Grimes
George Grizzard
John Guare
Otis L. Guernsey Jr.
Tyrone Guthrie
Uta Hagen
Lewis Hallam
T. Edward Hambleton
Oscar Hammerstein II
Walter Hampden
Otto Harbach
E.Y. Harburg
Sheldon Harnick
Edward Harrigan
Jed Harris
Julie Harris
Rosemary Harris
Sam H. Harris
Rex Harrison
Kitty Carlisle Hart
Lorenz Hart
Moss Hart
Tony Hart
June Havoc
Helen Hayes
Leland Hayward
Ben Hecht
Eileen Heckart
Theresa Helburn
Lillian Hellman
Katharine Hepburn
Victor Herbert
Jerry Herman
James A. Herne
Henry Hewes
Al Hirschfeld
Raymond Hitchcock
Hal Holbrook
Celeste Holm
Hanya Holm
Arthur Hopkins
De Wolf Hopper
John Houseman
Eugene Howard
Leslie Howard
Sidney Howard
Willie Howard
Barnard Hughes

Henry Hull
Josephine Hull
Walter Huston
Earle Hyman
Henrik Ibsen
William Inge
Bernard B. Jacobs
Elsie Janis
Joseph Jefferson
Al Jolson
James Earl Jones
Margo Jones
Robert Edmond Jones
Tom Jones
Jon Jory
Raul Julia
Madeline Kahn
John Kander
Garson Kanin
George S. Kaufman
Danny Kaye
Elia Kazan
Gene Kelly
George Kelly
Fanny Kemble
Jerome Kern
Walter Kerr
Michael Kidd
Richard Kiley
Sidney Kingsley
Kevin Kline
Florence Klotz
Joseph Wood Krutch
Bert Lahr
Burton Lane
Frank Langella
Lawrence Langner
Lillie Langtry
Angela Lansbury
Charles Laughton
Arthur Laurents
Gertrude Lawrence
Jerome Lawrence
Eva Le Gallienne
Canada Lee
Ming Cho Lee
Robert E. Lee
Lotte Lenya
Alan Jay Lerner
Sam Levene
Robert Lewis
Beatrice Lillie
Howard Lindsay
Frank Loesser
Frederick Loewe
Joshua Logan
Pauline Lord
Lucille Lortel
Alfred Lunt
Charles MacArthur
Steele MacKaye
Judith Malina
David Mamet
Rouben Mamoulian
Richard Mansfield
Robert B. Mantell
Fredric March
Nancy Marchand
Julia Marlowe
Ernest H. Martin
Mary Martin
Raymond Massey
Siobhan McKenna
Terrence McNally
Helen Menken
Burgess Meredith
Ethel Merman
David Merrick
Jo Mielziner
Arthur Miller
Marilyn Miller
Liza Minnelli
Helena Modjeska
Ferenc Molnar
Lola Montez
Victor Moore
Robert Morse
Zero Mostel
Anna Cora Mowatt
Paul Muni
Tharon Musser
George Jean Nathan
Mildred Natwick
Nazimova
Patricia Neal
James M. Nederlander
Mike Nichols
Elliot Norton
Sean O'Casey
Clifford Odets
Donald Oenslager
Laurence Olivier
Eugene O'Neill
Jerry Orbach
Geraldine Page
Joseph Papp
Osgood Perkins
Bernadette Peters
Molly Picon
Harold Pinter
Luigi Pirandello
Christopher Plummer
Cole Porter
Robert Preston
Harold Prince
Jose Quintero
Ellis Rabb
John Raitt
Tony Randall
Michael Redgrave
Vanessa Redgrave
Ada Rehan
Elmer Rice

Lloyd Richards
Ralph Richardson
Chita Rivera
Jason Robards
Jerome Robbins
Paul Robeson
Richard Rodgers
Will Rogers
Sigmund Romberg
Harold Rome
Lillian Russell
Donald Saddler
Gene Saks
William Saroyan
Joseph Schildkraut
Harvey Schmidt
Alan Schneider
Gerald Schoenfeld
Arthur Schwartz
Maurice Schwartz
George C. Scott
Marian Seldes
Irene Sharaff
George Bernard Shaw
Sam Shepard
Robert E. Sherwood
J.J. Shubert
Lee Shubert
Herman Shumlin
Neil Simon
Lee Simonson
Edmund Simpson
Otis Skinner
Maggie Smith
Oliver Smith
Stephen Sondheim
E.H. Sothern
Kim Stanley
Jean Stapleton
Maureen Stapleton
Frances Sternhagen
Roger L. Stevens
Isabelle Stevenson
Ellen Stewart
Dorothy Stickney
Fred Stone
Peter Stone
Tom Stoppard
Lee Strasberg
August Strindberg
Elaine Stritch
Charles Strouse
Jule Styne
Margaret Sullavan
Arthur Sullivan
Jessica Tandy
Laurette Taylor
Ellen Terry
Cleon Throckmorton
Tommy Tune
Gwen Verdon
Robin Wagner
Nancy Walker
Eli Wallach
James Wallack
Lester Wallack
Tony Walton
Douglas Turner Ward
David Warfield
Ethel Waters
Clifton Webb
Joseph Weber
Margaret Webster
Kurt Weill
Orson Welles
Mae West
Robert Whitehead
Richard Wilbur
Oscar Wilde
Thornton Wilder
Bert Williams
Tennessee Williams
Lanford Wilson
P.G. Wodehouse
Peggy Wood
Alexander Woollcott
Irene Worth
Teresa Wright
Ed Wynn
Vincent Youmans
Stark Young
Florenz Ziegfeld
Patricia Zipprodt

THE THEATER HALL OF FAME FOUNDERS AWARD

ESTABLISHED IN 1993 in honor of Earl Blackwell, James M. Nederlander, Gerard Oestreicher and Arnold Weissberger, The Theater Hall of Fame Founders Award is voted by the Hall's board of directors to an individual for his or her outstanding contribution to the theater.

1993 James M. Nederlander
1994 Kitty Carlisle Hart
1995 Harvey Sabinson
1996 Henry Hewes
1997 Otis L. Guernsey Jr.
1998 Edward Colton
1999 No Award
2000 Gerard Oestreicher
2000 Arnold Weissberger
2001 Tom Dillon
2002 No Award
2003 Price Berkley

MARGO JONES CITIZEN OF THE THEATER MEDAL

PRESENTED ANNUALLY TO a citizen of the theater who has made a lifetime commitment to theater in the United States and has demonstrated an understanding and affirmation of the craft of playwriting.

1961 Lucille Lortel
1962 Michael Ellis
1963 Judith R. Marechal
George Savage
1964 Richard Barr,
Edward Albee
Clinton Wilder
Richard A. Duprey
1965 Wynn Handman
Marston Balch
1966 Jon Jory
Arthur Ballet
1967 Paul Baker
George C. White
1968 Davey Marlin-Jones
1968 Ellen Stewart
1969 Adrian Hall
Edward Parone
1969 Gordon Davidson
1970 Joseph Papp
1971 Zelda Fichandler
1972 Jules Irving
1973 Douglas Turner Ward
1974 Paul Weidner
1975 Robert Kalfin
1976 Gordon Davidson
1977 Marshall W. Mason
1978 Jon Jory
1979 Ellen Stewart
1980 John Clark Donahue
1981 Lynne Meadow
1982 Andre Bishop
1983 Bill Bushnell
1984 Gregory Mosher
1985 John Lion
1986 Lloyd Richards
1987 Gerald Chapman
1988 No Award
1989 Margaret Goheen
1990 Richard Coe
1991 Otis L. Guernsey Jr.
1992 Abbot Van Nostrand
1993 Henry Hewes
1994 Jane Alexander
1995 Robert Whitehead
1996 Al Hirschfeld
1997 George C. White
1998 James Houghton
1999 George Keathley
2000 Eileen Heckart
2001 Mel Gussow
2002 Emilie S. Kilgore

MUSICAL THEATRE HALL OF FAME

THIS ORGANIZATION WAS established at New York University on November 10, 1993.

Harold Arlen
Irving Berlin
Leonard Bernstein
Eubie Blake
Abe Burrows
George M. Cohan
Dorothy Fields
George Gershwin
Ira Gershwin
Oscar Hammerstein II
E.Y. Harburg
Larry Hart
Jerome Kern
Burton Lane
Alan Jay Lerner
Frank Loesser
Frederick Loewe
Cole Porter
Ethel Merman
Jerome Robbins
Richard Rodgers
Harold Rome

2003–2004 NEW PUBLICATION OF PLAYS, ADAPTATIONS, TRANSLATIONS, COLLECTIONS AND ANTHOLOGIES

○○○○○

Compiled by Rue E. Canvin

PLAYS

Adult Entertainment. Elaine May. Samuel French (acting ed.). $6.50

Anna in the Tropics. Nilo Cruz. Theatre Communications Group (paper). $12.95

Antigone. Sophocles. Oxford. $25.00

Bad Dates. Theresa Rebeck. Samuel French (acting ed.). $6.50

The Band Plays. Mart Crowley. Alyson Publications. $13.95

Big Bill. A.R. Gurney. Broadway Play Publishing. $12.95

Black Monk. David Rabe. Samuel French (acting ed.). $6.50

Boys and Girls. Tom Donaghy. Dramatists Play Service. $6.50

The Carpetbagger's Children and The Actor. Horton Foote. Overlook Press (paper). $14.95

The Cavalcaders. Billy Roche. Dramatists Play Service (acting ed.). $5.95

The Chemistry of Change. Marlane Gomard Meyer. Dramatists Play Service (acting ed.). $6.50

The Coast of Utopia. Tom Stoppard. Grove Press (boxed set). $49.95

The Coming World. Christopher Shinn. Dramatists Play Service (acting ed.). $6.50

Complicite! Complicite. Methuen (paper). $24.50

Crowtet 2. Mac Wellman. Green Integer (paper). $12.95

The Dazzle. Richard Greenberg. Dramatists Play Service (acting ed.). $6.50

The Deatherians. John O'Keefe. Green Integer (paper). $10.95

Dirty Story. John Patrick Shanley. Dramatists Play Service (acting ed.). $6.50

Enchanted April. Matthew Barber. Dramatists Play Service (acting ed.). $6.50

The Exonerated. Jessica Blank and Erik Jensen. Faber and Faber (paper). $13

Frozen. Bryony Lavery. Faber and Faber (paper). $13

Franny's Way. Richard Nelson. Broadway Play Publishing (acting ed.). $7.95

The General From America. Richard Nelson. Samuel French (acting ed.). $6.50

Getting Frankie Married – And Afterwards. Horton Foote. Dramatists Play Service (acting ed.). $6.50

The Gigli Concert. Tom Murphy. Methuen (paper). $11.95

Gum and The Mother of Modern Censorship. Karen Hartman. Dramatists Play Service (acting ed.). $6.50

Hard Time for These Times. Heidi Stillman. Northeastern University Press (paper). $14

Henry IV. William Shakespeare. Adapt. Dakin Matthews. Andak Theatrical Services (paper). $10
Hitchcock Blonde. Terry Johnson. Methuen (paper). $14.95
Hold Please. Annie Weisman. Dramatists Play Service (acting ed.). $6.50
House Arrest. Anna Deavere Smith. Dramatists Play Service (acting ed.). $6.50
House Arrest and Piano: Two Plays. Anna Deavere Smith. Random House (paper). $13
How We Talk in South Boston. David Lindsay-Abaire. Playscripts (acting ed.). $7
The Illusion. Tony Kushner. Broadway Play Publishing (paper). $7.95
I Am My Own Wife. Doug Wright. Faber and Faber (paper). $13
The Importance of Being Earnest and Four Other Plays. Oscar Wilde. Barnes and Noble (paper). $6.95
Inherit the Wind. Jerome Lawrence and Robert E. Lee. Ballantine (paper). $6.99
Is He Dead? Mark Twain. University of California Press. $24.95
Inventing Van Gogh. Steven Dietz. Dramatists Play Service (acting ed.). $6.50
The Jero Plays. Wole Soyinka. Methuen (paper). $13.95
Kimberly Akimbo. David Lindsay-Abaire. Overlook Press (paper). $14.95
Last Dance. Marsha Norman. Samuel French (acting ed.). $6.50
The Last Sunday in June. Jonathan Tolins. Dramatists Play Service (acting ed.). $6.50
Little Fish. Michael John LaChiusa. Dramatists Play Service (acting ed.). $7.50
The Love of Three Oranges. Carlo Gozzi. Lulu Press (paper). $17.98
Las Meninas. Lynn Nottage. Dramatists Play Service (acting ed.). $6.50
Midsummer Nights's Dream. William Shakespeare. Eds. Edward Hall and Roger Warren. Oberon (paper). $16.95
Monster. Neal Bell. Broadway Play Publishing (acting ed.). $7.95
Mrs. Farnsworth. A.R. Gurney. Broadway Play Publishing (paper). $12.95
The Mystery of Attraction. Marlane Gomard Meyer. Dramatists Play Service (acting ed.). $6.50
The Notebook. Wendy Kesselman. Dramatists Play Service (acting ed.). $6.50
Omnium Gatherum. Theresa Rebeck and Alexandra Gersten-Vassilaros. Samuel French (acting ed.). $6.50
The Oresteia. Aeschylus. Random House. $22
Oroonoko. Aphra Behn. Ed. Janet Todd. Penguin (paper). $9
Our Town. Thornton Wilder. HarperCollins (paper). $9.95
Polish Joke. David Ives. Dramatists Play Service (acting ed.). $6.50
Reckless and Other Plays. Craig Lucas. Theatre Communications Group (paper). $16.95
The Retreat From Moscow. William Nicholson. Random House (paper). $11
Rocket Man. Steven Dietz. Dramatists Play Service (acting ed.). $5.95
Saint Lucy's Eyes. Bridgette Wimberly. Samuel French (acting ed.). $6.50
Samuel Beckett Trilogy. Samuel Beckett. Riverrun (paper). $19.95
Scattergood. Anto Howard. Dramatists Play Service (acting ed.). $6.50
Semi-Monde. Noël Coward. Methuen (paper). $13.95
Snow Angel. David Lindsay-Abaire. Playscripts (acting ed.). $12.75
String Fever. Jacquelyn Reingold. Dramatists Play Service (acting ed.). $6.50
Take Me Out. Richard Greenberg. Faber and Faber (paper). $14
Ten Unknowns. Jon Robin Baitz. Dramatists Play Service (acting ed.). $6.50
36 Views. Naomi Iizuka. Overlook Press (paper). $14.95

This Thing of Darkness. Craig Lucas and David Schulner. Dramatists Play Service (acting ed.) $6.50

Three One-Act Plays. Woody Allen. Random House (paper). $13.95

Topdog/Underdog. Suzan-Lori Parks. Theatre Communications Group (paper). $12.95

A Touch of the Poet and More Stately Mansions. Eugene O'Neill. Ed. Martha Gilman Bower. Yale (paper). $15.95

The Violet Hour. Richard Greenberg. Faber and Faber (paper). $14

What Didn't Happen. Christopher Shinn. Dramatists Play Service (acting ed.). $6.50

What Mama Said: An Epic Drama. Osonye Tess Onwueme. Wayne State University Press (paper). $19.95.

Wonder of the World. David Lindsay-Abaire. Dramatists Play Service (acting ed.). $6.50

ADAPTATIONS

Dance of Death. August Strindberg. Adapt. Richard Greenberg. Dramatists Play Service (acting ed.). $6.50

Fortune's Fool. Ivan Turgenev. Adapt. Mike Poulton. Overlook Press (paper). $14.95

Miss Julie. August Strindberg. Adapt. Richard Nelson. Broadway Play Publishing (paper). $7.95

Misanthrope. Molière. Adapt. Constance Congdon. Broadway Play Publishing (paper). $7.95

Plays by Anton Chekhov. Anton Chekhov. Adapt. Richard Nelson. Broadway Play Publishing (paper). $14.95

Tattoo Girl. Naomi Iizuka. Playscripts (acting ed.). $7

The Shoemaker's Holiday. Thomas Dekker. Adapt. by Bernard Sahlins. Ivan R. Dee (paper). $7.95

TRANSLATIONS

The Castle. Franz Kafka. Trans. Donald Fishelson and Aaron Leichter. Dramatists Play Service (paper). $5.95

Chekhov: The Essential Plays. Anton Chekhov. Trans. Michael Henry Heim. Random House (paper). $8.95

The Church. Louis-Ferdinand Celine. Trans. Mark Spitzer and Simon Green. Green Integer (paper). $13.95

The Figaro Trilogy. Beaumarchais. Trans. David Coward. Oxford (paper). $12.95

Faust. Goethe. Trans. John R. Williams. Wordsworth Editions (paper). $5.95

Fear and Misery of the Third Reich. Bertolt Brecht. Trans. John Willett. Methuen (paper). $16

Fragments of the Artwork. Jean Genet. Trans. Charlotte Mandell. Stanford University Press (paper). $19.95

The Methuen Book of Latin American Plays. Mario Vargas Llosa; Egon Wolff; José Triana. Trans. Gwynne Edwards. Methuen (paper). $24.95

The Recognition of Sakuntala. Kalidasa. Trans. Arthur W. Ryder. Dover (paper). $2.50

R.U.R. (Rossum's Universal Robots). Karel Capek. Trans. Claudia Novack. Penguin (paper). $8

COLLECTIONS

The Birds and Other Plays. Aristophanes. Trans. David Barrett and Alan H. Sommerstein. Penguin (paper). $11

The Castle of Otranto and The Mysterious Mother. Horace Walpole. Ed. Frederick S. Frank. Broadview Press. (paper). $9.95

Ibsen's Selected Plays: Norton Critical Edition. Henrik Ibsen. Ed. Brian Johnston. Norton (paper). $20

The Labor of Life: Selected Plays. Hanoch Levin. Trans. Barbara Harshav. Stanford University Press (paper). $27.95

Misadventure: Monologues and Short Pieces. Donald Margulies. Dramatists Play Service (acting ed.). $6.50

Our Lady of 121st Street and Other Plays. Stephen Adly Guirgis. Faber and Faber (paper). $15

The Portable Arthur Miller. Arthur Miller. Ed. Christopher Bigsby. Penguin (revised; paper). $17

Selected Plays of Arthur Laurents. Arthur Laurents. Watson-Guptill (cloth). $19.95

Terry Johnson: Plays 3. Terry Johnson. Methuen (paper). $24.99

Ward No. 6 and Other Stories. Anton Chekhov. Barnes and Noble (paper). $7.95

Women in Turmoil: Six Plays by Mercedes de Acosta. Mercedes de Acosta. Ed. Robert A. Schanke. Southern Illinois University Press (cloth). $40

ANTHOLOGIES

The Broadview Anthology of Romantic Drama. Ed. Jeffrey N. Cox and Michael Gamer. Broadview Press (paper). $29.95

Four Roman Comedies. Ed. Michael J. Walton. Methuen. (paper). $19.95

Five Comedies From the Italian Renaissance. Trans. Laura Giannetti and Guido Ruggiero. Johns Hopkins University Press (paper). $19.95

Holy Terrors: Latin American Women Perform. Ed. Diana Taylor and Roselyn Costantino. Duke University Press (paper). $23.95

The New American Musical Theatre: Libretti. Ed. Wiley Hausam. Theatre Communications Group (paper). $18.95

Plays and Playwrights 2004. Ed. Martin Denton. New York Theatre Experience (paper). $16

Plays for the Theatre: A Drama Anthology. Oscar G. Brockett and Robert J. Ball. Thomson Learning (eighth edition; paper). $56.95

Russell Simmons' Def Poetry Jam on Broadway . . . and More. Eds. Danny Simmons, Russell Simmons and Stan Lathan. Simon and Schuster. $20

Short Arabic Plays: An Anthology. Ed. Salma Khadra Jayyusi. Interlink Books (paper). $25

Voices Made Flesh: Performing Women's Autobiography. Ed. Lynn C. Miller, Jacqueline Taylor and M. Heather Carver. University of Wisconsin (paper). $26.95

The Wadsworth Anthology of Drama. Ed. W.B. Worthen. Thomson Learning (fourth edition; paper). $75.95

IN MEMORIAM

MAY 2003–MAY 2004

○○○○○

PERFORMERS

Adams, Cecily (46) – March 3, 2004
Anderson, Carl (58) – February 23, 2004
Barnett, Etta Moten (102) – January 2, 2004
Bates, Alan (69) – December 27, 2003
Berry, Fred (52) – October 21, 2003
Bettger, Lyle (88) – September 24, 2003
Bradlee, Frederic (84) – July 12, 2003
Brown, Charles (57) – January 8, 2004
Capers, Virginia (78) – May 6, 2004
Carney, Art (85) – November 9, 2003
Chaikin, Joseph (67) – June 22, 2003
Chitnis, Leela (89) – July 13, 2003
Clarke, David (95) – April 18, 2004
Cloutier, Suzanne (80) – December 2, 2003
Cronyn, Hume (91) – June 15, 2003
Cusack, Richard "Dick" (77) – June 2, 2003
Dawson, Ronnie (64) – September 30, 2003
Ebsen, Buddy (95) – July 6, 2003
Elam, Jack (87) – October 21, 2003
England, Hal (71) – November 6, 2003
Evans, David Dillon (83) – March 21, 2004
Falkenhain, Patricia (77) – January 5, 2004
Farrell, Tommy (82) – May 2, 2004
Flanagan, Pauline (77) – June 28, 2003
Fonaroff, Nina (89) – August 14, 2003
Gray, Spalding (62) – March 7, 2004
Goz, Harry (71) – September 6, 2003
Hackett, Buddy (78) – June 30, 2003
Hagen, Uta (84) – January 14, 2004
Harris, Jeff (68) – February 2, 2004
Hemmings, David (62) – December 3, 2003
Hepburn, Katharine (96) – June 29, 2003
Hindman, Earl (61) – December 29, 2003
Hines, Gregory (57) – August 9, 2003
Hope, Bob (100) – July 27, 2003
Kilpatrick, Lincoln (73) – May 18, 2004
King, Alan (76) – May 9, 2004
Lange, Hope (70) – December 19, 2003
Lee, Anna (91) – May 14, 2004
Leonard, Lu (77) – May 14, 2004
Loudon, Dorothy (70) – November 15, 2003
McCambridge, Mercedes (87) – March 2, 2004
Manning, Irene (91) – May 28, 2004
Marshall, William (78) – June 11, 2003
Miller, Ann (80) – January 22, 2004
Miner, Jan (86) – February 15, 2004
Mitchell, Gordon (80) – September 20, 2003
Moran, Michael P. (59) – February 4, 2004
O'Connor, Donald (78) – September 27, 2003
O'Neal, Ron (66) – January 14, 2004
Pastorelli, Robert (49) – March 8, 2004
Paulsen, Albert (78) – April 25, 2004
Peck, Gregory (87) – June 12, 2003
Punsly, Barnard (80) – January 20, 2004
Raize, Jason (28) – February 6, 2004
Randall, Tony (84) – May 17, 2004
Randolph, John (88) – February 24, 2004
Redwood, John Henry III (60) – June 17, 2003
Ritter, John (54) – September 11, 2003
Rivas, Carlos (78) – June 16, 2003
Robbins, Rex (68) – September 23, 2003
Rule, Janice (72) – October 17, 2003
Singleton, Penny (95) – November 12, 2003
Stanley, Florence (79) – October 3, 2003
Trenier, Claude (84) – November 17, 2003
Ustinov, Peter (82) – March 28, 2004
Waymire, Kellie (36) – November 13, 2003
Welch, Elisabeth (99) – July 15, 2003
White, Barry (58) – July 4, 2003
Winde, Beatrice (79) – January 3, 2004
Winfield, Paul (62) – March 7, 2004
Wright, Brian (42) – July 29, 2003
Ziegler, Anne (93) – October 13, 2003

PLAYWRIGHTS

Axelrod, George (81) – June 21, 2003
Evans, Don (65) – October 16, 2003
Gardner, Herb (68) – September 24, 2003
Lawrence, Jerome (88) – February 29, 2004
Newman, David (66) – June 27, 2003

COMPOSERS, LYRICISTS, SONGWRITERS

Berger, Arthur (91) – October 7, 2003

Curet, Catalino "Tite" (77) – August 5, 2003
Guerin, John (64) – January 5, 2004
Karlin, Fred (67) – March 26, 2004
Kempel, Arthur (58) – March 3, 2004
Kupferman, Meyer (77) – November 26, 2003
Mantooth, Frank (56) – January 30, 2004
Matlovsky, Samuel "Sandy" (82) – February 17, 2004
Small, Michael (64) – November 25, 2003
Smith, Elliott (34) – October 21, 2003
Wing, Jessica Grace (31) – July 19, 2003
Warren Zevon (56) – September 7, 2003

PRODUCERS, DIRECTORS, CHOREOGRAPHERS

Allen, Lewis M. (81) – December 8, 2003
Arthur, Hartney J. (86) – March 24, 2004
Broccoli, Dana (82) – February 29, 2004
Cullman, Joan S. (72) – March 18, 2004
Estess, Jenifer (40) – December 16, 2003
Gaither, Gant (86) – February 16, 2004
Gutierrez, Gerald (53) – December 30, 2003
Jiranek, David (45) – August 17, 2003
Karp, Beverly Bailis (72) – June 10, 2003
Kazan, Elia (94) – September 28, 2003
O'Donnell, May (97) – February 1, 2004
Savage, Lesley (90) – October 8, 2003
Schwartz, Bernard (85) – October 17, 2003
Stark, Ray (88) – January 17, 2004

MUSICIANS

Baker, Julius (87) – August 6, 2003
Bennett, William (49) – October 7, 2003
Bey, James Hawthorne (91) – April 8, 2004
Carter, Benny (95) – July 12, 2003
Cash, Johnny (71) – September 12, 2003
Fontana, Carl (75) – October 9, 2003
Henderson, Luther (84) – July 29, 2003
Hucko, Michael "Peanuts" (85) – June 19, 2003
Istomin, Eugene (77) – October 10, 2003
Jackson, Chubby (84) – October 1, 2003
Knepper, Jimmy (75) – June 14, 2003
Lowe, Frank (60) – September 19, 2003
Mann, Herbie (73) – July 1, 2003
Marcus, Marie (89) – October 10, 2003
Mitchell, Grover (73) – August 6, 2003
Ramone, Dee Dee (50) – June 5, 2003
Wilburn, Teddy (71) – November 24, 2003

ARTS WRITERS AND CRITICS

Norton, Elliot (100) – July 20, 2003
McCulloh, T.H. (69) – March 28, 2004
Taylor, Markland (67) – July 6, 2003
Warfield, Polly (89) – October 2, 2003

OTHERS OF NOTE

Bryant, Mary (71) – February 22, 2004 Broadway press agent
Cooke, Alistair (95) – March 29, 2004 Journalist and commentator
Falkenberg, Jinx (84) – August 27, 2003 Radio and television host
Gersh, Phil (92) – May 10, 2004 Founder of the Gersh Agency
Harth, Robert (47) – January 30, 2004 Carnegie Hall artistic and executive director
Henline, Darrell (75) – September 25, 2003 Publisher of *Cabaret Scenes*
Kassel, Tichi W. (77) – March 8, 2004 Publisher emeritus of *The Hollywood Reporter*
Keeshan, Bob (76) – January 23, 2004 Title character in television's *Captain Kangaroo*
Klavan, Gene (79) – April 8, 2004 New York radio personality
Orrell, John. (68) – September 16, 2003 Globe Theatre historian
Paar, Jack (85) – January 27, 2004 Talk show host
Phillips, Sam (80) – July 30, 2003 First to record Elvis Presley
Rigler, Lloyd E. (88) – December 7, 2003 Arts philanthropist
Samuelson, Carl (77) – April 20, 2004 Founder of Stagedoor Manor
Stevenson, Isabelle L. (90) – December 28, 2003 Chairman of the American Theatre Wing, actor and dancer
Tisch, Laurence (80) – November 15, 2003 Arts and education philanthropist
Tremayne, Les (90) – December 19, 2003 Noted radio actor and voiceover artist
Wojtasik, George (69) – April 30, 2004 Former managing director of Equity Library Theatre

THE BEST PLAYS AND MAJOR PRIZEWINNERS 1894–2004

OOOOO

LISTED IN ALPHABETICAL order below are all works selected as Best Plays in previous volumes of the *Best Plays* series, except for the seasons of 1996–97 through 1999–2000. During those excluded seasons, *Best Plays* honored only major prizewinners and those who received special *Best Plays* citations. Opposite each title is given the volume in which the play is honored, its opening date and its total number of performances. Two separate opening-date and performance-number entries signify two separate engagements when the original production transferred. Plays marked with an asterisk (*) were still playing June 1, 2004 and their number of performances was figured through May 31, 2004. Adaptors and translators are indicated by (ad) and (tr), the symbols (b), (m) and (l) stand for the author of the book, music and lyrics in the case of musicals and (c) signifies the credit for the show's conception, (i) for its inspiration. Entries identified as 94–99 and 99–09 are late-19th and early-20th century plays from one of the retrospective volumes. 94–95, 95–96, 96–97, 97–98, 98–99 and 99–00 are late-20th century plays.

PLAY	VOLUME	OPENED	PERFS
Abe Lincoln in Illinois—Robert E. Sherwood	38–39	Oct. 15, 1938	472
Abraham Lincoln—John Drinkwater	19–20	Dec. 15, 1919	193
Accent on Youth—Samson Raphaelson	34–35	Dec. 25, 1934	229
Adam and Eva—Guy Bolton, George Middleton	19–20	Sept. 13, 1919	312
Adaptation—Elaine May; and Next—Terrence McNally	68–69	Feb. 10, 1969	707
Affairs of State—Louis Verneuil	50–51	Sept. 25, 1950	610
After the Fall—Arthur Miller	63–64	Jan. 23, 1964	208
After the Rain—John Bowen	67–68	Oct. 9, 1967	64
After-Play—Anne Meara	94–95	Jan. 31, 1995	400
Agnes of God—John Pielmeier	81–82	Mar. 30, 1982	599
Ah, Wilderness!—Eugene O'Neill	33–34	Oct. 2, 1933	289
Ain't Supposed to Die a Natural Death—(b, m, l) Melvin Van Peebles	71–72	Oct. 20, 1971	325
Alien Corn—Sidney Howard	32–33	Feb. 20, 1933	98
Alison's House—Susan Glaspell	30–31	Dec. 1, 1930	41
All My Sons—Arthur Miller	46–47	Jan. 29, 1947	328
All in the Timing—David Ives	93–94	Feb. 17, 1994	526
All Over Town—Murray Schisgal	74–75	Dec. 29, 1974	233
All the Way Home—Tad Mosel, based on James Agee's novel *A Death in the Family*	60–61	Nov. 30, 1960	333
Allegro—(b, l) Oscar Hammerstein II, (m) Richard Rodgers	47–48	Oct. 10, 1947	315
Amadeus—Peter Shaffer	80–81	Dec. 17, 1980	1,181

Bride of the Lamb, The—William Hurlbut .... 25–26 ..... Mar. 30, 1926 109
Brief Moment—S.N. Behrman .... 31–32 ..... Nov. 9, 1931 129
Brigadoon—(b, l) Alan Jay Lerner,
(m) Frederick Loewe .... 46–47 ..... Mar. 13, 1947 581
Broadway—Philip Dunning, George Abbott .... 26–27 ..... Sept. 16, 1926 603
Broadway Bound—Neil Simon .... 86–87 ..... Dec. 4, 1986 756
Burlesque—George Manker Watters, Arthur Hopkins .... 27–28 ..... Sept. 1, 1927 372
Bus Stop—William Inge .... 54–55 ..... Mar. 2, 1955 478
Butley—Simon Gray .... 72–73 ..... Oct. 31, 1972 135
Butter and Egg Man, The—George S. Kaufman .... 25–26 ..... Sept. 23, 1925 243
Butterflies Are Free—Leonard Gershe .... 69–70 ..... Oct. 21, 1969 1,128

Cabaret—(b) Joe Masteroff, (m) John Kander, (l) Fred
Ebb, based on John van Druten's play *I Am a*
Camera and stories by Christopher Isherwood .... 66–67 ..... Nov. 20, 1966 1,165
Cactus Flower—Abe Burrows, based on a play
by Pierre Barillet and Jean-Pierre Gredy .... 65–66 ..... Dec. 8, 1965 1,234
Caine Mutiny Court-Martial, The—Herman Wouk,
based on his novel .... 53–54 ..... Jan. 20, 1954 415
California Suite—Neil Simon .... 76–77 ..... June 10, 1976 445
Caligula—Albert Camus, (ad) Justin O'Brien .... 59–60 ..... Feb. 16, 1960 38
Call It a Day—Dodie Smith .... 35–36 ..... Jan. 28, 1936 194
Camping with Henry & Tom—Mark St. Germain .... 94–95 ..... Feb. 20, 1995 88
Candide—(b) Lillian Hellman, based on Voltaire's satire,
(l) Richard Wilbur, John Latouche, Dorothy Parker,
(m) Leonard Bernstein .... 56–57 ..... Dec. 1, 1956 73
Candle in the Wind—Maxwell Anderson .... 41–42 ..... Oct. 22, 1941 95
Caretaker, The—Harold Pinter .... 61–62 ..... Oct. 4, 1961 165
*Caroline, or Change—Tony Kushner .... 03–04 ..... Nov. 30, 2003 106
03–04 ..... May 2, 2004 32
Case of Rebellious Susan, The—Henry Arthur Jones .... 94–99 ..... Dec. 20, 1894 80
Cat on a Hot Tin Roof—Tennessee Williams .... 54–55 ..... Mar. 24, 1955 694
Cats—(m) Andrew Lloyd Webber, based on T.S. Eliot's
Old Possum's Book of Practical Cats, (add'l l)
Trevor Nunn, Richard Stilgoe .... 82–83 ..... Oct. 7, 1982 7,485
Celebration—(b, l) Tom Jones, (m) Harvey Schmidt .... 68–69 ..... Jan. 22, 1969 109
Chalk Garden, The—Enid Bagnold .... 55–56 ..... Oct. 26, 1955 182
Changelings, The—Lee Wilson Dodd .... 23–24 ..... Sept. 17, 1923 128
Changing Room, The—David Storey .... 72–73 ..... Mar. 6, 1973 192
Chapter Two—Neil Simon .... 77–78 ..... Dec. 4, 1977 857
Chicago—Maurine Dallas Watkins .... 26–27 ..... Dec. 30, 1926 172
Chicago—(b) Fred Ebb, Bob Fosse, (m) John Kander,
(l) Fred Ebb,based on the play by Maurine Dallas
Watkins .... 75–76 ..... June 3, 1975 898
Chicken Feed—Guy Bolton .... 23–24 ..... Sept. 24, 1923 144
Children of a Lesser God—Mark Medoff .... 79–80 ..... Mar. 30, 1980 887
Children's Hour, The—Lillian Hellman .... 34–35 ..... Nov. 20, 1934 691

Play	Season	Opened	Perfs.
Creation of the World and Other Business, The—Arthur Miller	72–73	Nov. 30, 1972	20
Creeps—David E. Freeman	73–74	Dec. 4, 1973	15
Crimes of the Heart—Beth Henley	80–81	Dec. 9, 1980	35
	81–82	Nov. 4, 1981	535
Criminal Code, The—Martin Flavin	29–30	Oct. 2, 1929	173
Crucible, The—Arthur Miller	52–53	Jan. 22, 1953	197
Cryptogram, The—David Mamet	94–95	Apr. 13, 1995	62
Curtains—Stephen Bill	95–96	May 21, 1996	64
Cynara—H.M. Harwood, R.F. Gore-Browne	31–32	Nov. 2, 1931	210
Da—Hugh Leonard	77–78	May 1, 1978	697
Daisy Mayme—George Kelly	26–27	Oct. 25, 1926	112
Damask Cheek, The—John van Druten, Lloyd Morris	42–43	Oct 22, 1942	93
Dance and the Railroad, The—David Henry Hwang	81–82	July 16, 1981	181
Dancing at Lughnasa—Brian Friel	91–92	Oct. 24, 1991	421
Dancing Mothers—Edgar Selwyn, Edmund Goulding	24–25	Aug. 11, 1924	312
Dark at the Top of the Stairs, The—William Inge	57–58	Dec. 5, 1957	468
Dark Is Light Enough, The—Christopher Fry	54–55	Feb. 23, 1955	69
Darkness at Noon—Sidney Kingsley, based on Arthur Koestler's novel	50–51	Jan. 13, 1951	186
Darling of the Gods, The—David Belasco, John Luther Long	99–09	Dec. 3, 1902	182
Daughters of Atreus—Robert Turney	36–37	Oct. 14, 1936	13
Day in the Death of Joe Egg, A—Peter Nichols	67–68	Feb. 1, 1968	154
Dazzle, The—Richard Greenberg	01–02	Mar. 5, 2002	80
Dead End—Sidney Kingsley	35–36	Oct. 28, 1935	687
Deadly Game, The—James Yaffe, based on Friedrich Duerrenmatt's novel	59–60	Feb. 2, 1960	39
Dear Ruth—Norman Krasna	44–45	Dec. 13, 1944	683
Death of a Salesman—Arthur Miller	48–49	Feb. 10, 1949	742
Death Takes a Holiday—Alberto Casella, (ad) Walter Ferris	29–30	Dec. 26, 1929	180
Deathtrap—Ira Levin	77–78	Feb. 26, 1978	1,793
Deburau—Sacha Guitry, (ad) Harley Granville Barker	20–21	Dec. 23, 1920	189
Decision—Edward Chodorov	43–44	Feb. 2, 1944	160
Déclassée—Zoë Akins	19–20	Oct. 6, 1919	257
Deep Are the Roots—Arnaud d'Usseau, James Gow	45–46	Sept. 26, 1945	477
Delicate Balance, A—Edward Albee	66–67	Sept. 22, 1966	132
Deputy, The—Rolf Hochhuth, (ad) Jerome Rothenberg	63–64	Feb. 26, 1964	109
Design for Living—Noël Coward	32–33	Jan. 24, 1933	135
Designated Mourner, The—Wallace Shawn (special citation)	99–00	May 13, 2000	30+
Desire Under the Elms—Eugene O'Neill	24–25	Nov. 11, 1924	208
Desperate Hours, The—Joseph Hayes, based on his novel	54–55	Feb. 10, 1955	212
Destiny of Me, The—Larry Kramer	92–93	Oct. 20, 1992	175

Enchanted, The—Maurice Valency, based on Jean Giraudoux's play *Intermezzo* ..... 49–50 ..... Jan. 18, 1950 45
End of Summer—S.N. Behrman ..... 35–36 ..... Feb. 17, 1936 153
Enemy, The—Channing Pollock ..... 25–26 ..... Oct. 20, 1925 203
Enough, Footfalls and Rockaby—Samuel Beckett ..... 83–84 ..... Feb. 16, 1984 78
Enter Madame—Gilda Varesi, Dolly Byrne ..... 20–21 ..... Aug. 16, 1920 350
Entertainer, The—John Osborne ..... 57–58 ..... Feb. 12, 1958 97
Epitaph for George Dillon—John Osborne, Anthony Creighton ..... 58–59 ..... Nov. 4, 1958 23
Equus—Peter Shaffer ..... 74–75 ..... Oct. 24, 1974 1,209
Escape—John Galsworthy ..... 27–28 ..... Oct. 26, 1927 173
Ethan Frome—Owen and Donald Davis, based on Edith Wharton's novel ..... 35–36 ..... Jan. 21, 1936 120
Eve of St. Mark, The—Maxwell Anderson ..... 42–43 ..... Oct. 7, 1942 307
Excursion—Victor Wolfson ..... 36–37 ..... Apr. 9, 1937 116
Execution of Justice—Emily Mann ..... 85–86 ..... Mar. 13, 1986 12
Extra Man, The—Richard Greenberg ..... 91–92 ..... May 19, 1992 39
Extremities—William Mastrosimone ..... 82–83 ..... Dec. 22, 1982 325

Fair Country, A—Jon Robin Baitz ..... 95–96 ..... Oct. 29, 1995 153
Fall Guy, The—James Gleason, George Abbott ..... 24–25 ..... Mar. 10, 1925 176
Falsettoland—William Finn, James Lapine ..... 90–91 ..... June 28, 1990 215
Family Business—Dick Goldberg ..... 77–78 ..... Apr. 12, 1978 438
Family Portrait—Lenore Coffee, William Joyce Cowen ..... 38–39 ..... May 8, 1939 111
Famous Mrs. Fair, The—James Forbes ..... 19–20 ..... Dec. 22, 1919 344
Far Country, A—Henry Denker ..... 60–61 ..... Apr. 4, 1961 271
Farmer Takes a Wife, The—Frank B. Elser, Marc Connelly, based on Walter D. Edmonds's novel *Rome Haul* ..... 34–35 ..... Oct. 30, 1934 104
Fatal Weakness, The—George Kelly ..... 46–47 ..... Nov. 19, 1946 119
Fences—August Wilson ..... 86–87 ..... Mar. 26, 1987 526
Fiddler on the Roof—(b) Joseph Stein, (l) Sheldon Harnick, (m) Jerry Bock, based on Sholom Aleichem's stories ..... 64–65 ..... Sept. 22, 1964 3,242
5th of July, The—Lanford Wilson ..... 77–78 ..... Apr. 27, 1978 159
Find Your Way Home—John Hopkins ..... 73–74 ..... Jan. 2, 1974 135
Finishing Touches—Jean Kerr ..... 72–73 ..... Feb. 8, 1973 164
Fiorello!—(b) Jerome Weidman, George Abbott, (l) Sheldon Harnick, (m) Jerry Bock ..... 59–60 ..... Nov. 23, 1959 795
Firebrand, The—Edwin Justus Mayer ..... 24–25 ..... Oct. 15, 1924 269
Fires in the Mirror—Anna Deavere Smith ..... 91–92 ..... May 12, 1992 109
First Lady—Katherine Dayton, George S. Kaufman ..... 35–36 ..... Nov. 26, 1935 246
First Monday in October—Jerome Lawrence, Robert E. Lee ..... 78–79 ..... Oct. 3, 1978 79
First Mrs. Fraser, The—St. John Ervine ..... 29–30 ..... Dec. 28, 1929 352
First Year, The—Frank Craven ..... 20–21 ..... Oct. 20, 1920 760
Five Finger Exercise—Peter Shaffer ..... 59–60 ..... Dec. 2, 1959 337
Five-Star Final—Louis Weitzenkorn ..... 30–31 ..... Dec. 30, 1930 175

GOLDEN BOY—Clifford Odets .... 37–38 ..... Nov. 4, 1937 250
GOOD—C.P. Taylor .... 82–83 ..... Oct. 13, 1982 125
GOOD DOCTOR, THE—(ad) Neil Simon, suggested by stories by Anton Chekhov .... 73–74 ..... Nov. 27, 1973 208
GOOD GRACIOUS ANNABELLE—Clare Kummer .... 09–19 ..... Oct. 31, 1916 111
GOOD TIMES ARE KILLING ME, THE—Lynda Barry .... 90–91 ..... May 21, 1991 207
GOODBYE, MY FANCY—Fay Kanin .... 48–49 ..... Nov. 17, 1948 446
GOOSE HANGS HIGH, THE—Lewis Beach .... 23–24 ..... Jan. 29, 1924 183
GRAND HOTEL—Vicki Baum, (ad) W. A. Drake .... 30–31 ..... Nov. 13, 1930 459
GRAND HOTEL: THE MUSICAL—(b) Luther Davis, (m, l) Robert Wright, George Forrest, (add'l m, l) Maury Yeston, based on Vicki Baum's *Grand Hotel* .... 89–90 ..... Nov. 12, 1989 1,077
GRAPES OF WRATH, THE—(ad) Frank Galati from the novel by John Steinbeck .... 89–90 ..... Mar. 22, 1990 188
GREAT DIVIDE, THE—William Vaughn Moody .... 99–09 ..... Oct. 3, 1906 238
GREAT GOD BROWN, THE—Eugene O'Neill .... 25–26 ..... Jan. 23, 1926 271
GREAT WHITE HOPE, THE—Howard Sackler .... 68–69 ..... Oct. 3, 1968 556
GREEN BAY TREE, THE—Mordaunt Shairp .... 33–34 ..... Oct. 20, 1933 166
GREEN GODDESS, THE—William Archer .... 20–21 ..... Jan. 18, 1921 440
GREEN GROW THE LILACS—Lynn Riggs .... 30–31 ..... Jan. 26, 1931 64
GREEN HAT, THE—Michael Arlen .... 25–26 ..... Sept. 15, 1925 231
GREEN JULIA—Paul Abelman .... 72–73 ..... Nov. 16, 1972 147
GREEN PASTURES, THE—Marc Connelly, based on Roark Bradford's *Ol' Man Adam and His Chillun* .... 29–30 ..... Feb. 26, 1930 640
GROSS INDECENCY: THE THREE TRIALS OF OSCAR WILDE—Moisés Kaufman .... 97–98 ..... June 5, 1997 534
GUS AND AL—Albert Innaurato .... 88–89 ..... Feb. 27, 1989 25
GUYS AND DOLLS—(b) Jo Swerling, Abe Burrows, based on a story and characters by Damon Runyon, (m, l) Frank Loesser .... 50–51 ..... Nov. 24, 1950 1,200
GYPSY—Maxwell Anderson .... 28–29 ..... Jan. 14, 1929 64

HADRIAN VII—Peter Luke, based on works by Fr. Rolfe .... 68–69 ..... JAN. 8, 1969 359
HAMP—John Wilson, based on an episode from a novel by J.L. Hodson .... 66–67 ..... Mar. 9, 1967 101
HAPGOOD—Tom Stoppard .... 94–95 ..... Dec. 4, 1994 129
HAPPY TIME, THE—Samuel Taylor, based on Robert Fontaine's book .... 49–50 ..... Jan. 24, 1950 614
HARRIET—Florence Ryerson, Colin Clements .... 42–43 ..... Mar. 3, 1943 377
HARVEY—Mary Chase .... 44–45 ..... Nov. 1, 1944 1,775
HASTY HEART, THE—John Patrick .... 44–45 ..... Jan. 3, 1945 207
HE WHO GETS SLAPPED—Leonid Andreyev, (ad) Gregory Zilboorg .... 21–22 ..... Jan. 9, 1922 308
HEART OF MARYLAND, THE—David Belasco .... 94–99 ..... Oct. 22, 1895 240
HEIDI CHRONICLES, THE—Wendy Wasserstein .... 88–89 ..... Dec. 11, 1988 81
88–89 ..... Mar. 9, 1989 621
HEIRESS, THE—Ruth and Augustus Goetz, suggested by Henry James's novel *Washington Square* .... 47–48 ..... Sept. 29, 1947 410

Leah Kleschna—C.M.S. McLellan ... 99–09 ... Dec. 12, 1904 ... 131
Left Bank, The—Elmer Rice ... 31–32 ... Oct. 5, 1931 ... 242
Lend Me a Tenor—Ken Ludwig ... 88–89 ... Mar. 2, 1989 ... 481
Les Liaisons Dangereuses—Christopher Hampton, based on Choderlos de Laclos's novel ... 86–87 ... Apr. 30, 1987 ... 148
Les Misérables—(b) Alain Boublil, Claude-Michel Schönberg, (m) Claude-Michel Schönberg, (l) Herbert Kretzmer, add'l material James Fenton, based on Victor Hugo's novel ... 86–87 ... Mar. 12, 1987 ... 6,680
Lesson From Aloes, A—Athol Fugard ... 80–81 ... Nov. 17, 1980 ... 96
Let Us Be Gay—Rachel Crothers ... 28–29 ... Feb. 19, 1929 ... 353
Letters to Lucerne—Fritz Rotter, Allen Vincent ... 41–42 ... Dec. 23, 1941 ... 23
Life, A—Hugh Leonard ... 80–81 ... Nov. 2, 1980 ... 72
Life & Adventures of Nicholas Nickleby, The—(ad) David Edgar from Charles Dickens's novel ... 81–82 ... Oct. 4, 1981 ... 49
Life in the Theatre, A—David Mamet ... 77–78 ... Oct. 20, 1977 ... 288
Life With Father—Howard Lindsay, Russel Crouse, based on Clarence Day's book ... 39–40 ... Nov. 8, 1939 ... 3,224
Life With Mother—Howard Lindsay, Russel Crouse, based on Clarence Day's book ... 48–49 ... Oct. 20, 1948 ... 265
Light Up the Sky—Moss Hart ... 48–49 ... Nov. 18, 1948 ... 216
Liliom—Ferenc Molnar, (ad) Benjamin Glazer ... 20–21 ... Apr. 20, 1921 ... 300
Lion in Winter, The—James Goldman ... 65–66 ... Mar. 3, 1966 ... 92
*Lion King, The—(b) Roger Allers, Irene Mecchi, (m, l) Elton John, Tim Rice, (add'l m, l) Lebo M, Mark Mancina, Jay Rifkin, Julie Taymor, Hans Zimmer ... 97–98 ... Nov. 13, 1997 ... 2,768
Lips Together, Teeth Apart—Terrence McNally ... 91–92 ... June 25, 1991 ... 406
Little Accident—Floyd Dell, Thomas Mitchell ... 28–29 ... Oct. 9, 1928 ... 303
Little Foxes, The—Lillian Hellman ... 38–39 ... Feb. 15, 1939 ... 410
Little Minister, The—James M. Barrie ... 94–99 ... Sept. 27, 1897 ... 300
Little Night Music, A—(b) Hugh Wheeler, (m, l) Stephen Sondheim, suggested by Ingmar Bergman's film *Smiles of a Summer Night* ... 72–73 ... Feb. 25, 1973 ... 600
Living Out—Lisa Loomer ... 03–04 ... Sept. 30, 2003 ... 40
Living Room, The—Graham Greene ... 54–55 ... Nov. 17, 1954 ... 22
Living Together—Alan Ayckbourn ... 75–76 ... Dec. 7, 1975 ... 76
Lobby Hero—Kenneth Lonergan ... 00–01 ... Mar. 13, 2001 ... 40
00–01 ... May 8, 2001 ... 136
Loman Family Picnic, The—Donald Margulies ... 89–90 ... June 20, 1989 ... 16
Long Christmas Ride Home, The—Paula Vogel ... 03–04 ... Nov. 11, 2003 ... 27
Long Day's Journey Into Night—Eugene O'Neill ... 56–57 ... Nov. 7, 1956 ... 390
Look Back in Anger—John Osborne ... 57–58 ... Oct. 1, 1957 ... 407
Look Homeward, Angel—Ketti Frings, based on Thomas Wolfe's novel ... 57–58 ... Nov. 28, 1957 ... 564
Loose Ends—Michael Weller ... 79–80 ... June 6, 1979 ... 284
Lost Horizons—Harry Segall, revised by John Hayden ... 34–35 ... Oct. 15, 1934 ... 56

Play	Season	Opened	Perfs.
Ohio Impromptu, Catastrophe and What Where—Samuel Beckett	83–84	June 15, 1983	350
Oklahoma!—(b, l) Oscar Hammerstein II, based on Lynn Riggs's play *Green Grow the Lilacs,* (m) Richard Rodgers	42–43	Mar. 31, 1943	2,212
Old Maid, The—Zoë Akins, based on Edith Wharton's novel	34–35	Jan. 7, 1935	305
Old Soak, The—Don Marquis	22–23	Aug. 22, 1922	423
Old Times—Harold Pinter	71–72	Nov. 16, 1971	119
Old Wicked Songs—Jon Marans	96–97	Sept. 5, 1996	210
Oldest Living Graduate, The—Preston Jones	76–77	Sept. 23, 1976	20
Oleanna—David Mamet	92–93	Oct. 25, 1992	513
Omnium Gatherum—Theresa Rebeck and Alexandra Gersten-Vassilaros	03–04	Sept. 25, 2003	78
On Borrowed Time—Paul Osborn, based on Lawrence Edward Watkin's novel	37–38	Feb. 3, 1938	321
On Golden Pond—Ernest Thompson	78–79	Sept. 13, 1978	30
	78–79	Feb. 28, 1979	126
On Trial—Elmer Rice	09–19	Aug. 19, 1914	365
Once in a Lifetime—Moss Hart, George S. Kaufman	30–31	Sept. 24, 1930	406
Once on This Island—(b, l) Lynn Ahrens, (m) Stephen Flaherty, based on the novel *My Love My Love* by Rosa Guy	89–90	May 6, 1990	24
	90–91	Oct. 18, 1990	469
One Sunday Afternoon—James Hagan	32–33	Feb. 15, 1933	322
Orpheus Descending—Tennessee Williams	56–57	Mar. 21, 1957	68
Other People's Money—Jerry Sterner	88–89	Feb. 16, 1989	990
Otherwise Engaged—Simon Gray	76–77	Feb. 2, 1977	309
Our Country's Good—Timberlake Wertenbaker	90–91	Apr. 29, 1991	48
Our Lady of 121st Street—Stephen Adly Guirgis	02–03	Sept. 29, 2002	15
	02–03	Mar. 6, 2003	166
Outrageous Fortune—Rose Franken	43–44	Nov. 3, 1943	77
Our Town—Thornton Wilder	37–38	Feb. 4, 1938	336
Outward Bound—Sutton Vane	23–24	Jan. 7, 1924	144
Over 21—Ruth Gordon	43–44	Jan. 3, 1944	221
Overture—William Bolitho	30–31	Dec. 5, 1930	41
P.S. 193—David Rayfiel	62–63	Oct. 30, 1962	48
Pacific Overtures—(b) John Weidman, (m, l) Stephen Sondheim, (add'l material) Hugh Wheeler	75–76	Jan. 11, 1976	193
Pack of Lies—Hugh Whitemore	84–85	Feb. 11, 1985	120
Painting Churches—Tina Howe	83–84	Nov. 22, 1983	206
Parade—(b) Alfred Uhry, (m,l) Jason Robert Brown	98–99	Dec. 17, 1998	85
Paris Bound—Philip Barry	27–28	Dec. 27, 1927	234
Passion—(b) James Lapine, (m) Stephen Sondheim, based on the film *Passione D'Amore*	93–94	May 9, 1994	280
Passion of Joseph D., The—Paddy Chayevsky	63–64	Feb. 11, 1964	15

Play	Season	Opened	Perfs.
Prisoner of Second Avenue, The—Neil Simon	71–72	Nov. 11, 1971	780
*Producers, The—(b) Mel Brooks and Thomas Meehan, (m, l) Mel Brooks	00–01	Apr. 19, 2001	1,294
Prologue to Glory—E.P. Conkle	37–38	Mar. 17, 1938	70
Proof—David Auburn	00–01	May 23, 2000	79
	00–01	Oct. 24, 2000	917
Quartermaine's Terms—Simon Gray	82–83	Feb. 24, 1983	375
R.U.R.—Karel Capek	22–23	Oct. 9, 1922	184
Racket, The—Bartlett Cormack	27–28	Nov. 22, 1927	119
Ragtime—(b) Terrence McNally, (m) Stephen Flaherty, (l) Lynn Ahrens, based on E.L. Doctorow's novel	97–98	Jan. 18, 1998	861
Rain—John Colton, Clemence Randolph, based on the story by W. Somerset Maugham	22–23	Nov. 7, 1922	648
Raisin in the Sun, A—Lorraine Hansberry	58–59	Mar. 11, 1959	530
Rattle of a Simple Man—Charles Dyer	62–63	Apr. 17, 1963	94
Real Estate—Louise Page	87–88	Dec. 1, 1987	55
Real Thing, The—Tom Stoppard	83–84	Jan. 5, 1984	566
Rebel Women—Thomas Babe	75–76	May 6, 1976	40
Rebound—Donald Ogden Stewart	29–30	Feb. 3, 1930	114
Red Diaper Baby—Josh Kornbluth	92–93	June 12, 1992	59
Rehearsal, The—Jean Anouilh, (ad) Pamela Hansford Johnson, Kitty Black	63–64	Sept. 23, 1963	110
Remains To Be Seen—Howard Lindsay, Russel Crouse	51–52	Oct. 3, 1951	199
*Rent—(b,m,l) Jonathan Larson	95–96	Feb. 13, 1996	56
	95–96	Apr. 29, 1996	3,370
Requiem for a Nun—Ruth Ford, William Faulkner, adapted from William Faulkner's novel	58–59	Jan. 30, 1959	43
Reunion in Vienna—Robert E. Sherwood	31–32	Nov. 16, 1931	264
Rhinoceros—Eugene Ionesco, (tr) Derek Prouse	60–61	Jan. 9, 1961	240
Ritz, The—Terrence McNally	74–75	Jan. 20, 1975	400
River Niger, The—Joseph A. Walker	72–73	Dec. 5, 1972	120
	72–73	Mar. 27, 1973	280
Road—Jim Cartwright	88–89	July 28, 1988	62
Road to Mecca, The—Athol Fugard	87–88	Apr. 12, 1988	172
Road to Rome, The—Robert E. Sherwood	26–27	Jan. 31, 1927	392
Rockaby—(see *Enough, Footfalls* and *Rockaby*)			
Rocket to the Moon—Clifford Odets	38–39	Nov. 24, 1938	131
Romance—Edward Sheldon	09–19	Feb. 10, 1913	160
Rope Dancers, The—Morton Wishengrad	57–58	Nov. 20, 1957	189
Rose Tattoo, The—Tennessee Williams	50–51	Feb. 3, 1951	306
Rosencrantz and Guildenstern Are Dead—Tom Stoppard	67–68	Oct. 16, 1967	420
Round and Round the Garden—Alan Ayckbourn	75–76	Dec. 7, 1975	76
Royal Family, The—George S. Kaufman, Edna Ferber	27–28	Dec. 28, 1927	345
Royal Hunt of the Sun—Peter Shaffer	65–66	Oct. 26, 1965	261
Rugged Path, The—Robert E. Sherwood	45–46	Nov. 10, 1945	81

Play	Season	Opened	Perfs.
6 Rms Riv Vu—Bob Randall	72–73	Oct. 17, 1972	247
Skin Game, The—John Galsworthy	20–21	Oct. 20, 1920	176
Skin of Our Teeth, The—Thornton Wilder	42–43	Nov. 18, 1942	359
Skipper Next to God—Jan de Hartog	47–48	Jan. 4, 1948	93
Skriker, The—Caryl Churchill	95–96	May 12, 1996	17
Skylark—Samson Raphaelson	39–40	Oct. 11, 1939	256
Skylight—David Hare	96–97	Sept. 19, 1996	116
Sleuth—Anthony Shaffer	70–71	Nov. 12, 1970	1,222
Slow Dance on the Killing Ground—William Hanley	64–65	Nov. 30, 1964	88
Sly Fox—Larry Gelbart, based on *Volpone* by Ben Jonson	76–77	Dec. 14, 1976	495
Small Craft Warnings—Tennessee Williams	71–72	Apr. 2, 1972	192
Small Tragedy—Craig Lucas	03–04	Mar. 11, 2004	22
Soldier's Play, A—Charles Fuller	81–82	Nov. 20, 1981	468
Soldier's Wife—Rose Franken	44–45	Oct. 4, 1944	253
Speed-the-Plow—David Mamet	87–88	May 3, 1988	278
Spic-O-Rama—John Leguizamo	92–93	Oct. 27, 1992	86
Split Second—Dennis McIntyre	84–85	June 7, 1984	147
Squaw Man, The—Edward Milton Royle	99–09	Oct. 23, 1905	222
Stage Door—George S. Kaufman, Edna Ferber	36–37	Oct. 22, 1936	169
Staircase—Charles Dyer	67–68	Jan. 10, 1968	61
Star-Wagon, The—Maxwell Anderson	37–38	Sept. 29, 1937	223
State of the Union—Howard Lindsay, Russel Crouse	45–46	Nov. 14, 1945	765
Steambath—Bruce Jay Friedman	70–71	June 30, 1970	128
Steel Magnolias—Robert Harling	87–88	June 19, 1987	1,126
Sticks and Bones—David Rabe	71–72	Nov. 7, 1971	121
	71–72	Mar. 1, 1972	245
Stone and Star—Robert Ardrey	61–62	Dec. 5, 1961	20
Stone Cold Dead Serious—Adam Rapp	02–03	Apr. 7, 2003	35
Stop the World–I Want to Get Off—(b, m, l) Leslie Bricusse, Anthony Newley	62–63	Oct. 3, 1962	555
Storm Operation—Maxwell Anderson	43–44	Jan. 11, 1944	23
Story of Mary Surratt, The—John Patrick	46–47	Feb. 8, 1947	11
Strange Interlude—Eugene O'Neill	27–28	Jan. 30, 1928	426
Streamers—David Rabe	75–76	Apr. 21, 1976	478
Street Scene—Elmer Rice	28–29	Jan. 10, 1929	601
Streetcar Named Desire, A—Tennessee Williams	47–48	Dec. 3, 1947	855
Strictly Dishonorable—Preston Sturges	29–30	Sept. 18, 1929	557
Subject Was Roses, The—Frank D. Gilroy	64–65	May 25, 1964	832
Substance of Fire, The—Jon Robin Baitz	90–91	Mar. 17, 1991	120
SubUrbia—Eric Bogosian	93–94	May 22, 1994	113
Sugar Babies—(ad) Ralph G. Allen (special citation)	79–80	Oct. 8, 1979	1,208
Sum of Us, The—David Stevens	90–91	Oct. 16, 1990	335
Summer of the 17th Doll—Ray Lawler	57–58	Jan. 22, 1958	29
Sunday in the Park With George—(b) James Lapine, (m, l) Stephen Sondheim	83–84	May 2, 1984	604
Sunrise at Campobello—Dore Schary	57–58	Jan. 30, 1958	556

Titanic—(b) Peter Stone, (m, 1) Maury Yeston .... 96–97 .... Apr. 23, 1997 804
Toilet, The—LeRoi Jones (a.k.a. Amiri Baraka) .... 64–65 .... Dec. 16, 1964 151
Tomorrow and Tomorrow—Philip Barry .... 30–31 .... Jan. 13, 1931 206
Tomorrow the World—James Gow, Arnaud d'Usseau ..... 42–43 .... Apr. 14, 1943 500
Topdog/Underdog—Suzan-Lori Parks .... 01–02 .... Jul. 26, 2001 45
01–02 .... Apr. 7, 2002 144
Torch Song Trilogy—Harvey Fierstein (*The International Stud, Fugue in a Nursery, Widows and Children First*) .... 81–82 ..... Jan. 15, 1982 117
82–83 ..... June 10, 1982 1,222
Touch of the Poet, A—Eugene O'Neill .... 58–59 ..... Oct. 2, 1958 284
Tovarich—Jacques Deval, (tr) Robert E. Sherwood .... 36–37 ..... Oct. 15, 1936 356
Toys in the Attic—Lillian Hellman .... 59–60 ..... Feb. 25, 1960 556
Tracers—John DiFusco (c); Vincent Caristi, Richard Chaves, John DiFusco, Eric E. Emerson, Rick Gallavan, Merlin Marston, Harry Stephens with Sheldon Lettich .... 84–85 ..... Jan. 21, 1985 186
Tragedie de Carmen, La—(see *La Tragédie de Carmen*)
Translations—Brian Friel .... 80–81 ..... Apr. 7, 1981 48
Travesties—Tom Stoppard .... 75–76 ..... Oct. 30, 1975 155
Trelawny of the Wells—Arthur Wing Pinero .... 94–99 ..... Nov. 22, 1898 131
Trial of the Catonsville Nine, The—Daniel Berrigan, Saul Levitt .... 70–71 ..... Feb. 7, 1971 159
Tribute—Bernard Slade .... 77–78 ..... June 1, 1978 212
Tuna Christmas, A—Jaston Williams, Joe Sears, Ed Howard .... 94–95 ..... Dec. 15, 1994 20
Twilight: Los Angeles, 1992—Anna Deavere Smith .... 93–94 ..... Mar. 23, 1994 13
93–94 ..... Apr. 17, 1994 72
Two Blind Mice—Samuel Spewack .... 48–49 ..... Mar. 2, 1949 157
Two Trains Running—August Wilson .... 91–92 ..... Apr. 13, 1992 160

Unchastened Woman, The—Louis Kaufman Anspacher ..... 09–19 ..... Oct. 9, 1915 193
Uncle Harry—Thomas Job .... 41–42 ..... May 20, 1942 430
Under Milk Wood—Dylan Thomas .... 57–58 ..... Oct. 15, 1957 39
Urinetown—(b) Greg Kotis, (m) Mark Hollmann, (l) Greg Kotis, Mark Hollmann .... 00–01 ..... May 6, 2001 58
01–02 ..... Sept. 20, 2001 965

Valley Forge—Maxwell Anderson .... 34–35 ..... Dec. 10, 1934 58
Valley Song—Athol Fugard .... 95–96 ..... Dec. 12, 1995 96
Venus Observed—Christopher Fry .... 51–52 ..... Feb. 13, 1952 86
Very Special Baby, A—Robert Alan Aurthur .... 56–57 ..... Nov. 14, 1956 5
Victoria Regina—Laurence Housman .... 35–36 ..... Dec. 26, 1935 517
View From the Bridge, A—Arthur Miller .... 55–56 ..... Sept. 29, 1955 149
Violet—(b,1) Brian Crawley, (m) Jeanine Tesori, based on *The Ugliest Pilgrim* by Doris Betts .... 96–97 ..... Mar. 11, 1997 32
Violet Hour, The—Richard Greenberg .... 03–04 ..... Nov. 6, 2003 54

WISTERIA TREES, THE—Joshua Logan, based on Anton Chekhov's *The Cherry Orchard* ..... 49–50 ..... Mar. 29, 1950 165
WIT—Margaret Edson ..... 98–99 ..... Oct. 6, 1998 545
WITCHING HOUR, THE—Augustus Thomas ..... 99–09 ..... Nov. 18, 1907 212
WITNESS FOR THE PROSECUTION—Agatha Christie ..... 54–55 ..... Dec. 16, 1954 645
WOMEN, THE—Clare Boothe ..... 36–37 ..... Dec. 26, 1936 657
WONDERFUL TOWN—(b) Joseph Fields, Jerome Chodorov, based on their play *My Sister Eileen* and Ruth McKenney's stories, (l) Betty Comden, Adolph Green, (m) Leonard Bernstein ..... 52–53 ..... Feb. 25, 1953 559
WORLD WE MAKE, THE—Sidney Kingsley, based on Millen Brand's novel *The Outward Room* ..... 39–40 ..... Nov. 20, 1939 80

YEARS AGO—Ruth Gordon ..... 46–47 ..... Dec. 3, 1946 206
YELLOWMAN—Dael Orlandersmith ..... 02–03 ..... Oct. 22, 2002 64
YES, MY DARLING DAUGHTER—Mark Reed ..... 36–37 ..... Feb. 9, 1937 405
YOU AND I—Philip Barry ..... 22–23 ..... Feb. 19, 1923 178
YOU CAN'T TAKE IT WITH YOU—Moss Hart, George S. Kaufman ..... 36–37 ..... Dec. 14, 1936 837
YOU KNOW I CAN'T HEAR YOU WHEN THE WATER'S RUNNING—Robert Anderson ..... 66–67 ..... Mar. 13, 1967 755
YOUNG MAN FROM ATLANTA, THE—Horton Foote ..... 94–95 ..... Jan. 27, 1995 24
YOUNG WOODLEY—John van Druten ..... 25–26 ..... Nov. 2, 1925 260
YOUNGEST, THE—Philip Barry ..... 24–25 ..... Dec. 22, 1924 104
YOUR OWN THING—(b) Donald Driver, (m, l) Hal Hester and Danny Apolinar, suggested by William Shakespeare's *Twelfth Night* ..... 67–68 ..... Jan. 13, 1968 933
YOU'RE A GOOD MAN CHARLIE BROWN—(b, m, l) Clark Gesner, based on the comic strip *Peanuts* by Charles M. Schulz ..... 66–67 ..... Mar. 7, 1967 1,597

ZOOMAN AND THE SIGN—Charles Fuller ..... 80–81 ..... Dec. 7, 1980 33

CONTRIBUTORS TO *BEST PLAYS*

○○○○○

Lenora Inez Brown has developed new plays at various regional theatres including Madison Repertory Theatre and Crossroads Theatre in New Jersey. She also has been a dramaturg for development workshops and was a member of the artistic team for the 2000 and 2001 Sundance Theatre Lab. Brown is a freelance theater critic for the Chicago Sun Times and assistant professor of dramaturgy at the Theatre School, DePaul University. She serves on the board of ASSITEJ/USA and earned an MFA in dramaturgy from the Yale School of Drama.

Rue E. Canvin worked at the *New York Herald Tribune*, first as a secretary in the advertising department and then as an editorial assistant in the drama department for 15 years where she worked with the editors and the arts critics until the demise of the newspaper in 1966. She also worked at the *World Journal Tribune* until it closed in 1967. Canvin has served as an assistant editor of *The Best Plays Theater Yearbook* series since 1963. She has also transcribed taped interviews for the Dramatists Guild and Authors League.

Tish Dace, chancellor professor emerita at the University of Massachusetts Dartmouth and winner of its 1997 Scholar of the Year Award, has published several books, thousands of play reviews, and more than 200 essays, articles and book chapters. She chaired the American Theatre Wing's Henry Hewes Design Awards—earlier known as the Maharam Awards and as the American Theatre Wing Design Awards—for nearly 20 years. Dace served six years as a member of the executive committee of the American Theatre Critics Association, and still serves on the executive committee of the International Association of Theatre Critics. She has been a theater critic for 30 years and the New York critic for *Plays International* since 1986. She has published in such periodicals as the *New York Times*, *The Times* of London, *New York*, *The Village Voice* and *American Theatre*.

Christine Dolen has been the *Miami Herald*'s theater critic since 1979. She holds bachelor's and master's degrees in journalism from Ohio State University and was a John S. Knight Journalism Fellow at Stanford University in 1984–85. In 1997, she was a member of the Pulitzer Prize drama jury; in 1999, she was a senior fellow in the National Arts Journalism Program at Columbia University. Currently, she is on the advisory council of the American Theatre Critics Association. Before becoming the *Herald*'s theater critic, she was arts editor and pop music critic. Her awards include the Green Eyeshade in criticism from the Atlanta Chapter of the Society of Professional Journalists and first place in arts writing in the Missouri Lifestyle Journalism Awards. Dolen received the George Abbott Award for Outstanding Achievement in the Arts at the 2001 Carbonell Awards.

Michael Feingold has worked in the theater for more than three decades as a translator, playwright, lyricist, director, dramaturg and literary manager. A graduate of Columbia University and the Yale School of Drama, he has translated more than 50 plays and operas. Feingold has held literary posts at the Yale Repertory Theatre, the Guthrie Theater and the American Repertory Theatre. He has been an O'Neill Conference playwright and is a "Usual Suspect" at New York Theatre Workshop. He is best known as the chief theater critic for *The Village Voice*, for which he received the George Jean

Nathan Award. In 2001, he was named a senior fellow of the National Arts Journalism Program. He has taught dramatic literature, criticism, and dramaturgy at Columbia, NYU, and the O'Neill Critics Institute.

Mel Gussow, a cultural writer for *The New York Times*, is the author of the biography, *Edward Albee: A Singular Journey*, and of *Conversations With Miller*, as well as books about Harold Pinter, Tom Stoppard and Samuel Beckett. He has also written *Theater on the Edge: New Visions, New Voices*, a collection of theater reviews and essays, and was co-editor of the Library of America's two volume edition of the plays of Tennessee Williams. In 2002, he was awarded the Margo Jones Medal and, in previous years, the George Jean Nathan Award for Dramatic Criticism and a Guggenheim Fellowship.

Paul Hardt of Stuart Howard Associates works in casting for theatre, television and film. His casting credits include the national tours of *The Who's Tommy*, *Leader of the Pack* and *Game Show*. Stuart Howard Associates currently casts *I Love You, You're Perfect, Now Change*, *On Golden Pond* starring James Earl Jones and Leslie Uggams, and the upcoming revival of *Pajama Game* starring Harry Connick Jr.

Charles Isherwood is a theater critic for *The New York Times*. He served as chief theater critic for *Variety* from 1998 to 2004, and worked as a Los Angeles-based critic and editor for the publication since 1993. He has also written about theater for *The Times* of London and contributed arts writing to other publications including the *Advocate* magazine.

John Istel has edited and contributed to a variety of performing arts, general interest and reference publications over the last 20 years including *American Theatre*, *The Atlantic*, *Back Stage*, *Contemporary Playwrights*, *Elle*, *Mother Jones*, *Newsday*, *New York*, *Stagebill* and *The Village Voice*. He has taught at New York University, Medgar Evers College and currently teaches English at Manhattan Theatre Lab High School in Harlem, a New Visions school, which he helped create in partnership with Roundabout Theatre Company.

Jeffrey Eric Jenkins is the sixth editor of *The Best Plays Theater Yearbook* series founded by drama critic Burns Mantle in 1920. He has served as theater critic, contributor and editor for a variety of newspapers, magazines and journals. Since 1998, he has been a faculty member in the Department of Drama at New York University's Tisch School of the Arts, where he has taught theater studies—with an emphasis in United States drama and theater. Jenkins has also taught at Carnegie Mellon University, the University of Washington, and SUNY–Stony Brook. He received degrees in drama and theater arts from Carnegie Mellon University and San Francisco State University, and he has directed more than two dozen productions in professional and educational theaters across the United States. Jenkins is a former board member of the American Theatre Critics Association (1995–2001) and served as the association's chairman from 1999 to 2001. He chairs the American Theatre Wing's Henry Hewes Design Awards, is a board member of the American Theatre and Drama Society and serves on the executive committee of the Theater Hall of Fame. Jenkins serves on the advisory committees of the American Theatre Wing and the William Inge Theatre Festival.

Vivian Cary Jenkins spent more than twenty years as a healthcare administrator and teacher before focusing on editorial work for *The Best Plays Theater Yearbook* series. Prior to her work in healthcare, she was a dancer and a Peace Corps volunteer in Honduras.

Chris Jones reports on and reviews theater for the *Chicago Tribune*. He has contributed reviews and articles to *Variety* for the past 15 years, specializing in out-of-town tryouts and the Broadway road. His reviews, interviews and commentary also have appeared in *American Theatre* and *The New York Times*, along with numerous other arts publications. Born in Manchester, England, Jones holds a PhD in theater criticism from Ohio State University.

Robert Kamp is the owner I Can Do That Productions, Inc., a graphic design company in New York City. Prior to starting his own business, Bob worked for several arts and entertainment publications including *Stagebill* and *City Guide Magazine*. Bob designed the *Best Plays* logo, and has worked on the book's photos and graphic images since the 2000–2001 edition.

Lara D. Nielsen is a writer and theater studies faculty member in the Department of Drama at New York University. She has published in *Theatre Journal*, *Women & Performance*, *Contemporary Theatre Review* and *Studies in Law, Politics and Society*. Nielsen holds an MA in comparative literature, cultural studies and feminist theory from the University of Minnesota, Twin Cities, and a PhD in performance studies from NYU. Her research examines relationships between aesthetics and the technologies of the state. She lives in Brooklyn, where she's working on several forthcoming manuscripts in the arts and in criticism.

Rick Pender is arts and entertainment editor for *Cincinnati CityBeat*—an award-winning alternative newsweekly. He is also the newspaper's theater critic and columnist. Pender is managing editor of *The Sondheim Review* and a regional correspondent for *Back Stage*, covering Cincinnati, Louisville and Indianapolis. In 2002 the Ohio Society of Professional Journalists named him "Best Critic in Ohio." Pender serves as 2004–05 chairman of the American Theatre Critics Association.

Christopher Rawson has been since 1983 drama critic and (more recently) drama editor of the *Pittsburgh Post-Gazette*. Along with local reviews, features, news and columns, he also reviews regularly in New York, London and Canada. His love of theater is partly inherited from his father, actor Richard Hart, but he started professional life teaching English literature at the University of Pittsburgh, where he still teaches Shakespeare and critical writing. His BA is from Harvard and his PhD from the University of Washington. A former chairman of the American Theatre Critics Association, he is a member of the executive committee of the Theater Hall of Fame, managing the selection process with Henry Hewes.

Michael Sommers is the New York theater reviewer and reporter for *The Star-Ledger* of Newark, NJ, and other Newhouse Newspapers. He is the vice president of the New York Drama Critics' Circle.

Anne Marie Welsh is theater critic for the *San Diego Union-Tribune*. She earned an MA and a PhD in literature and drama from the University of Rochester. She co-edited *The Longman Anthology of Modern and Contemporary Drama*, co-authored *Shakespeare: Script, Stage & Screen* (with David Bevington and Michael Greenwald) and is completing a study of war plays since the Greeks, *Theater of War*. A visiting lecturer in theater history, dance history and criticism at the University of California, San Diego, Welsh has also published many poems and stories for children.

Charles Wright has been a contributor to four editions of the *Best Plays Theater Yearbook* and to the recently published *Theatermania Guide to Musical Theater Recordings*. A native of Tennessee and a long-time resident of New York City, he holds degrees from Vanderbilt, Oxford, and the University of Pennsylvania. As a business affairs executive at A&E Television Networks for the past decade, Wright has been involved in hundreds of hours of nonfiction programming, including *The Farm: Angola, USA*, which received the 1998 Grand Jury Prize at Sundance and was nominated for an Academy Award as Best Documentary Feature the following year, and such primetime series as *Growing Up Gotti* and *Intervention*.

Index

Titles in bold are play titles.
Page numbers in italic indicate essay citations.
Page numbers in bold italic indicate Broadway and Off Broadway listings.
Nouns or numbers in parentheses delineate different persons or entities.